D0401245

CALIFORNIA BEACHES

The Complete Guide to More Than 400 Beaches and 1,200 Miles of Coastline

Parke Puterbaugh
and Alan Bisbort

Foghorn Press
BOOKS BUILDING COMMUNITY™

ISBN 0-935701-00-1
51995
9 780935 701005

Copyright © 1996
by Parke Puterbaugh and Alan Bisbort

All rights reserved. This book may not be reproduced in full or in part without the written permission of the publisher, except for use by a reviewer in the context of a review. Inquiries and excerpt requests should be addressed to:

Publishing Manager
Foghorn Press
555 DeHaro Street, Suite 220
San Francisco, CA 94107

To order individual books, please call Foghorn Press:
1-800-FOGHORN (364-4676) or (415) 241-9550.

Foghorn Press titles are distributed to the book trade by Publishers Group West, based in Emeryville, California. To contact your local sales representative, call 1-800-788-3123.

No liability is assumed with respect to the information or content of this book. No one should participate in any of the activities described in this book unless they recognize and personally assume the associated risks.

Library of Congress ISSN Data:
June 1996
California Beaches
The Complete Guide to More Than 400 Beaches and 1,200 Miles of Coastline
1996–1997 Edition
ISSN: 1088-0704

The Color of Commitment

Foghorn Press has always been committed to printing on recycled paper, but up to now, we hadn't taken the final plunge to use 100 percent recycled paper because we were unconvinced of its quality. And until now, those concerns were valid. But the good news is that quality recycled paper is now available. We are thrilled to announce that Foghorn Press books are printed with Soya-based inks on 100 percent recycled paper, which has a 50 percent post-consumer waste content. The only way you'd know we made this change is by looking at the hue of the paper—a small price to pay for environmental integrity. You may even like the color better. We do. And we know the earth does, too.

Printed in the United States of America

We dedicate this book to our wives, Carol Hill Puterbaugh and Tracey O'Shaughnessy Bisbort. They have been as tolerant as angels of our extended absences and inveterate beachcombing. Because of them, we're actually glad the summer isn't an endless one.

Preface

We are beach bums. In our more jocular or self-important moments (take your pick), we humor ourselves with the notion that we are America's beach bums. And why not? We have spent a fair portion of our adult lives dodging gainful employment in order to visit and write about beaches. It's a tough job, but somebody's gotta do it, as we've been told by a few hundred would-be comedians over the years. (Our retort: If it's so easy, why has no one else done it before?) This is our third book on beaches, but our first for Foghorn Press, and also the first devoted to a single state.

We needn't go into great detail about why we've kicked off a series of beach books with the state of California. One simple statistic says it all: California lays claim to 1,264 miles of coastline—beautiful and changeable coastline, at that. Beaches have insinuated themselves into the psyche of Californians like nowhere else. Much of the state's population is pressed up against the coast, which means they live near the beach or play there with great frequency. Others cross mountains and valleys to get to them on a more occasional basis. Many cross state lines—and even international borders—to vacation on the Golden State's beaches.

California Beaches is aimed at all who are curious to learn more about the greatest coastline in America. Whether you're planning a vacation or simply want to do some armchair beachcombing, you can vicariously visit just about every publicly accessible beach in the state—about 420 of them, by our count—with us as your hosts. We regard this book as both a travelogue and a travel guide. It is a travelogue in the sense that you can wander up the coast with us—from south to north, from beach to beach—and find continuity in the journey and a spirit of close cultural observation in the writing. It is a travel guide in that we've provided the reader with plenty of service information, such as phone numbers, entrance fees, and hours of operation. We've also liberally spiked the book with sidebars—some full of practical information, others anecdotal accounts of various and sundry encounters—to break up a very long trip with the reader's equivalent of rest stops. Our idea is that *California Beaches* should be both a useful tool and an entertaining read. With no false modesty, we believe we've succeeded on both counts.

And we could not have had a better time putting this book together. You'd have to be as crusty as a barnacle not to have a blast on the beaches of California. Having long ago traded dress shoes for flip-flops, we eagerly embarked on yet another border-to-border, beach-by-beach pilgrimage. As for omens, you couldn't beat this one: at the outset of one summer-long trek for this book, a sequel to the great '60s surfer flick *Endless Summer* had just been released and was playing at small theaters along the coast. Fitting, we thought, because our own aims were not far from those of the beach-blond, well-tanned dudes who followed the sun in search of the perfect wave. The only difference between us and the guys in the film is that instead of carrying surfboards on our heads, we toted notebooks in our hands.

To be honest, we came looking for a few more things than the surfers were: not just waves and beaches for surfing but striking scenery, other beach activities (volleyball, biking, hiking, etc.), a bit of coastal geology, and a touch of local history, plus worthwhile places for sleeping, eating, and having fun after the sun goes down. *California Beaches* covers a lot of ground. We've written about every coastal community between the Mexican and Oregon borders, including each beach that can be safely and legally reached by foot, car, or ferry. For more miles and months than you can imagine we were the enthralled captives of the Pacific Coast Highway and U.S. 101. But enough of all this—time to pile in the car and hit the beach.

—Parke Puterbaugh and Alan Bisbort

Table of Contents

How to Use This Book

California Beaches proceeds from south to north, covering the state's 15 coastal counties. The book is divided into three regions: Southern, Central, and Northern California. If you know the name of the community, park, or beach you want to visit, look for it in the index beginning on page 600.

Each chapter begins with a map of the coastal area and features numbers indicating the location of each beach within the county. Next come the actual write-ups of individual communities and their beaches. These begin with the name of a community or beach area (when the latter falls outside a municipality), plus its population, area code, and zip code. An introductory essay orients the reader to the area's history, attractions, and ambience. Additional information follows under these headings: Beaches, Bunking Down (accommodations), Coastal Cuisine (restaurants), and Night Moves (nightlife).

Beaches

Under the Beaches heading, we give the lowdown on what you can expect to see and do at each beach. This includes a description of its natural features and any other observations that seem relevant or interesting. Beach descriptions are accompanied by a listing of practical information for each beach, including how to get there, where to park, hours, facilities, and a contact number.

What the Symbols Mean

Each beach listing features symbols indicating what can be found at or along the beach, or in its immediate vicinity:

Bike path · Camping · Food and drink · Hiking · Nude

Pier · RVs allowed · Surfing · Volleyball

Here are some explanatory notes:

- The biking symbol indicates there is a bike path along the beach.
- The food-and-drink symbol indicates there is a food concession or store on or near the beach.
- The hiking symbol signifies that there are trails in the park, a path to the beach, or good beach hiking.
- The RV symbol shows that RV camping is permitted; it does not guarantee the availability of electrical or sewage hookups.
- The volleyball symbol shows that sand courts with standards are located on the beach.

What the Ratings Mean

Following the symbols, we've rated each beach on a one-to-five scale. The first rating is an indication of how crowded it is:

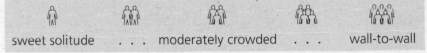

sweet solitude . . . moderately crowded . . . wall-to-wall

The second, and vastly more subjective, category is our overall rating. This is an aesthetic judgment that rates each beach according to its overall appeal. It is our attempt to answer the question "How desirable is this place to visit?" The scale is as follows:

don't bother . . . worth a visit . . . beach heaven

These ratings represent nothing more than the informed opinions of two well-traveled beach bums. If you disagree, please write to us in care of Foghorn Press and let us know why. It will help with future editions.

Bunking Down

The Bunking Down section offers a look at what kind of accommodations you can expect to find in a given locale, plus commentary on hotels, inns, or resorts that we deem worthy. It is by no means an exhaustive list.

Room rates fluctuate according to the day of week, time of year, special events, and the economy—all factors that determine what price the market will bear at a given time. Our $ to $$$$ price range is a general indication of the nightly cost of a standard room with two beds (during the peak season). The range is:

$ = inexpensive (less than $60)
$$ = moderate ($60 to $120)
$$$ = expensive ($120 to $180)
$$$$ = extravagant ($180 and up)

Coastal Cuisine

Our $ to $$$$ price range for restaurants indicates the cost of an average à la carte dinner entrée. The range is:

$ = inexpensive (less than $6)
$$ = moderate ($6 to $12)
$$$ = expensive ($12 to $18)
$$$$ = extravagant ($18 and up)

Night Moves

Night Moves means nightlife, and to us nightlife means people congregating to relax or blow off steam after the sun has set. Our listings run the gamut from hole-in-the-wall surf bars to rock clubs with live music. We didn't write about lounge pianists or high culture. Essentially, we wrote about bars—beach bars and coffee bars, where you can kick back and hang ten after the sun has slipped beneath the salty rim of the Pacific Ocean.

For More Information

We've provided addresses and phone numbers for sources, such as chambers of commerce and tourist bureaus. For areas outside of municipalities, we've provided addresses and phone numbers for national, state, or county park headquarters.

Every effort has been made to ensure that the information in California Beaches *is as up to date as possible. However, details such as fees and telephone numbers are liable to change. Please contact the parks, lodgings, and restaurants you plan to visit for the latest information.*

Introduction

California, if one word were used to describe it, is abundant: abundant in people, abundant in nature, abundant in variety, and abundant in beaches. It is a seemingly endless state in which there's always another beach around the next bend in the highway. In our travels, we've set foot on nearly every saltwater beach in America—East, West, and Gulf Coasts—but California remains our state of choice. It's our good fortune in *California Beaches* to rhapsodize about every beachside community in the Golden State's 15 coastal counties.

Beaches are the raison d'être of this book. Everything else we've written appears solely because of its bearing on or proximity to the beach. The beach itself is the object, the destination, the pot of golden sand at the end of the asphalt rainbow. In the following pages, we offer candid impressions of and practical information about more than 400 beaches. We can't say enough good things about California's coast, although God knows we've tried, expending a quarter million words on the subject. In our humble opinion, it is the most beautiful, varied, and fascinating coastline in the world.

Our write-ups include descriptions of the area surrounding the beach (lodgings, restaurants, and nightlife) and information and observations to help you get a handle on each place: its history, attractions, and activities; the look of the community; things we saw and overheard; and things we think you ought to know (e.g., are the natives friendly?). Our methods are simple: we dig around, get our hands dirty, mull over our experiences, and then tell it like we saw it. We make no bones about being opinionated. People spend a lot of money on trips and vacations, so they deserve to hear the truth—or at least a candid and informed opinion—before ransoming their time and money.

It made sense to us to organize the book from south to north, beginning in Southern California, the land where beaches occupy an almost mythic stature. This is where the majority of people live, play, and vacation, and where the ocean water is warm enough to swim in without a wet suit (at least in the summer). Starting at Border Field State Park by the Mexican border, we proceed up the coast, ending at Pelican State Beach on the Oregon state line.

California Beaches is divided into three sections—Southern, Central, and Northern California—which reflect the natural geographic divisions found along the coast. Southern California offers a warmer climate, less dramatic topography, and the quintessential look of a warm-weather playground by the sea. Its beaches and the activities enjoyed on them—surfing, volleyball, sunbathing—are the standards by which all other beaches are judged.

Farther up the coast, the beaches take on a more rugged, wild look. The Santa Lucia Mountains plunge down to the ocean in Big Sur, where the only sand beaches are small ones nestled into coves. Central California has a different social climate as well—one that is less gregarious and activity-crazed than the heavily populated fast-lane free-for-all of the Southland. This is even more true as one moves into Northern California. From the windswept Point Reyes Peninsula to the black-sand beaches at the base of the King Range in Humboldt County, this coast bears a timeless, primeval look.

California's coastline exists along the margin between two enormous crustal plates—the oceanic Pacific plate and the continental North American plate—that are sliding past one another. It is a young, erosional coast that is still geologically active. Unlike the East Coast, it is not so much a finished product as a work in progress. Its endless evolution is part of what makes it such a fascinating place to visit, study, and (most of all) play.

Getting to the Beach

The only qualification for a beach's inclusion in this book is public access—that is, the public must legally be able to reach it. Making beaches accessible is the business of the California Coastal Commission (CCC), the agency that evolved after the passage of Proposition 20 (the Coastal Initiative) in 1972. The enactment of the California Coastal Act of 1976 accorded the

CCC permanent status as a state agency. Its stated mission is to protect, maintain, and enhance the quality of the coastal environment.

Since its inception, the California Coastal Commission has fought to democratize a coastline increasingly walled off by private development. A controversial entity, at times it has been a political football subject to the whims and special interests of Democrats and Republicans alike (depending on who was wielding power). Providing public access across private land has rubbed some big-money interests the wrong way. Even non-wealthy coastal landowners balk at the idea of granting easements across their property to allow the public to beat a path to the beach. In a way, you can't blame them.

The issue pits individual property rights against the public's collective ownership of the beaches. Technically, the part of the beach shoreward of the mean high-tide line is classified as "public trust lands," held in trust by the government on behalf of the public. It is a concept that dates back to English common law. In other words, the beach is open to and owned by all. Anyone has a legal right to be there.

The hitch is getting onto the beach, which often involves crossing private property. For years the CCC required public easements as a precondition for granting permits to landowners in the coastal zone. The strategy was challenged in a well-publicized court case (Nollan v. California Coastal Commission) and struck down by the U.S. Supreme Court in 1987. The tide of public sentiment and legal judgment has subsequently risen against the CCC as the property-rights movement has gained steam in the 1990s.

During the past three decades, the California Coastal Commission has somehow managed to open access points all along the California coast. The agency has also compiled several fine reference works, including the indispensable *California Coastal Access Guide* (Berkeley: University of California Press, 4th ed., 1991). It makes an excellent companion to the more anecdotal, opinionated travel guide you hold in your hands.

Some beaches are accessible by little more than a trail or walkway across private property (e.g., the access trails through Sea Ranch in Sonoma County). Happily, many beaches and the land behind them belong to the state, county, or city. One-fourth of the California coastline is state owned and maintained as state parks or beaches. Entry fees are generally charged to get to them. They range from $4 to $6 per vehicle at the more developed and popular sites to $2 or no fee at some remote locations where there are few or no facilities.

It might surprise many who take beaches for granted to discover to what extent the wide, sandy swaths, particularly those in Southern California, require "beach renourishment"—the trucking or pumping in of sand—to maintain an acceptable width. This is because much of the natural beach gets carried into offshore canyons by currents and storms, while natural supplies of sand that would normally replenish the narrowed beaches have been cut off by dams, roads, and development.

Coastal engineers argue that renourishing the beaches of Southern California makes economic sense when you consider the revenue generated by the people who visit the beaches. Most of the time, renourishment passes the cost-benefit test. However, it's interesting to realize that some of California's most celebrated beaches are a bit of a mirage. That is, they exist only because sand has been trucked in and beach-widening structures such as groins and jetties have been built to hold them in place.

Throughout this book, we feature symbols illustrating what can be done on a given beach: camping, biking, hiking, surfing, playing volleyball, snacking, and hanging out in the buff. We do not have symbols for some popular coastal activities—namely fishing, tidepooling, and diving. We made the logical assumption that every ocean beach offers an opportunity for some type of fishing. Anglers eager to obtain a copy of the latest California sportfishing regulations can drop by any bait-and-tackle shop or write to the California Department of Fish and Game, 1416 Ninth Street, Box 944209, Sacramento, CA 94244-2090. Pay particular attention to chapter 4 of the regulations ("Ocean Fishing"), which lists marine ecological reserves, marine life refuges, and ocean waters with restricted fishing; prohibitions and restrictions are imposed on taking fish, mollusks, crustaceans, and other forms of marine life at these locales.

We've excluded tidepooling from the book because we don't want to encourage any more disturbance of marine life in the intertidal zone than already takes place. That's just the curmudgeonly cut of our jib, mate.

Anyone interested in information about diving on the California coast should pick up *California Diving News* at dive shops or order a subscription by writing to P.O. Box 11231, Torrance, CA 90510. It includes comprehensive listings of dive trips, events, and shops throughout California. To obtain an informative brochure about diving in California State Parks (whose holdings account for a quarter of the state's coastline), request a copy of "Dive In!" from California State Parks, Office of Marketing and Public Affairs, P.O. Box 942896, Sacramento, CA 94296.

Bunking Down by the Beach

We've provided a general overview of accommodations at or near the beach, with some specific choices at a range of prices. Generally, we didn't stray east of the Pacific Coast Highway or Highway 101. You should be able to see or at least sense the beach from the places we've mentioned, be it a campground or five-star resort.

As a rule, we're more willing to recommend chain hotels and motels than chain restaurants. Whereas chain restaurants guarantee little more than consistent mediocrity, chain lodgings often assure a far more desirable commodity: a consistent level of cleanliness and comfort. We believe there is a solid case to be made for sticking with name brands when it comes to choosing where you lay your head at night. You are better off dropping your bags and body in a Holiday Inn than some roadside fleabag where the mattress springs are squeaky, the carpet stained, the pillows and walls precariously thin, and the odors unsavory.

At the beach there are, of course, other options such as posh private resorts and upscale bed-and-breakfast inns (B&Bs). These provide a welcome opportunity to savor either unique architecture and furnishings (as is often the case at cozy, commodious B&Bs) or a class of amenities that's a cut above the name-brand pack (as you will find at the tonier beach resorts). We have endeavored to pick out a helpful sampling of beachside B&Bs, resorts, name-brand motels, and one-of-a-kind hotels worth considering when planning a California-coast vacation. If you have a favorite hideaway that isn't mentioned, drop us a line and we'll check it out for the next edition of *California Beaches*.

On the subject of saving money, we've got a few tips when it comes to bunking down. By all means, ask for a AAA or AARP discount when making reservations. In many cases, this can knock a minimum of 10 percent off the cost of a room, and special promotions can mean an even deeper discount. At times we've gotten nearly a 50 percent discount, thanks to special rates advertised in AAA's California guidebook. The benefits of a AAA membership—discounts, maps, guidebooks, roadside service—make it well worth the modest annual fee. You might also try booking rooms through a travel agent, as these professionals are often privy to special rates. Try traveling in the off-season, after prices have dropped and crowds have thinned. This strategy works particularly well in California, whose coast boasts a pleasant climate most of the year.

Another way to slash prices is to use discount coupons found in booklets at state welcome centers, rest areas, gas stations, and fast-food restaurants along interstate highways. The most widely distributed is the green *California-Nevada Travelers Guide,* published by EXIT Info, Inc. Though you can't make advance reservations with these coupons, the savings can be substantial if you've got some flexibility and are willing to gamble on last-minute availability.

Watch out for pricey perks. A continental breakfast can add to the value of a room, but don't be swayed by this minor freebie. After all, if you're paying $15 more a night than you would at the place next door for canned orange juice, office-quality coffee, and a packaged Danish worth $1.50, you've lost on the deal. Don't overpay for a setup that offers amenities you won't use or don't need (e.g., exercise room, pool, tennis or golf course, swank terrycloth robes, and a phone beside the toilet).

Be sure to ask for the kind of room you want when making reservations: smoking or nonsmoking, ground level or upper floor, king-sized bed or two doubles, poolside or ocean view. Don't be afraid to request another room if the one you've been given doesn't meet with your satisfaction. The squeaky wheel gets the best rooms, while the quiet malcontents suffer in silence.

A brief word on a pet peeve of ours: hotel phone charges. This is where hotel guests really pay unnecessarily. It seems the more expensive the hotel, the more shameless the add-ons. Local calls made from a room phone can cost up to $1. Direct-dialed long-distance calls amount to out-and-out extortion. Unless you have a reputable long-distance carrier's access code and a personal identification number (PIN), you might wind up with some fly-by-night carrier or the hotel itself charging an arm and a leg. Our advice: make local calls with quarters at lobby pay phones, and use an access code from one of the big three carriers (AT&T, Sprint, MCI) before placing long-distance calls from your hotel room. The codes are as follows:

AT&T: 1-0-288-0
Sprint: 1-0-333-0
MCI: 1-0-222-0

The restaurant-style à la carte approach to hotel charges seems to be catching on. Some places assess separate fees for such things as parking and use of on-site exercise facilities. It would seem logical and fair that a room rate would include a space to park your car, but such a thing becomes just another profit center in a corporate world that is endlessly inventive in its ability to furtively embellish a basic charge.

Finally, upon leaving the lodging, be sure to review the bill to verify all charges. Question things that don't look right. Insist on a satisfactory accounting and the removal of disputed charges. Vacations are expensive, and there's no sense paying for more than you have to.

Coastal Cuisine: Where to Cast a Mealtime Net

Eating well is one of the major pleasures of any California beach vacation. The Golden State is a seafood lover's cornucopia, with such native catches as halibut, snapper, ling cod, petrale sole, and ahi, not to mention plump Pacific oysters and incomparable king and queen crab from cold Alaskan waters. Thanks to the healthy California nouvelle style of cooking that's popular these days, you can find a wealth of fresh fare deliciously prepared almost anywhere along the coast.

Our restaurant write-ups single out particular spots for praise and recommendation; however, while we've tried to be as thorough as possible, we make no claims of being exhaustive. Quite simply, we looked for a decent sampling of restaurants specializing in seafood and/or regional

California cuisine located at or near the beach. The restaurant scene is highly changeable, with new ones popping up and old ones closing all the time. This is particularly true along the coast, where the tourist-driven economy is notoriously volatile.

We cast a favorable eye upon restaurants that have been around for a while and have maintained a consistently high reputation and level of quality. Philosophically, we are bullish on the notion of eating at nonfranchise restaurants, as opposed to predictable chains where Americans dine on the run (which is most of the time). We've got no use for the visually blighted corporate grease pits crammed side by side on major roadways from sea to shining sea. We'd rather give our business to individually owned restaurants than those garish places where cooking is not an art but a minimum-wage job and ingredients are delivered frozen on tractor-trailer trucks.

We urge you to support honest regionalism and innovation in cooking by dining at nonfranchised restaurants where the money that's received is returned to the community, not some distant corporate headquarters. Franchised operations are rarely mentioned here, since everyone knows what they look like, what's on the menu, and so on. Instead, we've chosen to spotlight restaurants where the love of doing things well is as important as the bottom line. We welcome your comments, particularly if a favorite restaurant has been overlooked.

Night Moves: Having Fun After the Sun Sets

After checking out the beaches, we still had enough energy at the end of each day to peruse the nightlife. Don't believe that we weren't exhausted and sleepless by the time we reached the Oregon border. But it was all for a worthy mission: our self-appointed task to get a bead on everything along the coast, including the nightlife. This was both the hardest and the most fun aspect of beach life to write about: hard, because too much late-night carousing can make it difficult to get up early and jump into beach-researching mode; fun. . . well, for obvious reasons. We hope you enjoy reading about our after-dark research as much as we did conducting it. Our proudest moment was hooking up with a bunch of bar-hopping surfers in Pacific Beach, who, at the end of a long, liquid evening, gave us the thumbs-up and a benediction: "You guys are a couple of real party dudes." To which we can only add, "Cowabunga!" Whatever that means.

California Coast

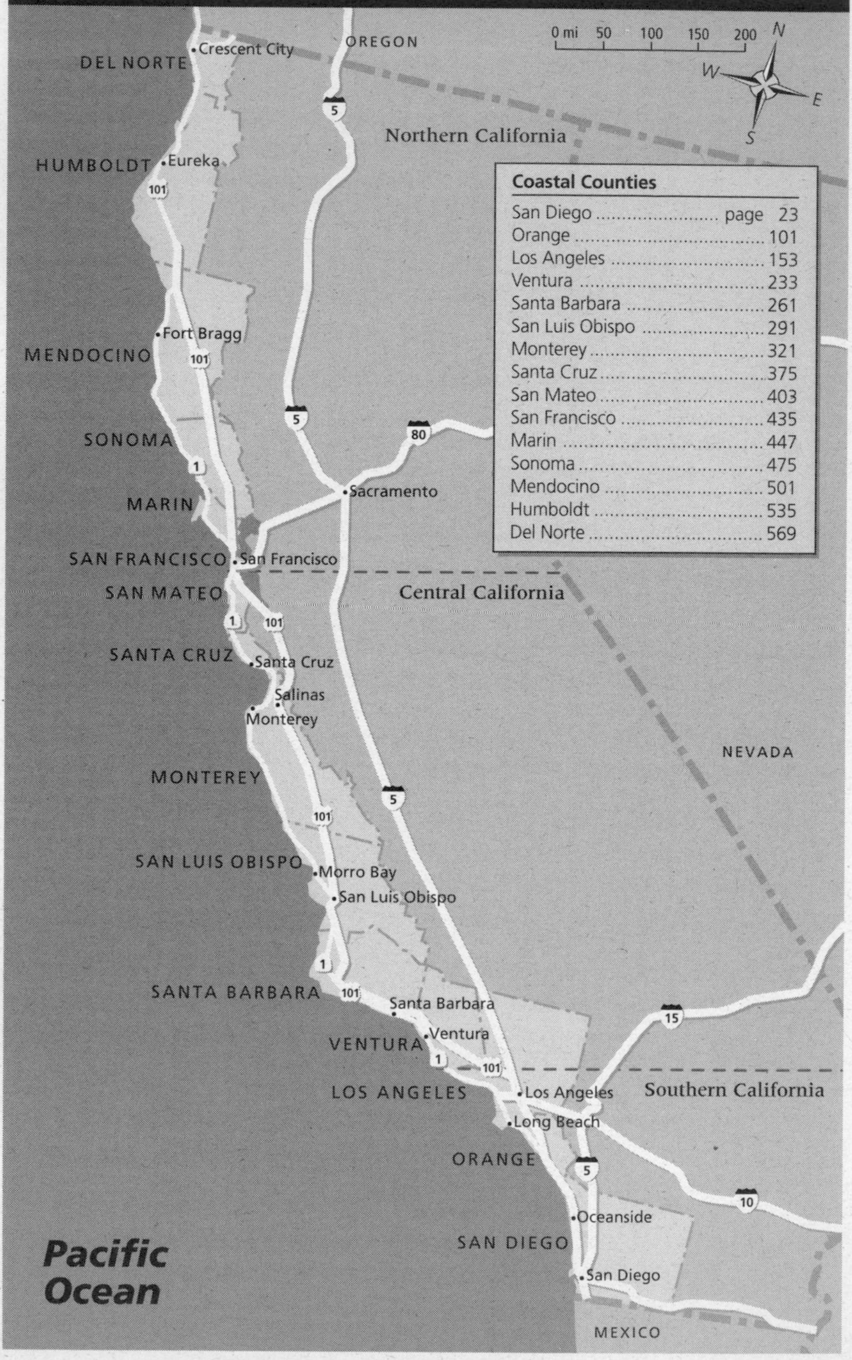

0 mi 50 100 150 200
N
W
E
S
OREGON
Northern California
DEL NORTE
Crescent City
HUMBOLDT
Eureka
MENDOCINO
Fort Bragg
SONOMA
MARIN
Sacramento
SAN FRANCISCO
San Francisco
SAN MATEO
Central California
SANTA CRUZ
Santa Cruz
Salinas
Monterey
MONTEREY
NEVADA
SAN LUIS OBISPO
Morro Bay
San Luis Obispo
SANTA BARBARA
Santa Barbara
VENTURA
Ventura
LOS ANGELES
Los Angeles
Southern California
Long Beach
ORANGE
Oceanside
SAN DIEGO
San Diego
MEXICO
Pacific Ocean
5
80
101
1
15
10
Coastal Counties
San Diego .... page 23
Orange 101
Los Angeles 153
Ventura 233
Santa Barbara 261
San Luis Obispo 291
Monterey 321
Santa Cruz 375
San Mateo 403
San Francisco 435
Marin 447
Sonoma 475
Mendocino 501
Humboldt 535
Del Norte 569

Southern California Beaches

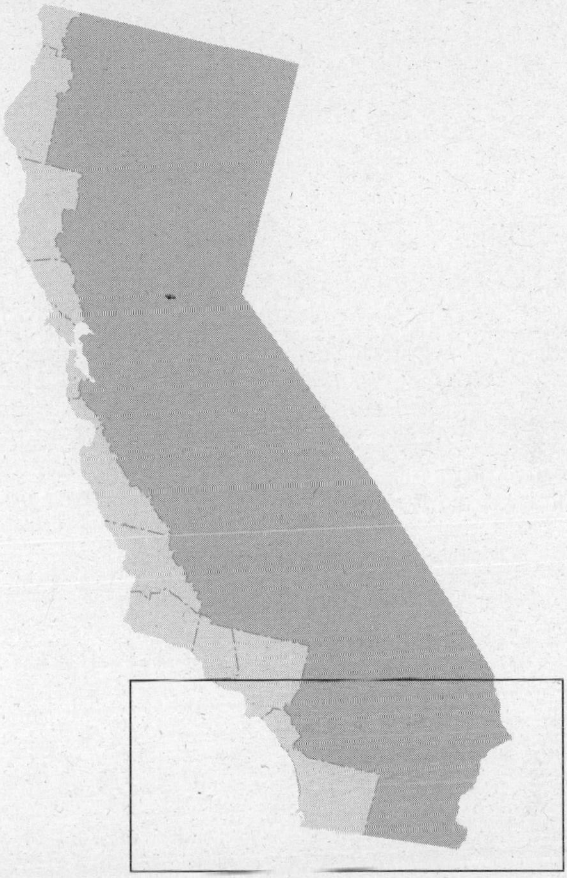

Key to the Symbols

Bike path · Camping · Food and drink · Hiking · Nude

Pier · RVs allowed · Surfing · Volleyball

Crowd Rating

sweet solitude . . . moderate crowds . . . wall-to-wall

Overall Rating

1 don't bother . . . 2 . . . 3 worth a visit . . . 4 . . . 5 beach heaven

Southern California

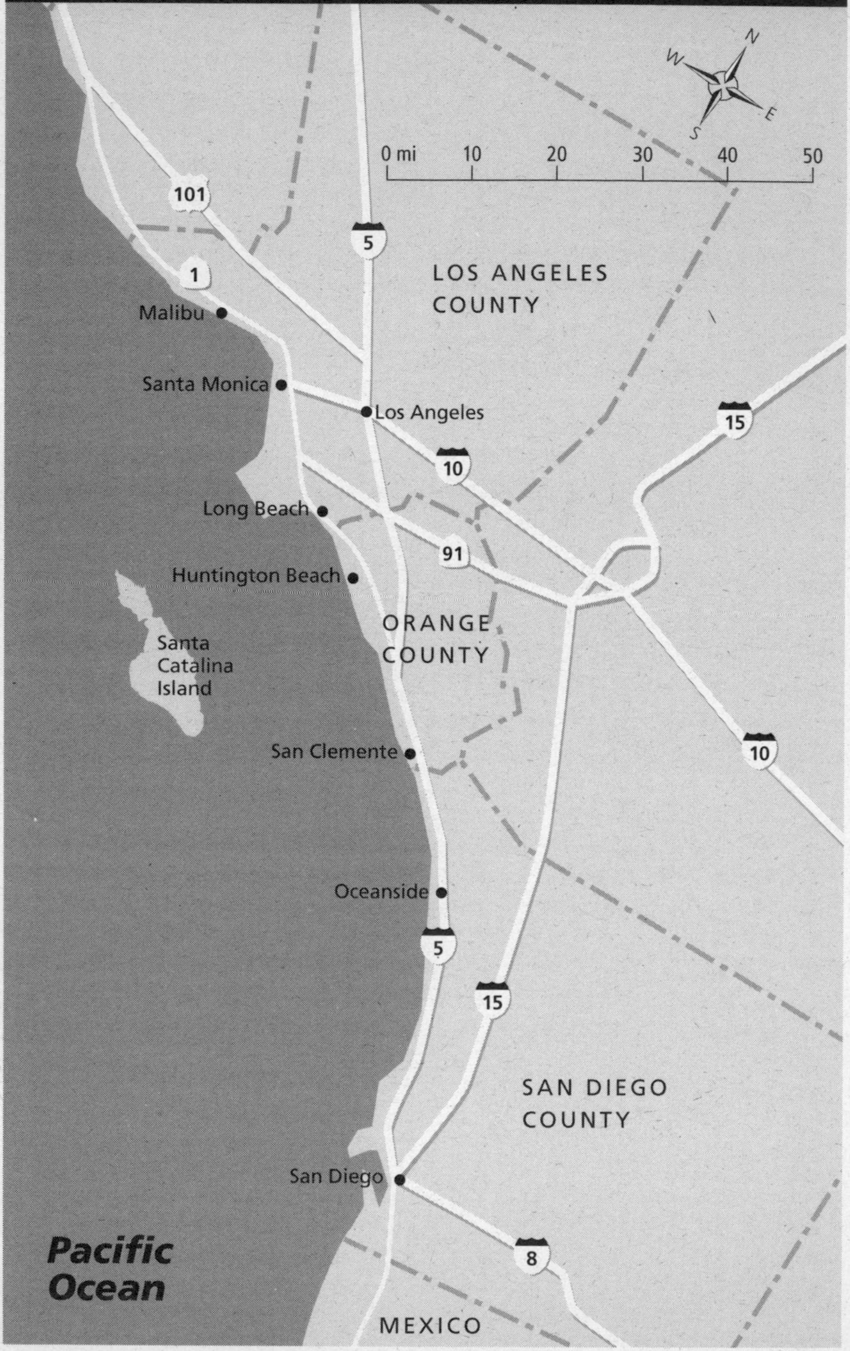

0 mi
10
20
30
40
50
N
E
S
W
101
1
5
LOS ANGELES COUNTY
Malibu
Santa Monica
Los Angeles
10
15
Long Beach
91
Huntington Beach
ORANGE COUNTY
Santa Catalina Island
San Clemente
10
Oceanside
5
15
SAN DIEGO COUNTY
San Diego
8
Pacific Ocean
MEXICO

Southern California

San Diego County

The United States of America could not have rolled out a welcome mat more inviting than San Diego County's 76 miles of beaches. From the wide-open Mexican border to the sandstone cliffs of Torrey Pines and points north, they cover a range of settings: long, wide stretches of soft sand; thin, silvery strands of hard-packed sand; rocky, hidden coves; sea caves and cliffs; bays, wetlands, and lagoons; and underwater reserves for divers. These coastal locales play host to every manner of activity that inveterate beach lovers like ourselves take for granted as American birthrights: surfing, swimming, sunbathing, biking, bird-watching, surf casting, boating, beach camping, volleyball playing, beer drinking, taco scarfing, flirting, partying.... You get the idea.

No other county in California—or in the country, for that matter—compares to San Diego County. In fact, in our eyes it is the home of the quintessential Southern California beach experience. This was symbolically brought home to us on the Fourth of July one recent summer. At *(continued on page 26)*

Coastal San Diego County's Climate

San Diego Averages

	Daily High Temp. (°F)	Daily Low Temp. (°F)	Rainfall (inches)	Relative Humidity	Sunshine (% of day)
January	65	46	1.9	52%	83%
February	66	48	1.5	52%	77%
March	66	50	1.6	60%	60%
April	68	54	0.8	67%	54%
May	70	57	0.2	62%	71%
June	71	60	0.1	67%	69%
July	75	64	0	69%	78%
August	77	66	0.1	68%	74%
September	76	63	0.1	67%	81%
October	74	58	0.3	56%	75%
November	70	52	1.2	43%	86%
December	66	47	1.7	42%	75%
Yearly Average	**70**	**55**	**9.5**	**59%**	**74%**

Source: National Weather Service data, National Oceanographic and Atmospheric Administration.

Map of San Diego County beaches—page 24

San Diego County

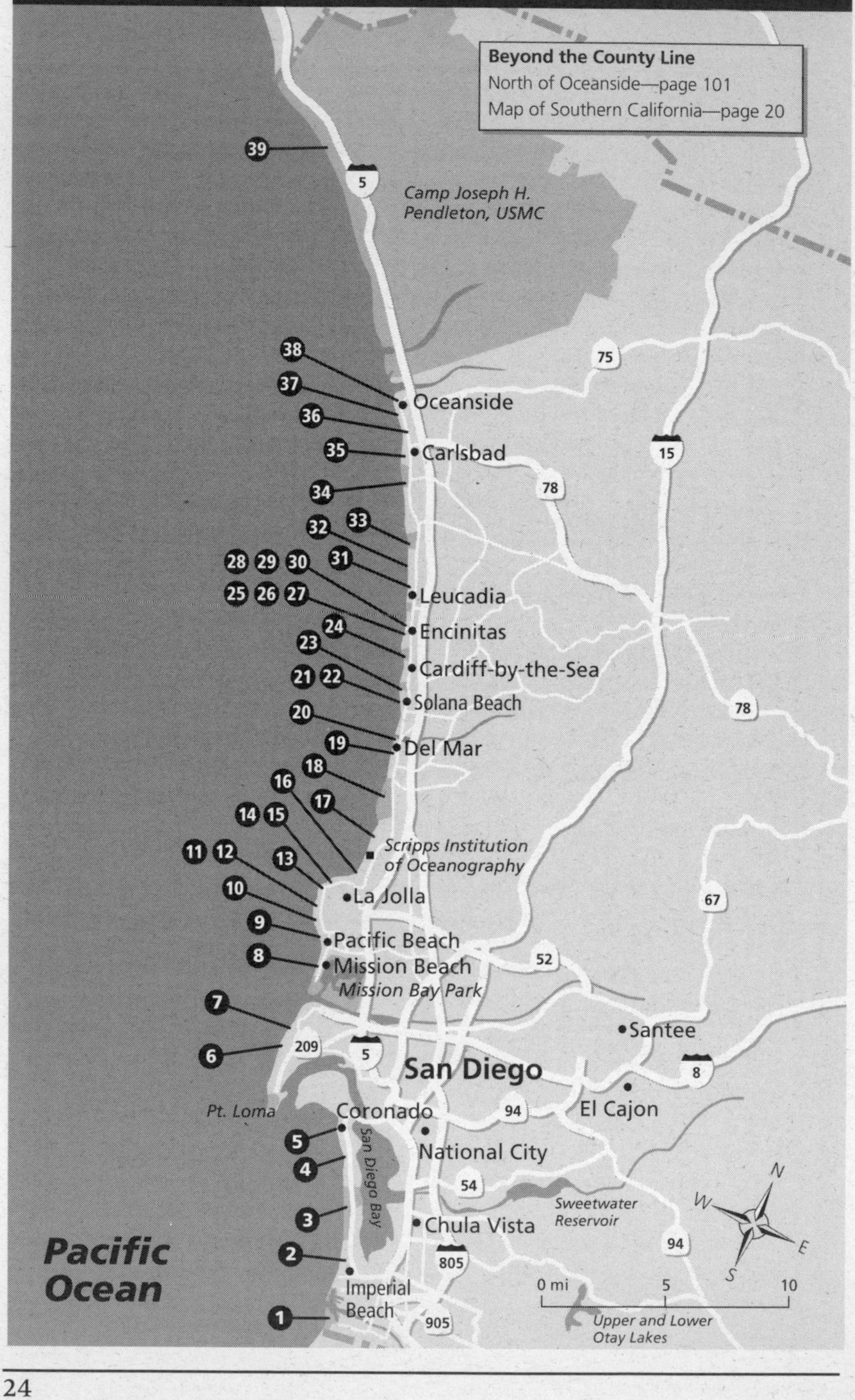

Beyond the County Line
North of Oceanside—page 101
Map of Southern California—page 20
Camp Joseph H. Pendleton, USMC
Oceanside
Carlsbad
Leucadia
Encinitas
Cardiff-by-the-Sea
Solana Beach
Del Mar
Scripps Institution of Oceanography
La Jolla
Pacific Beach
Mission Beach
Mission Bay Park
Santee
San Diego
El Cajon
Pt. Loma
Coronado
National City
San Diego Bay
Sweetwater Reservoir
Chula Vista
Imperial Beach
Pacific Ocean
Upper and Lower Otay Lakes
0 mi
5
10
N
W
E
S
5
75
15
78
67
52
209
8
94
54
805
905

San Diego County Beaches

Map of Southern California—page 20

(continued from page 23) midnight, on some inexplicable impulse, we found ourselves wandering out to Windansea Beach in La Jolla. The surfers had all gone to their favorite dive bars and overcrowded apartments, but the waves continued to roar. On a nearby jut of sand, a young couple was interfacing. We sat on a stony ledge, inhaling huge draughts of fine, salt-sprayed air while staring at the dark, endlessly churning sea. It could have been the setting for everything from *Endless Summer* to more sixties flicks than you could shake a beach blanket at. *Whoosh, splash, boom, roar.* The waves kept coming, and we continued breathing the briny brew. This single short trip to Windansea Beach invigorated us for days thereafter, like a contact high with a vast, saline Fountain of Youth.

Key to the Symbols

Bike path · Camping · Food and drink · Hiking · Nude

Pier · RVs allowed · Surfing · Volleyball

Crowd Rating

sweet solitude . . . moderate crowds . . . wall-to-wall

Overall Rating

1 don't bother . . . 2 . . . 3 worth a visit . . . 4 . . . 5 beach heaven

Border Field State Park

Location: On the California-Mexico border. From Interstate 5, take the Dairy Mart Road exit and follow the signs.

Depending on how you look at it, **Border Field State Park** is either the beginning or the end of California. Some folks might say Border Field is the end of the world, and not because it's hard to find. In fact, Border Field is incredibly easy to find, which is part of the problem. The people who find it most frequently are illegal aliens—that is, immigrants who either scale the 10-foot fence that separates the U.S. from Mexico or brazenly wade out beyond the restraining wall at low tide and walk into the U.S., as if they were beachcombing.

For those fun-seekers who visit Border Field legally, this makes for an intriguing sociological study but a bummer of a beach trip. The effect is one of stark dichotomies: the lulling sound of crashing waves...suddenly interrupted by the screech of an Immigration Service paddy wagon lurching from behind a clump of dried grass to snag another undocumented alien. Another contrast: a gorgeous stretch of wild, windswept sand surrounded by wildflowers, marshlands, and jagged geological formations...dotted with signs warning that swimming is prohibited indefinitely due to raw sewage spills washing northward from Tijuana.

Yes, Border Field State Park is a party pooper. The area, however, is not without historic and environmental interest. The border, which runs from Border Field east for 1,952 miles, was established on October 10, 1849, the date California was officially whisked away from Mexico to become a part of the United States. A cement monument to this event stands nearby, and informative placards are strewn about the park that recount both nations' histories and prehistories (one rather curiously refers to Native Americans as "the first emigrants"). Other signs offers tidbits about the ancient geological uplift that created this ruggedly beautiful beach and the wildlife that presumably still roams it.

Unfortunately, the words on most of the markers have been worn away by sun, sand, and surf. The spray-painted Spanish graffiti on the walls is more legible. More overwhelming than anything nature might devise is the sprawl of Tijuana, which is separated from the park by only a fence. Tijuana is a city twice the size of San Diego that is growing at an alarming rate. It is the land of last hope for rural Mexicans who come looking for work or wait until dark to make the illegal stroll north.

A flying saucer–shaped bullring looms less than 100 yards away and cries of "*Olé*" are heard on weekends, as another beast bites the dust for the sadistic pleasure of man. Across from the bullring, less than 50 feet from where we stood, a group of sunbaked men passed a bagged bottle among themselves, staring back at, or perhaps through, us. The overall feeling we got was that an entire nation had spread its buttocks against the fence that separates it from its neighbor. ***(continued on page 30)***

Border Field State Park

Location: Take the Dairy Mart Road exit off Interstate 5 near the Mexican border. Follow signs to the end of Monument Road.

Parking: $4 entrance fee per vehicle if kiosk is attended; free otherwise.

Hours: Wednesday through Sunday, 10 AM to 5 PM.

Facilities: Rest rooms, picnic tables, and fire pits.

Contact: For beach information, contact the Tijuana Estuary Visitors Center at (619) 575-3613.

See number 1 on page 24.

On the Border

All the issues that plague California have been compressed onto the beaches near the Mexican border. You name it, they got it: illegal immigration, sewage disposal, farm runoff, ocean contamination, shoddy development, erosion, vandalism, overpopulation, psychotic behavior, litter, language barriers....

We learned this on a visit to Border Field State Park and the Tijuana River Estuary. The trip started out promisingly enough, with green irrigated fields of sod bordering Dairy Mart and Monument Roads and rugged, dry hills in the distance suggesting a raw, lunarlike landscape. It did not take long for things to turn nasty.

Hand-lettered signs soon sprang up on the side of Monument Road as we headed west toward the ocean. One announced: "Environmentalists Destroy Human Lives." And another, farther along, trumpeted: "Welcome to No Man's Land. Environmentalists. Illegal Aliens. Smuggling. Flooding. Sewage. Garbage." A series of signs, arrayed Burma Shave–style down Monument Road, blamed environmentalists for hurting the economy, for the suffering of "desperate animals caught in the mud," and for the drowning deaths of 24 illegals in the estuary. At the bottom of one such sign were spray-painted the ominous words: "Remember Waco, Texas."

On the Mexican side, shoddily built villas could be seen dotting the dry brown hillsides, some clinging treacherously to their high perches. Police vehicles could also be seen, secreted behind clumps of dry weeds and dirt. Like enormous metal insects, the four-by-four paddy wagons lie in wait for fence-hoppers who might try their luck a little inland from the more popular Border Field State Park. This entire end of the U.S.–Mexico boundary is the most sievelike in the country, accounting for nearly one-third of all illegal alien arrests. As many as 80,000 arrests are made in the peak months of April and May, when seasonal employment lures migrant workers.

To the north, along the vandalized barbed-wire boundaries of the estuary, more signs are seen: "Contaminated with Sewage. Keep Out." Things did not improve at the beach. The state park ranger who took our fare was as beat as the scene around him. "Do you ever get busy at the park?" we asked, cheerful naifs that we are.

"We used to," he said, ever so slowly, "but not no more."

Then he sighed and, as if cutting off further questions, said, "It's a long story.... It has nothing to do with the park."

Indeed, the parkland at first seemed a splendid setting and didn't gibe with his defeated manner. Then we pulled into the parking lot. It was filled with vehicles sporting either Mexican license plates or no plates at all. One group of Mexicans wearing cowboy hats had completely disassembled a car, leaving the engine's parts strewn about on the asphalt. They didn't seem to be in any hurry to reassemble them.

Mexican radio stations blared from every direction like a musical EKG. The stares we received were as cold as the beers being tilted back every few seconds. The families ate food from plastic bags, bickered and laughed, and fell asleep on the grass and walls, hands resting on well-sated stomachs. Screaming packs of kids were running everywhere—none, curiously, ventured down to the ocean, where the waves seemed much more enticing than the hot asphalt. Pregnant women fanned themselves with the lids of take-out fried-chicken boxes. One young couple groped passionately in the grass while an infant lay napping beside their intertwined bodies. At this point, we realized we weren't at the beach. We were in a documentary film.

We asked one of the friendly tykes why he wasn't playing in the ocean.

"I used to but not no more."

"Why? Too cold?" No answer. "Smell bad?"

Big smile and a nod. Then holding his nose, he spewed, "Pee-yoo!"

Indeed, we soon learned, the ocean waters for several miles north of the border smell bad most of the time. The Mexican sewage treatment plants can't keep up with the load from the burgeoning population and periodically the system breaks down, sending raw sewage into the surrounding Tijuana River Estuary and, ultimately, into the ocean. This creates what the Mexicans call *aguas negras* (black waters)—as much as 20 million gallons of it in a single day.

Then the San Diego health officials step in and declare the water unfit for swimming until tests prove otherwise. Bingo. End of summer vacation for anyone within 50 miles. And to treat the spills costs $500,000 a month in San Diegans' tax money.

This happens so frequently that it has become a running joke (or a sore one) to San Diegans. A local cartoonist shows Uncle Sam hugging a Mexican government official, then making an announcement to the city: "Our friends in Tijuana have decided to wait until after July 4th to have their annual multi-million gallon sewage spill!" The sewage issue has been forthrightly addressed by a new "bi-national" border sewage treatment plant, which began operating in 1995 but won't be complete until 1998. Whether it will be able to handle the increasing demands of a growing border population is still unclear. Imperial Beach is holding its nose until the verdict comes in.

And every day the region continues to face the larger issues of overpopulation and immigration. Random immigration checkpoints are administered not just at the border, but on Interstate 5 throughout San Diego County and into Los Angeles. Like speed traps, the police cordon off the highway. As traffic slows, they peer inside each vehicle, and any that look suspicious are waved off to the side, where immigration agents check them out. This is another issue, like contamination of the estuary, where everybody has his or her own solution. The most controversial is the construction of an unscalable, impenetrable wall along the southern border of San Diego County.

In the seven years between our visits, things have gotten worse at Border Field. We had thought that was impossible. Now we think they will get worse still.

(continued from page 27)

While we were combing the coast in 1994, the biggest issue in the California senate and gubernatorial campaigns was immigration. So flogged and flummoxed has the state become by this that consensus is impossible, and mere discussion of the matter makes for an unpleasant experience. So does a visit to Border Field, sad as it is to report.

One of the few pleasant pastimes that can be enjoyed at Border Field is riding horses. Horses can be rented and ridden on designated trails in the adjoining Tijuana River National Estuarine Reserve. Several stables along Monument Road rent out horses. Hilltop Stable (Monument Road, 619-428-5441) offers serviceable mounts at reasonable rates of $4 per hour, with the third hour free.

For More Information

Call Border Field State Park at (619) 428-3034, or write the California Department of Parks and Recreation, P.O. Box 942896, Sacramento, CA 94296-0001.

Imperial Beach

Location: Directly south of San Diego, via Interstate 5, taking the Palm Avenue or Coronado Avenue exit.
Population: 26,500
Area Code: 619 **Zip Code:** 91932

Forget Border Field. America really begins at Imperial Beach, the southernmost beach town in California. Here you'll find the southernmost shopping malls, condos, homes, lawns, burger stands, pool halls, libraries, baseball fields, running and bike paths, skateboard ramps, and "Born in the USA" T-shirts. You'll also find a modest-sized community of mostly middle-class and mostly legal citizens trying hard as heck to ignore the shanty-town presence of Tijuana, so close by that on smog-free days the bullring is visible from the beach.

It is perhaps more accurate to say that Southern California begins at Imperial Beach, because everything here seems tailor-made for summer fun: a beautiful wide beach that runs for 2.5 miles, a long and sturdy pier, a healthy surf, an army of surfers, a 17-man lifeguard crew, nearly year-round sun, and pleasant natural backdrops to both the east (distant hills and mesas) and the south (Tijuana Slough National Wildlife Refuge)—which brings welcome visual relief *and* ensures that the town will not get much bigger. On top of that, folks here make a concerted effort to sell the town as a placid resort, billing it as the "South Coast Hide Away."

Yes, Imperial Beach has it all. So why the hangdog expressions?

Well, this is the resort beach most impacted by the sins of Tijuana. In 1993, for instance, the beach was closed for 193 days due to sewage contaminants in the ocean. To book a room or rent an apartment in advance here would seem a risky venture, though matters improved in the feces-covered-sand department in 1994 and 1995. Things might even be brighter in 1996 and 1997, as a campaign by a number of local community governments, led by the mayor of Imperial Beach, has implemented an aggressive sand-replenishment program on the beaches of southern San Diego County. This, they hope, will assure not only cleaner sand but more of it. No more encouraging words could be heard, in our opinion.

If you catch Imperial Beach at the right time, you are in for some pleasant surprises. The surf here is among the most challenging in San Diego County. Surfers—male and female, young and old—vie for space near the pier, which provides an excellent vantage point from which spectators can view their prodigious skills. After one particularly nice run by a blond surfer—during which he did several 360-degree spin moves to keep abreast of his chosen wave—the grandfatherly chap next to us shouted down to him, "Good show!" The surfer shrugged and said, "No, I blew it!" But he was obviously pleased someone had noticed. We soon realized that half the excitement, for spectators and surfers alike, was the wonderment over how these brave souls kept from cracking their crania on the pier's barnacle-covered underpinnings.

The downside to this churning surf is its dangers to the uninitiated. Despite the fact that the beach was closed for half of 1993, the lifeguards in Imperial Beach made 455 rescues (there were no drownings). The only beach in the county with more rescues was South Mission Beach (with 615), which was open every day that year. In addition to powerful waves, rip currents, some extending out as far as three-quarters of a mile, are capable of pulling even the strongest swimmer under. This only adds to the appeal for surfers and lifeguards, who are often one and the same. As one lifeguard said, "We are one of the last truly open beaches. You can surf anywhere."

As long as the refuse stays put in Tijuana, that is.

Beaches

Two main drags, Palm and Coronado Avenues, lead to the ocean. These parallel routes are the commercial corridors for vacationers and day-tripping inlanders, a hodgepodge of liquor stores, taco huts, shacklike bars, pool halls, and mobile homes. Also in the mix are new condos and apartments trying to gentrify the flotsam out of existence, but they seem to have to resort to outrageous enticements ("First three months rent free") to sell their upscale wares. Seacoast Drive parallels the ocean.

The beach at **Imperial Beach** was extended a few years back by a massive infusion of sand from nearby San Diego Bay. Dredgings were deposited in front of what was once a seawall and a few rocks, leaving the town with a wide sandy swath of brownish gold suitable for framing a beach towel (with you as the reclining sunscreened seminude). At the center of the beach is the pier. Though architecturally sound, sections of the pier have been periodically destroyed by rough surf.

Swimming can be exciting but treacherous. To add to the thrill, the ocean floor drops off dramatically where the dredged sand ends. Advisories are issued daily and, on particularly rough days, lifeguards will temporarily suspend swimming.

Bunking Down

The nicest place to stay in Imperial Beach is at its southern end, a finger of land that lies between the Tijuana Slough National Wildlife Refuge and the ocean, where well-tended vacation homes and apartments abound. When the water quality improves once and for all, this will be the place to come for weeklong rentals. Otherwise, the best and beachiest motel is the **Seacoast Inn** (800 Seacoast Drive, 424-5183, $$), just north of the pier. It is the

Imperial Beach

Location: In the town of Imperial Beach. Take the Palm Avenue or Coronado Avenue exit off Interstate 5 and continue west into Imperial Beach. The beach runs along Seacoast Drive from Palm to Encanto Avenues.

Parking: Metered lot and street parking.

Hours: Open 24 hours.

Facilities: Lifeguards, rest rooms, and showers.

Contact: For beach information, call the Imperial Beach Lifeguard Station at (619) 423-8328.

See number 2 on page 24.

very essence of what we conceive a beach motel to be. It faces a wide beach, and if the ocean's too rough, cold, or polluted, they have a baby lima-shaped pool ringed with palm trees out back. Beyond this, a string of budget motels lines the Interstate 5 off-ramps, with rooms going for bottom-dollar prices, often as low as $30. But who wants to hear the drone of cars all night when, for a few dollars more, you can hear the ocean roar?

Coastal Cuisine

Close to the ocean is a welcome addition to the seafood scene, **Brendory's By the Sea** (710 Seacoast Drive, 423-3991, $$). It's a small local chain, more in line with the leaner, "liter" fare favored by the belly-conscious. Brendory's has a slightly upscale tone, with a good lunch menu of salads, sandwiches, and, best of all, barbecue with homemade cornbread. We didn't have to wander far to find two tolerable

Tough Times on the Tijuana River Estuary

As you watch any of the 340 species of birds that have been spotted in the Tijuana River Valley, you'd never know that a raging controversy runs through the beautiful estuary. The Tijuana River Estuary is an integral part of California's remaining coastal wetlands, 90 percent of which have been lost to dredging, development, and pollution. More pertinent to this densely populated area, the Tijuana River National Estuarine Reserve (which also encompasses the Tijuana Slough National Wildlife Refuge to the north) is a vital natural buffer between the urban behemoths of Tijuana and San Diego. Located between Border Field State Park and Imperial Beach, it is among the last wetlands in San Diego County. First, let's define a few terms:

- An *estuary* is a coastal marine area, usually—but not always—a river that is alternately bathed by fresh water (through rain and river flow) and salt water (from the ocean's tides).
- *Wetlands* refer to land surfaces inundated with water all or part of the time. They are a rich haven for birds, mammals, and fish. As a placard at the nearby Border Field State Park says: "Two-thirds of all fish and shellfish found in coastal waters spend part of their lives in estuaries like this one."
- An *estuarine reserve* is a designation by the federal government that permanently protects an estuary. It is not a park, per se, but a reserve—land set aside and protected in perpetuity.

Most of the Tijuana River runs through Mexico, draining 1,700 square miles. The final five miles of the river cuts across the U.S. border and snakes through San Diego County, where it meets the ocean. Those five miles and the 3,000 acres of federal and private land drained by it have been battled over as intensely as any five miles of the western front in World War I.

The 3,000 acres are owned by private parties, the city of San Diego, the county of San Diego, the state of California, and the federal government, which administers

 Map of San Diego County beaches—page 24

taco huts: **Gustavo's Tacos II** (805 Seacoast Drive, 423-3031, $) and **El Tapatio's** (260 Palm Avenue, 423-3443, $). Both establishments sent us hat-dancing out the door, happy that for under $4 we each had a combination plate with taco, burrito, rice and beans, chips, and soda. The meat was shredded and the hot sauce volcanic. And if we wanted, we could have ordered some, according to one sign, "Foot to Go."

Night Moves

Beer joints and pool halls line Palm and Coronado Avenues. **Ye Olde Plank Inn** (24 Palm Avenue, 423-5976) is the most inviting and beach-bum-friendly of the lot.

For More Information

Contact the Imperial Beach Chamber of Commerce, 600 Palm Avenue #221, Imperial Beach, CA 91932; (619) 424-3151.

the majority of it (2,531 acres). Each has an idea about how best to save the estuary from the many slings and arrows constantly hurled at it, including raw sewage, agricultural runoff, flood from winter rains, drought, vandalism, and poaching.

In the grand laissez-faire manner that defines Southern California's real estate cartel, the private landowners blame the bureaucrats for the ills that have befallen the area. This attitude is usually couched in terms of "all those much-needed jobs that are lost because of the evil environmentalists who are playing God." The environmentalists, in turn, blame the Mexican bureaucrats. The tourists don't blame anyone because they stopped coming here years ago.

Regardless of who did what to whom and why, everyone agrees that some sort of intervention is needed to protect the reserve. Unclear on what sort of intervention is best? So are the experts. Meanwhile, each night the cat-and-mouse game between cops and illegals goes on in the shrubbery, as does the dumping of chemicals and sewage. Somehow the birds and the bees and the fish and the fleas try to make the best of it.

All this is a double crying shame because the best way to see the estuary is on foot, without the extra political baggage of the ongoing dispute. To help with this, a free walker's guide to the Tijuana River National Estuarine Reserve is available from the Southwest Wetlands Interpretive Association (P.O. Box 575, Imperial Beach, CA 92032; 619-435-5184). This useful tool reveals the lay of the land from footpaths and horse trails to hitching posts and overlooks. We recommend a look-see at this wonderful, threatened spot to anyone concerned about coastal ecology. There is no better learning lab than the Tijuana River Estuary. Here you will discover the difference between mudflats, tidal sloughs, uplands, riverbeds, and low, middle, and high marshes. Then there are the hundreds of species of plants and animals that live here. One of the tips in the walker's guide should be mandatory etiquette at every beach in the world: "Feel free to pick up as much litter as you like!"

San Diego

Location: 20 miles north of the Mexican border, along Interstate 5.
Population: 1,150,000 **Area Code:** 619
Zip Codes: 92101 through 92109

A thousand years ago, the land on which San Diego now stands was a paradise inhabited by the Kumeyaay Indians. They thrived along the bountiful waters of this big bay, one of the largest natural harbors in the world. With Point Loma to the west, fish- and wildlife-rich marshlands to the south, and protective mountains to the east, they must have thanked the gods many times for their good fortune.

Of course, fortunes like this don't remain secret for long. Almost 500 years ago, the Portuguese explorer Juan Rodríguez Cabrillo stumbled upon the Kumeyaays' bay. The last of the conquistadors, Cabrillo came in search of gold. Instead, he found this perfect harbor and claimed it for his royal patrons. Then he sailed away. This one quick visit earned Cabrillo the distinction of having "discovered" the West Coast.

Cabrillo brought his knowledge of the Kumeyaays' paradise back to Europe with him. Even so, it would not be until July 16, 1769, that another European would settle here. On that date, the Franciscan mystic-priest Father Junipero Serra established the town of San Diego de Alcala along this bay, the first European settlement on the West Coast. More a visionary than a humble padre, the charismatic Serra inaugurated an ambitious plan for his town, blending a military battalion and a Catholic parish that would become known as the "mission system." His "mission" was clear enough—to convert the heathen natives—and his "system" eventually spanned 21 settlements, a network that subjugated the native populations of California.

Serra's recruitment method was known as "the cross or the sword." By the time the Spanish overlords were finished, the Kumeyaay had been left either dead by the sword or dependent on the mercy of the cross. Today, Serra's settlement, called Old Town, stands in testament to his achievement. Though it's mostly a shopping mall set among period buildings, Old Town is home to Serra's original mission and chapel, where mass is still held every Sunday.

San Diego remained a relatively quiet town until more than a century ago, when the gold Cabrillo craved was found in the mountains to the east. A boomtown ensued, and with it a sudden rise in real estate prices and crime. The railroad arrived soon after, further inflating land speculation. A fast-talking Easterner named Alonzo Horton purchased the entire waterfront and laid out a grid of streets upon which the business district was built. Even today, Horton's "new town" looks new, dominated by nondescript skyscrapers. A plaza stands in tribute to Horton—another upscale shopping and hotel area, with an art museum adding a note of culture.

Ninety years ago, the U.S. Navy landed here, building shipyards and installations on every available scrap of oceanfront land and creating a gray military presence that dominated the architecture of San Diego until recent times. Because of the harbor, San Diego soon became the permanent base for the nation's largest West Coast fleet, numbering well over 100,000 personnel. This, of course, attracted private military contractors such as General Dynamics, who subsisted on the government tab for years. It and many other private contractors are now downsizing, creating a negative turn in San Diego's fortunes. When we visited, 1,900 employees had just been let go by General Dynamics, and Convair had released a few hundred more. Now Convair is down to 1,922 employees, compared with a one-time peak of 46,859.

 Map of San Diego County beaches—page 24

In some ways, San Diego is still a navy town, but it is looking elsewhere for its identity. And, as the seventh largest metropolitan area in the country and with a bayfront that is the envy of the world, it certainly has the resources to draw upon. In fact, the area has swelled like a dry sponge dropped in a tidepool. Many people are retiring here, while others sail in as part of the leisure-boat crowd. Throughout the 1980s, the city received 30,000 new residents annually and boasted almost 30 million visitors a year.

There is a reason for this prodigious migration. The weather in San Diego is ideal for anyone who doesn't crave variety. Temperatures year-round rarely stray from the seventies. It seldom rains in the summer, and when it does, according to a local resident, people stare at the heavens as if witnessing a solar eclipse. (The winter rains sometimes make up for this, causing occasional flooding of the Tijuana River and other area waterways.) Within easy reach are beautiful mountains and unique desert communities (including one by the intriguing name of Plaster City). There are zoos, museums, and theaters galore. And, of course, there are 70 miles of ocean beaches in the county.

San Diegans love their city. Almost everyone we met in San Diego was so upbeat and friendly we thought they were hirelings of the

Dropping the Population Bomb on California

Along the southern coast, on rest-room walls and in other public spaces, we noticed a lot of graffiti. Among the ivylike tagging we kept seeing this same message: "Stop Breeding." Though somewhat overstated, we couldn't help but understand the frustration that would drive someone to such extremes. Indeed, in California, the population bomb has hit with a resounding and furious fallout. And it is in your face if you look for it at the beaches of Southern California. The numbers say it all:

- California's population has tripled since 1950. Given current trends, it will double in 25 years.
- Even without illegal immigration, California is the chosen home of 35 percent of the nation's legal immigrants. Between 1980 and 1990, Los Angeles alone had two million legal immigrants, one million of whom were from Mexico and El Salvador. Los Angeles County is now 40 percent Hispanic and 10 percent Asian.
- Of the state's 32 million residents, Southern California is home to almost half of them, and 90 percent live within 100 miles of the beach.
- Due to population growth and ever expanding private development, the state's wetlands have almost vanished. The state animal, the grizzly bear, is gone. The state ranks first in the U.S. in the number of endangered and threatened species.
- Air pollution from urban areas costs state farmers $100 million in lost crops annually.
- Between 1971 and 1991, the number of motor vehicles in California rose from 12 million to 21 million; vehicle-driven miles rose 146 percent, and gasoline usage doubled.

Skeptics in Paradise

Despite the rosy prose of San Diego's tourist brochures, "America's Finest City" is beginning to show some wear and tear. Part of this is due to circumstances beyond San Diego's control—illegal immigration, for example, saps the local tax base to pay for things like the 4,100 babies delivered each year to Mexican women who sneak over the border in their ninth month. The crush of humanity on both sides of this border also contributes to the sprawl that never ends. The land boom in San Diego, in fact, has spawned a religion of growth, with 30 pages in the Yellow Pages devoted to real estate. The result: new condos, new faux adobes, new fast-food franchises, new resorts as far as the eye can see (which isn't far on smoggy days). And still there's a purported housing shortage, which an army of homeless would seem to verify.

Yet despite its reputation for pro-growth, head-in-the-sand conservatism, San Diego is an enlightened city in many ways. The rumblings of healthy skepticism and honest discourse about urban issues can be found everywhere. Perhaps the oddest place we found them was in the *Golden Triangle Metropolitan*, a local publication devoted to "a business lifestyle," wherein developers and CEOs are regularly profiled as "visionaries," and their high-rise buildings and planned communities are depicted as acts of the gods. In a column called "Golden Triangle Dreamer," several average citizens were asked: "If you could have one wish for the city, what would it be?" Here are some random responses:

- "I wish we had more of a village feeling."
- "I wish I didn't have to drive everywhere."
- "I wish the city was hipper."
- "I wish the city had more soul."
- "I wish we had more public art."
- "I wish we could get out of our cars."
- "Everything is part of a development or a mall.... It's sterile."

These answers fly directly in the face of what the editors perhaps intended. It's the "business lifestyle" they suck up to that worships the gleaming chrome, mirrored-glass, and exhaust-plumed asphalt that defines the "new" San Diego, as created by its urban "visionaries."

But the unanimous response from those who are forced to reside in the communities built by such visionaries is one of frustration and a desire to see cities and beach resorts become more livable and human scaled. We couldn't agree more.

 Map of San Diego County beaches—page 24

Chamber of Commerce, ticking off local attractions like auctioneers at a tobacco warehouse. So eager to please are San Diegans that they have adopted all of the following titles for their town: Sports Town USA, Golf Land USA, America's Finest City, California's Oldest City, The Place Where California Began, California's Plymouth Rock.

Even areas of dubious history or merit are trumped up into Disneyesque attractions, carrying touristy names such as Seaport Village, Gaslamp Quarter, the Embarcadero, New Town, and Horton Plaza. Then there are the genuinely worthwhile attractions like Balboa Park and about 90 museums. All of the happy interfacing that takes place here requires a maze of superhighways. These interstates intertwine across the scorched brown terrain like seaweed, giving a novice driver headaches, twinges of anxiety, and watery eyes. (You may be told otherwise, by the locals, but there is smog in San Diego.)

The pace of life here is deceptive. Though leisurely on the surface, the city positively throbs with an undercurrent of manic activity, with the main contestant in the high-stress sweepstakes being the automobile. Cars are in constant motion, glittering like metallic bugs in the dry heat as they roll along the freeways. Bicycles, in-line skates, skateboards, unicycles, and even pogo sticks hound the heels of sedate pedestrians. Joggers blip past the harborfront. Sailboats and yachts cut through the bay like stilettos. The race is on among the new blood of San Diego, even if you can't figure out where the finish line is or what you get if you win. Perhaps an eternal round of golf.

Once a novice driver gets acclimated to the pace, the lure of San Diego is obvious. It starts at the water, with its appealing and ever expanding harborfront. Over the past decades, separate islands (Shelter, Harbor, Vacation, and Fiesta) have been constructed from materials dredged from the bay bottom. These are meticulously planned, manicured, sculpted, and coifed pockets of wealth, metaphorically breaking away from the once paradisiacal city that is now beset with many of the urban problems facing its nemesis, Los Angeles (about which San Diego seems to suffer a chronic hang-up). If you can swing it, the best way to visit downtown San Diego is by boat. There are 2,000 berths on Shelter Island and 1,000 more on Harbor Island, and San Diego now gears its big beautiful bay to wealthy boat owners.

Because our yacht was repossessed in a previous lifetime, we spent less time on the bay—except for a meal, a stroll along the Embarcadero's Marina Park, and a visit to Balboa Park—and drove straight to the beaches of San Diego. This is where we encourage our readers to start and finish their experiences of this remarkable city. Each of San Diego's beach communities—Coronado, Point Loma, Ocean Beach, Mission Beach, Pacific Beach—is given a chapter in the following pages. Each has its own unique flavor. Each is worth a separate summer vacation. We only wish we had additional lifetimes to devote to that pursuit.

For More Information

Contact the San Diego Visitors Information Center, 11 Horton Plaza, San Diego, CA 92101; (619) 236-1212; the Greater San Diego Chamber of Commerce, 402 West Broadway, San Diego, CA 92101; (619) 232-0124; or the San Diego Visitor Information Center, 2688 East Mission Bay Drive, San Diego, CA 92109; (619) 276-8200. The last of these is the closest to the beaches.

Coronado

Location: Just southwest of metropolitan San Diego, via the San Diego-Coronado Bridge. Silver Strand Boulevard (Highway 75) and Ocean Boulevard run alongside the ocean. The main beach is Coronado City Beach, located west of Ocean Boulevard.
Population: 27,000
Area Code: 619 **Zip Code:** 92118

Coronado gleams with a gilded, moneyed loveliness that stands in stark contrast to the border-town blues of nearby Imperial Beach. Driving north from Imperial Beach along Silver Strand Boulevard, you pass from a land of no money to a land of new money. First you notice the yachts that fill the Glorietta Bay Marina, their long masts standing as tall and straight as a fistful of pencils jammed in a cup. Then you realize that the price of gas has jumped 25 cents a gallon in the space of 10 miles. Finally, turning onto Orange Avenue, which leads into downtown Coronado, you roll by a palatial old resort hotel and rows of opulent private homes fronted by lawns that are better tended than country-club putting greens.

The rich have perched alongside the naval air base on this spit of land enfolding San Diego Bay. They have erected high-rise condos, private estates, and tropical gardens where flowers of flaming crimson add a splash of color to what would be, in its natural state, an arid landscape. Coronado is a verdant garden-by-the-sea, an oasis made possible by sprinkler systems and big money. The story of Coronado's founding is emblematic of how it went in the glory days of California's birth: some wealthy guy would get an idea, and all of a sudden a desert would magically become a Technicolor resort in year-round bloom. Coronado's past is linked with some of the wealthiest figures in California's history, and their presence sets a standard of luxurious living that endures to this day.

The founding fathers of Coronado were railroad tycoon Elisha Babcock, Jr., and piano magnate H. L. Story. The two spent time hunting on the wild, majestic Coronado peninsula, enjoying the place so much that they eventually switched their quarry from rabbits and quail to tourist dollars. The pair formed a syndicate, the Coronado Beach Company, and bought the entire peninsula for $110,000 in 1885. On January 12, 1887, ground was broken on the Hotel del Coronado, which they envisioned as a wondrous resort that would become the "talk of the Western world." Barely a year later, the "Del," as it is informally known, was open for business.

Babcock and Story were later joined in their venture by John D. Spreckels, a wealthy San Francisco–reared heir to a sugar fortune who sailed his yacht down to San Diego in 1887, dropped anchor, and essentially brought the city to life. He built the first wharves in San Diego's natural harbor, and linked the city with the outside world with the construction of the San Diego, Arizona, and Eastern Railway. He also bought newspapers, installed streetcars, and founded a bank. To his eternal credit, he ensured that the development of San Diego proceeded along pleasingly aesthetic lines, seeing to it that the city was generously laid out with parks and that the parks were planted with his favorite flowers: geraniums. His financial stake in the Del grew to the point that he bought out the other partners by the turn of the century. There have been only four other owners since Spreckels, and the Hotel del Coronado of the mid-1990s projects a casually lavish splendor, much as it did a century ago.

The centerpiece of Coronado, the Del is vast but unpretentious, a rambling, capacious, and funky-but-chic structure that's far more comfortable and inviting than your average marble-filled corporate high-rise hotel. The grounds

 Map of San Diego County beaches—page 24

are impeccably well maintained, with walkways that meander among tropical greenery and such exotica as the rare "dragon tree" (imported from China in the 1920s). The Del lives up to its top-of-the-line reputation without straining to swath its visitors in garish creature comforts. They know that merely laying out on a breezy deck in a chaise lounge, with a dog-eared paperback, an icy drink, and a gaggle of musicians tooting jazz on a small bandstand is what a vacation is all about. The code words are rest and relaxation, not tie-your-tie and hurry-hurry.

If you can afford it, Coronado is the ideal vacation town, as tourism is the only industry (unless you count retirement). There's evidence of money everywhere. Even the sand on Coronado's beaches is speckled with what looks like gold dust, glittering every time it's overwashed by a wandering wave. The feel-good feeling radiates outward from the Hotel del Coronado to the downtown area, wherein a graceful S curve carries motorists through a squeaky-clean shopping district of modestly upscale shops and restaurants along Orange Avenue. Coronado's cafés and stores service the needs of locals and tourists alike. Everyone casually strolls the sun-dappled streets in search of swimwear, surfboards, frozen yogurt, and real estate.

Continue away from the beach along Fourth Avenue and soon you'll be headed out of town via the narrow San Diego-Coronado Bridge, a breathtaking span that arches like a roller coaster. It's high enough to allow navy destroyers to pass through, and also to attract would-be jumpers, judging from the numerous signs lining the bridge that offer a phone number for suicide counseling. The naval presence is everywhere. The North Island Naval Air Station can claim to be the birthplace of naval aviation (in 1911). From its airstrip, Charles Lindbergh took off for New York, where he embarked upon his famous transatlantic flight in 1927. Today, it occupies 2,500 acres and employs 29,000 personnel. A few miles south, recruits are trained at the U.S. Naval Amphibious Base, along San Diego Bay.

Beaches

Heading north from Imperial Beach along Silver Strand Boulevard, you begin to see the pipe rooftops of Coronado Cays, clustered together so tightly that the development looks like one continuous orange roof. Along the south side of the bay is the South Bay Marine Biological Study Area, a wildlife refuge that affords visitors an upclose look at a wetland environment. A nature trail leads into the study area, where bird-watching is excellent. On the ocean side of the highway, **Silver Strand State Beach**, a long beach occupying a skinny splinter of land no more than two football fields wide, connects Imperial Beach with Coronado. Inside the park, we saw a plaque of RVs jammed together as close as possible while still allowing its occupants to open the doors. Without shade or much in the way of vegetation, it didn't look like our idea of camping fun. Being so far south, the waters here are as swimmable as any in California, from a temperature standpoint—topping off at around 70 degrees by late summer—and less swimmable than many, from a pollution standpoint. (A hearty

Coronado City Beach

4

Location: In Coronado, at Ocean Boulevard and F Avenue.

Parking: Metered street parking.

Hours: 5 AM to 11 PM.

Facilities: Lifeguards, rest rooms, picnic area, and fire rings.

Contact: For beach information, contact Coronado Recreation Services at (619) 522-7342.

See number 5 on page 24.

gracias to our neighbors to the south for the gift of untreated sewage, which flows north with the current.) On another sour note, from the beach we couldn't even see the town of Chula Vista to the east because of the obscuring haze of automotive smog rising out of San Diego.

Coronado City Beach runs for a mile from the Hotel del Coronado up to the airstrip at the North Island Naval Air Station. The beach is wide and flat, dimpled with halfhearted dunes that look like termite mounds. To our inquiring eyes, the early-summer waves were tame, and the beachgoers were similarly benign. A wall of boulders stands where the beach meets Ocean Boulevard, which has plentiful on-street parking. In Coronado, parking doesn't seem to be as horrific a problem as it does elsewhere in Southern California beach towns. On a gorgeous Saturday over a Fourth of July weekend, we found metered, on-street parking that was both available and reasonably priced at a quarter an hour. A good omen. Away from the beachfront, roughly between Sixth and Ninth Streets along Orange Avenue, free three-hour street parking can be found bordering a lovely green park.

Coronado Shores Beach fills the breach between Silver Strand and the city beach; it's accessible via the Coronado Shores condo development, and is widely used by surfers, swimmers, shell collectors, and anglers. Beaches, in fact, abound on both the bay and the ocean—28 miles of them in all. Renting a bike is a good way to check them out, as 15 miles of bike paths wind their way around Coronado and down Silver Strand.

Bunking Down

On the outdoor deck of the **Hotel del Coronado** (1500 Orange Avenue, 435-6611, $$$), a quintet was playing a mix of blues and jazz. An elderly black man was singing, "I got the blues." He had to have been the only one within earshot who did, as the crowd—a well-heeled lot who were either reclining on chaise lounges amid a sea of red-and-white umbrellas, playing tennis, or swimming in the Olympic pool—were having the time of their lives. A food kiosk offered "super burgers," "yummy hot dogs," and "healthy chicken breasts." It was quite a sight: a herd of happy people renting a small piece of paradise, basking in the midday sun. On another deck speakers blared

Coronado Shores Beach

Location: At the south end of Coronado, at the Coronado Shores condo complex, on Silver Strand Boulevard (Highway 75).

Parking: Free parking lot.

Hours: 5 AM to 11 PM.

Facilities: None.

Contact: For beach information, contact Coronado Recreation Services at (619) 522-7342.

See number 4 on page 24.

Silver Strand State Beach

Location: Between Imperial Beach and Coronado, along Silver Strand Boulevard (Highway 75).

Parking: $4 entrance fee per vehicle.

Hours: 8 AM to 8 PM PDT (8 AM to 7 PM PST).

Facilities: Lifeguards, rest rooms, showers, picnic area, and fire pits. There are 125 RV campsites. Fees are $12 to $14 per night. For camping reservations, call Destinet at (800) 444-7275.

Contact: For beach information, contact Silver Strand State Beach at (619) 435-5184.

See number 3 on page 24.

Best Reads on San Diego

The hippest people in San Diego are, of course, at the beach. Take our word for it. However, if you want to learn about what makes this city tick, politically and culturally, or if you want to find the screen times for *Endless Summer II* or learn where to go for a mug of home brew, the best reads are not the daily newspapers. No, the second largest city in California has a couple of mediocre dailies. Not only are they ultraconservative, but most of the stories—even on the front page—are from wire services. Also, compared to the local weeklies, the daily papers seem out of touch, catering to reactionary elements of the population. That's the bad news.

The good news is that the best paper in San Diego is free. It's the *San Diego Reader*, published weekly and distributed all over the beachfront. Ostensibly an entertainment tabloid, the *Reader* is thick with alternative listings, literate writing, incendiary politics, and irreverent wit. We read it cover to cover, and find rewarding beach nuggets on every page. Grab a copy on arrival and read on!

Frank Sinatra, who was belting out the words "I'm king of the hill, top of the heap, A Number One. . . ." His lyrics were reaching the right audience, bathing the upscale resort crowd in positive reinforcement.

The Del claims to be the largest full-service beachfront resort on the Pacific Coast. We've certainly seen nothing in our travels to dispute that. The resort encompasses 689 rooms, and every one is different. Built in 11 months according to plans that were not written down but improvised day by day, the hotel is one of the architectural wonders of the Western world. At the time of its construction, it was the largest electrically lighted structure outside of New York City. Four hundred rooms are originals, dating from 1888, the rest are in a wing constructed in the 1960s. By all means try to stay in the main part of the hotel. This four-story marvel rambles around in a rectangle that surrounds a green courtyard filled with palm trees and brightly colored flowers. The on-premises amenities include two giant outdoor pools, six tennis courts, a pair of volleyball nets, and a croquet green.

More impressive than the statistics is the feeling of informal, Old World elegance that fills the place. It's not in the least stuffy. Rambling around the Del is like exploring a rich old relative's mansion. If you come here, you'll no doubt be living above your station (as were we), but you'll be made to feel right at home. "You've stayed with us before?" asks a bellhop as you arrive, as if assuming you've returned to renew an old friendship. The hotel's brick-red turrets and gleaming white Victorian exterior make it look less like a hotel than a castle. Indeed, it is a national landmark that has played host to 11 U.S. presidents. Hollywood seems to like the place, too. *Some Like It Hot*, starring Marilyn Monroe, was filmed here, and the city of Oz in *The Wizard of Oz* was patterned after the Hotel del Coronado's castlelike design.

Across the street is the mission-style **El Cordova** (1351 Orange Avenue, 435-4131, $$), whose 40 rooms are actually like small apartments, tucked into stairwells around a brick courtyard of ground-level shops and restaurants. Originally a private mansion built in 1902, when the area was still relatively rural, El Cordova opened as a hotel in 1930 and is currently maintained as one of the most homey and nicely appointed suite-style hotels we've encountered in our coastal travels.

Over on the bay, the family mansion of sugar king John D. Spreckels is the centerpiece of the **Glorietta Bay Inn** (1630 Glorietta Boulevard, 435-3101, $$), a relaxed but regal inn. Many rooms overlook the bay, while others face out on gardens. Despite the quiet setting, downtown Coronado is just a few blocks away.

Coastal Cuisine

We had our first encounter with healthy, low-fat Mexican cuisine (no, that's not necessarily an oxymoron) in Coronado, courtesy of a fast-food chain called **La Salsa!** (1360 Orange Avenue, 435-7778, $). The legend printed on the beverage cups relates the chain's culinary phi-

Beach Flicks

Endless Summer II, released in 1994, didn't capture the imagination of young America the way the original *Endless Summer* did in 1966. Of course, the Beach Boys, the Ventures, and Jan and Dean had musically paved the way for Bruce Brown's first documentary on surfing, as Jack Kerouac's *On the Road* had put the car in gear before that.

Even before Brown's watershed flick, there were several attempts to capture the burgeoning surf culture on celluloid. Most were lame, stilted, and inaccurate—as are all attempts by adults to understand "youth culture." One thing these movies did accomplish—for which we're personally grateful—was to infuse California (and, to a lesser extent, Hawaii) with a sort of mythical, sirenlike power. As a result, everyone in America at one time or another has wanted to live beside a California beach. Here are capsule summaries of some of the best and worst of the beach flicks:

- *Beach Ball* (1964)—Alleged to be truly awful (sadly, we never got the chance to see it), the flick stars Edd "Kookie" Byrnes and features performances by the Walker Brothers, Jerry Lee Lewis, the Four Seasons, the Nashville Teens, the Righteous Brothers, and the Supremes. How awful could it be with that soundtrack?
- *Beach Blanket Bingo* (1965)—Erich Von Zipper makes an appearance, rescuing this Frankie Avalon and Annette Funicello farce.
- *Beach Party* (1963)—The first in the Frankie and Annette beach sagas, this had the redeeming presence of Dick Dale and the Deltones performing "Surfin' and A Swingin'" and "Secret Surfin'," plus some of the world's first surf punks, led by the notorious Erich Von Zipper. This movie also had an original plot idea: an anthropologist studies surf culture through a telescope. Hey, maybe this is where Tom Wolfe got his inspiration for *The Pump House Gang*!
- *Bikini Beach* (1964)—Here's another Frankie and Annette vehicle lacking a full tank of gas, although it turns on a potentially hilarious idea—spoofing the Beatles via a teen idol named the Potato Bug. Little Stevie Wonder performs "Fingertips."
- *Blue Hawaii* (1961)—King Elvis stars in this sandy epic, the most intriguingly perverse aspect of which is the soundtrack, boasting winners like "Slicin' Sand," "Beach Boy Blues," and "Ito Eats." (That's what the credits say, Judge!)

 Map of San Diego County beaches—page 24

losophy: "No can openers. No microwaves. No freezers. No lard. Skinless chicken. Lean steak." We ordered vegetable tacos and watched the cook carefully slice onions and tomatoes, grill and place them on a soft taco, slather on black beans and top it all off with shredded cheese, lettuce, avocado wedges, and fresh cilantro. Customers can ladle on salsa from a salsa bar, choosing from four grades of heat. While the California Burrito has got 18 grams of fat in it (it's the avocado's fault), by Mexican food standards even this is lean cuisine. La Salsa has five other franchises in the San Diego area, as well as locations in La Jolla, Pacific Beach, and

- *Catalina Caper* (1967)—Set on the island jewel off the coast of Los Angeles, this film has the all-time greatest musical concept: Little Richard singing "Scuba Party."
- *Clambake* (1967)—The King bakes some clams, makes some clams, and goes to Las Vegas afterward to make even more. He's a water-ski instructor in this one.
- *Ghost in the Invisible Bikini* (1966)—Monsters go to the beach, with Boris Karloff and Basil Rathbone trading spooky taunts amidst the beach blankets. Gnarly.
- *Girls on the Beach* (1965)—A sorority tries to raise funds with a rock concert. They want the Beatles to perform, but they have to settle for the Beach Boys, with equally happy results. It includes songs by the Beach Boys, the Crickets, and Leslie Gore.
- *How to Stuff a Wild Bikini* (1965)—Frankie, Annette, and Erich Von Zipper reprised. In this one, Frankie hires a witch doctor to keep an eye on Annette while he is in the Navy Reserves. Mickey Rooney and Buster Keaton make cameos. You figure it out.
- *It's a Bikini World* (1967)—Tommy Kirk is sort of a poor man's Frankie Avalon, which says a mouthful in itself. The Animals perform "We Gotta Get Out of This Place" (were they talking about this film?), plus "Peanut Butter and Jam" by the Gentrys.
- *Muscle Beach Party* (1964)—Frankie and Annette (again) meet bodybuilders, and the only winners are Dick Dale and the Deltones and Little Stevie Wonder.
- *Paradise-Hawaiian Style* (1966)—Although the hula dancers were required by film code to cover their navels under their hula skirts, the movie does have Elvis singing "Queenie Wahine's Papaya." For that, the world is eternally grateful.
- *Surf Party* (1964)—Set in Malibu, with songs by the Astronauts, the Routers, Bobby Vinton, and Jackie DeShannon.
- *Wild on the Beach* (1965)—The best thing about this beach-sploitation flick is the music: songs by the Astronauts ("Little Speedy Gonzalez," "Rock the World," "Snap It") and "Drum Dance" by the great Sandy Nelson.

Newport Beach, for coastal travelers craving a Mexican meal that won't send them down the road to a bypass operation.

Good-quality Mexican food in a sit-down environment is served at **Miguel's Cocina** (1351 Orange Avenue, 437-5237, $$), in the courtyard of El Cordova Hotel. They're known for their fish tacos, which we can unhesitatingly recommend. Also very good are the Calamari Torta and the Chicken Torta: sautéed squid steak and charbroiled free-range chicken, respectively, served on a torta roll with avocado, tomato, lettuce, and sauces. On the upper end of scale, the best bets for seafood are **Azzura Point** at Loews Coronado Bay Resort (4000 Coronado Bay Road, 424-4000, $$$) and **Chez Loma** (1132 Loma Avenue, 435-0661, $$$), which specialize in California seafood dishes served in a romantic setting. Chez Loma has the added advantage of history, occupying a landmark dating from 1889. More down to earth is the **Fish Company** (1007 C Avenue, $$), a fresh-fish market and outdoor café with catch-of-the-day specials and a sushi bar.

Over at the Hotel del Coronado, the **Crown-Coronet Room** (1500 Orange Avenue, 435-6611, $$$) has served kings, presidents, movie stars, sheiks, and tycoons from all over the world. It is the largest of six restaurants on the premises. The room is as long as a football field, and the ceiling is 33 feet high, making it one of the largest free-standing wood structures in North America. At ground level, the menu tends toward "progressive continental" preparations, and the panoramic view is as delectable as the food. The most formal dining room at the Del is the **Prince of Wales Room** (1500 Orange Avenue, 435-6611, $$$$). We were advised of the dress code by our bellhop: "California formal—which means coat and tie and shoes."

Night Moves

Don't come to Coronado expecting nightlife. In fact, you can expect to be free of it (sometimes this is a blessing). Your choices on the Coronado side are pretty much limited to a handful of Irish pubs along Orange Avenue. The busiest of these is **McP's Irish Pub & Grill** (1107 Orange Avenue, 435-5280), which bills itself as "Coronado's hottest night spot." It does get pretty raucous, at least for low-key Coronado.

For some serious whoopee, head over the bridge to San Diego, which will deposit you on Harbor Drive. Then proceed north to Fifth Avenue, which will lead into downtown San Diego and its bustling Gaslamp Quarter district. There you'll find an abundance of restaurants and nightclubs.

For More Information

Contact Coronado Visitor Information, 1111 Orange Avenue, Suite A, Coronado, CA 92118; (619) 437-8788. Or contact the Coronado Chamber of Commerce, P.O. Box 396, Coronado, CA 92118; (619) 435-9260. Upon request, they will send you a "Coro-Kit." (Just try not to have a "Coro-nary"!)

 Map of San Diego County beaches—page 24

Point Loma

Location: Point Loma Peninsula is attached to San Diego. To reach it, take Harbor Drive or Rosecrans Street and then follow Route 209 through the naval installations and out the peninsula to Cabrillo National Monument. Harbor Island is located off Harbor Drive, and Shelter Island can be accessed via Shelter Island Drive, off Rosecrans Street.
Population: 22,000
Area Code: 619 **Zip Code:** 92106

Heading out Point Loma from Ocean Beach, the land rises—first gently, then steeply—until you're high above the beaches and the bay. From this promontory the ocean glitters like a diamond choker and the cliffs take on a deep red hue at dusk. The area of Point Loma that enjoys these views, roughly between Ocean Beach and the Naval Ocean System Center, looks to be one of the choicest places to live in San Diego.

For a free glimpse of some of the most dramatic scenery on the peninsula, drive along Sunset Cliffs Boulevard for 1.25 miles from Point Loma Avenue to Ladera Street. The entire area is known as Sunset Cliffs Park; rather than an actual picnic-and-Frisbee green space, it is a series of parking areas and dirt trails that run along cliffs, allowing you to scuttle down like a crab to the edge of a heart-stopping drop-off. Some determined surfers and divers actually make their way down the steep paths to the sandy and rocky coves below. Be cautious, however: cliffs here are succumbing to wave-driven erosion at an alarming rate. Several parking turnouts have been closed, and signs warn visitors to keep a safe distance at others.

To continue out Point Loma, turn off Sunset Cliffs Boulevard onto Hill Street—an aptly named vertical grade—and then hang a right onto Catalina Boulevard (Route 209). This becomes Cabrillo Memorial Drive and leads all the way to Cabrillo National Monument at the tip of the peninsula. The peninsula narrows as you pass through the gates of the Naval Ocean System Center and past an endless military cemetery of small white crosses. For a fee of $4 per car, visitors are treated to a stone statue of the Spanish conquistador and explorer Juan Rodríguez Cabrillo, views over San Diego Bay and Coronado, and the Old Point Loma Lighthouse, a harbor light and coastal beacon that illuminated the coast from 1855 to 1891. A skylit visitor center houses exhibits on Cabrillo's voyage and a well-stocked bookstore and gift shop. For those up for a bit of exertion, there's a one mile (one-way) trail on the bay side and tidepools on the ocean side.

Also on the bay side, inside the crook formed where Point Loma bends south out of San Diego, are two islands created in the 1960s from dredge spoil. (That's the stuff hauled off the bay floor to deepen the channel for boat traffic.) The resulting sandbanks were christened Shelter Island and Harbor Island, and private investors poured millions into developing them, building high-rise resorts, restaurants, and yacht basins. Familiar hotel and motel chains (Sheraton, Best Western, Travelodge) have perched upon this artificial paradise. Both are primarily oriented to boaters and convention crowds, though Shelter Island has the added advantage of a sandy beach.

For More Information

Write Superintendent, Cabrillo National Monument, P.O. Box 6670, San Diego, CA 92106; (619) 557-5450.

Ocean Beach

Location: Immediately west of San Diego, Ocean Beach can be reached by taking the San Diego Freeway (Interstate 5) to the Ocean Beach Freeway (Interstate 8); continue to Sunset Cliffs Boulevard. Activity is centered around Ocean Beach City Beach, which can be accessed by turning west off Sunset Cliffs Boulevard onto any street between Niagara and Pescadero and following it to the end. Sunset Cliffs Boulevard itself hugs the coast between Point Loma Avenue and Ladera Street, where it ends.

Population: 28,000

Area Code: 619 **Zip Code:** 92107

In the medical profession, it's a maxim that a patient's condition either improves or worsens over time, which is another way of saying that nothing remains the same for very long. The same bit of wisdom holds true for beach towns. Having taken the pulse of the California coast at different times over the years, we've discovered that it's possible to come back to a community after several years' absence and sense immediately whether it's gone up or down on the community health-o-meter. Ocean Beach, happily, has gone up. During our previous visits, we found it to be a low-rent DMZ (demilitarized zone, that is) by the sea. In an earlier book, we bluntly described it as "a sub-Coney Island maze of dirty streets, litter-strewn parking lots, sun-faded storefronts, and rough-looking bars." That no longer is true. Ocean Beach—or "OB" for short—has gotten a much-needed makeover. And while no one will mistake it for La Jolla just yet, it's a comfortably funky beach town with just enough upscale refurbishing to inspire visitors to stick around rather than hurry away.

That is to say, Ocean Beach has improved in much-needed ways, but not to the point that it has become unrecognizable. The community is a mix of the raunchy and the respectable. On one side of a street will be a decrepit bungalow occupied by folks who look like remnants of the Haight-Ashbury, drinking and grunting at one another in the yard. On the other side will sit a well-tended house with a neatly clipped lawn and a new coat of paint. The two opposing sensibilities—upscale and downtrodden—are literally staring each other down, though apparently coexisting peaceably.

The heart of Ocean Beach is along Newport Avenue from Sunset Cliffs Boulevard to its terminus at the beach. What used to be an ugly array of failed or failing liquor stores and five-and-dimes now runs the gamut from decent, lively burger joints for the surfer crowd to trendy restaurants with neon-scripted names. The sidewalks are clean and litter-free. The pier has been recently refurbished. Where was once a liquor store is now a fitness center. Even the local tattoo parlor seems vaguely respectable, offering custom tattooing "in the San Diego tradition." Aqua-colored tiles have been glued in a line along the curb with the names of local businesses inscribed on them. Cute. Likable. Two words we never thought we'd associate with Ocean Beach.

Beaches

Ocean Beach has gone to the dogs. We mean that literally and, oddly enough, positively. At a parking lot located where Voltaire Street runs out at the beach is **Ocean Beach Park**. At this end of the park is Dog Beach, a stretch of sand given over to the frolics of our canine friends. The sign reads: "Welcome to Dog Beach. This is a dog 'FREE' beach. Leashes are not required." (Even for rottweilers and pit bulls? we wondered.) Dogs do indeed have the run of the place. Their owners stand off to the side like helpless chaperones at a party gone haywire. The canine revelers scamper and yap; dig holes as if tunneling to China; sniff one another, fore and aft; relieve themselves indis-

 Map of San Diego County beaches—page 24

criminately; and run in and out of the water with tails wagging. In other words, they generally behave no differently than humans do at the beach. We saw no fights, no snarling territorial disputes—just a happy pack of mutts and purebreds alike set free by their owners to romp to their heart's content. We should all get along so well.

Just up from Dog Beach is Tot Beach. Or so it seemed. Families recreate on **Ocean Beach City Beach** in much the same spirit of good, clean fun as their canine counterparts. These days it's more of a family beach than a party beach. All the same, it is unquestionably dangerous—unquestionably, because a sign planted in the sand, festooned with a skull and crossbones, reads: "No Swimming." People, however, were heedlessly jumping in the water. According to the head of lifeguard operations for San Diego County, "My impression is that Imperial Beach and Ocean Beach and the south end of Black's Beach are the most treacherous in San Diego. They have the strongest rip currents that are consistently pulling." Don't say we didn't warn you.

Surfers congregate around the T-shaped Ocean Beach Municipal Pier. The concrete pier is long and sturdy, with a food shack at the end. We walked out on it and watched a group of surfers waiting for the right wave. To us, watching surfers in action is nearly as much fun as surfing itself. They bob up and down on the swells in their wet suits, making small talk until... here comes a monster. Just before it starts to curl, they steer into it, emerging astride their boards in a shower of flying foam and negotiating the sloping face of the spilling wave with perfect body English. Before it breaks on the beach the surfers U-turn out of it and resume a belly-down position on the board again, paddling back out to wait on another ride.

Bunking Down

The choices are limited and, cool as Ocean Beach may be for a day trip, you probably are better off staying elsewhere in San Diego. Still, the **Ocean Beach Motel** (5080 Newport Avenue, 223-7191, $) is a surfer's dream: plain, utilitarian, and cheap. The **Ocean Villa Motel** (5142 West Point Loma Boulevard, 224-3481, $) is a bit nicer and takes pains to enforce a "no pets/no parties" policy.

Coastal Cuisine

Set in a typical bungalow that is the architectural trademark of Ocean Beach, **The Bungalow** (4996 West Point Loma Boulevard,

Ocean Beach City Beach

Location: In Ocean Beach, between the west ends of Niagara and Pescadero Avenues.

Parking: Metered lot and street parking.

Hours: Open 24 hours.

Facilities: Rest rooms and lifeguards.

Contact: For beach information, contact the San Diego Coastline Parks Division at (619) 221-8900 or the San Diego Lifeguard Service at (619) 221-8899. For a surf report, call (619) 221-8884.

See number 6 on page 24.

Ocean Beach Park

Location: In Ocean Beach, at the end of Voltaire Street.

Parking: Metered parking lot.

Hours: Open 24 hours.

Facilities: Lifeguards, rest rooms, showers, and picnic area.

Contact: For beach information, contact the San Diego Coastline Parks Division at (619) 221-8900 or the San Diego Lifeguard Service at (619) 221-8899. For a surf report, call (619) 221-8884.

See number 7 on page 24.

224-2884, $$) offers French/Continental cuisine at moderate prices. The house specialty is duck, but fish and chicken dishes are good as well. At the other end of the scale, **Hodad's** (5010 Newport Avenue, 224-4623, $) claims to serve the world's best burgers, proudly hanging a McDonald's-dissing sign that reads: "Under 99 billion sold." Another sign conveys the hang-loose atmosphere of the place: "No shirt, no shoes, no problem." The burgers are great

Wringing Out the Old in Ocean Beach

The motley old guard in Ocean Beach is being displaced grain by grain with an incoming tide of more respectable inhabitants. At this point in time, it may appear to be a Mexican standoff, but sure as the sun sets in the west, the eventual elbowing aside of the decaying hippie-biker contingent will be complete. Their sad, addled likes still can be seen drifting about town, muttering distractedly and occasionally creating a public spectacle, but their numbers are steadily dwindling through attrition and displacement. We view it as a kind of yuppie-led manifest destiny, having seen it happen all over the coast, for good or ill.

We arrived at Dog Beach just in time to watch one of the old-timers being handcuffed by a gentle contingent of police and lifeguards. The onerous character responsible for the disturbance was totally drunk and disorderly. His hair was scraggly as seaweed, his drink- and drug-fueled countenance way beyond the pale. There is no point, beyond that of political correctness, to give him the benefit of the doubt. He was a public menace. People recoiled in fear. Even the dogs kept their distance.

He delivered his rap as the authorities tried to restrain him with handcuffs.

"What are you guys doin', man?" he bellowed hoarsely. "I love my dog. If I lose my dog, you know what? I'll kill ya."

Apparently his dog had wandered off in the fracas.

A good samaritan, overhearing the melee, ambled over and offered to help. "If the guy's got a dog, I'll be glad to go look for it," he said.

The offending character jerked his head back and began yelling: "No you won't, but I will! [Begins quaking in his cuffs.] I will get nervous! I will get nervous! I will get nervous!"

Policeman [gently]: "Relax, we just wanna talk.'

"Buttheads! You made me cry. Motherf__ers made me cry. Better get my dog, man, or I'm gonna go off. I'm gonna go off. [Thoughtful pause.] F__ life. I don't like life. Sonofabitch, you hurt me. Know what? I've been through three years of pain, man...."

The bellowing went on and on. We walked away, our absorption in this grisly spectacle hovering between pity and disgust.

Minutes later the wagon rolled away, subject in custody, no doubt to be dried out and turned loose again. Another walking time bomb, loose on the streets and beaches of California.

 Map of San Diego County beaches—page 24

messy slabs of beef stuck between a big bun and served in a basket. One table was fashioned from the sawed-off front of a VW bus. A buzzing hive of surfers chomps away at all hours, making a racket while gnawing on burgers the size of boogie boards.

Night Moves

Across the street from Hodad's, the **South Beach Bar and Grill** (5059 Newport Avenue, $$) is a great place to eat and/or down a few. We downed a few, eyeing the action on the pier from barstools pulled up to the picture window. The brew of choice is Hale's Pale Ale (say that three times fast), poured frosty cold from the tap. The restaurant serves fresh grilled thresher shark tacos for $2.25, Baja fish tacos for $1.75, and a ceviche cocktail for $3.95, among a full menu of other tasty seafood appetizers and entrées. While we were there, reggae king Bob Marley was playing on the sound system, while the hapless San Diego Padres were losing on the boob tube. At a stool adjacent to ours, a prototypical beach girl with sun-damaged hair and reddened face remarked to her male consort, in reverent tones: "The ocean—what an amazing thing." We toasted this truism with raised mugs as the last rays of the day glinted off the distant waves.

For More Information

Contact the San Diego Peninsula Chamber of Commerce, P.O. Box 7018, San Diego, CA 92107; (619) 223-9767.

Mission Beach

Location: West of downtown San Diego, it can be accessed via the Grand Avenue exit off Interstate 5 or via Mission Bay Drive.
Population: 6,000
Area Code: 619 **Zip Code:** 92109

Mission Beach looks more and more like Pacific Beach every day. We mean that as a compliment. These neighboring communities—wedded by a paved, three-mile "ocean walk"—do indeed complement one another. Along with Ocean Beach, which has seen vast improvements in recent years, these stretches of San Diego's shoreline epitomize what a trip to a Southern California beach ought to be.

It is not until you walk down Garnet Avenue toward the Crystal Pier and then turn left (toward Mission Beach) or right (toward Pacific Beach) that you actually feel as if you're entering the pumping aorta of a true California beach town. You know, the kind you've always heard the Beach Boys sing about: skateboards, roller skates and in-line skates, volleyball on the beach, surfboards, surf shops, surf bars, surf bums, surf bunnies, and more bronzed flesh than you'll see in any 10 MTV videos. Mission Beach is a great, relaxed party town where college students from San Diego State and other nearby schools live the beach life to its fullest, majoring in sun, surf, sand, suds, and sex, in addition to whatever it is they're purportedly studying up the hill in La Jolla. Our theory is that because surfers and other twenty-somethings are so unmaterialistic, living in the outdoors beside the ocean, they don't steal, making this a relatively safe community. Life can be lived with a few pairs of cutoff jeans and a diet of cheap tacos. Who needs more?

Although both towns are, as their signs proclaim, "communities of San Diego," they have more in common with the monkey cages at the San Diego Zoo than with the straitlaced corporate enclaves that define the rest of the city. They are also sizable towns in their own right. Pacific Beach has a population of over 40,000 and Mission Beach, though limited in area as a peninsula, is wall-to-wall real estate.

Map of San Diego County beaches—page 24

Until recent years, Mission Beach seemed like Pacific Beach's lovable but sloppy younger brother. In our eyes, this reputation was epitomized by a self-proclaimed "guide to the night life" whom we met here in the mid-1980s. After having had his driver's license revoked, he simply equipped his banana bike handlebars with a "beer-can holder" (a Maxwell House coffee can held in place with electrician's tape) so that he could continue his bar-hopping unabated. We must admit he was one knowledgeable lad.

By now our guide is no doubt climbing the Twelve Steps of AA. We certainly have toned down our own acts, and Mission Beach has improved its manners to some degree as well. That is to say, either Mission Beach has grown into Pacific Beach's shoes, or the latter has slid into to the former's flip-flops. Either way, they've met in the middle. The figurative beer-can holders are still here, as is the army of nocturnal revelers who live their rites of summer passage on these streets and beaches.

Added to the eclectic mix of types who come here—from families and preppies to punks and the homeless—is a veneer of understated civility and good, clean fun that wasn't always evident before. This renaissance was ushered in by the 1993 reopening of Belmont Park, an amusement park and shopping center with a mountainous red, white, and blue roller coaster (the 70-year-old Giant Dipper) that defines the revived spirits of the town. More moms, pops, and kids are coming to Mission Beach, yet it still retains a tolerant attitude toward fun in the sun—and no less an authority than Sir Kenneth Clark proclaimed tolerance to be the key element of all civilizations.

For example, the beat cops are in remarkably good physical shape. They wear shorts, ride bikes, mingle, laugh, and eat ice cream cones like everyone else. They don't needlessly provoke confrontations; in fact, they spend a good deal of time defusing them. Even the homeless have found a haven of sorts in Mission Bay Park, a nice swath of green across from Belmont Park where they loll on the grass next to their shopping carts. Tanned redder than rare roast beef, they chat, drink from bags, and pass out without fanfare. Again, tolerance is the key.

Perhaps Mission Beach can be magnanimous because it has double the beachfront of other beach towns. That is, two different waterfronts are available to visitors here—the ocean and the bay. They are obverse images of each other, offering opposing but equally appealing beach styles.

The oceanfront was, is, and always will be *Animal House* and *American Graffiti* rolled into one. Strolling along Ocean Front Walk on any summer day is like walking along fraternity row during Rush Week. Shirtless guys clutch tall beers and lean off the balconies of their rented apartments, passing judgment on the human parade below or squirting one another with water guns, while bikini-clad beauties casually lean back in chaise lounges and toy with mixed drinks and sunscreen, lathering their lithe bodies while the guys leer and yelp and yahoo. There was even a pet pig (frat mascot?) strutting on someone's patio, wagging its tail like a dog.

Life goes on without pause on Ocean Front Walk below, as people jog or whiz by, oblivious under their Walkmans to the raucous racket above. One sun-bronzed fellow calmly stood atop his skateboard while two leashed, panting dogs gamely pulled him along like miniature huskies. Mission Beach is not unlike Mardi Gras, except that it goes on for months instead of days. The parade passing along Mission and Pacific Beaches provides endless hours of spectator sport available only in Southern California.

The scene on Mission Bay is more middle-class than back-of-the-class. Executive types and their families play badminton on the putting green-type grass along the water. Barbecue grills are on display, as are American flags. Catamarans are lashed to the dock or pulled onto the sand. Another three-mile paved track,

 Map of San Diego County beaches—page 24

Bay Side Walk, runs parallel to Ocean Front Walk, but the pace is more leisurely, less chaotic. It is most popular with joggers, who no doubt appreciate the safety. The houses and villas are a pleasant and eclectic blend of architectural styles, making for great window shopping while strolling beside the bay.

Our advice to novice visitors is to leave the car at the motel and rent bikes at one of the outfitters on Ocean Front Walk. Mission Beach has devoted only a limited amount of its precious open space to parking. If you do drive in Mission Beach, try to park on the bayfront, at Mission Bay Aquatic Center. To get there, turn east toward the bay on Santa Clara Place and follow it into the free lot. It is within walking distance to the beach, as well as a host of great bars and restaurants.

Beaches

Mission Beach runs the entire length of Ocean Front Walk and has designated areas for board surfing, bodysurfing, and swimming. The water conditions are updated on a board outside the lifeguard station (e.g., "Lots of rip currents and deep holes on the inside of the surf zone. Ask us where to swim."). Mission Beach ends around the Crystal Pier, where Pacific Beach picks up the chain of sandy command. We waded along the ocean's edge for a good distance. The water, at first cold to the touch, felt good and warmed quickly. Mission Beach, incidentally, appears friendly to surfers of all skill levels. The surf is more forgiving to beginners than La Jolla's storied beaches, but under the right swell conditions Mission Beach also presents challenges for experts.

On the Ocean Front Walk, the paved promenade that faces the beach, a *Comédie Humaine* that would have impressed Balzac glides past on bikes, in-line skates, shopping carts, and anything else to which wheels can be affixed. Somehow they don't collide, even though all are traveling at different speeds. In the midst of all this sauntered an old crone with a Hefty sack full of returnable cans and bottles, riffling through the trash cans for more. A gang of sun- and booze-battered longhairs of late 1960s vintage came riding around the corner on low-to-the-ground banana bikes that looked like something our sisters played on when they were six. It is all in the spirit of Mission Beach, a town where the laugh track runs continuously.

Mission Beach

4

Location: In Mission Beach, along Mission Boulevard, between Mission Bay Channel and Santa Rita Place.

Parking: Metered lot and street parking.

Hours: Open 24 hours.

Facilities: Lifeguards and rest rooms.

Contact: For beach information, contact the San Diego Coastline Parks Division at (619) 221-8900 or the San Diego Lifeguard Service at (619) 221-8899. For a surf report, call (619) 221-8884.

See number 8 on page 24.

Bunking Down

The rents on the bayfront are higher than those on the oceanfront, but the noise factor has to be considered. You do want to go to sleep eventually, right? We saw a cozy little cottage on the bay side that rented for $650 a month, but next door to it was a chic *Architectural Digest* centerfold that was going for closer to $650 a week. The scuttlebutt is that all the good (read: cheap) ones are booked months, if not years, in advance, usually by people who faithfully return each summer. We can't blame them.

This leaves motels, of which there aren't many in Mission Beach. The largest and best is the **Catamaran Resort Hotel** (3999 Mission Boulevard, 488-1081, $$), with 312 units, many with bay views. They have a safe bay beach at the back, where you can rent sailboats and get windsurfing lessons, and there's a pool on the premises. Things occasionally get hopping at the on-premises lounge, if you're looking for a little *après du sail.*

Coastal Cuisine

As if to reinforce the twin themes of fun and nourishment, the best places to eat in Mission Beach are often the best places to drink, too. Our favorites are the **Guava Beach Bar and Grill** (3714 Mission Boulevard, 488-6688, $$) and the **Santa Clara Grill** (3704 Mission Boulevard, 488-9484, $$), situated side by side one block back from the beach. With doelike innocence, the friendly waitresses at both places hustle about, making small talk and refilling drinks within seconds of last sips. Their menus are also similar, with a Mexican flavor to most of the staples and all items reasonably priced and perfectly unfancy. Guava Beach offers "Baja Bargains" every day, happy-hour specials like the Cabo Quesadilla with Sour Cream, Spicy Rosarito Fish Taco, and Brie & Calypso Salsa Quesadilla. Drink and eat up!

Santa Clara is equally good-humored, with the added dimension of a patio from which you can easily eavesdrop on the packs of baying revelers on the sidewalk behind the palm trees. Here are excerpts from the menu: "If you want something that is not on the menu, ask for it. The waiter will discuss it with the dishwasher.... If you must sing, please refer to the *Anderson Book of Etiquette* as to the type of music best suited for an establishment specializing in great beach food. Pink Floyd and Devo are not acceptable. Whistling is permitted."

Night Moves

There are two camps in Mission Beach's nightlife: those who are preparing to party and those who are already partying heartily. The prelude to a party animal's evening in Mission Beach is to watch the sunset from one of several Ocean Front Walk bars. The hottest one during our expedition was **Chillers** (3105 Ocean Front Walk, 488-2000). If you can find the roller coaster, you can find Chillers, which practically sits in its shadow. Formerly one of the legendary Red Onion clubs, Chillers revives the ghost of that now-defunct chain. The **Open Bar** (4302 Mission Boulevard, 270-3221) is one block off the beach, but equally popular with locals for preludes to serious partying. Ditto for the **Pennant** (2893 Mission Boulevard, 488-1671), located at the south end of the peninsula. It is a sloppy hut with a wooden bar and booths, plastic cups of draft beer, boisterous and sometimes slurred conversations, and a clientele that leans toward slacker attire. If you don't wear your baseball cap backward, you probably won't get served here. **Acapulco Joe's Cantina** (3840 Mission Boulevard, 488-2340) is yet another friendly tavern that also serves full meals. Most Mission Beachers who don't hunker down for the duration at one of these spots end up browsing the even more boisterous bars in Pacific Beach.

For More Information

Contact the San Diego Visitor Information Center, 2688 East Mission Bay Drive, San Diego, CA 92109; (619) 276-8200.

Mission Bay

Location: Northwest of downtown San Diego, behind Mission Beach.

Mission Bay is a kinder, gentler echo of San Diego Bay. Tucked behind the peninsula of Mission Beach, it is a world unto itself and a beach haven that, though popular, remains nicely out of the way. The beaches here are on the bay, of course, and many of the visitors come here to sail out on the water, not splash about the calm shoreline. This 4,600-acre aquatic park—the largest on the West Coast—can be accessed via numerous ramps, landings, and marinas to the north and west and on Fiesta Isle, the largest of the two man-made islands in the bay itself. Watery activities pursued here include fishing, sailing, windsurfing, waterskiing, and swimming, and the sight of people doing all of these things at once gives the scenic (and unpolluted) bay a sort of relaxed elegance, not unlike a Seurat painting of a scene along the Seine.

Mission Bay is also a living lesson in democracy. Everyone comes here, from the wealthy, relaxing on deck in sailor suit and cap, to camping anglers, bunking in tents and RVs at the two campgrounds on the north shore. The bay is, in fact, appealing in so many ways that it's almost a shame it has to "compete" with the ocean beaches just a Frisbee toss to the west. But that only means there's plenty for everyone in San Diego.

The centerpiece of Mission Bay Park from a tourist's standpoint is Sea World (226-3901). This 150-acre marine zoo "stars" Shamu (a two-ton killer whale), Baby Shamu, dolphins, otters, walruses, sharks, eels, and stingrays. There's also "A Penguin Encounter" and "Beach Blanket Ski Show" (featuring show-offs on water skis). It isn't cheap ($23 for adults, $17 for kids), but it's open from 9 AM to 11 PM in the summer (9 AM to dusk the rest of the year), so if you hang out long enough you might get your money's worth. Who knows? Maybe you can have a private audience with Baby Shamu, as one of us did. (There was a lot of mutual head-wagging—not your typical backstage encounter with a celebrity.)

Beaches

They're not ocean beaches, but there's a bevy of sandy bay beaches to be found on Vacation and Fiesta Islands, as well as Mission Bay's mainland shoreline. Probably the best among half a dozen of them is to be found at **De Anza Cove**, on the bay's northeast flank. Here you'll find a well-equipped public park as well as private campgrounds for tents and trailers (see below).

Bunking Down

The best seat in the house at Mission Bay is a sleeping bag. Two excellent, if somewhat pricey, campgrounds are available. **De Anza Harbor Resort**, off North Mission Bay Drive, has 250 spaces for RVs ($27 to $44 per night, 273-3211). The much larger and more scenic **Campland on the Bay** has 750 spaces for both tents and RVs ($35 to $45 per night, 800-422-9386). If it's creature comforts you're wanting, try the **San Diego Princess Resort** (1404 West Vacation Road, 274-4630, $$$), on Vacation Island in Mission Bay. It's stocked to the gills with everything you could possibly want, including five pools and a bayside beach.

Coastal Cuisine

For dinner we ventured over to the San Diego Princess Resort, located on the smaller of two man-made isles in the heart of Mission Bay. In a setting of tropical gardens the **Dockside Restaurant** (1404 West Vacation Road, 274-4630, $$) serves superb and affordable seafood-oriented cuisine, offering a dining experience that's tough to top in San Diego. Every table in the spacious and casually elegant dining room has a postcard-perfect view of the bay. The food, breads, appetizers, seafood entrées, and desserts are freshly prepared in a creative but unpretentious manner. The eggplant salad appetizer, for instance, consisted of thick, meaty layers of grilled eggplant, fresh mozzarella, and prosciutto, served in a vinaigrette dressing. It tasted like a healthy Big Mac. The grilled salmon and pan-seared ahi were also very good. So take your time, chew slowly, enjoy the view, and count your blessings. It's open for dinner only, beginning at 6 PM daily.

Night Moves

Vacation Island seems to be a lively place, at least judging from the commotion coming from the **San Diego Princess Resort**'s nightclub (1404 West Vacation Road, 274-4630) on a balmy Friday night. What piqued our curiosity was hearing a Steppenwolf song being played in the distance by a cover band. We ambled over to check it out. Were we not gorged with food and out of it, feeling more like addled John Belushis than agile John Travoltas, we might have stuck around for more than a cursory look at the bubbling, dance-happy crowd.

For More Information

Contact the San Diego Visitor Information Center, 2688 East Mission Bay Drive, San Diego, CA 92109; (619) 276-8200.

Pacific Beach

Location: West of San Diego, via the Grand Avenue exit off of Interstate 5. Mission Boulevard runs along the oceanfront. Pacific Beach is the name of the city and the beach, which occupies the space between Mission Beach and La Jolla.

Population: 40,000

Area Code: 619 **Zip Code:** 92109

Any beach town that names itself after the world's largest ocean better have the waves to back it up. Happily, Pacific Beach (or "PB" as it is known to locals) has waves upon waves of great surf, great beaches, great weather, great bars, and great cheap eateries. In short, Pacific Beach is the quintessential Southern California beach town and is among our favorites on either coast. All the same, PB's fortunes have receded in recent years, due mostly to the lingering effects of the California recession. Although the downward signs are undeniable—shirtless drunks with bad attitudes, a growing contingent of street people, litter-strewn streets—PB is still the place to go if you want to have serious fun in San Diego.

There is an unstated rivalry between Pacific Beach and La Jolla, the jewel on the hill four miles north. Natives have bemoaned the gentrification that has trickled down from their wealthier neighbor. They've mockingly dubbed themselves "Baja La Jolla" for all the rich preppies who come here to party. And, indeed, some overly trendy boutiques have muscled onto the scene. Still, it seems unlikely that any business that charges $32 for designer T-shirts is going to last long in PB.

The irony about this give-and-take between the two towns is that PB itself, beyond the commercial corridors of Garnet Avenue and Mission Boulevard, is a well-tended, suburban, and relatively pricey place in which to live. Where do all the wasted Marky Mark look-alikes go at the end of the night, we wondered?

Of course, none of this really matters once you are ensconced here and splashing happily about in the surf near the Crystal Pier. Surfers in particular like PB, rising with the sun to catch the early-morning waves. Part of the reason for this is that surfing is off-limits after 11 AM on many local beaches. The other explanation

 Map of San Diego County beaches—page 24

is that surfers are masochistic. One ex-surfer told us he was now into "body whomping." Body whomping requires the practitioner to roll into the hollow tube of a large wave. Surfers and whompers alike refer to this as "entering the green room." The whompers then allow the force of the breaking wave to pound them senseless against the ocean floor. Our surfer friend described the one last moment before the wave collapsed as "magical." He also confessed to having back problems.

Beaches

The beach at **Pacific Beach** runs along the Ocean Front Walk, picking up where Mission Beach leaves off. The same large crew of lifeguards surveys the scene at both beaches. Just north of the main beach, before hitting La Jolla's curvaceous coves, is **Tourmaline Surfing Park**, which is off-limits to swimmers but Nirvana to surfers. Waves are notoriously large at Tourmaline and break a good distance from shore. The old guard of the historic surfing scene congregates here. The purists are distinguished from the come-latelies by steadfastly adhering to the dying tradition of long boards with single fins and no leg lines. "A good surfer never loses his board," a good surfer informed us.

Bunking Down

The **Pacific Terrace Inn** (610 Diamond Street, 800-344-3370, $$$) is still the best place to stay along this five-mile stretch of coast. The three-story, pink and brown hotel blends as unobtrusively with the sand as a 73-room inn possibly can, and the location, just north of the Crystal Pier on the beach, is unsurpassable. Built on the site of what used to be a transient flophouse, the Pacific Terrace is a modern "luxury" hotel, comfortable and clean without being stuffy. Many of the rooms have balconies overlooking the ocean and the large heated pool. Purchased in 1989 by a large "property management corporation," the Pacific Terrace has tentatively embraced some La Jollan affectations in recent years (valets in safari outfits, Gucci freebies), but no place on the beach in San Diego can match it. However, with rooms starting at $160 a night in the summer, it is not for beach bums on a budget.

In contrast to the Pacific Terrace Inn, the **Crystal Pier Motel** (4500 Ocean Boulevard, 483-6983, $) is right in the heart of PB. The name does not lie. It is set directly on the short, historic Crystal Pier (dating from 1927). The rooms are actually separate cottages affixed like a row of white window boxes to both sides of

Pacific Beach

Location: In Pacific Beach, along Ocean Boulevard, from Thomas Avenue to Diamond Street.

Parking: Metered street parking.

Hours: 9 AM to 6 PM.

Facilities: Lifeguards and rest rooms.

Contact: For beach information, contact the San Diego Coastline Parks Division at (619) 221-8900 or the San Diego Lifeguard Service at (619) 221-8899. For a surf report, call (619) 221-8884.

See number 9 on page 24.

Tourmaline Surfing Park

Location: In southern La Jolla, at the end of Tourmaline Street.

Parking: Free parking lot.

Hours: Open 24 hours.

Facilities: Lifeguards, rest rooms, showers, and picnic area.

Contact: For beach information, contact the San Diego Coastline Parks Division at (619) 221-8900 or the San Diego Lifeguard Service at (619) 221-8899. For a surf report, call (619) 221-8884.

See number 10 on page 24.

the weather-beaten pier. Each cottage has a different sea creature carved into the cute blue shutters (in case you forget your room number, just remember "sea horse"). The Crystal Pier Motel is most popular with fishing families, members of which drop their line in the water from the windows of their rooms. It's not luxurious, but it is unique.

Coastal Cuisine

Restaurant-wise, PB is a battle royale between burgers, burritos, and fish-and-chips, with no clear winner. Too many franchises have muscled their way onto the scene in recent years, but it does leave one alternative: buy the same fare from the locals. For example, the best burgers in town are served at **Cass Street Bar and Grill** (4612 Cass Street, 270-1320, $), which is also a great watering hole for locals, many of whom eat here so often it might as well be an extension of their refrigerators. We were happy to find **Ramiro's** (4525 Mission Boulevard, 273-5227, $), a comfortably ramshackle take-out hut that serves three rolled tacos for $1.60. Nothing on the menu is over $4.60. It's great rib-spackling Mexican fare. Because it's open 24 hours a day, Ramiro's attracts all kinds of comers. As we waited for a 2 AM snack after a night on the town, a sexy woman in a miniskirt stood in line in front of a shirtless old drunk who had trouble standing long enough to order. Another old PB favorite is **Sheldon's Café** (4711 Mission Boulevard, 273-3833), which is also open 24 hours and serves American fare: chicken-fried steaks, soups, salads, and a popular breakfast buffet.

Night Moves

In the immortal words of a local PB party animal, "For me there's living at the beach. Then there's middle age. And then there's death." Perhaps this deep philosophical musing best captures the transcendent wildness of the nightlife here. The town merchants encourage unbridled frivolity by offering a package deal called the "VIP card." For $20, this card allows you immediate entry (in front of everyone else in line) to all of the bars. On busy summer nights, it's your only hope if you're desperate to be shoehorned inside.

On our several visits here we've toured enough places to fill a scorecard and even managed, once, to get pulled over by the cops, the result of making a rolling "California stop" at a four-way intersection. The officer turned on his flashers and got on the bullhorn, yelling "pull over, goddamn it" loud enough to be heard in La Jolla. After our driver passed the coordination test with Baryshnikov-like grace, the officer was all sweetness and light, shaking hands and praising us for having the good sense to appoint a designated driver.

The old reliables—**Cass Street Bar and Grill** (4612 Cass Street, 270-1320) and **Kahuna's Surf Bar** (873 Turquoise Street, 488-6201)—are still around. The latter is perhaps the ultimate unrefined surf bar on the Southern California coast. Like the pipeline of a wave, only dauntless surfers venture inside. Surf music plays on the jukebox, longboards hang from the ceiling, surfing footage plays continuously on video monitors, and the place is packed with rowdies, especially on the "rage nights" of Friday and Saturday. When we last visited, the place was run by the "head Kahuna," a scary-looking guy with a gray beard and soiled baggy trunks. Throughout the evening he taunted and regaled the crowd over a microphone, offering free shots of tequila to any woman who'd bare her breasts for him, leaping over the bar to referee a fistfight, and leading cheers of "Kahuna! Kahuna! Kahuna!" as he paced behind the bar like a caged panther. **Moondoggies** (4479 Everts Street, 581-0149), a tamer surf bar that caters more to surfer wannabes, has opened in PB; there's one in La Jolla as well.

Two other longtime reliables on the PB scene are **Hennessey's Tavern** (4650 Mission Boulevard, 483-8847) and the **Pacific Beach**

 Map of San Diego County beaches—page 24

Bar and Grill (860 Garnet Avenue, 272-4745). The former, though part of a chain, has been adopted by locals mainly because it occupies the site of a late, lamented Mexican cantina. The latter has an excellent jukebox, an outdoor patio, and a line out the door all night long. The best place for live music is **Offbeat** (832 Garnet Avenue, 483-4520), which features national acts at reasonable prices. If disco posing is your thing, try **Tremors** (860 Garnet Avenue, 272-7278). Like luscious lemmings who come to honor a monument to their own narcissism, guys and dolls crowd into Tremors on hot summer nights, primped and preened and mirror-conscious. Formerly the trendy Club Diego's, it's a massive multimedia complex. It costs a $4 cover to hear taped hip-hop music played at a volume that would scare the gulls circling over nearby Ramiro's.

Our choices for best new entries on the scene are the **Plum Crazy Saloon** (1060 Garnet Avenue, 270-1212) and **Café Crema** (1001 Garnet Avenue, 273-3558). The former is an extremely friendly place, with good taped music, countless drink specials, and delirious locals, typified by a blond woman who pantomimed every song played, replete with pelvis and lip twitches and tabletop leg kicks, as well as a men's room "convenience center" that sells everything from "chocolate fudge condoms" to Bayer aspirin. Café Crema is the part of the latest coffeehouse craze, which has even overtaken beery PB. Open 22 hours a day, they bake their own pastries and offer an excellent array of rich coffees, plus treats like "Latte of the Month" and "Creme De La Crema" (44 ounces of espresso, ice cream, whipped cream, chocolate, and banana). Books and magazines are strewn about, card and chess games are in progress, and folk music is earnestly strummed. All in all, it's a civilized alternative to the beer battles being waged beyond the picture windows.

For More Information

Contact the San Diego Visitor Information Center, 2688 East Mission Bay Drive, San Diego, CA 92109; (619) 276-8200.

Feeding the Pigeons in PB

While dining alfresco at Ramiro's, a fine, inexpensive Mexican food stand occupying the site of a former gas station along Mission Boulevard, we discovered that the pigeons of Pacific Beach (not to be confused with the swallows of San Juan Capistrano) love to hang around for a neighborly handout. Alfred Hitchcock never conjured a flock of birds as brazen as these garbage eaters. A pack of them numbering in the dozens fearlessly hopped on our table and waddled at our feet, demanding in birdspeak that we share our bounty. They were more insistent and in-your-face than the spare-changers jangling down the sidewalks of this be-all and end-all of beach towns. We obliged our feathered friends, tearing hunks from an enormous chicken chimichanga and tossing them into the gutter. The delirious birds merrily flung the flour tortilla pieces into the air from one to another, as if playing a madcap avian version of "Capture the Flag." The grasping and flinging of the tortilla and its innards enabled the birds to reduce it to edible morsels. We amused ourselves with birds and burritos for longer than reason might have deemed prudent, but hey, we'd been in the sun all day and were a little delirious ourselves.

Bad Vibes After Dark

Southern Californians are unabashedly sensual. They are children of the sun, as Jim Morrison dubbed them, physically fit and mentally uncomplicated. The state of profligate fun that colors their every waking activity is played to an unending soundtrack of laughter and rock and roll, and they never seem to tire of each other's presence. This is never more evident than at night when they come out to play after a hard day of hanging out in the ever-present sun.

On the surface, the nocturnal rites of Southern California unfold in a relaxed and thoroughly appealing state of anarchy, an anarchy that somehow manages to stay within the bounds of civilization most of the time. Perhaps this is simply due to the fact that every day is perfect here. (This is no myth.) Since every day is a clean slate, tomorrow is always one party away, if things don't work out today. Southern Californians owe this sunny outlook to the fact that they are always engaged in some physical activity and therefore don't have time to develop the dark pathologies of sedentary folks who stir up trouble at night in other places. Of course, all this fun in the sun also leaves little time to develop the mind, beyond periodic dabblings in the latest New Age manifesto. (*The Celestine Prophecy* was hot during our latest summer sojourn.) Hey, if there's an awesome happy hour at Chillers or the Green Circle or Plum Crazy, who's got time to get serious? And, more important, who needs to?

Okay. If it all seems too good to be true, it is. The pressure to perpetually live it up to the max produces its own pathologies, and we saw this dark side rear its surly head one night in Pacific Beach, the party town of San Diego County. Actually, it was the Fourth of July, of all symbolic days, and the festivities had come to a begrudging end around 2 AM, at which point a hungry contingent of beach bums descended on one of several Mexican fast-food outlets that stay open all night in PB. We did likewise.

At the first outdoor hut we visited, a sad-comic scene ensued. While we studied the hand-lettered menu outside the taco parlor, a grocery cart entered from stage right, listing like a rusty galleon with a tall load of empty cans and Hefty plastic bags. The cart was pushed by a sun-pulverized woman of indeterminate age, perhaps 35, perhaps 70. (Who can tell, really, about people who live in public parks?) She was wearing a grease-stained miniskirt, a fluorescent orange fanny pack, dirty knee socks, and torn, untied sneakers that looked too small for her swollen feet. From out of the shadows staggered her consort, a shirtless, shoeless man with tattoos covering his bare belly. He answered to the name of "Bear," a sobriquet the woman hurled at him to get his attention as he stumbled across the street.

The woman loudly begged Bear for a dollar, the modest sum of money needed to buy some rolled tacos. Bear growled and extended his paw, proffering a moist, wadded bill extracted from the unfathomable folds of his soiled blue jeans. While she approached the window to order, he proceeded to gruffly panhandle the other people in line, who were no more than two feet away from the woman to whom he'd just

 Map of San Diego County beaches—page 24

given a dollar. We left at that point, figuring the all-too-familiar scene would deteriorate into more pathos than we could stomach after a night of prowling among the Barbies and Kens of San Diego.

As it happened, the second Mexican fast-food joint we visited provided the actual violence that had only been hinted at by the first. After ordering our chicken quesadillas, we retreated to a booth in the corner, feeling bad for the Mexican-American behind the counter. Before taking our order he had been verbally abused by a Surfer Joe-type who accused him, in mock Mexican dialect, of withholding the sour cream from his burrito. The place was as loud as the bar we'd just left; the revelry just never seems to die down in Pacific Beach.

We set about trying to enjoy our food, though the helping was so large that it seemed to multiply like protoplasm with each bite. As we were finishing, an odd, indescribable series of events took place. (It made no sense to us at the time, and we witnessed it!) Suffice it to say that like a row of dominos stood back to back, it only took one jolt to send them all tumbling down. The "jolt" was provided by a skateboarding local and his companion, a blond woman whose expanding girth was covered by a pair of overalls. Her mate took offense at something he heard in line. This ignited a bizarre scene that ended with another person—an athletic African-American who was not even involved in the original dispute—punching the woman in overalls so hard in the face that her head hit the front window of the Mexican restaurant with a sickening thud. A college kid with grunge rocker's facial hair ran outside to break up the fight, during which a heavy wooden trash can got overturned. He ended up being pummeled by the black athlete, as was the original wastrel who'd set things off. After leaving the parking lot strewn with at least four prone, moaning bodies, most of whom were just trying to make peace, the assailant took off down Garnet Avenue. The cops arrived at that point, trying to sort out something that had no rationale beyond suppressed rage and unreleased testosterone. The final grace note was provided by one of the original disputants, the oblivious guy in line whose chance remark had touched off the fracas. Exiting the restaurant with his take-out order, he surveyed the parking lot and exclaimed, with a combination of disgust and humor, "I started all this, and I didn't even get punched!"

The quesadillas weighed heavy on our stomachs as we rehashed this turn of events. In a way, we felt like we'd lost some of our innocence about Southern California. For all the paradisiacal trappings—and the day at the beach that was now ending had been one of the most perfect we've encountered in our many years of coastal combing—we detected an underlying dissatisfaction, the ennui of the pampered American psyche that wants more of everything: sex, money, power, sun, surf, good times.

La Jolla

Location: 14 miles north of metropolitan San Diego, it can be reached via exits off the San Diego Freeway (Interstate 5). La Jolla Boulevard is the main drag through town, paralleling the coast. Coast Boulevard and Neptune Place run directly alongside the ocean in La Jolla proper. Camino Del Oro and La Jolla Shores Drive run along or close to the beach in La Jolla Shores. La Jolla is dotted with small beaches carved into its cliffs. The most popular of these are Windansea, Children's Pool, and La Jolla Cove Beaches.

Population: 37,000

Area Code: 619 **Zip Code:** 92037

On May 3rd, 1987, the town of La Jolla celebrated its centennial. In its coverage of the event, the *La Jolla Light* recounted the glorious spring afternoon in 1887 when La Jolla came into being. The first line of the story said it all: "It could not have been a better day for selling real estate." It was boom time in California, and settlers scurried westward to join in the land grab. One historical account claims they were sold a false bill of goods: "The plots were touted as having water mains and convenient telephone and rail service, none of which was true." It didn't matter. The setting was so much like paradise, perched high above the ocean on tawny, pine-covered bluffs, that no one was about to quibble over phone lines.

La Jolla (pronounced *la HOYa*) means "the jewel" in Spanish. Indeed, La Jolla does look like a jewel—maybe the prize bauble on the marble-topped vanity of coastal California. Wealth is palpable, both in the natural bounty of a marvelous setting and the material prosperity evident in the cars residents drive, the clothes they wear, the houses they live in, and the shops that cater to their every caviar whim. They make their money hawking real estate and trading stocks, occupations that allow them to bask in a perfect environment, squired away in upscale, uphill semiexclusivity. The tone is set by signs that welcome visitors with the warning: "No shouting within city limits."

Technically, La Jolla is a community belonging to San Diego, but in every imaginable way it is a world removed. The freeway cacophony of downtown San Diego is miles away. La Jolla is distanced by attitude and altitude from rabble-rousing Pacific and Mission Beaches. Every attempt is made to cultivate a village atmosphere. La Jollans boast of having a "significantly high standard of living." It is a community whose residents lead a life of the senses. They are impeccably attired. They appreciate good food, wine, and art. They are masters at landscaping. Their hair is perfect. And, like all busy people pursuing wealth and privilege in the '90s, they often appear to be harried as they bustle around their little seaside sanctuary.

The heart of La Jolla is the intersection of Prospect and Fay Streets, which looks like a bonsai version of Wall Street. Outside the offices of Paine Webber and Merrill Lynch are arrayed gleaming rows of Mercedes and BMWs—foreign-made cars for patriotic free-enterprise capitalists. The working women, who tend toward real-estate professions, likewise fix their steely gazes on the pot of gold at the end of the corporate rainbow. We actually overheard a couple of them at a seaside café discussing, over lunch, the origin and meaning of the company name "Re/Max."

The men all look to be some indeterminate, forever-young 30, resembling those perfectly coifed leading men of daytime-TV melodramas. They include gray-haired bon vivants driving racy red convertibles, consorting with blonde gold diggers half their age. We spied one younger, upwardly mobile professional, whose long dirty-blond hair was heavily moussed and neatly swept back, pecking furiously at a calculator while nursing a tall coffee and scone at

 Map of San Diego County beaches—page 24

the local Starbucks. We could just imagine him changing out of his office attire into baggies and sandals, grabbing his board and making for the waves at Windansea when 5 PM rolls around.

The ocean exerts a near-mystical pull upon all who live in La Jolla. At day's end, they gravitate to the ocean's edge, gazing over the broad expanse at the setting sun like bedouins engaged in prayer rituals. They watch from porches and balconies. They pull up to curbs in cars and vans with surfboards jammed in back or tethered on top. They jog along Coast Boulevard. Some bring picnic baskets, crawling onto sandstone shelves to toast the rosy sun as it slides into the crystal goblet of the Pacific.

The scene at sundown is emblematic of the Southern California experience. On an especially lovely late afternoon in midsummer, we set up camp at Windansea to watch the unfolding parade. Vans lined the street, their doors slid open to reveal fur-covered seats, carpeted floors, and knee-high card tables at which guys sat cross-legged, cracking jokes and sipping beer. A trio of divers with yellow tanks strapped to their backs waded into the water, caucusing briefly before disappearing beneath the surface. An apple-cheeked beauty with shiny blond hair jogged by in a turquoise sweatshirt and coral sweatpants. A surfer in a wet suit came sprinting down a side street, board tucked under one arm, anxiously scanning the waves. Peopled assumed the lotus position on rock ledges, hands shielding eyes from the harsh glare of the dimming sun as they gazed seaward. A girl in a bulky sweater, her guitar slung over a shoulder, strummed and strolled out onto the rocks as if serenading the sea. On the water, a surfer caught an amazing ride, tunneling through the foam and down a sloping wave until he was shooting the curl. Moment by moment, the setting sun slowly turned the buff-colored sandstone to golden honey.

Despite its lofty perch, La Jolla has not been entirely immune to the effects of the California recession, and cracks in the facade have begun to emerge. Prospect Street has seen a gradual incursion of less tony shops. In the midst of all the jewelers, perfumeries, and art galleries displaying Miro lithographs have come low-rent T-shirt stores and bargain rug merchants. Even McDonald's—designated a "McSnack" and mercifully lacking in golden arches—has stiff-armed its way onto a prime block of Prospect Street. We saw a few occasional panhandlers wandering the streets, a further blight to La Jolla's formerly unalloyed brilliance. They were upscale panhandlers, to be sure, like the well-attired beggar who sat bolt upright, arm slung jauntily over the back of a bench outside the post office. His English was the most formal we'd ever heard from an indigent. "Might you be able to spare any change today?" he inquired with a gentlemanly lilt in his voice. His shoes were nicer and newer than our own. His hair looked styled. Our change remained in our pockets.

Top Ten Things to Do on the Fourth of July

On our nation's birthday, this was listed on the blackboard by the lifeguard shack at La Jolla Cove:

10. Watch fireworks.
9. Drink a beer.
8. Look for a parking space.
7. Eat veggie burgers and tofu dogs.
6. Drink another beer.
5. Yell at the guy who "stole" your parking space.
4. Swim at the Cove.
3. Drink another beer.
2. Ask the lifeguard a question.
1. Feel very patriotic.

One evening, we followed the incongruous sound of banjo-picking to a downtown street corner, where a fake hillbilly whose hat lay upturned at his feet played bluegrass for the well-to-do Californians who strolled around him. A few paid polite attention and tossed him a coin, but most shuffled away as if avoiding a foaming dog. On the street, a woman sat at a small folding table she'd set up, offering Tarot readings and on-the-spot counseling for those wandering by. She gazed deeply into the eyes of a customer, holding her hand while consulting the cards. We tried to read her lips; it looked like she was saying, "I feel your pain."

We could read further signs of slippage along the fault line dividing the haves from the have-nots in La Jolla. While after-dinner crowds milled and window-shopped on a Saturday night, a pack of unwashed teen derelicts and their mangy cur took up residence on the sidewalk, loudly reminiscing about their misspent afternoon: "We been drinking all day, man, got a case of beer and went to work on it...." (Who says the young lack ambition?) A smattering of homeless had taken up residence at key intersections, brandishing signs offering to work for money. One offered prospective employers this bargain: "Will work for five days, you pay me for four." Up the hill along Torrey Pines Road, swinging away from the beach, units in a condo complex gone bust were being auctioned off. A real-estate failure in La Jolla—can this be? Hired honeys in Uncle Sam top hats stood at strategic intersections, waving arms and holding arrows that pointed the way to the auction. Bids began at $179,000—a pittance for a piece of La Jolla, and a sign of the times.

In the meantime the ocean churns away, infinitely impervious to all the human turmoil in Southern California's premier ocean-resort community. Meanwhile, "the jewel," though slightly tarnished, still possesses a setting as splendid as any on the coast.

Beaches

The ruddy sandstone cliffs of La Jolla are a perpetual work-in-progress; at this point, the humans who scamper along the sandy, erodible rocks overlooking the sea are probably contributing as much to its sculpted form as the force of the waves that batter it from below. The beaches of La Jolla are among the most varied and striking on the Southern California coast, ranking with the coves of Laguna Beach. Around the knob of La Jolla, numerous small beaches are tucked into folds in the undulating rock. Along Coast Boulevard, from the lifeguard stand at La Jolla Cove south to its

Children's Pool Beach

5

Location: In La Jolla, at Coast Boulevard and Jenner Street.

Parking: Free street parking.

Hours: Open 24 hours.

Facilities: Lifeguards.

Contact: For beach information, contact the San Diego Coastline Parks Division at (619) 221-8900 or the San Diego Lifeguard Service at (619) 221-8899. For a surf report, call (619) 221-8884.

See number 14 on page 24.

La Jolla Cove

4

Location: In La Jolla, at Coast Boulevard and Girard Avenue.

Parking: Free street parking.

Hours: Open 24 hours.

Facilities: Lifeguards and rest rooms.

Contact: For beach information, contact the San Diego Coastline Parks Division at (619) 221-8900 or the San Diego Lifeguard Service at (619) 221-8899. For a surf report, call (619) 221-8884.

See number 15 on page 24.

intersection with Prospect Street, are arrayed a number of small beaches and inviting green spaces for your swimming, sunning, surfing, and picnicking pleasure.

The beach at **La Jolla Cove** is the most popular, and it's invariably choked with a thick tide of beach blankets and bodies at the height of summer. It is manned by lifeguards who post the daily swimming and diving conditions on a blackboard, such as, "Surf: Picking up slightly 1-2' west with a southern component that is spuratically [*sic*] trying." During our visit in early July, the water temperature hit 69.2 degrees, and the locals were exultant. To them, this was bathwater, and very close to the yearly high of 71 degrees Fahrenheit, reached in August and September. Further cause for celebration was this note, posted on an information board near the lifeguard stand: "Ocean water testing at the cove and shore will be suspended until October. Results have shown that water off the cove is generally excellent during the summer and early fall months."

The beach at La Jolla Cove lies at the southern end of the gigantic cove, which stretches in a broad, tongue-shaped curve all the way up to Scripps Pier, at which point the coast resumes its northwesterly course. The area has

La Jolla Shores Beach

Location: In La Jolla Shores, at Camino Del Oro and Calle Frescota.
Parking: Metered parking lot.
Hours: Open 24 hours.
Facilities: Lifeguards, rest rooms, showers, picnic tables, and fire pits.
Contact: For beach information, contact the San Diego Coastline Parks Division at (619) 221-8900 or the San Diego Lifeguard Service at (619) 221-8899. For a surf report, call (619) 221-8884.

See number 16 on page 24.

Marine Street Beach

Location: In La Jolla, at the end of Marine Street.
Parking: Free street parking.
Hours: Open 24 hours.
Facilities: None.
Contact: For beach information, contact the San Diego Coastline Parks Division at (619) 221-8900 or the San Diego Lifeguard Service at (619) 221-8899. For a surf report, call (619) 221-8884.

See number 13 on page 24.

La Jolla Strand Park

Location: In La Jolla, at Neptune Place and Palomar Avenue.
Parking: Free street parking.
Hours: Open 24 hours.
Facilities: None.
Contact: For beach information, contact the San Diego Coastline Parks Division at (619) 221-8900 or the San Diego Lifeguard Service at (619) 221-8899. For a surf report, call (619) 221-8884.

See number 11 on page 24.

Windansea Beach

Location: In La Jolla, at Neptune Place and Bonair Street.
Parking: Free street parking.
Hours: Open 24 hours.
Facilities: None.
Contact: For beach information, contact the San Diego Coastline Parks Division at (619) 221-8900 or the San Diego Lifeguard Service at (619) 221-8899. For a surf report, call (619) 221-8884.

See number 12 on page 24.

been designated the La Jolla Ecological Reserve: a boat-free zone in which spears, floats, dogs (between 9 AM and 6 PM), and glass are also prohibited. The beach at La Jolla Cove is protected and calm, and therefore gets quite crowded. The cove itself fills with scuba divers, snorkelers, and long-distance swimmers, some of whom are over 60. They paddle the chilly two miles across the cove, emerging like fearless amphibians at La Jolla Shores. Then they shake themselves off until presentably drip-dried and hitchhike back to La Jolla, wearing only their Speedos. The locals know them on sight, so the rides come easily.

You can hike to **La Jolla Shores Beach** from La Jolla Cove via a "coast walk" that starts out promisingly, clinging to and winding along the cliff faces. Beautiful though it is, the trail is precarious, narrow, and dangerous. Besides, it peters out, requiring walkers to finish along the streets. Our first impression of the vast, heavily peopled beach at La Jolla Shores was that it looked more like a refugee camp than a recreational spot. It was wall to wall, with packs of children throwing black-sand mudballs at one another and screaming as they braved the pounding surf. The beach is flat and the waves can be huge.

Some beach property in the La Jolla Shores area is conspicuously private. We encountered several young men brandishing clipboards who were posted at either end of property belonging to the La Jolla Beach and Tennis Club. Their job was to make sure nonmembers did no more than walk through. The club's real estate is not much of a beach to begin with—people sunbathed in chairs pressed against the back wall of the building as waves lapped at their feet. Kayakers put in at a nearby restaurant called the Marine Room, which is aptly named as waves wash into its base. Fortunately the main expanse of La Jolla Shores Beach, along with Kellogg Park, a grassy picnic and play area behind it, belong to the people—and the people do indeed turn out to frolic on it.

The west-facing beaches of La Jolla proper are a varied lot, having in common the fact that they receive the full brunt of the ocean's energy. Around the point from La Jolla Cove is Boomer Beach, a popular spot for body-surfing. (Boards are forbidden, because of dangerous rip currents.) Above it is Ellen Scripps Park, a bluff-top green covering several acres that's perfect for picnicking, Frisbee tossing, or simply lying on your back and looking up at the sky. As it was the Fourth of July, we saw people doing all these things and more. Windswept trees form a canopy over the sidewalk, sculpted so that their limbs grow horizontally. A broad, brown band of kelp floated 100 yards offshore. Those who are so inclined can stroll out onto a staircase of sandstone ledges and watch the sunset. At the park's south end stairs lead to Shell Beach, a small, sandy pocket tucked into a cove. It is a steep, sloping beach with coarse brown sand—an indication of a rough and active surf zone. The beach was packed with sunbathers, but few were venturing beyond the point where the waves break.

The crème de la crème of La Jolla's beaches is **Children's Pool Beach**. A small breakwater curves out and around, protecting the beach's inner flank from waves and creating an ideal place to swim or sun. Apparently, the local population of sea lions agrees. They've got their own designated parcel of the beach, roped off from humans, who discreetly watch and take pictures from a short distance. One summer afternoon we counted 44 of the mammals sunning themselves on Children's Pool Beach, arrayed in the sand like fat sausages. Barking, cuddling, rolling over, and occasionally flapping into the water for a cooling lap, they seemed perfectly content and at home in the company of humans. Not surprisingly, this pie-shaped wedge of beach is popular with families. Children shriek as they dart from the path of spilling waves like sandpipers. Waves slam into rocks at the base of the breakwater, which has a handrailed walk-

 Map of San Diego County beaches—page 24

way, and spray—sometimes soak—people standing on it. Seabirds and their guano cover the rocks farther out.

Continuing south along Coast Boulevard, you come upon a series of vest-pocket parks and paths leading to cove beaches. The parks are equipped with benches and huts that people use for barbecues or as places to erect an easel and paint the coastal scenery. The seaside walk runs out when Coast Boulevard curves inland to meet Prospect Street at its origin, but the public beaches resume in short order. An impressive trio of them—**Marine Street Beach**, **Windansea Beach**, and **La Jolla Strand Park**—occupy an approximately one-mile stretch of prime beachfront real estate. The beaches are flatter, sandier, and more expansive here. These in-town favorites draw

"Did You Giggle Together?"

The high-pressure lifestyle of making and spending money in volatile economic times is bound to take a toll that no amount of tennis or scuba diving can adequately soothe. This perhaps explains why La Jolla, a village of 30,000, lists five pages of state-licensed psychiatrists in its Yellow Pages, not to mention the usual array of psychic problem-solvers. Stress remains a hot topic of conversation. Signs of trouble in paradise are evident and even audible, as we discovered one afternoon while strolling past a gorgeous estate in La Jolla only to hear its occupants screaming so loudly at each other that we thought the stucco was going to crack.

Relationships are casually psychoanalyzed down to the most intimate details. At dinner one night, we were seated near a medical specialist and his date (whose occupation went undivulged). Both were in their early 40s, recently divorced, and talkative to the point of indiscretion. We certainly heard every word they said.

The male interrogated his partner with highly personal questions whose premises were either incredibly profound or terribly silly, depending on which side of the New Age fence you sit. "Did you ever get to the point where you dug each other on a soul level, or was it all fantasy?" he earnestly queried. "Did you giggle together?" he asked with deep concern. By this time we were giggling together, heads buried in our plates so as not to draw undue attention. The conversation proceeded to a lengthy recounting of some sort of tongue-lashing he'd received from a psychic nutritionist with whom he had consulted. Despite his wounded ego, he generously interpreted her insults as "a loving gesture." Only in California.

Such snippets of dialogue always send us flashing back to *The Serial*, writer Cyra McFadden's brilliant '70s spoof on California-speak, of which we are affectionate connoisseurs. Which brings up another true story, related to us by a transplanted Easterner who was hired to work at the Hotel del Coronado. The new arrival attempted to organize a reading circle with his neighbors in San Diego. He enthusiastically explained the concept to his well-tanned but apparently little-read enlistees. One of them looked perplexed. "You mean we'd read books and then sit around and talk about them?" he piped up. That's right, he was told. "Indoors?" he asked incredulously. Well, he has a point, you know?

Map of San Diego County beaches—page 24

sizable numbers of surfers, anglers, swimmers, and divers. The fabled locale of Tom Wolfe's *Pump House Gang*, Windansea is legendary to this day among Southern California's surf elite. The waves are equally impressive at La Jolla Strand and Marine Street Beaches, offshore of which lie Big Rock Reef and Horseshoe Reef, respectively.

We ended our Fourth of July ramble at Windansea, winding up on the beach after ducking out on a nearby party to which some surfers had invited us. It had sounded promising: the waiter/surfer/college student who told us to come described life at his apartment complex, a few short strides from Windansea, as a nonstop episode of *Melrose Place*. Apparently,

The World According to Surfer Jeff

We had just finished swimming laps and lifting weights at our hotel's pool and exercise area, building the Olympic stamina that allows us to keep pace with the surfing, swilling, and scene-making triathletes of Southern California once the sun goes down. Heading for the Jacuzzi, we spotted a tow-headed lad, who from a distance looked about eight or nine years old. He turned out to be a surf bum in his mid-20s named Jeffrey. He hailed us as we approached, offering a congratulatory pep talk about keeping in shape while handing us each a beer—lukewarm Bud Lights plucked from a 12-pack that was well on its way to being demolished. He was not a registered guest at the hotel, just a local who'd wandered onto the property to dangle his feet in the hot tub and knock back some brews.

His worldview was a mixture of hedonism and pathos, an outlook common to those who outwardly "have it all" and yet feel a spiritual void inside themselves. It is the animus behind just about every song the Eagles have ever written, including "Hotel California," the ultimate anthem to the have-everything, feel-nothing, paradise-sucks state of spiritual torpor that most hedonists eventually wind up espousing, if only to make themselves feel less guilty for having so much fun. We refer to it as "sunny angst."

Surfer Jeff was the peroxide-blond embodiment of sunny angst. After handing over the beer, he struck up a friendly monologue, quickly informing us total strangers that "it's time for me to get my life together." He paused, then confessed, "I'm getting old.... I'm almost 25." He'd like to get out of La Jolla, he said, a town where "your life is everyone else's business," where tongues wag and people stab you in the back to get ahead. He admitted to having family problems; his folks were less than thrilled that their high-school dropout son was still perfecting his form on the waves but had no career prospects. In addition, he intimated that among the townsfolk he was widely regarded as a wastrel who'd worn out his welcome. "I've got a bad reputation around here," he candidly confessed. "I don't know why, but I do."

Outwardly, he was an exemplary specimen of young California manhood, neatly massaged by sun, wind, and waves to a lean, statuesque ideal of perfection. His skin was burnished to a ruddy brown, while his windblown hair was the color of Midwestern hay. He positively glowed with the boisterous virility of a life lived out-of-

 Map of San Diego County beaches—page 24

we came too late. By the time we arrived, it looked more like an episode of *Sanford and Son*. Trash cans full of empties were already being dragged to the curb, and except for a rap record playing in the apartment and a girl skating in the driveway, the party was over. We kept walking down Bonair Street till it ended at the beach. Then we perched on a sandstone ledge, brews in hand, listening to the soothing sounds of the sea in the aftermath of the holiday fireworks.

Bunking Down

The inns and hotels of La Jolla tend to be on the sumptuous (read: expensive) side, so don't come looking for a budget Best Western here.

doors. But now he found himself an unwilling adult with no career and no life beyond that of hanging ten and then guzzling at least that number once out of the water. "I've got no tools," he lamented, holding up his hands as if to display his lack of real-world skills.

He possesses nothing beyond an ability to ride the waves and, in the words of Prince, to party like it's 1999. That may be all you need to get by while in the throes of a reckless California youth, but it won't pay the bills or feed the family past age 30. Not that he's got (or wants) a family or that he will ever succumb to the rat race of working to acquire things he doesn't really covet or require, however forcefully they're urged on him by a consumption-oriented culture that won't take no for an answer. In Surfer Jeff's worldview, who really needs anything more than a warm day, a nice southern swell, and a tall, cool can of brew?

Beneath the veneer of gotta-get-my-life-together beats the heart of a guy who's basically content, periodically offering hand-wringing displays of regretful sensitivity in order to convince himself and others that he's "serious" about the future. His philosophy is not far from that of Henry Miller, who opened the novel *Tropic of Cancer* with these lines: "I have no money, no resources, no hopes. I am the happiest man alive." Surfer Jeff cast that sentiment in his own words: "I've tried to get away, but the beach keeps calling me back. There's just something about it. It's so much fun that there's no real incentive to think of doing anything else. Just when you get bored with the whole scene, there's always somebody new who will wander down the beach with a cooler full of beer. It's like, 'Where's the next pool? Where's the next party? Where are we going now?'"

At this point a friend of his who waited tables in the hotel restaurant wandered into the pool area for a smoke. Surfer Jeff instantly switched out of his introspective mode and loudly greeted his friend with a series of birdlike squawking noises that recalled Jerry Lewis in one of his more demented and sophomoric film roles. They gave each other a mighty high-five, and the new arrival accepted the beer reflexively shoved at him, even though he was still on-duty and wearing a tuxedo. They talked about their plans for later that evening. "If you come up with something to do," pleaded Surfer Jeff, "please drag my sorry ass along with you, man."

The nicest are the European-style hotels located downtown or overlooking the cove. Our pick of the litter is the **Colonial Inn** (910 Prospect Street, 454-2181, $$$), a mannerly and well-appointed hostelry that dates from 1913. Rooms are plush, and amenities include a heated pool in a gorgeous courtyard setting and free valet parking. Then there's the lavishly appointed **La Valencia** (1132 Prospect Street, 454-0771, $$$), a salmon-colored stucco wonder that feels like the old California, if not the Old World. The beach at La Jolla is just steps away out the backdoors of the Colonial Inn and La Valencia.

Even closer is **La Jolla Cove Motel** (1155 Coast Boulevard, 459-2621, $$), a four-story modern that trades what it lacks in architectural distinction for a prime location directly overlooking La Jolla Cove and a few steps away from Ellen Scripps Park. Oceanfront balconies, a heated pool, and proximity to La Jolla's downtown shopping district are added pluses. Another of the fancy in-town hotels, the **Empress Hotel of La Jolla** (7766 Fay Avenue, 454-3001, $$$), swaddles its guests with Old World elegance and contemporary luxury. Large, comfortable rooms are appointed with marble-tired baths, well-stocked minibars and terrycloth robes that hang inside mirrored closet doors. Mauve cloth napkins are placed next to a gilt-edged ice bucket. (You get the idea.) On the lobby level is a gourmet Italian restaurant called Manhattan; in the basement, an exercise room, spa, sauna, and showers.

Being partial to beachside locations, we've found the **Sea Lodge** (8110 Camino Del Oro, 459-8271, $$$) to be the best combination of location and comfort in the area. Its 128 rooms surround a tropical plant–filled terra-cotta courtyard. All rooms have balconies or lanais, and La Jolla Shores Beach is literally steps away. The feeling out here is more outdoorsy, rustic, and recreational than it is in La Jolla's business district. With its arched, wood-plank ceilings, it feels more like a ski lodge than a sea lodge—until you sniff the salt air blowing off the ocean. Recreational facilities include a heated outdoor pool and tennis courts; the hotel also will provide guests with beach equipment, such as chairs, umbrellas, and volleyball equipment. It's highly recommended.

The **Summer House Inn** (7955 La Jolla Shores Drive, 459-0261, $$) is a modern, 11-story high-rise located four blocks from La Jolla Shores Beach. In addition to panoramic ocean views from the rooms, the Summer House boasts a world-class restaurant, **Elario's** (459-0541, $$$), on its top floor. Dress is semiformal; the menu is continental, with a seafood emphasis; the wine list is world-class. Finally, for corporate chain-hotel partisans there's the top-of-the-line **Sheraton Grande Torrey Pines** (10950 North Torrey Pines Road, 558-1500, $$$), a 400-room resort that's adjacent to a golf course and overlooks the ocean. A perfectly adequate and reasonably priced **Radisson Hotel** (3299 Holiday Court, 453-5500, $$) reposes in the hills west of the town center, where Interstate 5 meets La Jolla Village Drive.

Coastal Cuisine

La Jolla's restaurant scene is dominated by **George's at the Cove** (1250 Prospect Street, 454-4244, $$$), a three-story restaurant that offers diners the option of semiformal indoor dining downstairs or a more casual setting on an outdoor deck that overlooks La Jolla Cove. Since it was midsummer, we took the latter option, enjoying the extensive view out to sea and up the coast. We dined on grilled marinated swordfish and a mixed grill of three fish, both of which tasted of the grill and were absolutely delicious—especially as they were accompanied by "George's Handmade Margarita" before and glasses of River Road Chardonnay during. The third-level deck seats 115 and looks out on the ocean as if from the bow of a ship. Plexiglas panes keep the wind at bay, and heat lamps provide a note of warmth to counter the chill. Yes, we were dining on the beach in Southern California in July, and heat lamps were needed. For those who doubt, there's a pronounced fall-like tang in the air even in midsummer along the California coast, thanks to the ocean's giant cooling engine.

Downstairs, the more formal dining room specializes in creative seafood preparations done with a California flair—i.e., apple-smoked salmon served with fennel, miso, and Hawaiian pesto, and halibut in chicken fumet with poached leeks, garlic, and shallots. George himself can be seen bustling around the premises, impeccably attired and super-competent, yet possessing a dry, I've-seen-it-all wit straight out of *Fawlty Towers*. George's at the Cove is a bona fide La Jolla landmark and a must-try for visitors.

Another good choice with a comparable view and decided seafood emphasis is the **Crab Catcher** (1298 Prospect Street, 454-9587, $$), which serves a fine menu of reasonably priced offerings. For lunch, we had an excellent Dungeness crab sandwich that came with bow-tie pasta salad and red-cabbage cole slaw. On the Mexican side, you'll find some good sit-down Spanish and Mexican restaurants along Prospect Street, such as **Jose's Court Room** (see Night Moves below).

In the morning, we headed like all good gourmet coffeeholics to **Starbucks Coffee** (Prospect Street, 551-5526, $). In addition to the best cup of coffee this side of Java, they've got first-rate pastries to bolster your cholesterol count (but in a good way). We're bullish on the raisin scones and cranberry apple pop-over muffins.

Night Moves

In recent years, La Jolla has lost some of its cultivated politesse, which has helped liven up its formerly stultifying nightlife. Today the multilevel minimalls of Prospect Street contain the likes of a **Hard Rock Café** (909 Prospect Street, 454-5101) and a brand-new **Moondoggies** (909 Prospect Street, 454-9664), one of a small but growing chain of spacious, upscale surf bars (find the oxy-moron). However, in our judgment **Jose's Court Room** (1037 Prospect Street, 454-5655) is the place. A combination Mexican restaurant and bar, it was by far the liveliest joint we encountered in La Jolla. A loud CD jukebox sprayed its decibels upon a throbbing, three-deep crowd of beautiful people surrounding the oval island of the bar. The Mexican grub is good, but folks really crowd in for the company. So call out for an ice-cold Pacifico, one of the best of the Mexican beers, and join in the brew-ha-ha. Incidentally, we kept bumping into a character in the downtown bars whom we dubbed "Mr. Photo Op of La Jolla." He apparently makes his living trotting from place to place with a camera on his shoulders, clicking pictures of people willing to pay for a visual record of their "special occasions" (drunkenness and adultery excepted).

For More Information

Contact the La Jolla Town Council, 1055 Wall Street, Suite 110, La Jolla, CA 92037; (619) 454-1444.

Black's Beach and Torrey Pines State Beach

Location: Between La Jolla and Del Mar, reachable via exits off the San Diego Freeway (Interstate 5).

A few miles north of La Jolla, just above the Scripps Institution of Oceanography and the Scripps Aquarium and Pier, lies one of the real gems of the state park system: Torrey Pines State Reserve. Its setting is so peaceful and untrammeled you'll easily forget it brushes against a city of over a million people. Trails lead into stands of the rare Torrey pine, which grow only in this park and on Santa Rosa Island, 175 miles to the northwest. Several overlooks offer breathtaking views of the beach 300 feet below. An old lodge, dating from 1902, serves as a visitor center. Some 436 plant and animal species are native to the park, including 144 birds, 110 invertebrates, 85 plants, 39 mammals, 28 reptiles, 23 fish, and 7 amphibians. In addition to its flora, fauna, and spectacular geology, the reserve is rich in fossils, and is close to where archeologists discovered the bones of Del Mar Man, believed to be the oldest human remains yet discovered in North America. The tranquillity of the park is interrupted only by rustling breezes and the occasional sight of a gopher breaking open a Hottentot fig. The park offers a truly homeopathic remedy for urban stress: an oasis of calm set beneath an awesome canopy of *Pinus torreyana*.

The shore below Torrey Pines is **Black's Beach**, probably the most infamous nude beach in the country, found at the southern end of Torrey Pines State Beach. It is set at the

Black's Beach

Location: In La Jolla. Walk down to the beach via the steep, gated, paved path that begins at the junction of La Jolla Farms Road and Blackgold Road. Or walk north along the beach from Scripps Pier or south from Torrey Pines State Beach.

Parking: Limited free street parking on and around La Jolla Farms Road. A better option is to park at Torrey Pines State Beach and walk south.

Hours: Open 24 hours.

Facilities: None.

Contact: For beach information, contact the San Diego Coastline Parks Division at (619) 221-8900 or the San Diego Lifeguard Service at (619) 221-8899. For a surf report, call (619) 221-8884.

See number 17 on page 24.

Torrey Pines State Beach

Location: In Torrey Pines. Take the Carmel Valley Road exit off Interstate 5, five miles north of La Jolla. Turn onto McGonigle Road and follow it to the beach.

Parking: $4 entrance fee per vehicle.

Hours: 8 AM to 10 PM.

Facilities: Lifeguards, rest rooms, and picnic tables.

Contact: For beach information, contact Torrey Pines State Beach at (619) 755-2063.

See number 18 on page 24.

base of the high bluffs between Scripps Pier and Los Penasquitos Lagoon, and is as controversial as it is hard to reach. It is so out of the way we wonder why anyone would bother to get uptight about people enjoying the sun, surf, and sand au naturel. Yet the dimensions of the feud have occasionally plunged Black's Beach into the national news.

The Scripps Institution of Oceanography

Founded as an independent research lab in 1903 by a University of California, Berkeley, biology professor, the Scripps Institution of Oceanography is one of the oldest centers for marine research in the world. It was named the Scripps Institution for Biological Research in 1912, owing to the munificence of its benefactors, Ellen Browning Scripps and E. W. Scripps. As time passed, it came to focus its research efforts on the sea—an evolution that was recognized in 1925 when it was rechristened the Scripps Institution of Oceanography. The Institution's assets include: a fleet of four oceanographic vessels and two research platforms; classrooms and laboratories; shoreline and underwater reserves; a seismological observatory and a satellite oceanography facility; a pier and aquarium/bookstore; a major marine sciences library; and faculty and staff numbering more than 1,000. At any given time there may be 250 research programs under way, ranging from beach erosion to the physiology of invertebrates. If study in the fields of oceanography, marine biology, and earth sciences interests you, Scripps is the place to go for graduate training.

Even if doctoral studies in the geomorphology of ocean basins or manganese-nodule formation is not in your future, Scripps still has something to offer: an aquarium that's open to the public free of charge (though a measly $2 donation is suggested) from 9 AM to 5 PM daily. The Scripps Aquarium and Pier are located in La Jolla Shores, just up from Kellogg Park and La Jolla Shores Beach. The glass tanks of the aquarium contain everything from a 12-foot spiny lobster to an old gray grouper who cowers grumpily in a corner. Highlights include rainbow-colored exotics from Micronesia and the frozen-in-glass coelacanth, a nearly extinct relic from an ancient biological regime that looks like a battered piece of luggage.

As a free museum attached to a university-funded research facility, it's not nearly as vast and "oh, wow" as, say, the Monterey Bay Aquarium up the coast. But Scripps does offer a squid's-eye view of everything from kelp beds to coral reefs, plus a taste of the important research being conducted at the institution. On that last note we'd like to lob this bit of wisdom at our readers, copied years ago from one of the exhibits, as we've seen evidence of its truth on every coast we've traveled: "Man has interfered with nature's supply of sand to our beaches, thus compounding the erosion problem, and we are now seeing the results of this intervention. Putting it bluntly, we are losing are beaches."

For more information, contact the Scripps Aquarium and Pier, 8602 La Jolla Shores Drive, La Jolla, CA 92037; (619) 534-3474.

After 5,000 frolicsome nudists partied naked on the Fourth of July, 1977, the good citizens of San Diego voted that October to ban nudity at Black's Beach. But the clothing-optional sun worshippers were not to be denied. In defiance of the law, nudity still prevails at Black's Beach, although it is best described as occasional rather than pervasive.

Our experiences have borne out that observation. On a sparkling June afternoon several years back—Mother's Day, as fate would have it—all we saw were half a dozen men wandering the beach wearing only white socks and tennis shoes. More recently, on a warm afternoon in mid-July the sum total of bathers in the buff consisted of an overweight couple of AARP age and several bearded male loners. We were finally able to decode the putative partitioning of who disrobes where along Black Beach's two-mile stretch, thanks to a gatekeeper at Torrey Pines. Here's the lowdown: the north end is for men only, the middle part is coed, and the south end is for surfers. "It's our Hawaii," said the gatekeeper, whose attention had to be pried away from a pod of dolphins whose offshore movements he was monitoring with a pair of binoculars. A surfer himself, he added: "The waves are good all over the coast, but for some reason they're particularly big down there."

It's a long, albeit beautiful and rugged, hike to Black's Beach. Getting there is actually easier from above. A stairway descends from the Glider Port (off Scenic Torrey Pines Road). Steeply etched into the cliffs, this point of entry comes with a warning: "Stairway and cliffs unsafe and unstable due to 1993 rains." The warning goes unheeded, and the foot of the staircase roughly demarcates the surfer's zone from the coed nudists' encampment. The safest way down, however, is via the service road that begins where Blackgold and La Jolla Farms roads meet. You can't drive a car down it, but your own two feet will deposit you on the beach in 10 minutes or so. Free on-street parking is available, and there are a sufficient number of spaces (with two-hour limits) to handle demand most of the time, summer weekends and holidays excepted. The road to the beach drops steeply in a series of switchbacks, passing warning signs ("Danger: Hazardous Cliffs Subject to Landslide") and irreverent graffiti ("Do Not Eat or Feed Nudists") before flinging walkers out at the south end of Black's Beach, with the Scripps Pier in plain view.

Alternatively, you can park up at **Torrey Pines State Beach** and hike south along the beach. The longer, ground-level Torrey Pines route offers a Kodak carousel's worth of dramatic scenery: enormous toppled boulders, giant piles of talus at the base of the towering cliffs, and huge sheets of blackboard-smooth rock. The whole landscape has a wild, otherworldly appearance. Hikers will want to keep a watchful eye on incoming tides, which could potentially strand the unwary in a cove as they rise.

The less adventurous will prefer to stay put in the middle section of Torrey Pines State Beach, a better-than-adequate day-use beach. An ample parking area abuts Los Penasquitos Lagoon. Arrive early if you want a parking spot on a good beach day. The cobble-filled beach itself is inferior to the sandy, scenic, and less crowded expanses of Black's Beach.

For More Information

Write the Torrey Pines Association, P.O. Box 150, La Jolla, CA 92037, or Torrey Pines State Reserve, P.O. Box 38, Carlsbad, CA 92008. Call Torrey Pines State Beach at (619) 755-2063.

 Map of San Diego County beaches—page 24

Del Mar

Location: 20 miles north of downtown San Diego, it can be reached by taking exits off the San Diego Freeway (Interstate 5). Del Mar Heights Road is the most direct point of access. The main street through town is Camino Del Mar, which parallels the ocean from a few blocks away. Del Mar City Beach is the most popular beach in the area.
Population: 5,100
Area Code: 619 **Zip Code:** 92014

The boutiquing of Southern California reaches a modest crescendo in Del Mar. It is not as loud as the cymbal crash heard in places like Dana Point and Huntington Beach, but the drums are beating all the same. It's getting to the point where Del Mar sometimes seems undeserving of its self-decreed "village" status, even with a population of only 5,100. These days Del Mar is a trendy, buzzing little hive in town and a jazzed-up mall-o-drama out by its famous racetrack. The pace of traffic has picked up, giving Camino Del Mar a taste of the fumey, bumper-to bumper backup that congests Laguna Beach. That's not to say the place has lost its charm, just that it's experiencing growing pains. But this is par for the coast; there's scarcely an available acre within sight of water in Southern California that hasn't been built up or targeted for development.

All the same, Del Mar is the closest you will come to finding a true village atmosphere in coastal San Diego County. Thanks to the vigilant attempts of the populace to keep development under control, coupled with the breezy, relaxed atmosphere of the racetrack that is the town's centerpiece, Del Mar has the air of a less harried time in California's past. To a great extent, it has geography to thank. Del Mar is situated on a hill between two lagoons, with a canyon to the east and ocean to the west. The land thins to precipitous strips at the lagoons: Los Penasquitos to the south (at Torrey Pines State Reserve), and San Dieguito, behind and around the river mouth at the north end of town. There's only so much you can build out here that hasn't already been constructed or attempted. In the mid-1980s, environmental prerogatives saved the San Dieguito Lagoon from boneheaded plans to construct a cluster of hotels, shops, and freeway access ramps.

In town, the only major new project that's survived the legal gauntlet has been the L'Auberge Del Mar, a $45 million luxury hotel and spa built on the site of the old Del Mar Hotel (which was demolished in 1967). Even so, it took the developer, a Del Mar resident, more than a decade to gain approval of the plan. The heart of the village, along Camino Del Mar from about Sixth to Fifteenth Streets, is a cavalcade of small shops catering to a consumer's every whim. Folks mosey from cafés to shops, grazing and browsing, as traffic moves in fits and starts along Camino Del Mar while drivers scour the streets for parking spaces.

The town is best known for the thoroughbred racing season at the Del Mar Thoroughbred Club. The brief, 43-day season runs from late July to early September, packing the town with racing buffs. The racetrack was built in the 1930s as the brainchild of local celebrities Bing Crosby, Jimmy Durante, and Pat O'Brien. Their cosponsor in the venture was the Works Progress Administration, which pulled out midway through construction. Crosby and O'Brien were left holding the bag, having to borrow funds to bring the track to completion. Der Bingle wrote and recorded a song to commemorate the track's opening in 1937. "Where the Surf Meets the Turf" is still played before the first race with all the dewy-eyed solemnity of the National Anthem. Grandstand seats run from $3 to $10 at the track, which lies inside a triangle formed by Via de la Valle, Camino Del Mar, and Jimmy

Durante Way. The grounds are also the site of the annual Del Mar Fair, a June/July to-do that draws three-quarters of a million San Diegans. The rest of the year is given over to horse shows, trade shows, and concerts.

Before the first "... and they're off!" echoed around the track, Del Mar was already trotting along on an initially shaky but eventually well-heeled course. In 1883, developer Jacob Taylor Shell bought the strip of coastline upon which Del Mar sits today. He built a seaside spa on his 338 acres that included the Casa Del Mar Hotel, a dance pavilion, a bathhouse and pool, and a railroad depot. It briefly thrived before succumbing to bankruptcy, flood, and fire (in that order) by 1890. The town received a facelift during the Roaring Twenties: a renovated hotel, a rebuilt pier, and new roads into town. The fairgrounds came in 1936, the racetrack a year later. Del Mar has grown slowly but steadily ever since, trying its best to remain—as a *Newsweek* article described it a quarter of a century ago—"a sleepy little seacoast town."

Beaches

Del Mar City Beach is a sunbather's paradise, quickly filling to capacity on summer days. A grassy play area, Seagrove Park, sits on the short bluffs overlooking the beach from the south end. The park, coastal walkway, and beach are separated from town by railroad tracks. It's an extremely popular beach, attracting a mix of students from UC-San Diego, teens from all over, and families who have come to town for the county fair or horse races. All find room to roam on this extremely wide, well-lifeguarded beach. Finding a spot on the beach is less of a problem than finding a place to park close by. There's on-street metered parking along Coast Boulevard, as well as a few pay lots. The early bird gets the parking spot while the loser cruises; July and August parking is wall to wall. The beach itself is good for swimming and body surfing.

Beyond Del Mar City Beach lies the mouth of the San Dieguito River, which is dry at low tide, and Del Mar Bluffs City Park. A steep wooden staircase laden with sand leads to a spectacular overlook from the top of the bluff. The 360-degree panorama encompasses the ocean, the racetrack, and the town. Straddling Del Mar and neighboring Solana Beach is **Seascape Shores**, a sandy stretch of beach reachable from stairways near the 500 and 700 blocks of South Sierra Avenue. These beaches are popular with locals and tourists alike, not the least reason being that in season you might catch trainers working their horses on the beach.

Del Mar City Beach

4

Location: In Del Mar, at the west end of Camino Del Mar and 15th Street.

Parking: Metered parking lot.

Hours: Open 24 hours.

Facilities: Lifeguards, rest rooms, and showers.

Contact: For beach information, contact Del Mar Community Services at (619) 755-1524.

See number 19 on page 24.

Seascape Shores

3

Location: In Solana Beach, between the 500 and 700 blocks of South Sierra Avenue.

Parking: Free street parking.

Hours: 6 AM to 10 PM.

Facilities: Lifeguards.

Contact: For beach information, contact the Solana Beach Department of Marine Safety at (619) 755-1569.

See number 20 on page 24.

Bunking Down

Some things never change. The **Del Mar Motel On the Beach** (1702 Coast Boulevard, 755-1534, $$) is where it's always been: smack dab on the beach. A charmingly unpretentious place that's been around since 1946, it's the only place in the area that can make that claim. Such homey motels are more the exception than the rule, as Del Mar and other North Coast communities are more typically represented these days by places like **L'Auberge Del Mar** (1540 Camino Del Mar, 259-1515, $$$$). You'll pay through the nose to be pampered at this resort spa. Visitors can select seaweed body packs, aromatherapy, reflexology, Shiatsu massage, and the ever-popular "Balneo Therapy Revitalizing Bath" from a menu of spa services more extensive than the list of ice-cream flavors at Ben & Jerry's. It's a splendid resort, to be sure, with beautiful interiors, an inviting pool area, multilevel decks, and walkways that meander among walled-in gardens that suggest a place far removed from the reality of a busy street corner. Large and well-landscaped grounds confer that all-important sense of splendid isolation that justifies room rates that run from $165 to $250 a night ($325 to $700 for suites).

And yet we hesitate. There's something a little off-putting about a too-fancy resort by the beach that bends over backward to target rich executives. It's the sort of place that revels in its own exclusivity. "Entertaining business clients or friends unfolds smoothly in salons that offer a sense of intimacy and grace" reads one line from a L'Auberge brochure, accompanying a picture of a grand piano in a faux library-cum-dining room. What about the beach a few short paces away? The sun? Real life?

We are partial to the **Stratford Inn of Del Mar** (710 Camino Del Mar, 755-1501, $$), located a few steps from the center of town. It burrows low into a hillside, with rooms that are set into cul-de-sacs off a main catwalk that winds around the building. Constructed of gray, weathered wood, the Stratford Inn blends nicely into its environment. The grounds are invitingly quiet, featuring two heated pools and underground parking, and the large rooms come with private balconies and patios.

Coastal Cuisine

Down by Del Mar City Beach, a pair of restaurants with picture-window views of the ocean do a brisk business. **Jake's Oceanfront Restaurant** (1660 Coast Boulevard, 755-2002, $$$) and the **Poseidon Restaurant** (1670 Coast Boulevard, 755-9345, $$$) are the places to go if you want to dine by the water. Jake's offers a menu of seafood prepared any number of ethnically diverse ways: Chinese (Fresh Ahi Szechwan), New Orleans (Fresh Fish Cajun Style), and Spanish (Shrimp and Scallops Valencia). Their Pacific Seafood Chowder (with fish, clams, and diced veggies) is rated among the best on the coast. The Poseidon sticks more closely to baked or broiled seafood basics. Both restaurants are overpriced—the cheapest entrée at Jake's, for instance, is $13.95—but you're paying a premium for location and ambience. The Poseidon has an especially inviting modern interior of varnished pine walls, tile floor, and big panoramic windows facing the ocean.

The **Fish Market** (640 Via De La Valle, 755-2277, $$) is an unpretentious, bustling sure bet for fresh seafood. If you're in a quandary about what to order, walk up to the fresh-fish counter, decide what looks good to you, and order it back at your table. They smoke their own fish—the salmon/albacore combo is a must-try appetizer—and fresh seafood entrées range from Utah rainbow trout to local thresher shark, plus skewers of scallops, oysters, ahi, and more. The Fish Market is close by the track.

Choices in town include **Carlos & Annie's Café** (1454 Camino Del Mar, 755-4601, $$), a Southwestern-themed restaurant that regularly wins "best breakfast" awards on the strength of such offerings as Carlos' Omelette (chicken, salsa, avocado, cheese, Spanish sauce). On the other side of the street, **Café Del Mar** (1247 Camino Del Mar, 481-1133, $$) serves brick-oven pizza and creative pasta dishes, such as sautéed salmon with dill vodka sauce over penne, all priced very reasonably.

Night Moves

Generally, the night moves made in Del Mar are the sort of stretching and yawning calisthenics performed immediately before crawling into bed. As in most professedly quiet towns, there's not much to do beyond eating well, strolling a few blocks through the village after dinner, or maybe downing a highball in one of the "salons" at L'Auberge Del Mar to the polite accompaniment of a tinkling piano. You might find a little action in the bar at **Bully's** (1404 Camino Del Mar, 755-1660), a prime-rib palace with an outdoor patio that's open till midnight. Otherwise, if you want nightlife you'll just have to roll up to Solana Beach, which has plenty of it.

For More Information

Contact the Greater Del Mar Chamber of Commerce, 1442 Camino Del Mar, Suite 214, Del Mar, CA 92014; (619) 755-4844.

Solana Beach

Location: 25 miles north of downtown San Diego, between Del Mar and Cardiff-by-the-Sea. Sierra and Pacific Avenues run alongside the beachfront. Fletcher Cove is the best of Solana Beach's meager lot of beaches.
Population: 13,000
Area Code: 619 **Zip Code:** 92075

Solana Beach is one of a conglomerate of communities lined up end to end along the corridor between Old Highway 101 and the San Diego Freeway (Interstate 5) in north San Diego County. Old Highway 101 literally explodes with commercial developments in these north-county communities, except for areas occupied by state beaches. In terms of personality, the towns blend into one another. Cookie-cutter strip malls do not endow a community with discernible character; in fact, they tend to suffocate the qualities that make a town unique.

Solana Beach's traditional claim to fame has been as party headquarters for north San Diego County. The townsfolk, whose per capita income is said to be even greater than that of Del Mar, haven't exactly been thrilled that their community traditionally has been the one to play Pied Piper to a hip-hopping party crowd. They've been working to change their image with tighter permitting and more vigilant law enforcement. As a result, the nightlife has gradually become more evenly spread around this end of the county, spilling into Cardiff and up into Carlsbad. Ultimately, it's all one big overflow valve for the city of San Diego anyway. Solana Beach calls itself "the best spot under the sun." It's got two miles of beach, a number of decent restaurants and delis, and one of the best clubs in the country for live music (see Night Moves below).

Beaches

Access to Solana Beach's beaches is blocked, to a great degree, by residential housing. There's a teeny-tiny municipal parking lot at Del Mar Shores Terrace and Sierra Avenue, site of Seascape Shores (see the Del Mar Beaches entry on page 74). Sierra Avenue eventually dumps into a large free parking lot at Fletcher Cove, site of a run-down community center, a basketball hoop, and two shuffleboard courts. It's an attractive natural setting, especially from the bluff-top vista point, which looks out over the crumbling cliffs to the churning ocean below. It was here that we saw an old codger, a postal employee, taking a midday siesta on a park bench. You could hardly blame him. The cove was blasted into being by early settlers, who dynamited the cliff bases. (Can you imagine the environmental furor that would cause today?) The sandy beach at **Fletcher Cove** is the best that's available within city limits, so it is a popular place with the locals. The southern end is good for shelling; the northern end for surfing. A half mile north is **Tide Beach Park**, which is located at the base of a bluff reachable by a stairway; it's good for tidepooling, spear fishing, surf casting, and scuba diving.

Bunking Down

The best choice is the **Ramada Inn** (717 South Highway 101, 792-8200, $$), an attractive hotel from which you can walk to the beach that lies on the other side of Sierra Avenue.

Coastal Cuisine

A good spread of Mexican food can be had at **Fidel's** (607 Valley Avenue, 755-5292, $$), a crowded cantina with an unpretentious atmosphere. The local franchise of **California Pizza Kitchen** (437 South Highway 101, 793-0999, $$) offers 28 kinds of pizza in an internationally flavored menu that includes toppings such as Thai chicken, shrimp pesto, and tandoori chicken. All pizzas are baked in wood-fired ovens. The place is as large as a car dealership and seems to be a popular hangout.

Night Moves

The **Belly Up Tavern** (143 South Cedros Avenue, 481-8140) enjoys a national reputation and is beloved by musicians and music fans alike. A roomy club, it is typical of other well-run, similarly sized nightclubs around the country that provide a living to musicians who might otherwise be applying for unemployment benefits. These include ghosts of the 1960s who have gone from stardom to cult status, as well as current up and comers. We caught a droll, low-key set by Dan Hicks, the San Francisco Scene pioneer and jazz-pop stylist whose justifiably cynical disenchantment with the music business made for entertaining between-song patter. Well-traveled journeymen like Richie Havens and Jorma Kaukonen, along with reconstituted groups of varying vintages that can still boast a few original members—such as the Tubes, the Blasters, and the Band—make up the bulk of

Fletcher Cove Park

Location: In Solana Beach, at 111 South Sierra Avenue.

Parking: Free parking lot.

Hours: 6 AM to 10 PM.

Facilities: Lifeguards, rest rooms, and picnic tables.

Contact: For beach information, contact the Solana Beach Department of Marine Safety at (619) 755-1569.

See number 21 on page 24.

Tide Beach Park

Location: At Pacific Avenue and Solana Vista Drive.

Parking: Free street parking.

Hours: 6 AM to 10 PM.

Facilities: Lifeguards.

Contact: For beach information, contact the Solana Beach Department of Marine Safety at (619) 755-1569.

See number 22 on page 24.

the entertainment calendar at the Belly Up. The acoustics are great throughout, and the whole operation is first-class. In short, it is one of the top clubs in the country.

For More Information

Contact the Solana Beach Chamber of Commerce, 210 West Plaza Street, Solana Beach, CA 92075; (619) 755-4775.

Cardiff-by-the-Sea

Location: Between Solana Beach and Encinitas, along Highway 101. The main beach is Cardiff State Beach, which can be reached via Old Highway 101.
Population: 15,000
Area Code: 619 **Zip Code:** 92007

Cardiff-by-the-Sea, which takes its name from the Welsh seaport city, is the most unassuming of the north San Diego County beach towns. Its chief attractions are the state beaches on opposite ends of town. However, the arrival of several trendy bistros on the beach and some fairly new seaside lodges attest to Cardiff's growing popularity. Still, the governing philosophy is that quality of life, not size, is to be preferred. The only industry that Cardiff has ever had dates back to 1912; it was a kelp-processing operation that closed down three years later.

Beaches

Cardiff State Beach lies west of the San Elijo Lagoon, separated from it by Old Highway 101. The large, soft, sandy beach is great for board surfing, swimming, windsurfing, and surf casting. There are boat launches at the north end and tidepools at the south end. Visitors enter the beach from a dusty, bumpy, pothole-ridden parking lot. Plans have been in the works for a $1.5 million asphalt lot that will accommodate 500 cars, but the project is not without critics. The issue of landscaping (or, rather, lack of it) was being hotly debated by the Cardiff-by-the-Sea town council when we passed through. The town is known

Cardiff State Beach

Location: In Cardiff-by-the-Sea, along Old Highway 101 at San Elijo Lagoon.
Parking: $4 entrance fee per vehicle.
Hours: 6 AM to 11 PM.
Facilities: Lifeguards and rest rooms.
Contact: For beach information, contact San Elijo State Beach at (619) 753-5091.

See number 23 on page 24.

San Elijo State Beach

Location: On north side of Cardiff-by-the-Sea, along Old Highway 101 at Chesterfield Drive.
Parking: $4 entrance fee per vehicle.
Hours: 7 AM to 10 PM.
Facilities: Lifeguards, rest rooms, showers, and picnic tables. There are 171 campsites for tents and RVs. Fees are $14 to $16 per night. For camping reservations, call Destinet at (800) 444-7275.
Contact: For beach information, contact San Elijo State Beach at (619) 793-5091.

See number 24 on page 24.

for its palm trees, and the residents wanted some palms planted among the black asphalt desert. "It's going to be an awful lot of asphalt out there cooking in the summer sun," crowed a local real-estate broker. "I can't believe they're not going to do anything for landscaping." The argument runs that the lot sits in a basin that is subject to flooding, and that any vegetation planted would be washed away. It's hard enough to hold the beaches and roadway in place, let alone palm trees. Already 10,000 tons of riprap have been installed as shore protection.

San Elijo State Beach is best known for camping, being the southernmost developed campground in the state system. Set high atop a jagged cliff, San Elijo's 171 sites fill up quickly. Reserve early, especially for the summer months. The campground is nicely laid out, with scraggly hedges providing some shade and privacy. The sites closest to the cliff's edge are the best. From these spots you can hear the waves crashing at night. You're also closer to the wooden stairs that lead to the beach. It is a long, lifeguarded beach and a good place to savor a gorgeous California sunset.

Bunking Down

If camping in the sand at **San Elijo State Beach** (see above) is too primitive for you, try the **Countryside Inn** (1661 Villa Cardiff Drive, 944-0427, $$). It's a 102-room Colonial-style hotel with bed-and-breakfast amenities.

Coastal Cuisine

Cardiff has its own little beachside "Restaurant Row" along Old Highway 101. The place to dine in Cardiff is the **Beach House** (2530 South Highway 101, 753-1321, $$$), a pricey, glitzy seafood restaurant so close to the beach the fish could practically swim from the ocean to the broiler. The parking lot attests to its popularity, as an army of young valets in tennis shorts and monogrammed pullovers take turns running the 40-yard dash, car keys jangling, to park or retrieve diners' vehicles. The ocean views are fantastic, so try to come at sunset. For those on a budget, there's an old reliable Mexican eatery, **Los Olas** (2655 South Highway 101, 942-1860, $), on the dry side of the highway, facing the beach.

Night Moves

The **Kraken Bar & Restaurant** (2531 South Highway 101, 436-6483) bills itself as "the bar by the beach...where the locals still and probably always will party." They've got pool and pinball tables, six color TVs, and two (count 'em!) satellite dishes. Summer happy hour runs from 4 PM to 7 PM. What more can we say but "let it rip, dude!"

For More Information

Contact the Cardiff-by-the-Sea Chamber of Commerce, P.O. Box 552, 2017 San Elijo Avenue, Cardiff-by-the-Sea, CA 92007; (619) 436-0431.

Beach Games

The play's the thing in Southern California, at least at the beach. Most career choices, in fact, revolve in some way around outdoor activities. If one is not involved in real estate—selling or developing chunks of oceanfront that are the leisure set's most precious commodity—one is connected to the service fields that minister to the whims or needs of a populace that worships the sun.

Although nonacquisitive surfers would appear to be immune to this buy-and-sell world, even they get sucked into it, as do construction workers, waitpersons, motel maintenance staff, barkeeps, and salespeople. We figured that if we lived in Southern California we might make pretty good yardmen, sculpting yucca plants into likenesses of the legendary surfer Duke Kahanamoku.

That said, let the beach games begin, and may they never end! The following are some of the most popular games we've witnessed on our beach journeys:

- **Frisbee**: What can we say? The equipment is cheap, and the only rule is not to throw it out to sea. Any game in which a dog can participate is one we feel safe playing. Not to mention those times when the little plastic saucer gets away from you and lands near a babe straight out of *Baywatch*.

- **Hacky-sack**: The Rubik's cube for beach slackers, this is mostly a solitary pastime, although you sometimes see circles of shirtless guys (never girls) kicking the hacky-sack around. Basically, the object is to keep a leather bean bag in the air with the use of your feet. It requires dexterity, concentration, endurance, and a lack of anything better to do. Presumably the "score" is kept by counting the number of times the little bag is kicked before it hits the ground.

- **Over The Line (OTL)**: This exciting combination of softball, volleyball, and cricket is played on the hot, golden sand in bare feet. The only equipment needed is a bat, a mushy softball, and gloves (the latter is optional for real OTL studs). The OTL field is paced off, 60 feet in width (or 22 paces), with no limit on the length. Two teams, each with three players, compete. As in softball, teams alternate batting and fielding, with three outs per at-bat, but the game lasts only five innings. Another switch: the pitcher throws to his or her own teammates, kneeling three feet away in the sand and lobbing the ball into an optimum swinging zone (not unlike setting up a spike in volleyball). A "hit" is required to land "over the line" (about 55 feet, or 20 paces, from the batter), and between the foul lines.

- **Paddleball**: A combination of tennis, handball, and ping-pong, this terrific game is played as either singles or doubles on a miniature tennis court. The rules are the same as tennis, with the exception of the racket, which is a wobbly-centered thing that looks like an oversized ping-pong paddle. The paddle cuts down on the range of a struck ball and presumably its velocity (although it looked plenty fast to us). When the sport is played well—as it is on the courts in Venice Beach and Santa Monica—it can be as exciting as center court at Wimbledon (well, close). In the limited space of a paddleball court, doubles requires a series of movements as intricate as kabuki dance. Check it out.

- **Skee-ball**: Okay, so it's not a beach game, per se. But it is the only beach arcade game on either coast at which we excel. The key: a secret bounce-move off the side cushion when the arcade attendant isn't looking. The best part of skee-ball is the choice of prizes you "earn" by scoring big—such as plastic spider rings, harmonicas shaped like crabs, and pirate eye patches. Where else but at the beach can you land such booty? Another confession: once, in Salem, Massachusetts, we were so good at skee-ball that the proprietor asked the security guards to make us leave because we were intimidating the younger lads with our prodigious skills. This was a truly great moment for us. Almost as good as the time we knocked someone completely out of their vehicle on the bumper cars.
- **Volleyball**: If you don't already know the rules of volleyball, move to the back of the bus. Basically, you knock the thing playfully in the air a couple of times and then you try to ram it down the throat of someone on the other side of the net. What makes this game so "California" are the two-man and -woman teams that play on the beach. How, you find yourself wondering in awe, do two people in bare feet cover that much ground? Will that bikini top stay on? And most important, how can anyone ever hope to return one of those spikes, routinely clocked at over 100 miles per hour? (Answer: They rarely do, which is why those games move so swiftly.) In some places, two-man or -woman volleyball is not a game but an entire subculture. It's also a professional sport, one that in recent years has been embraced by advertisers, fashion designers, and ESPN.
- **Whiffleball**. You always feel like Phil Niekro or curveball artist Bert Blyleven with one of these plastic bad boys in your hand. You can make any batter look as foolish as you want, especially if you're tossing one of those whiffleballs with the wacky waffle holes. The rest of the game is played just like baseball, though no gloves are needed. If you want, you can make the rules up as you go (e.g., must catch ball with teeth). The best rule we found was one we observed at Mission Beach: put your beer-laden cooler near home plate, and use the ocean as the outfield. If the batted ball goes beyond where the waves break, it's a home run. If it lands in the waves, it's a double. The object is to bat and drink from the cooler as much as possible.

Encinitas and Leucadia

Location: 22 miles north of San Diego, off Highway 101. Moonlight Beach is the most popular beach in Encinitas, while Beacon's Beach (formerly Leucadia State Beach) is the place to go in Leucadia.
Population: 57,000 (combined)
Area Code: 619 **Zip Code:** 92024

Like any coastal community with a beautiful, if treacherous, shoreline and relatively modest real-estate prices, Encinitas has learned that when one problem is licked, another one pops up to take its place. The ebb and flow of the ocean seems to parallel the ebb and flow of daily life in Encinitas and neighboring Leucadia more dramatically than anywhere else in Southern California.

Several years ago, on our first visit, we found raw sewage—it was grosser than that, actually—on the sands of Moonlight Beach, the town's centerpiece. Twin cement culverts empty their effluent from the Encinitas Sanitary District Treatment Plant at the north end of the popular beach. This is beach business as usual, according the *California Coastal Access Guide*, which reports: "Sewage treatment plants use the ocean as a location for disposal of treated effluent." Like other beach towns, Encinitas occasionally has trouble treating the effluent.

That problem appears to have been solved in the past few years, judging from our inspection of the beach. Today the biggest problem is the sand at Moonlight Beach. It's disappearing. In 1993 the city spent $22,000 to dump 1,100 tons of clean sand at Moonlight, but by 1994 that load needed to be replenished, a problem seemingly solved free of charge. A contractor building a bridge inland wanted to give 8,000 cubic yards of displaced sand (actually dirt) to Encinitas rather than dispose of it another way.

The California Coastal Commission—a beneficent bureaucracy that is responsible for, among other things, the coastal access points we all depend on—must examine the proffered soil first to determine if it's free of contamination and compatible with existing grain size of the sand on the beach. Otherwise, the whole caboodle will wash out to sea. Of course, the locals don't see it that way. In their view, the CCC is the evil government that exists only to thwart their grandest schemes.

But Encinitas residents need more than just sand. They need ways to get to their beaches. Much of the town's coastal access is denied by private-property owners and by the crumbling cliffs upon which their homes sit (many are second homes, tax write-offs for those who got rich in the 1980s). At one time, there was a Sixth Street and most of a Fifth Street in Encinitas. Maps clearly show they existed. They do not exist now, having been annexed by the Pacific Ocean. A local geologist, using old surveys and maps, has determined that 800 feet of Encinitas' shoreline has disappeared in the last hundred years. The cliffs are made of sandstone, shale, and siltstone, and constant assault by waves, opens cracks, and fissures eventually cause the cliff tops to pitch forward.

Despite the obvious folly, homes are still being built on the cliffs. Some are already listing noticeably. "For Sale" signs are not uncommon along the aptly named Neptune Avenue. Some coastal access points have washed out, and their precipitous stairwells are off-limits. One state beach access in Leucadia washed out in 1983 and has never reopened.

This is not to say Encinitas's beachfront does not have appeal to novice visitors. Despite the obstacles, the beaches are popular, primarily with teenagers (many from the inland communities) who occasionally exhibit threatening behavior and upset residents and families who have been coming here for years. The biggest story in town during our visit concerned "drunken abuse" taking place along the stairwell to Stone Steps Beach, where beer-drinking

 Map of San Diego County beaches—page 24

slackers from the valley were trying to intimidate families into leaving "their" beach, forcing them to join the crowds down at Moonlight Beach. Ah, the "teen problem," another unsolvable beach issue.

Despite its municipal attachment to Encinitas, the community of Leucadia retains a distinct identity. It is a place where alternative lifestyles (read: vegetarians and old VW bugs) go to roost. It is also a somewhat ugly town, from the vantage point of the highway, that's welded to Encinitas above the point where the strip malls of the latter give way to unmoored (that is, un-malled) businesses that look one season away from bankruptcy.

Founded by English spiritualists in 1888, Leucadia is a congenial and slightly run-down stretch of Highway 101 that runs along the crumbling sea cliffs. Leucadia means "isle of paradise" in Greek, and the streets here are named for Greek deities (Daphne, Diana, Phoebe, Glaucus). But as in the Elysian Fields, not much goes on here. The number-one industry appears to be the selling of used merchandise, with seemingly every business along Highway 101 from here back to Encinitas involved in the secondhand trade (thrift shops, consignments, used clothing, etc.). Our favorite was a yellow U-Haul contraption on whose sides was inscribed an offer to buy used blue jeans from 10 AM to 3 PM on Sundays. A roadside motel called the Ocean View offered no such view at all, being situated at the foot of a hill blocks from the ocean. A generic trailer park

Self-Realization Fellowship Retreat, Gardens, and Hermitage

The most intriguing spot in Encinitas is a place of worship. The 17-acre grounds of the Self-Realization Fellowship Retreat, Gardens, and Hermitage (215 K Street, 619-753-1811) cling to the cliffs at the southern end of town, visually dominated by three towers that loom above Highway 101 like hallucinations. The lotus towers were designed by Paramahansa Yogananda (1893–1952), the spiritual leader who founded the center in 1937 and built the temple in 1938; at the time it was the largest building on the Southern California coast. Yogananda dedicated his life to uniting East and West through the ancient practice of meditation. He lived in the hermitage for several years and helped design the cliff-side meditation gardens. The guru also planted the ancient ming tree on the site of his favorite pond, which was drained when the cliffs collapsed in 1941.

Yogananda made a name for himself internationally with his *Autobiography of a Yogi*, which he completed here in 1946 and is now considered a spiritual literature classic. The lively, detailed text traces the spiritual awakening of this gentle man whose teachings had a profound effect on the lives of many Westerners, including Greta Garbo, Leopold Stokowski, and Christopher Isherwood. Perhaps the best indication of the spiritual openness of Yogananda is that his special place, the retreat and gardens, has always been open to visitors. You are free to stroll and meditate to your heart's content, with no attempts by anyone to proselytize or judge. To us, this is what religion was meant to be.

Yes, the Self-Realization Fellowship is quite a refreshing place. And it is just a leap away from a great beach in Encinitas called Swami's.

bore the misleadingly pastoral name, "Mobile Village—Valley of Dreams."

People in Leucadia live and let live, work construction jobs when available, eat tacos and brown rice, use environmentally safe products, and stare unconcerned as cars pass through town. They simply don't need vacationers in Leucadia, which is just as well, because the beaches aren't big enough to attract them and the cliffs are eroding away. The sign at one washed-out beach access had this spray-painted addendum: "No tourists. Go home." It might as well have read: "No beach. Go home."

The issues facing Encinitas spill over to its neighbor, especially since Encinitas, Leucadia, Cardiff-by-the-Sea, and Olivenhain have become municipally joined at the hip. In 1986, they collectively came together as "the city of Encinitas," with a combined population of 57,000. Still, each community faces problems peculiar to it. Symptomatic of Leucadia's trying issues is the controversy over the construction of a seawall along the base of the bluff upon which its oceanfront homes sit. If it is to be built, everyone in Leucadia will have to chip in equally—about $50,000 a household. Obviously, those with older and smaller homes get the shaft. One longtime resident described it as "a country-club situation," in which the needs of a few impact on the many. "Obviously, we've lost the beach," he said. "Some homeowners, like those who have built up to the edge of the bluff...they have problems." And how.

Beaches

Starting from the south, **Swami's** is located below Seacliff Roadside Park (free parking, day-use only), a bluff-top city park at the south end of the Self-Realization Fellowship Retreat, Gardens, and Hermitage. During the winter, this is "surfer heaven," and during the summer it's still plenty of rough fun. A long stairwell—topped by white wooden crests, emulating the lotus towers of the adjoining meditation center—

Beacon's Beach

Location: In Leucadia, at 948 Neptune Avenue.
Parking: Free street parking.
Hours: 5 AM to 2 AM.
Facilities: Lifeguards.
Contact: For beach information, contact Encinitas Community Services at (619) 633-2880.

See number 31 on page 24.

Boneyard Beach

Location: In Encinitas, north of Swami's Beach, between E and J Streets.
Parking: Free street parking.
Hours: 5 AM to 2 AM.
Facilities: None.
Contact: For beach information, contact Encinitas Community Services at (619) 633-2880.

See number 26 on page 24.

D Street Viewpoint

Location: In Encinitas, at 450 D Street.
Parking: Free parking lot.
Hours: 5 AM to 2 AM.
Facilities: Lifeguards.
Contact: For beach information, contact Encinitas Community Services at (619) 633-2880.

See number 27 on page 24.

leads along the cliff face to the small but lovely beach. Surfers were bobbing a good distance from shore while a lifeguard named Jeb looked on. He was the most contented guy we've ever seen. Perhaps he was meditating. The cliff face has been reinforced with plantings since our last visit, and the stretch of bluff from here north to D Street has been designated a Marine Life Refuge. Don't pull out any plantings. The house you save may be your own.

Just above Swami's, and accessible only on foot from it, is **Boneyard Beach**. At low tide, small, protective coves afford romantics, nudists, and surfers privacy for their various activities. Just don't get caught by a rising tide with your drawers down.

The **D Street Viewpoint** is in the town of Encinitas, the access at the end of D Street. Steps lead down to a rock-backed city-run beach not unlike Swami's, with a lifeguard. We did see a few dead-enders looking for trouble, but they posed no threat to a couple of muscular studs such as ourselves. Besides, we left the area quickly.

Just a hop down the coast at the foot of Encinitas Boulevard, is **Moonlight Beach**, the city's large-scale beach. At Moonlight you'll find a free municipal parking lot, plenty of facilities, volleyball nets, recently pumped-in sand, and a bunch of happy sunbathers. While we encountered effluent here on our last visit, the only waste we found this time was a harmless

Encinitas Beach

Location: In Encinitas, north of Stone Steps Beach.

Parking: Free street parking at Stone Steps Beach.

Hours: 5 AM to 2 AM.

Facilities: None.

Contact: For beach information, contact Encinitas Community Services at (619) 633-2880.

See number 30 on page 24.

Moonlight Beach

Location: In Encinitas, at Fourth and B Streets.

Parking: Free parking lot.

Hours: 5 AM to 2 AM.

Facilities: Lifeguards, rest rooms, showers, picnic tables, and fire rings.

Contact: For beach information, contact Encinitas Community Services at (619) 633-2880.

See number 28 on page 24.

Stone Steps Beach

Location: In Encinitas, at Neptune Avenue and El Portal Street.

Parking: Free street parking.

Hours: 5 AM to 2 AM.

Facilities: Lifeguards.

Contact: For beach information, contact Encinitas Community Services at (619) 633-2880.

See number 29 on page 24.

Swami's

Location: In Encinitas, at 1298 First Street, below Seacliff Roadside Park.

Parking: Free parking lot.

Hours: 5 AM to 2 AM.

Facilities: Lifeguards, rest rooms, picnic area, and barbecue grills.

Contact: For beach information, contact Encinitas Community Services at (619) 633-2880.

See number 25 on page 24.

rusted deck chair sitting square in the creek bed beneath the twin cement culverts of the sanitary district. Did someone flush the chair down their toilet?

The access to **Stone Steps Beach** is located on Neptune Avenue. Park for free in the quiet neighborhood along Neptune's curbs and climb down the steep stone steps, paying homage to a mural of the mermaid on the half-shell. A lifeguard stand, marked with surf and tide advisories, is at the bottom of the stairwell. The beach is rocky toward the bluffs but otherwise fine, attracting a score of surfers. If you walk north from Stone Steps Beach, you'll reach the similar **Encinitas Beach**. There is no other direct coastal access to it from shore, which makes it secluded enough to please space-seeking swimmers, surfers, and solitary sorts.

Formerly Leucadia State Beach but now a city-managed area, **Beacon's Beach** lies at the foot of a yellow sandstone cliff and can be reached by hiking down a trail of sandbags, stairs, and switchbacks. You can park for free at the Beacon's Beach access and walk down the steep stairwell to the thin, two-mile strip of blackened sand and cobblestones; the beach seems to shrink with each wave, replaced with kelp that washes prodigiously ashore to be entangled with the equally abundant litter. When we asked a girl who waited tables in Encinitas about how all the rounded stones wound up on the beaches of Leucadia and Carlsbad, she said she heard from some people who'd lived there in the 1960s that "one night, they just showed up." You could look up and down the coast from the base of the cliffs at Beacon's Beach and see the same things: steep, eroding cliffs and no beach to speak of.

Above the beach, in the lot, a roving surfing instructor (his van was emblazoned "Kahuna Bob's Surf School") was giving preliminary lessons to a group of youngsters who looked so eager to hit the water that they were positively shivering with excitement. Beyond them, another Leucadia resident, also a surfer, stared wistfully at Beacon's rugged waves. He'd suffered a shoulder injury in a nasty spill some weeks earlier and found himself beached until it healed. In the meantime, he pedaled a bike to stay in shape, but it just wasn't the same. Leucadia was his alternative to Pacific Beach, where he'd been living until he was squeezed out by mounting crowds and rents. Pacific Beach had, in turn, been his alternative to Ocean Beach, which had been his alternative to Imperial Beach. Gradually, he said, he will make his way north to the magic land of Santa Barbara. "I want to live at the beach forever," he announced with no solicitation. For now, Leucadia is home; relaxed, uncrowded, untrendy, it is his isle of paradise. Besides, he knows someone with private access to the beach.

Bunking Down

Beware of motels with "Ocean" or "Beach" in their names that are located on a highway bypass nowhere near a beach. In particular, they must be avoided in Encinitas and Leucadia, where flyblown motels tout "sea breezes" and "views" when the only views they offer are of the gun shop on one side and the consignment shop on the other. The most expensive motel in town is located four nonsidewalked blocks from the water and overlooks the sewage treatment plant. The only place actually on the beach in either town is the **Moonlight Beach Motel** (233 Second Street, 753-0623, $), a functional and affordable three-story place with balcony views of the town's biggest beach. Other viable options close by are the campground at **San Elijo State Beach** in Cardiff-by-the-Sea (see the Cardiff-by-the-Sea entry on page 78) and a **Holiday Inn Express** (607 Leucadia Boulevard, 944-3800, $) in Leucadia.

Coastal Cuisine

Along Highway 101 to the south, Encinitas is top heavy with semifancy Italian and Mexican cafés; although bedecked with carved wooden signs, suggesting a "classy" image, their shopping-plaza backdrops are better indicators of the predictable fare they offer. Keep driving until you get to the town center. There you will find several more than serviceable dining spots. The best seafood in town is at **Shrimply Delicious** (559 Old Highway 101, 944-9172, $$), which serves, to quote from a menu, "live fresh fish steamed in spices from the Deep South. If you are looking for a quick bite, this is definitely not for you." They take cash only here, and the names of entrées, including "Sons of the Beaches" and "Love at First Bite," reflect the friendly ambience. They're open for lunch and dinner.

Just up the road, **DB Hackers** (101 Old Highway 101, 436-3162, $), serves the quick bite of seafood Shrimply eschews. The entrées are mostly fried and the outdoor patio treats you to car noise and construction, but the staff is friendly and the food is relatively cheap. We were more than sufficiently rejuvenated by the fish tacos and the Jimmy Cliff tape that was playing. For breakfast, go to **George's Restaurant** (641 South Highway 101, 942-9549, $), a legendary place that was the original home of the California Surf Museum (now in Oceanside). Their specialty is "Surf's Up," a no-nonsense feed with scrambled eggs, ham, American cheese on an English muffin, and hash browns.

Night Moves

The friendliest bar in town is the **Full Moon Saloon** (485 First Street, 436-7397), which

Karaoke Is King in North San Diego County

Karaoke is "air guitar" for singers. Basically, you get up on stage and warble along to the instrumental tracks of popular tunes, from which the vocals have been wiped off. It's so popular in the towns north of La Jolla that there's a local publication devoted exclusively to it. Leave it to Southern California to come up with a new twist to this ubiquitous (and we thought waning) national trend: strip karaoke.

Yes, it was in the aforementioned periodical that we came across an article by the "queen of strip karaoke." She wrote: "Nudity is not the object. A perfect body is not necessary.... As an added benefit to those of us without partners... in these SAFE SEX '90s... it's a great outlet for all that unused libido!"

They also have their own karaoke lingo in Southern California. Here are some sample terms:

- Barber—a drunk patron who, unsolicited, sings along with every tune (presumably from *The Barber of Seville*).
- Flipper—a singer who, while on stage, flips his or her head around a lot.
- Phantom—a sober patron who, unsolicited, sings along with every tune (presumably from *Phantom of the Opera*).
- Shred—to butcher a song in performance (presumably from ex-marine Oliver North's propensity for shredding damaging evidence against himself).

Okay, pop quiz! Explicate the following sentence: "The flipper accused the barber of shredding his 'Stairway to Heaven.'" By God, you've got it!

offers live music most nights and a game room for the excess crowd. Our best band name award goes to Semisi and the Fula Bula Band, a reggae contingent playing the Full Moon during our stopover. More live music can be found at **First Street Bar** (656 First Street, 944-0233), which is popular with locals. Encinitas and Leucadia have, over the years, attracted a sizable contingent of New Age groupies and ex-hippies, some of whom can be found knocking back a house decaf at the **Naked Bean Coffee Co.** (1126 First Street, 634-1347), which also features live music on weekends. We opted for a movie: *Endless Summer II*, the sequel to the '60's surfing classic. During our visit, it was held over by popular demand at the local theater, the charming old La Paloma, which also features Surf Movie Night every Monday.

For More Information

Contact the Encinitas Chamber of Commerce Visitor Center, 345-H First Street, Encinitas, CA 92024; (619) 753-6041.

Carlsbad

Location: 35 miles north of San Diego, 86 miles south of Los Angeles, along Highway 101. Ocean Street runs along the beach through the heart of Carlsbad. The main beach is Carlsbad State Beach.
Population: 68,000
Area Code: 619 **Zip Code:** 92008

Carlsbad is an anomaly. Of all the towns that cling to the Southern California coast, it is the only one not founded by a Spaniard or profoundly shaped by Latin influences. Instead, Carlsbad was the brainstorm of Gerhard Schutte, a German who came west via Nebraska to found a town of "small farms and gracious homes." His dream was made possible in 1883, when the Arizona Eastern Railway was completed, linking Southern California with the rest of civilization. This line also opened the land between Los Angeles and San Diego to homesteaders. Schutte headed up the list and moved on out.

Spanish and Native American influences are not entirely absent from the historical record. For centuries prior to Schutte's arrival, the Luseino Indian tribe lived on the land between the two lagoons that form the boundaries of Carlsbad. However, they were quickly run off or subjugated by the missions when, in 1769, the conquistador Gaspar de Portola arrived with his faith-filled sidekick, Father Juan Crespi. Even though the entire area was under Spanish rule, the only lingering trace of their influence today is Agua Hedionda, the name given to one of the local lagoons. It means "stinking waters."

By the time Schutte arrived, the mission system was destroyed and the land grab was on. Schutte and his followers purchased a chunk of land and began planting eucalyptus trees and squaring off lots for a town. In the process, they discovered that the mineral water from their wells was identical to that found at the renowned Ninth Spa in Karlsbad, Bohemia (now Karlovy Vary, in the Czech Republic). The town took its name and identity from that happenstance, becoming a bastion of Old Europe in the New World. When word got out about the water, settlers began arriving. Humble, hardworking, and mostly English, these folks built their town to reflect their no-nonsense values.

Surprisingly little of the town has changed to this day. Original buildings are restored, and the subsequent growth of the town adheres

 Map of San Diego County beaches—page 24

to an established code, allowing Carlsbad to justifiably call itself a "village by the sea." With its Victorian, Dutch, and Bohemian architecture, Carlsbad has retained an appealingly antiquarian personality. This is remarkable when you consider the huge military city of Oceanside next door and the concrete jungle of San Diego to the south.

Some of the local buildings—such as Magee House, Twin Inns, and the Santa Fe Railway Station—have been designated National Historic Landmarks. The best place to orient yourself to town history is the Chamber of Commerce office, located inside the Santa Fe Railway Station on Carlsbad Village Drive. Built in 1887, it's the oldest commercial structure in town.

Another must-see is the Alt Karlsbad Haus, on Carlsbad Boulevard. Built in 1964 on the site of the first mineral well, the house soon to be converted into a 20 room resort looks like an architectural escapee from *Monty Python and the Holy Grail*. It's actually an exact replica of Antonin Dvorák's house in Prague. The great composer, who never visited Carlsbad but whose patriotic "New World Symphony" had achieved national notoriety when the town was founded, is honored by a plaque on one wall; on the other wall is a second plaque that reads: "The formation of the Hanseatic League in the 13th Century gave birth to modern civilization, and through commerce and trade lifted Europe out of the Dark Ages." Dvorák was a Bohemian who, out of love for his adopted home, offered to write a new national anthem for America. His spirit is a fitting one to symbolize the village of Carlsbad, which has lifted itself above the Dark Ages of the late twentieth century by holding fast to civilized values.

Today, Carlsbad seems to have everything going for it. Its public school system is one of the best in the country. The unemployment rate is the lowest in San Diego County. The public library is larger than some college libraries. The average temperature is a comfortable 60 degrees. The young people look healthy, happy, and well groomed. ("Hey, John," one Beaver Cleaver look-alike yells out a car window to a pal, "your new haircut looks great!") The old folks who choose to live out their years here look contented, too. After a few hours, you begin to wonder if this isn't the town Norman Rockwell was painting all those years.

Quail Botanical Gardens

Before the land around Encinitas was sold to developers, the town was known for its rolling green hillsides. But in 1986, Encinitas grew by annexation, incorporating the communities of Leucadia, Cardiff by the Sea, and Olivenhain to become the "big-time city of North County" with 57,000 residents. To bolster its image, the city now refers to itself as the "Flower Capital of the World." In the surrounding hills, an enormous nursery and greenhouse industry grows most of the carnations dyed and sold on city streets around the world.

Another throwback to those green days is the Quail Botanical Gardens (230 Quail Gardens Drive, 619-436-3036), a 30-acre collection of plants and trees native to California, as well as exotic tropicals, palms, and bamboos. The botanical gardens offer a self-guided and educational tour of the premises, which includes a chaparral grove, a bird sanctuary, and more than 5,000 species of botanical life. Admission is about $2 for adults and $1 for children, and it's open daily year-round.

Yes, Carlsbad is not just a place to vacation. It's a place to settle down and attend the church of your choice. Religious diversity is a hallmark of the town. Lutheran rest homes stand hard by humble Hispanic Pentecostal churches. We passed one of the latter, a sort of Quonset hut with a steeple, while strolling over the railroad tracks on the way to dinner. The door was open to the street and we heard the congregation singing while banging drums and tambourines. Two hours later, on our return stroll, they were still at it, now being exhorted by a minister who was fervently shouting at the congregation like a Hispanic Jimmy Swaggart.

This is how Carlsbad shall remain, apparently. Of the 37 square miles that fall within the city limits, only a third has been developed. According to a venerable resident, "We're putting the screws on too much more growth." Of course there's always something pesky nipping at those Utopian heels. Here, it's a children's theme park called Lego Land, which is being built on Carlsbad Ranch, east of town. Though local businessmen are in favor of it, calling tourism "clean growth," old-timers are concerned about what the influx of out-of-towners will do to their tiny corner of paradise. Why don't the developers just "Lego" the land, for a change?

Beaches

Carlsbad has one long beach that is broken into different domains; the first, **South Carlsbad State Beach**, starts four miles south of town. A good deal of the beach in the Carlsbad area has eroded since the construction of Oceanside Harbor to the north. Some of the sand is blackened by natural causes, necessitating the use of the "Tar-Off" packets that turn up in every motel room. The beaches are still popular with day-use visitors from the inland valley and Encinitas. South Carlsbad is especially popular with surfers, who brave the cobblestone-strewn shoreline to get at the monster waves. The beach has a campground with over 200 sites. It's one of the most popular in the State Park System, and reservations are filled well in advance. Lifeguards are on duty. A relatively new unit of South Carlsbad State Beach, named **Ponto Beach**, has been established by the Batiquitos Lagoon, between Carlsbad and Leucadia. Its arrival has pissed off the surfers, who now have to pay to get to a revered surfing spot of longstanding.

Carlsbad City Beach

Location: In Carlsbad, along Carlsbad Boulevard at Ocean Street.

Parking: Free lot and street parking.

Hours: 6 AM to 11 PM.

Facilities: Lifeguards and rest rooms.

Contact: For beach information, contact South Carlsbad State Beach at (619) 438-3143.

See number 35 on page 24.

Carlsbad State Beach

Location: In Carlsbad, along Carlsbad Boulevard at Tamarack Avenue.

Parking: $4 entrance fee per vehicle.

Hours: 6 AM to 10 PM.

Facilities: Lifeguards, rest rooms, and picnic tables.

Contact: For beach information, contact South Carlsbad State Beach at (619) 438-3143.

See number 34 on page 24.

South Carlsbad State Beach runs into **Carlsbad State Beach**, which in turn meets **Carlsbad City Beach**. Again, despite the fact that the waves practically lick the seawalls at high tide, these are heavily used beaches. The state beach is popular with all sorts: bodysurfers, boogie boarders, swimmers, divers, and surf casters. Because of its restricted hours, however, the city beach is less beloved by surfers.

Carlsbad is a great town for walking, especially along its beaches. Wide concrete walkways run a good distance along the state beach. People jog, stroll, and in-line skate at all hours—even at night, thanks to good lighting. The only problem is the beach itself. As the crone in the Wendy's commercial used to say, "Where's the beach?" It's a precipitously narrow strand that gets overwashed by incoming waves, leaving little room for sunning or beachcombing. A volleyball net pegged in the sand appeared useless, as there was not enough dry sand to have a game. Smooth, rounded cobblestones noisily roll around in the waves, and 100-pound clumps of kelp wash up on the beach. It's all a little disconcerting. Nonetheless, we easily made a total immersion, getting knocked around in the big waves that were baptizing us. It was, as Brian Wilson of the Beach Boys once described it, like being in a giant washing machine. And, if all goes as planned, Carlsbad should have a wide, new beach in the near future, thanks to the emplacement of millions of cubic yards of sand dredged from the bottom of San Diego Harbor.

Believe it or not, the "stinking waters" at Agua Hedionda Lagoon (east of Carlsbad City Beach) are popular with swimmers and waterskiers. Boats and water skis can be rented at Snug Harbor Marina (4215 Harrison Street, 434-3089). A nice hiking/biking trail runs along the shore of the lagoon, in case you want to look at, but not touch, the stinking waters.

Bunking Down

It's not cheap to stay in the "village by the sea." The village mentality can be a little tough on the wallet if you're not a corporate moneybags riding into town waving a five-iron. There's a big-time, 500-room golf and tennis resort, **La Costa Resort & Spa** (Costa del Mar Road, 438-9111, $$$$), that attracts celebrities by the Lear jet load and hosts golf and tennis tournaments.

A few steps down in price and many steps closer to the beach is the **Carlsbad Inn Beach**

Ponto Beach (a part of South Carlsbad State Beach)

Location: Just north of Leucadia. Take the La Costa Drive exit off Interstate 5 and follow it until it ends at the Old Highway 101 at the Batiquitos Lagoon.

Parking: $4 entrance fee per vehicle.

Hours: 6 AM to 10 PM.

Facilities: Rest rooms, showers, picnic tables, and barbecue grills.

Contact: For beach information, contact South Carlsbad State Beach at (619) 438-3143.

See number 32 on page 24.

South Carlsbad State Beach

Location: Four miles south of Carlsbad, along Carlsbad Boulevard at Poinsettia Lane.

Parking: $4 entrance fee per vehicle.

Hours: 6 AM to 10 PM.

Facilities: Lifeguards, rest rooms, showers, picnic tables, and fire pits. There are 222 developed tent and RV campsites. Fees are $14 to $16 per night. For camping reservations, call Destinet at (800) 444-7275.

Contact: For beach information, contact South Carlsbad State Beach at (619) 438-3143.

See number 33 on page 24.

Resort (3075 Carlsbad Boulevard, 434-7020, $$), an appealing beach and tennis complex built in the center of town under the community's watchful Old World architectural guidelines. Another worthy beachfront choice is the **Tamarack Beach Resort** (3200 Carlsbad Boulevard, 729-3500, $$$), which is more like a time-share condominium than a motel. Each suite has a washer and dryer, a full kitchen, and a stereo.

Front and center on the beach, you can't do any better than the **Best Western Beach Terrace Inn** (2775 Ocean Street, 729-1078, $$). Located in a quiet residential neighborhood, the Beach Terrace has as sunny a disposition as you'll find at the beach. Plus, you can practically jump off the balcony into the ocean, though we'd advise against it. Nearly as appealing is the **Best Western Bach View Lodge** (3180 Carlsbad Boulevard, 729-1151, $$), which lies close to but not quite on the ocean.

Coastal Cuisine

If you like fried seafood, you can order it by the basket at **Harbor Fish South** (3179 Carlsbad Boulevard, 729-4161, $), an outdoor-patio joint beside the ocean and next to a surf shop. The clientele is young and less discriminating than the folks at La Costa. The "Surfer's Special," for instance, is a cheeseburger and fries. But the view and ambience are perfectly beachy.

The best local seafood we found was at the **Fish House Vera Cruz** (417 Carlsbad Villa Drive, 434-6777, $$), a pleasant stroll over the railroad tracks just east of town center. The name derives from a fishing boat that scours the Pacific coast from Baja to Alaska to nab the goodies they serve here. Everything is mesquite-grilled to perfection and prices are moderate. The place even looks like the hold of a fishing vessel, with lots of nautical knickknacks.

Niemans (2978 Carlsbad Boulevard, 729-4131, $$$) is worth visiting because it's housed in the oldest Victorian structure in town, formerly the Twin Inns. If you're not inclined toward "proper attire," you can at least stroll the grounds and pretend to be studying the menu. The menu at Niemans' **Seagrill** ($$) is worth checking out, and the bar/brasserie looks to be a happening place.

Night Moves

In a Norman Rockwell kind of town, you're lucky to find a place that serves even something as harmless as frozen yogurt after dark. Carlsbad, fortunately, does have a semblance of nightlife. The primary source of activity is the **Sand Bar Café** (3878 Carlsbad Boulevard, 729-3170), which sits across the street from the roaring ocean surf and is home to live entertainment on most nights. It draws from miles around. Another hopping haunt is the local **Hennessey's Tavern** (2777 Roosevelt Street, 729-6951), which has live music on weekends. For more low-key good times the **Kafana Coffee Shop** (3076 Carlsbad Boulevard, 720-0074) offers warbling folkies and good, stiff belts of caffeine.

For More Information

Write the Carlsbad Convention and Visitors Bureau, P.O. Box 1246, Carlsbad, CA 92008; (619) 434-6093. Or try the Carlsbad Chamber of Commerce, 5411 Avenida Encinas #100, P.O. Box 1605, Carlsbad, CA 92008; (619) 931-8400. You can also drop by the Visitors Information Center, located in the Old Santa Fe Train Depot on Carlsbad Village Drive.

 Map of San Diego County beaches—page 24

Oceanside

Location: 40 miles north of San Diego, off Highway 101. Pacific Street and "the Strand" run alongside the ocean. Oceanside City Beach is the main beach in the area, and it is adjacent to Oceanside Pier.
Population: 128,000
Area Code: 619 **Zip Code:** 92054

For decades, Oceanside has been regarded as something of a sprawling military/urban wasteland. Though the reputation hasn't changed much over the years, the city lately appears to be on the upswing. To fully understand the fluctuating fortunes of Oceanside, it's necessary to do like the Marines and hit the beaches.

You would expect a town with a name like Oceanside to be blessed in that department. From South Oceanside Beach and Linear Beach to Oceanside City Beach and Harbor Beach, this unpretentious place has been adopted by beachgoers from as far afield as Encinitas. They come to Oceanside because their own beaches are either crowded or disappearing, and because parking is easy to find, the hassles are fewer, prices cheaper, and attitudes more conducive to casual enjoyment.

Even given these enviable conditions, Oceanside has a tale of woe all its own regarding the beach that sits on either side of the formidable Oceanside Pier (at 1,942 feet, it's the longest on the West Coast). According to the still-angry locals, the main culprit is the U.S. Army Corps of Engineers. In the 1960s, having conducted only minimal study of the impact on the surrounding coastline, the Corps created a harbor at Oceanside. This one is big, slick, and modern, with 1,000 berths for pleasure craft and yachts, a marina, upscale restaurants, and condominiums. Oh yes, and there's a shopping plaza designed along the lines of a Cape Cod village.

Before the architectural surgery, Oceanside had one of the widest, longest, and best-loved beaches on the southern coast, a Sahara of sand that was especially attractive to surfers. Imagine, if you will, a sea monster coming ashore and taking a five-acre bite out of the center of this beach, then spitting the sand back into the water several miles offshore. This, essentially, is what has happened in Oceanside. According to one local historian who was in high school at the time, he and his classmates, as a science project, conducted a study of the proposed harbor project. They foresaw the horror that would be done to their beloved beach. They presented their study to the Corps and were basically told, "Beat it, kids, you don't know what you're talking about."

Alas, they did know. Photographs of Oceanside City Beach taken in 1946 show an uninterrupted swath of sand as wide and straight as any we've seen on either coast. The same beach today is certainly lovely to behold, but it's nowhere near the size of the beach of 1946. The jetty that was meant to ward off rough waters from the precious luxury vessels in the harbor was built at the wrong angle. The sand that normally flowed down with the longshore currents in years past is now blocked and winds up at the bottom of an offshore canyon, lost forever. To make this tale even more shameful, the Army Corps of Engineers still has to dredge the harbor two or three times a year just to keep it navigable. "It's amazing that Carlsbad doesn't sue the Corps," opined our local historian, referring to the devastating residual effects of the erosion to areas south of town. "It's a pretty big thing to lose your beach."

Thankfully, a new sand bypassing operation has been developed that has begun to replenish the shoreline. It involves shooting sand through six-inch tubes located around the harbor, where it can then resume its natural southerly drift with the currents. In a sense, Oceanside has lost and found its beach.

Map of San Diego County beaches—page 24

Happily, the city is gearing up for another boom. The 100 acres behind the pier—except for the California Surf Museum (see sidebar, "California Surf Museum")—have been slated for development. The Marriott hotel chain has already signed on, and four 10-story buildings are on the drawing board. But, unlike the residents of most coastal towns, the natives aren't opposed to a massive facelift in Oceanside. "It won't be Cement City, like they did to Huntington Beach," a longtime local told us. "It will be more like a seaport village, made of wood, with an educational Sea Center. We want it." No, after all it's been through, the dauntless, rough-and-tumble city of Oceanside *deserves* it.

Prior to this juncture, the main reason for Oceanside's rapid growth, and almost the sole reason for its existence, was Camp Pendleton, the world's largest U.S. Marine base. Camp Pendleton is literally next door to Oceanside, its back gate opening onto Oceanside Harbor. A total of 45,000 Marine personnel work and train at the camp. Those who don't live on base reside in Oceanside with their families. At first glimpse, Oceanside doesn't look like the stereotypical military town. Great pains have been made to disguise this fact. Still, at its core, it is a military town. It may not be a bona fide war zone, as many landlocked military towns are. But as you pull away from the upscale harbor you begin to notice the broken-bulb saloons, the low-rent food stands, the thrift shops full of Persian Gulf war relics, the discount clothiers, and the chockablock flat-roofed duplexes—all signs of a military lifestyle that has remained virtually unchanged since World War II. No slight intended—one of us was an army brat who spent the happiest years of his childhood on and around military bases.

Beaches

The past is behind Oceanside and the future's so bright you gotta wear shades. The present is pretty nifty, too, starting with **South Oceanside Beach**. You can park in the neighborhood along an enormous cement embankment and go enjoy the sand to the west. More easily accessed is nearby Buccaneer Park, which is also in the residential neighborhood. The beach here is a tiny pocket of sand that is completely free of rocks and debris. It's nice, but nicer still is pondering what the beach would be like if it weren't hogged by all the houses built right on top of it. Also quite nice is the Loma Alta Marsh, a small lagoon to the east of the beach, with a trail that leads under a rail-

Harbor Beach

Location: In Oceanside, at the end of Harbor Drive, off Pacific Street.

Parking: $5 entrance fee per vehicle.

Hours: Open 24 hours.

Facilities: Lifeguards, rest rooms, picnic areas, and fire rings. There are RV campsites. The fee is $15 per night. No camping reservations.

Contact: For beach information, contact the Oceanside Department of Harbors and Beaches at (619) 966-4535.

See number 38 on page 24.

Oceanside City Beach

Location: In Oceanside, along Pacific Street, between Witherby Street and the San Luis River.

Parking: Metered lot and street parking.

Hours: Open 24 hours.

Facilities: Lifeguards, rest rooms, showers, picnic tables, and barbecue grills.

Contact: For beach information, contact the Oceanside Department of Harbors and Beaches at (619) 966-4535.

See number 37 on page 24.

road trestle, along which birds can be seen chirping happily.

The beach lengthens, and strengthens, at Linear Park, which can be reached via four separate access point along Pacific Street (Fourth Street, Third Street, Tyson Street, and Mission Avenue). A walkway has been placed along the bluff top, whose benches afford lovely views of sand and sea. The promontory blends into the Strand, a grassy park with benches that runs the rest of the length of town. It's great for family strolls or lonely naps in the grass. Flanking the massive pier are **Oceanside City Beach** (a.k.a. Oceanside Pier Beach) and **Harbor Beach**. The former is the longest beach in town and the latter is the widest, as it receives constant replenishment from harbor dredging. The sand is soft and white and well patrolled by lifeguards. Our favorite access point is along Mission Avenue next to the pier. You can park along the avenue for 50 cents an hour—a bargain, by beach standards.

No license is needed to fish off the pier, and a trolley runs to and from it. A community center is attached to the pier at the Strand Pier Plaza; its gym is open to the public. Just behind the pier sits the California Surf Museum, which is a required stop for people who like people who like beaches (see sidebar). Finally, there's the Buena Vista Lagoon Ecological Reserve, located south of town, behind South Oceanside Beach and just north of Carlsbad. This large natural wetland—one of the few left in Southern California—is a habitat for birds and vegetation (including rare species of both). A trail along the shoreline makes for pleasant sightings. If you mistrust your self-guided instincts, the Buena Vista Audubon Nature Center on Hill Street (439-2473) provides exhibits, lectures, and group tours. They're open from 10 AM to 2 PM, Tuesday to Saturday.

Oh yes, one extra-credit foray is available for those willing to drive four miles inland on Route 76 to see the "King of the Missions," Mission San Luis Rey de Francia (4050 Mission Avenue, 757-3651). Founded in 1798 by Father Fermin de Lasuen, it was named for King Louis XI of France. The largest of the Franciscan-run missions, it was lavishly decorated and was something of a showpiece. Today, it houses an active order of Franciscan monks and a museum, open to the public for viewing and souvenir-buying. A fiesta is held here every year in the third week of July. Of particular interest are the paintings done by local Native Americans.

South Oceanside Beach

2

Location: In Oceanside, at Cassidy and Pacific Streets.
Parking: Free street parking.
Hours: Open 24 hours.
Facilities: None.
Contact: For beach information, contact the Oceanside Department of Harbors and Beaches at (619) 966-4535.

See number 36 on page 24.

Bunking Down

At the moment, Oceanside is sorely lacking in motels as accommodating as its beaches. The closest motel to the beach is **Sandman Motel** (1501 Carmelo Drive, 722-7661, $$), a fairly ordinary place near the harbor. Coming soon will be a holy host of hotels behind the Oceanside Pier. Until then you're probably best off staying at the **Best Western Oceanside Inn** (1680 Oceanside Boulevard, 722-1821, $$), a well-appointed motel adjacent to Interstate 5; it offers pools, saunas and large, clean rooms.

Coastal Cuisine

Meals here are gotten mostly to go, or casually eaten in picnic-table ambience. Our favorite bite in town is **Johnny Mañana's** (308 Mission Avenue, 721-9999, $), a great quickie take-out or

California Surf Museum

As everyone knows, surfing is more than a sport. In Southern California, perhaps more than anywhere else, it is a religion. And the church of choice is the California Surf Museum in Oceanside (308 North Pacific Street, 619-721-6876), located near the Oceanside Pier.

The museum's history is not unlike that of a wandering religious mystic. Founded in 1985 by Jane Schmauss and Stuart Resor, the museum was originally housed at George's Restaurant in Encinitas. It was then moved to Pacific Beach, then back to Encinitas's Moonlight Plaza. Finally it arrived at its Canaan—a former VFW hall and beach bar that sits in the heart of surfer country. When all the new development goes in, the museum will have its final resting place in a brand-new location close to where it now sits.

The California Surf Museum is a delight for both devotees of the sport and the merely curious. Here the history and lore of surfing are lovingly told with original relics, informative placards, vintage photographs, clothing, clippings, books, and even shrines to dead surfers. Exhibits are changed regularly and various events celebrate the sport's history, which is particularly rich in this locale. For example, in 1994 they celebrated the 80th birthday of Lorrin "Whitey" Harrison, a lifelong surfer who still surfs daily at San Onofre. Another event featured the work of LeRoy "Granny" Grannis, a 76-year-old whose surfing pictures are the pinnacle of action photography. But the most sacred moments, and mementos, are devoted to the pantheon of greats who've taken the great pipeline to heaven. Their stories read like the lives of saints. They include:

- Duke Kahanamoku, the Polynesian who popularized surfing worldwide. He also reintroduced surfing to Hawaii after missionaries forbade it. He took his nickname from the Duke of Edinburgh and won three gold medals in swimming at the 1912 Olympics. One of the Duke's long redwood boards is on display at the museum.

- George Freeth, the Hawaiian who introduced surfing to California and then became a lifeguard in Oceanside. Freeth died of pneumonia in 1910 after rescuing several people in the rough waters off the Oceanside Pier.

- Bob Simmons, whose only possessions were a 1937 Ford sedan and a longboard. He was a daredevil who developed the "spoon nose" (a lift at the front of the board that helps avoid nose-dives) and was the first surfer to use rope hand grips. He was inexhaustible, surfing from sunup to sundown. On September 27, 1954, while surfing off Windansea Beach in La Jolla, Simmons caught a wave bigger than even he could handle. His board made it to shore. He never did.

Anecdotes like these and the countless items for perusal and sale bring surfing alive, even for the uninitiated. Hang ten here. Tell 'em we sent you.

 Map of San Diego County beaches—page 24

eat-in joint where heaping helpings of Mexican fare are served at low prices in a pleasant beachy atmosphere. The house special is a BLT burrito, served with lettuce, tomato, bacon, mayonnaise, guacamole, and salsa. It's hard to spent more than four or five bucks here, and you can make off with a plain cheese quesadilla for a mere $1.65. A cold Pacifico beer, served with complimentary salsa and chips, is just $1.35. *¡Arriba!* Similar in spirit to Johnny Mañana's is the **Beach Break Café** (1902 Hill Street, 439-6355, $), which serves a more diverse menu, including bagels and croissants.

Night Moves

The nightlife here can be a bit...raw. After a week of sweating in the hills of Camp Pendleton, a feller can work up a big thirst. But when the feller is a Marine, his thirst isn't just heavy—it's profound. To quench it, he heads into Oceanside. Typical of the kind of joints catering to them is one called the Prides Inn, which had this sign affixed to the outside wall: "Welcoming Those Who Have Served and Those Serving." Besides drinking and, perhaps, an inebriated fight or two, the only other entertainment in Oceanside worth mentioning is karaoke. Several different bars are devoted to this art form on different nights of the week. On the other nights they offer "adult contemporary" music. The best of the lot are the **Flying Bridge** (1103 North Hill Street, 722-1904), the **Back Room Cocktail Lounge** (2677 Vista Way, 721-5400), and **Monterey Bay Canners** (1325 Harbor Drive North, 722-3474).

For More Information

Contact the Oceanside Chamber of Commerce, 928 North Hill Street, P.O. Box 1578, Oceanside, CA 92054; (619) 722-1534. Or contact the Oceanside Visitors Information Center, Interstate 5 and Route 76, Oceanside, CA 92054; (619) 721-1101.

Surf Writers

Because of the good surf, hidden coves, and affordable prices, Encinitas and Leucadia are popular with surfers, especially older ones who can afford homes on the coast. Among the best known is Chris Ahrens, the 46-year-old publisher of *Longboarder* magazine and author of a book of true surf stories called *Good Things Love Water*. It's a sympathetic, if somewhat sentimental, collection of tall tales and profiles; one surfer described it as "someone standing around a fire ring talking with other surfers." His *Longboarder* magazine still lives, too, and shares the magazine rack with *Surfers' Journal* (by general consensus, the best surfing mag, edited by Steve Pezman), *Longboard Quarterly* (edited by Guy Motil), *Surfer* magazine, and *Tracks*, an Australian periodical of surf worship.

In an interview for a local paper, Ahrens nailed down the surfer's raison d'être: "Once you're out in the water, the rules of the land are left behind. A whole new government takes place. It's a kind of peaceful anarchy."

Other recent surf writers of distinction include Greg Noll, whose *Da Bull: Life Over the Edge* is an oral history of this big-wave cat. Mike Doyle, a surfing legend in his own right, has published a memoir called *Morning Glass*, which captures the halcyon days of surfing. The diarylike entries are written chronologically and thus make a good historical reference tool. Finally, a note about the notorious *Pump House Gang* by Tom Wolfe, his 1966 attempt to capture the manners and mores of a group of surf bums who made their home on the beaches of La Jolla. His sneering portrait is universally reviled by all surfers. Here is a sample excerpt:

"Their backs look like some kind of salmon-colored porcelain shells.... They were staring out to sea like Phrygian sacristans looking for a sign.... I foresaw the day when the California coastline would be littered with the bodies of aged and abandoned Surferkinder, like so many beached whales."

As much as we enjoy Tom Wolfe's writing, we suggest he run that one by Chris Ahrens, Greg Noll, or Mike Doyle. Perhaps they can provide the crow he so richly deserves to eat.

The following eclectic selection of books should be on any California beach lover's list:

- *Big Sur,* by Jack Kerouac.
- *Big Sur and the Oranges of Hieronymus Bosch,* by Henry Miller.
- *Book of Waves,* by Drew Kampion.
- *California Coastal Access Guide*, compiled by the California Coastal Commission. A great resource for the coast. Indispensable.
- *California Hiking,* by Tom Stienstra and Michael Hodgson. Not exclusively devoted to beach locales, this book nonetheless offers the best shoreline trails among its 1,000 suggested hikes.

 Map of San Diego County beaches—page 24

- *California Surfriders,* by John Heath "Doc" Ball. First published in 1946 and now reprinted, this pictorial record of "thrills, spills, personalities and places of California surfing" was lovingly put together by Doc Ball, the first professional surf photographer.
- *City of Quartz: Excavating the Future in Los Angeles,* by Mike Davis.
- *Cowabunga: A History of Surfing,* by Lee Wardlaw. While not as definitive as *Surfing: The Ultimate Pleasure* (see below), it has its charms.
- *Fiberglass Ding Repair,* by Franklin Pierce. The best guide to repairing your surfboard. For nonsurfers, a "ding" is a divot, scratch, cut, smash, shark bite, or blemish on the surface of your best friend, the board.
- *Hawaiian Surfriders 1935,* by Tom Blake. This is the first book ever written on the history of the sport. Blake, the author, is the inventor of the paddle board and a surfing legend in his own right.
- *Learning Hawaiian Surfing: A Royal Sport at Waikiki Beach, Honolulu, 1907,* by Jack London. Yes, this is *the* Jack London, who learned the sport in the summer of 1907 from the great George Freeth. This pamphlet was compiled from London's diaries of that summer and is a blast to read. Is there anything Jack London didn't do?
- *Surfer's Start Up,* by Doug Warner. The only how-to guide to the sport.
- *Surfing California,* by Bank Wright. A guide to the best surfing beaches, written in inimitable surf speak.
- *Surfing Terms and Surfspeak: A Surfinary Compiled,* by Trevor Cralle. You may not believe us, but this dictionary of surfing lingo is an inch and a half thick.
- *Surfing: The Sport of Hawaiian Kings,* by Ben R. Finney and James D. Houston.
- *Surfing: The Ultimate Pleasure,* by Leonard Lucernos. By general consensus, this is the best book on the history of the sport.
- *Waikiki Beach Boys,* by Grady Timmons. A chronicle of the original 12 or so Hawaiians who gave the world the sport of surfing. It includes a chapter on Duke Kahanamoku.

The California Surf Museum (next to the Oceanside Pier) is a good place to begin your hunt for many of these titles. Rich Watkins, the museum director, is in contact with all the small presses that publish them, and he knows many of the authors. Unfortunately, some of the titles are out of print, which means that some sleuthing may be required to find them.

San Onofre State Beach

Location: Alongside San Clemente, San Onofre can be reached via the Basilone Road exit off Interstate 5. It offers 3.5 miles of wide, sandy beach and two campgrounds.

The last stop in San Diego County, **San Onofre State Beach** buts up against the Orange County line. It's a great spot for surfers and campers who don't mind recreating close to a nuclear power plant. The beach at the south end of San Onofre, known as Bluffs Beach, can be accessed via six numbered trails that descend steeply to it. It is a three-mile beach, with three miles of campsites running along the abandoned stretch of coastal highway above it. There's nothing fancy about San Onofre Bluffs Campground, whose 221 sites don't receive much in the way of shade. The main day-use beach at San Onofre is Surf Beach, a popular spot for surfing north of Bluffs Beach off Basilone Road. San Mateo Campground, a recent addition to the state beach, has 161 sites (69 with electrical and water hookups) and lies east of Interstate 5. A paved 1.5-mile trail leads from this campground to Trestle's, a famous surfing beach to which die-hards willingly trek with boards on head, so outstanding is the wave action.

A few things about San Onofre might make some visitors uneasy. First, it's in the shadow of the San Onofre Nuclear Generating Station, whose twin peaks are visible from the park. Second, San Onofre is surrounded by Camp Pendleton, the largest U.S. Marine base in the country. In fact, the park lies on Marine Corps land that has been leased to the state. Camp Pendleton occupies a staggering 125,000 acres, and you never know what might whiz by this deceptively empty landscape. We were enjoying the view from a freeway vista point when an amphibious tank came roaring across the terrain, kicking up dust. (We also heard a few jets breaking the sound barrier.) Third, the area is full of rattlesnakes. They are the only venomous snake in all of California, but they do sink their fangs into roughly 200 unlucky Southlanders a year. Other snakes native to San Onofre include red racer, gopher, and king. Even so, the most common animal-related injury is the bite of the stingray, which is known to settle in the sand close to shore.

San Onofre State Beach

Location: Take the Basilone Road exit off Interstate 5, three miles south of San Clemente.

Parking: $6 entrance fee per vehicle.

Hours: 6 AM to 10 PM.

Facilities: Lifeguards, rest rooms, showers, picnic tables, and fire pits. There are 383 developed tent and RV campsites. Fees are $14 to $16 per night. For camping reservations, call Destinet at (800) 444-7275.

Contact: For beach information, contact San Onofre State Beach at (714) 492-4872.

See number 39 on page 24.

For More Information

Contact San Onofre State Park Headquarters, 3030 Del Presidente, San Clemente, CA 92672; (714) 492-4872 (San Onofre Bluffs) or (714) 361-2531 (San Mateo Campground).

Orange County

Although the oranges are mostly gone and the county government walks a tightrope over a self-made fiscal nightmare, the glorious beaches of Orange County are here—we hope and pray—forever. They start pleasantly, and with understatement, at San Clemente, one of the few beach towns in America where you can hop off an Amtrak train and walk 100 feet to the ocean's edge.

Most of Orange County's oceanfront was invitingly low-key only two decades ago. Many of the beaches singled out for praise in the Beach Boys' classic "Surfin' USA" are in Orange County. But in the years since the Beach Boys celebrated the area, a real-estate land rush, led by the Irvines and the Disneys, has effectively walled off much of the prime beachfront in Orange County for the private enjoyment of...God knows who. (Nobody *we* consort with, that's for sure!) The worst sins were committed at Dana Point, Huntington Beach, and south *(continued on page 104)*

Coastal Orange County's Climate

Laguna Beach Averages

	Daily High Temp. (°F)	Daily Low Temp. (°F)	Rainfall (inches)
January	65	42	2.8
February	66	43	2.3
March	66	44	1.9
April	67	46	1.2
May	69	51	0.3
June	71	55	0.1
July	75	58	0
August	77	59	0.1
September	77	57	0.3
October	74	53	0.3
November	70	46	1.4
December	66	42	1.6
Yearly Average	**70**	**50**	**12.3**

Newport Beach Averages

	Daily High Temp. (°F)	Daily Low Temp. (°F)	Rainfall (inches)
January	63	46	2.6
February	63	47	2.1
March	63	49	1.7
April	65	51	1.2
May	66	55	0.2
June	69	58	0.1
July	72	62	0
August	73	63	0.1
September	73	61	0.3
October	71	57	0.2
November	67	51	1.3
December	64	47	1.5
Yearly Average	**67**	**54**	**11.1**

Source: National Weather Service data, National Oceanographic and Atmospheric Administration.

Orange County

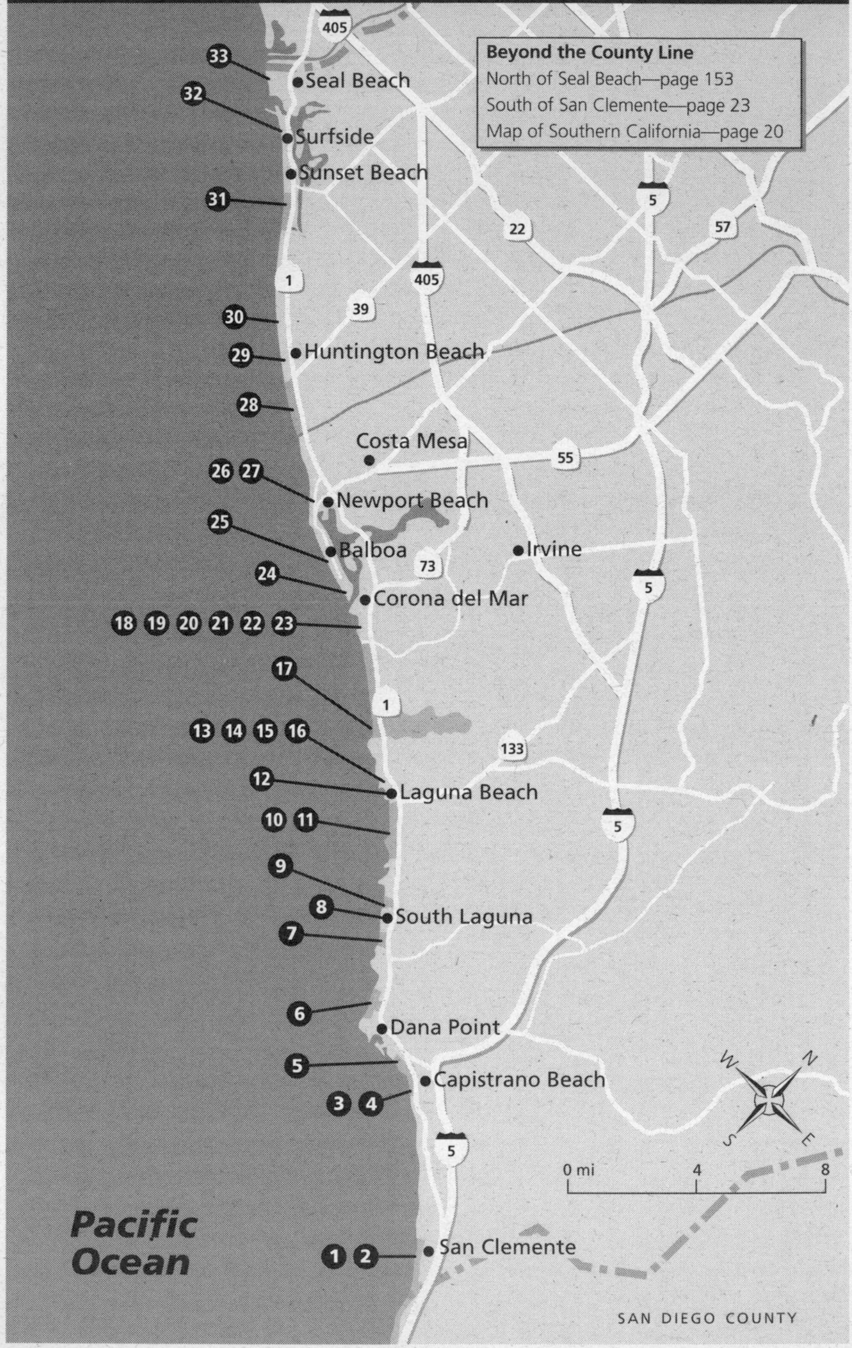

Orange County Beaches

Map of Southern California—page 20

(continued from page 101) of Laguna Beach, where those who most loved the shoreline (and had the least impact upon it) are now persona non grata. They're the ones living with memories of how these places used to be.

The county's current fiscal woes might be blessings in disguise by revealing the viciously destructive capacity of the greedhead agenda. That, in turn, might help protect the remaining beaches of Orange County's lovely shoreline from additional developmental desecration. (Okay, it's a far-fetched theory, but we're eternal optimists who are not above grasping at straws.) First, the underlying cause of the bankruptcy—speculating in dubious stock-market investment schemes with taxpayer's money—will be exposed for the shortsighted business transaction it really is. Second, with no money to bully others, the beach desecraters and their cronies in banking and local government will have to go elsewhere. And most of them already have.

In the past several decades, Orange County has earned a legendary reputation as a bastion of starchy conservatism. While the rap is justified, the county's conservative bent has also given rise to its attitudinal opposite: a culture of noisy punk-rock bands that loathe authority. This at least portends a healthy—or unhealthy, but who cares—counterbalance to all the stuffed-shirt bottom-liners. Regardless of Orange County's intractable conservative politics, the beaches here are treasures as succulent as any navel orange we've ever bitten into. And two of its beach towns—Laguna Beach and Newport Beach—are among our all-time favorites. We hope to keep returning to them, year after year—if they'll have us!

Key to the Symbols

Bike path · Camping · Food and drink · Hiking · Nude

Pier · RVs allowed · Surfing · Volleyball

Crowd Rating

sweet solitude . . . moderate crowds . . . wall-to-wall

Overall Rating

1 2 3 4 5

don't bother . . . worth a visit . . . beach heaven

San Clemente

Location: Approximately halfway between San Diego (55 miles) and Los Angeles (60 miles), with Interstate 5 bisecting it. The main street through town is El Camino Real. No single street runs along the ocean for very far, but Avenida del Mar will deliver you to San Clemente State Beach, at the municipal pier.
Population: 43,500
Area Code: 714 **Zip Code:** 92672

Nestled in the hilly contours of the California coast between Dana Point and Camp Pendleton, San Clemente is fully removed—by geography and sensibility—from the sprawl that slithers toward it from all directions. It has very little in common with the worlds that bear down upon it from metropolitan Los Angeles and exurban Orange County. It is likewise distant from the collision of boutique chic and surfer funk that characterize the chain of resort towns beaded along the coast of north San Diego County. San Clemente is an entity unto itself, rather like a small-scaled SoCal version of Santa Barbara.

Promoting this sense of cozy self-containment is the arrangement of the city streets, which take their cue from the geography of the area. San Clemente is a city whose roads meander in awkward semicircles, following topographical contours. The layout confuses one's sense of direction and forces visitors to play closer attention to their surroundings than they would if driving some boring old grid. And pay attention you do: to the beautiful houses, to the verdant shrubs and gorgeous flowers, and finally to the surrounding hills that plunge dramatically to the sea.

The town is built above some striking beaches, with weathered bluffs and scantily vegetated hills rising behind it. Avenida del Mar links El Camino Real (the main drag, which parallels the Interstate 5 freeway) with the municipal pier and beach. Along the way, it passes through the heart of town, a shopping and business district that could pass for Anytown, U.S.A. Think of it as a stucco version of Mayberry R.F.D. For every cutesy boutique there's a plain old mom-and-pop store serving some basic community need for things like prescription drugs, camera equipment, stationery, and "notions." (When was the last time you heard that word used?) You can sip a civilized cup of coffee at an outdoor café and watch folks amble by, betraying none of the stressful hysteria that sends the rest of us to shrinks, doctors, and an early grave.

Perhaps it is this sense of restful calm that inspired a sitting U.S. president to build a second home in San Clemente. The late Richard Nixon put this small town on the map in 1969 by turning a Spanish-style, red-roofed estate at the south end of town, known as Casa Pacifica, into the "Western White House." Built in 1927 by one Hamilton Cotton, Casa Pacifica served as Nixon's home away from the White House for one-and-a-half terms during the tumultuous era of Vietnam and Watergate. Oddly enough, the estate faces one of the best surfing spots in all of California (Cotton Point, informally known as "Cotton's"), and surfer lore is filled with tales of fearless board bums trying to outfox the Secret Service in their efforts to gain access to it. The way to the waves is more easily negotiated these days, though it's still no picnic, as surfers have to hike a half mile down a path of scalding sand with boards hoisted atop their heads. There's nothing to suggest the Prez attempted the feat himself, but maybe he was actually hipper than we ever gave him credit for. During a tape-recorded tour of the Nixon Library (it's 40 miles from San Clemente, in Yorba Linda), the late president allows that "if there had been a good rap group around in those days, I might have chosen a career in music instead of politics." What would he have called the act: "Tricky Dick and DJ Watergate"?

(continued on page 108)

Golf Course Living— or Selling Orange County by the Hook and Slice

Orange County is California's cradle of Republican values. Beyond its beautiful beaches, the county has all the lingering appeal of a luxury hotel lobby or a bank waiting area. Every man-made structure is replete with fake fountains and forests of weeping figs. The words "May I help you?" spoken by an Orange County service operative usually can be translated to: "How much money do you intend to spend here?"

Orange County's local cultural heroes are Mickey Mouse and John Wayne. The local political heroes are Richard Nixon, whose library and grave are in Yorba Linda, and Bob Badham, who cited "the arms build-up" as the highlight of his multiterm tenure in the U.S. Congress and who pronounced Dan Quayle "very competent and bright."

The irony of all this staunch conservatism is that 30 years ago Orange County was a sleepy rural retreat from Los Angeles. Cities such as Anaheim were the sorts of places little old ladies dreamed of going to get away from the fast-moving City of Angels. Most of the land was either grazed by livestock or graced by orange groves.

Not soon thereafter, the little old ladies passed away. In their place came a glad-handing battalion of budding Bob Badhams—mall designers, entrepreneurs, interstate makers, and commercial developers. All put pressure on pliable government officials to do their bidding. It's the American way, right?

No, it was the will of the Irvine Company, who orchestrated the whole onslaught. The Irvine Company is the mysterious, SMERSH-like realty octopus that owns most of the undeveloped land in Orange County. It holds assets worth $10 billion, and its owner, Donald Bren, is one of the richest men in North America. (Not surprisingly, he is also one of the largest contributors to Republican candidates in the state.) It has built its empire on an equally mysterious real-estate plan. Instead of selling land, it is leased in 99-year increments, thereby ensuring that no one but they actually own it. What the company doesn't lease, it sits on, waiting as market forces drive up land values. It's estimated that the Irvine Company makes $630,000 a year in equity on every acre of undeveloped land it owns.

Originally, most of Orange County was a land grant called Irvine Ranch, a huge slab of what was then Mexico wrested by Spaniards from the Native Americans. Irvine Ranch is five times the size of Manhattan, the largest private real-estate holding in a major U.S. metropolitan area. Just the name "Irvine Ranch" evokes the *Father Knows Best* patriarchy that governs every square foot of Orange County. (But does father really know best? The whole damn county went bankrupt in 1994!)

Instead of cows, Irvine Ranch is grazed by golfers. Instead of orange trees, palm trees have been geometrically arranged around climate-controlled corporate campuses. To the east, the faceless, interchangeable towns that orbit them have been erected. For

 Map of Orange County beaches—page 102

example, 110,000 people live in a city called Orange. Ever heard of Orange? Does it evoke any tangible associations—natural, historical, cultural, whatever? Another 110,000 people live in Irvine, a "planned community" that is livable and safe but as antiseptic as Listerine. Ditto Costa Mesa, clocking in with 100,000 residents. Another 300,000 live in Santa Ana, 300,000 more in Anaheim, and 132,000 in Pasadena. It is a sprawl that is best summed up by this headline from a local newspaper: "Coto de Caza set to open five new neighborhoods."

It goes without saying that the money in Orange County is made primarily through real-estate transactions. In fact, land development is still the most lucrative industry, with annual profit margins of as much as 50 percent (in comparison, the oil industry's yearly profit margins are a relatively paltry 12 percent). You cannot go far without seeing one sign or another boasting "Phase 4 Now Selling" or "Starting at $350,000" (for a condo!) or some sordid variation on this theme. Indeed, if Northern California and the Western states are wondering where all their water is going, just come to Orange County and have a look. Every swath of green that doesn't have a hacienda plopped onto it (with the requisite backyard pool) is devoted to the unnaturally lush contours of a golf course. They've even devised a euphemism for their surreal lifestyle: "Golf Course Living."

A typical excerpt from a local publication reads: "Life in this grand region has become a lot-line-to-lot-line existence. That's why golf courses are so appealing. The yawning fairways and lush greens offer visual and physical relief from the closed-in world we all race to compete in." More philosophy: "Even for nonplayers, golf course living affords something often missing in today's fast-lane lifestyles: open space. Orange County has some of the best in golf course living."

Okay, enough of this bashing. To us, the beaches are the only areas of Orange County that retain any vestiges of or links with the historical and geological past. Despite the fact that the moneyed minions have succeeded in snuffing out the Old California feel of former beach haunts such as Dana Point and Huntington Beach, the towns of San Clemente, Laguna Beach, Newport Beach, and Seal Beach have retained much of their original charm.

Huntington Beach and Dana Point lost their battles because they were meccas for surfers—nonspenders who are run off the land whenever big money snakes its way into town. Still, some very important lessons about coastal development have been learned in Orange County. As we see it, Orange County represents an endpoint of greed and despoliation against which the rest of America's coastal communities need to be on guard.

(continued from page 105)

The return to pre-presidential calm after Nixon left office has suited San Clemente just fine. It's a lovely, unassuming town that looks much as it did when it was advertised to prospective buyers in 1925 as "a village done in the fashion of Old Spain." Named in 1602 by the explorer Sebastian Viscaino in honor of Saint Clement—whose feast day coincided with the date of discovery—San Clemente was one of California's first planned communities. The founder was Ole Hanson, a former mayor of Seattle. In 1925, Hanson and three partners purchased and designed a 2,000-acre parcel in the classic Spanish style, hoping to attract folks who'd grown sick and tired of big city living to "San Clemente by the Sea." Somewhat more of an aesthetic visionary than the developers of today, Hanson rhapsodized: "San Clemente is just a painting five miles long and over a mile wide...its foreground the sea, its background the hills. We use for our pigments flowers and shrubs and trees and red tile and white plaster." Some 70 years later, the painting remains so impressive that it could make an art lover out of any visitor.

Mud on the Tracks

In 1993 and 1994, more than jurisdictional boundaries separated San Clemente from Capistrano Beach. After a period of heavy rain, a February 1993 landslide completely rendered the stretch of the Pacific Coast Highway between the two towns impassable. A rain-soaked bluff gave way, dropping boulders the size of cars and a house the size of...a house...onto the highway and railroad tracks. The dimensions of the slide left a pile of debris two-and-a-half stories high and 200 yards long on the roadway. Hillside homes had to be evacuated for fear of more rain and mudslides.

The questions we have to ask in the wake of such events are: Was this truly a natural disaster or a man-made one? Would the bluff have collapsed had it not been weakened by the houses built on it, which denuded vegetation and increased runoff? In any case, would the bluff's collapse have been an issue if a highway and railroad track hadn't been laid on the precariously thin ribbon of sand between the ocean and the bluff?

When all is said and done, it is really more of an economic disaster than a natural one. Humans continue to build in places they shouldn't, laying the groundwork for natural disasters that translate into economic hardships. In the meantime, 17 months passed before crews began cleaning up the 44,000 tons of rubble that had fallen and, worse, appeared to be supporting what remained of the hillside. The clearing of the highway and construction of a bluff-side retaining system began in July 1994, to the relief of those who felt stranded.

"Seventeen months is a ridiculous amount of time to wait for them to finally do something, especially when you consider that it took only 66 days to repair the Santa Monica Freeway," grumbled one local, who apparently forgot that the Santa Monica Freeway bears a bit more daily traffic than the Pacific Coast Highway between San Clemente and Capistrano Beach. Oh well. The road finally reopened for business in March 1995.

Beaches

San Clemente is a town so full of civic pride that it has its own "city song," entitled "On the Beach of San Clemente." We can't claim to know that little ditty, but we'll happily sing the praises of San Clemente's beaches. Avenida del Mar slaloms to an end right at **San Clemente City Beach**, where there's a historic 1,200-foot pier dating from the 1920s, a municipal parking lot (as well as metered parking on the surrounding streets), bathrooms and showers, plus all the usual provisions of a well-tended city beach. The beach is accessible not only from the terminus of Avenida del Mar, but from numerous street ends and paths along the two-mile stretch from the Ole Hanson Beach Club (a public pool and playground overlooking the beach) south to San Clemente State Beach.

A small, hutlike Amtrak station sits next to railroad tracks so close to the ocean they practically get a licking from the waves. The surf is strong all along the coast around here, drawing an enthusiastic knot of surfing devotees. At high tide, large breakers slam into the pier pilings, turning the frothing water a milky green. The soft, brown-sand beach draws a young, healthy-looking crowd, with the surfers congregating around the pier.

Some inviting seaside bed-and-breakfasts and outdoor cafés face the beach in a line along the dry side of Avenida Victoria, which runs beside the water a short distance before looping up, up, and away. On a nice summer day—and all the ones we've ever spent in San Clemente have had ideal weather—the area in the vicinity of San Clemente City Beach has the charmingly upscale aura of a Mediterranean villa, with climate to match. You couldn't ask for better weather: average highs of 68 degrees in June, 73 degrees in September (the "hot" month), and 66 degrees in December. There are less than 10 inches of rain a year and 342 days of sunshine each year. In a word, it's perfect.

Then there's the "ah"-inspiring **San Clemente State Beach**, which offers some of the best coastal camping along the coast. Whereas the municipal beach is wide and hospitable to swimmers and surfers, the state beach is narrow, prone to rip currents and almost primevally wild. A campground overlooks the mile-long beach. Trees afford some protection from the summer sun, and the place looks more like the national parks of

San Clemente City Beach

Location: In San Clemente, on Avenida del Mar at Avenida Victoria.

Parking: Metered street parking.

Hours: 4 AM to midnight.

Facilities: Lifeguards, rest rooms, showers, picnic area, and fire pits.

Contact: For beach information, contact the San Clemente Department of Marine Safety at (714) 361-8219. For a surf report, call (714) 492-1011.

See number 2 on page 102.

San Clemente State Beach

Location: In San Clemente, on Avenida del Presidente.

Parking: $6 entrance fee per vehicle.

Hours: 6 AM to 10 PM (6 AM to 8 PM from December to February).

Facilities: Lifeguards, rest rooms, showers, picnic areas, and fire pits. There are 160 tent and RV campsites; hookups are available. Fees are $14 to $20 per night. For camping reservations, call Destinet at (800) 444-7275.

Contact: For beach information, contact San Clemente State Beach at (714) 492-3156.

See number 1 on page 102.

the Southwest—Bryce or Zion Canyons, for instance—than some of the flatter and more exposed coastal state parks, such as nearby San Onofre State Park (see the entry on page 100 in the San Diego chapter). An asphalt trail leads down a steep, dramatically eroded ravine to the beach. Railroad tracks run extremely close to the water, protected for the time being by riprap. Near the water's edge, the sand slopes sharply. Breakers scurry up the slope, and an occasional tongue of foam licks the dry sand above it. It's a great beach to hike; the sense of solitude and the scenic backdrop are stunning. Divers plumb the depths for spiny lobster and abalone. Swimming is discouraged, and surfers choose to hotfoot it

Getting Around the Big Orange

By car, Orange County is a waking nightmare. This reality was brought home to us by our attempt to go to a California Angels–Baltimore Orioles baseball game in Anaheim. The city of Anaheim was a paltry 18 miles east of our motel in Newport Beach. Shucks, 18 miles to see Bo Jackson and Cal Ripken, Jr.? No problem. Or so we thought.

This is the same route that leads to Disneyland, the same route driven from the coast by every other beachgoer who blithely imagines a pleasant day trip to that Mickey Mouse trap during their summer vacation. Personally, we can't imagine anything more pleasant than the beaches of Newport Beach, but people do feel duty-bound to visit Disneyland (about $28 for adults, $23 for kids).

Our venture mired us in an unmoving traffic jam both before and after the ball game. Although we thought we had allowed plenty of time for the commute to the stadium, we missed the first inning. Afterward, at 11 PM on a weeknight, traffic was backed up even worse than before the game. We found ourselves sitting stock still on the freeway for 15 minutes. The delay wasn't due to wrecks or a departing game crowd (hell, only 15,000 people attended). It was due partly to road construction—the widening and repairing of the roads that never seem to end in Southern California. Even so, as midnight approached, the delay became absurd. An hour and a half to go 18 miles?

Road building has reached such an unutterable state of lunacy in Orange County that a new plan is afoot to alleviate traffic where Interstates 5 and 405 meet. It would create a highway *26 lanes wide!* Happily, an alternative to driving a car exists, as Orange County has led an effort to implement a viable public transit system in Southern California. Regular Amtrak trains run from San Clemente to Fullerton. Plans are under way to expand rail service, but for now, the most beach-friendly mode of conveyance is the excellent bus system run by the Orange County Transportation Authority. One dollar gets you as far south as San Clemente, as far north as Long Beach, and as far east as Anaheim and Yorba Linda. One route on this system traverses the entire length of Highway 1 in Orange County, paralleling the coast and stopping at every town. Coupon books and reduced-rate monthly packages are available.

For a copy of the bus system's free *Map and Ride Guide*, contact the Orange County Transportation Authority, P.O. Box 14184, Orange, CA 92613; (714) 560-6282.

down to better waves at Cotton's and San Onofre's Trestle's beaches, which straddle the San Diego County line from opposite sides of San Mateo Point. If you happen to see a surfer or two studying the distant waves from a freeway off-ramp south of town, they're weighing the pros and cons of whether the day's surf is worth the long walk to the water.

Bunking Down

Across the street from San Clemente Municipal Pier is a charming block with a smattering of bed-and-breakfasts offering wonderful beach views at top-end prices. One is **Casa Tropicana** (610 Avenida Victoria, 492-1234, $$$), whose theme rooms (e.g., "Out of Africa," "Emerald Forest," and "South Pacific") overlook the pier at prices that will quickly bring you down to earth ($140 to $350 a night). Another is the **Villa del Mar Inn** (612 Avenida Victoria, 498-5080, $$$), whose condo-style suites offer beach-facing sundecks, big living rooms, and fully equipped kitchens. Rooms run from $150 to $199 in the high season and drop by $70 a night in the rest of the year. Since the weather barely changes from month to month, the off-season rates are a real bargain.

Many visitors put up at the **San Clemente Inn** (2600 Avenida del Presidente, 492-6103, $$), which is beside San Clemente State Park. It operates as a hotel condominium, offering homey apartment-style suites set amid grounds that include a pool and spa, shuffleboard courts, and gargantuan pineapple trees. Among hotel chains, the **San Clemente Holiday Inn Resort** (111 South Avenida del Estrella, 361-3000, $$) is a posh oceanside retreat that's got the competition beat when it comes to amenities: heated pool, spa, fitness center, sundeck with a view, and a location convenient to the beach.

Coastal Cuisine

Look no farther than the San Clemente Municipal Pier for dinner. You have two choices: the **Fisherman's Restaurant** (611 Avenida Victoria, 498-6390, $$) on the left side of the pier, and **Fisherman's Bar** on the right. They serve good, fresh Pacific seafood at both places. The full dinners menu at the restaurant ranges from fish-and-chips to whole Dungeness crab. If you're toting a huge appetite, they offer all-you-can-eat feasts of clams, halibut, salmon, swordfish, or crab, served with salad, rice pilaf, sourdough bread, and Fisherman's chowder. Yum! The bar tends more toward heavy appetizers.

In the same vicinity, on the opposite side of the street, the **Beach Garden Café** (685 1/2 Avenida Victoria, 498-8145, $) is a cute, modern eatery serving a good selection of omelettes, sandwiches, pizzas, and entrées such as fish-and-chips. If you're looking for something a little fancier, there's **Etienne's** (215 South El Camino Real, 492-7263, $$$), a French restaurant of long-standing that puts a healthy, Cal-nouvelle twist on classic European gourmet cuisine, with a particular emphasis on fresh fish.

Night Moves

After sunset (best watched from the pier, sundowners), San Clemente gets quieter than an orange grove. Laguna Beach and San Juan Capistrano are the nearest outposts of serious nightlife. A cocktail waitress at the San Clemente Pier tipped us off to a particularly lively club up the coast where it was supposedly reggae night. "Have you ever heard of reggae music?" she asked, as if she were an elementary school teacher introducing a new vowel sound. We didn't feel like letting our dreadlocks down that night and happily opted to remain glued to our bar-side perches and enjoy the pier's relative tranquillity.

For More Information

Contact the San Clemente Chamber of Commerce, 1100 North El Camino Real, San Clemente, CA 92672; (714) 492-1131.

Capistrano Beach

Location: Halfway between San Diego and Los Angeles (roughly 60 miles from each), along and between Interstate 5 and the Pacific Coast Highway. Doheny State Beach and Capistrano Beach Park are the main beaches in an unbroken stretch that runs along the Capistrano Bight up to Dana Point.
Population: 7,500
Area Code: 714 **Zip Code:** 92624

Enfolding the coastline between Dana Point and San Clemente, the Capistrano Beach area has been marketed—rather overoptimistically—as "California's Riviera." In the words of the rap group Public Enemy, "Don't believe the hype." In actuality, Capistrano Beach is a small and relatively uncrowded oceanfront sanctuary. That quality of spaciousness has become a virtual novelty in Southern California, and it is what sets Capistrano Beach apart from its neighbors to the north and south. For instance, San Juan Capistrano—a larger town that has scared away the swallows by building malls and boxy stucco homes on every available square inch—lies behind it and offers what less jaded travel writers than we would refer to as "fabulous shopping opportunities." To us, it's just another infernal gash in the landscape that was made to bleed the unconscious consumer. (Much of Orange County, particularly its interior sprawl, has come to resemble a Hieronymous Bosch vision of hell, with groaning condominiums and howling land speculators instead of shrieking harpies filling the canvas.)

Stick to the beach; it's pleasant out here, and there's lots of it to go around. Capistrano Beach has got a sweet, unhurried way about it. Whether you're looking out to sea from the beach or the palisades above, it's a pianissimo passage in the Wagnerian symphony of overdevelopment that otherwise characterizes much of the coast between San Diego to Los Angeles.

Beaches

On a nice day, the beaches here almost look too good to be true: a mirage of white sand and emerald water gleaming beneath a bright blue sky. But this vision is for real. Down on the shoreline, Capistrano Beach boasts a wide, unblemished public beach. A road called the Palisades drops down from steep residential hills to meet the Pacific Coast Highway. The entrance to **Capistrano Beach** is near this

Capistrano Beach

3

Location: In Capistrano Beach, on El Camino Real at Palisade Drive.
Parking: Metered parking lot.
Hours: 6 AM to 10 PM.
Facilities: Lifeguards, rest rooms, showers, and picnic tables.
Contact: For beach information, contact the South Beaches Operation Office of Orange County Harbors, Beaches, and Parks at (714) 661-7013.

See number 4 on page 102.

Poche Beach

3

Location: In Capistrano Beach, on Camino Capistrano at the Pacific Coast Highway.
Parking: Free street parking.
Hours: 6 AM to 10 PM.
Facilities: None.
Contact: For beach information, contact the South Beaches Operation Office of Orange County Harbors, Beaches, and Parks at (714) 661-7013.

See number 3 on page 102.

intersection. A large parking lot with inexpensive metered parking—no small bargain for a California beach—faces the ocean. The beach is popular but seldom overrun. At 7 AM on a drizzly May morning, a group of teenage girls were enthusiastically engaged in a little preschool volleyball practice. Meanwhile, cars were parked along the lip of the lot, their drivers lost in meditative contemplation before heading off to a hard day of hammering nails or making deals.

The parking lot runs beside the beach for a good distance, and people were aerobicizing along its length in jogging shoes or in-line skates. By midmorning a furious full-court basketball game was in progress. In the distance, surfers congregated off Doheny Point. Just another day in the life of a prime Southern California beach. For those staying on the inland side of the Pacific Coast Highway, pedestrian overpasses cross the highway at several points. At the south end of Capistrano Beach, where Camino Capistrano runs out at the Pacific Coast Highway, an underpass for walkers leads out to **Poche Beach**, a sandy surfing beach just above the landslide that closed a stretch of the PCH in 1993. Incidentally, the magazine *Surfer* is published in Capistrano Beach, and surfboards are manufactured here.

Bunking Down

Out along the Pacific Coast Highway, staring at the beach from the landward side, there is a

Where Have All the Swallows Gone?

The story of the swallows of San Juan Capistrano is a major chapter in California's legend and lore. Each year the swallows, ever-reliable in the constancy of their reappearance, make the 6,000 mile trip from Goya, Argentina, to Mission San Juan Capistrano. They arrive on March 19, build nests and hatch their chicks, then depart for the winter on October 23. You can set your calendar by them. The date of their spring arrival is known as St. Joseph's Day (a.k.a. Swallow Day). Large numbers of tourists turn out to greet the swallows, a ritual highlighted by the 8 AM ringing of the mission bells by the 100-year-old town patriarch Paul Arbiso. Everybody oohs and ahs over the return of the little five-inch gliding birds. It's a great day for birds and bird-watchers alike.

However, the truth of the matter may be a little harder to, uh, swallow. In 1993, for instance, an estimated 25,000 tourists doubled the town's population over the weekend. Thousands turned out in the early morning to witness the flapping of four startled birds who were roused from the mission eaves by the aged bell-ringer. The swallows of Capistrano were outnumbered, according to published accounts, by pigeons. Nonetheless, a celebratory parade of 4,000 people, many on horseback, took place in the afternoon. That's a parader-to-bird ratio of 1,000 to 1. Does something seem cuckoo about all this? Still, the feeder roads get clogged and the hotels and restaurants are booked solid over the St. Joseph's Day weekend. The irony is that one annual migration (i.e., the birds) may well have been displaced by another (i.e., humans). In 1991, flocks of swallows passed over San Juan Capistrano and instead set up housekeeping on the campus of Pepperdine University, in Malibu.

row of vacation time-share condos that also operate like hotels. That is, you can either buy a week or two a year in perpetuity for a large sum or simply drive up and spend the night, with no strings attached, for a not-unreasonable sum. We tried the **Capistrano Surfside Inn** (34680 Pacific Coast Highway, 240-7681, $$$) and found it quite comfortable. The units are one- and two-bedroom suites that come with full kitchens and outdoor balconies stocked with furniture and gas grills. The inn arranges a daily schedule of activities for those so inclined, including day trips to beaches on the Baja Peninsula. There's a pool on the premises, or you can cross the street to the beach. Close by is the **Capistrano Edgewater Inn** (34744 Pacific Coast Highway, 240-0150, $$$), which offers comparable prices, views, and amenities.

Coastal Cuisine

A famous Mexican restaurant called **Olamendi's** (34660 Pacific Coast Highway, 661-1005, $$) does a big business in burritos across the street from the beach. Its popularity is easy to gauge from the parking lot, which is frequently full, even in midafternoon. Inside, moderately priced Mexican food of good quality is served at padded, semicircular booths. Tacos, burritos, and enchiladas are served every conceivable way (stuffed with shredded beef, sirloin steak, chicken, fish, pork, cheese—seemingly everything but burro meat). The menu carries a one-word endorsement from the late Richard Nixon: "Excellent." Up by the cash register hangs a picture of El Presidente, nervously posed with the kitchen staff. If you're hankering for something a little more high-end, nearby Dana Point and San Juan Capistrano offer a range of gourmet Italian, French, and California options.

Night Moves

The after-hours options in Capistrano Beach are as weak as the glow from a child's night-light, but you stand a good chance of catching some great music at the **Coach House** (33187 Camino Capistrano, 496-8927) in nearby San Juan Capistrano. It's one of the vital links in the chain of clubs that keeps good musicians in work (see the entry on the Belly Up Tavern, in Solana Beach, on page 77). "San Juan Cap" (as it's known to locals) is a formerly quaint, Mission-style community now beset with endless malls whose acreage rivals that of a cattle ranch. The train station is the hub of weekend nightlife. Everyone from wandering minstrels on down performs for the assembled masses, some of whom even ride the rails from L.A. just to be part of the crowd.

For More Information

Contact the Capistrano Beach Chamber of Commerce, P.O. Box 2335, Capistrano Beach, CA 92524; (714) 496-1017. For information about San Juan Capistrano, which is just slightly inland, write or visit the San Juan Capistrano Chamber of Commerce, 31882 Camino Capistrano, Suite 218, San Juan Capistrano, CA 03675; (714) 493-4700.

Dana Point

Location: Between Capistrano Beach and South Laguna, 50 miles south of Los Angeles. Take Interstate 5 to Highway 1 (Pacific Coast Highway) and turn left on Dana Harbor Drive, which runs out to the yacht basin, Mariner's Village, and Lookout Park. The main beaches in the vicinity of Dana Point are Doheny State Beach, just south of the yacht basin, and Salt Creek County Beach, just north of Dana Point.
Population: 31,900
Area Code: 714 **Zip Code:** 92629

A nine-foot bronze statue of seaman and writer Richard Henry Dana, Jr., looks out over the harbor that's named after him. Dana came here in the 1830s aboard the square rigger *Pilgrim*. He recorded his experiences as a naïf on the high seas in the autobiographical narrative *Two Years Before the Mast*, a California literary classic. He also described the cliff-backed cove at Dana Point as "the only romantic spot in California." We beg to differ with the estimable writer on this point. Number one, there are plenty of romantic spots in California. Number two, Dana Point is no longer one of them.

Of course, Dana himself had nothing to do with the artificial facelift that turned the rugged environment he knew and loved into a sanitized playground for the wealthy, so we won't hold him accountable on this last point. Instead, we'll direct our venom toward those dissemblers of public-relations jive who use his words to promote the arid development that calmed the waves and transformed the landscape. The refashioning of Dana Point into a 2,500-slip yacht harbor—which began in 1969 when the Orange County Board of Supervisors approved construction of a jetty, harbor, and harborside community—is the sort of tale that would have inspired a salty young sailor like Dana to mutiny. Indeed, were Dana around to see the area today, he would scarcely be able to comprehend the changes that have taken place since his time. The man-made Dana Harbor has stilled the waves for yuppie yachts, while the Mariner's Village developers have erected a faux New England fishing village that is a facile mockery of the real thing.

The brotherhood of surfers is still steamed about what the addition of the 1.5-mile jetty did to the surf at Doheny State Beach. "The mellow lines of Doheny are all but gone, replaced by the calm water of Dana Point Harbor," lamented surfing historian and chronicler Allan "Bank" Wright. Lifelong surfer, beach aficionado, and journalist John McKinney nearly aborted a planned hike of the California coastline because he grew so disgusted with the barricading of Dana Point. Stranded outside a gated residential community, McKinney wrote: "As I stand with Dana's memorial...the sun, which I cannot see, drops toward the ocean, which I cannot see, showering golden light on sandstone cliffs, where I cannot legally walk." Of the yacht basin, he wrote: "I walk across the acres of hot asphalt comprising the Dana Harbor parking lot. The sight of the huge plasticky and antiseptic marina takes the wind out of my sails. A favorite surfing spot of my adolescence has been totally destroyed." The name of McKinney's essay says it all: "The Boutiquing of the California Coast."

It's not only the squeaky clean fake seaport experience that rankles. The Pacific Coast Highway has become clogged on both sides through the Dana Point/South Laguna corridor with strip malls, slowing traffic and congesting the area. Colorful, ceremonial nylon flags fly from shops and subdevelopments alike, but their gaiety seems a fraudulent joke played on the vanquished environment. The buildup along the highway has been torrential since the mid-1980s, with the result that there isn't much unviolated "outdoors" visible anymore. Despite efforts to promote and trade on that very quality, it is vanishing.

Beaches

Two great Orange County coast beaches flank Dana Point. **Doheny State Beach** is enfolded by the long arm of the south jetty that protects Dana Harbor. Although the surf has been tamed, all has not been lost. It's a great beginner's beach for surfers and still gets some decent peelers on a south swell. Swimmers, meanwhile, can enjoy the relative calm of Doheny's white, wide, three-quarter-mile-long beach. It's very popular, and an early-morning arrival on summer days is recommended. An interpretive center offers a touch tank and five aquariums. A wooded campground, grassy picnic area, and bike path make this 62-acre park an exceptional unit in the state-park system.

North of Dana Point is **Salt Creek County Beach**. Salt Creek preserves a long stretch of beach, extending from the point up toward South Laguna—at least this is some consolation for the damage done at Dana Point. Situated on the bluffs above and behind the beach is Bluff Park, a section of the county beach that has just about everything you could ask for: trails, picnic tables, rest rooms and outdoor showers, grills and fire rings, basketball courts, and views out to Catalina Island. It is also a good onshore spot for whale watching during the peak season of February and early March.

Bunking Down

Posh and pricey are the bywords at Dana Point. The **Ritz-Carlton Laguna Niguel** (33533 Ritz-Carlton Drive, 240-2000, $$$$) will swaddle you in five-star comfort: It is probably the premier resort on the Southern California coast. We are hard-pressed to think of one more imposing in its roll call of amenities: four tennis courts, three restaurants, two heated pools, and an 18-hole golf course—everything but the proverbial partridge in a pear tree. And the view, from a bluff 150 feet above the ocean, is unparalleled. As they put it, "We overlook nothing but the Pacific." The other twin peak in the hotel opulence sweepstakes is the **Dana Point Resort** (25135 Park Lantern Drive, 661-5000, $$$$), a sprawling pleasure dome that occupies some 12 acres offering biking and jogging trails. All 350 rooms are ocean-view. In addition to health clubs, tennis courts, and spas, it's got one of the finest gourmet restaurants in the state, Watercolors (see page 117).

Doheny State Beach

5

Location: At Dana Harbor, along Del Obispo and the Pacific Coast Highway.

Parking: $5 entrance fee per vehicle.

Hours: 6 AM to 10 PM.

Facilities: Lifeguards, rest rooms, showers, picnic areas, and fire rings. There are 120 tent and RV campsites. Fees are $14 to $20 per night. For camping reservations, call Destinet at (800) 444-7275.

Contact: For beach information, contact Doheny State Beach at (714) 496-6171.

See number 5 on page 102.

Salt Creek County Beach

4

Location: In Dana Point, off Ritz-Carlton Drive.

Parking: Metered parking lot.

Hours: 6 AM to midnight.

Facilities: Lifeguards, rest rooms, showers, picnic tables, and fire rings.

Contact: For beach information, contact the South Beaches Operation Office of Orange County Harbors, Beaches, and Parks at (714) 661-7013.

See number 6 on page 102.

Boutiquing the California Coast

We use the term "boutiquing" throughout this book in a pejorative way, taking our cue from the informed rancor of West Coast writer John McKinney on the subject of shoreline desecration: "A unique coastal history is cheapened when the marketable is substituted for the memorable. Coastal architecture suffers when the frivolous is substituted for the functional. Coastal ecosystems are degraded when the expensive replaces the priceless. In short, economically and ecologically, what we are witnessing…is the boutiquing of the California coast."

Those words were written in 1984. More than a decade later, there is no end in sight. From the perspective of a condo owner, a community such as Dana Point might seem like a wonderfully cloistered paradise, but to a visitor who just wants some reasonable beach access its aesthetic seems phony, overcrowded, out of place: the New England "seacoast village" motif employed in countless waterfront developments; the ornate, ersatz Victorian constructions that, set against the originals, appear cheap and cutesy; and the ubiquitous pipe-roofed, stucco-walled imitation of the gracious Mission style, evident in subdevelopments thrown up in tight clusters on land that can scarcely bear another iota of construction.

For budget accommodations, head a few miles up the coast to South Laguna, which has some less swank beachside motels along the Pacific Coast Highway.

Coastal Cuisine

We stated our biases against the exclusivity and landscape-shattering development at Dana Point up front. That doesn't mean we don't admire several of the properties that have gone up out there, particularly the Ritz-Carlton and the Dana Point Resort, both of them first-class resorts that live up to every expectation. **Watercolors**, the restaurant at the Dana Point Resort (25135 Park Lantern Drive, 661-5000, $$$), went way beyond expectations. Had we never eaten another morsel after our feast at Watercolors, we could have died happy men. The meal commenced with a pair of appetizers—tuna tartare and spring rolls filled with meaty slices of grilled duck—so artistically rendered that we almost didn't dare disturb them. They proved as delicious to eat as they were to look at. Entrée preparations were similarly sumptuous. The room is light and airy, done in peach tones and brass accents, and the prevailing style is contemporary American cuisine: healthy, attractive, creative, and oh so good.

Night Moves

The lounges at the hotel resorts—particularly the Ritz-Carlton, with its nightclub offering live entertainment—are your primary options in upscale Dana Point. After a day of tennis and/or sailing and a good meal, you might not feel like much more than a civilized nightcap in any case.

For More Information

Dana Point Chamber of Commerce, 24681 La Plaza, Suite 120, Dana Point, CA 92629; (714) 496-1555.

Laguna Beach and South Laguna

Location: Approximately 50 miles south of Los Angeles. Laguna Beach can be reached from points north and south via the Pacific Coast Highway, which passes through it, and from the west via Laguna Canyon Road, which connects with Interstate 5 (San Diego Freeway). Highway 1 (Pacific Coast Highway) runs alongside the ocean. More than 30 beaches are scattered among the coves of Laguna Beach, but the busiest, broadest, and sandiest of these is Main Beach, located where Laguna Canyon Road meets the Pacific Coast Highway
Population: 25,000
Area Code: 714 **Zip Code:** 92651

When people hear the name Laguna Beach, they tend to think of faraway places: the French Riviera, the Greek Isles, the coast of Italy. They think of anywhere but Orange County, California, where the town is an anomaly: an impressionistic seaside village that attracts free spirits. It is a cultural oasis in a land of fume-choked freeways, soulless suburban sprawl, and fiercely unforgiving arch-conservatism. As those who live here will argue, it is in many ways an island. Not literally an island, but figuratively so, set apart from the rest of Orange County by geography—hills and canyons on three sides, ocean to the west—and by the disposition of its inhabitants, which is more creative than mercenary. The argument was stated by a resident in a local publication, who may have revealed more than she intended when she wrote: "Whatever you do, the waves will take your troubles far out to sea, leaving you mindless."

Above all else, Laguna Beach is an artist's colony. There were 55 galleries in Laguna Beach at last count, the lion's share arrayed along the Pacific Coast Highway. While other beach towns in Southern California host surfing competitions, lifeguard races, and volleyball tournaments, Laguna Beach sponsors three art festivals every summer, among them a nationally renowned event called the Pageant of the Masters (see sidebar, "Laguna Beach's Summer-Long Art Affairs"). Easels are as plentiful as palm trees, especially around sunset, when artists strive to capture the gold fire that illuminates the town's myriad coves and beaches.

South Laguna begins around Ocean Vista Drive (just below Victoria Beach) and extends south to Salt Creek County Beach. The differences between South Laguna and Laguna Beach are strictly jurisdictional and nomenclatural. In the words of a longtime resident, "It's all Laguna Beach to me." Indeed, they blend into one another so thoroughly that only a mapmaker can tell them apart. It's all Laguna Beach to us, too.

People who call Laguna Beach home love everything about it except the traffic. They revere the intellectual camaraderie that encourages self-expression and abides eccentricity; the cool, even climate; the striking beauty of cliffs that plunge to a dramatic shoreline (sometimes taking homes with them); and the quasi-European manners of the place, with its emphasis on high culture and old money. There's even room for surfers, skateboarders, and all the less intellectual flotsam that washes ashore. Their presence keeps the community from becoming swamped by its own pretensions.

That's not to say there hasn't been trouble in paradise of late. AIDS has decimated the gay population in Laguna Beach, as it has in gay coastal strongholds the country over, like Fire Island, Provincetown, and Key West on the East Coast. Recession has cut into the local economy, as it has everywhere. Fire consumed a lot of property in Laguna Beach in October 1993, scarring canyons and destroying hundreds of millions of

 Map of Orange County beaches—page 102

dollars worth of homes. (Fortunately, no lives were lost.) The Laguna Beach fire was viewed the world over on CNN newscasts, and European tourist numbers declined the following summer. Apparently, they were under the impression that the town had been thoroughly incinerated. According to one local innkeeper, "German TV news maps made it appear as if all of Southern California was on fire."

Though 70,000 acres were charred in six Southern California counties, most of the damage in Laguna Beach was confined to the canyons and homes that were ill-advisedly built in them. But that wasn't the end of the story. Torrential October rains were followed by November mudslides that, among other things, inundated the grounds where the annual Festival of Arts is held. Today, the scars left by the fire and mudslides are barely visible up the canyons east of Laguna Beach, and the town center appears physically none the worse for its trial by fire and rain. In fact, the townsfolk valiantly rallied around their tribulations, rebounding with renewed vigor and survivalist spirit.

Laguna Beach has always marched to the beat of a different drummer. Unlike much of California, which was parceled out in the form of land grants by the rulers of Spain and Mexico to friends of the throne, Laguna was homesteaded by tree-planting pioneers following the region's annexation by the United States. It was initially called Lagonas, from the Shoshone word for lakes, because of the freshwater lagoons situated behind the beaches where creeks pour into the ocean. The first arrivals were Mormons, who were followed by Methodists. Laguna's first hostelry opened in 1886 and has been operating ever since as the Hotel Laguna.

Artists began forming an enclave here in the early 1900s, around which time the name was changed to Laguna Beach. Gradually, a style known as California impressionism began to evolve here after an artist named Lewis Botts painted his famous *Girl of the Golden West* in 1914. Much in the style of Monet's

Laguna Beach's Summerlong Art Affairs

If you come to Laguna Beach in the summer, chances are you'll spend as much time looking at paintings of the ocean as you will at the actual thing. These three art festivals keep things hopping all summer long in Laguna Beach:

Art-A-Fair (777 Laguna Canyon Road, 714-494-4514) and the **Sawdust Festival** (935 Laguna Canyon Road, 714-494-3030) run from June 30 through August 28. Art-A-Fair is a juried art show that also features demonstrations and workshops. The Sawdust Festival is more of the same, plus food and entertainment, such as a juggler of fiery batons who wouldn't be out of place on Venice Beach.

The venerable **Festival of Arts** (650 Laguna Canyon Road, 714-497-6582) and its highlight, the **Pageant of the Masters**, runs from July 8 through August 28. It has been an annual feature of Laguna Beach life for more than 60 years. The Pageant of the Masters brings to life approximately 40 pieces of classic art using live, human subjects. Actors and locals three-dimensionally re-create paintings by the likes of Matisse, Van Gogh, Magritte, and Seurat for staged, 90-second sittings that take several hours (if not months) to prepare. The evening culminates in a grand *tableaux vivant* setting of Da Vinci's *Last Supper*. The effect is both lifelike and eerily two-dimensional, thanks to creative lighting techniques.

French Impressionist school, they painted the natural surroundings with rapid brush strokes and an eye for how the sunlight bathed the landscape. The Laguna Beach Art Association was founded in 1918, and thereafter art galleries began popping up all over. Today small galleries hang signs in their front windows such as this one: "We buy Old Laguna and Old European paintings."

The artistic imperative meanders all the way down Laguna Canyon Road to the water. At Main Beach, an art-deco chess table done in a colorful mosaic of ceramic tiles sits in the grassy picnic area for all to admire or use. Don't be surprised to see eye-catching models posing and preening on the beach for a professional fashion shoot. A lot of models and film-industry types live in Laguna Beach. The former estate

Beach Curfews: Night Time Is the Wrong Time

It's all the rage in California—even trendier than coffee bars and Rollerblades. We're talking about beach curfews. Towns up and down the California coast, particularly from Long Beach south, have opted to address their beachfront noise and crime problems by imposing curfews. Coronado, Laguna Beach, and Huntington Beach are just three beach communities that keep people from making trouble on the sand by denying them after-hours access. In a sense, these ordinances reverse the push to democratize the beaches, a mandate that has been a guiding philosophy of the California Coastal Commission since its founding in 1972. A true sign that the times are a-changin' is that in 1994 the commission approved a nighttime curfew for Coronado.

We don't disagree that curfews are a right and necessary thing. While it is noble to want universal public access, drunken and even homicidal behavior—such as the shootings that have occurred at the Huntington Beach and Newport Beach piers—have necessitated imposing limits. In the name of public safety, you can't really blame the communities.

The curfew in Coronado is year-round, effective from 11 PM to 4 AM in the fire-ring area along its public beaches, where crime is most concentrated. In July 1994, Laguna Beach's town council set a 10 PM curfew for all youths under 18 years of age. It was a move prompted by gatherings of outsiders who'd come to Laguna from other Orange County towns with earlier curfews. The ordinance prohibits minors from idling or loitering in public places between the hours of 10 PM and 6 AM unless accompanied by a responsible adult.

It is similar to curfews in force throughout the county, inland as well as on the coast. Huntington Beach imposed curfews after a gang fight at Bolsa Chica State Beach in 1992 resulted in injuries to lifeguards who attempted to intervene. For several years, Long Beach has attempted to check crime by closing its beachfront parking lots at night.

The California Coastal Commission challenged the legality of the Long Beach curfews. The debate turned into a Mexican standoff, with the commission acting in

 Map of Orange County beaches—page 102

of Bette Davis is a local landmark. From the earliest days, it's been a gathering place for the jet set. Celebrity residents have included Charlie Chaplin, Judy Garland, Rudolph Valentino, and Gregory Peck.

The main artery through Laguna Beach is the Pacific Coast Highway, which unfortunately snakes right through the center of town. The steady stream of traffic mars the town's otherwise genteel village atmosphere. There is simply no other way to get from Dana Point to Newport Beach. A proposed freeway bypass located a few miles inland was nixed years ago. All the whizzing traffic makes getting in and out of your parked car a sport as hazardous as surfing. If traffic were rerouted away from town, Laguna Beach would be a more pleasant place.

the interest of public access, the Long Beach city government acting in the interest of public safety, and both sides claiming jurisdiction. The commission subsequently issued an order prohibiting communities from passing curfews without its approval. They haven't ruled out curfews, but insist that evidence sufficient to justify them be submitted. In other words, the communities have in effect been told to wait until more people are injured, and then curfew approval may be granted. The situation was likened by one observer to waiting until enough wrecks had occurred at an intersection before putting up a stoplight.

Here are the curfews in effect on the beaches of Southern California. This information is, of course, subject to change.

City or Beach	Public Beaches (hours closed)	Beach Parking Lots (hours closed)
Bolsa Chica State Beach	8 PM to 5 AM	7 PM to 5 AM
Cabrillo City Beach (San Pedro)	10:30 PM to 5 AM	10:30 PM to 5 AM
Corona del Mar	10 PM to 6 AM	10 PM to 6 AM
Coronado	11 PM to 4 AM	
Doheny State Beach (Dana Point)	8 PM to 6 AM	
Huntington City Beach	8 PM to 5 AM	one-half hour after dusk to 5 AM
Huntington State Beach	8 PM to 6 AM	7 PM to 6 AM
Laguna Beach	10 PM to 6 AM	
Long Beach	midnight to 5 AM	10 PM to 5 AM
Newport Beach	10 PM to 6 AM	
San Clemente City Beach	midnight to 4 AM	
San Clemente State Beach	8 PM to 6 AM	
San Onofre State Beach	8 PM to 6 AM	
Seal Beach	10 PM to 4:30 AM	

As it is, though, Laguna has atmosphere, culture, scenic beauty, and fantastic beaches. Renowned for its friendliness, the town at one time even had an unofficial greeter, Eiler Larson by name. This friendly, shaggy mountain man would stand at the city limits, hollering "How are you?" to those coming and "Leaving so soon?" to those going for eight hours a day. After he died, numerous tributary wood likenesses began appearing on the town's sidewalks.

You've got to love a community that has its own activist beautification council, which successfully battled outside business interests that wanted to refashion Laguna Beach into a convention center during the 1970s. The would-be developers were sent packing and the threatened town center was instead turned into the landscaped, open-air Main Beach Park. Along the coastline, such happy endings are all too rare. This one deserves a standing ovation.

Beaches

Laguna Beach comes stocked with beaches—30 or so of them, tucked into coves along a hilly, undulating coastline. (To give you an idea of its ruggedness, the elevation within this small

1,000 Steps Beach

3

Location: In South Laguna, at Ninth Avenue and the Pacific Coast Highway.
Parking: Metered street parking.
Hours: 6 AM to 9 PM.
Facilities: Lifeguards.
Contact: For beach information, contact the South Beaches Operation Office of Orange County Harbors, Beaches, and Parks at (714) 661-7013.

See number 7 on page 102.

Aliso Creek County Beach

2

Location: In South Laguna, along the 31,000 block of the Pacific Coast Highway, across from the Aliso Creek Inn.
Parking: Metered parking lot.
Hours: 6 AM to 10 PM.
Facilities: Lifeguards, rest rooms, showers, picnic tables, and fire pits.
Contact: For beach information, contact the South Beaches Operation Office of Orange County Harbors, Beaches, and Parks at (714) 661-7013.

See number 9 on page 102.

Brooks Beach

3

Location: In Laguna Beach, at the end of Brooks Street, off the Pacific Coast Highway.
Parking: Metered street parking.
Hours: 6 AM to 10 PM.
Facilities: None.
Contact: For beach information, contact the South Beaches Operation Office of Orange County Harbors, Beaches, and Parks at (714) 661-7013.

See number 11 on page 102.

Crescent Bay Point Park

3

Location: On the north side of Laguna Beach, at the end of Crescent Bay Drive.
Parking: Free street parking.
Hours: 6 AM to 10 PM.
Facilities: Lifeguards and rest rooms.
Contact: For beach information, contact the South Beaches Operation Office of Orange County Harbors, Beaches, and Parks at (714) 661-7013.

See number 17 on page 102.

town's limits ranges from sea level to 1,039 feet.) **Main Beach** (a.k.a. Laguna Beach Municipal Park) is just that: the main place to congregate and recreate in Laguna. In a town of tiny coves and pocket beaches, this is the big enchilada. Two gas stations face the beach like beefeaters at the gates of Buckingham Palace. Balls are bounced and batted during every daylight hour. With its volleyball and basketball courts, picnicking green, and long, sandy beach bordered by a winding boardwalk, Main Beach is a buzzing hive of activity.

Beyond Main Beach, plenty of smaller beaches can be found in both directions along the Pacific Coast Highway. It seems that every side street ends at the cliffs, with a stairway leading to a fan-shaped cove. We'll survey the more noteworthy ones, starting in South Laguna, a seemingly independent community (though only a surveyor would know where to divide it from Laguna Beach). To begin with a fun one, check out **1,000 Steps Beach**. It's located where Ninth Avenue meets the Pacific Coast Highway in South Laguna. You'll have to park a few blocks away on the highway's asphalt shoulder, since all the curbs are red in the immediate vicinity, but the walk from your car to the top of the stairs will warm up your

Diver's Cove

Location: In Laguna Beach, along the 600 block of Cliff Drive.

Parking: Metered street parking.

Hours: 6 AM to 10 PM.

Facilities: None.

Contact: For beach information, contact the South Beaches Operation Office of Orange County Harbors, Beaches, and Parks at (714) 661-7013.

See number 15 on page 102.

Main Beach

Location: In the center of Laguna Beach, at Laguna Canyon Road and the Pacific Coast Highway.

Parking: Metered street parking.

Hours: 6 AM to 10 PM.

Facilities: Lifeguards, rest rooms, showers, and picnic tables.

Contact: For beach information, contact the South Beaches Operation Office of Orange County Harbors, Beaches, and Parks at (714) 661-7013.

See number 12 on page 102.

Picnic Beach

Location: In Laguna Beach, below Heisler Park, where Myrtle Street meets Cliff Drive.

Parking: Metered street parking.

Hours: 6 AM to 10 PM.

Facilities: Lifeguards and picnic tables.

Contact: For beach information, contact the South Beaches Operation Office of Orange County Harbors, Beaches, and Parks at (714) 661-7013.

See number 13 on page 102.

Rockpile Beach

Location: In Laguna Beach, below Heisler Park, where Myrtle Street meets Cliff Drive.

Parking: Metered street parking.

Hours: 6 AM to 10 PM.

Facilities: None.

Contact: For beach information, contact the South Beaches Operation Office of Orange County Harbors, Beaches, and Parks at (714) 661-7013.

See number 14 on page 102.

calf muscles for the trek down the lengthy cement staircase to the beach.

At the bottom of the stairs you'll find a small beach pinned against steep cliffs, Gibraltar-sized rocks that frame the cove, and huge waves that run up on the beach with great force. Houses cling precariously to the eroding cliffs, each with its own set of stairs that looks more like a ladder. Climbing out of this grotto is the real acid test—and that's an apt choice of words, since Timothy Leary and his LSD-imbibing gang frequented this beach in the 1960s. The ascent actually numbers 219 steps, and you can amuse yourself on the return trip by reading the obscene graffiti that has been scrawled onto the vertical face of each step.

Shaw's Cove

Location: In Laguna Beach, at Fairview Street and Cliff Drive.

Parking: Metered street parking.

Hours: 6 AM to 10 PM.

Facilities: None.

Contact: For beach information, contact the South Beaches Operation Office of Orange County Harbors, Beaches, and Parks at (714) 661-7013.

See number 16 on page 102.

Victoria Beach

Location: In Laguna Beach, along Victoria Drive, off the Pacific Coast Highway.

Parking: Metered street parking.

Hours: 6 AM to 10 PM.

Facilities: None.

Contact: For beach information, contact the South Beaches Operation Office of Orange County Harbors, Beaches, and Parks at (714) 661-7013.

See number 10 on page 102.

West Street Beach is one of the better bodysurfing spots in a town renowned for its waves. Shoehorned into a small cove at the base of a stairwell at the end of West Street, about 10 blocks north of 1,000 Steps Beach, it's also got a volleyball court and is seasonally popular with locals.

Aliso Creek County Beach lies along the heart of the motel/burger stand/gas station corridor of South Laguna. Ample metered parking draws the summertime masses here, as does the fine board and bodysurfing. The beach slopes steeply down to where the waves break, making for hazardous swimming. All the same, it's packed with families. The beach is supposed to have lifeguards, but we didn't see any. You'll find just about everything else here, though: a playground, fire rings, benches, bathrooms, and a short pier with snack bar. When pushed along by a powerful south swell, the waves appear taller than the people playing in them. They break with a thundercrack, sending cascades of foam running up the brown, sandy beach. We saw happy packs of kids building communal sand castles and getting knocked over by the waves.

The lagoon formed where Aliso Creek empties into the ocean is a popular bird-bathing spot, for all you gull-watchers. The creek becomes steep-sided on its southern bank as it approaches

West Street Beach

Location: In South Laguna, at West Street and the Pacific Coast Highway.

Parking: Metered street parking.

Hours: 6 AM to 10 PM.

Facilities: None.

Contact: For beach information, contact the South Beaches Operation Office of Orange County Harbors, Beaches, and Parks at (714) 661-7013.

See number 8 on page 102.

the ocean, sculpting a 10-foot shelf of sand outside of its meanders. Don't climb into the creek yourself, as its near-constant contamination is an issue that continues to plague Laguna Beach. Nonpoint source pollution from developments up the canyon fouls the creek, necessitating warning signs. But what to do? Officials haven't figured that out yet, despite much head-scratching, finger-pointing, and public debate. Parents, keep an eye on your young ones here. If the creek is contaminated, it stands to reason that the ocean into which it empties is polluted, too, in the immediate vicinity. The twin threats of water quality and water safety make this a less than ideal family beach, when all is said and done.

The prettiest beach in Laguna, **Victoria Beach**, is also one of the hardest to find. Given the lack of signs, it would appear that the locals want to keep it that way. The beach can be entered at several points along Victoria Drive, a street off the Pacific Coast Highway that's lined with homes built as close together as any block of Victorians in San Francisco. Residents have sacrificed space in exchange for easy access to a common, sandy front yard along the Pacific Ocean. Hiking down from the walkway and stairs at the north end, you pass private homes set behind a yellow cinder-block wall. A final curve deposits you on one of the nicest beaches in Southern California, and one that's especially beloved by bodysurfers. It is broad and uncrowded, known mostly by locals, an inviting-looking spot to drop a towel that is one of the more awesome and hidden beaches in all of Southern California.

At the end of Brooks Street in Laguna Beach, facing Halfway Rock, is **Brooks Beach**, a rocky beach that surfing authority Bank Wright says serves up "the cleanest, best-shaped big wave in Laguna Beach." Have it your way.... Would you like some southern swell on that wave? Maybe a garland of kelp? A shark-fin appetizer? Of course, everyone has their own favorite, and there are potentially as many beaches out here as there are street ends. Don't expect locals to divulge their secret coves to a stranger, but feel free to scavenge around—you might stumble upon an unpeopled cove if you're lucky. We remind and beseech you, however, to respect private property and, as a policeman once scolded while ejecting us from a pro-wrestling match where we misbehaved, "act like you got some sense."

North of Main Beach, lovely Heisler Park serves as a point of entry to **Picnic Beach** and **Rockpile Beach**. Heisler Park looks down on it all from its cliff-hugging perch. The foremost feature here is the walkway that lines the coastal bluffs for about a mile. At dusk, it's a magical sight. As the fog settles in, the town's twinkling lights come on, rendering a real-life canvas as fanciful as any Impressionist's pointillistic study. Picnic Beach and Rockpile Beach are accessible from Heisler Park via a ramp and a stairway, respectively, that lead down to them. Picnic tables are nestled among the trees of Heisler Park, giving Picnic Beach its name. Rockpile is a good surfing beach located in front of the Laguna Art Museum, where Jasmine Street meets Cliff Drive. Up in the 500 block of Cliff Drive, at the north end of Heisler Park, is **Diver's Cove**, which draws the scuba divers. A few blocks up is picturesque **Shaw's Cove**, another diver's dream that has the added bonus of tidepools at its south end.

The procession of beaches ends up by **Crescent Bay Point Park**, a bluff-top green with views of Seal Rock and Laguna Beach and a beach below, whose big, tubular waves make for great—but sometimes scary—bodysurfing. At the north end of Laguna Beach, the erodable sandstone coast gives way to sturdier volcanic rocks that form points, with bays cut into the softer shales.

Bunking Down

You can expect to pay three figures a night for the finer European inn–style lodgings in Laguna Beach. The **Surf and Sand Hotel** (1555 South

Pacific Coast Highway, 497-4477, $$$$) is the hostelry of first choice. For starters, it is situated right on a private beach. It has two gourmet restaurants on the premises. Rooms are pleasantly and airily appointed. The price is up there ($150 to $290 a night), but hey—it's your money. South Laguna is the site of the **Aliso Creek Inn** (31106 South Pacific Coast Highway, 499-2271, $$$). Aliso Creek runs through the property, and you can follow it to the beach of the same name, which is only a thousand feet away via a pedestrian underpass. Despite its proximity to the ocean, the inn feels like it is set in another world. With views up a canyon and out on mountains, its grounds are woodsy, wild, and secluded—a rare atmosphere to find in the midst of a beach town. There's truly no finer setting on the Southern California coast. All rooms are spacious one- and two-bedroom townhouses. The grounds include a nine-hole golf course, a large heated pool, and **Ben Brown's Restaurant**, which serves traditional continental fare. Wildlife, especially deer and raccoons, wander the property, and even bobcats and mountain lions have been spotted.

A string of park-at-your-door motels cut from plainer cloth can be found in South Laguna. The **Best Western Laguna Reef Inn** (30806 South Pacific Coast Highway, 499-2227, $$) looks to be the nicest of these, offering clean

Hanging Out with the Surf Addicts

We arrived in Laguna Beach exhausted from our nighttime rambles around the coastal party towns of San Diego County. After a big meal and an after-dinner walk, we were ready to call it a night when the sounds of live music came wafting across the street. Seduced by the siren call of electric guitars, we followed the noise to its origins: a blurry cacophony created by three bands playing simultaneously at three open-doored bars in proximity. The nightlife of Laguna Beach is compacted into the midtown area near Main Beach. That seems a logical enough arrangement, but rarely are beach clubs laid out so conveniently close to one another.

The contenders in this Thursday night battle of the bands consisted of Low Tolerance, your basic functional rock-and-roll bar band, playing at the White House Restaurant; the Missiles of October, a folksy, bluesy band of local stalwarts who packed the house and sidewalks outside the Marine Room Tavern; and the Surf Addicts, a surf-punk trio who were blasting away at Hennessey's Tavern. We opted for the Surf Addicts, as their music sounded the most original and fun. Their story, and their sound, is fairly typical of the Southern California experience. They write witty songs about the archetypal SoCal surfer/party-dude lifestyle. They sing about living hard, having fun, and taking chances but getting out alive. "I want to live on the edge without falling over," explained guitarist/singer Drew while downing a shot glass filled with cinnamon liquor.

For him, surfing is an activity as reflexive as breathing. He's found his own private slice of wavy heaven, a cove beach in South Laguna that few others know about. (We won't give away his secret.) Drew's idea of a perfect day begins with a hard bout of surfing, followed by a chow-down at Papa's Tacos (a cheapie Mexican food joint beloved by locals) and a gig with the Surf Addicts that evening. Early in his musical

 Map of Orange County beaches—page 102

rooms and a heated pool for half of what you'll pay for a room in Laguna Beach proper. If you want to pay a little more to be where the action is, a place like the **Inn at Laguna Beach** (211 North Pacific Coast Highway, 497-9722, $$$) is the ticket. It's got an unbeatable location—just above Main Beach on a bluff next to the best restaurant in town, Las Brisas. Your biggest problem will be deciding how to best allocate your time: hanging out on Main Beach, sitting on your private ocean-facing balcony, sunbathing on the rooftop sundeck, or strolling along Cliff Drive. Moreover, the Inn at Laguna Beach has an amenity that is worth its weight in gold in Laguna Beach: an on-site underground garage.

Finally, if you're feeling sentimental for the Old California, you can always stay at the **Hotel Laguna** (425 South Pacific Coast Highway, 494-1151, $$$), a midtown treasure whose beginnings date back to the very founding of Laguna Beach.

Coastal Cuisine

For fine dining and *fun* dining, nothing can top **Las Brisas** (361 Cliff Drive, 497-5434, $$$). The indoor dining room and outdoor patio overlook Main Beach and the ocean from the bluff top at the south end of Heisler Park. Its house specialty is seafood with a south-of-the-border flair—everything from fresh sea-bass

career he wanted to join a reggae band, but his style was too distinctive to fit into the music and he kept getting turned down. Then one day it occurred to him—as it eventually does to all true artists—to write, sing, and play music about what he knows. In his case, he knows about surfing and partying in Laguna Beach. "We always partied with tourist girls," Drew said, "so I wrote a song called 'Tourist Girls.' I grew up partying in Laguna, so I wrote a song called 'Party in Laguna.' I've always imagined what it would be like to surf Hawaii. I thought it would be kind of scary facing waves of that size, so I wrote a song around the line 'Don't hair out'—meaning don't chicken out—'in Wainea.'"

The Surf Addicts are to the 1990s what bands like the Beach Boys were to the 1960s. They encapsulate a lifestyle in music. It's fun to listen and dance to them. Their songs are about real, recognizable things. They play well; their tunes take interesting and unexpected turns, and they're solid instrumentalists. To us, they sounded like the Police, the Beach Boys, and the Clash all riding on the same surfboard. While their tapes are sold in surf shops and local record stores, they rarely play outside the area. They have a solid local following and no idea of how to break out beyond the scene in their immediate vicinity. In a postshow confab over a table full of beer mugs, they wondered out loud, after their bracing, breakneck set, if the rest of the country would find anything they do worth hearing.

Hell yes, we say! The Surf Addicts are an authentic slice of Americana (or at least Californiana), uncorrupted by blind ambition about making it in the corporate music biz. They take the feeling of riding a wave or chugging a beer and turn it into music that makes you want to do both. They made us glad to be wide awake and rocking at the beach at 2:00 in the morning. What more can you ask of a rock-and-roll band?

ceviche to Mexican lobster. The lunch ensaladas are too good to be true. Save room for dessert, which is not to be missed. The restaurant serves breakfast (a buffet), lunch, and dinner, with an out-the-door-popular, five-course weekend brunch.

The **Beach House Inn** (619 Sleepy Hollow Lane, 494-9707, $$$) is another fine dining option. The glass-walled dining room faces the ocean, so try to book a reservation at sunset. The menu selections tend toward creative, California nouvelle-style preparations of seafood. The broiled filet of sole, for example, is accompanied by bananas sautéed in butter and brown sugar, plus chutney and grated coconut. Set in an old house that used to belong to actor Slim Summerville (one of the original Keystone Cops), the Beach House Inn has retained its original architecture, and a relaxed air pervades the dining room.

The **White House Restaurant** (340 South Pacific Coast Highway, 494-8088, $$) is a local institution with a schizophrenic personality. It's a cozy, romantic room at the dinner hour that turns into a popular night spot afterward. The interior of this 1918-vintage restaurant, once patronized by the likes of Bing Crosby, is filled with Tiffany lamps and varnished wood tables. Specialties include fresh pastas and Halibut Maison. Later on, the "maison" shakes to everything from reggae bands to local rockers.

Down in South Laguna, your best bets are Mexican. At least ours were. A surfer/rocker who grew up here turned us on to **Papa's Tacos** (31622 Pacific Coast Highway, 499-9822, $), and after feeding on their fish tacos and blackened shrimp quesadillas, all we can do is add a hearty "come to Papa's." Another local favorite is the **Coyote Grill** (31621 Pacific Coast Highway, 499-4033, $$), whose motto is "A Taste of Baja at the Beach." A message on their menu says, "When we open our doors, we open our hearts." When we opened their doors, we opened our mouths for things like Lobster Puerto Nuevo (whole lobster grilled with all the fixings) and Pescados Frescos. That's fresh fish to all of you who don't *habla español*, and it changes here daily according to what's available. Coyote Grill is a three-meal-a-day restaurant whose outdoor deck makes a pleasant spot to enjoy a late-afternoon drink.

Night Moves

As the dinner hour wanes, several of Laguna's more popular restaurants metamorphose into nightspots. The **White House Restaurant** (340 South Pacific Coast Highway, 494-8088) is popular with locals. Bar bands on weekends and reggae during the week seem to be the rule of thumb here. Las Brisas also attracts a sizable crowd who come to the bar to meet and mingle. The **Marine Room Tavern** (214 Ocean Avenue, 494 3027) draws a mixed bag of bands, anything from country-rock to alternative. People were crammed into the place to hear local favorites Missiles of October and even filled the sidewalks in front of the place. Across the street **Hennessey's Tavern** (213 Ocean Avenue, 494-2743) is the kind of place that does good business no matter what. On one of our visits, the band that was playing finished a poor second, in terms of patron interest, to the daredevil boating video on the big-screen TV. It all depends on the band, the night, and the mood as to which club is packing 'em in. The Marine Room, Hennessey's, and the White House are without question the Big Three in Laguna Beach, closely quartered down by Main Beach. Competition breeds excellence, and the nightlife here is living proof of that. Party!

For More Information

Contact the Laguna Beach Visitor Information Center, 252 Broadway, Laguna Beach, CA 92651; (714) 497-9229 or (800) 877-1115. The center will assist callers with complimentary hotel and restaurant reservations.

 Map of Orange County beaches—page 102

Crystal Cove State Park

Location: Between Laguna Beach and Corona del Mar, approximately four miles from each, on Highway 1.

This state park, located between Laguna Beach and Corona del Mar, is one of the best surprises on the Orange County coast. Stretching from the ocean into the wooded San Joaquin Hills, its 2,791 acres provide excellent hiking opportunities, three separate coastal accesses (Pelican Point, Los Trancos, and Reef Point), three miles of beautiful golden-sand beach, and an "underwater park," the Irvine Coast Marine Life Refuge. With all this bounty, **Crystal Cove State Park** is not exactly a secret to swimmers, surfers, sunbathers, and divers.

Crystal Cove State Park

Location: Along the Pacific Coast Highway, between Laguna Beach and Corona del Mar.

Parking: $6 entrance fee per vehicle.

Hours: 6 AM to sunset.

Facilities: Lifeguards and rest rooms.

Contact: For beach information, contact Crystal Cove State Park at (714) 494-3539.

See number 18 on page 102.

As if it didn't offer enough already, another 3,400-acre parcel of land adjoining the present state beach will be added to Crystal Cove in the next few years. This land, west of Laguna Canyon Road, will eventually interconnect with Crystal Cove and be named Irvine Coast Wilderness Park.

Reef Point is the southernmost access to Crystal Cove, with a stairway to a beach, a hiking trail, a bike path, and rest rooms. Los Trancos has the largest parking lot, located on the east side of the Pacific Coast Highway, with a tunnel leading under the highway to a sandy beach. Pelican Point is the northernmost access, with a bluff-top trail leading to a beach access ramp. Day-use fees are charged at all three units.

One sour note to all this pristine coastal glory is the Newport Coast development just north of Pelican Point. Bought by the obsessively acquisitive Disney Corporation, this new private community is devoted to luxury timeshare condominiums for the loophole-loving rich who will write off the cost of these second homes on their taxes. Disney is trying to disguise their affiliation with this venture, which is no doubt causing Uncle Walt to roll over in his vault.

For More Information

Contact Orange Coast District, Crystal Cove State Park, 18331 Enterprise Lane, Huntington Beach, CA 92648; (714) 494-3539.

Corona del Mar

Location: Two miles south of Newport Beach, along the Pacific Coast Highway. Corona del Mar State Beach is the main beach.
Population: 15,000
Area Code: 714 **Zip Code:** 92625

This small, mostly residential suburb of Newport Beach is blessed with a sweeping vista of the ocean that visitors encounter as they approach Newport Beach on the Pacific Coast Highway. The town's financial standing is evident in the Lamborghini car dealership and the chic boutiques that do a buzzing business along the main drag. It's a shame there's really nowhere viable to stay in Corona del Mar, because it would make an excellent alternative to the aridity of Newport Beach's Fashion Island high-rises.

Beaches

The beach at Corona del Mar is gorgeous, as are the people who go there. Located at the end of Marguerite Avenue, **Corona del Mar State Beach** is a gigantic sandbox, wider at

Bayside Drive County Beach

Location: In Corona del Mar, at 1901 Bayside Drive.
Parking: Free street parking.
Hours: 6 AM to 10 PM.
Facilities: Rest rooms.
Contact: For beach information, contact the North Beaches Operation Office of Orange County Harbors, Beaches, and Parks at (714) 723-4511.

See number 23 on page 102.

China Cove Beach

Location: In Corona del Mar, at Ocean Boulevard and Fernleaf Avenue.
Parking: Free street parking.
Hours: 6 AM to 10 PM.
Facilities: None.
Contact: For beach information, contact the Newport Beach Marine Department at (714) 644-3044. For a surf report, call (714) 673-3371.

See number 22 on page 102.

Corona del Mar State Beach

Location: In Corona del Mar, at Ocean Boulevard and Iris Avenue.
Parking: $6 entrance fee per vehicle.
Hours: 8 AM to 10 PM PDT (8 AM to 8 PM PST).
Facilities: Lifeguards, rest rooms, showers, picnic tables, and fire pits.
Contact: For beach information, contact the Newport Beach Marine Department at (714) 644-3044. For a surf report, call (714) 673-3371.

See number 20 on page 102.

Little Corona del Mar Beach

Location: In Corona del Mar, at Ocean Boulevard and Poppy Avenue.
Parking: Free street parking.
Hours: 6 AM to 10 PM.
Facilities: None.
Contact: For beach information, contact the Newport Beach Marine Department at (714) 644-3044. For a surf report, call (714) 673-3371.

See number 19 on page 102.

the north end, where eight volleyball nets have been set up. All year-round, like some kind of fertility rite, tanned bruisers and their svelte, aerobicized sweeties get physical with the white ball. Many others prefer to camp comfortably on beach blankets, readying their tans for unveiling at happy hour. We were content to just sit and drink in this real-life version of *Baywatch*.

If you can pull yourself away from the action, a pleasant stroll south will bring you to **Little Corona del Mar Beach**, a wonderfully secluded cove that is part and parcel of the larger state beach. It's a miniparadise for snorkeling, scuba diving, and tidepooling. Logically enough, there's also a **Big Corona del Mar Beach**, where you'll find fire rings, a snack bar, a rest room, and volleyball nets.

Climbing the rocks at the north end of Corona del Mar State Beach, in defiance of the "Don't Climb the Rocks" sign, will net you a nifty vantage point from which to study Newport Harbor. Corona del Mar forms one side of the harbor's mouth, and if you scramble down the protective rocks to the sandy cove below (known as **Rocky Point**, also as Pirates Cove), you can watch the boats come and go in relative solitude.

Up the neck of the bay from Rocky Point is **China Cove Beach**, which is actually a pair of cove beaches that are easily accessible via Shell and Cove Streets or via the stairwell at Ocean Boulevard and Fernleaf Avenue. You can hike to Rocky Point and China Cove from Corona del Mar Beach; it's worth the huffing and puffing and hugging the shore to get there. Much farther into the harbor is **Bayside Drive County Beach**, a bay beach with rest rooms, located beside the Harbor Patrol Bureau.

Rocky Point
(a.k.a. Pirates Cove)

Location: In Corona del Mar, at Ocean Boulevard and Harbor Channel.
Parking: Free street parking.
Hours: 6 AM to 10 PM.
Facilities: None.
Contact: For beach information, contact the Newport Beach Marine Department at (714) 644-3044. For a surf report, call (714) 673-3371.

See number 21 on page 102.

Coastal Cuisine

While it lacks lodging options, Corona del Mar has some of the glitziest restaurants in Orange County. Among the most notable are the posh, contemporary **Trees** (44 Heliotrope Avenue, 673-0910, $$$) and the British-themed, jacket-required **Five Crowns** (3801 East Pacific Coast Highway, 760-0331, $$$$). The latter is an elegant re-creation of England's oldest inn, Ye Old Bell, that's faithful in every detail, right down to the Elizabethan garb worn by the wait staff.

For More Information

Contact the Corona del Mar Chamber of Commerce; 2843 East Pacific Coast Highway, Corona del Mar, CA 92625; (714) 673-4050.

"Catch a Wave": A Brief History of Surf Music

In the early 1960s, the state of California infiltrated rock and roll with a sound that could have come from nowhere else: surf music. The Beach Boys, Jan and Dean, and Dick Dale launched an indigenous music scene out of the sun-dappled wonderland of Southern California. It was a movement that was well established before the Beatles made their first stateside splash with "I Want to Hold Your Hand."

The Beach Boys are generally deemed responsible for spinning the California myth—a harmony-rich musical outlook based on the holy trinity of sun, surf, and fun—although Jan and Dean (with "Surf City") and the Mamas and the Papas (with "California Dreamin'") certainly warbled a few anthems of their own. The promise of a beatific adolescence in the Golden State transcended the foursquare suburban reality of cow towns like Hawthorne and Torrance. As Brian Wilson, the Beach Boys' founder, explained in 1976, "It's not just surfing; it's the outdoors and cars and sunshine; it's the society of California; it's the way of California." Southern California—the Los Angeles basin in particular—was the wellspring of the California myth.

For those who made their living plowing acreage in the Plains states or who were buried up to their knees in winter snows in the Northeast, it was a potent come-on. The California myth promised everything; health and longevity beneath a bountiful sun that shone warmly year-round; prosperity in a job-filled environment catering to the burgeoning aeronautics and communications industries; and, finally, a relaxed approach to life that had "fun, fun, fun" as its first commandment.

Until the Beach Boys came along, surf music was the domain of hotshot instrumentalists such as Dick Dale, the undisputed king of surf guitar. According to Dale, "Real surfing music is instrumental, characterized by heavy staccato picking on a Fender Stratocaster guitar." A surfer could listen to one of his fast-fingered solos and feel the surging power of the ocean as it hurtled him toward shore. Such numbers as "Let's Go Trippin'," "Surf Beat," and "Miserlou" promoted a sense of identity within the surfers' ranks.

Although surf music was primarily designed for dancing at beach parties, amusement parks, and surfers' clubs, the genre left its mark on the national charts with songs by the Surfaris ("Wipe Out") and the Chantays ("Pipeline"). Both were released in 1963. The Chantays, a five-man garage band from Santa Ana, rode "Pipeline" all the way to Number Four. The Surfaris, a quintet from Glendora, saw "Wipe Out" soar to Number Two. "Wipe Out," a tumbling wave of tom-tom rolls and frenzied guitar breaks, remains the premier instrumental surf hit of all time.

But that was just the tip of the iceberg. The Routers took a song called "Let's Go," adapted it to a new dance craze—the pony—and had a hit with "Let's Go (Pony)," whose familiar clap and chant has since become a cheerleaders' staple. The Marketts made their mark with "Surfer's Stomp," "Balboa Blue," and "Out of Limits"—the latter based on the theme from the *Outer Limits* TV show. Then there were the Pyramids, from Long Beach, who recorded the surf classic "Penetration" and stretched the outer limits as personalities, performing with shaved heads and arriving at shows in helicopters and atop elephants, and the Ventures, who were neither a surf band nor from California.

However, it was the arrival of the Beach Boys that signaled the imminent flowering of surf and hot-rod music. The sport's foremost cultural emissaries, the Beach Boys spread the gospel of surfing "even in places where the nearest thing to surf is maybe the froth on a chocolate shake!" (to quote the liner notes of *Surfin' USA*, their second album). With their earliest songs, "Surfin'" and "Surfin' Safari," the Beach Boys made a magical, intuitive leap—bridging Chuck Berry and the Four Freshmen and adding their own libretto about surfing and the California way of life.

The duo of Jan (Berry) and Dean (Torrance) were the other minstrel demigods in the car-and-surf-song sweepstakes. With "Surf City," a tune cowritten by Brian Wilson and cut with his help during the summer of 1963, Jan and Dean had the first Number One surfing song. The real-life surf city they had in mind was Huntington Beach, which promotes itself with that handle to this day.

The Californians' summer fever became a national contagion. Surf music began turning up in such unlikely places as Colorado, which produced the Astronauts, and Minnesota, home of the Trashmen, whose "Surfin' Bird" went to Number Four. Another Midwestern band, the Rivieras, delivered the West Coast tribute "California Sun." Even sooty old New York turned out the Trade Winds. Their big hit line: "New York's a lonely town when you're the only surfer boy around."

Back on the West Coast a small cadre of writers, producers, and performers kept turning out the real thing (or at least turning it out in the real environment). In addition to the Beach Boys and Jan and Dean, singing surf/car groups included the Fantastic Baggys ("Tell 'Em I'm Surfing," "Summer Means Fun"), the Rip Chords ("Hey Little Cobra," "Three Window Coupe"), and the Sunrays ("I Live for the Sun"). At mid-decade, a new wave of Southern California based acts swept the Top 10. Among them were the Turtles, Gary Lewis and the Playboys, Paul Revere and the Raiders, the Mamas and the Papas, Johnny Rivers, the Byrds, and the Monkees.

In 1967, California would enter a whole different stage: acid rock, the Summer of Love, the Monterey Pop Festival, the San Francisco Sound, and a wave of bands based around the Sunset Strip of Los Angeles. The seeds of this revolution can be traced back to five Pendleton-shirted Beach Boys and the idea they got to sing about surfing. As Beach Boy Carl Wilson recalled, "People wanted to hang out at the beach. It was really an early hippie thing." In a way, it still is.

Newport Beach and Balboa

Location: 50 miles south of Los Angeles and 85 miles north of San Diego, along Highway 1 (Pacific Coast Highway). To get onto the Balboa Peninsula, where the beaches are, take the Newport Boulevard exit off the Pacific Coast Highway. There are more than six miles of ocean beach in Newport Beach. The main beach on the peninsula is Newport Beach Municipal Beach, which runs for two-and-one-quarter miles from the Santa Ana River Jetty to Newport Pier.
Population: 70,000
Area Code: 714 **Zip Code:** 92663

Newport Beach has been mislabeled. The goods are in order, but the writing on the can is all wrong. Before our initial visit 10 years ago, we'd been led to believe that it was "Nouveau Beach," a land of conspicuous consumption that looked down on anyone in flip-flops and cutoffs. We came expecting manic wheeler-dealers and bored women dripping with Lloyds of London–insured jewelry. After all, Newport Beach was modeled on and named after Newport, Rhode Island, an exclusive community for the old-money yachting set. Indeed, Newport west has a few of that older community's amenities, most notably the second largest pleasure-craft harbor in the country (with 10,000 berths). But Newport Beach also has an unpretentious, accommodating side that just doesn't jibe with its designer reputation. After several happy visits here, we've come to realize that Newport Beach is, at heart, a fun and funky beach town.

First of all, Newport Beach is not a small town, nor is most of it truly on the beach. Many Newport Beach residents drive expensive imported cars with vanity plates, but they tend to live in walled-in or gated condo complexes to the east. The heart and soul of the city is out on Balboa Peninsula, a thin finger of land that reaches into the Pacific, then bends around to protect the beautiful harbor. Back bays and waterways have been sculpted into the peninsula, and two small inhabited islands, Balboa and Lido, sit close by. Newport Beach is almost always sunny, relaxed, and dominated by watery pastimes. Boats dock right up against the back doors of houses.

The fun begins when you turn off the Pacific Coast Highway onto Newport Boulevard or Balboa Boulevard (Route 55 South). Like the spine of a fish, these two merge into one boulevard that runs the length of Newport Beach's peninsula. It's a six-mile stretch ending at the Wedge, the south jetty of the harbor mouth. To oversimplify, the big money is on the harbor side and all the fun is on the ocean side. Most beachgoers assemble in the general vicinity of the peninsula's ocean piers, Newport Pier and Balboa Pier.

The most boisterous activity can be found at and around Newport Pier. The first pier on this site was built in 1888 by the McFadden brothers, who founded the town and for whom the pier was originally named. Local history lingers here in the form of the beloved Dory Fleet, a fishing contingent who have launched their wooden dories from this spot since 1891. Each day, the Dory Fleet leaves before dawn and returns by 9:30 AM to sell their fresh catch in the sands beside Newport Pier. Their motto: "Our fish is the freshest fish on earth." A childlike wooden sculpture pays tribute to these stout-hearted laborers, and their method of selling fish right on the beach creates an authentic California atmosphere. Nearby, ancient street performers address the crowd. A balloon sculptor sings spirituals in an operatic tenor while a long-haired sea dog takes Polaroids of passersby posing with his beautifully plumed parrots.

 Map of Orange County beaches—page 102

In the 1980s, Newport's nouveau-riche elite—exhibiting the shortsightedness that brought them wealth and wound up bankrupting Orange County in 1994—wanted to do away with the Dory Fleet and give the Newport Pier area a corporate sprucing up. They were quickly shot down, offering further proof that Newport Beach's ordinary townsfolk possess the sense and spirit that its more moneyed mullet-brains lack.

Balboa Pier lies two miles farther out the peninsula. Here, things are a little less crazy. On the harbor side behind Balboa Pier is Balboa Pavilion, a Victorian landmark that dates from 1906. A renowned hot spot during the Big Band era, the pavilion still hosts events. You can catch a harbor-cruise boat on this spot (see the former homes of John Wayne, King Gillette, and Ron Popeil, inventor of the "pocket fisherman"), as well as a whale-watching boat and passenger ferry to Catalina Island. The best ride of all might just be the cute little quarter-a-ride ferry that runs continuously to Balboa Island. It is mostly residential, tightly packed with the homes of wealthy people whose car alarms chirp like crickets as they approach and exit. The island has a sprinkling of

Doin' Wheelies in Newport Beach

People of all ages and persuasions flock to the streets around the Newport Beach piers and jam the Balboa Peninsula with traffic. During the peak season, it's not unusual to find traffic slowed to a standstill on Balboa Boulevard all the way out to Ocean Highway. Traffic is a continuous thorn in Newport Beach's side, partly the result of a decision made years ago not to have Interstate 5 built closer to the coast here. (Ironically, the decision was made in order to preserve the peace and quiet of the community.) The strategy worked for a while but backfired when Newport Beach exploded with development in the 1980s.

It goes without saying that driving here can be as gnarly as swimming through a kelp bed. Parking tickets come with stiff fines, and parking at most meters costs 25 cents for 15 minutes, with a six-hour limit. If our calculations are correct, six hours costs six bucks, and who carries 24 quarters in their pocket? If you park illegally on Lido or Balboa Islands, we presume you get the gas chamber.

Thus, the best way to see Newport Beach is on bicycle, coasting to and fro on the Ocean Front promenade. The terrain is flat and the city is bicycle-friendly. A local outfit called Bikeways (330 Newport Boulevard) carries an excellent map of trails in the vicinity, with detailed tips and rules of the road that are useful anywhere, as well as local points of interest, license information and fees, hazards, and bike lanes along highways. Bike trails run as far east as Irvine, traversing the Back Bay Ecological Reserve, one of the few natural areas that the Irvine Company has left alone.

Several bike and skate outlets are located close to the Ocean Front promenade, including Oceanfront Wheelworks at Balboa Pier (714-723-6510), and the Pedal Pusher near Newport Pier (118 23rd Street, 714-675-2570). The latter is run by the friendly folks who gave Pee Wee Herman the bicycle he used in his epic *Pee Wee's Big Adventure*. They have a fleet of similarly lovable two-wheeled flivvers that are available at reasonable rates.

upscale boutiques and tourist shops, too, but its most appealing feature is the walkway around it, with views of the bay and harbor.

Newport Beach is a quintessential California beach town by day and a rock-and-roll party zone at night. Despite the nonstop crunch of humanity, the peninsula is a friendly place. The most violent blows result from the affectionate pounding of backs, and the loudest shouts are those of approval for some minuscule sashaying bikini. The pedestrian's best friend here is the Ocean Front promenade, an asphalt trail that parallels the Pacific for nearly the full length of the peninsula. It is the primary route for bicyclists, joggers, and in-line skaters, and the human parade along this walkway is an intoxicating sight in and of itself.

Beaches

On the beachfront, Newport Beach has the best of everything. There are several long beaches, each delineated by big-bouldered jetties and massive piers. Starting at the south end of the peninsula, **West Jetty View Park** (a.k.a. the Wedge) is the El Dorado for body surfers. Extremely rough surf, with waves as high as 20 feet, make the Wedge unsafe for board surfing and suitable only for highly experienced bodysurfers. Just across the harbor from the Wedge is Corona del Mar State Beach (see the Beaches

Balboa Beach

5

Location: Along Balboa Boulevard, at Balboa Pier in Balboa.
Parking: Metered street parking.
Hours: 6 AM to 10 PM.
Facilities: Lifeguards, rest rooms, showers, picnic tables, and barbecue grills.
Contact: For beach information, contact the Newport Beach Marine Department at (714) 644-3044. For a surf report, call (714) 673-3371.

See number 25 on page 102.

Newport Beach Municipal Beach

5

Location: In Newport Beach, along Oceanfront at Newport Pier.
Parking: Metered lot and street parking.
Hours: 6 AM to 10 PM.
Facilities: Lifeguards, rest rooms, showers, picnic tables, and fire pits.
Contact: For beach information, contact the Newport Beach Marine Department at (714) 644-3044. For a weather and surf report, call (714) 673-3371.

See number 26 on page 102.

Santa Ana River County Beach

3

Location: In Newport Beach, at Seashore Drive between Summit and 61st Streets.
Parking: Metered street parking.
Hours: 6 AM to 10 PM.
Facilities: Lifeguards.
Contact: For beach information, contact the North Beaches Operation Office of Orange County Harbors, Beaches, and Parks at (714) 723-4511.

See number 27 on page 102.

West Jetty View Park (a.k.a. The Wedge)

4

Location: On the tip of Balboa Peninsula, at the end of Channel Road in Balboa.
Parking: Free parking lot.
Hours: 6 AM to 10 PM.
Facilities: None.
Contact: For beach information, contact the Newport Beach Marine Department at (714) 644-3044. For a weather and surf report, call (714) 673-3371.

See number 24 on page 102.

entry on page 130). Do not try to swim across. It may look like a short distance, but the water is treacherous.

The stretch of sand from the Wedge to Balboa Pier is **Balboa Beach**. The dune structure along here is exceptionally healthy, an indication of what the Orange County coast looked like in the 1950s when it was an escape for the hoi polloi of Los Angeles. Families congregate on Balboa Beach for relaxed sunbathing and swimming.

The two-mile stretch of sand from Balboa Pier to the end of the peninsula has been proclaimed **Newport Beach Municipal Beach**. Along this golden strand, surfers prefer the beaches at 52nd Street, North Jetty, and from 61st Street Beach all the way to **Santa Ana River County Beach**, which lies on both sides of the river mouth, just south of Huntington Beach. All beaches on the Newport Beach peninsula are subject to a 10 PM curfew.

Bunking Down

Nightly lodgings directly on the beach are scarcer than gulls' teeth. A particularly nice and fairly pricey one located only a few bare feet from the surf is the **Portofino Beach Hotel** (2306 Ocean Front, 673-7030, $$$). Formerly a surf shop, it's got 20 elegant rooms that you wouldn't be surprised to find along the Italian Riviera. Just off the Balboa Peninsula, the most reasonably priced ($57 to $65 in season, $40 to $50 off season) and beach-accessible of the motels that line the Pacific Coast Highway is the **Newport Channel Inn** (6030 West Pacific Coast Highway, 642-3030, $). The staff is helpful and informed about the area. The motel is across the street—the "street" being Pacific Coast Highway—from a wide, sandy beach at the north end of Newport Beach.

The friendly tone of the town and the easy proximity to the sand makes a weekly (or monthly) apartment rental an appealing prospect here. Two agencies that specialize in beachfront rentals are **Villa Rentals** (675-4912) and **Property House Realtors** (642-3850). The rental units that sit on Balboa Beach are more family-oriented, with a casual ambience. Rates range from $750 for a weeklong stay to $2,500 for a whole month. People recline in chaise lounges on the back patio, reading newspapers and drinking highballs or coffee, oblivious to the parade passing by mere feet away on the Ocean Front promenade. The wildest characters you'll run across are adolescents trying to act raunchy. One 12-year-old sported a T-shirt that read "Will Work For Sex." Very funny, junior.

On either side of Newport Pier and continuing to the north end of the peninsula, rentals are snapped up by college kids or groups of party-minded guys whose spartan pads are open to the scrutiny of passersby. Shirtless, tanned, smiling, and perpetually holding beers, they hang loose on every balcony and porch.

Coastal Cuisine

The Crab Cooker lives! This, one of our favorite eateries in the universe, has been serving its patented smoked and grilled fish for 45 years in a building that was once a bank. "We're the only seafood joint that keeps its fish in a vault," jokes the owner, Bob Roubian. Mr. Roubian is an expert on the subject of fish. More than that, he is obsessed with them. He thinks about fish all day. He dreams about fish at night. He poeticizes about fish, sculpts fish, and writes songs about fish. He offers one of the songs he penned, "Who Hears the Fishes When They Cry?," for sale at his restaurant. (He sounds a bit like Tom Waits.) Music and fish have a lot in common, he tells us: both have scales. He encourages everyone to "Eat Lots A Fish" (his motto, emblazoned on the front of the building).

Located near Newport Pier, the **Crab Cooker** (2200 Newport Boulevard, 673-0100, $$) is a local institution for several reasons, not the least of which is that. Roubian enforces strict standards on the fish he serves. He buys only fish

Newport's Fashion Faux-Pas

Fashion Island is as Orange County as it gets. Since its name is misleading, we offer this description to set the record straight: Fashion Island is not an island and it is not on the water. It is not even fashionable, unless your tastes run to gray concrete and black asphalt. A huge hub of commerce and finance built far from the harbor, Fashion Island is a perfect symbol of soulless corporate power thrilled with itself. From the east side of the Pacific Coast Highway, it looms over Newport Beach, flexing its muscles like a Mr. Universe contestant. Often it is the only glimpse of the city that passersby take with them.

At the empty heart of Fashion Island is a posh shopping mall, outside of which is a sculpture entitled *Joining Hands*. The similarities to Michelangelo's Sistine Chapel ceiling are embarrassingly obvious, even to amateur art buffs such as ourselves. Three figures swirl in the air, reaching out to one another but not quite extending their hands far enough. Maybe the sculptor should have had them extending their American Express cards—to salesclerks at Neiman-Marcus, Fiorucci, the Posh Potato, and all the other boutiques with silly names. We assume the symbolism behind this sculpture is that shopping at Fashion Island is a religious experience. The ultimate act of faith, then, must be plunking down a wad of money for a totally useless piece of merchandise—say, $100 for a tiny rag doll stuffed inside a glass egg.

Surrounding Fashion Island's shopping mall in a perfect circle are the various corporate cathedrals that make all this possible. The architecture is in the numbingly unimaginative skyscraper style, which can deaden the soul if studied too long. If Fashion Island is an island, then it is a desert isle surrounded by an asphalt ocean, with Mercedes for sand dunes, sidewalks for beaches, real-estate agents for lifeguards, and valets for horseflies.

There is another contender on the Orange County shopping front. In 1994, a new shopping experience opened. Dubbed the "Anti-Mall," it's an "experiment in niche shopping" built in Costa Mesa, five miles from Fashion Island. Its official name is "The Lab," and it is aimed at "dual-channel people," the new generation of "mall rats" (their words) who glean their worldview from CNN and MTV. Stores such as Urban Outfitters (described as "The Gap's Evil Twin") studiously cop anti-style poses. There's also Tower Alternative and a clothier called "The Philosophy of Comfort." The intention is to create an ambience of urban grit in sterile Orange County. Yet the county is so lacking in that quality that they had to hire New York designers to give The Lab the authentically squalid feel of an urban nightmare.

As an alternative to a worthless afternoon spent browsing Fashion Island and The Lab, how about donating some of your surplus income to a worthy cause, such as the Surfrider Foundation, and spending the day on the beach?

 Map of Orange County beaches—page 102

that's caught by the hook-and-line method and is eviscerated (bled and cleaned) within five minutes of being pulled from the water, thus assuring its freshness. Fresh fish never smell fishy, he insists; if anything, it smells a little sweet, like watermelon. His fish, shrimp, crab, and scallops are cooked on wooden skewers over a charcoal grill, because that's the way his mother did it. All dinners come with homemade bread, cole slaw, and Romano potatoes. While waiting for your order, you'll snack on the best breadsticks in Christendom. The food is served on paper plates, like a picnic, and it is beyond compare in quality and price.

This wonderfully ramshackle place is always packed, but don't try to call for reservations or pay with plastic. Just show up and wait your turn in line. To Roubian, this is democracy, and he'll make no exceptions—not for a U.S. president, not for his grandmother, not even for himself. John Wayne, a longtime regular, always had to wait his turn, as did Richard Nixon. Sometimes the wait can be long but just settle back on the wooden benches outside, have a cup of the Crab Cooker's famous seafood chowder, write someone a postcard. (Roubian provides cards and postage, if mailed from the restaurant.) Try the smoked salmon or albacore appetizer for lunch, then get a combination plate (the best way to sample the menu) for dinner. But by all means "eat lots a fish" here as often as possible.

Newport is doubly blessed in the seafood department. Another top-sail restaurant, the **Cannery** (3010 Lafayette Avenue, 675-5777, $$$) is a step up in decor and manners, and serves excellent fare. The calamari appetizer is the most tender we've ever had, and the grilled swordfish tomatillo was a catch. It's located in a converted cannery, with implements of the trade hung on the wall: wheels, pulleys, conveyer lines, boilers, and processing machines. You can either eat inside or out on the deck overlooking the water. At night, after the dinner hour, the Cannery does a quick-change into one of the livelier night spots in Newport Beach.

For a quick bite with a nice view, hit **Ruby's** at the end of Balboa Pier (1 Balboa Pier, 675-7829, $). Okay, so the fare is mostly burgers and the atmosphere is faux '50s diner, rimmed with neon. But the location is the best in town and the food is fine as far as burgers and dogs go.

Night Moves

Most of the action after dark takes place on and around the piers. At Balboa Pier, set the wayback machine to the 1950s and step into a world of flirtatious adolescents on parade. Around and around the Balboa Pavilion circles an army of Annettes and Frankies too young to drink but too blitzed out on raging hormones to sit still. Dressed to thrill, they circle about, creating human log jams, broken up by friendly beat cops on patrol. They walk around the pavilion again and return to the same log jam—cruising without cars, as it were.

The crowd is older, noisier, and more unpredictable at Newport Pier. Motorcycles and muscle T-shirts replace high fashion, and voices get raised a bit louder. The same cops survey the scene, but in a somewhat less friendly manner. Mostly, though, the chaos has a certain California etiquette to it, with lots of backslaps, handshakes, high-fives, and hang tens.

Near here is **Blackie's** (21st Street and Ocean Front), the beer bar equivalent of the Crab Cooker. It is a timeless, changeless throwback to the days of the Dory Fleet, located directly on Ocean Front promenade. On the walls are mounted hammerhead sharks, team pennants, three TVs (each tuned to a different station), pool tables, and a jukebox. It is a classic oasis at any time of the day or night. We'd give you the phone number, but it's unlisted—part of its homey charm.

Just down the Ocean Front to the north we found **Mutt Lynch's** (23rd Street and Ocean Front, 675-1556), a raucous corner joint serving passable pizza, sandwiches, and sports-bar munchies, plus geysers of beer. We were served by a lovely waitress in a Spandex outfit that may as well have been a Ziploc bag. Around the corner, off the Ocean Front, is the **Stag Bar** (121 McFadden Place, 673-4470). It is not, however, a stag bar. That is to say, women are welcome here, and most seem welcoming, especially if you're wearing your college logo on a piece of clothing. Reflecting a cutting-edge collegiate atmosphere, the Stag Bar is hip, loud, and wild, with a great jukebox (R.E.M., Jane's Addiction), pool tables, and no pretensions.

Just across the plaza is **Rumplestiltskin's** (114 McFadden Place, 673-5025), the best venue for live rock and roll. It's catch as catch can on the music, some nights leaning more toward heavy metal than we like. (You know, guitarists with shag haircuts whose trousers pinch a bit tightly in the loins.) During one visit we found ourselves surrounded by GIs on weekend leave who took turns puking their guts out in the john. On other nights, you might catch a band like Dreamworld, an all-woman pop quartet that exemplified all the enduring appeal of rock and roll as we like it. They reminded us of what a wonderful world this could be if decent live music were the norm at the shore. Taking their name from a Midnight Oil song, they played clean, well-oiled pop with great harmony vocals.

Just down the street is **Woody's Wharf** (2318 Newport Boulevard, 675-0474). It's another wild hangout with live music (mostly blues and boogie) that is mobbed on weekends. The clientele seems a bit, shall we say, wanton. It's got an outdoor patio and a harborfront dining area, but the main part of the club is configured all wrong and we wound up being wedged against the bar like sardines. Still, it's a hopping place if you want to frolic with the locals, who have been doing so here for 30 years.

Swindlin' USA

(sung to the tune of "Surfin' USA")

If every realtor had an ocean
There would be hell to pay
They'd be sellin' off the coastline
Like California
You'd see 'em building marinas
Time-sharing condos, too
Goofy goofy golf courses
Swindlin' USA

You'll catch 'em boutiquing Del Mar
Up to Orange County Line
Installing spas and Jacuzzis
And pouring vintage wine
All over the Southland
Like down Doheny way
Developers gone bonkers
Swindlin' USA

We'll all be planning out a ruse
We'll pay some bribes real soon
We're shaking down our bankers
We can't wait for loot
We'll be bulldozing all summer
Phase One by fall, hooray!
Tell the surfers we're comin'
Swindlin' USA

At Huntington and Newport
We always get our way
We're draining Bolsa Chica
More homes and green fairways
All over the coastline
We're wrecking beach and bay
Developers gone loony
Swindlin' USA

For More Information

Contact the Newport Beach Visitors Bureau, 366 San Miguel, Suite 200, Newport Beach, CA 92660; (800) 942-6278 or (714) 644-1190. Or try the Newport Harbor Area Chamber of Commerce, 1470 Jamboree Road, Newport Beach, CA 92660; (714) 729-4417.

 Map of Orange County beaches—page 102

Huntington Beach

Location: Huntington Beach is 38 miles southeast of Los Angeles and 97 miles northwest of San Diego. Both Interstate 405 (San Diego Freeway) and Highway 1 (Pacific Coast Highway) pass through it, with the latter running beside the ocean. Three public beaches run for 8.5 continuous miles in Huntington Beach. They are, from south to north, Huntington State Beach, Huntington City Beach, and Bolsa Chica State Beach.

Population: 182,500

Area Code: 714 **Zip Code:** 92648

Once upon a time Huntington Beach was just another cow town close to Los Angeles with a beautiful beach that was much beloved by the surfing cult. They knew it then as "Surf City"—and still do now. Here, as the surf-music duo Jan and Dean sang in their 1963 number-one national hit, the surf was always up and there was the added incentive of "two girls for every boy." During the golden era of surfing of the 1950s and 1960s, the surfers pretty much had the place to themselves. As recently as the mid-1980s, Huntington Beach remained a pretty sleepy sprawl along the Pacific Coast Highway with unpretentious food shacks (usually Mexican), surf shops, and one-story motor courts. The town would awaken only for the annual Labor Day surfing tournament and the de rigueur riot that often accompanied it.

All that has changed with the arrival of (drumroll, please) "the Waterfront," a controversial 12-story, 293-room Hilton hotel that has forever altered the character of Huntington Beach. And that's just a taste of what's on the way. It has been joined by places like the Pierside Pavilion and Promenade complex—clusters of trendy stores, restaurants, theaters, and office space that chased off a lot of funky junk in the vicinity of the beach. On the horizon is a 500-room conference hotel (for those stressed-out business types who always convene at nice places but rarely get to enjoy them), a 250-unit "all-suites" hotel, a 400-unit luxury hotel, and behind the hotel, 500 or so pricey residential units. The target date for completion of all this razing and reconstruction is 1998. After having remained sleepy for so many years, this flat, foursquare cow town has woken up a raging Godzilla, insofar as development is concerned. And it is the beach that is getting beaten up.

With a bit of imagination, the eye can trace its way across the current landscape and imagine what Huntington Beach must have looked like at some remote point in the presettlement past: fields of large, fully vegetated dunes extending for a good distance off the beach, backed by lagoons and wetlands. In the early years of this century, it was actually named "Pacific City" by a developer who wanted to see it become the West Coast's answer to Atlantic City. It was sold to a group who renamed the town Huntington Beach, hoping that by paying railroad magnate H. E. Huntington this nominal tribute he would extend his Pacific Electric Railroad to the young city. (He did.) In 1919, Standard Oil leased 500 acres from the Huntington Beach Company; a year later, a well came in with a roar literally heard for miles. To this day, nine million gallons a year are pumped out of Huntington Beach. Oil derricks are everywhere you look (except tourist brochures): along the highway, in backyards, on the beach, atop offshore platforms. They rise and fall as far as the eye can see, like an aerobics class of giant black magpies playing "touch your toes."

It's kind of heartbreaking to ponder the changes that have been wrought upon the landscape, from power plant and oil derricks that visually blight it to the bricked-in shopping malls and colossal resorts that have stolen its very soul. Yet despite all the new development, Huntington Beach doggedly remains a people's beach, having long served the recreational needs of families, surfers, and everyday folks. Those same elements still crowd the city and state beaches that run for a great distance in either direction from town. (Main Street, where it meets the Pacific Coast Highway at the Huntington Beach Pier, is the heart of the action.) But the retail scenery around these beaches has changed drastically.

At one extreme, there's the Hilton vacation monolith. At the other extreme, fast-food chains now rule the waterfront where once humble but lovable nonfranchise burger and taco huts used to stand. The Main Street/Pacific Coast Highway intersection is the site of the Pierside Pavilion and Promenade, a two-story mega-boutique full of cute shops meant to amuse those whose idea of a day at the beach consists of shopping close to it. Lest we sound too harsh in our condemnation of such places, experience has shown that the shops filling these nouveau malls generally have a life span of only a few of years, while they displace less trendy stores and restaurants that might have been there for decades. In the process, we've lost—and continue to lose—many of the forgotten shanties that stood sentry throughout the decades when *American Graffiti* was being lived instead of marketed. A generation from now, will anyone remember what the beach life was really like?

The old Huntington Beach—a motley but likable cluster of surf shops, dive bars, and food stands—has fallen to the wrecking ball. "Another safe, quality demolition" read a sign we saw hooked to a fence in 1987, when the ball was just beginning to do its damage. City officials referred to the forced uprooting and relocation of local residents, in *1984*-style doublespeak, as a "conversion procedure." We have no delusions here: we are not lamenting the passing of great architectural landmarks or businesses with any great utility in the 1990s marketplace. It's just sad to see something so grandly unimaginative and, by design, exclusive go up in their place.

It's an attitude thing. For example: Dean Torrance, of Jan and Dean fame, suggested to the Huntington Beach City Council in 1991 that they consider copyrighting the name "Surf City" for promotional purposes. "People from Iowa want to come here to the beach," noted Torrance. "All the city has to do is grab onto the coattails of this idea." A great and legitimate hook for reeling in the tourists, no? Not in the eyes of one councilman, who whined, "We want people who will spend several hundred dollars a day in our hotels and restaurants. With inland California surfers, we're lucky if they spend $10 or $15 a day." This is how minds work in Orange County: with a resolutely stony eye fixed on the bottom line at all times.

Whether you're spending $10 or $300 a day, the only part of Huntington Beach that matters is its coastal frontage. The town that sprawls behind it, arrayed along wide arteries that link the Pacific Coast Highway and Interstate 405, offers the transient visitor little that can't be found on or close to the beach. Huntington Beach is certainly pleasant enough, from all outward appearances. With a population of over 180,000, it is the 13th-largest city in California. From the beach, the town fans east, giving way to neat rows of white stucco homes in quiet, palm-shaded residential neighborhoods. Beach Boulevard is the Big Kahuna of commerce in the area, offering a lengthy corridor of gas stations, cheap motels, franchise food stands, ATM machines, and strip malls. You can venture down this sun-beaten ribbon of concrete in search of drive-through grub, suntan lotion, film, flip-flops, or a more affordable motel, if you like, but you're better off staying close to the beach. There's not much to distinguish the interior of Huntington Beach from Fresno or Des Moines.

The city itself is a quandary: on the one hand so outwardly normal and Beaver Cleaver clean, and yet on the other hand wracked with

 Map of Orange County beaches—page 102

issues that continue to divide the populace. From battles over construction of "the Waterfront" to a debate over what to do with the wetlands of Bolsa Chica (to develop or not to develop, that was the question), Huntington Beach has found itself in the hot seat a lot lately. Even the old reliable surfers, source of the "Surf City" drawing card, have seemed like a scourge, on occasion. Back in 1987, the same year in which Huntington Beach was declared the safest city in the United States, a major riot erupted on the beach during the Labor Day surfing tournament, making national headlines. A few boneheads tried to remove some girls' bikini tops. Their boyfriends took umbrage. Fists started flying, the crowd began chanting, and earthquakelike tremors spread across the beach. Innocent bystanders were injured,

Legend of the Duke

There's another "Duke" besides John Wayne who left his mark on Orange County. We are talking about Duke Kahanamoku, a Waikiki wave rider who became a California legend. More than anyone else, he spread the word about Huntington Beach, turning a withering, would-be resort into a bustling beach mecca. Duke was a Hawaiian native, an Olympic swimmer, and a world-class surfer—one of the first, in fact, to make a living at these things. Way back at the turn of the century, this Pied Piper of the waves publicly promoted the sport, gracefully skiing the sloping surf on his favorite plank. His salary was paid by railroad mogul H. E. Huntington, who wanted to give the public new incentives to travel his freshly laid stretch of track from Los Angeles to Huntington Beach. He wowed the locals in the 1920s by surfing *under* the pier—a dangerous but impressive feat.

Following Duke's lead, a small but growing surfing cult began pointing their longboards toward Huntington Beach. In the early 1960s, surfing seized the national imagination. When the Beach Boys, Jan and Dean, and the Surfaris took the sport into the Top Forty with a string of catchy surfing anthems, the entire nation suddenly craved coastal access. While surfers trekked the entire West Coast in search of the perfect wave, it was Huntington Beach that became known far and wide as "Surf City," after Jan and Dean's chart-topping hit. The first major surfing competition, the Pacific Coast Surfboard Championships, was held here. Since the early 1970s, the U.S. Surfboard Championships have drawn hundreds of thousands to the brown-sugar beach at Huntington.

For many years, a small bust of Duke Kahanamoku stood at the foot of the Huntington Beach Pier, his beneficent gaze turned seaward. In recent years, it has been moved inside the Huntington Beach International Surfing Museum. Today, the late Duke—he died in 1968 (at the ripe old age of 78)—is recognized, along with fellow Hawaiian native George Freeth, as one of the fathers of surfing. Remnants and relics of surfing's golden age fill the museum, including everything from wildly adorned Hawaiian shirts to a 12.5-foot, 135-pound wooden longboard. There's also memorabilia from the Huntington Beach Surf Theater, a bygone 1960s-era film house that showed *only* surf movies. Ah, yes, those were the days.

private property was destroyed, and lawsuits flew around for years afterward. As a result, the surfing championships have been moved from Labor Day to early summer in an attempt to cut down on the crowd size.

Beaches

Santa Cruz and Huntington Beach have been squabbling for years over which community has earned the right to the title of "Surf City," but based on all the available evidence, it's not even a contest. Huntington Beach rules! Summer surfing championship meets have been held here since 1928, and it is widely known as the International Surf Capital of the World. In August it holds the U.S. Open of Surfing, and in June the Op Pro Surfing Championships. But there's always something going on here, surfing-wise.

People flock to Huntington Beach on weekends from the surrounding valley towns, as well as from surf-deprived Long Beach, with boards strapped to the roofs of everything from boat-sized woodies to old VW bugs. The beach is so extensive, sandy, and clean, and the tumbling waves that roll ashore so well formed for surfing, that Huntington was voted the sixth best beach in the world in a poll conducted by (of all things) Lifestyles of the Rich and Famous. Surfers tend to get a far-off look in their eyes when they ponder the unobstructed south swells that spill forward in perfect curls of wave and foam (known as "rooster tails"), sometimes reaching 12 feet.

The beach is gorgeous. It runs for more than eight miles, encompassing **Huntington State Beach**, **Huntington City Beach**, and **Bolsa Chica State Beach**. The offshore breezes are refreshing, and the beaches are among the widest in Southern California—at least along the state and city beaches. Around Bolsa Chica the beach starts narrowing, only to widen again at the state beach's north end. Fences have been put up to keep people back from unstable, crumbling cliffs where the beach has severely eroded. The beach at Bolsa Chica is usable only at low tide. Except for this, however, the beaches of Huntington Beach are pretty much archetypal Southern California experiences, both in the way they look and what you can do on them, such as surf, picnic, and swim. Another beach tradition, grunioning, lives on here as well. (People come out to watch the

Bolsa Chica State Beach

Location: In Huntington Beach, along the Pacific Coast Highway, from Main Street to Warner Avenue.

Parking: $5 entrance fee per vehicle.

Hours: 6 AM to 10 PM.

Facilities: Lifeguards, rest rooms, showers, picnic areas, and fire pits. There are 50 RV campsites. The fee is $14 per night. For camping reservations, call Destinet at (800) 444-7275.

Contact: For beach information, contact Bolsa Chica State Beach at (714) 846-3460.

See number 30 on page 102.

Huntington City Beach

Location: In Huntington Beach, along the Pacific Coast Highway, from Beach Boulevard to Main Street.

Parking: $6 entrance fee per vehicle.

Hours: 7 AM to 10 PM.

Facilities: Lifeguards, rest rooms, showers, picnic tables, and fire rings. There are 25 en route RV campsites. The fee is $15 per night. No camping reservations are accepted.

Contact: For beach information, contact Huntington City Beach at (714) 536-5280.

See number 29 on page 102.

spawning rituals of the grunion, which emerge from the surf en masse to leave their eggs in the sand under certain lunar/tidal conditions.) Camping is available at Bolsa Chica in an "en route" campers' parking lot.

When you've had enough fun on the beach, make your way to the Huntington Beach International Surfing Museum (411 Olive Street, 960-3483) and the Surfing Walk of Fame (at the intersection of Main Street and the Pacific Coast Highway). The former facility opened in 1988 and claims to be the largest of a growing number of surfing museums. Only at a place like this could you hope to learn that the first documentation of surfing occurred in 1778, when Captain James Cook of the British Navy witnessed Hawaiian natives riding the waves on crudely fashioned longboards. The Walk of Fame starts at Jack's Surfboards, a surf shop that's so much of a fixture that a Republican Congressman-cum-surfer set up his reelection campaign at the back of the shop. The walk consists of a line of 12 stone monuments up Main Street, dedicated to surfers who have been inducted in various categories, including Surf Pioneer, Surf Champion, and Woman of the Year.

Huntington State Beach

Location: In Huntington Beach, along the Pacific Coast Highway, from the Santa Ana River to Beach Boulevard.

Parking: $5 entrance fee per vehicle.

Hours: 6 AM to 10 PM PDT (6 AM to 8 PM PST).

Facilities: Lifeguards, rest rooms, showers, picnic areas, and fire rings.

Contact: For beach information, contact Huntington State Beach at (714) 536-1454.

See number 28 on page 102.

Bunking Down

The **Waterfront Hilton Beach Resort** (21100 Pacific Coast Highway, 960-7873, $$$) really isn't so bad, price-wise. Rooms start at $115 a night, which is not unreasonable for the creature comforts proffered, and top off at around $260. It claims to be the only hotel right on the surf between Laguna Beach and Redondo Beach. If you're after something a little more down to earth, the **Quality Inn** (800 Pacific Coast Highway, 536-7500, $$) has got location (three blocks north of the Huntington Beach Pier, across from the beach), price (significantly less than the Waterfront), and looks (contemporary, clean) going for it. Nothing much else worth mentioning can be found as close to the beach as these two choices, but Beach Boulevard is chockablock with cheap motels all the way out to Interstate 405.

Coastal Cuisine

During this period of transition, the restaurant scene at Huntington Beach is largely up in the air. Our impression is that it is, like the town itself, essentially undistinguished. In recent years some favorite food stands along the Pacific Coast Highway have been washed away by the incoming tide of high-stakes development. Parts of the Huntington Beach Pier have literally been washed away, in 1983 and 1987, taking with it the End Café, an end-of-the-pier eatery set to rise again from the ashes. At the dry end of the pier, a decent seafood dinner awaits you at **Maxwell's** (317 Pacific Coast Highway, 536-2555, $$$). Entrées are overpriced, but eating here is arguably worth it for the view over the water. Adjoining the pier, Maxwell's generally offers half a dozen fresh fish a day and just as many ways to prepare them, from Cajun spiced to smothered in Mexican sauce to the simple (and probably preferable) sautéed or broiled options.

At the less pricey end you can always "run for the border." The local Taco Bell is crawling with surfers. They stand on the tiled floor, topless, shoeless, shirtless, and dripping wet, waiting for their orders to be called. The Huntington Beach Taco Bell on the Pacific Coast Highway is something of a landmark. It was among the first in the chain to serve Baja fish tacos (or so we were told by a seemingly credible surfer with a lean and hungry look). As for the fast-food fish taco, it is a pale fast-food imitation of the more substantial fare to be found at 1,001 authentic Mexican food stands between Mission Beach and Malibu. The price is right, but it tasted to us like a Mrs. Paul's fish stick wrapped inside a soft taco that was about as appetizing as boiled parchment.

Night Moves

The surfers and party dudes are still lamenting the passage of the Golden Bear, a great

A Surfer Looks at 50

We overheard a fellow named Brian Goodman talking to a waitress at Woody's Diner in Sunset Beach. She was having a bad day, and he, mimicking a New Age therapist, urged her to "fluff up her aura" and "receive some of our positive vibes, 'cause we're full of happiness." He was sitting with his 15-year-old son, plotting the future (surfing adventures on the Baja Peninsula) and leisurely downing a plateful of Super Spuds: hash browns fried in a skillet with mushrooms, onion, green peppers, and cheese. This stick-to-your-ribs concoction has been warming surfers' tummies at this location since the 1950s. We engaged him in conversation, and he openly shared his life story and opinions on what's been happening along the California coast in recent decades.

Of Huntington Beach, on whose sands he learned to surf, he said: "We're disgusted with it. We don't go there anymore. We don't go to Main Street anymore." As thick as the development of Huntington Beach's shoreline has grown since the arrival of the unsightly colossus known as "the Waterfront," Goodman revealed that plans are in the works to make it much, much worse—plans that he, as an active member of the Surfrider Foundation and a concerned resident, has been diligently battling at the grassroots level. For 20 years, a company called Signal Land Properties has gobbled up oceanfront real estate while hatching a long-term blueprint for a massive waterfront development. They envision a 1,000-foot breakwater and 4,000 new home sites surrounding the harbor. The Pacific Coast Highway would be elevated 100 feet in the air in this area. Sounds like fun, eh?

Thus far, the developer has been enjoined in court by citizen's-action groups such as the Surfriders. It may just be a matter of time before some sort of scaled-down and compromised—yet no doubt disruptive—development gets under way. Goodman is quick to point out that rules can be bent when influential Orange County businessmen want their bidding done. The "build first, ask questions later" mentality extends right down to the water. How, Goodman asks rhetorically, did the Hilton Waterfront resort get around Proposition 13, which clearly forbids the further construction of high-rise fortresses along the ocean?

 Map of Orange County beaches—page 102

old hangout that got nuked by the redevelopment prerogative. Most of the bars in the vicinity of the beach, many of which we remember as being a little rough, have met a similar fate. In many cases, it was no great loss. If you're up for entertainment, head to **Music City** (18774 Brookhurst Street, Fountain Valley, 963-2366). Located at a shopping mall in Fountain Valley, about five miles inland, it draws a bubbling crowd of all ages and dance steps.

For More Information

Contact the Huntington Beach Conference and Visitors Bureau, 2100 Main Street, Suite 190, Huntington Beach, CA 92648; (714) 969-3492.

Goodman has been doggedly leading the good life while fighting the good fight, but for him the "Old California" of the 1950s and 1960s is a waning memory. He speaks fondly of nights spent sleeping sitting up in a Jeep at Bolsa Chica (known to locals as Tin Can Beach) in order to rise with the sun and go surfing. A wearying day on the waves would be followed by a hearty plate of Super Spuds at a bait and donut shop on the site of what is now Woody's Diner. Today, here he is, decades later, still surfing waves and scarfing spuds on the same spot, but disenchanted with the corporate makeover of his beloved California coast. He mourns the loss of Dana Point as a surfer's mecca, especially now that the man-made harbor eliminated one of the most challenging point breaks on the West Coast. These days he's got his eyes pointed south, beyond California, where he'll stake his claim in "some Third World nation." There he'll scan the horizon for the perfect wave that will carry him to a beach where he won't have to look at some moneyed bigwig's vacation home.

Goodman is like a surfing Fred MacMurray: he's middle-aged, and he speaks fondly of "my three sons," whom he has looked after responsibly and well. The youngest is almost out of high school. Upon his graduation, Goodman feels he will have fulfilled his responsibility as a parent and can turn his attention to his own adventures. Already, he shares a year-round lease on a shack at a beach on the Baja, well south of anything that could be described as Americanized. A paltry $900 gets it for the whole year. Divide that by six tenants, and you're talking next to nothing in living expenses. It's a sweet life. The locals like the gringos, and vice versa. Goodman has got his sights set on a full-time move in that direction, after he quits a job that he has held for seven years (the longest uninterrupted stretch of gainful employment in his life).

His smile is genuine and constant, the sense of pleasure he derives from his largely nonmaterialistic life an inspiration as he stares at age 50 without the self-imposed baggage that imprisons millions. Unlike those who are fretting over adjustable rate mortgages on their Huntington Beach condos, Goodman is living free and easy, able to pull up anchor and move on at a whim. "I've still got places to go and things to see and waves to ride," he concludes with a gleam.

Bolsa Chica Ecological Reserve, Huntington Harbor, Sunset Beach, and Surfside

Location: Adjoining Huntington Beach to the northwest, via the Pacific Coast Highway. Sunset Beach is the principal beach in this area of wetlands, man-made harbors, and private residential communities.
Population: 5,000
Area Code: 310 **Zip Code:** 90742

Huntington Harbor is a ritzy marina and residential development that split a significant wetland in two. Some of the remains of that wetland have been preserved as Bolsa Chica Ecological Reserve, southeast of Huntington Harbour, and as the Seal Beach National Wildlife Refuge, just inland of Sunset Beach and Seal Beach. Be that as it may, a significant amount of wetlands acreage is still under private ownership, with plans to develop it further. For years, the Koll Real Estate Group pushed forward a plan to build 4,286 homes on a 1,700-acre wetlands tract. They met with opposition from such grassroots environmental groups as the Bolsa Chica Land Trust and Amigos de Bolsa Chica.

In August 1994, the Orange County Planning Commission (a misnomer, if ever there was one) readied a proposal to rezone the Bolsa Chica wetlands from agricultural to residential use. The county's environmental impact statement was challenged by the city of Huntington Beach, which threatened to sue. By November, the California State Coastal Conservancy, the cities of Huntington Beach and Seal Beach, the Sierra Club, and the League of Women Voters had all weighed in with pro-preservation opinions, lobbying Secretary of the Interior Bruce Babbitt and U.S. Senator Dianne Feinstein. One of the arguments mustered was that, in addition to its inherent value as a wetland, Bolsa Chica is a valuable archeological site. More "cogged stones"—used in Native American rituals between 6,000 and 3,500 B.C.—have been found here than anywhere else. "It is the mother of cogged-stone sites," said Pat Ware, president of the Pacific Coast Archeological Society.

The depressing denouement to the Bolsa Chica controversy came in mid-January 1996, when the California Coastal Commission granted Koll permission to proceed with its plans to build homes in the wetlands. Having destroyed 95 percent of its coastal wetlands, the state of California can ill afford to lose another acre. Yet it appears that in Huntington Beach, money talks and wetlands walk. Chalk up another victory for business interests.

Shoreward of the Bolsa Chica reserve are the small communities of Sunset Beach and Surfside. The latter is a private beach colony accessible only to pedestrians and bicyclists through a gate at the end of Anderson Avenue. Sunset Beach is more in line with the old, surfer-friendly ways of Huntington Beach back when board bums had the run of this stretch of the coast. Remnants of that time are still evident in some of the funky restaurants and bars lining the Pacific Coast Highway.

Beaches

While the developers make their move on Bolsa Chica, life goes on at Huntington Harbor and **Sunset Beach**. The first of these is a private marina that has some public docks and overnight slips for rental. The community of Sunset Beach, arrayed like a centipede along the Pacific Coast Highway, has a linear park, complete with rest rooms and volleyball nets, that runs along its public beachfront between

 Map of Orange County beaches—page 102

Anderson and Warner Avenues. A small beach is also accessible through the gates of the private **Surfside** community, which is appended to the north end of Sunset Beach. But the beaches at Sunset and Surfside are probably not worth the trouble it takes to get to them, as parking is limited at the former and nonexistent at the latter. Neither beach has much to commend it to visitors, who are better off setting their sights on the massive city and state beaches in Huntington Beach proper.

Coastal Cuisine

Vestiges of the area's comfortably unglamorous past can be seen in places like the **Harbor House Café** (16341 Pacific Coast Highway, 592-5404, $) and **Woody's Diner** (16731 Pacific Coast Highway, 592-2134, $). The Harbor House has been around since 1939, and the site occupied by Woody's has a long and storied history as well. Both have menus heavy on omelettes and seafood and burger variations, offering something for everyone in pleasant surroundings.

For More Information

Contact the Huntington Beach Conference and Visitors Bureau, 2100 Main Street, Suite 190, Huntington Beach, CA 92648; (714) 969-3492.

Sunset Beach

Location: In Sunset Beach, at the end of Pacific Avenue.

Parking: Limited free street parking.

Hours: 6 AM to 10 PM.

Facilities: Lifeguards and rest rooms.

Contact: For beach information, contact the North Beaches Operation Office of Orange County Harbors, Beaches, and Parks at (714) 723-4511.

See number 31 on page 102.

Surfside Beach

Location: In Surfside, a short hike from the gated community at Anderson Avenue and the Pacific Coast Highway.

Parking: This beach is accessible only to pedestrians and bicyclists through a gated entrance at the end of Anderson Avenue, off the Pacific Coast Highway, or by walking north from Sunset Beach.

Hours: 6 AM to 10 PM.

Facilities: None.

Contact: This is a private community; no contact number is available.

See number 32 on page 102.

Seal Beach

Location: Just south of the Los Angeles County line, north of Sunset Beach off the Pacific Coast Highway, via Seal Beach Boulevard. Seal Beach and its municipal pier are the center of activity.
Population: 26,000
Area Code: 310 **Zip Code:** 90740

Seal Beach was named for the flappy sea mammal that was once so popular with the garment trade. By Orange County standards it's a modest town in the best sense of the word. It could have just as easily been named for its good fortune at having been "sealed" off from its neighbors. Located at the north end of the county, just over the San Gabriel River from Los Angeles County, Seal Beach is a seal among sprawling sea monsters.

The Pacific Coast Highway passes wide of Seal Beach, sparing the town center the nonstop wall of traffic headed to and from Long Beach. One must vigilantly search for the turnoff (Seal Beach Boulevard) or miss the town completely. Like the fictional village of Mayberry, Seal Beach is a world unto itself, existing primarily for those who live here. It has a Main Street that looks like a Main Street should—shaded with trees, cobbled with bricks, and as civilized as one of Grandma's bedtime stories. It has a grassy park named for an American president, Dwight D. Eisenhower, whose memory is synonymous with a more reassuring past. There's a tiny historical museum housed in an antique railroad car, an art-deco movie house with a Wurlitzer organ, an Irish pub, a couple of seafood restaurants, a municipal pier, a city beach—and that's about it for Seal Beach.

The main intersection at the beachfront is not your typical surf-culture strip. It underwhelms you with its lack of gratuitous commerce. The hottest ticket in town on our last visit was the Lion's Club fish fry. The community bulletin board was filled with solicitations for recipe-swapping and pen pals. We quickly signed up for the latter.

Beaches

For all its small-town charm, **Seal Beach** is not completely undiscovered, as the surf here is middling popular. Many of the surfers who make the trek are too young to drive, so they ride the bus from Long Beach, boards tucked under their arms like briefcases. At 9:30 on a Monday morning, we counted 78 surfers on the north side of Seal Beach Pier. Looking like tropical fish in their fluorescent wet suits, they sat passively on their boards and stared west, bobbing up and down, not speaking to one another, just waiting for the perfect wave.

The wait can be a long one. The surf here approaches the beaches that run for half a mile on each side of the pier at a southerly angle. Sometimes this produces ideal waves, sometimes not. The surf's erratic quality keeps the town from becoming another Huntington Beach. Even when the waves aren't rocking and rolling, though, the currents and crosswinds are swift and potentially treacherous. Signs warn: "Beware of Beach Hazards, Long Shore Currents, Rip Currents, Inshore Holes, Sand Bars, Underwater Objects, Pier Seawall and Rock Structures."

Seal Beach

Location: In Seal Beach, at Main Street and the Seal Beach Pier.
Parking: Metered street parking.
Hours: 4:30 AM to 10 PM.
Facilities: Lifeguards, rest rooms, and showers.
Contact: For beach information, contact the Seal Beach Lifeguard Station at (310) 430-2613.

See number 33 on page 102.

"Our Filthy, Stinking Beaches"

The following letter to the editor first appeared in the *Long Beach Press-Telegram* under the above headline on August 27, 1993. It passionately states the frustrations felt by one eloquent coast-dweller over the mounting offenses wrought by beach-hardening schemes (jetties, in this case) and pollution brought by population pressures and a lack of caring. It serves as testimony to the problems faced by Seal Beach in particular and Southern California in general, and needs no further elaboration.

To the Editor:

Seal Beach is an extremely sentimental place to me and probably to thousands of people who learned to surf there as I did 19 years ago. Back then, the jetty smelled like wet sand and it had healthy kelp growing with large, greenish leaves. There were pelicans all over the rocks because of the abundance of fish. I used to collect pretty little shells on the sand and tried to catch the crabs as they climbed in the rocks.

Well, I went back to surf there recently and was horrified. In place of my pretty little shells were trash and debris, including jagged tin can lids. The water was black and had a foul odor. Walking out in the water was difficult because of the trash and debris wrapping around my legs. Worst of all, I broke out in a rash on my face and neck that evening. I understand that the pollution is not the city's fault; it's coming from other sources. But it is the city's responsibility to have the water checked when it gets as bad as it was on August 5. It's also the city's responsibility to close the jetty when it's that polluted. The Health Department only checks twice a month and then only for *E. coli* bacteria, which would determine the percentage of sewage in the water. Who knows what else is in there?

Eventually, people will stop going to the beach. Word will spread through the community. People are ignorant of problems until the ocean looks, smells, and even feels bad from debris and trash, and when kids say, "Look, Mom, the water is black!" (as I heard one boy say). That's the beginning of the end of local tourism. Shops, restaurants, and parking fees will all suffer. The community would probably be willing to donate for the cleanup and search for the main source of the pollution. If most of the pollution comes from storm drains, then we need to start a campaign to educate people not to throw oil, paint, transmission fluid, etc., in the gutters. Whatever it takes, I'm willing to donate my time to help. I love Seal Beach. It has nothing but good memories for me. I would love to see it restored for our children and grandchildren. Maybe it is a lost cause, but I'm not willing to believe that. If it is eventually closed, I want to know that I tried my best to prevent it.

Marlene Falcioni
Buena Park

Okay, Seal Beach is not as dangerous as these signs make it seem, and a large contingent of lifeguards keep a close watch on everyone. Still, the unpredictable beach currents are partly caused by the concrete jetty that splits Seal Beach down the center. The sand is 50 yards narrower on the north side of the wall than on the south side. Planners who constructed the massive jetty did not intend this to happen—instead, the jetty was meant to hold the sand equally on both sides.

Surfing is allowed on the shorter stretch of beach north of the pier and on Surfside Beach, on the far side of the town's south jetty (and belonging, in actual fact, to the small community of Surfside; see the entry on page 149). The longest and widest stretch of beach, between the pier and the south jetty, is reserved for swimmers and sunbathers. The 1,885-foot pier was destroyed in January 1983 by the same storm that leveled Huntington Pier. The Seal Beach Pier was rebuilt the next year, with a placard to commemorate the town's industriousness and a cute bronze sculpture of a seal.

Oh, so you noticed the oil platforms offshore? Well, that's part of the scenery the town has no control over. Occasionally, in fact, Seal Beach is the unwilling recipient of an oil spill that closes the beach until it's cleaned up. During one of our previous visits, Seal Beach was hit by a small but nasty spill from a leaky pipe on an offshore platform. While the oil-company execs ducked culpability, the town mobilized with bulldozers and volunteers to clean up the mess. As we were leaving, the beach had been reopened. Meanwhile, angry letters to the editor began to appear. "The rigs not only besmirch the coastline," wrote one citizen, "they pose a constant threat to our beaches and sea life." Let's guess: next came the press release from the oil company publicists reassuring the townsfolk how environmentally conscious they are. Then local officials reminded the citizens about the money and jobs the oil companies bring the local economy. Everyone forgets for a while, then another small but nasty spill occurs, and the cycle beings anew.

Anyway, here's to the good folks of Seal Beach. May your sand remain eternally clean.

Bunking Down

In this homey town, there's really only one large motel, the **Radisson Inn Seal Beach** (600 Marina Drive, 493-7501, $$). Set far enough away from town center so as not to detract from the Main Street atmosphere, the Radisson is still an easy walk from the beach and pier. Two small pools are on the premises. You may wish to opt for the 23-room **Seal Beach Inn and Gardens** (212 Fifth Street, 493-2416, $$$), a restored 60-year-old inn with splendid gardens . It combines the best of bed-and-breakfast and hotel amenities under one roof.

Coastal Cuisine

Of the seafood places in Seal Beach, **Walt's Wharf** (201 Main Street, 598-4433, $$$) attracts the most devoted following. It's more upscale than most of the restaurants in town, drawing a large crowd of gregarious boat people in the late afternoon. There are nearly as many fish to choose from as there are imported beers on tap, and the seafood is as fresh as it comes around here.

Night Moves

Don't bother leaving **Walt's Wharf** (201 Main Street, 598-4433) if you're looking for something to do after dinner. It's got a great bar with a kick-back-and-relax ambience and excellent appetizers to go with the brew. Alternatively, there's a **Hennessey's Tavern** (140 Main Street, 598-4419) across the street. Hennessey's, a Southern California chain, is an old reliable watering hole no matter where the location.

For More Information

Contact Seal Beach Chamber of Commerce, 13820 Seal Beach Boulevard, Seal Beach, CA 90740; (310) 799-0179.

Los Angeles County

A separate book could be written about coastal Los Angeles County, home to everything from the Queen Mary ocean liner in Long Beach to the chainsaw jugglers in Venice Beach. Just the familiar ring of the names of its beaches is enough to evoke images of endless summers, bottomless margaritas, and topless—we mean incomparable—bathing beauties.

Who can resist the lure of Santa Catalina Island; Redondo, Hermosa, and Manhattan Beaches, down along the South Bay; Venice, Santa Monica, and Marina del Rey, all part of the pulse of daily life in L.A.; and Malibu's 27 miles, wherein the coast takes a turn for the wilder. As beleaguered as this county is, Los Angeles gets an "A" for making its beaches safe and accessible to a population of nine million (plus 65 million tourists a year). It's just the rest of L.A. that drives us batty (but we won't obsess). So pick a beach, stick to it, and let the world that lies east of your chosen Eden go about its clamorous business while you fine-tune your tan.

Coastal Los Angeles County's Climate

Long Beach Averages

	Daily High Temp. (°F)	Daily Low Temp. (°F)	Rainfall (inches)
January	66	44	3.0
February	67	46	2.5
March	66	48	1.7
April	71	51	0.8
May	73	55	0.2
June	77	59	0
July	83	63	0
August	84	64	0.1
September	83	62	0.2
October	76	57	0.2
November	73	50	1.4
December	67	45	1.6
Yearly Average	**74**	**54**	**11.5**

Santa Monica Averages

	Daily High Temp. (°F)	Daily Low Temp. (°F)	Rainfall (inches)
January	64	49	3.3
February	64	50	3.0
March	63	50	2.1
April	64	52	1.0
May	65	55	0.2
June	68	58	0
July	71	61	0
August	72	63	0.2
September	72	61	0.1
October	70	58	0.2
November	68	53	1.7
December	66	50	1.9
Yearly Average	**67**	**55**	**13.7**

Source: National Weather Service data, National Oceanographic and Atmospheric Administration.

Map of Los Angeles County beaches—page 154

Los Angeles County

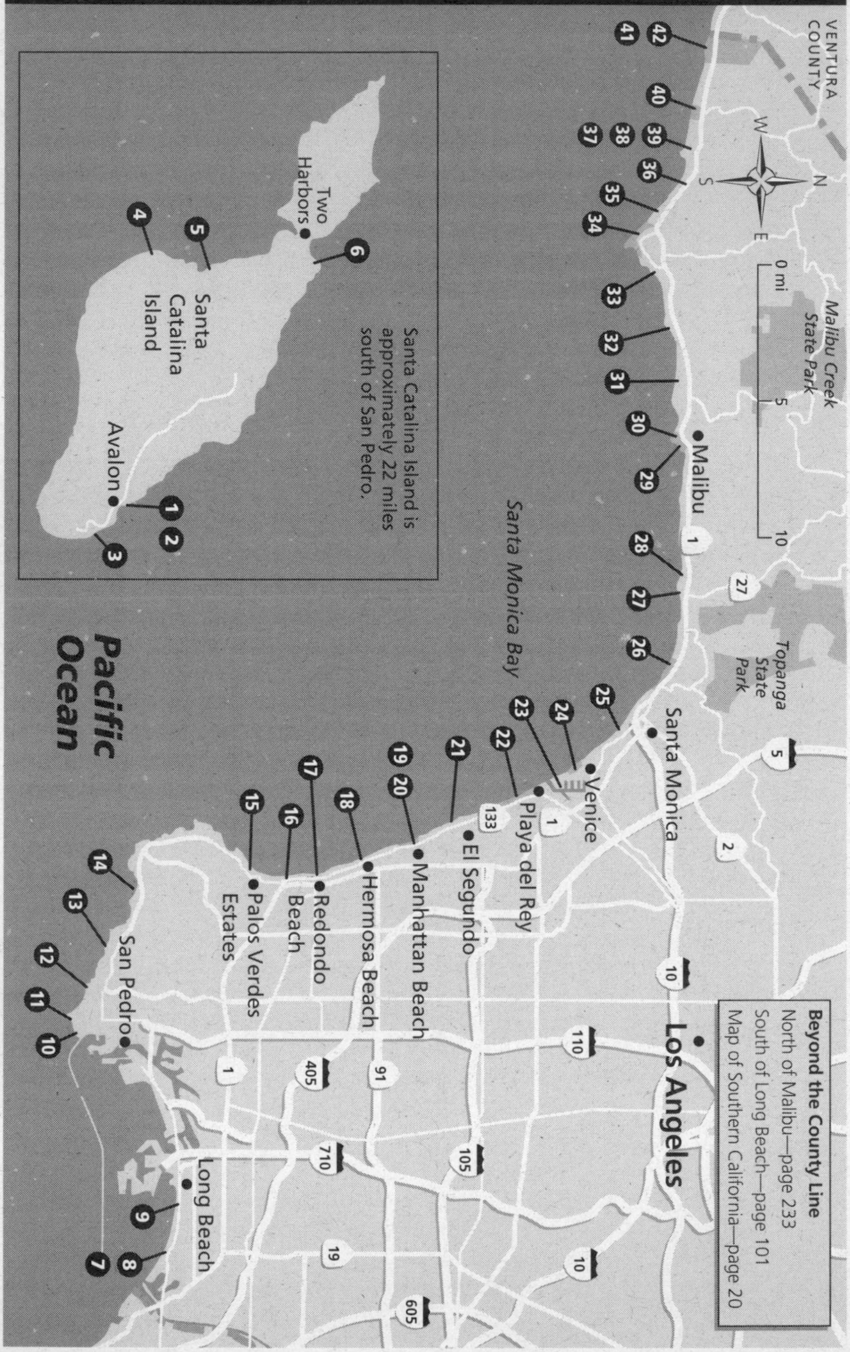

VENTURA COUNTY
Malibu Creek State Park
0 mi
5
10
N
S
E
W
Malibu
Topanga State Park
Santa Monica
Venice
Playa del Rey
El Segundo
Manhattan Beach
Hermosa Beach
Redondo Beach
Palos Verdes Estates
San Pedro
Long Beach
Los Angeles
Santa Monica Bay
Pacific Ocean
Two Harbors
Santa Catalina Island
Avalon
Santa Catalina Island is approximately 22 miles south of San Pedro.
Beyond the County Line
North of Malibu—page 233
South of Long Beach—page 101
Map of Southern California—page 20

Los Angeles County Beaches

(continued on page 156)

Map of Southern California—page 20

Los Angeles County

Key to the Symbols

Bike path · Camping · Food and drink · Hiking · Nude

Pier · RVs allowed · Surfing · Volleyball

Crowd Rating

sweet solitude . . . moderate crowds . . . wall-to-wall

Overall Rating

1 don't bother . . . 3 worth a visit . . . 5 beach heaven

 Map of Los Angeles County beaches—page 154

Santa Catalina Island

Location: 22 miles off the California coast and closest to the mainland city of San Pedro. The only communities on the island are at Avalon (the center of island activity) and Two Harbors. The best beaches, though difficult to reach, lie on the island's west side.
Population: 3,000
Area Code: 310 **Zip Code:** 90704

To visit Santa Catalina Island is to step back into the past. The prehistoric past, that is. Most of the island—86 percent of its 76 square miles, to be exact—is owned and protected by the Santa Catalina Island Conservancy, a nonprofit outfit that has maintained it as a wilderness preserve since 1972. Consequently, Catalina looks the way it did when sun-worshipping Native Americans inhabited it 4,000 years ago. Even the Spaniards, who arrived with Cabrillo in 1542 and again with Viscaino in 1602, didn't leave any scuff marks behind.

Catalina Island's Climate

Catalina Island Averages

	Daily High Temp. (°F)	Daily Low Temp. (°F)	Water Temp. (°F)
January	63	49	57
February	62	49	57
March	61	50	57
April	65	53	59
May	67	54	63
June	70	57	64
July	73	61	67
August	72	62	68
September	74	61	70
October	73	58	68
November	70	53	64
December	63	46	59
Yearly Average	**68**	**54**	**63**

Source: National Weather Service data, National Oceanographic and Atmospheric Administration.

Catalina is a rugged, rocky island that is 21 miles long and 8 miles wide. Its jagged green hills rise out of the Pacific Ocean. Mount Oriaba, at 2,069 feet, is the highest peak. On days when the Santa Ana winds blow Southern California's smog away, Los Angelenos can clearly see the island.

Because the natural order has been allowed to prevail, Catalina Island is a different world from mainland California. The ecosystem is unique, with several species of plants and animals endemic only to the island. The most celebrated flora is the Catalina ironwood, a tree that teeters on the brink of extinction; only two wild groves are left. A total of 395 species of plant life are native to Catalina, and a fascinating variety of animals make their home here. The island has its own subspecies of ground squirrel and fox, the latter a beautiful but elusive creature. Buffalo freely roam the island's interior. An original herd of 14 buffalo was brought here in 1924 for the filming of *The Vanishing American;* now it numbers 400. Wild pigs, goats, and deer also have the run of the place, and some of the world's finest purebred Arabian horses are raised at El Rancho Escondido, a private ranch that is separate from the conservancy.

Unfortunately for visitors (but fortunately, in the long run, for the wild plant and animal life here), the average Joe and Josephine can't reach many of the island's natural wonders, because human exploration is fairly restricted. Hiking, biking, backpacking, and camping are permitted on a limited basis. Free permits, trail maps, rules, and regulations are available at (and required by) the conservancy. You can obtain these at their headquarters (206 Metropole Avenue, 510-1421) or information center (302 Crescent Avenue, 510-2500). Los Angeles County runs three campgrounds on the island, and a separate permit is required for each one. Permits are available from (and required by) the L.A. County

Getting To and From Catalina

Although passenger ferries to Santa Catalina Island leave from three mainland points (Long Beach, San Pedro, and Newport Beach), the logistics are about the same. Round-trip fare for adults is approximately $21 to $25; for kids, $19 to $21; and for infants, $2. Parking on the mainland is not included and generally costs $7.50 a day at the terminal. The extremely relaxing passage over to Catalina takes about two hours one-way. It costs an additional $3 to $5 to bring a bike or a surfboard.

- Catalina Cruises: Boats depart daily from Long Beach to Avalon and Two Harbors. Call (310) 510-0325 or (800) CATALINA for reservations.
- Catalina Express Commuter: Boats run year-round from San Pedro and Long Beach terminals to Avalon and Two Harbors. Call (310) 519-1212 for reservations.
- Catalina Flyer: This catamaran departs Balboa Pavilion in Newport Beach daily. For reservations, call (714) 673-5245.
- Catalina-Vegas Airlines: A 40-minute flight from San Diego to Airport in the Sky at mid-island is available. Call (619) 292-7311 for reservations.
- Helitrans Air Service: Regular helicopter transport is available from Long Beach, San Pedro, and Costa Mesa. Call (310) 548-1314 for reservations.

Department of Parks and Recreation (P.O. Box 1133, 510-0688). The camps are Bird Park (near the harbor at Avalon), Black Jack Campground (nine miles inland from Avalon), and Little Harbor Campground (seven miles from Two Harbors, on the west side of the island). Trails to the campgrounds aren't exactly easy strolls through the clover, and the island is really too mountainous for bicyclists who don't regularly race in cross-country marathons. Unless you live here, driving a car on the island is out of the question. The ferries that bring you here are passenger-only.

All of these permits and prohibitions are sensible and laudable. They keep the island free of Jeep-driving bozos waving shotguns at the wild buffalo. The flip side to this, though, is that most visitors are off-loaded into the harborfront encampment of Avalon and see little more of the island. Avalon lies on the eastern side of Catalina, facing the mainland. Passenger ferries from San Pedro, Long Beach, and Newport Beach dock here, making the town something of a tourist side-pocket on the otherwise empty green billiard table of Catalina Island.

The first person we encountered at the end of the ferry gangplank at the Green Pleasure Pier in Avalon was a bearded son of a gun with a sailor's cap scrunched atop his gnarled web of red hair. With no encouragement from us—we were perfectly content to lug our bags—he pronounced himself "our man." This meant that for a modest fee he'd tote our bags to the hotel, which he warned was "all the way over on the other side of town." Avalon is all of one square mile, and many of its hotels are within easy walking distance of the harbor. Our man no doubt serves some useful purpose here. Just decide before being browbeaten by him or his like whether you can manage for yourself.

There are excellent ways to see other parts of the island without having to trek like sherpas.

Several different bus tours depart the Avalon Harbor area regularly, and taxis can be hired for private trips. The most reasonable of the bus tours is the Skyline Drive ($10.50 for adults, $7 for kids), a two-hour trip that ventures 10 miles into the heart of the conservancy. The Inland Motor Tour ($19.50 for adults, $12.50 for kids) is a four-hour version of the trip. Glass-bottomed boat tours ($5 for adults, $3.25 for kids) operate out of Avalon Harbor, offering eyewitness proof of the prodigious underwater life teeming in the blue-green waters. Other boat tours sail around the southern tip of Catalina to the western side of the island, where the only other "town," Two Harbors, is located. Two Harbors is a jumping-off point for some of the best hiking trails on Catalina. There are snorkeling tours, too, and buffet cruises. For information on tours, call or drop by the Catalina Island Visitors Bureau, located on the Green Pleasure Pier (510-1520), or Two Harbors Visitor Services (211 Catalina Avenue in Avalon and at the foot of the main pier in Two Harbors, 510-2800).

Many people travel to the island from the mainland on their own boats, at times turning the channel into a watery version of the Santa Ana Freeway. Some even swim over from Los Angeles. Each year, an Ocean Marathon is held; the record time is 7.5 hours.

The salvation of our visit was a golf cart. Everyone on Catalina uses them, and they can be rented for $15 to $20 an hour, or around $50 for an entire day. After two hours of exhilarating travel into the arrow-marked hills above Avalon, we had seen everything we wanted to see. We also got a sufficiently uplifting feel for the natural riches of the island's interior to make us fantasize about a backpacking expedition at some later date.

Steer your golf cart south out of Avalon on Pebbly Beach Road. This state route hugs the shoreline, revealing placid waters with a rocky bottom—perfect for snorkeling and scuba diving, not so hot for swimming (*brrrr*). After two miles, the road moves inland, up a steep and winding grade that peaks at Mount Ada and the Wrigley Mansion. Incredible as it may seem, Catalina Island used to belong to William Wrigley Jr., the chewing-gum magnate and owner of the Chicago Cubs. Upon his death, he deeded the island to the organization that now maintains it as a nature conservancy. Along this route, you'll pass the second oldest golf course in the country. It's a nine-holer wedged into a rugged canyon in 1892. The road also skirts the now-overgrown field where the Cubs held their spring training from 1921 to 1951 (with four years off for World War II). A piece of trivia: Ronald Reagan, the Cubs' radio broadcaster, often followed the team to Catalina.

The nicest of Wrigley's legacies are the William Wrigley Jr. Botanical Gardens. The Wrigley Memorial, set at the top of the gardens, is an imposing structure (232 feet by 130 feet) that dwarfs the surrounding Avalon Canyon like a misplaced Lincoln Memorial. The memorial took a year to build, and plaques attest to its tonnage, craftsmanship, and sturdiness. The plaque at the courtyard entrance reads: "The building is dedicated to William Wrigley Jr., who in 1919 recognized the potential of Santa Catalina as a nature preserve."

The gardens next to the memorial are a pleasure to stroll. Laid out in sections, they feature Catalina's indigenous plants, as well as oddities from around the world like South Africa's red-hot poker. The most intriguing part of the garden is the separate wing devoted to cacti, some of which are the strangest and most Freudian we've ever seen.

One other noteworthy attraction is the Casino, a Mediterranean-style structure built by Wrigley on Avalon harbor in 1929. It dominates the waterfront the way Wrigley's memorial overwhelms Avalon Canyon. At one time, big bands blew hot and cool in the ballroom of this nongambling casino, which has also been used as a backdrop in many Hollywood films. Today, the Catalina Island Museum, featuring historic artifacts of human habitation on the island, is housed in its basement, and first-run movies play on the first floor.

Beaches

Crescent Beach (in Avalon) and **Pebbly Beach** (just south of Avalon) provide access to chilly, waveless harbor water. Crescent Beach has a bathhouse at 228 Crescent Avenue with lockers and a laundry. The beach itself is a tiny line of sand upon which you might place towels. A private beach, **Descanso Beach**, can be accessed via the beach club near the casino. Nonmembers must pay for access to this safe, sandy beach and its cabanas. Cove beaches can also be found farther up the north side of the island, above Avalon. (Gallagher Beach, Lava Wall Beach, and Starlight Beach are among the ones

Ben Weston Beach

Location: On Santa Catalina Island, at the end of Middle Canyon Trail, 11.5 miles south of Two Harbors. The road to Ben Weston Beach was washed out during January 1995 rainstorms; it remained closed as this book went to press.

Parking: Cars are not allowed on Santa Catalina Island. Golf carts can be rented and driven within the city limits of Avalon and parked in designated spaces. Tour buses, biking, and hiking are the only means of exploring the island outside Avalon.

Hours: A hiking, camping, or biking permit is needed to travel anywhere more than a mile beyond the city limits of Avalon at any time. Hikers and bikers must return by dusk. Daily hiking permits are free. Biking permits are $50 per person and $75 per family and are good for a year (from May 1 through April 30). Overnight camping permits cost $6.50 per person, per night. Permits can be obtained at the Santa Catalina Conservancy office in Avalon, at Airport in the Sky (the island's airport), and at the Two Harbors Visitor Services Office.

Facilities: Picnic area.

Contact: For beach information, contact the Santa Catalina Island Conservancy at (310) 510-1421.

See number 4 on page 154.

Crescent Beach

Location: On Santa Catalina Island, along Crescent Avenue at the Green Pleasure Pier in Avalon.

Parking: Cars are not allowed on Santa Catalina Island. Golf carts can be rented and driven within the city limits of Avalon and parked in designated spaces.

Hours: Open 24 hours.

Facilities: Lifeguards and rest rooms.

Contact: For beach information, contact the Santa Catalina Island Conservancy at (310) 510-1421.

See number 2 on page 154.

Descanso Beach

Location: On Santa Catalina Island, at the Beach Club next to the Casino on Avalon Harbor. The fee to use the beach is $1.50 per person.

Parking: Cars are not allowed on Santa Catalina Island. Golf carts can be rented and driven within the city limits of Avalon and parked in designated spaces.

Hours: 9 AM to sunset.

Facilities: Rest rooms and showers.

Contact: For beach information, contact the Descanso Beach Club at (310) 510-7408.

See number 1 on page 154.

that have names.) This area is pocked with pebbly or sandy coves, offering environmental camping on a first-come basis. **Little Fisherman's Cove** is the site of a campground located right on the water close to Two Harbors, where you'll find a restaurant, bar, and dive shop.

The best pure ocean beaches are located on the western side of the island, necessitating a long walk, or a bus or boat ride from Two Harbors. At **Little Harbor** (see sidebar, "Paradise Found: Catalina Island's Little Harbor Beach"), a wide, sandy protected beach is a real jewel for swimmers, snorkelers, divers, and campers ($6.50 a night). Four miles south is **Ben Weston Beach**, a nice sandy cove. Again, it requires some advance planning to gain access to it—not to mention an 11.5-mile trek from Two Harbors.

Little Fisherman's Cove

Location: On Santa Catalina Island, at Two Harbors, 12 miles northwest of Avalon.

Parking: Cars are not allowed on Catalina Island. Golf carts can be rented and driven within the city limits of Avalon and parked in designated spaces. Tour buses, biking, and hiking are the only means of exploring the island outside Avalon.

Hours: A hiking, camping, or biking permit is needed to travel anywhere more than a mile beyond the city limits of Avalon at any time. Hikers and bikers must return by dusk. Daily hiking permits are free. Biking permits are $50 per person and $75 per family and are good for a year (from May 1 through April 30). Overnight camping permits cost $6.50 per person, per night. Permits can be obtained at the Santa Catalina Conservancy office in Avalon, at Airport in the Sky (the island's airport), and at the Two Harbors Visitor Services Office.

Facilities: Rest rooms, showers, picnic tables, and fire pits. There are 50 campsites for tents. Fees are $7.50 to $8.50 per person, per night. For camping reservations, call the Two Harbors Visitor Services Office at (310) 510-2800.

Contact: For beach information, contact the Santa Catalina Island Conservancy at (310) 510-1421.

See number 6 on page 154.

Little Harbor Beach

Location: Seven miles south of Two Harbors on the western side of Santa Catalina Island.

Parking: Cars are not allowed on Santa Catalina Island. Golf carts can be rented and driven within the city limits of Avalon and parked in designated spaces. Tour buses, biking, and hiking are the only means of exploring the island outside Avalon.

Hours: A hiking, camping, or biking permit is needed to travel anywhere more than a mile beyond the city limits of Avalon at any time. Hikers and bikers must return by dusk. Daily hiking permits are free. Biking permits are $50 per person and $75 per family and are good for a year (from May 1 through April 30). Overnight camping permits cost $6.50 per person, per night. Permits can be obtained at the Santa Catalina Conservancy office in Avalon, at Airport in the Sky (the island's airport), and at the Two Harbors Visitor Services Office.

Facilities: Rest rooms, showers, picnic tables, and fire pits. There are 17 campsites for tents. Fees are $7.50 to $8.50 per person, per night. For camping reservations, call Two Harbors Visitor Service Center at (310) 510-2800.

Contact: For beach information, contact the Santa Catalina Island Conservancy at (310) 510-1421.

See number 5 on page 154.

Bunking Down

First, for bicyclists and hikers, the campgrounds on Catalina are among the most secluded in California. Permits are required for bicycles and hiking, and separate permits are required for camping. The best conduit to campground reservations and hiking trails is Two Harbors Visitor Services Office (Two Harbors, 510-2800). For bike permits, contact the Catalina Island Conservancy (510-1421). The **Hermit Gulch Campground** (510-8368), a mile outside Avalon, is privately run. Two county-run campgrounds located within a reasonable hike of town—**Bird Park Campground** (75 sites) and **Black Jack Campground** (75 sites)—can be reserved through the County Parks and Recreation Department, but neither is anywhere near a beach.

Almost all of the lodgings on the island are in Avalon. In fact, Avalon seems like one large hotel. Our first night in town some years back reminded us of "Duncan," the Paul Simon song: "Couple in the next room bound to win a prize/They've been going at it all night long." We holed up in the Hotel Villa Portofino, a Mediterranean-style "villa," the brochure for which promised "a touch of Old World elegance and luxury." By "Old World," they apparently meant a windowless room with cots, a tiny shower stall, a sliding glass door for an entrance, and the thinnest walls this side of an eggshell. (If this is what the Old World was all about, we now understand why the Boston Tea Party took place.) For this, you pay over $100 or so a night. We've slept more peacefully on top of picnic tables.

The next night, we found sane and commodious sanctuary at the **Pavilion Lodge** (513 Crescent Avenue, P.O. Box 737, 510-2500, $$). The lodge spreads back from the harborfront street into a landscaped courtyard, replete with a two-ton piece of redwood that drifted from the mainland and was placed here with the aid of several trucks, tractors, and herniated laborers. The rooms are quiet and comfortable, too. Ah, golden slumbers.

The most venerable hotel in town is the **Glenmore Plaza Hotel** (120 Sumner Avenue, 510-0017, $$). This pastel-tinted beauty is over a century old and has hosted such eminences as Teddy Roosevelt (who hunted on the island) and Clark Gable. The wicker-filled rooms are airy and large, and the room rate includes wine and cheese in the courtyard each afternoon and a continental breakfast. However, the poshest of Avalon's hotels is the **Hotel Metropole** (205 Crescent Avenue, 510-1884, $$$), a three-story beauty set in the Metropole Marketplace, overlooking Avalon Harbor.

Over at Two Harbors, lodging can be found at the **Banning House Lodge** (Two Harbors, 510-2800, $$$), an 11-room B&B built in 1910 as a summer home for the Bannings, two island-owner siblings. This homey, unpretentious inn looks out over Two Harbors' Isthmus Cove from its hillside perch.

Crowds throng to Catalina Island in the summer, but the island is no less charming during its "undiscovered season," from September to April, when the room rates run con-

Pebbly Beach

Location: On Santa Catalina Island, along Pebbly Beach Road, one mile southeast of Avalon Harbor.

Parking: Cars are not allowed on Santa Catalina Island. Golf carts can be rented and driven within the city limits of Avalon and parked in designated spaces. Tour buses, biking, and hiking are the only means of exploring the island outside Avalon.

Hours: Open 24 hours.

Facilities: None.

Contact: For beach information, contact the Santa Catalina Island Conservancy at (310) 510-1421.

See number 3 on page 154.

siderably lower. Oh, and there's nary a chain hotel or motel to be found.

Coastal Cuisine

Around dinnertime one evening, an elderly gentleman with hearing aids and a cane stood wheezing in front of a seafood restaurant on Crescent Avenue, Avalon's waterfront thoroughfare. Winded from his search for a suitable meal—a stroll that had covered three blocks and several posted menus—he turned on his wife when she sweetly suggested they eat at a place with a "pot roast and potato pancake" special. "I'm not going to put that junk in my mouth!" he cried in frustration. Propped up by his cane, he turned and shuffled

Paradise Found: Catalina Island's Little Harbor Beach

Though most of Santa Catalina Island's visitors confine their explorations to Avalon, there is an up-island sanctuary that is well worth checking out. Little Harbor Beach is a palm-fringed, crescent-shaped semitropical paradise located midway down the windward, southwest-facing side of the island. Mountains rising to heights of more than 2,000 feet form a stunning backdrop for the wide, sandy cove. Little Harbor is actually three (click), three (click), three beaches in one: there's Little Harbor proper, which has a beachside campground; a small, unnamed cove that's a Gauguin-in-Tahiti paradise; and then Shark's Cove. The three adjacent coves, separated by rocky protrusions, amount to about one-third of a mile of wild, gorgeous beach out of range of civilization.

Getting to this end of the island is half the fun, particularly if you enjoy a long hike. The cross-island hike to Little Harbor can be undertaken from Avalon or Two Harbors, the island's two population centers. The trek from Avalon is longer and more arduous, following a calf-bruising 17-mile trail that ascends spiny ridges and drops into canyons. The 6.8-mile walk from Two Harbors can be made either along the main road, which passes by Little Harbor en route to Avalon, or via the Banning House Road Trail. The latter is more interesting and invigorating, hugging the coastline and making significant elevation changes.

The 17-site campground at Little Harbor comes equipped with outdoor showers, chemical toilets, and running water. Some visitors arrive via private boat, anchoring offshore and camping at Little Harbor. Anglers catch halibut and sun worshippers catch rays on the beach. Little Harbor is protected from the ocean by a small peninsula and offshore reef, making it excellent for snorkeling and scuba diving. Shark Harbor, which adjoins Little Harbor, gets the wave action and is good for bodysurfing and boogie boarding. Have no fear of the name, however. Shark Harbor is named for a rock that looks like the dorsal fin of a great white.

Kayaks, diving gear, backpacking equipment, and more can be rented at the Two Harbors Visitor Services (310-510-2800), at the foot of the main pier in Two Harbors. The same outfit runs buses out to Little Harbor, arranges interisland and cross-channel transportation, assists in travel planning, and issues camping and hiking permits.

farther down the street, bound and determined to find something more to his liking.

Most visitors to Catalina Island find themselves in the same, ahem, boat. A hungry army, they wander the quaint Mediterranean streets of Avalon at sundown, studying one menu after another for some clue as to the cuisine. Much of the seafood here is brought over from the mainland. Even the little pier-side food hut serves a pretty bland paper boatload of fish-and-chips. They also offer Abalone Burgers and Buffalo Burgers, which were described to us by a buffalo-booster as being "leaner than beef." Even the restaurant touted as the best seafood place in Avalon seemed suspect. Upon close inspection, the posted review upon which the place built its reputation turned out to be a thinly veiled pan.

Solomon's Landing (101 Marilla Street, 510-1474, $$) at least offers a nice indoor/outdoor patio and a few fresh seafood entrées mingled among the Mexican specialties. The best bet for seafood—and the only seafood restaurant on Avalon Bay—is **Armstrong's Fish Market & Seafood Restaurant** (306 Crescent Avenue, 510-0113, $$).

One night years ago during our first visit to the island, we settled on **Antonio's Pizzeria & Cabaret** (230 Crescent Avenue, 510-0008, $) because of the intriguing sign in the window: "This restaurant has been declared a genuine Catalina bomb shelter—come on in and bask in the ambience of the decaying '50s while the world passes on." The place has moved from its original Sumner Street haunt to Crescent Avenue, into a building that is not bomb-proof, but where the spirit of the original lives on.

Night Moves

Unless you know someone at the members-only Catalina Yacht Club or the Tuna Club—the latter of which was founded in 1898 and has boasted Winston Churchill, Richard Nixon, King Olaf, and Hal Roach as members—your night moves will be as humble as the lonely buffalo. The only live music we could scare up around town was a guitar strummer named Tony Baloney, a self-professed human jukebox who claims to know 500 songs and takes requests. The best places to drink sans entertainment are the lounge inside **Solomon's Landing** (101 Marilla Street, 510-1474) or at **J.L.'s Locker Room** (126 Sumner Street, 510-0258), a sports bar. Rams, Angels, and Dodgers photos adorn the walls, some inscribed to J.L. himself by players who have come all the way to Catalina to quaff a cold one at his pub.

For More Information

Contact the Catalina Island Chamber of Commerce and Visitors Bureau, 1 Green Pleasure Pier, P.O. Box 217, Avalon, CA 90704; (310) 510-1520.

Long Beach

Location: Long Beach is situated in southern Los Angeles County, 22 miles south of Los Angeles and northeast of Catalina Island. Both Interstate 405 and Highway 1 (Pacific Coast Highway) pass through Long Beach, while Ocean Avenue runs alongside its beachfront. Long Beach City Beach is the main ocean beach in the vicinity, running for four miles between downtown Long Beach and the San Gabriel River.
Population: 442,000
Area Code: 310 **Zip Code:** 90802

This is a city whose fortunes rise and fall with those of a humongous British cruise ship. The Queen Mary is to Long Beach what London Bridge is to Lake Havasu City, Arizona: a grand relic of the crumbling British empire purchased and brought to America to confer a borrowed identity upon a place that has little of its own. In 1967, the ailing city of Long Beach welcomed the arrival of the Queen Mary, the world's largest ocean liner, which had itself fallen on hard times. (By then, people much preferred the convenience of flying to making the passage by water.) The old boat was docked in the Port of Long Beach and refurbished into a combination hotel and tourist attraction. More important, perhaps, was the symbolism of the luxury liner. Laid to rest in Long Beach after 1,001 transatlantic crossings, the grand dame of the high seas became the city's beacon for a hopeful future.

It hasn't quite worked out that way. The Queen Mary has had good years and bad years, in terms of generating tourist revenue, but it's become more like an albatross than a savior. When the boat was rechristened on September 26, 1994, exactly 60 years after being launched on its maiden voyage in Clydebank, Scotland, the grandson of the vessel's namesake broke a bottle of champagne on her hull. Only a few hundred people bothered to show up for the occasion. The previous year, an editorial in the *Long Beach Press-Telegram* posed the question, "Who will save the Queen?" Citing maintenance problems, declining attendance, and the need for massive capital improvements at a time when no funding could be found, the editorial concluded: "The signal coming from the Queen Mary isn't all that clear, but it's beginning to sound like an S.O.S."

We can only second that opinion. The Queen Mary was eerily deserted during our stay in mid-July of 1994. It was a time when the World Cup Soccer playoffs were in progress a stone's throw away in Los Angeles, and business should have been brisk. But we saw precious few other paying customers aboard the boat during our stay: two elderly couples dancing to a jazz trio that was playing for an otherwise empty house at the Observation Bar; a smattering of foreigners as confused as we were about the layout of the boat; and the Hispanic housekeeping staff, who could not tell us how to get from point A to point B.

We were assured that the Queen Mary, like the Long Beach Convention Center and all the surrounding hotels and restaurants that serve business travelers, does the bulk of its business from August to November, the designated convention season. Even so, the historic vessel—a living museum that served both as a luxury liner "where the rich and famous took their ease" and as a World War II troop carrier—should be hauling aboard at least a moderate catch of tourist business during summer months. Though it proudly holds onto its regal bearing, these are not the best of times for the grounded Queen or the community that sprawls at her feet.

The truth hurts, but Long Beach is simply not a prime vacation destination. Beyond the Queen Mary, this is a town ruled by its harbor, which exists to serve naval and shipping interests first and foremost. Away from the harbor,

Queen Mary Facts 'n' Figgers

Number of workers involved in construction: 300,000

Date work began: December 1, 1930

Date launched: September 26, 1934

Maiden voyage: May 27, 1936

Date retired: September 19, 1967

Number of transatlantic crossings: 1,001

Period of wartime service: 6.5 years (March 1940 to September 1946)

Number of troops transported in World War II: 765,429

Number of miles sailed in World War II: 569,429

Bounty placed on ship by Adolf Hitler: $250,000

World War II nickname: "The Gray Ghost"

Passenger capacity: 1,957

Officers and crew: 1,174

Number of decks: 12

Number of lifeboats: 24

Number of portholes: 2,000

Number of rivets: 10 million

Length of ship: 1,020 feet

Weight of ship: 90,985 tons

Height of ship (keel to top deck): 92 feet

Cruising speed: 34 mph

Fuel consumption: 0.0025 miles per gallon (13 feet per gallon)

Fuel consumed per crossing (from Southampton, England, to New York City): 1,267,600 gallons

Fresh meat consumed per crossing: 77,000 pounds (38.5 tons)

Capacity of wine cellar: 15,000 bottles

Record number of passengers carried at one time: 16,683 (during World War II)

Record time, Atlantic crossing: 4 days, 10 hours, 6 minutes (August 24–29, 1966)

The Queen Mary is open year-round from 10 AM to 6 PM. It is located at the south end of Interstate 710 (Long Beach Freeway). Self-guided tours cost about $7 for adults, $6 for seniors 55 and up, and $4 for children ages 4 to 11. For more information, contact the Queen Mary Seaport, 1126 Queens Highway, Long Beach, CA 90802; (310) 435-3511.

it is a big city (the fifth largest in California) with big-city problems and without sufficient big-city compensations to make it tolerable or interesting. Local pundits and public-relations people are essentially reduced to touting entertainment and recreational options that surround Long Beach rather than Long Beach itself: Disneyland, Santa Catalina Island, Knott's Berry Farm, and (hey ho!) the Movieland Wax Museum. Worse, the Queen Mary's companion in tourism—the Spruce Goose, a gargantuan wooden airplane that never flew, built by Howard Hughes before he began growing his fingernails—was sold off in 1992 and hauled away to Oregon. In its place, we were told by a proud Mary staffer, they were erecting sets for the filming of *Batman Forever*. After the Queen Mary has been talked up and talked out, antsy visitors find themselves in figurative dry dock, their remaining options running to things like driving past the world's largest whale mural, which covers the Long Beach Sports

Arena. A local columnist, attempting a feel-good rah-rah on behalf of downtown, wrote the following, which confirmed our worst suspicions: "Anything can happen downtown. If it rains, you get wet. If it's hot out, you sweat. Panhandlers may ask you for money. A few people get mugged. Downtown is life. And it appears to be on the rebound."

Well, at least it appears to be trying. The downtown intersection of Broadway and Pine Avenue is the center of an urban island that is in the process of being gentrified. The concentration of music clubs, restaurants, movie theaters, and coffeehouses into a compact area is a theme we saw repeated elsewhere in metropolitan Southern California (such as in Santa Monica). There's safety and strength in numbers, it seems, and yet the sleaze element can still violate the permeable borders. The entire neighborhood throbs in hot pink and purple neon, implicitly buzzing the message "class and cool" but instead saying "trendy urban cliché." But at least there is good food and music to be had in downtown Long Beach, and it felt reasonably secure—or so we thought. Our walk to a destination well within the borders of this safe haven required a hasty U-turn when a crowd of menacing homeboys appeared to be blocking the sidewalk. An ashen-faced couple came sprinting up the street from their direction, so we decided to bail out as well, rather than risk becoming another crime statistic.

Since 1975, more than $1.3 billion has been pumped into redeveloping Long Beach's shoreline and downtown. The principal drawing card is the Long Beach Convention and Entertainment Center—192,000 square feet of meeting and exhibit space. More revitalization is on the way in hopes of turning around the stagnant local economy. The Queensway Bay project, which has a $566 million price tag, would revitalize the downtown waterfront by moving the Queen Mary from its current berthing place to a more accessible site by a pier at the foot of Pine Avenue. What is now the Shoreline Aquatic Park would be turned into a new downtown harbor, including a five-berth cruise-ship terminal and a $40 million aquarium. As big as these plans may seem, they're a mere consolation prize compared with the $3 billion "DisneySea" theme park that was planned for the same site and abandoned by Disney because of opposition from the California Coastal Commission.

In the meantime, the area is hurting—especially Shoreline Village, a complex of shops constructed in New England fishing-village chic. People can't easily drive to it because of various construction projects, and it is too far from the downtown area to be reached on foot. Without something like the Queensway Bay redevelopment, the downtown waterfront area may well go bust before long.

As if all that weren't discouraging enough, the city took a direct hit on June 23, 1995—a day referred to as "Black Friday" by the *Long Beach Press-Telegram*—when the Defense Base Closure and Realignment Commission announced the scheduled 1997 closing of the Long Beach Naval Shipyard. What Long Beach will lose, aside from a critical piece of its history and identity, is 3,100 military jobs, which will trigger the further loss of an estimated 6,000 civilian jobs and about $757 million a year in lost wages and spending. Ouch. The announcement came a year after the Long Beach Naval Station and the Long Beach Naval Hospital closed their doors, taking a staggering 17,500 military and civilian jobs from the community. That shutdown had first been announced in 1991, during an earlier round of downsizing. Presently plans are afoot to build a huge shopping center and entertainment complex on the site of the former naval hospital. The question is, who will have any money to buy anything?

Though most visitors never see it, there's more to Long Beach than the downtown waterfront. Miles and miles of poor, ethnic neighborhoods roll inland. One blighted ghetto bears the nickname "Dogtown." On a brighter note, Belmont Shore, a quasi-self-contained neighborhood along the water in south Long Beach, boasts excellent ocean and bay-beach access and lively shopping and nightlife along Second Street. It you find yourself priced out of the high-rise hotels near the Long Beach Convention and Entertainment Center, Belmont Shore is a viable place to stay. We prefer it, in fact. Long Beach, when all is said and done, is really more oriented to convention business than pleasure travelers. It is better described as a jumping-off point for attractions in the surrounding area than a bona fide destination in and of itself.

Beaches

Away from the downtown waterfront redevelopment zone, which looks as if it will be under construction well into the next century, there are some fine neighborhoods to be found along the water in Long Beach. Heading south along Ocean Boulevard from the Long Beach Freeway to its end at Alamitos Bay in Belmont Shore, you pass miles of beautifully landscaped, architecturally varied homes facing the green, linear Bluff Park that runs along the oceanfront. Long Beach has its own sandy, extensive city beach, but water quality can be poor and the offshore breakwater keeps the waves at bay, so to speak. Yes, the same breakwater that makes Long Beach's man-made harbor the busiest port on the West Coast cuts off the surf completely. The ocean is calmer than a farm pond. No waves roll ashore here, forcing natives to head to points north and south to surf and swim. Over a Memorial Day weekend, the beach was all but empty. Those who could afford to had high-tailed it out of Long Beach for Santa Catalina Island or the Baja Peninsula. The rest simply threw surfboards and wet suits in the back and pointed their wheels to Huntington Beach.

Long Beach City Beach runs for four miles, between First Place and 72nd Place seaward of Ocean Avenue. It's a nice expanse of sand, but there are much better ocean beaches in the vicinity—for instance, Seal Beach (see the entry on page 150) or the beaches of the South Bay Peninsula. The city beach is bisected by Belmont Pier, a 1,620-foot pier used by locals who appear not to be fishing for recreation but out of necessity, angling for their dinner. Looking across the rippled waters of Long Beach Harbor, one spies what appears to be a series of small resort islands with 10-story hotels built on them. They are, in fact, oil derricks, dressed up to be more appealing from

Alamitos Bay Beach
(a.k.a. Horny Corners)

4

Location: In the Belmont Shore area of Long Beach, along Bayshore Drive and Second Street.

Parking: Free street parking.

Hours: 5 AM to 10 PM.

Facilities: Lifeguards and rest rooms.

Contact: For beach information, contact Long Beach Marine Services at (310) 594-0951.

See number 7 on page 154.

Belmont Shore

3

Location: In the Belmont Shore area of Long Beach, along Ocean Boulevard between 39th and 54th Places.

Parking: Metered street parking.

Hours: 5 AM to 10 PM.

Facilities: Lifeguards and rest rooms.

Contact: For beach information, contact Long Beach Marine Services at (310) 594-0951.

See number 8 on page 154.

the vantage point of the shoreline. These artificial islands received their designer look from the Disney organization. Named after dead astronauts (e.g., Island Grissom, Island Chaffee), hidden behind high-rise camouflage and bathed in peach and green lighting, Long Beach's offshore oil industry is nothing if not innovative, at least in its exterior design.

The best beach in Long Beach turns out to be on the bay—specifically, the inner flank of **Alamitos Bay** in **Belmont Shore**. It's a calm-water strip of sand that runs along Bay Shore Drive between Ocean Avenue and Second Street. Locals refer to this bayside beach with an informal nickname: Horny Corners. Old folks, young kids, hot babes from Cal State Long Beach, scarlet-skinned dudes with yellow hair—all are content to lay prone on a beach towel, greased with tanning oil. Some fling Frisbees, others read or gawk at the flesh parade, and a few rent kayaks and paddle around. Some even swim in the bay's glass-smooth waters. Bay Shore Drive is blocked off all summer, in deference to walkers, in-line skaters, and others who are traveling and playing *à pied*.

Bunking Down

There are too many high-rise hotels and not enough bodies to fill them in Long Beach. The $80 million, 398-room, 15-story **Long Beach Hilton World Trade Center** (2 World Trade Center, 90831, 983-1200, $$$), which opened in 1991, contributed further to what was already a soft, saturated hotel market. Already, plans for further new hotel construction have fallen through. Take your pick of the brand names, all of them towering above the action in the area of the convention center, downtown, and waterfront. Other impressive contenders for your lodging dollar include the **Sheraton Long Beach at Shoreline Square** (333 East Ocean Boulevard, 436-3000, $$$) and the **Hyatt Regency Long Beach** (200 South Pine Avenue, 491-1234, $$$). If you've got a yen to stay on the beach at a budget price, the **Edgewater Beach Motel** (1724 East Ocean Boulevard, 437-3090, $), fits the bill, offering views of Catalina from its deck and five-minute proximity to the downtown hubbub.

Then there's the **Hotel Queen Mary** (1126 Queens Highway, 499-3511, $$). Her 365 staterooms are the largest ever build aboard a ship. While they might have been a blast to stay in on a high-seas voyage four decades ago, today they are substantially less commodious than the rooms you'll find at one of the downtown high-rises (or even at a generic Travelodge). There's but a single porthole in each standard room that faces the water, providing a small, circular shaft of light onto the harbor. The rooms are dark and mildly claustrophobic, the bathrooms are small (and the plastic shower stalls scandalously cheap), yet the beds are comfortable and the unique experience of bunking down aboard a grand old ocean liner compensates for some of the drawbacks. To be perfectly honest, however, we'd recommend taking a daytime tour of the Queen Mary and laying your head elsewhere in Long Beach.

Long Beach City Beach

Location: In Long Beach, along Ocean Boulevard, from Belmont Pier to Alamitos Avenue.

Parking: Metered lot and street parking.

Hours: 5 AM to 10 PM.

Facilities: Lifeguards, rest rooms, and showers.

Contact: For beach information, contact the Long Beach Department of Marine Services at (310) 594-0951.

See number 9 on page 154.

Coastal Cuisine

Fine dining is a relatively recent concept in Long Beach, and one that *(continued on page 172)*

Shooting Hoops with the Toast of the Coast

We came to the Acapulco Inn looking for a Pop-a-Shot machine, a game found in many bars that allows you to fire little basketballs at a miniature net six feet away. For two guys who'd spent their college years in North Carolina, where basketball is king, an opportunity to shoot hoops, even in as scaled down a fashion as this, was a welcome diversion. Fortunately, these stand-up shooting galleries are found in all the best bars and pool halls in Southern California.

With a mound of quarters in our pockets and frosty mugs in hand, we prepared to fritter away another five bucks or so feeding our basketball jones in the corner of the Acapulco Inn, a way-cool beer bar in Belmont Shore. It is so relaxed in terms of dress code that at one time they would scissor the tie right off your neck if you dared to come here so attired. One entire wall of the place used to be covered with the remains of fancy neckwear. It's all since been taken down, but a token tie remains hung upon the wall, with this printed legend: "Jeff Sims is pissed because he lost an Oscar de la Renta."

We were beaten by a millisecond to the hoops game by a pair of dudes named Kevin and Greg. The latter was a construction foreman, the former a construction worker and one-time marine. They'd just gotten their paychecks and were spending them as quickly as possible on draft beer and miniature basketball. They asked us to join them, so we had a nightlong round-robin, four-man basketball shoot-out that grew so noisy we would have been thrown out of any other bar but this one. Kevin wore a baseball cap, smoked fat cigars, made pitchers of beer disappear like magic, and had a wicked set shot. When he found his rhythm, he racked up the points.

A nonstop talker and self-promoter, he would lapse into a deadly accurate Dick Vitale impersonation after scoring a particularly high game. "Oh, bay-bee!" he hollered, audible from inside a locked bathroom. "He's shooting out the lights to-night! Rock and roll!" He scored an evening-high 46, leaving the rest of us in the dust, and gloated to all within earshot that his score was unbeatable. That is, until one of us came along and entered what sports commentator Vitale would have referred to as "a zone," swishing one after another and mounting up a final score of 54. It silenced Kevin for a little while. He gnawed on his cigar, looking annoyed. Then he tried to top it, feverishly popping quarters, game after game, until he bounced a ball so hard in frustration that it hit the ceiling. Then he declared he had finally had enough.

At this point, he took a seat at the bar and shared with us his wisdom on any subject we cared to name. He knew everything about everything, challenging us to stump him and offering to fill in the holes in our impoverished fund of knowledge. Elvis Presley, surfing, world geography, sports, the fairer sex, bar brawling—he was a walking Jeopardy game who knew all the answers. An affable guy, likable almost in spite of himself, he embodied a good-natured self-centeredness that we'd seen across Southern California. This expressed itself in boundless braggadocio and a glaring lack of curiosity about anything outside his sphere of experience. He was the Sun King; the world revolved around him. He also made a blanket offer to drop whatever he was doing at any time to share with us his firsthand knowledge of the coast on behalf of our book. He'd be glad to take us around. In fact, we'd *better* call him, he said, jabbing a finger at us for emphasis.

Would he remember any of this in the morning? Probably not. He was a decorated marine who'd served honorably in the Persian Gulf. He also claimed to be the world's biggest Elvis Presley expert, challenging us to stump him with trivia. On one of his many trips to Graceland, he claimed, he loudly broke wind on the premises, thereby cementing some sort of spiritual bond with the King. He was very proud of this accomplishment.

He matter-of-factly gave us the lowdown on sexual mores in Southern California during the age of AIDS: "You can't just pick up women and have one-nighters anymore. They won't let you have sex for one, two, three months. You'll have to go out with them awhile and prove you're serious before they'll let you into bed with them. While you're waiting, you just have to look at your videos or skin mags or whatever gets you off."

As the beer flowed, so did his rhetoric.

- "You want to know about surfing? I've surfed up and down the coast since I was a kid. You name it: County Line. Oil Piers. Rincon. I finished sixth out of 12 in my first amateur competition. I'll take you anywhere you want to go. I can get you onto places you won't believe. I've got three boards. Used to have four. Sold one of them. Son-of-a-bitch still hasn't paid me for it."
- "I don't like fighting, I'm a Christian person, but I won't walk away from a fight. I've been in 14 bar fights and never lost once. You want to try me? [*Flexes biceps*] See that bartender? [*Motions to a strapping guy with the physique of Arnold Schwarzenegger*] I've taken down guys bigger than him. No problem."
- "What do you want to know about Elvis Presley? You wanna know Elvis? I know Elvis. I'm the biggest Elvis fan there is. I'm only 24 and I've got records, actual vinyl records, by Elvis. The Beatles? The Beach Boys? What do you want to know? I know it all." [*Puffs chest*]

We concluded that he must be the wisest man in the world, or at least in the Acapulco Inn. After all, any person who claims to have farted in the hallowed halls of Graceland can only be one miracle away from sainthood.

(continued from page 169) tends to thrive inside the pricey new convention hotels. The restaurant scene here has labored to keep pace with the city's fast-breaking redevelopment program, but these things take time. How do you convince a three-star chef to move to Long Beach—tell him that the offshore oil platforms look like the Eiffel Tower? Nonetheless, it is possible to ante up for more than fish-and-chips and saloon burgers, thanks to places like **Dominick's East Village** (555 East Ocean Boulevard, 437-0626, $$$), a New York–style Italian eatery—modeled, in fact, after Carmine's—that is housed in a downtown bank building. It's a great place to eat, with lots of atmosphere and hearty food. We defy you to go home hungry after a lunch or dinner here. Many entrées are available in half or full orders. No lightweights in the appetite department, neither of us could entirely finish even a half order (on top of soup and appetizers, granted), delicious though they were. We recommend Putanesca with Fresh Tuna, Spaghetti with Mixed Seafood, and Sautéed Calamari with Tomato Sauce and Garlic. Baked fish are served whole in a sauce of lemon, olives, and olive oil. What more can we add but "*mangia, mangia.*"

Parker's Lighthouse (435 Shoreline Village Drive, 432-6500, $$) serves some of the best seafood around. A solid reputation has ensured its survival amidst the economic vicissitudes of beleaguered Shoreline Village. Downtown, the **Pine Avenue Fish House** (100 West Broadway, 432-7463, $$$) is a terrific choice for grilled or broiled fish served with light, creative, and tasty sauces, such as Chilean Sea Bass with Dill Chardonnay Sauce (a house favorite) or Blackened Halibut with Corn Relish and Red Pepper Coulis. The award-winning cioppino—a tomato-based fisherman's stew with clams, mussels, shrimp, crab, squid, and fish—is another winning choice.

All manner of varied ethnic cuisine is available in Long Beach, but we were most surprised to find a place that served real Southern-style barbecue. The down-home fare at **Johnny Reb's Southern Smokehouse** (4663 Long Beach Boulevard, 423-7327, $$)—pit-cooked barbecue, crackling fried chicken, cole slaw, and hush puppies—sent this pair of erstwhile rebels home happier than a cold hog in warm mud.

We can't quit without mentioning **Joe Jost's** (2803 East Anaheim Avenue, 439-5446, $). It's the oldest continuously operating bar in California, and it has been run by three generations of Jost's. Papa Joe, God rest his soul, invented a deli sandwich that has become a local institution. Called Joe's Special, it consists of a hunk of Polish sausage surrounded by a slice of Swiss cheese with a pickle spear stuck into a V-shaped slit, all stuffed between mustard-slathered pieces of rye bread and wrapped in a waxed-paper handle. Joe Jost's serves hundreds of them every day, and just as much of the other house specialty, a basket of pretzels, peppers, and pickled eggs. As for what's on tap at Joe Jost's, they pump ice-cold Blitz beer, brewed in Oregon, in 20-ounce schooners.

Night Moves

The centerpiece of the Broadway/Pine Avenue downtown renaissance is a 16-screen AMC cineplex at **Pine Square** (245 Pine Avenue, 435-1355). Surrounding it are a neon galaxy of munchie parlors, coffeehouses, restaurants, and clubs. The **System M Caffe Gallery** (213-A Pine Avenue, 435-2525) is the gathering place for Long Beach's new bohemians, with gentlemen on the outdoor patio affecting pince-nez, goatees, and Kramer-like explosions of hair while sucking contemplatively on cigarettes and watching the smoke curl against the fuchsia glow of the restaurant's neon. Food, drinks, coffee, and art are served within.

In the same vicinity, the **Blue Café** (210 Promenade, 983-7111) pays homage to the electric guitar along a largely undeveloped pedestrian promenade. Regionally popular blues, rock, and alternative musicians perform here for a modest cover charge. We paid $4 apiece on a

Monday night to see a local band called Standard Fruit and had a fine time. Bathed in ubiquitous neon, it is, like every other business on this embryonic scene, an outpost of civility trying to stay afloat in a sea of economic uncertainty. Since our last visit a downtown jazz club—Birdland West, affiliated with the fabled New York City nightclub—had already bitten the dust, so who knows what lies ahead.

From there, we felt like getting rowdy, so we proceeded down to Belmont Shore, a livelier and more organic community in south Long Beach. We've always had a good time rambling around the bars and taverns of Second Street. They are jam-packed with friendly and fun-loving college kids, neighborhood residents, and navy guys out for a brew. Take your pick and pull up a bar stool. There's **Legends** (5236 East Second Street, 433-5743), a sports bar that's always abuzz with folks ogling the action on the big screen; **Panama Joe's** (5100 East Second Street, 434-7417), an upscale "meet market" that gets good bands on weekends; and our personal favorite, the **Acapulco Inn** (5283 East Second Street, 439-3517). The latter is a collegiate dive bar that's wilder than any toga party John Belushi ever attended. At the "AI," students from nearby Cal State Long Beach cut loose in a party environment so out of control on big nights that it's almost a caricature of hell-raising. The jukebox leans heavily on 1960s party favorites, while an assortment of games—including a Pop-a-Shot concession that nearly cleaned out our wallets—gives you something to do besides clutch a beer. If you can keep up with this crowd, you deserve whatever you wake up with the next morning: a hangover, a fellow party animal, or both.

For More Information

Contact the Long Beach Area Convention & Visitors Bureau, One World Trade Center, Suite 300, Long Beach, CA 90831; (310) 436-3645 or (800) 452-7829.

San Pedro

Location: 21 miles from downtown Los Angeles. Take the San Diego Freeway (Interstate 405) south to the Harbor Freeway; follow the Harbor Freeway to its end.
Population: 71,000
Area Code: 310 **Zip Code:** 90731

Tucked behind the protective, ever-changing Palos Verdes Peninsula is San Pedro, the port town for the city of Los Angeles. In 1889, after heavy competition with other bay towns like Redondo Beach, it was chosen to house Los Angeles Harbor, thanks to the good offices of Senator Stephen M. White (after whom a main drag in town is named). Before it was enlarged to its present size, the harbor was so shallow that oceangoing vessels had to be anchored offshore and loaded and unloaded from there. Today it is known as "Worldport L.A." The harbor covers 7,000 acres and 28 miles of waterfront, making it one of the largest artificial ports in the world.

Overlooking San Pedro Harbor is formidable Fort MacArthur, once an integral part of our West Coast defense posture. San Pedro is home to 70,000 people, many of whom make their living on the docks. It was also the home of one of our favorite writers, the late Charles Bukowski. He came to live in San Pedro in 1978, leaving Los Angeles after 58 years of a squalid hand-to-mouth existence. According to biographer Neeli Cherkovski, Bukowski chose San Pedro because "unlike some of the other beach towns, the spirit of the '60s hadn't settled on it." That much is true. The real lure of San Pedro for Bukowski was its proximity to the freeways, which afforded a quick escape from anonymous middle-class respectability to the racetracks at Hollywood Park and Santa Anita. Bukowski died here in 1993.

Despite the relative lack of beaches, elbowed out by the harbor, there's plenty of waterfront activity in San Pedro. The Cabrillo Marine Museum (3720 Stephen M. White Drive, 548-7562) has 38 aquariums with marine life native to Southern California, as well as a multimedia show for kids, seasonal grunion tours, and whale-watching expeditions. It's free, but parking costs $5.50. Down on the docks is the Los Angeles Maritime Museum (Berth 84, Sixth Street, 548-7618), which presents an assortment of maritime equipment, memorabilia, and historical photographs detailing the construction of the harbor and the old ferry days. In addition, you can take several tours out of San Pedro Harbor, including ferries to Santa Catalina Island and dinner and harbor cruises.

Beaches

There are a few beaches in San Pedro worth seeking out if you're in the area. The main one—and the only sandy beach in San Pedro—is **Cabrillo City Beach**, located east of Point Fermin on either side of the San Pedro Breakwater. The "harbor" side of the beach is protected and calm, with a boat-launching ramp. The "ocean" side, on the other side of the harbor fortification, receives the full force of the ocean—real waves for board surfing and windsurfing. Attached to the breakwater at Cabrillo City Beach is a 1,000-foot municipal fishing pier. **Point Fermin** is a park and lighthouse situated on a bluff overlooking the ocean; steep trails lead to the rocky shore below.

West of Point Fermin is a beach that has been split into two jurisdictions. The parking lot that lies below the cliffs at White Point is divided into **White Point County Park** (left) and **Royal Palms County Beach** (right). It's all the same beach, though: a rugged, rocky shoreline that's popular with shell collectors and surf casters. Surfers like it, too, in winter. The most unique feature of White Point/Royal Palms, though, is the presence of mineral springs that lie offshore, which divers explore. When you tire of the beach, you can always

Cabrillo City Beach

3

Location: Along Stephen M. White Drive at 40th Street in San Pedro.

Parking: $5 entrance fee per vehicle.

Hours: 5 AM to 10:30 PM.

Facilities: Lifeguards, rest rooms, showers, picnic tables, and barbecue grills.

Contact: For beach information, contact the Los Angeles County Lifeguard Service, Southern Section, at (310) 832-1179. For a surf report, call (310) 379-8471.

See number 10 on page 154.

Point Fermin Park

3

Location: Follow Interstate 110 (Harbor Freeway) south into downtown San Pedro, where it becomes Gaffey Street. Continue to its end at Paseo del Mar near the Point Fermin Lighthouse.

Parking: Free parking lot.

Hours: 6 AM to sunset.

Facilities: Rest rooms, picnic tables, and barbecue grills.

Contact: For beach information, contact the Los Angeles County Lifeguard Service, Southern Section, at (310) 832-1179. For a surf report, call (310) 379-8471.

See number 11 on page 154.

wander around the grounds of the old Royal Palms Hotel, which was washed away in a storm seven decades ago, though the royal palm trees remain.

Bunking Down

The **Best Western Sunrise Hotel** (525 South Harbor Boulevard, 548-1080, $$) is the closest hotel in town to the harbor. Rooms look out on the harbor; amenities include deluxe continental breakfast, a pool, and a Jacuzzi.

Coastal Cuisine

The **22nd Street Landing Seafood Grill & Bar** (141 West 22nd Street, 548-4400, $$$) serves more than a dozen types of fresh fish daily in a dining room that looks right out on the harbor. For seafood, it's the best choice for miles around. There's also some excellent Italian restaurants in the area. Tops among them is **Madeo Ristorante** (295 Whaler's Walk, 831-1199, $$$), adjacent to the Doubletree Hotel at Cabrillo Marina.

Night Moves

Most of the restaurants on the harbor have cocktail lounges. For a nonalcoholic alternative, duck into the **Sacred Grounds Coffee House & Art Gallery** (399 West Sixth Street, 514-0800) where art, live entertainment, and cappuccino is the house blend.

For More Information

Contact the San Pedro Peninsula Chamber of Commerce, 360 West Seventh Street, San Pedro, CA 90731; (310) 832-7272.

Royal Palms County Beach

3

Location: Take Western Avenue (Highway 213) south to its end at Paseo del Mar and turn left. Continue a quarter mile and turn right on Kay Fiorentino Drive to get to the beach. The left side of the parking lot is White Point County Park, the right side Royal Palms County Beach.

Parking: $5 entrance fee per vehicle.

Hours: 6 AM to sunset.

Facilities: Lifeguards and rest rooms.

Contact: For beach information, contact the Los Angeles County Lifeguard Service, Southern Section, at (310) 832-1179. For a surf report, call (310) 379-8471.

See number 13 on page 154.

White Point County Park

4

Location: Take Western Avenue (Highway 213) south to its end at Paseo del Mar and turn left. Continue a quarter mile and head right on Kay Fiorentino Drive to get to the beach. The left side of the parking lot is White Point County Park, the right side Royal Palms County Beach.

Parking: $5 entrance fee per vehicle.

Hours: 6 AM to sunset.

Facilities: Rest rooms.

Contact: For beach information, contact the Los Angeles County Lifeguard Service, Southern Section, at (310) 832-1179. For a surf report, call (310) 379-8471.

See number 12 on page 154.

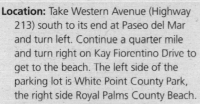

Palos Verdes Peninsula

Location: 20 miles southwest of Los Angeles, and west of San Pedro via Palos Verdes Drive or south from Torrance via Highway 107.
Population: 62,000
Area Code: 310 **Zip Code:** 90274

The enormous landmass known as the Palos Verdes Peninsula, located in the southwest corner of Los Angeles County, is one that will (as Muhammad Ali used to say) "shock and amaze ya." As is the case in the northern part of the county—with the Santa Monica Mountains, the Malibu Peninsula, and the Hollywood Hills—the Palos Verdes Peninsula is an example of the incredible diversity of landforms found in and around the City of Angels.

This craggy, lunarlike peninsula is no party to the smog dish of the Los Angeles Basin. Even though its jagged, cliff-lined shore embraces 15 miles of Pacific coastline—from San Pedro to Torrance—the Pacific Coast Highway doesn't come near it. Instead, it moves inland, leaving the tough, shifting terrain of the peninsula to the hermitic wishes of the folks who live out here on the edge of the planet.

Driving around this wondrous peninsula entails following a series of small, winding back roads that pass through a quaking, unsettled landscape. Along this Jell-O-like terrain, a road sign warns of "Constant Land Movement Next 8 Miles." What could this mean? we wondered. A road that jiggles like the 25-cent "magic fingers" in our motel room? It means that sections of the road, particularly in the vicinity of Portuguese Bend, look like they've just been removed from a waffle iron and have more dips in them than an amusement-park roller coaster. The land here actually moves at a rate of one to six inches a month and has been doing so since the mid-1950s, when highway blasting caused the top layer of rock to separate from and slip over the lower layer (a phenomenon known as "block-glide").

You will find yourself holding your breath for reasons other than fear, however, as one seductive panorama of sky, sea, and headlands follows another until you work your way off the peninsula at Torrance. Depending on how you approach it, the drive is either an unexpectedly nice side trip or the most unique way to enter the backdoor of Los Angeles. At one time, the entire peninsula was the *rancho* of the Sepulveda family, until they sold it in 1914 to a company with plans to develop it as a "millionaire's colony." To that end, they called in the landscape firm of Olmstead and Olmstead (sons of Frederick Law Olmstead, designer of New York's Central Park). The Olmstead brothers planted trees on the barren lands and built houses among them, and the millionaires dug in for the long haul. They're still dug in out here, although the nerve-jangling land movement has driven many to abandon the sloping Portuguese Bend area. The houses that didn't slip into the drink have been sold off for a song to intrepid souls unafraid to live in them. Yet the neighborhoods behind the falling ridge remain some of the most exclusive properties in Los Angeles.

Beaches

The small, sandy coves on the Palos Verdes Peninsula are difficult to get to, but they are among the most prized in the county, due partly to their very inaccessibility. The most visited are **Malaga Cove** and **Abalone Cove Beach**. Malaga Cove—also known as RAT (for "Right After Torrance")—is the only true sand beach on the peninsula. It's popular with surfers and swimmers who climb down with their boards and towels from the paved access point at Via Arroyo, off Palos Verdes Drive West. There's a small, free parking lot. Abalone Cove, which straddles the legendary Portuguese Bend off Palos Verdes Drive South, can be reached via a pay parking lot.

 Map of Los Angeles County beaches—page 154

Even if you don't take the plunge to the beaches, the cliff-hugging route along the outer rim of Palos Verdes makes for an exciting afternoon drive. Particularly appealing is Paseo del Mar, a loop road that leaves Palos Verdes Drive and cuts through Palos Verdes Estates Shoreline Preserve, which runs for 4.5 miles and comprises 130 city-owned acres above a bluff top. Several precipitous paths leave the bluff top and zigzag down to cove beaches at Lunada Bay, Bluff Cove, and Malaga Cove. On the southwestern corner of the peninsula, the small Point Vicente Park offers free parking, rest rooms, a whale-watching deck, and displays that interpret local history and ecology. At the park's pullout is a dirt trail leading to Point Vicente Fishing Access. This magical fishing hole draws skin and scuba divers as well as anglers. South of Point Vicente Park is the Point Vicente Light house, which was built in 1926 and is now closed to the public.

The splendid architecture on the peninsula is worth checking out from a car window. It is something every developer should witness and learn from. Hidden among the trees and hills, the human habitations don't try to compete with the grandeur of the landscape. This philosophy of architectural noninterference reaches a zenith with the Wayfarers Chapel (5755 Palos Verdes Drive South, 377-1650), located on the mainland side of the road just beyond Portuguese Bend. Built in 1946 by Lloyd Wright (son of Frank), the predominantly glass edifice allows worshippers (devotees of the theologian Emanuel Swedenborg) to feel as if they're outdoors among the redwoods and gardens that surround the chapel. It is open to the public daily from 11 AM to 4 PM. A small museum on the grounds has exhibits about "Swedenborgianism" and Helen Keller, a practitioner thereof.

One final note: it was on Palos Verdes that Marineland of the Pacific was built in 1954. Once the home and playpen for a small navy of Flippers, Orcas, and Jaws, the three-ring aquatic circus is long gone. The park's inaccessibility is the reason for its financial demise. The property was sold off, presumably to an eccentric millionaire with a penchant for large swimming pools.

For More Information

Contact the Palos Verdes Peninsula Chamber of Commerce, P.O. Box 2484, Palos Verde, CA 90274; (310) 377-8111.

Abalone Cove Beach

Location: On the southwest corner of the Palos Verdes Peninsula, along Palos Verdes Drive at Narcissa Drive.

Parking: $4 entrance fee per vehicle.

Hours: 6 AM to sunset.

Facilities: Lifeguards, rest rooms, and picnic area.

Contact: For beach information, contact the Los Angeles County Lifeguard Service, Southern Section, at (310) 832-1179. For a surf report, call (310) 379-8471.

See number 14 on page 154.

Malaga Cove

Location: On the northwest corner of the Palos Verdes Peninsula, along Paseo del Mar at Via Arroyo.

Parking: Free parking lot.

Hours: 6 AM to sunset.

Facilities: Lifeguards, rest rooms, and showers.

Contact: For beach information, contact the Los Angeles County Lifeguard Service, Southern Section, at (310) 832-1179. For a surf report, call (310) 379-8471.

See number 15 on page 154.

Redondo Beach

Location: Redondo Beach is south of metropolitan Los Angeles, six miles from the Los Angeles International Airport (LAX). It is bisected by Highway 1 (Pacific Coast Highway). Harbor Drive runs along the waterfront. Redondo County Beach and Torrance County Beach, which run contiguously for approximately 2.5 miles, are located south of the Redondo Beach Municipal Pier.
Population: 65,000
Area Code: 310 **Zip Code:** 90277

Of the triumvirate of beach towns that are conjoined in the South Bay area of Los Angeles, Redondo Beach has been spiked the hardest by economic recession and natural disaster. Whereas its sisters in sand and sun, Hermosa Beach and Manhattan Beach, are primarily residential communities and only secondarily tourist-oriented, Redondo Beach—at least that part of town seaward of the Pacific Coast Highway—seeks and depends on visitor dollars. The lineup of waterfront attractions in Redondo Beach includes the marinas at King Harbor (there are four of them), the International Boardwalk, the town's famous "horseshoe pier," and several resort hotels. You can gauge Redondo's dependence on visitors by the size of the parking decks. Whether you're berthing a yacht in one of the basins or wheeling a rented Escort into one of the garages, Redondo Beach is glad to have you and your pocketful of pesos jingling around town. For this reason, it is the most outsider-friendly of the South Bay communities.

Nonetheless, in some aspects it is a rather sad-looking, beaten-down place. You can sense the mood of weary surrender. Redondo Beach is not the bustling, beach-happy mecca it used to be. Today it is a tourist town down on its heels. The recent downturn dates back to 1988, which was a banner year for disaster on the waterfront—so much so it's amazing they've found the will to piece the place back together at all. Here's what the first half of that cruel year brought Redondo Beach:

- A raging mid-January storm blew down from the Arctic, heavily damaging seaside restaurants and knocking out 20 pier pilings. Waves from the high surf crashed through a window of the Blue Moon Saloon, injuring seven people. Fifty lodgers at the Portofino Inn had to be evacuated by helicopter because it was surrounded by water. Parked cars were inundated by waves washing onto the Yacht Club parking lot. Total damage: $17 million.

- Later in January, part of a parking structure weakened by the storm collapsed during an awards ceremony for a 10K race, killing one person and injuring nine others.

- On April 30, massive waves wrecked a 155-foot promenade that connected two parts of the Pier Complex—Monstad Pier and Fisherman's Wharf—causing $1.25 million in damage.

- On May 27, an electrical fire delivered a crowning bow, destroying even more of the pier and its businesses than the January storm. Thirteen shops and two restaurants were ravaged as the fire, feeding on the pier's creosote-treated planks, sent flames leaping 100 feet into the air. There was no sprinkler system in operation on the pier, and a water main for fire fighting fell into the sea early in the blaze. All totaled, 34,000 square feet of commercial property were wiped out, and damage estimates again soared to upward of $17 million.

Four disasters of this magnitude in less than six months would seem to signal that the gods were not pleased. The long-term effects of these episodes—bolstered by the statewide recession, which has slowed the pace of re-

 Map of Los Angeles County beaches—page 154

construction—have been well-nigh insurmountable. Today the waterfront complex is a catacomb of nearly empty parking decks; food stalls along the concrete boardwalk that are boarded up and out of business or doing iffy business; and a handful of pier-based restaurants that are open but holding on for dear life. Strolling around one bright July afternoon, we observed clumps of foreign tourists wandering aimlessly, confused and unsure of where to go or how to get there. Repairs to the piers and environs are ongoing and the sound of saws and power tools fills the air, but it almost seems like a lost cause. What happens the next time the Arctic sends another unforgiving squall Redondo's way? How long can this cycle of destruction and rebuilding continue—or has the cycle already been broken?

With this streak of misfortune has come an inevitable downscaling of the types of businesses found on the pier. The quality restaurants that were lost to the sea—the Breakers, the Cattleman's Wharf Restaurant, and the Edge—have not reappeared. With few exceptions, the food stands that remain open serve edibles on the order of "hot dogs on a stick," generic slabs of pizza, and frozen foodstuffs lobbed into bubbling vats of grease. One Korean restaurant offered a dinner entrée of "sea squirts and sea cucumbers," but the out-of-focus picture that displayed these, uh, delicacies convinced us that their proper place was on the ocean floor, not on a plate. More ominously, official signs posted by the seafood restaurants on the pier bore the warning: "Mussels from these waters are unfit for consumption from May 1st to October 31st." Also: "No eating of white croaker. Found with trace elements of DDT and PCB." *Bon appétit!*

A small arcade on ground level has the usual low-rent boardwalk kiddie rides. Upstairs, children of all ages and depressed IQs can buy Three Stooges T-shirts at a cut-rate emporium better suited to Venice Beach. Just down the road, the local Red Onion—part of a restaurant/nightclub chain that had a lock on Southern California nightlife in the 1980s—has gone out of business. The entire chain went belly up, leaving a void where the collective SoCal party-animal libido used to dwell. We rode our rented bikes through the empty parking lot, where signs for valet parking and nightly food specials were left standing, bringing to mind evenings of bacchanalian frenzy we'd once spent on these very premises. The sight seemed emblematic of Redondo's faded glory.

On a cheerier note, one of the most best-loved features of the waterfront, the South Bay Bicycle Trall, endures. A 20-mile paved path that extends from Torrance County Beach (just south of Redondo) to Will Rogers State Beach (in Malibu), it is a two-way concrete freeway for cyclists, in-line skaters, skateboarders, and joggers. Even the odd walker can be spotted, although mere strolling is a little too undemanding for this high-speed crowd. If you're not in shape, this isn't the place to reveal your unseemly bulges. The bike path is part aerobic runway, part fashion runway, and always crowded—the place to see and be seen.

Traveling south from Hermosa Beach, the trail swings onto the streets of Redondo for a few blocks before entering the innards of the King Harbor-Pier Complex. Once past this maze, through which you're asked to walk your bike, the path resumes a straight and steady course south along Redondo County Beach, giving cyclists a superb view of the rugged bluffs of the Palos Verdes Peninsula. Cruising the South Bay is a popular pastime, and bikes can be rented at local shops, the best of which are in Hermosa Beach. The local climate almost mandates outdoor activity. The mercury rarely falls below 45 degrees in January or rises above 75 degrees in July. Los Angeles's chronic halo of smog doesn't choke the beaches of the South Bay. Cooling offshore breezes ensure that the air is generally clean and the skies blue.

And so Redondo Beach sits at the edge of the Pacific like a tarnished jewel in a splendid setting. It has been knocked around by Mother Nature and is still somewhat punch-drunk, yet its residents doggedly regroup, rebuild, and persevere. There's an element of precedent figuring in all this. Redondo Beach is a town that has fancied itself a vacation destination since the 1890s, when a trio of Spanish sisters sold the sand dunes they inherited to developers. Shipping was an important early industry, but after Redondo Beach unsuccessfully vied to have the Port of Los Angeles located here (San Pedro won), the town turned to tourism. A huge luxury hotel, along with tent cities for the fiscally challenged, drew vacationers to the pristine beach. The Hotel Redondo—which opened in 1890 and was stupidly torn down in 1926—actually was the sister establishment of the splendid Hotel del Coronado down the coast. During Redondo's heyday, folks would ride the fabled Pacific Electric "red cars" from downtown Los Angeles to the beach.

At one time, Redondo Beach had it all: big-band ballrooms, offshore gambling ships reached by water taxis, and a huge, heated indoor saltwater pool called "the Plunge." A Hawaiian native named George Fresh demonstrated the strange new sport of surfing to curious onlookers behind the Hotel Redondo. (Fresh was described biblically by developer Henry Huntington as "the man who could walk on water.") Redondo's glory days are documented in the Redondo Beach Historical Museum (320 Knob Hill Avenue, 543-3108), operated by the Redondo Beach Historical Commission. Residents would no doubt like to see those golden days return, but that will take a long reprieve from the forces of nature and economics—and that is one tall order.

Beaches

The beach at Redondo Beach maintains a respectable width south of the pier, but it is narrow and eroded north of it. Erosion is the result of harborfront construction, including a breakwater that diverts sand into a submarine canyon just offshore from Redondo Beach. The same canyon causes wave crests to refract in a way that concentrates their energy onto the beaches north of the canyon, occasionally wrecking beaches and the houses built along them. In severe storms, such as a series that occurred in the winter of 1983, the breakwater has been overtopped and damaged. Signs warn people away from what's left of the beach in the vicinity of the harbor, where the ocean angrily slaps walls of riprap that have been erected to protect the construction behind it.

Redondo County Beach

2

Location: In Redondo Beach, at Torrance Boulevard and Esplanade.

Parking: Metered street and lot parking.

Hours: 6 AM to sunset.

Facilities: Lifeguards, rest rooms, and showers.

Contact: For beach information, contact the Los Angeles County Lifeguard Service, Southern Section, at (310) 832-1179. For a surf report, call (310) 379-8471.

See number 17 on page 154.

Torrance County Beach

4

Location: In Torrance, along Paseo de la Playa.

Parking: $4 entrance fee per vehicle.

Hours: 6 AM to sunset.

Facilities: Lifeguards, rest rooms, and showers.

Contact: For beach information, contact the Los Angeles County Lifeguard Service, Southern Section, at (310) 832-1179. For a surf report, call (310) 379-8471.

See number 16 on page 154.

The beach scene improves markedly on the south side of the pier along the strand encompassing **Redondo County Beach** and **Torrance County Beach**. Redondo County Beach runs for about 1.5 miles from the pier south to some rest rooms, on the other side of which it becomes Torrance County Beach, continuing down to the Palos Verdes Peninsula for three-quarters of a mile. It's the same beach—a flat swath of sand that widens between pier and peninsula, and a nice place to come for a little more nature and a little less in the way of crowds than you'll find at Hermosa or Manhattan Beaches. To the delight of surfers, this stretch is serviced by the west swells of winter.

Bunking Down

To oversimplify, Redondo Beach has the hotels, Manhattan Beach has the restaurants, and Hermosa Beach has the nightlife. Numerous chain motels are located along and west of the Pacific Coast Highway, only one-third of a mile from the beach. Down along the harbor are the two top choices: the **Portofino Hotel and Yacht Club** (260 Portofino Way, 379-8481, $$$) and the **Holiday Inn Crowne Plaza** (300 North Harbor Drive, 318-8888, $$). The latter is an especially attractive property, an airy and spacious five-story resort hotel overlooking King Harbor from the dry side of Harbor Drive. It qualifies as a real at-the-beach deal with room rates under $100. Private balconies, an outdoor heated pool and sundeck, exercise facilities, a sports bar, a piano bar, an on-premises restaurant and more make this the prime place to lay in when visiting Redondo Beach. Another option is the **Palos Verdes Inn** (1700 South Pacific Coast Highway, 316-4211, $$$), located only three blocks from the beach along a curve on the coastal highway, where it begins to skirt the uplands of the Palos Verdes Peninsula. The hotel is a self-contained city, with an excellent continental restaurant (Chez Melange, 542-1222, $$$), a gourmet deli (Chez Allez, $), a popular supper club with a big-band theme (The Strand Supper and Dance Club, 316-1700) and a half-acre pool, spa and gardens on the premises. Rooms are comfortably furnished and many come with ocean-view balconies.

Coastal Cuisine

For seafood, try the Breakers—ah, sorry, washed out to sea. For the best steaks in town, try the Cattleman's Wharf Restaurant—oops, it's somewhere down there with the sea anemones. In Redondo Beach, restaurants aren't closed down by bad reviews or word of mouth. Big waves wreck them. Still, the harborside restaurant scene survives, particularly the **Blue Moon Saloon** (207 North Harbor Drive, 373-3411, $$$), a casual seafood eatery in the Redondo Beach Marina that has endured wind and wave to emerge as a long-lived institution on the waterfront. The International Boardwalk is home to **Quality Seafood** (130 South International Boardwalk, 374-2382, $$), a seafood market and snack bar that displays and prepares all manner of fresh, colorful seafood: local crab and fish, plus Louisiana crawdads and New Zealand eel. They'll steam a crab for you on the spot, which you can take to a table and crack to your heart's content. Then there's **Sitar by the Sea** (125 West Torrance Boulevard, 376-9447, $$), which isn't the name of a Ravi Shankar album—though it ought to be—but an excellent Indian restaurant in the pier complex.

Night Moves

The nightlife is over in Hermosa Beach, and with the Red Onion having bitten the dust Redondo Beach is pretty quiet after hours. There's a **Hennessey's Tavern** (1710 South Catalina Avenue, 316-6658) in Riviera Village, a shopping area set back from the beach. Come to think of it, there's a Hennessey's in each of the three South Bay beach towns: Redondo, Hermosa, and Manhattan. You can also find a decent cocktail lounge at one of the seafood restaurants in King Harbor: the old reliable **Chart House** (231 Yacht Club Way, 372-3464) or the **Blue Moon Saloon** (207 North Harbor Drive, 373-3411). You might wander into a decent jam at **Papa Garo's** (1810 South Catalina Boulevard, 540-7272), a Mediterranean restaurant and music club where you'll find live blues music in a smoke-free environment—as incongruous as that might seem. Then there's **The Strand Supper and Dance Club** (1700 South Pacific Coast Highway, 316-1700), a party palace for the older set. Finally, we must mention **Moose McGillycuddy's** (179 Harbor Drive, 372-9944), the only dance club in the South Bay and the heir apparent to the "meet market" tradition forged by the late Red Onion.

For More Information

Contact the Redondo Beach Chamber of Commerce, 200 North Pacific Coast Highway, Redondo Beach, CA 90277; (310) 376-6911.

Hermosa Beach

Location: Hermosa Beach is between Redondo Beach and Manhattan Beach. The smallest of the three South Bay beach communities, it is located 17 miles southwest of Los Angeles, at the south end of the Santa Monica Bay, and four miles from Los Angeles International Airport (LAX). Hermosa Avenue runs parallel to Hermosa City Beach, a two-mile public beach.

Population: 18,200

Area Code: 310 **Zip Code:** 90254

In Spanish, *hermosa* means "beautiful," and it's an apt description of this unpretentious community, which seems light-years removed from the smoggy hubbub of Los Angeles, against which it brushes. The more things change around it, the more Hermosa Beach remains the same. It is the most relaxed and laid-back of the South Bay communities, a town full of coffee bars, bookstores for serious readers, and shops catering to the healthful prerogatives of a physically fit populace. Living beside the ocean in an almost perfect climate tends to make people look after themselves. Even a place like the Rocky Cola Café, a 1950s-style burger-jukebox joint, offers a healthy menu, analyzing its food items in terms of fat grams and calories; they leave things like egg yolks out of their omelettes and serve black beans and brown rice as side dishes. But this is par for the course in a community that has a solid sense of itself and has plotted its destiny well.

In 1901 the beach was surveyed for a boardwalk, in 1904 the first pier was built, and in 1907 the town of Hermosa Beach was incorporated. At that time the city gained ownership over its two-mile oceanfront in a deed mandating that it be held in perpetuity as "beach playground, free from commerce, and for the benefit of not only residents of Hermosa, but also for the sea lovers of Southern California." Those ideals remain in force today. It is an aesthetically attractive town with a gleaming, well-maintained beach.

What's most magical about Hermosa Beach is the descent down Pier Avenue toward the ocean. Rounding a curve, it yields a spectacular view of the ocean. The light sea breeze is constant, the environment feels clean and continuously refreshed, and you just can't help but stroll around Hermosa Beach in a state of grateful rejuvenation. If you want to get out of the sun, you can always duck into a good bookstore: the Either/Or, a sizable, well-stocked, New Age–themed reader's paradise, or Nations

 Map of Los Angeles County beaches—page 154

Travel Bookstore, a shop specializing in travel guides, maps, and videos.

You won't want to leave town without renting a bike or a pair of in-line skates at one of the shops down on the Strand (the paved boardwalk connecting the beach communities). From here you can take off for a spin along the bike path—up to Malibu, down to Redondo, anything's possible. And the unfolding beach scenery is worth the legwork.

Parking remains the one big bugaboo in Hermosa Beach. There's barely enough of it for those who live here, much less for visitors. Street parking is hard to find and expensive, and parking-meter charges are enforced 24 hours a day. Hotel guests are covered, but day trippers be advised: come via rapid transit, on foot, or via bicycle, if possible. Otherwise you might find yourself incurring some degree of expense and/or hassle. In the words of a letter to the editor of the *Easy Reader*, a free local paper: "The nemesis of Hermosa Beach that there's just no getting around is parking." We can second that emotion. Still, we like everything else about Hermosa Beach and recommend it highly.

Beaches

Hermosa City Beach stretches for two unblemished miles, part of the continuous strip of sand that runs along the Santa Monica Bay before slamming to a halt at the Palos Verdes Peninsula. The 1,328-foot-long Hermosa Pier is its centerpiece, offering year-round angling in the waters of Santa Monica Bay. At the foot of the pier is a statue of a surfer poised in mid-ride. Beneath the frozen surf rider's impassive gaze, swarms of people whiz by on the South Bay Bicycle Trail, which sometimes appears to be the busiest thoroughfare in Hermosa Beach. Although everyone moves at different speeds and in different directions, this complex symphony of motion somehow plays through without a lot of serious spills or collisions. Just get on your bike or 'blades and groove, dude.

In addition to all the hell-on-wheels aerobicizing along the South Bay Bicycle Trail, sand rats play volleyball and paddleball out here on the ample beach, which we have yet to see in a condition that could be described as overcrowded. You never know what might be going on here. During our stay, members of the U.S. and Brazilian national soccer teams played an exhibition game in the sand, drawing a few thousand onlookers. One pastime that's not too big, oddly enough, is surfing. Apparently, the breakwater that protects Redondo Beach's harbor knocks the waves here down to a size for which only novices and locals have much use.

Hermosa City Beach

5

Location: In Hermosa Beach, along Pier Avenue at Hermosa Avenue.

Parking: Metered street parking.

Hours: 6 AM to sunset.

Facilities: Lifeguards, rest rooms, and showers.

Contact: For beach information, contact the Los Angeles County Lifeguard Service, Southern Section, at (310) 832-1179. For a surf report, call (310) 379-8471.

See number 18 on page 154.

Bunking Down

Because this is a residential community, and a small one at that, there are only four motels in Hermosa Beach—and just one of these is directly on the beach. But it's a goodie—a funky, down-to-earth place called the **Sea Sprite Ocean Front Motel** (1016 Strand, 376-6933, $$) that's perfect for a true beach lover. The Sea Sprite is an informal yet well-tended motel that rents rooms and apartment-style cottages. From the second-floor pool deck you can watch the world skate by on the bike path below or just enjoy the misty breezes rolling off the ocean. They've even

Eavesdropping in Hermosa Beach: "I'm Very There"

(A real-life play in one act. All conversation is reported verbatim.)

Scene: The bright stucco interior of the Hermosa Beach Post Office on a summer afternoon at midweek.

He: A slouching, unshaven male of indeterminate age who could be anywhere from 25 to 45 years old. His face is stubbly, his hair short but unkempt. He is wearing soiled cutoffs, sandals, and a T-shirt that has grayed from one too many unsorted washings. He looks as if he has just rolled out of bed.

She: A former California beach queen, now gone to seed as she approaches 40. Her skin has been worn to the texture of alligator hide by the sun, her face is creased with age and worry lines, and her thighs sag with cellulite. Her hair is dirty blonde, and she wears Spandex bike shorts and a loose-fitting T-shirt. Her eyes are concealed by designer sunglasses.

[They meet at a counter in the front room of the post office, where He is addressing a package.]

He: You look great!

She: Thanks. I feel great. [*Pauses*] But it just ain't enough. [*Emits a hoarse, jaded cackle, then continues*] People are so goddamned superficial out here. Everybody is chasing that big white cloud, and I don't know what it is.

He: Yeah, I know. I'm so busy, I'm just running around all the time. This is what my day looks like: I get up, go to work, look for a place to park, and work for eight hours. I don't even have time to eat. I'll call to have some food delivered, then I shove it down when I can grab a moment. Then it's off to classes, then I get home, and call for more takeout food while I'm doing my homework and

managed to shoehorn in a parking space for every room, a perk that's worth its weight in parking tickets. There's nothing fancy about the Sea Sprite, but when you're right on the ocean—and you couldn't be any closer except on a surfboard—who needs marble bathrooms and turn-down service?

For something a little more upscale, the **Hotel Hermosa** (2515 Pacific Coast Highway, 318-6000, $$) is an attractively landscaped property five blocks away from the beach. A recent arrival, it's a Spanish-style three-story hotel with a heated pool, a Japanese garden, workout facilities, and comfortable rooms, many with ocean-facing balconies. We also got a nice room for a fair price at the **Travelodge** (901 Aviation Boulevard, 374-2666, $). A large room with two beds that was spacious, well appointed, and clean for only $55 at the height of summer qualifies as a deal in our book—and you're only a bracing, 10-minute walk to the beach.

Coastal Cuisine

Restaurants are as abundant in Hermosa Beach as hotels are scarce. Boasting the highest per capita income in the South Bay, the town is sufficiently cosmopolitan to support a high-

whatever *work* work I've had to take home. I'm beat all the time. The harder I work, the more I fall behind. I just don't know what's wrong.

She: I know what you mean. I spent six years in therapy, and all I wanted to know was how to find peace. Now I've found it, but I'm in the minority.

He: I'm very there.

She: I just don't need it anymore.

He: Good for you! I've been there, done that.

She: I'm going to Costa Rica to look for work. I've had it with L.A., it's just too crowded for me. Everyone running around, getting in each other's way. You know what I mean? No one wants to admit it, but it's over. L.A. is over. I've had it.

He: Are you going to Costa Rica with your mate?

She: No. [*Thoughtful pause*] We're taking a second look at where we're at right now. If it happens, it happens. We'll see.

He: I was talking to my mate about this, too. A relationship starts out with a certain amount of mass, and once that mass begins falling away, you're forced to interface with one another. [*Pauses to reflect*] You know, I like that phrase.

She: That's so true. Well, gotta go. Gotta get back to work. We'll hook up sometime.

He: Bye.

She: Bye-bye.

[*Both walk away.*]

quality, ethnically diverse restaurant scene. You can take your pick of Thai, Italian, Mexican, French, Peruvian, Greek, Japanese, Indian, Cajun, Middle Eastern, macrobiotic, and more in this village. The crowds really seem to gravitate to the Italian eateries like **Buona Vita** (439 Pier Avenue, 379-7626, $$), a popular restaurant serving a broad variety of creative pasta dishes befitting a restaurant whose name translates as "good life." Prices are very reasonable: $11.95 and under for almost everything.

Yet sushi just might be the most favorite food of all. There are more sushi bars in Hermosa Beach than you can shake a chopstick at. **Sushi Sei** (50 Pier Avenue, 379-6900, $$) is the consensus choice of raw-fish fans in the South Bay, offering sushi, soup, loud music, and comedic sushi chefs. It's hard to miss; just look for the enormous Japanese mural over the door. You can't beat **Paradise Sushi** (53 Pier Avenue, 274-0123, $$) for value, especially between 5:30 and 6:30 PM, when you can order all-you-can-eat sushi for $14.90. They make some great rolls here: the Punk Roll (yellowtail, crab, avocado) for those with an attitude problem and/or a skateboard; the Rock 'n' Roll (scallops, crab, avocado); and the Ninja Roll (taken verbatim from the menu, you be the judge: "deep fried egg skin, fish"). Around the corner, **California Beach Rock 'n Sushi** (934 Hermosa Avenue, 374-7758, $$) is another good place to eat it raw. But just exactly what is the connection between rock and roll and sushi here? Beats us.

We had a hearty, healthy lunch at **Rocky Cola Café** (1025 Pacific Coast Highway, 798-3111, $), a combination 1950s-style diner and health-food restaurant. Amid the standard fare of burgers, floats, and onion rings they have a "bodybuilder fitness menu," including such things as Ahi Tuna Tacos (dolphin-safe, of course) and Egg White Veggie Omelette. Just think how much tougher "the Fonz" could have been if he'd had these dining options back in the era of *Happy Days*. Close by, we dropped into **El Pollo Inka** (1100 Pacific Coast Highway, 372-1433, $$) to sample the Peruvian-style grilled chicken. It's a good, inexpensive, rotisserie-style plate of chicken, served with salad and rice or French fries. If you're feeling a bit more adventurous, you can ante up for one of the seafood dishes, such as Saltado de Camarones: sautéed shrimp, onions, tomatoes, and red pepper. Excellent!

Coffeehouses are big in the South Bay (as they are all over California). At a place called **Java Man** (157 Pier Avenue, 379-7209, $), we sipped on big mugs of the coffee of the day (macadamia nut) and munched pastries with the other clientele, who were similarly absorbed in the *Los Angeles Times*. One serious and sensitive fellow, though, was drawing psychedelic swirls onto paper with colored pencils, attentively rendering paisley blobs in an abstract, Romper Room-on-acid style. He accompanied these with poetic thoughts and lyric fragments. When he made a trip to the bathroom, we sauntered over to inspect his drawing pad. Sample verse: "I am looking for my vision/A sight to set me free." We returned to our java, muffins, and newspapers, burying our beaks in the latest revelations on the O.J. Simpson front.

Night Moves

The nightlife never changes here. The same places are located at the same addresses on the south side of the last block of Pier Avenue before it ends at the Strand. We've rarely seen a row of bars and clubs as entrenched as this one. Such consistency is unheard of at the beach, where places open and close like a banker's briefcase. Like a stack of dominoes, four clubs are arrayed in a row. It might be you, however, that's falling over by the end of the evening. Your choices are **Hennessey's Tavern** (8 Pier Avenue, 374-9203), an Irish pub-style bar/restaurant that never fails to draw a crowd; the **Lighthouse Café** (30 Pier Avenue, 372-6911), a former jazz club turned rock-and-roll bistro; the **End Zone** (22 Pier Avenue, 374-1717), a clubby sports bar with pool tables; and **Pier 52** (52 Pier Avenue, 376-1629), a loose, cheap, and rowdy beer joint.

The Lighthouse Café has been supporting "the art of live entertainment" for four decades. It showcases local and regional acts on a small stage that faces a long bar. The acts aren't always the sort that will set your socks on fire, but there's a down-home feeling about the place—one of friends playing for friends—that's appealing. We saw a couple of dudes with heavy-metal haircuts who were taking a busman's holiday from their loud rock band to have a Tuesday night "unplugged" session. The musical choices were galling, running the gamut from Peter Frampton covers to the title song from *Hair*. Then there were the originals, such as a histrionic number about "American heroes" who "take a fall" but turn out to be "human after all," sentiments no doubt triggered by the Simpson murders. But there was no cover, and the beer was cold, so what the heck? We downed a few and had fun people-watching.

Hennessey's Tavern is the least franchise-like unit in this chain, having been Hermosa'd into a relaxed, unpretentious beach bar. Around the corner from this estimable string of taverns, facing the beach itself on the Strand, is the old reliable **Poop Deck** (1272 Strand, 376-3223), a well-worn and unfancy place where well-worn and unfancy types come to slake their thirsts on a daily basis. It's a good place to head for a celebratory brew at sundown.

Then there's the back-alley institution known as **Bestie's** (1332 Hermosa Avenue, 318-3818). Once owned by British soccer legend George Best, a player second only to Pele in the annals of the sport, Bestie's faithfully recreates a British pub atmosphere. The menu is filled with staples of British cuisine like lamb stew and bangers and mash. They'll pull you a long, cool mug of inky Guinness draft, and you can play pool, toss darts, or watch sports on one of a dozen or so TVs strung up around the premises. On weekends, a back room is opened up and miraculous metamorphoses into **DBC**, a hip dance club that plays alternative music. Though the address is listed as being on Hermosa Avenue, you must enter from an alley behind it. Because you must know what you're looking for, it's popular with locals and all but unknown to outsiders.

Finally, where best to party at the beach than a café and nightspot owned by the Beach Boys? We jest not. The **Beach Boys Café**, a.k.a. the California Grill and Beach Club (2701 Pacific Coast Highway, 379-3395), is one place to go in the South Bay for "Fun Fun Fun." You might even meet some knockout "California Girls." At the very least, you'll enjoy the "Good Vibrations." Surf's up!

For More Information

Contact the Hermosa Beach Chamber of Commerce, 323 Pier Avenue, Hermosa Beach, CA 90254; (310) 376 0951.

Manhattan Beach

Location: Manhattan Beach is located 19 miles southwest of Los Angeles near the south end of the Santa Monica Bay. To get there, take Interstate 405 to the Manhattan Beach Boulevard exit. The main beach is Manhattan State Beach.

Population: 33,500

Area Code: 310 **Zip Code:** 90266

The view of the sand in either direction from Manhattan Beach Pier is enough to convince anyone that living in Los Angeles is worth every hassle—meteorological, seismic, automotive—just to have access to such splendor. Volleyball nets are strung out to the south as far as the eye can see. Surfers bob in the water, waiting for the wave that will carry them shoreward. Hot, hard-bodied babes oil down and catch rays on the beach. Weather-beaten anglers stand poised against the pier railings, their poles and lines an excuse for sitting all day in the golden sun. One old bird in an electric wheelchair had foregone the pretense of fishing. Between satisfying slugs from his thermos, he trained his binoculars on the nubile bodies lying on the sands below. Succumbing to temptation—and too ashamed to ask the old dude for a look-see—we dropped quarters into the pay telescopes mounted on the wooden railings of the pier and conducted our own on-site inspection. Why else are these telescopes here—so you can check out the oil refineries of El Segundo?

You could almost flip a coin to discern the difference among the three beach towns—Redondo, Hermosa, and Manhattan—strung out along the southern edge of Santa Monica Bay. The three have more similarities than differences. For starters, they're linked by the South Bay Bicycle Trail, which also serves as a boardwalk, and they all strive to cultivate as low-key a personality as possible, given their proximity to Los Angeles.

If there is any difference between Manhattan Beach and the others, it is evident away from the water. Manhattan Beach is the most moneyed, family-oriented, and residential of the three. Its 2,300 acres are as developed as a suburban community can be, crowded with smallish homes and yards that typically consist of a square foot of bleached pebbles and a dark green bush. The line of natural dunes hasn't been bulldozed away, and building heights have been held down to a bearable level. These facts, coupled with the town's sudden roller-coaster plunge toward the ocean, allow nearly all who live here an invigorating view of the Pacific Ocean. You *feel* the ocean in Manhattan Beach. It's like a permanent drive-in movie to help relieve the stress of the gridlock to the east.

There are, however, a few nagging signs that Manhattan Beach may be losing its grip on growth. A 187-acre business park has been relegated to the eastern edge of town in the flight path of Los Angeles International Airport and next to a smoke-belching power plant. With it have arrived an army of nouveau riche who have driven up land values with their real-estate schemes. This has caused longtime residents to skirmish with developers. Their battle is perhaps typified by this rebuttal from a homeowner in the local paper, the *Beach Reporter*, to a proposal put forth by one of many real-estate speculators: "Mr. B_ states that the current trend of residential development in the city is purely a matter of economics... that long-time residents should cash in their chips and move elsewhere, preferably to a place where land values are low.... Once there, they could buy a larger house on several acres of wasteland, where they could spend the rest of their days counting the profits derived from the sale of the home in which their children grew up enjoying the beaches, the trees, and the picturesque atmosphere that has made Manhattan Beach such a desirable place to live."

Indeed, it is desirable. Inside the snug city limits are 13 churches, 5 parks, and 2 libraries; one of the parks provides the setting for Sunday afternoon concerts during the summer. Most of the commerce is concentrated around the intersection of the two main drags, Manhattan Beach Boulevard and Highland Avenue. The local businesses squeezed in here are the sort of nonfranchise shops that obsessive consumers love to believe they've discovered for themselves, bearing such names as "Pour Moi-La Boutique," "Foote Fetish," and "Le Chat." (The last of these is next door to an animal hospital... hmm.) Parking isn't necessarily a problem, but it isn't cheap. Street meters run 24 hours and cost 25 cents for 15 minutes, with a 5-hour limit. They take quarters only.... Where is somebody supposed to come by that many quarters?

A young woman who lives in Manhattan Beach told us that the town has developed an attitude that is lacking in the more laid-back Hermosa Beach. That attitude, one supposes, comes from the money it costs to live here. One local realtor—whose slogan is "I have the right energy to sell your house"—advertised this bargain: "A classic beach home on the walk streets with fabulous ocean views." Translation: a modest wooden box with an upstairs balcony located blocks off the ocean. Asking price: $699,000.

Still, as you near the beach, all pretensions disappear in a blaze of tanned, libidinous glory. Relaxed bars, taverns, and restaurants near the pier on Manhattan Boulevard help sustain the friendly cacophony that is at the heart of the Southern California beach experience.

Beaches

Manhattan Beach's two-mile oceanfront is completely residential (e.g., no motels, few affordable rentals). The clean, sandy **Manhattan County Beach** is bisected by a 900-foot pier (at the west end of Manhattan Beach Boulevard) and backed by a seawall adorned with tasteful murals and less tasteful graffiti. The water is subject to occasional rough currents but is well patrolled by a bevy of lifeguards. Beach volleyball is not just a sport but a religion here. From the pier, sand volleyball courts and nets extend down toward Hermosa Beach. North of Manhattan Beach is **El Porto Beach**. You can walk to it from Manhattan Beach or park near the ramps at 41st and 44th Streets. El Porto has full facilities and volleyball nets, but the scene here tends to be loud and uninviting.

Bunking Down

Lodging isn't Manhattan Beach's strong suit. The closest you can get to the beach is three steep uphill blocks away from the action on Highland Avenue. The **Sea View Inn** (3400 Highland Avenue, 545-1504, $) is the most appealing of a handful of choices. They only have eight rooms, but these surround a swimming pool away from the noise of the busy thoroughfare.

Coastal Cuisine

The most celebrated restaurant in town is **H20** (401 Manhattan Beach Boulevard, 545-6220, $$$), as in the chemical formula for water. The food is sumptuous and meticulously prepared nouvelle cuisine on overdrive (e.g., sautéed duck breast, bacon garlic fig sauce, with sweet potato confit hash). At night, H20 doubles as an upscale club. A quick bite of fried fish can be had at the **Saltwater Café** at the end of Manhattan Beach Pier (2 Manhattan Beach Boulevard, 372-6383, $). The café's menu is written on a surfboard mounted above the takeout counter. It's nothing fancy and a tad pricey by end-of-the-pier fast-food standards. Grab a magazine off the rack out front and sit down on the bench beside the railing.

Night Moves

A clear sign of the upscaling of Manhattan Beach is the fate of La Paz, once considered to be the "king of the beach bars" and "Animal

El Porto Beach
(a part of Manhattan County Beach)

Location: At the end of 45th Street, north of Manhattan Beach Pier in Manhattan Beach.

Parking: Metered street parking.

Hours: 6 AM to sunset.

Facilities: Lifeguards, rest rooms, and showers.

Contact: For beach information, contact the Los Angeles County Lifeguard Service, Southern Section, at (310) 832-1179. For a surf report, call (310) 379-8471.

See number 20 on page 154.

Manhattan County Beach

Location: Along the Strand at Manhattan Pier in Manhattan Beach.

Parking: Metered street and lot parking.

Hours: 6 AM to sunset.

Facilities: Lifeguards, rest rooms, and showers.

Contact: For beach information, contact the Los Angeles County Lifeguard Service, Southern Section, at (310) 832-1179. For a surf report, call (310) 379-8471.

See number 19 on page 154.

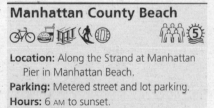

Getting Around the South Bay

The quality of life in the triad of South Bay beach communities—Hermosa, Redondo, and Manhattan—is about as good as it gets in metropolitan L.A. In fact, it's not like living in L.A. at all, as the locals will assure you. There is no smog problem, as the ocean breezes blow it inland. It is a little Shangri-la that enjoys breathing room from the freeway madness to the east, with a truly laid-back pace in comparison to the free-for-all fast lane of L.A. Whether you're just visiting or want to squeeze on in and live here, the South Bay is a delectable slice of seaside paradise awaiting your perusal.

The most immediate hassle is parking. It's a pain in the posterior whether you're living here or just visiting. Consequently people tend to walk, in-line skate, or bicycle from place to place whenever possible. The clerk at our Hermosa Beach hotel was typical. She works in Hermosa but lives at the south end of Redondo, a distance of five miles. She commutes to her job and back home again on in-line skates, via the South Bay Bicycle Trail and the Pacific Coast Highway. The advantages are numerous: there are no parking spaces or traffic tie-ups to worry about; it costs nothing to skate to work; you pass spectacular scenery and inhale fresh ocean air; and you acquire a lean, muscular physique, and healthy glow. She was the archetypal California girl, the sort of tanned, leonine goddess that prompted the Beach Boys to sing—and the world to agree—"I wish they all could be California girls."

If, unlike our skating heroine, you're driving a car, there still doesn't have to be a problem. Park it at your motel or a long-term lot, forget about it, and rent a bike, tooling around the peninsula courtesy of your own two feet. You can rent wheels at Hermosa Cyclery for about $6 an hour (or $18 for a full day). That's for a one-speed, but who needs more than one gear to pedal along a gradeless bike trail that runs at sea level? We biked the trail from the Manhattan Beach Pier south to its terminus at the south end of Torrance State Beach, where it faces the rising topography of the Palos Verdes Peninsula. That's a distance of about seven miles, and it is packed with California specimens who have fined-tuned their bodies to bronzed, sculpted perfection. The passing scenery is magnificent—and the beaches aren't bad to look at, either. The concrete ribbon sticks to the beachfront, sometimes splitting into separate pathways for cyclists and pedestrians.

Down in Redondo, you are wheeled off the beach and onto the roadway (you still have your own lane), through a parking garage, and across the King Harbor-Pier Complex. Signs ask you to walk your bike through the area. Use the respite to savor the aroma of fresh fish at Quality Seafood and soak up the people-watching fun. It's an unforgettable ride, one of the quintessential Southern California experiences. One word of warning: on weekends the bike path is so jam-packed that you really need to know what you're doing to negotiate the wheeled parade of humanity. The path, incidentally, stretches north all the way up to Will Rogers State Beach, some 20 miles away, if you're up for a serious bike hike.

House at the beach" by the usual reliable sources of surfers and local beach bums. It was a sloppy, wonderful, ramshackle place that we feel privileged to have visited on a previous trip. La Paz is gone now, replaced by a municipal parking lot beside the pier. Picking up the slack are the **Manhattan Beach Brewing Company** (124 Manhattan Beach Boulevard, 798-2744), with designer home brew, and the **Shellback Tavern** (116 Manhattan Beach Boulevard, 376-7857), which is the closest in spirit to La Paz you'll find in town. They serve pretty good tacos and burgers, too.

For More Information

Contact the Manhattan Beach Chamber of Commerce, 425 15th Street, Manhattan Beach, CA 90266; (310) 545-5313.

El Segundo

Location: Five miles southwest of Los Angeles, via Interstate 405 to the Imperial Avenue exit. The main beach in El Segundo is Dockweiler State Beach, one of Los Angeles County's largest and most popular beaches.
Population: 16,000
Area Code: 310 **Zip Code:** 90245

Like San Pedro, El Segundo is an integral part of Los Angeles, but it is mostly overlooked or ignored. It is home to a sprawl of oil refineries, an oil pier, and the Hyperion Sewage Treatment Plant (the Grand Coulee Dam of sewage plants) and the Scattergood Steam Generating Station. El Segundo is also directly beside Los Angeles International Airport. This bathes the town in a toxic-industrial-aeronautic cacophony that blends perfectly with the boom boxes that reign along the shore.

Beaches

In spite of the surrounding environment, El Segundo has two of the broadest beaches in the Los Angeles area: **Dockweiler State**

Dockweiler State Beach

Location: Along Vista del Mar Boulevard from El Segundo north to Del Rey Lagoon in Playa del Rey.
Parking: $5 entrance fee per vehicle.
Hours: 6 AM to 10 PM.
Facilities: Lifeguards, rest rooms, showers, a picnic area, and fire pits. There are 117 campsites for RVs. The fee is $15 to $25 per night. For camping reservations, call Destinet at (800) 444-7275.
Contact: For beach information, contact the Los Angeles County Lifeguard Service, Southern Section, at (310) 832-1179. For a surf report, call (310) 379-8471.

See number 22 on page 154.

El Segundo Beach (a part of Dockweiler State Beach)

Location: In El Segundo, at the end of Grand Avenue at Vista del Mar Boulevard.
Parking: $4 entrance fee per vehicle.
Hours: 6 AM to 10 PM.
Facilities: Lifeguards and rest rooms.
Contact: For beach information, contact the Los Angeles County Lifeguard Service, Southern Section, at (310) 832-1179. For a surf report, call (310) 379-8471.

See number 21 on page 154.

Beach and **El Segundo Beach**. Together they comprise a six-mile stretch of sand that would make any other beach town sorely envious. Although there's beach access and large pay public parking lots off El Segundo Boulevard and at the end of Grand Avenue, the best way to see El Segundo and Dockweiler State Beaches is by bicycling along the shoreline-hugging South Bay Bicycle Trail. Almost anywhere along this stretch you can pull off the bicycle trail and the beach is all yours.

It's an odd sensation to be on a beach so huge on a picture-perfect summer day, all of five miles from the center of Los Angeles, and find the place nearly deserted. As long as you don't look shoreward at the oil refineries and sewage plant, or fret too much over the gangsta rap blaring from the direction of the parking lot, you'd swear this was as perfect a beach as you could hope to find. Dockweiler State Beach has the added incentive of a 117-site campground for RVs only at its south end. Dockweiler is so long that it encompasses the oceanfront in both El Segundo and neighboring Playa del Rey.

For More Information

Contact the El Segundo Chamber of Commerce, 427 Main Street, El Segundo, CA 90245; (310) 322-1220.

Playa del Rey

Location: Along the oceanfront three miles north of El Segundo and one mile southwest of Marina del Rey. Dockweiler State Beach is the vast beach that stretches out before it.
Population: 10,000
Area Code: 310 **Zip Code:** 90045

Playa del Rey is a largely residential town built along streets that dead-end into a lagoon at sea level and run on top of towering bluffs that look out over the beach. The chief calling card is Dockweiler State Beach, a wide, white-sand beach that extends from Del Rey Lagoon south to the park's RV campground in El Segundo. Across the lagoon lies Venice Beach; behind it, along constructed waterways, Marina del Rey. It is due west of Los Angeles International Airport.

Beaches

The word "wide" does not even begin to describe the sandy expanse at **Dockweiler State Beach**, which is shared by Playa del Rey and neighboring El Segundo (see the preceding entry for more detail). Dockweiler and adjacent beaches in Los Angeles County have been extended seaward with sand dredged from the site of the Hyperion Sewage Treatment Plant and the Scattergood Steam Generating Station. They can handle all eager beachgoers, all summer long. Even with all of mighty Los Angeles knocking at the back door, such beaches as Dockweiler, Venice, and Santa Monica seldom reach the saturation point. Not that they're terrifically attractive—but they are indisputably large. They are also prone to closure when the waters of the Santa Monica Bay become polluted with nasty storm-drain runoff.

For More Information

Contact the Marina del Rey Area Chamber of Commerce, 4519 Admiralty Way, Suite 206, Marina del Rey, CA 90292; (310) 821-0555.

Marina del Rey

Location: Marina del Rey is 15 miles southwest of Los Angeles via Route 90 (Marina Freeway). A circular boulevard known as Admiralty Way runs around the marina. Although Marina del Rey has no ocean frontage, there is a lagoon beach located at Basin D.

Population: 11,000

Area Code: 310 **Zip Code:** 90292

Marina del Rey can be summed up in two words: yachting and eating. It is the world's largest recreational small-craft harbor, consisting of eight basins that collectively contain 6,000 boat slips. It also claims to have the greatest concentration of restaurants in a single square-mile area this side of New York City. The place is like a magnet for money.

It's hard to imagine that until the mid-1950s the area was a swampy lagoon at the mouth of Ballona Creek. Progress, you say? Well, maybe. The construction of the marina has not been without problems. Although the East Coast has an abundance of natural harbors, the California coast has few of them, necessitating the construction of man-made harbors involving jetties, breakwaters, and the dredging of marinas. After opening, Marina del Rey faced a series of design-related problems. First, under a certain set of wave conditions outside the marina, the original design enabled the spread of destructive standing waves inside the marina, resulting in damaged boats and lawsuits. To rectify this, designers hastily added a 1,200 foot, detached offshore breakwater in 1962. The marina has also seen the recurring problem of sand shoaling up against the north jetty and forming a bar across the southern entrance channel, which has required expensive dredging on a regular basis.

All the same, the marina generates more money than it costs to maintain, so most everyone is happy, especially L.A. boat groupies. Like a hand with eight fingers, the yacht basin at Marina del Rey reaches inland, grabbing Los Angeles by the seat of the pants. In addition to the 6,000 boats in the water, it can store another 3,000 vessels in dry dock. There are nearly as many boats in Marina del Rey as there are residents. Admiralty Way runs in a semicircle around the harbor. It connects with Via Marina (on the west side) and Fiji Way (on the south side) to form a great horseshoe around the octet of boat basins. It is in this watery world-within-a-world that the moneyed heart of Marina del Rey can be heard to beat. Condos average in the $300,000 range. Apartment rentals are $1,500 and up, depending on what floor you're on and whether you look out on the city, ocean, or yacht basin. Some people live on their boats. A few have died on them. Dennis Wilson of the Beach Boys drowned here while diving for discarded souvenirs in a boat slip where he used to live with a former wife. .

Over the past three decades, Marina del Rey has blossomed like a cactus flower out of its desertlike surroundings. An impressive retail industry of waterfront restaurants, luxury hotels, dance clubs, and specialty shops has grown around the harbor. In Marina del Rey you can, as a brochure proclaims, browse for everything "from socks to solid gold." Signs heralding one's arrival in Marina del Rey offer this menu of options: "Apartments, Berths, Chandlery, Hotels, Launching, Maintenance, Moorings, Motels, Restaurants, Shops, Sportfishing, Town Houses, Yacht Sales." As you spiral closer to Admiralty Way from the outside world—passing through the buffer zones that isolate Marina del Rey from the less glamorous neighboring communities of Culver City, Playa del Rey, and Venice—an oasis of boats, buildings, and greenery emerges out of nowhere. If you look and listen closely, you might even hear ducks quacking and waddling around a large lake that's part of a nature preserve. Off-road bike paths wind around the marina. The South Bay Bicycle Trail leaves the beach at the mouth of Ballona Creek and passes through the marina, reemerging by the ocean at Venice Pier. Four small parks within the marina add a note of greenery and tranquillity. Burton Chase Park, at the end of Mindinao Way, is a six-acre green space from which one can watch boats enter and exit the marina. The retail area known as Fisherman's Village is one of the more convincing of the nautical-themed, New England-style shopping complexes we've seen, right down to its cobblestone walks. The whole of Marina del Rey has the privileged, dreamlike aura of a mirage. It's a great mirage, if you've got the means to enjoy it.

Beaches

In this case, the proper heading would be the singular "beach." Because it is a protected inland harbor, Marina del Rey by definition has no ocean beaches. The marina does have one beach at the end of Basin D: **Mother's Beach**, where water-lovers can swim, windsurf, and sail on a sandy, lifeguarded stretch of sand where no waves roll ashore. Maybe that's why choosy mothers choose Mother's as a place to bring their kids to frolic in relative safety. In any case, this mushroom-shaped lagoon enables both calm-water swimming and wind-free sunbathing. The drawback is water quality. Would you want to swim in a man-made lagoon routinely fouled by boat fuel, bilgewater, and storm runoff? Finally, Del Rey Lagoon is not a beach but it is a park overlooking the ocean by the south jetty at Marina del Rey, and it offers access to the northern end of Dockweiler State Beach. Facilities on this grassy, 13-acre park include picnic tables, a playground, basketball courts, and baseball diamonds.

Mother's Beach

Location: In Marina del Rey, at Basin D on Panay Way.

Parking: Metered parking lot.

Hours: Sunrise to 10 PM.

Facilities: Lifeguards, rest rooms, showers, and picnic tables.

Contact: For beach information, contact Marina del Rey Parks, Beaches, and Harbors at (310) 305-9503.

See number 23 on page 154.

Bunking Down

The selection of hotels and restaurants in Marina del Rey makes it the Neiman-Marcus of beach communities. Starting from the top, the vaunted **Ritz-Carlton** (4375 Admiralty Way, 823-1700, $$$$) brings a touch of Old World elegance to the land of new money. This 14-story masterpiece affords a choice of harbor or ocean views, swaddling guests in comfort (for a price) in a veritable island of first-class amenities: lighted tennis courts, a heated outdoor pool, yacht charters, and so on. **The Marina Beach Marriott** (4100 Admiralty Way, 301-3000, $$$$) offers comparable upscale accommodations in a 10-story tower that looks like a giant sand dune from the street. The balcony views—of the Malibu coastline to the north, of the Palos Verdes Peninsula to the south—are majestic, especially around sunset. With a ninth-floor cocktail lounge, ground-floor California-cuisine restaurant (Stones), an outdoor garden café and pool, and sumptuous rooms decorated in muted pastels and accented with brass and marble, you won't lack for pampering here. It's expensive to stay in Marina del Rey, but if you're going to do it, you might as well go straight to the top. If saving money is a consideration, nearby Culver City is loaded with cheaper chains, such as the **Culver City Travelodge** (11180 Washington Place, 839-1111, $), where you'll save a bundle, which you can blow on dinner and nightlife in the marina.

Coastal Cuisine

A few years back one of us had Sunday dinner with rock-and-roll pioneer Little Richard at **Aunt Kizzy's Back Porch** (4325 Glencoe Avenue, 578-1005, $$), a soul-food eatery located in the Villa Marina Shopping Center. Not only can Richard sing and pound the piano, the man knows how to pick a restaurant. The culinary style is Deep South and down-home: mounds of fried chicken, pork tenderloin, homemade mashed potatoes, stewed vegetables, fruit cobblers, and other fresh desserts. Aunt Kizzy's food is so good it's enough to give you religion, if you haven't got it already.

On the waterfront, **Edie's Diner** (4211 Admiralty Way, 823-5341, $) does a big business in burgers, fries, and pie. It's done up in diner chic, from the gleaming ceramic tile to the retro rock tunes on the booth-side jukeboxes—and the burgers are everything you'd want in a slab of ground cow: big, sloppy, and good. They do breakfast, as well. If burger fare or soul food isn't in the cards, the **Dining Room at the Ritz-Carlton** (4375 Admiralty Way, 823-1700, $$$$) offers a sublime culinary experience at the other end of the scale: in formal surroundings (jacket required) with a French accent and fresh California ingredients.

Then there's the **Cheesecake Factory** (4142 Via Marina, 306-3344, $$), an enormously popular franchise restaurant overlooking the marina. The menu you're handed is as thick as a small-town phone directory. The number of choices and the size of the servings are almost overwhelming. If you can narrow your preference down to a single category—salads, sandwiches, pastas, seafood, or other entrées—you're off to a strong start. But how can you make a final choice between, say, a spicy house jambalaya served over spinach-and-egg linguine (the most popular item) or Pasta del Mare, consisting of scallops, mussels, shrimp? Then there are the namesake cheesecakes. The problem is, who has room for dessert after a meal of the sizes they serve here? Solution: get a piece boxed to go. Coffee-holics will want to head over to the **Coffee Roaster Café** (552 Washington Street, 305-7147, $$), a favorite gathering place of Venice-Marina bohemians. In addition to espresso, cappuccino, and pastries, they offer healthful breakfasts, lunches, and dinners.

Night Moves

A night on the town in Marina del Rey begins with a fruitless search for a parking space. The way they've got it rigged, there's next to nothing in the way of legal street parking, leaving one with no choice but to hand the keys to a (gulp) valet at the club or restaurant of your choice. We despise valet parking. Why should you pay some scampering young man in tennis shorts to strip the gears on your car while moving it a few feet from the spot in which you disembarked? Our pet theory is that valet parking is a state-funded make-work project designed to keep high school–age California males off the streets and out of trouble. We will go to any lengths to avoid handing our car keys to a valet.

In this vexatious spirit we drove around Marina del Rey looking for parking. After cruising for a while, we tried the lot at a shopping center just outside the marina, but it was filled with signs warning that all cars belonging to noncustomers would be towed. We took our chances all the same and left the car, hiking to a place called—God, it hurts just to type a name this stupid—**Moose McGillycuddy's** (3535 Mindinao Way, 574-3932). Moose's is an indoor/outdoor pub, grub, and disco franchise that claims the same sort of crowd that used to jam the Red Onion, a now-defunct singles-bar chain that, in its own way, helped speed along the 1980s population boom in Southern California.

At Moose's a young crowd of mixed singles hopped to the fascistic beat of the latest synthetic dance hits. Some lined up to be plastered with free temporary tattoos, which was that evening's big promotion. A salty dog who looked like the Skipper on *Gilligan's Island* circulated with a wicker basket full of plastic-wrapped Moonie roses, cutting an odd figure. In the bathroom, a guy removed the sweaty T-shirt in which he'd arrived and changed into a trendier leisure-wear ensemble, looking like a discofied Clark Kent who'd come to dazzle the ladies with his sartorial Kryptonite. At one table a mutually infatuated couple took turns grooming each other, like Rhesus monkeys, with combs and brushes. We stationed ourselves at the Pop-a-Shot concession, vainly trying to impress the locals with our shooting ability and finally retreating to the outdoor patio.

Heat lamps were working hard to take the chill out of the summer night's air. Apparently we hit L.A. at the height of an unseasonable summer cold snap. Temperatures averaged in the 70s by day and plunged into the 60s at night, keeping the heat-seeking Angelinos at home and indoors. It felt heavenly to us, although the bars and clubs were seeing significantly reduced numbers as a result. Though it was only July, it looked like the summer had already ended at the **Endless Summer Sports Bar & Restaurant** (300 Washington Boulevard, 821-3577). However, our comely cocktail waitress assured us that the place would be packed tighter than a tin of sardines once the mercury returned to normal levels.

Across the street, the **Baja Cantina** (311 Washington Boulevard, 821-2252) was hopping all night long. Maybe it was all those hot chilis that were warming up the patrons in this popular Mexican restaurant and watering hole. You come in, put your name on the list, belly up to the bar, grab a Mexican beer, and wait for a table in tight quarters with what seems like half of Los Angeles. The Baja Cantina is noisy and fun, with its sociocultural ambience best suggested by two of the celebrities whose framed, autographed pictures hang on the wall: the actor Tony Danza and the porn star Christy Canyon.

For More Information

Contact the Marina del Rey Area Chamber of Commerce, 4519 Admiralty Way, Suite 206, Marina del Rey, CA 90292; (310) 821-0555.

Venice

Location: Venice is located 12 miles west of downtown Los Angeles. It can be reached by taking the Washington Boulevard exit off Interstate 405. Venice City Beach is among the most crowded, popular, and lively beaches in Los Angeles County.
Population: 52,000
Area Code: 310 **Zip Code:** 90291

In the 1993 film *Falling Down*, the Michael Douglas character—an everyman driven to psychopathy by the stress of living in Los Angeles—cuts a swath westward across the city to Venice, committing a rash of demented crimes on his way. The police track him down, forcing a final stand at the end of Venice Pier. As he dies, falling over the pier railing after absorbing a point-blank blast from Robert Duvall's service revolver, he gives Venice a last befuddled backward glance and then splashes into the beautiful blue Pacific.

In Venice, life doesn't just imitate art. It defines it. If it's cutting edge, chances are it started in Venice... and it probably will end here, too. Venice is many things: a fascinating human zoo, a nasty urban war zone, and just about everything in between.

Take the pier, for example. Though it was used for this Hollywood film shoot, it has been closed to public use for several years. Like the Michael Douglas character, many alienated people gravitate to Venice in order to make an escape. On the other hand, many who come here—us, for example—have given it a befuddled backward glance as they headed out of town.

It's easy to trash Venice. Not for nothing is it known as the home of $2 sunglasses, $3 T-shirts, $4 Tarot readings, and $5 stress massages. New Age prophets walk shoulder to shoulder with the old-age homeless. Runaway children seek shelter in group houses, and gangs bring their hideous territorial squabbles to the shore. Cops walk the beat, half amused and half afraid.

It's easy to allow preconceptions to unfairly blind a first-time visitor to Venice's peculiar appeal. The source of that appeal goes right back to the town's roots. Venice began as the dream of a man named Abbot Kinney, who made his millions on cigarettes and spent them all in 1900 purchasing 160 acres of marshland south of Santa Monica. For some reason (nicotine frenzy perhaps), he saw similarities between his new property and the site on which Venice, Italy, was built. He commissioned two architects to design a "thoroughly equipped" city with streets, hotels, houses, and canals—15 miles of cement-bottomed canals. By June 1905, the canals were filled with water. All Kinney needed for his new Venice were people to build their dream homes beside his man-made waterways.

Like any good businessman, Kinney lured folks here with a gimmick: gondolas and gondoliers. He imported some of Italy's finest oarsmen and had them serenade prospective buyers while rowing them up and down the canals to inspect the empty lots. He persuaded merchants to build hotels, restaurants, and shops in the architectural style of the Venetian Renaissance. He also oversaw the construction of a lecture hall, pavilion, and theater. Provocative speakers were brought in, first-rate plays were staged, and blue-ribbon orchestras performed. All the while, the gondoliers kept singing.

Kinney's noble experiment failed, culminating in a poorly attended and abbreviated run of *Camille* starring Sarah Bernhardt, the greatest stage actress of her day. Visitors to Venice, it turned out, preferred sand and sidewalks to the interior of a concert hall. To salvage his enormous investment, the dauntless Kinney did an about-face, filling in a number of his festering, plant-choked ***(continued on page 200)***

The Fall and Rise of L.A. Culture

Like anything that never stops moving, Los Angeles is hard to get a bead on. Here are some random snippets of L.A. culture we caught on our last pass through town.

* * *

Montel Williams, the host of a daytime-TV talk show based in L.A., devoted a full hour-long segment to "catfighting," a new craze among the fetishist set. Shapely, lithe young lionesses decked out in suggestive garb (Spandex drawers, Victoria's Secret push-up bras) engage in physical combat, during which they rip each other's clothes off, claw each other's bodies, and yank at their prodigious manes of hair. All of this is videotaped and sold at exorbitant fees to weirdos with too much time on their hands.

The largest producer of these videos is a woman who allegedly has a degree from Harvard (an English major, no less!). Her long-winded defense of her handiwork included the catch-all excuse that justifies all forms of excess—i.e., that it's "meeting a real need." The "male perspective" was provided by the quintessential slick playboy. (You know, gleaming coifed toupee, too-white capped teeth, and a Hawaiian shirt open to the sternum.) His justification for enjoying catfighting videos was even more pathetic. He liked it because "it was real." Would this sleazeball enjoy catfighting as much if the participants were even closer to reality—say, a bunch of tired, middle-aged harridans fighting over handbags at a rummage sale?

* * *

A Los Angeles comedian addressing a local crowd: "Nine out of ten porno films are made right here in Los Angeles. Who says we don't have culture?"

* * *

We always make it a habit to study the Yellow Pages in every beach town. Often the listings provide the most revealing glimpse of a community outside of a guided tour by a longtime resident. In Los Angeles, on the verso of the page we wanted (for "Laundries—Self Service"), we found listings for "Lecture Bureaus." Of the 20 bureaus listed, the most intriguing was this one: "Zen of Hype Presentation." What could this be? Months later, we are still pondering the possibilities. Which is probably the point. A koan in the Yellow Pages. What a concept.

* * *

The hottest art exhibit in town when we passed through was for a celebrated Angelino whose mid-career retrospective featured a one-room conceptual sculpture that was titled *Eviscerated Corpse*. The art critic for the *L.A. Weekly*, a hip tabloid, wrote this in his review: "K_'s activity has been characterized as playing with his own shit, and in a sense, it's true.... But the fundamental, and surprisingly often missed, difference with K_ is that he is not simply demonstrating his fecal interest, but is actually doing something with it." One of us has a cat about which we could say the same thing.

* * *

A local cartoonist concocted a tableau in *Buzz* magazine entitled "The Rise and Fall of the L.A. Art Scene." It included such commentary as: "Once upon a time there was surfing, the Beach Boys, and a handful of Beat poets." And: "New York had Warhol and Lichtenstein. So we got Ruscha and Kienholz. New York had lofts. So we got lofts, too. New York had bad boys. So we got bad boys, too." And: "After a year or two in the dumpster, it looks as if the fickle L.A. art market may be coming back to life."

* * *

Two ads sitting side by side in the *L.A. Reader*, a local alternative weekly, offered these coming attractions: (1) a band called Human Waste Project playing at a venue called Club Ugly; (2) a Fetish Ball featuring a Mistress of Ceremonies named "Eva Destruction" as well as a "mandatory dress code of latex, leather, PVC, cross-dress, uniforms, corsets, high heels."

* * *

Of the 50 largest metropolitan areas in the country, Los Angeles ranked 48th overall in donations to charities. Here is how L.A. fared specifically in giving to some of the larger charitable organizations:

- American Cancer Society (38th)
- American Red Cross (48th)
- Boy Scouts (49th)
- Girl Scouts (50th)
- Habitat for Humanity (46th)
- Jewish Federations (42nd)
- United Way (47th)

* * *

Excerpt from an article in *Buzz*. We think it speaks for the silent majority of sane Los Angelinos we've met and befriended during our many visits to the city. The author notes, "L.A. parties always seem to fall into three basic categories:

"1. Parties held by and for people far more famous than you. Flashbulbs going off at the door are a pretty good indication you will be regarded as chattel inside. Beware of German or French male hairstylists/photographer assistants/blah-blahs.

"2. Parties held by and for your social peers. . . . [T]his means everyone standing around rehashing their work week while voraciously consuming room-temperature Trader Joe's products.

"3. Parties held by people a few years and pieces of furniture behind you. Expect to faithfully BYOB only to be greeted with a single bowl of Nacho Cheese Flavored Doritos under a bare light bulb, people in bicycle pants screaming and sweating around them."

What could we possibly add—except that we've been there, too.

(continued from page 197) canals and bringing in sideshow freaks, street theater, and a roller coaster. A miniature railroad was built to run along with the Ocean Front Walk, turning the town into an amusement park by the sea. In 1925, the little town became part of Los Angeles. By 1939, Kinney's conversion was complete, with Venice known as "the Playland of the Pacific" and "the Coney Island of the West."

Venice has since undergone other transformations. It was covered with oil wells, low-income housing, and boarded-up slums in the 1940s. It was adopted by beatniks in the 1950s, hippies in the 1960s, artists and fitness freaks in the 1970s, and gentrified homeowners—the original audience Kinney had dreamed of for Venice—in the 1980s. In the 1990s, Venice still lives in a dream, as it always has, perceiving itself as some sort of impervious Left Bank, but one beset by problems.

Granted, certain aspects of Venice's surreal sideshow are real and fascinating. There's the endless parade of oddballs who entertain for spare change along Ocean Front Walk, the cement boardwalk that runs along the backside of Venice Beach. Although this pedestrian thoroughfare is only 0.7 miles long, it is light-years beyond whatever else passes for cutting edge elsewhere in America. The best place to start a walk-through is at the Windward Avenue access, the halfway point in the human parade. Here, you'll find the classic *Venice on the Half Shell* mural, which captures the spirit of the procession. It may sound like a cliché, but you really are likely to see anything out here. The following are just some of the things we've witnessed: a guy in a turban chewing glass... a guy on a unicycle juggling knives... another unicyclist juggling chainsaws...a legless, armless dwarf dancing on his stumps to Latin disco music... an assortment of Michael Jackson impersonators, with proud mamas pocketing the donations... a "post tribal artist"... a cabalistic Tarot reader... a village shaman offering a spoken "love revival"... a gypsy performing "three-day dissolving marriage ceremonies"... folk performers with purple hair... an ancient black woman shrieking incoherent blues while strumming an electric guitar lent her by a well-meaning college kid... body piercers... hair braiders... X-rated comedians... conceptual artists... mural artists... caricaturists... acrobats... animals performing stupid pet tricks... transvestites... leather freaks... Rastafarians... punks, drunks, and punch-drunks... and some people who are really and truly insane.

Along this same route, you'll find a few passable bars, some decent take-out food stalls, a good book shop, and a museum of Native American art. Hang around long enough and you'll also absorb the prevailing Venetian outlook: a healthy and well-cultivated disregard for chicness, big money, and normal ways of doing things.

Away from the curious clamor on Ocean Front Walk, Venice reveals another side of itself—a pleasant residential community filled with proud homeowners who casually enjoy the placid life along the town's back canals. In the past few years, the more secluded canals have been cleaned up and fish are even seen in the no-longer-murky waters. The Canal Walk—between Washington Boulevard and Rose Avenue—is part of the Venice Canal Historic District, which is listed on the National Register of Historic Places. Walking here is an enjoyable and quiet diversion, as you observe the fascinating and eclectic architecture and the commendable lengths that the residents have gone to turn the tiniest plots of land into gardening masterpieces.

To these good souls, the biggest crisis of late was the great duck controversy of 1993. The health department, disregarding the vehement protests of residents, exterminated several diseased ducks that had made their home in the canals. The quacking over this issue has since died down, but still it's enough to ruffle one's feathers. Community leaders regularly organize cleanups, and ad hoc action, block parties, and neighborhood watches have made inroads on crime prevention. Venice is not about to let the town go to seed, as it did in the past.

The best way to see the full tableau that Venice has to offer is to book a walking tour through the Venice Historic Society (392-1014). They cost around $7.50, and reservations must be made ahead of time.

Unfortunately, Venice still has a long way to go. There are parts of town that even the police are hesitant to patrol. During our visit, a group of L.A.'s finest staged a protest at being transferred to the Venice beat. In the previous nine months, an ongoing gang war had resulted in 17 deaths and 55 woundings in Venice alone. Ironically, the transfer was orchestrated by City Councilwoman Ruth Galanter, who had won a 1987 election while in a coma—the result of a near fatal stabbing by a stranger in her Venice home.

We were warned repeatedly about a new trend in urban crime that has been particularly prevalent in Venice: "bike-jacking." The pavilion smells of human waste and is so thick with graffiti that you have to look closely to make out this sign: "Notice—Defacing Park Property May Result in a Maximum Penalty of $500 Fine and Six Months in Jail." At the south end of Venice Beach, the gazebos along Ocean Front Walk have not been closed down but might as well be to anyone who doesn't regularly urinate outdoors. A lunatic fringe has set up a defiant beachhead in Venice, roasting like almonds in the sun and heckling passersby. We met a Dutch fellow who had a word for the less savory side of Venice: *onguur*. Though he claimed it was untranslatable, his facial expression told us all we needed to know. Venice can be real *onguur* sometimes.

None of this stems the flow of onlookers in Venice. Perversely, the sense of forbidden danger seems to add to its appeal. And so goes Venice, into the setting sun of the California dream, once delicious and golden, and now.... Well, we'll close with a quote from one of Venice's stellar residents, Orson Bean, who wrote in *Venice* magazine: "Venice of America dares you to be happy. Someone once wrote that the most revolutionary act possible might be three straight days of continuous happiness. People walk in Venice. They roller-skate and bicycle and skateboard. They rally to save ducks. They don't mind looking like fools. They figure everyone else enjoys it when they look like fools, so why shouldn't they?"

Beaches

Venice City Beach has never looked better. It is an amazingly wide sheet of sand, running for two miles north from Venice Pier to Santa Monica Pier, that largely goes to waste. Literally. People use it for an outhouse. Maybe this accounts for the fact that while people use this beautiful, wide porch of sand for all the normal activities—swimming, sunning, hanging out—the numbers are relatively small. The few people we saw on it had been lured there by a free concert to benefit the homeless.

The beach itself is spiked by three enormous jetties and was widened by sand dredged from the site of the massive Hyperion Sewage Treatment Plant. The most intriguing part of the

Venice City Beach

3

Location: In Venice, along Washington Boulevard at Ocean Front Walk.

Parking: Metered street parking.

Hours: 5 AM to 10:30 PM.

Facilities: Lifeguards, rest rooms, showers, and picnic areas.

Contact: For beach information, contact the Los Angeles County Lifeguard Service, Central Section, at (310) 394-3264. For a surf report, call (310) 578-0478.

See number 24 on page 154.

beach is at the north end, where a weightlifting area attracts body freaks. Some incredible games of basketball are played on the nearby blacktop, with occasional visits from pro stars. The paddle-tennis games are as intense as any matches at Wimbledon. The beach can be accessed from any of the main east-west streets in Venice (Washington Street, Venice Boulevard, Rose Avenue, Windward Avenue, Park Boulevard) or from anywhere on the Ocean Front Walk promenade. Metered parking is available along any of these thoroughfares as well.

Bunking Down

No matter how cutting edge you feel, you do not want to stay in Venice. For one thing, it's unpredictable and sometimes unsafe after dark. For another, there's really not much to choose from in the way of accommodations, unless you rent a beachfront villa by the week (and that is shockingly expensive). Visit for the day and buy a T-shirt, a hot dog, and a slab of pizza. Watch the street performers, then quietly take your leave, preferably back to the hotels of Marina del Rey (see the entry on page 193).

Crosstown Traffic: Driving in Los Angeles

It is nearly impossible to visit Los Angeles without spending a lot of time inside a car. If you wish to view the dubious baubles of ancient or current celebrity—Aaron Spelling's mansion, Grauman's Chinese Theatre, the condo where Nicole Brown Simpson was brutally murdered—you will have to drive and drive…and drive some more.

Despite the amount of lip service people pay to it, public transportation is piecemeal, almost discouraged. A Blue Line light rail makes regular 22-mile runs from Los Angeles to Long Beach. A Metro Red Line, the city's first subway, opened in January 1993, but as of this writing only one line is open—from Union Station to MacArthur Park. (For updates and schedules, call 800-252-7433.) By the year 2010, they hope to have 400 miles of track in place, carrying half a million passengers a day.

Los Angeles is too spread out over its 462 square miles to make riding the bus anything but a poverty-induced exercise in masochism. And forget walking the city's streets. Pedestrians are a low priority in Southern Californian city planning. Walking across any street is an adventure. Crossing a busy multilane boulevard is a dare. Few drivers will voluntarily stop for anyone in a crosswalk.

So drive you must. Interstates loop into each other like asphalt pretzels. The surrounding development looks much the same, a blight of ill-planned growth that beggars the imagination. Our first rule of thumb for beach travel in California is to stay on the Pacific Coast Highway. Nothing of interest lies more than five miles inland or is worth the trouble it takes to get there. Through this simple rule we have already spared you Disneyland, not to mention the Reagan and Nixon presidential libraries.

The corollary to this is to avoid Interstate 5 and Interstate 405 unless you have to make a long north-south haul. Built to ease car traffic, both roads are always backed up.

Perversely, the car-pool lanes on both interstates through Los Angeles and Orange Counties are nearly always clear. The number of passengers constituting a High Occupancy Vehicle (HOV) has been dropped. Now you need only two passengers per

Crosstown Traffic: Driving in Los Angeles *(continued)*

car. And still the carpool lanes are empty. That is because nearly everyone in Southern California is a "Lindbergh"—a solo driver. So the roads stay jammed.

Here are two indispensable driving tips (abridged) culled from *Los Angeles* magazine:

- Plan ahead. Know your destination in terms of points south and north, east and west. Directional signs on Interstate 405 read "Sacramento" to indicate north and "Long Beach" to indicate south. Learn the name and number of the freeways you'll be traveling:

Highway 2	=	Glendale Freeway
Highway 10	=	Santa Monica or San Bernardino Freeway
Highway 90	=	Marina Freeway
Highway 101	=	Ventura or Hollywood Freeway
Highway 110	=	Pasadena or Harbor Freeway
Highway 170	=	Hollywood Freeway
Interstate 5	=	Golden State or Santa Ana Freeway
Interstate 405	=	San Diego Freeway

- Keep track of traffic over the air waves. Many radio stations offer traffic reports. The stations with the best coverage are KNX (1070 AM) and KFWB (980 AM).

KNX, an all-news radio station, gives traffic reports *every six minutes, 24 hours a day!* A typical traffic update sounds like this (imagine a fast-talking, mellifluous deejay voice): "It's stop and go all the way from Santa Monica to Pasadena, but the good news is there are no accidents blocking the road." (This is good news?)

When an explanation for a traffic tie-up is warranted (what is called a "sigalert"), the tone of the deejay's voice doesn't modulate, and his update sounds like this: "There's a bus on top of a car near the Avalon exit on I-405. Ouch, that must smart!"

Further coloring the experience of driving in L.A. is the haze of smog, the vast wasteland of junkyards and metal salvage lots, the oil refineries, and the Smog Express inspection stations where, if you fail, you don't pay. After any amount of driving here you inevitably find yourself asking the obvious question: is this the wisest use of the land? Of course not.

But Los Angeles keeps on growing and, after each earthquake, the roads are rebuilt before the homes are, inviting more cars and rubes to drive them. A 1988 study by the Southern California Association of Governments warned that if the population continued to rise, $110 billion in new road construction would be needed just to stabilize existing congestion.

What's the answer? In the big picture, reconfigure society and the economy to encourage sustainable growth and to lower the birth rate. For the smaller purposes of a beach visit, our advice is to get down to the beach and stay there. Rent a bicycle or a pair of skates. Jog. Walk. But before crossing the street, look both ways...twice.

All things considered, we fared okay the one time we did stay in Venice. The room that we found, as forbidding as it looked from the outside, was at the **Venice Beach Cotel** (25 Windward Avenue, 399-9914, $). "Cotel" is short for "community hotel," and it is primarily for international travelers on a tight budget. A hostel, if you will, only a notch nicer. The rooms are spartan but clean, with no TV or air-conditioning and shared bathrooms, and the security is reassuringly tight (you must be buzzed in). Most of the foreigners we met at the Cotel claimed to be afraid to leave it. They weren't shrinking violets, by any means; we're talking hale and hearty Europeans in their 20s who had seen their share of world travel. After experiencing Venice at night, though, they preferred the Cotel hospitality's room to the bars and clubs on the streets below. After a few night moves of our own around Venice, we saw their point and gladly joined them. A good time was had by all, as we helped promote world unity by buying a group of Swedes, Aussies, Dutch, and Swiss round after round of Mexican beer. Cheers, Tomas and Gunnard, wherever you are.

Coastal Cuisine

In Venice, you take the bad with the good. And some good old reliables are still around. During the day, the **Sidewalk Café** (1401 Ocean Front Walk, 399-5547, $) is the best vantage point from which to observe the human circus. The items on the menu have been given literary names, because the café adjoins the excellent Small World Bookstore. Breakfast, for example, can consist of an omelette named after Gertrude Stein, Carlos Castaneda, or Jack Kerouac. Lunch could be a burger named for Charles Dickens, Pablo Neruda, or James Michener. (The latter, logically enough, features pineapples and ham.)

Two recent arrivals in Venice worth considering are the **West Beach Café** (60 North Venice Boulevard, 823-5396, $$$) and **72 Market Street** (72 Market Street, 392-8720, $$$). The former is a crowded, casual establishment specializing in California cuisine. 72 Market Street features "good-old American classics with a twist," even though it's co-owned by a famous Englishman, Dudley Moore.

Night Moves

We first read about aromatherapy, a New Age form of healing, in a Venice weekly devoted to planetary health. This therapy is based on the belief that your nose takes in "essential oils" vital to your well-being. When unhealthy, you simply need to inhale the proper mix of oils until you're good as new. Depression, for example, can be cured by inhaling the following herbs: basil, bergamot, chamomile, clary, lavender, marjoram, rosemary, and ylang-ylang.

After sampling Venice both by day and night, we have devised our own form of aromatherapy, which we'd like to share with anyone who has grown sick and tired of life back home. Go to the south end of Venice City Beach at the end of a long, hot summer day. Stand anywhere along Ocean Front Walk and breathe deeply, keeping your mouth closed so as to maximize the essential oils your nose takes in. We promise that you'll be exclaiming "there's no place like home" in short order.

If you wish to pick through the olfactory minefield of Venice after dark, the **Town House** (52 Windward Avenue, 392-4040) is the place to rock out. Large and loud enough for the rowdiest bike gang, the Town House features live rock and roll most nights in summer. If you're looking for a more civilized alternative, amble up Washington Street in the direction of Marina del Rey, where you'll find coffeehouses, sports bars, and cantinas galore.

For More Information

Contact the Venice Area Chamber of Commerce, 13470 Washington Boulevard, Suite 206, Venice, CA 90291; (310) 827-2366.

 Map of Los Angeles County beaches—page 154

Santa Monica

Location: 13 miles west of downtown Los Angeles, 8 miles northwest of Los Angeles International Airport. Ocean Avenue runs along the beach. A number of major east-west boulevards—Pico, Colorado, Santa Monica, Wilshire—end at Ocean Avenue. Santa Monica State Beach is among the largest and most popular beaches in Los Angeles County.
Population: 91,000
Area Code: 310 **Zip Code:** 90401

The most "urban" of Los Angeles's beach communities, Santa Monica is a showcase for much of the best, and some of the worst, that the city has to offer. The town has a temperate, even climate—perfect for those who live outdoors and those who only come out to play. After the "June gloom" has run its course, the weather in Santa Monica is dependably good the rest of the year.

Santa Monica's beach is where the heart and soul of Los Angeles comes to have fun in the summer. It serves as the steam-release valve for L.A.'s vast and diverse population, a no-frills playland that attracts close to 15 million visitors a year. That's about a quarter of the total load borne by all the beaches in Los Angeles County. Santa Monica is easily accessible to all. Perhaps for this reason, it suffers in comparison to its more glittery neighbors up toward Malibu and down by Manhattan Beach. At Santa Monica, it's just good people having a high old time at the beach, many of whom speak English only as a second language. Without Santa Monica in the summertime, Los Angeles would be one big, smog-laced pressure cooker.

In the process of serving as the city's back door to the beach, Santa Monica somehow manages to maintain a character and charm all its own. Grandeur and squalor are mixed here in unequal proportions, creating an appealing blend of tropical rot and urban cool that Raymond Chandler captured in his detective novels. (His fictional "Bay City" was modeled after Santa Monica.) Chandler's subterranean *noir* universe is but a flickering image now, seen in the architectural splendor of some of the older apartment buildings and the art-deco facades of the theaters. The city is in what might be called a period of transition, as it has been for several years. Many buildings are boarded up, some are being torn down, and other marginal properties await the inevitable.

An attempt has been made to revive downtown Santa Monica, adding pedestrian shopping malls and multiscreened cinemas in hopes of bringing back the healing plasma of money that fled to the hills in the 1980s. The epicenter of this downtown renewal is the Third Street Promenade. It is a brick pedestrian walkway that courses through four blocks of storefronts, from Colorado Avenue to Wilshire Boulevard, running parallel to the beach from three blocks back.

Though this mall dispenses the usual trendy consumer flotsam, the experience of walking through it is spiced by some unique street performers. In fact, these performers lend the promenade a flavor more distinctive than the shops. The Third Street brigade is more talented, and less scatological and dangerous, than the ragtag army in Venice. A string quartet composed of conservatory students plays Vivaldi beautifully. A small ensemble cranks out a huge big-band sound. A lonely jazzman offers a mournful blues on the vibes. An old man with an ashen face sings Willie Nelson's "On the Road Again" and yodels while standing on his head in a chair. Awesome.

The overwhelming feeling one gets while strolling Third Street is nostalgia for the grandeur that Santa Monica once represented. Many of the promenade businesses trade on nostalgia, re-creating the 1950s and '60s with glittery, antiseptic revisionism. The most popular eatery is a faux '50s diner. The hippest clothier is a thrift shop *manqué* that sells used clothing at boutique prices. (Ragged-looking T-shirts for $18—what a concept!) The bars are upscale pool halls filled with yuppies slumming as bikers. The nicest theater is a beautifully restored 1940s film palace. Of the 20 movies that were being shown at the multiplexes during a recent visit, fully two-thirds were sequels or remakes of old television shows. Third Street is ultimately a mirage of fake evocations: the upscale, chrome-railed pool hall serves gourmet pizza, the '50s diner gleams with an antiseptic aura, and the mock-bohemian coffeehouses collect 15 dimes (instead of one) for a cup of coffee.

Only the presence of the homeless milling about soils the mood of sentimental yearning (unless you're nostalgic for the Great Depression). The collision of Santa Monica's downward mobility with its last-ditch attempts at creating an urban island of crime-free consumerism makes for an odd melange on the streets. We saw some strange scenes indeed. An executive in a designer running outfit was spitting orders into a mobile phone while rollerskating past a haggard woman on a bench who was flicking at invisible bugs, her belongings arrayed in bulging bags at her feet. It was hard to tell which of these two characters was more insane. Then there was the wraithlike, barefoot woman who punched the air like Fred Sanford, intimidating a striding stream of Docker shorts and Polo shirts into stepping out of her way. At a yogurt café she walked in, looked around, saw what she wanted, and snatched it right off the plate of a startled German tourist.

In many ways, Santa Monica remains the most appealing and unique place in Los Angeles. Certainly, it is among the last bastions of kindness, egalitarianism, and liberalism. Still, it is life lived at its extremes. On the one hand, homeless occupy the parks and promenades, and proletarian hordes roam the beach and pier. On the other, luxury hotels overlook the ocean and stores cater to people with too much disposable income. As is the case in most American cities these days, there is no longer much in the way of a happy medium.

Beaches

Santa Monica State Beach is easily accessible from downtown Los Angeles via the Santa Monica Freeway (Interstate 10) or one of several primary east-west arteries (Pico, Wilshire, Santa Monica). Any number of bus lines start and end here as well. The dimensions of this beach are amazing: it is 3.3 miles long and several football fields wide. Generally it attracts a close-packed crowd of Hispanic families who bring beach towels and picnic baskets. South of Santa Monica Pier the blankets and bodies thin out. Two concrete walkways run parallel some distance back from the ocean. One ferries pedestrian traffic, while the other transports those on wheels. An army of mobile twenty- and thirty-something cyclists and inline skaters can be seen leaving vapor trails on the South Bay Bicycle Trail. You can park in state-run fee lots or take your chances feeding the meters on the streets.

The center of the action is Santa Monica Pier, which is among the best in the Golden

Santa Monica State Beach

4

Location: In Santa Monica, along Ocean Avenue at Colorado Avenue.

Parking: $6 entrance fee per vehicle or metered street parking.

Hours: 6 AM to sunset.

Facilities: Lifeguards, rest rooms, showers, and picnic tables.

Contact: For beach information, contact the Los Angeles County Lifeguard Service, Central Section, at (310) 394-3264. For a surf report, call (310) 578-0478.

See number 25 on page 154.

State. The pier is an antiquated slice of Americana, a West Coast Coney Island stocked with gaming arcades, T-shirt vendors (four for $10, rivaling Venice for, uh, value), fast-food stalls and incongruously chic restaurants. Built in 1909, it's a rickety wooden structure, sections of which must regularly be rebuilt due to the beating it takes from the waves. Tiny arcades flare off from the main concourse, creating an atmosphere not unlike the midway at a state fair. All the ingredients are here for kids to have a good time and for parents to get nostalgic about their own gloriously misspent youth: skee-ball, basketball shoots, Wedges/Hedges, bumper cars, rocking horses, an antique carousel, and a gift shop where one can purchase a plaster cast of Elvis stranger than any to be found in Memphis.

Once part of a huge playland, replete with a glamorous ballroom and famous "Blue Streak Racing Coaster," the old outlying structures fell to the wrecking ball some years ago, and all that remains is the pier. New cafés are planned for the future. For now, the fast-food stands are guaranteed to bring back memories of indigestion. Step right up for tacos, hot dogs, cotton candy, fried dough, and fish-and-chips. Then head home for a large, cool drink of Alka-Seltzer.

We took our skee-ball prizes (two tiny plastic rats and a thimble-sized trophy) and headed Back On the Beach. Yes, that's the name of a wonderful piazza on the sand an invigorating half-mile hike north of the pier. A former private beach club and now a café with a seating capacity of 200, Back On the Beach (see Coastal Cuisine below) is a quintessential L.A. beach experience. You can eat a salad as an antidote to the pier food or simply sit back with a beverage and watch the passing parade on the South Bay Bicycle Trail. President Clinton chose this spot for his morning jog when he was in the city, and Al Pacino is regularly seen here. Even more telling is the fact that several episodes of *Beverly Hills 90210* were filmed here. Volleyball nets and playground equipment are nearby, for further diversions.

As for swimming, the waves at Santa Monica State Beach are sufficient to excite the tiny tots on their Styrofoam boards but not large enough to attract serious surfing. Several hundred yards south of the pier is the real Muscle Beach, where Conan-like men and women hoist barbells all day long while lesser mortals stand around in the sand and applaud. Down toward Venice, you'll come to a sprawl of basketball and paddle-tennis courts, with grandstands beside them. Rest a spell and marvel at the athleticism of the men and women sweating in the sun.

The physical setting of the beach is almost as muscular as the weight lifters. Backed by a long, undeveloped bluff, Santa Monica's beach somehow seems tranquil even when thousands are jammed on the sand below—a glorious sight! Atop the bluff is Palisades Park, a shaded 26-acre jewel that runs for 14 city blocks from Colorado Avenue to Adelaide Drive. This green, shady buffer between the sand and the city is filled with benches and shuffleboard courts, and it's popular with Santa Monica's large contingent of senior citizens. It is also popular with the homeless. The two groups seem to coexist peacefully, though.

Given a city the size of L.A., there are bound to be problems with its most popular beach. In the late 1980s, Santa Monica became a colostomy bag for the city's then sick body. The Hyperion Sewage Treatment Plant, a gargantuan facility that serves four million people and was once the pride and joy of L.A. (earning rapturous accolades from Aldous Huxley, of all people), broke down. Millions of gallons of raw sewage poured directly into Santa Monica Bay. This set off a chain reaction that brought the county sewage system and city government to near collapse. The mayor called for voluntary water conservation, but the filthy rich in Westside and the San Fernando Valley didn't go along with it, filling pools and watering lawns in protest. Water became even scarcer, exacerbating tensions with Arizona and Northern California. But, on the bright side, the pollution of the Santa Monica Bay provided the impetus for a slow-growth and eco-minded grassroots movement that has gained strength ever since.

Bunking Down

It is possible to stay near the beach in Santa Monica. Many hotels and motels, large and small, line Ocean Avenue a block or two from the pier and a pedestrian bridge away from the beach. Staying here also solves your biggest beach problem—parking. Leaving your wheels in a hotel garage sure beats battling experienced, have-you-hugged-my-bumper-today natives, who will beat you to any available slot. There's only one drawback. Ocean Avenue can be loud, even at night. We learned this the hard way one year, taking a room at the least expensive motel on the strip: a $40 jobbie. The price was cheap because it was a four-walled cell with rancid bedcovers and thin, lifeless pillows. *Caveat emptor.* These fleabags litter the roadside like yesterday's papers. There are no bargains; you get what you pay for. Of all the smaller motels on Ocean Avenue, the **Breakers** (1501 Ocean Avenue, 451-4811, $$$) is the best. Of course, it is a bit expensive but solid as a rock and set off a bit from the traffic noise on the street.

A money transfusion in recent years has transformed the beachfront. Along with the older, dependable **Holiday Inn at the Pier** (120 Colorado Avenue, 451-0676, $$), high-rise luxury hotels now tower over the Santa Monica Beach south of the pier. The cream of the crop is the **Loews Santa Monica Beach Hotel** (1700 Ocean Avenue, 458-6700, $$$$). It's an attractive corporate-style lodge that somehow manages to exude a casual sort of class. (The additional parking charges aren't classy or casual, though.) The lobby alone is worth a look-see. You can hear the waves roll in from your balcony at Loews Santa Monica Beach Hotel and watch the human parade roll by on the bike paths. All in all, it's a very soothing sight. At night, milk and cookies are brought to guests' doors. The milk is served in tiny juice glasses placed inside a big cow mug that's been iced down. The cookies are huge chocolate-chip wedges, dipped in more chocolate and dusted with cocoa powder, providing a nice bedtime touch worthy of Mom.

Coastal Cuisine

The best quick bite is down at **Back On the Beach** (445 Palisades Road, 393-8282, $$) and the best quick morning hit is at **Starbucks**, in the Third Street Promenade (260-9947). At the latter, Charles Bukowski wannabes nurse a bottomless mug and work on their angst. Dinner is another matter. Santa Monica is home to some of Los Angeles's finest dining. Famed chef Wolfgang Puck's **Chinois On Main** (2709 Main Street, 392-9025, $$$$) is a celebrated bastion of *haute cuisine* blending French, Chinese, and Japanese elements. **Rocken Rolls**, chef Hans Rockenwagner's fast-food kiosk at the Third Street Promenade, is as popular as the French contemporary cuisine at his **Rockenwagner's** restaurant and bakery (2435 Main Street, 399-6504, $$$$). But we wanted seafood. We found it, sort of, at **Chez Jay** (1657 Ocean Avenue, 395-1741, $$). It's a longtime popular beach hangout run by a guy who once hunted pirate treasure. His signature dish is "spuds fried with bananas"—real surfer food, that—and his steaks, chops, and seafood have been pleasing palates for 35 years. Nearby, another oceanfront landmark, **Ivy at the Shore** (1541 Ocean Avenue, 393-3113, $$$) serves American fare in a tropical setting adjacent to the ocean.

We couldn't resist a drive inland for Cajun-style seafood at **Orleans** (11705 National Boulevard, 479-4187, $$$$). The fare is seafood and more, cooked the pure, unadulterated Paul Prudhomme way, with plenty of butter (although low-fat, low-sodium versions of dishes are offered). The blackened catfish, drum fish, salmon or redfish (from the Gulf), and the bronzed swordfish are seared in a hot pan and served with a simple sherry sauce. Before that arrives, there's irresistible homemade banana muffins and jalapeño rolls. For an appetizer, try the Cajun popcorn shrimp or seafood gumbo. Though the Cajun craze seems to have come and gone elsewhere, Orleans predates the trends, having served their étouffée and maquechoux for over a decade in a pleasant white house in a quiet neighborhood.

Night Moves

Santa Monica is only one boulevard (Sunset, Wilshire, or Santa Monica) away from Hollywood. Pick up the latest copy of *L.A. Weekly, L.A. Reader, L.A. Village View, Buzz* magazine, or the *Los Angeles Times* to find out what's doing in town. The detailed listings for each night of the week will give you some idea of what the term "free will" means. It's difficult to comment in much detail about a scene as extensive as the one in L.A. To a pair of beach bums who have been denied good music in more beach towns than we care to count, Santa Monica and Los Angeles are almost too much of a good thing. If only they could space out it evenly out over both coasts....

With that said, we direct your attention to the vicinity of upper Santa Monica Boulevard, where the old guard of clubs is still rocking the City of Angels—**Club Lingerie**, **Whiskey a Go-Go**, the **Roxy**, **McCabe's**, the **Palomino**. We unhesitatingly recommend the **House of Blues** (8439 Sunset Boulevard, 213-650-0476), less exuberantly the Johnny Depp–owned **Viper Room** (8882 Sunset Boulevard, 310-358-1881). Every night in L.A. is a who's who of musicians. Closer to the beach, your main alternative is to stroll the Third Street Promenade (between Colorado Avenue and Wilshire Boulevard). Nondrinkers will dig the outdoor cafés, used bookshops, street musicians, cinemas, and dessert places. Imbibers flock to **Yankee Doodle's** (1410 Promenade, 394-4632), a sports bar that epitomizes all that is faux-gettable about going out in the 1990s: overpaid yuppies affecting pirate kerchiefs and $1,000 leather jackets while playing pool and scarfing gourmet pizza. The drinks are overpriced. One large draft Fosters and a cranberry juice cost almost $10! Finally we retreated to a corner and shot at the electronic basketball concession until our quarters ran out. You would do better to walk a little farther and seek solace at **Anastasia's Asylum** (1028 Wilshire Boulevard, 394-7113), a hip coffeehouse in the best sense. There's no cover charge, the local atmosphere is genuine, and they have live entertainment and a vegetarian menu.

For More Information

Contact the Santa Monica Convention & Visitors Bureau, 2219 Main Street, Santa Monica, CA 90405; (310) 392-9631. Or try the Santa Monica Chamber of Commerce, 501 Colorado Avenue, Santa Monica, CA 90401; (310) 393-9825.

The Dandelion Under the Pillow

"Tell someone to put a dandelion under their pillow to cure dandruff and they'll elect you President...of anything."
—Henry Morgan, interviewed in *The Realist*, 1960

While we were combing the beaches of California, a local news story captured the nation's imagination. It seems that a Los Angeles woman lost her cat on a flight from New York's La Guardia Airport to LAX. A California psychic was called in for the cat hunt. The psychic picked up some feline vibes—our theory is litter-box odor—in the cargo bay. Tracking the vibes, the psychic pinpointed the cat's location. That is, the psychic pointed to the section of the cargo bay where the cat was later found. With that tail, er, tale, California's booming alternative industry racked up yet another success story.

California is the holy land for spiritual, medical, and political alternatives. This is the state that gave us the Summer of Love and the Monterey Pop Festival—but also the Altamont disaster and the Manson family. It has produced great alternative literature and groundbreaking music. It has also given rise to tax-payer revolts and Pebble Beach. It has coughed up Jim Jones and Ronald Reagan, the Black Panthers, Jerry Brown, and the SLA and Patty Hearst. It gave us former First Lady Nancy Reagan, whose reliance on a California astrologist directed the fate of the country for a spell. In a 1994 election, Michael Huffington spent a third of his $75 million fortune to buy one of the state's seats in the U.S. Senate—only to be revealed as a Manchurian candidate for his wife, who orchestrated his campaign. She follows the evangelical teachings of a man named, simply, John-Roger, a former high-school teacher who proclaims himself more powerful than Jesus.

A veritable smorgasbord of healers, shakers, counselors, therapists, holistic ministers, colon irrigators, Rolfers, fundamentalists, and other assorted gurus make their home in California. This is especially the case along the coast, where the sea breezes and unchanging weather help foster a meditative bent of mind. Every single one of these alternative healers is an expert on something. Though some are quacks, others have legitimately helped people beyond the reach of mainstream medicine while also serving to loosen the fascistic grip that the American Medical Association has on our nation's health care.

One way to get a handle on available alternative services is to consult the myriad free publications devoted to this subject. Reams of paper are given over to ads that are eerily similar to the personals in metropolitan "swinger" mags. How can so many people, we wondered, ply their trade in this alternative market? If indeed they do find enough customers to make a lucrative living at it, why is the state still so bedeviled? If Los Angeles, for instance, is filled to bursting with self-actualized, empowered, tanned, fit, Rolfed, and transcendentally meditated people, why is the city such a smog-strangled sprawl that its saner citizens can't wait to flee when an offer to work somewhere else comes along?

It's not our intent to knock alternatives. In fact, this guide is intended to be an alternative to the fulsome brochure copy that fills most travel books. Still, as one peruses the alternative reference tools, the notion begins creeping in that many of these experts are selling false hope. At their most innocuous, they provide an entertaining sideshow.

Here's a random line up of beach bhagwans:

- "OPENING TO THE GODDESS ENERGY: Explore and heal the denied feminne (sic) within.... $80 advance, $100 at the door."
- "SINGING, MOVING THROUGH THE FEAR, FOR NON-SINGERS WHO MUST SING: reasonable rates." (Don't karaoke bars provide this service free of charge?)
- "ENHANCED SEXUALITY TRAINING: Sexual meditation. Extended orgasm. Soul union and enlightenment. No overt sexual activity." (What a tease!)
- "PAST LIFE REGRESSION. Explore past lives for: Curiosity, Removing Blocks, Soul Cleansing. Affordable sessions. Sessions led by a metaphysical minister."
- "TRAVEL AROUND THE NATIVE AMERICAN AND CELTIC MEDICINE WHEEL... different journeys each week...$20 session."
- "AN EVENING WITH XANDO, channeled by G_. Donation. XANDO is a composite of six angelic beings."
- "POWER NEGOTIATION SKILLS. You will learn to: Formulate and dovetail outcomes for Win-Win results. Preserve the relationship while achieving your outcome. Apply these skills to business, personal and family issues... $250 at the door." (In other words, learn to manipulate others blind.)
- "GRANDFATHER OF THE NEW AGE REVEALS MYSTERIES: Now nearing 70 years of age, N_ is considered the leading expert on crystal skulls.... They are thought to be at least 10,000 to 20,000 years old. Three-day retreat will cost $149, plus transportation to and from Arizona, plus $25 a night at the Healing Center, plus $5 for breakfast and lunch, plus $7 dinner."
- "LOVESTAR INSTITUTE. Holistic Health Psychologist Thanatologist (Grief) Counselor." (Good grief!)

Heard enough? If not, contact The Whole Person, P.O. Box 2398, Santa Barbara, CA 93102; (800) 962-0338. Ask for the "Calendar of Events."

Pacific Palisades

Location: Between Santa Monica and Malibu along the Pacific Coast Highway and Sunset Boulevard. The only public beach in Pacific Palisades is Will Rogers State Beach.
Population: 23,100
Area Code: 310 **Zip Code:** 90272

This community, nestled in the foothills of the Santa Monica Mountains from Chautauqua Boulevard to Malibu, is not a beach town, but it does look down on one of the loveliest stretches of the Pacific coast. Originally populated in the 1920s by Methodists who founded it as their "new Chautauqua," Pacific Palisades is now the exclusive domain of the very rich. The streets, most of which branch off Sunset Boulevard, are winding, shaded routes, many ending in cul-de-sacs. Parts of Pacific Palisades are included on Hollywood celebrity bus tours.

We had another reason for visiting Pacific Palisades—a motive not unlike our quest for the ghost of Charles Bukowski in San Pedro (see the entry on page 173). Henry Miller retired here after Big Sur became too unnavigable for his frail body. He spent his happiest golden days riding "his best friend" (a bicycle) around these lovely streets. It was while pursuing the vision of this sweet old man that we stumbled upon the Self-Realization Fellowship Lake Shrine (17190 Sunset Boulevard, 454-4114), a 10-acre "wall-less temple," bird sanctuary, sunken garden, and altar to the "five major religions of the world." Fitting, somehow, that Henry Miller spent his final days nearby.

Beaches

Pacific Palisades puts its ocean frontage to good use. It is the site of a state beach named after our most famous cowboy-philosopher. **Will Rogers State Beach** is a sandy swath three miles long that's a favorite of sun-bronzed locals who are serious about their volleyball game and their tans. Its proximity to Hollywood makes it one of the more popular beaches in Los Angeles County. Furthermore, it is the starting point for the South Bay Bicycle Trail, which ends 20 miles later down at Torrance County Beach.

Incidentally, if you want to dig further into the life of the man who never met a man he didn't like, Rogers' 187-acre ranch is open to the public as Will Rogers State Historical Park (1501 Will Rogers State Park Road, 454-8212). Tours of the main house and grounds are offered daily, and one can also hike through the vast natural area or ride on equestrian trails.

Coastal Cuisine

Pacific Palisades has got little, if anything, to offer travelers in the way of accommodations and nightlife, being a predominantly ritzy and privacy-hoarding residential community. However, it's got a dandy restaurant on the beach that ranks high among the best to be found on the coast. **Gladstone's 4 Fish Restaurant** (17,300 Pacific Coast Highway, 454-3474, $$$$) is indeed the place to go "4 fish" in Los Angeles County. It's worth the drive, worth the wait, and worth the price. Barrels of unshucked peanuts are set out for waiting patrons to munch on, and the oceanside location makes

Will Rogers State Beach

Location: In Pacific Palisades, along the 16,000 block of the Pacific Coast Highway.
Parking: $5 entrance fee per vehicle.
Hours: 8 AM to 7 PM.
Facilities: Lifeguards, rest rooms, and showers.
Contact: For beach information, contact the Los Angeles County Department of Beaches and Harbors at (310) 305-9503.

See number 26 on page 154.

Pollution Report Card: L.A. County Beaches

A nonprofit environmental organization called Heal the Bay grades the beaches of Los Angeles County, which border the pollution-stressed Santa Monica Bay. They do this on a monthly basis in an effort to raise consciousness, alert beachgoers to health risks, and promote action that will "heal the bay." Heal the Bay celebrated its 10th anniversary in 1995. If you'd like to join or obtain volunteer information, call Heal the Bay at (310) 581-4188.

Most of the offending pollution comes from runoff near storm drains and by piers. The grades are much worse in wet weather than dry. In fact, during the wet weather, 41 of the 60 stations monitored by Heal the Bay received D or F grades in 1994. The report recommends that people do not swim in the ocean for three days after it rains, or swim within 100 yards of storm-drain discharges in any weather. Here are how some Los Angeles beaches fared, according to the 1995 report card:

Location	Summer (dry) grade	Winter (wet) grade
Cabrillo City Beach (Los Angeles Harbor)	F	F
Abalone Cove	A	A
Malaga Cove	A	F
Redondo Beach Municipal Pier (50 yards south)	C	F
Hermosa Pier (50 yards south)	A	A
Manhattan Beach Pier (50 yards south)	A	D
Marina del Rey Beach (lifeguard tower)	F	F
Venice Pier (50 yards south)	A	D
Santa Monica Pier (50 yards south)	F	F
Will Rogers State Beach	A	F
Surfrider Beach	F	F
Leo Carrillo State Beach	A	D

Source: Heal the Bay Pollution Report Card, 1995.

for superb sunset-watching. The portions are huge and the menu expansive at Gladstone's. Prime seafood entrées run in the $18 to $23 range and include such items as mesquite-grilled sea bass and ahi rolled in Cajun spices, then seared and cooked rare. Appetizers include plump, cold Pacific oysters, as well as ceviche salad and marinated calamari. A sashimi dinner offers a filling platter of raw seafood delights. King and Queen crab legs (the latter are slightly saltier and smaller, though still huge) are worth the $25 to $30 you'll plunk down for them. What you can't eat at Gladstone's will be wrapped by your server in gold foil and twisted to resemble a seabird or fish—a signature touch that completes a very satisfying dining experience.

For More Information

Contact the Pacific Palisades Chamber of Commerce, 15330 Antioch Street, Pacific Palisades, CA 90272; (310) 459-7963.

Malibu

Location: Beginning five miles north of Santa Monica, Malibu runs for 27 miles along the Pacific Coast Highway, from Coastline Drive up to the Ventura County line. Along its length are dozens of beaches. The most popular of these are Surfrider Beach, Paradise Cove, Zuma Beach, and Leo Carrillo State Beach.
Population: 28,000
Area Code: 310 **Zip Code:** 90265

Malibu might seem to the outside world to be some ultra-chic celebrity enclave accessible only to camera crews from *Lifestyles of the Rich and Famous*, but nothing could be further from the truth. The fact is, there are really two Malibus. The better known of these is the "inner" Malibu—the film colony, the celebrity sandbox, the glamorous private world behind locked gates about which the rest of the world likes to fantasize. The "outer" Malibu is a 27-mile stretch of rugged coastline, plunging canyons, and towering mountains, running along the Pacific Coast Highway from Coastline Drive to the Ventura County line. Local boosters refer to the PCH through Malibu as "the longest main street in America." We like to think of it as Little Big Sur. This side of Malibu—a wild, winding corridor physically bounded by the Santa Monica Mountains and Pacific Ocean—is accessible to all and yet is generally less familiar than the minuscule world of celebrity intrigue that makes Malibu an instant buzzword with readers and viewers of tabloid media.

The reality of Malibu is very different from popular conceptions of it. Much of it is unforgiving and desolate. Steep mountains plunge to the sea, which crashes angrily against the rocks. The elements hang in precarious balance here, not infrequently tilting over into destructive chaos. Malibu is particularly subject to what native Southern Californians wearily refer to as their four seasons: fire, flood, mudslide, and earthquake. One must drive through Malibu ever vigilant for fallen rocks. Some of the cliff faces along the Pacific Coast Highway are raw where mighty chunks have torn loose and crashed onto the roadway. Narrow ridgetops zigzag northward. Houses are hidden in the canyons between them. The hills are covered with dry, brown vegetation that turns green when the winter rains come. The threat of fire is constant. Lightning, arson, or a careless match can ignite a blaze that, propelled by hot Santa Ana winds, is capable of racing toward the seaside colony at speeds of 100 miles per hour. The other calamity is mudslides: slow, brown waves of muck, rock, and debris that swallow up everything in their path, houses included. The elements play no favorites here. No matter how much clout they may have in Hollywood, those who live in Malibu have no control over the periodic disasters that plague the seaside colony. Nature does not obey directors' cues.

Still, those who make their residence here derive a perverse sort of pleasure from the challenges of living on the edge. Writer Joan Didion captured its allure in her 1978 essay "Quiet Days in Malibu," in which she wrote: "I had come to see the spirit of the place as one of shared isolation and adversity, and I think now that I never loved the house on the Pacific Coast Highway more than on those many days when it was impossible to leave it, when fire or flood had in fact closed the highway." A dissenting opinion was rendered in an August 1983 *People* magazine cover story, which averred: "The plain truth is that [Malibu residents] are getting a noisy, shabby, perilous, and polluted pseudo-paradise."

The extent of the affront includes fecal pollution of the ocean (from untreated sewage and overflowing septic tanks) and not-infrequent offshore oil spills. A ruptured Chevron pipeline spewed jet fuel and diesel oil into the ocean in 1991, creating a floating puddle that moved onshore in the ritziest part of

 Map of Los Angeles County beaches—page 154

Malibu, near the seaside homes of such celebrities as Bruce Willis and Demi Moore. Spectacular firestorms raged down the canyons in 1982 and 1993, destroying hundreds of homes costing millions of dollars apiece. In the latter blaze, film star Sean Penn lost the $4 million mansion he once shared with ex-wife Madonna. Damaging waves from a winter storm was 1988's catastrophe, flooding homes in Malibu Colony, twisting piers, causing diners to flee seaside restaurants, and uprooting a homeless encampment. Erosion of the beaches east of Malibu Colony, where protective structures prevent the downward transport of sand, has become a serious problem.

Beach closures along Malibu's coast are not uncommon, due to high bacterial counts from human-generated sources of pollution. Breaches of Malibu Lagoon following heavy storms often send ribbons of foul, dark-stained water streaming into the waters near Surfrider Beach, causing mini-epidemics of nausea, vomiting, and diarrhea among surfers. One 21-year-old wave rider—Erik Villanueva, a student at Pepperdine University, on the hills above Malibu—believes he contracted Coxsackie B virus after paddling through a "dark stain" of pollution off Surfrider Beach in 1992. This bug generally causes gastrointestinal infections but in rare cases attacks the human

Art and History on Old Malibu

There are two offbeat Malibu attractions to justify an inland jaunt. The first is the J. Paul Getty Museum (17985 Pacific Coast Highway, 310-458-2003). The late oil billionaire created the world's largest endowment for a privately funded museum. Opened to the public in 1974, it reflects Getty's lifelong interests as a collector of Greek and Roman antiquities, Renaissance and Baroque paintings, and European decorative arts. The museum building is a recreation of the Villa dei Papiri, an ancient Roman country house, and the gardens are filled with plants and trees that might have been found there 2,000 years ago. The museum is open Tuesday through Sunday from 10 AM to 5 PM; admission is free, but you're asked to make a "parking reservation" at least one month in advance.

Another curious diversion worth checking out is the historic Adamson House and Malibu Lagoon Museum (23200 Pacific Coast Highway, 310-456-8432), located a quick left turn north of Malibu Pier. The house and grounds formerly belonged to the Adamson family, daughter and son-in-law of the last owners of the Malibu Spanish Land Grant. They are now state property, open to the public from Wednesday to Saturday, 11 AM to 2 PM. Built in 1929, the house is a classic Moorish-Spanish Colonial Revival–style residence that serves as a museum of ceramic art and design. The fantastic flower gardens on the premises were created by covering the natural dunes with a five-foot layer of humus. History buffs should note that a historical marker commemorates this establishment as the probable site of explorer Cabrillo's New World landing in 1542. He disembarked to greet the canoe-paddling Chumash Indians and to claim all the lands of "Alta California" in the name of the King of Spain. Large-scale real-estate transactions such as this one were apparently a simple matter back then. You just stepped up to the counter, so to speak, and ordered.

Want to Be an L.A. County Lifeguard?

If week after week of watching the flesh parade on *Baywatch* has you eager to join the ranks of Los Angeles County lifeguards, bear in mind that the reality of landing the job is a little tougher than showing up with a Screen Actors Guild card. In fact, to make it into rookie school at the Lifeguard Training Academy, you must meet the following conditions right off the bat: (1) you must have uncorrected vision of 20/30 or better; (2) you must be able to complete a 1,000-meter swim (approximately three-fifths of a mile); (3) you must be 18 years of age or older; and (4) you must have a valid California driver's license.

Lifeguard trials are held when more are needed. A trial in April 1994 drew 225 applicants, 20 percent of them women. Less than a third were invited for a follow-up oral interview and a physical exam. If chosen, new recruits begin as part-timers making $15 per hour and then attend 80 hours of "rookie school," where they learn First Aid and safety and rescue techniques. Recertification is required every year. For more information, call the Lifeguard Training Academy at (310) 577-5700.

However seriously you may or may not take it, *Baywatch* has indirectly saved lives. Widely viewed around the world, it has raised the level of lifeguard competence in cities such as Barcelona, Spain, which actually flew Los Angeles County lifeguards over for consultations. The meetings paid off. On one weekend in 1993 (before the consultations), there were 14 drownings on the beaches of Barcelona. During the first nine *months* of 1994, however, there were none.

heart. He has since had two heart-transplant operations and is convinced ocean pollution is to blame. Such events have led to a frenzy of heavily funded studies looking for sources of pollution in the Malibu Creek watershed, studying illness among beachgoers throughout the bay, and monitoring the genetic material of pathogens found in the lagoon. This is another way of saying that life is not always a beach in Malibu.

All of this is in large part a consequence of the accelerating pace of development in Malibu. The colony has changed considerably since the late 1970s, when author Joan Didion wrote (in the essay cited above): "In a way it seems the most idiosyncratic of beach communities, 27 miles of coastline with no hotel, no passable restaurant, nothing to attract the traveler's dollar." Now, like every other conquered corner of America, there are plenty of hotels, tons of passable restaurants, and lots of places to spend your money, including sprawling malls that would have been unthinkable only a decade ago.

In 1986, the California Coastal Commission adopted a land-use plan for Malibu that permitted significant retail growth in three areas: the Malibu Civic Center, the Point Dume/Paradise Cove area, and Pepperdine University. The same plan also okayed the construction of up to 6,582 new dwellings, nearly doubling the number that existed at that time. Many Malibu natives fought the plan, which pitted local and county governments against each other, with the coastal commission as referee. One local activist griped, "They want to allow undisciplined, unbridled growth in Malibu." That seems to be what they're getting, judging from the changes we've observed in recent years. In 1990, Malibu officially approved its incorporation as a city, something that had been rejected in ballot initiatives dating back to 1950, presumably so that residents could retain control over their own destiny in the volatile present.

The Malibu of today is a collage of the upscale and low-rent, plain and fancy, old and new. In certain ways Malibu has got an Old California feel to it, a wayback-machine aura evident in the unpretentious taverns and food stands that squat by the road, refusing to bend to trends. At the same time recent arrivals on the scene, most evidently the flashy Malibu Colony Mall, have altered the landscape with a dash of *nouveau* flair. The same, alas, cannot be said of the Malibu McDonald's, an oxymoron as inescapable as Ronald McDonald's idiotic leer.

The real appeal of the place remains the elemental collision of geological opposites—ocean basin and mountain ridge—separated by a precipitously narrow strip of barely habitable land subject to violent tantrums from both sides. A drive up the Pacific Coast Highway through Malibu—particularly above Point Dume, where the development subsides—is a stunning and humbling encounter with nature in the raw. The unfolding panorama of beaches yields one remarkable vista after another. Though you may never encounter a celebrity here, you will never lack for things to do, if you're the least bit resourceful and outdoor-oriented.

As for the highway, it's something of a bane in Malibu. At various points, especially along a four-mile stretch north of Topanga Canyon, it is subject to mass movements (rockfalls, landslides) from the unstable cliffs that were cut to build it. Traffic tramples through town on the four-lane Pacific Coast Highway like a stampede of heavy-hooved cattle. On weekends, the road jams to a standstill with carloads of Angelinos headed to their favorite north county beach or to play with the boats they keep in Ventura County's yacht basins. Parking lots at the state and private beaches fill up quickly, and the overflow lines the highway shoulders in both directions. For pedestrians, dashing across the highway can be a life-threatening kamikaze experience.

The beach access point we were attempting to reach at the time was actually a cement walk between buildings—one of the narrow accesses the California Coastal Commission has waged costly battles to establish, much to the chagrin of Malibu residents. Officially it is known as the Zonker Harris Accessway, after the *Doonesbury* cartoon character. On either side of it lies private property. You're reminded not to trespass, although California law does give citizens the right to walk along the beach up to the high-tide line. We did just that, ambling in the direction of the Malibu Pier past all manner of sunbathers (including some seminude beauties) who paid us no mind. The pier at Malibu is an old, broad-planked affair with a restaurant on the shore end. You can buy bait and tackle, obtain a fishing license, and charter a sportfishing boat at Malibu Sport Fishing Landing (23,000 Pacific Coast Highway, 456-8030). At one time the modest commercial heart of Malibu, it has been overtaken by all the new commercial development several miles north, around Point Dume, near the fabled and private Malibu Colony.

The canyons of Malibu are cut with torturous roads that wind through the Santa Monica Mountains. A drive up one of the canyon roads is a great way to pass a few hours, offering a mix of ocean vistas and mountain scenery as you make the jagged ascent. We went up Topanga Canyon Road and returned via Malibu Canyon Road, passing in a short time from cool sea level to broiling higher altitudes—a reverse of the normal situation. Lay hands on a map of Malibu and design your own up-and-back route.

Beyond these suggestions, you are more or less on your own in Malibu. Sometimes, you can be made to feel as unwanted as a stray dog shuffling along the side of the road. Unless you have a ton of money or know someone who lives here—say, Larry Hagman or Goldie Hawn—you'll have a hard time fashioning any sort of extended vacation on the Malibu coastline other than a camping trip. But hey, we'd rather be tenting beneath a stand of sycamores at Leo Carrillo State Park than attempting celebrity sightings at Paradise Cove any day. When we think of Malibu, we think of the land, not the famous landowners.

Beaches

Because the terrain is so rugged, with the Santa Monica Mountains plunging steeply into the sea, the geography of the coastline makes for some amazing beaches along Malibu's 27 miles. About half of the Malibu coast (12.5

Broad Beach

4

Location: In Malibu. Public-access stairways lead to the beach from Broad Beach Road, near the 31,200 block of the Pacific Coast Highway.
Parking: Limited free street parking.
Hours: 6 AM to sunset.
Facilities: None.
Contact: For beach information, contact the Los Angeles County Department of Beaches and Harbors at (310) 305-9503.

See number 36 on page 154.

County Line Beach (a part of Leo Carrillo State Beach)

3

Location: Along the Pacific Coast Highway at Yerba Buena Road, just south of the Ventura County line.
Parking: Limited free roadside parking.
Hours: 8 AM to midnight.
Facilities: None.
Contact: For beach information, contact Leo Carrillo State Beach at (818) 880-0350.

See number 42 on page 154.

Dan Blocker County Beach

3

Location: In Malibu, at 26,000 Pacific Coast Highway.
Parking: Limited free roadside parking.
Hours: 6 AM to sunset.
Facilities: Lifeguards and rest rooms.
Contact: For beach information, contact the Los Angeles County Lifeguard Service, Northern Section, at (310) 394-3264. For a surf report, call (310) 457-9701.

See number 31 on page 154.

El Matador State Beach

3

Location: Six miles north of Malibu, at 32,350 Pacific Coast Highway.
Parking: $2 entrance fee per vehicle.
Hours: 6 AM to sunset.
Facilities: Rest rooms.
Contact: For beach information, contact the Malibu Division of the Angeles District of the California Department of Parks and Recreation at (310) 457-8140.

See number 37 on page 154.

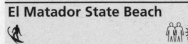

miles) is given over to state and county beaches, while the rest is under development. Surfrider, Zuma, and County Line are all names familiar to beachgoers and surfers worth their sea salt. But there are literally two dozen or so named beaches in Malibu. We'll hit the highlights.

Malibu's beach-erosion problems along the more developed areas east of Point Dume continue to worsen, as the ocean chomps hungrily at some of the most expensive real estate in the country. Out behind Gladstone's 4 Fish Restaurant, straddling the line between Pacific Palisades and Malibu, we watched three-foot breakers tenaciously whittle at the beachfront. A rock jetty built to keep the vanishing beach from retreating is fighting a losing battle as the sea steadily advances upon the establishment. This didn't deter a folksinger we spied one

El Pescador State Beach

3

Location: Seven-and-a-half miles north of Malibu, at 32,900 Pacific Coast Highway.

Parking: $2 entrance fee per vehicle.

Hours: 6 AM to sunset.

Facilities: Rest rooms.

Contact: For beach information, contact the Malibu Division of the Angeles District of the California Department of Parks and Recreation at (310) 457-8140.

See number 39 on page 154.

Escondido Beach

2

Location: Access to the beach is via a path at Escondido Creek (in the 27,200 block of the Pacific Coast Highway, near Malibu Cove Colony Drive). Public stairways to Escondido Beach can also be found in the parking lot of Geoffrey's restaurant and beside the Seacliff condominium complex.

Parking: Limited free roadside parking.

Hours: Sunrise to sunset.

Facilities: None.

Contact: For beach information, contact the Malibu Division of the Angeles District of the California Department of Parks and Recreation at (310) 457-8140.

See number 32 on page 154.

La Piedra State Beach

3

Location: Seven miles north of Malibu, at 32,700 Pacific Coast Highway.

Parking: $2 entrance fee per vehicle.

Hours: 6 AM to sunset.

Facilities: Rest rooms.

Contact: For beach information, contact the Malibu Division of the Angeles District of the California Department of Parks and Recreation at (310) 457-8140.

See number 38 on page 154.

Las Tunas County Beach

2

Location: In southern Malibu, at 19,400 Pacific Coast Highway.

Parking: Free parking lot.

Hours: 6 AM to sunset.

Facilities: Lifeguards and picnic tables.

Contact: For beach information, contact the Los Angeles County Lifeguard Service, Northern Section, at (310) 394-3264. For a surf report, call (310) 457-9701.

See number 28 on page 154.

evening around sundown. He was attempting to enjoy a communal moment with nature on the rocks, but instead was drowned out by the crash of foaming breakers that occasionally sprayed him and his guitar. It seemed a potent metaphor for the new tune that the denizens of Malibu and residents along the Santa Monica Bay are being forced to whistle, which goes by the name "Eco-tastrophe."

The first real beach in Malibu is **Topanga County Beach**, at the south end of Malibu, which runs for just over a mile. Like many in the area, it is narrow and rocky, set at the base of steep, eroding bluffs. Surfing is popular at the mouth of Topanga Creek, but there are too many rocks to allow for safe swimming along most of the beach. Above it is **Las Tunas County Beach**, a narrow, unimproved

Leo Carrillo State Beach

RV 5

Location: One mile south of the Ventura County line, at 36,000 Pacific Coast Highway.

Parking: $6 entrance fee per vehicle.

Hours: 8 AM to midnight.

Facilities: Lifeguards, rest rooms, showers, picnic areas, and fire pits. There are 138 campsites for tents and RVs. Fees are $14 to $16 per night. For camping reservations, call Destinet at (800) 444-7275.

Contact: For beach information, contact Leo Carrillo State Beach at (818) 880-0350.

See number 41 on page 154.

Malibu Lagoon County Beach

4

Location: North of Malibu Pier in Malibu, along the Pacific Coast Highway at Malibu Creek.

Parking: $5 entrance fee per vehicle. There is limited free roadside parking.

Hours: 6 AM to sunset.

Facilities: Lifeguards, rest rooms, showers, and picnic tables.

Contact: For beach information, contact the Los Angeles County Lifeguard Service, Northern Section, at (310) 394-3264. For a surf report, call (310) 457-9701.

See number 30 on page 154.

Nicholas Canyon County Beach

3

Location: Nine miles north of Malibu, at Nicholas Canyon Road and the Pacific Coast Highway.

Parking: $5 entrance fee per vehicle.

Hours: 6 AM to sunset.

Facilities: Lifeguards, rest rooms, picnic areas, and handicapped facilities.

Contact: For beach information, contact the Los Angeles County Lifeguard Service, Northern Section, at (310) 394-3264. For a surf report, call (310) 457-9701.

See number 40 on page 154.

Paradise Cove

4

Location: Near the Malibu Colony in Malibu, at 28,128 Pacific Coast Highway.

Parking: $15 entrance fee per car.

Hours: Sunrise to sunset.

Facilities: Lifeguards and rest rooms.

Contact: For beach information, contact Paradise Cove at (310) 457-2511.

See number 33 on page 154.

beach beneath the bluffs that held a special hazard for surfers, swimmers, and divers until recently: eight rusted 65-year-old groins placed here to keep the beach from moving. (They were finally removed in 1995, per court order.) The real attraction here is surf casting.

Surfrider Beach is located right up from the Malibu Pier. The beach covers 35 acres, including nearly a mile of ocean frontage. Its waves are perfectly formed and, even when small, carry surfers a good distance. The waves we've seen in summer are unspectacular in size but fascinating in form. Riding them, the surfers looked as if they were walking on water, almost moving in slow motion, gliding in on perfectly shaped, long-cycle waves for what seems like an eternity. The beach is situated at the head of a dramatic, U-shaped cove.

Point Dume County Beach

4

Location: Above Malibu, at the end of Westward Beach Road, on north side of Point Dume.

Parking: $5 entrance fee per car.

Hours: 6 AM to sunset.

Facilities: Lifeguards, rest rooms, and showers.

Contact: For beach information, contact the Los Angeles County Lifeguard Service, Northern Section, at (310) 394-3264. For a surf report, call (310) 457-9701.

See number 34 on page 154.

Surfrider Beach (a part of Malibu Lagoon County Beach)

4

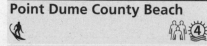

Location: In Malibu, along the Pacific Coast Highway at Malibu Pier.

Parking: $5 entrance fee per vehicle.

Hours: 6 AM to sunset.

Facilities: Lifeguards and rest rooms.

Contact: For beach information, contact the Los Angeles County Lifeguard Service, Northern Section, at (310) 394-3264. For a surf report, call (310) 457-9701.

See number 29 on page 154.

Topanga County Beach

3

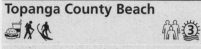

Location: In southern Malibu, at 18,500 Pacific Coast Highway.

Parking: $5 entrance fee per vehicle.

Hours: 6 AM to sunset.

Facilities: Lifeguards, rest rooms, and a picnic area.

Contact: For beach information, contact the Los Angeles County Lifeguard Service, Northern Section, at (310) 394-3264. For a surf report, call (310) 457-9701.

See number 27 on page 154.

Zuma County Beach

5

Location: Four miles north of Malibu, at 30,000 Pacific Coast Highway

Parking: $5 entrance fee per vehicle.

Hours: 6 AM to sunset.

Facilities: Lifeguards, rest rooms, and showers.

Contact: For beach information, contact the Los Angeles County Lifeguard Service, Northern Section, at (310) 394-3264. For a surf report, call (310) 457-9701.

See number 35 on page 154.

The Original Metal Heads

You've seen them. They're generally older people, fully clothed on hot summer days. They move slowly up the beach like lemmings, sweeping metal detectors over the golden sands at their feet. Every 10 yards or so they bend down to jab a pooper-scooper into the ground. They lift their implement, sift the sand therein, and inspect the latest treasure they've exhumed.

Have you ever wondered, as we have, what it is they find? Obviously, they must find something more valuable than bottle caps and beer tabs, right?

Well, we had our questions answered one beautiful summer afternoon at Zuma County Beach, in Malibu. One of the field marshals of this growing SWAT team—Arthur, a pleasant old chap from Orange County who sells metal detectors for a living—stopped and gave us the lowdown on the scoops. He said that you can easily and quickly recover the cost of a metal detector by combing any busy city beach in the hard wet sand near the water at low tide. That is where the most recently lost wedding bands, gold chains, earrings, pocket change—unknowingly jettisoned during body surfing, a playful swim, or even a jog in the shallows—are plucked from the sand like pirates' sunken treasure. On one recent day's work, this gentleman claimed to have found half a dozen gold rings (two with inlaid diamonds), collectively valued at $5,000—about 10 times the cost of the metal detector.

While speaking with us, this man—from all outward appearances a sane and solid citizen—suddenly leapt forward, bent down, and stabbed his pronged scooper into the sand a few yards from where we were sitting. He wrenched a spadeful of dirt upward, sifted it briskly, and reached in to grab a basket full of spare change. He thrust his palm toward us, admiring his booty. He was particularly proud to demonstrate this so close to where we were sitting.

Before parting, the man confessed to us that a week after he'd found his $5,000 haul of rings, they were stolen from his shop. He collected insurance on them nonetheless, as part of the settlement for the robbery.

Kiddies, bronzed Adonises, and big-bellied men, plus the usual crew of noble surfers, pack the place. Ravishing California girls watch the guys work out on the volleyball courts or in the waves, which are fought over and claimed by the most skillful surfers. Adjacent to Surfrider is the small Malibu Lagoon Museum and Adamson House. The museum, Malibu Lagoon (at the mouth of Malibu Creek), Surfrider Beach, and the 700-foot Malibu Pier all fall within the boundaries of **Malibu Lagoon County Beach**. Malibu Lagoon itself is subject to contamination, and though the warm, protected waters are attractive to young children, it can be pretty scummy. Not for nothing does the county post advisories against swimming here.

Between Malibu Lagoon and Point Dume lie several small beaches worthy of mention. **Paradise Cove** is a private-fee beach in the heart of Malibu Colony, offering the likeliest chance of celebrity sightings. Unlike whale-watching expeditions, however, a sighting is not guaranteed. The entrance fee lands you on a beach with a short pier and a wonderful view of the opposing sandstone bluffs of Point Dume and the Santa Monica Mountains. **Escondido Beach** can be reached via a stairway near Malibu Cove Colony Drive; situated at the mouth of Escondido Creek, it's a good diving area but otherwise not worth the trouble. Close by is **Dan Blocker County Beach** (formerly Corral State Beach), a lifeguarded beach (in season) that draws some surfers and divers. The beach is narrow and rocky, there are few facilities, and only roadside parking. But it's a great spot for scuba enthusiasts. Around the tip of Point Dume is **Point Dume County Beach** (a.k.a. Westward Beach), on Westward Beach Road. People park on the side of the road to save the entrance charge, but the local government seems intent on prohibiting on-street parking here to cut down on crowds, congestion, and litter.

Much like Laguna Beach's and La Jolla's oceanfronts, Malibu's coastline is intercut with coves, many of them accessible by stairways and paths if you know what you're looking for. Keep your eyes open for some of these spots between Topanga Beach and Paradise Cove (they are numerous). Also, be prepared to park on the highway and deal with hazardous crossings. Just for the record, there are public-access stairways to the beach on the following numbered blocks of the Pacific Coast Highway: 19,900; 20,300; 24,300; 24,400; 24,600; 24,700; 25,100; 31,000; and 31,300.

A more practical choice for those visiting the area on a short stay would be gigantic **Zuma County Beach**. (Go for the gusto, as the beer commercials say.) Zuma is the ultimate Southern California beach: wide, wild, extending for miles, and set in a stupendous natural setting. It is the largest county-owned beach with no fewer than eight parking lots and a $5 parking charge, avoided by many who use the shoulders of the Pacific Coast Highway. The beach here deserves its reputation for danger, as the waves form close to shore, rising out of nowhere to back-breaking height before crashing noisily and sending tongues of seawater and foam scurrying up the sloping beach face. It's the perfect recipe for rip currents, necessitating frequent heroics from the lifeguard stands. Contrary to notions that primo Malibu beaches such as this one are peopled only with perfect specimens awaiting casting calls from soap-opera producers, Zuma is chock full of families and normal-looking folks on summer weekends. With the invigorating clean air, the azure ocean's churning fury, and the breathtaking backdrop of steep-sided, brushy mountains, Zuma County Beach makes it possible to understand just why residents risk life, limb, and earthly possessions to live in Malibu. Zuma comes equipped with food stands at both ends of its four-mile expanse along the Pacific Coast Highway, from the western side of Point Dume to Broad Beach Road. West of Zuma, stairways along Broad Beach Road lead to secluded **Broad Beach**.

Proceeding westward, one encounters a trio of small state beaches that are accessible by path and stairway. The attraction here is isolation from the madding crowd. Parking is by the honor system; you're asked to stuff $2 into a collection box. The three beaches, proceeding westward, are **El Matador**, **La Piedra**, and **El Pescador**, occupying 18, 9, and 10 acres, respectively. Switchback paths are carved into the crumbly cliffs. No wonder Malibu has mudslides in the rainy season; the hills are nothing more than loosely consolidated dirt clods. The beaches and offshore waters are strewn with sizable, steep-sided sea stacks. Come here for a taste of the wild side of Malibu's coastal geology. Approximately two miles west of El Pescador is **Nicholas Canyon County Beach**, slightly larger (at 23 acres) than the trio preceding it. Keep your eyes out for the turnoff down to the fee parking lot, which is directly across from the Malibu Riding and Tennis Club. You can also hike down from Leo Carrillo State Beach, which adjoins it. Formerly known as Nicholas Beach—surfers referred to it as Point Zero—it is less crowded than many Malibu beaches and relatively free of wave-hogging surf punks. It is informally used as a nude beach, though authorities try to discourage it.

Malibu's marvelous procession of beaches reaches its crescendo with **Leo Carrillo State Beach**. The 3,000-acre park encompasses two sections of beach, separated by Sequit Point, and two campgrounds ($14 to $16 a night). One is located in the north beach area, while the other is set back on the landward side of the Pacific Coast Highway in Sycamore Canyon, amid the shade of eucalyptus and sycamore groves. The camping, particularly in the 138-site Sycamore Canyon Campground, is absolutely enthralling. Few other parks in the country can offer access to beach and mountains in such proximity. You are on the geological cutting edge of California's tectonic assembly line here. Carrillo's 1.5 miles worth of beaches are steeply sloped with coarse brown sand. When we visited, little kids were getting waxed on the beach by crashing breakers, while big kids who bobbed in the offshore kelp beds atop surfboards were also being slammed to the mat by the waves' decisive crashes. The surf here is not for the inexperienced or faint of heart, but the setting is as magnificent as any you'll find on either coast, offering sea caves and tidepools to explore, acres of sand to spread out on, and a scenic mountainous backdrop to gaze upon. For surfers, it gets good southerly swells, though the offshore and onshore rocks are intimidating.

Up by the Ventura County line vans and cars line the road, and surfers scamper down the steep, reddish-brown bluffs. **County Line Beach** is a favorite of surf-riders, sitting right up there with Rincon and Windansea. And this is where Malibu and Los Angeles County finally come to an end.

Bunking Down

Malibu has got exactly one luxury ocean hotel along its 27 miles, the fabulous **Malibu Beach Inn** (22878 Pacific Coast Highway, 456-6444, $$$$). This three-story, pink-stucco wonder is perched beside—and, at high tide, directly above—the ocean. When they say oceanfront, they're not exaggerating. You can open the balcony doors of your room and let the sounds of the churning, crashing ocean lull you to sleep. The complimentary breakfast buffet includes wonderful pastries, fresh fruit, cereal, and coffee. You can carry it to an outdoor sundeck and enjoy the morning meal over a copy of the *Los Angeles Times*. The rattan furniture and contemporary California decor, executed in muted pastels, enhance the sense of a relaxed getaway at the ocean's edge.

If you're going to pay top dollar for a place at the beach, you will find no nicer spot to do it than the Malibu Beach Inn. We have our own homemade souvenirs of the visit, incidentally: cassettes of waves breaking on the beach below, made with our portable recorders. The inn has won Robin Leach's seal of approval (check out the handwritten note just inside the lobby), and who better knows about refined lifestyles of idleness and pleasure than he? Situated a short distance down from Malibu Pier, the inn can, incidentally, arrange delivery of a meal from Alice's Restaurant, a long-standing landmark at the base of the pier. They also provide a "video menu" of movies for rent, with "comedies" for salads, "dramas" for entrées, and "adult XXX" for dessert. As incongruous as the latter category may seem in an inn as fine as this one, you must remember that this is, after all, Malibu—playground for the Hollywood film community and high-rolling libertines from L.A. With choices like *Taboo III* and *Tail Gunners*, we decided to pass on, uh, dessert.

Coastal Cuisine

Granita (23725 West Malibu Road, 456-0488, $$$) is the hands-down standout on the Malibu dining scene. This star attraction in celebrity chef Wolfgang Puck's arsenal of California restaurants has won over even the jaded

 Map of Los Angeles County beaches—page 154

Malibuites, who are wowed by its beachside proximity, its underwater fantasy decor (done in handmade ceramic tile and etched glass), and such dishes as Mediterranean fish soup, lobster club sandwich, spicy shrimp pizza, and seared scallops over black-pepper fettucine. Dress is Malibu casual: informal but neat. You may need to call up to a week in advance for a reservation, especially on weekends.

Another popular hangout is **Coogie's Beach Café** (23755 Malibu Road, 317-1444, $$), a spacious, high-ceilinged restaurant in a shopping center. Coogie's serves Malibu-style cuisine (indulgent and creative but healthy) for a very fair price. All the salads are good, as are items like fresh Alaskan salmon patties with dill, served with a plate of eggs any style, for only $7.50. It's a very Malibu kind of place, and you're likely to be surrounded by any number of Hollywood notables slumming in their casual wear. No one pays them (or you) any mind; that's part of the unspoken code of civility in celebrity-thick Malibu.

You can't get anything you want at **Alice's Restaurant** (Malibu Pier, 23000 Pacific Coast Highway, 456-6646, $$$), but your choices range to such satisfying selections as red snapper or shrimp sautéed with garlic, shallots, and tomatoes. Up at the opposite end of Malibu, directly across the street from County Line Beach, is a restaurant and fresh-seafood shop with the promising name **Neptune's Net** (42505 Pacific Coast Highway, 457-3095, $). It's stuck out in the middle of this beachy-keen nowhere and is packed with surfers assuaging hunger pangs on the outdoor deck. It's the kind of place that we tend to romanticize—off the beaten track, filled with local color, offering fresh, nonfranchised food. In reality, a meal here had us wishing that Neptune's Net had come up empty. A basket of tasteless, rubbery fried fish, scallops with the texture of pencil erasers, and "chips" (frozen French fries) was mediocre at best and no bargain at $6.55. They had the nerve to charge for extra tartar sauce. Even the fountain Coke tasted odd. To a bulletin board they had pinned Polaroids of petty thieves caught by hidden camera leaving the premises with unpaid booty (usually beer). Put simply, it struck us as a mediocre restaurant in a great location; much more could be done with it.

Night Moves

Nightlife has never been a big proposition up in Malibu, the whole idea of the place being an escape, an enclave for people who prefer not to be recognized. Nonetheless, a good time can be had at the **Malibu Inn** (22969 Pacific Coast Highway, 456-6106), a riotously fun restaurant and saloon. We hung out in the latter after the former closed for the night. Its ceiling is bedecked with a bizarre collage of metal wheels, surfboards (one serrated with shark teeth indentations), baseball mitts, and bric-a-brac. You can order your food, if you wish, through a huge, red pair of plastic lips. There's a pool table, a bar, some tables, and a sawdust-strewn, unfinished-wood floor in the main part of the saloon. The bartender cued up early Talking Heads and R.E.M. albums, which were a balm to ears that had been abused in one too many dance clubs. The Malibu Inn is as down to earth as it gets. Lest you think Malibu is all reclusive celebrities and pricey cafés, duck in here for a brew with the surfing clan.

For More Information

Contact the Malibu Chamber of Commerce, 23805 Stuart Ranch Road, Suite 100, Malibu, CA 90265; (310) 456-9025.

Close Encounters of the Turd Kind

So you've made it to Malibu and would love to lay eyes on one of the many celebrities from the entertainment community who make their home here. But you discover that their exclusive Malibu Colony is a gated and off-limits fortress. There's just no way for an ordinary average peon from Pasadena to slip past security. Not to worry! Just head on over to Surfrider Beach, one of Malibu's largest and most popular spots to surf and swim, and hop in the water. You may wind up indirectly having a close encounter with a celebrity, or a whole bunch of them, when fecal coliform bacteria from overflowing septic tanks in the private colony gets washed into the ocean and travels with the currents to the beaches that lie due south.

Gross as it sounds, this is exactly what is happening in the waters off Surfrider Beach, where a combination of sources that the government hasn't the time, money, or inclination to untangle has been fouling the water with bacteria and sickening those who swim here with a variety of ailments that range from ear and eye infections to gastrointestinal bugs. Samples of ocean water taken at Surfrider by the Los Angeles County Department of Health Services exceeded federal health standards for bacterial contamination for 13 of the first 21 weeks of 1994. The chief culprit is outflow from Malibu Lagoon, which serves as a catch basin for all sorts of disgusting muck. In addition to fecal matter from the septic tanks of Malibu Colony, culprits include doo-doo from waterbirds, urban runoff from within the 110-square-mile watershed that drains into Malibu Creek, runoff from soil tilling and animal waste, and refuse from homeless encampments near Malibu Civic Center. Unlike the vast majority of beaches that border Santa Monica Bay, bacterial levels at Surfrider generally remain high during both wet and dry weather.

The picture doesn't improve all that much as you move down the coast. Will Rogers State Beach, in Pacific Palisades, is another of the three pollution "hot spots" cited by the nonprofit Heal the Bay Foundation. The third is Dockweiler State Beach, just south of the jetties that protect Marina del Rey, which receives a heavy load of pollution from Ballona Creek.

For many years, industrial operations such as the Chevron oil refinery and Hyperion Sewage Treatment Plant were to blame. But under pressure from environmental groups like Heal the Bay, they've gone a long way toward cleaning up their act. Chevron voluntarily extended its wastewater discharge pipes from 300 to 3,000 feet offshore and also provided funding for a pilot epidemiological study to determine the causes and prevalence of illness among bay-area beachgoers. Hyperion has been forced to stop dumping sewage sludge into the bay. Now it is nearly in compliance with the terms of the Clean Water Act in the quality of the 330 million gallons of effluent it discharges daily into the bay. The guiltiest contributors to the bay's bacterial stew these days are the citizens of Los Angeles themselves. Fertilizer runoff from lawns, oil and antifreeze dumped into sewers, and garbage tossed into streets and gutters all find their way into the bay via storm drains during periods of rain. Piers are another source of human-generated contaminants that stress the bay. Eight native species of fish native have been found to be contaminated with DDT and PCBs, severe and persistent toxins that were dumped into the bay during the '60s. They are very slow to break down in the cold, mucky bay bottom where they reside and are still working their way up through the food chain.

As bad as Los Angeles County's problems are, the first annual Beach Closure Report—issued by the State Water Resources Control Boards in September 1994—pointed the most disapproving finger at San Diego County. More beach closures occurred in San Diego County in 1993 than in the rest of the state combined—62 of 92, or approximately two-thirds of all closures. Heavy rain damaged municipal sewage systems, a problem compounded by neighboring Tijuana's sewage problems. That's a lot of lost opportunities for recreation—not to mention a lot of opportunities for illness and infection.

Even national organizations such as the Natural Resource Defense Council (NRDC) have joined local advocacy groups like Heal the Bay and the Surfrider Foundation in calling for solutions to ocean pollution. As an attorney for NRDC noted in 1991, "A relaxing day at the beach may actually be a hazard to your health." If you're concerned, take a stand and get involved. By law, the beaches belong to everybody—and, by God, everyone should be upset about what's happening to them.

For more information, contact the following organizations:

American Oceans Campaign
725 Arizona Street, Suite 102
Santa Monica, CA 90401
(310) 576-6162

In 1987, Ted Danson founded this Santa Monica–based organization to warn people about ocean and beach pollution and to educate policy makers and the public about the need to preserve and restore our shorelines. "Oceans and beaches used to be visually pleasing," Danson said in a 1995 interview. "They took your breath away and made you feel good about being alive. Now they're lined with wall-to-wall condominiums. Because of the sheer number of people, water supplies are overburdened and breaking down." Danson first got involved with the beach nearest his home—magical Will Rogers State Beach—and after successfully fighting the oil companies on offshore drilling, he started AOC. Recently, Danson has taken his message to Congress to educate the pack of freshman pit bulls who want to disembowel environmental regulations.

(continued)

Close Encounters of the Turd Kind *(continued)*

Heal the Bay
2701 Ocean Park Boulevard
Santa Monica, CA 90405
(310) 581-4188

Heal the Bay is an increasingly powerful foundation that started out in a living room and grew to an organization with 10,000 volunteers, all upset with the condition of Santa Monica Bay. Their goal is to achieve a "fishable, swimmable, surfable" bay, and they do it by lobbying, public education, and barraging the media with disturbing facts, figures, and photographs. They were responsible for stopping the county of Los Angeles from dumping sewage sludge into the bay. "We know that if we get the word out that our beaches are threatened, people will take action and we will see results," executive director Adi Liberman has said.

Ocean Protection Coalition
P.O. Box 1385
Mendocino, CA 95460

This grassroots organization works to protect the ocean and coast from offshore oil drilling. Their guiding conviction, as stated in their brochure: "There has never been less need to plunder our country's spectacular West Coast or more need to protect it."

Surfrider Foundation
122 South El Camino Real, Suite 67
San Clemente, CA 92672
(800) 743-SURF

In 1984, this environmental action group was founded in Malibu by surfers who saw their beloved ocean growing filthier by the day. Today, their ranks have swelled to 25,000 and they operate out of offices in San Clemente. Their high-profile victories have included successfully suing pulp mills for polluting Humboldt Bay and halting plans to construct a mile-long breakwater off Imperial Beach. Their Blue Water Task Force collects ocean samples for water-quality testing. They'd rather be surfing (who wouldn't?), but they've responded to the mandate for action. As former executive director Jake Grubb told *Rolling Stone:* "When I started surfing these waters in the early 1960s, they were green and blue. Today they're gray or brown."

Central California Beaches

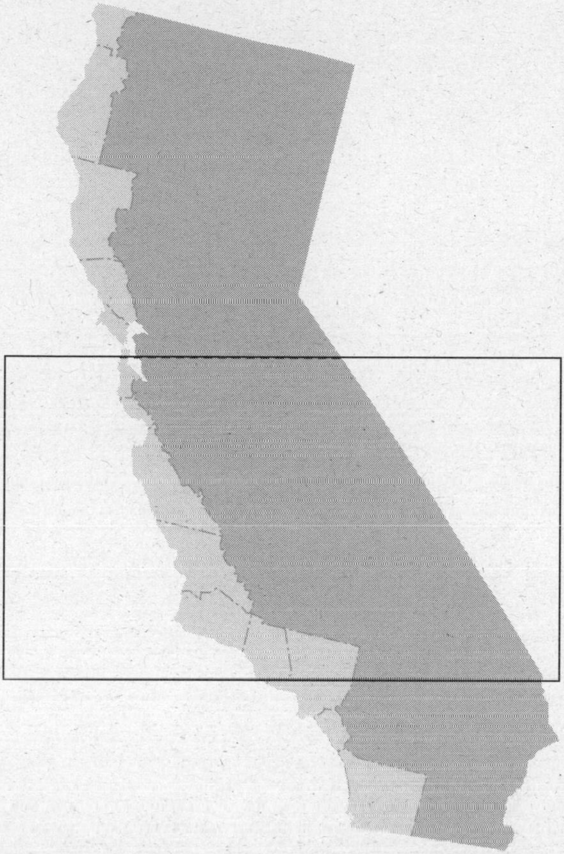

Key to the Symbols

Bike path   Camping   Food and drink   Hiking   Nude

Pier   RVs allowed   Surfing   Volleyball

Crowd Rating

sweet solitude . . . moderate crowds . . . wall-to-wall

Overall Rating

1 don't bother . . . 3 worth a visit . . . 5 beach heaven

Central California

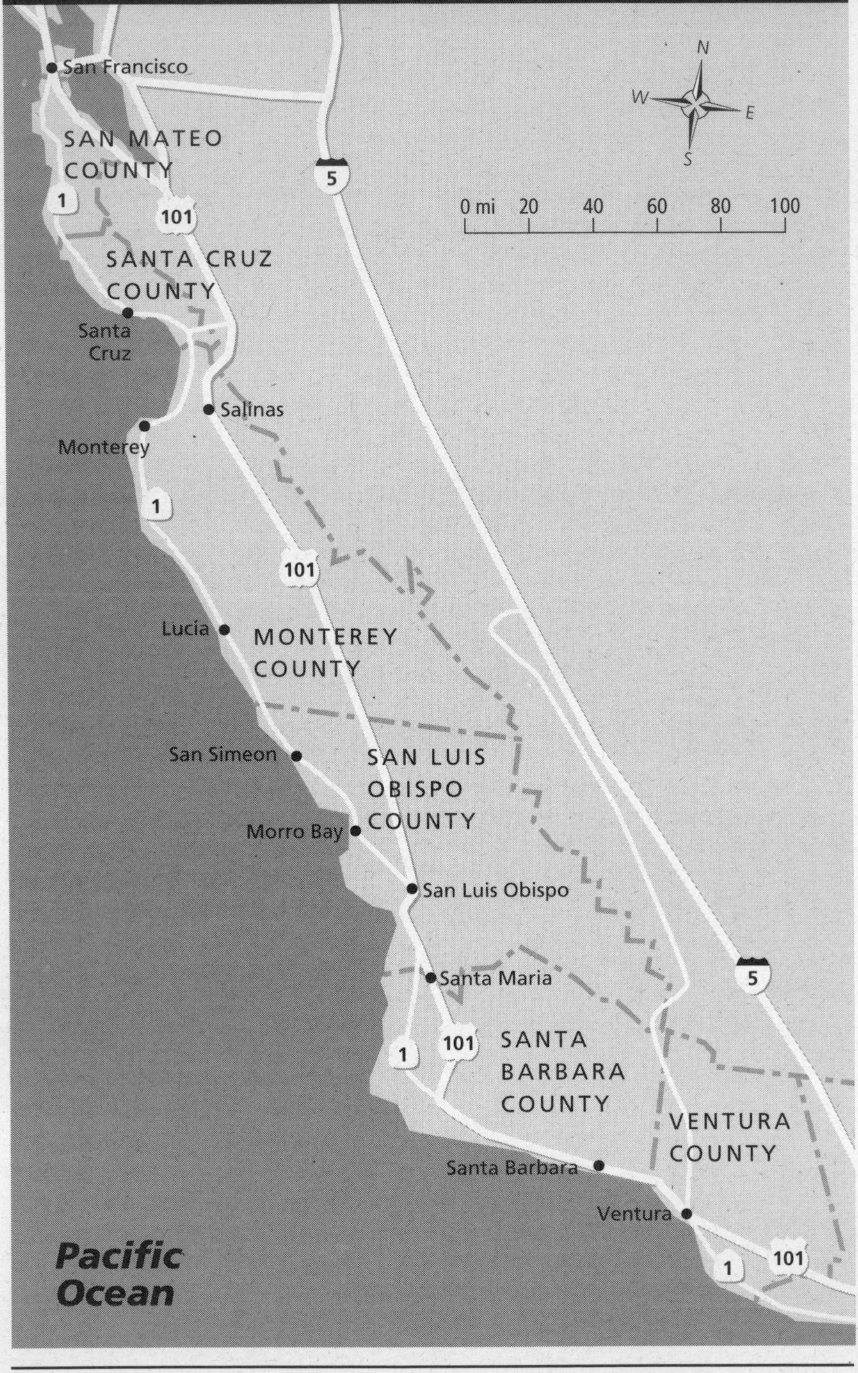

San Francisco
SAN MATEO COUNTY
1
101
5
N
W
E
S
0 mi 20 40 60 80 100
SANTA CRUZ COUNTY
Santa Cruz
Salinas
Monterey
1
101
Lucia
MONTEREY COUNTY
San Simeon
SAN LUIS OBISPO COUNTY
Morro Bay
San Luis Obispo
Santa Maria
5
1
101
SANTA BARBARA COUNTY
VENTURA COUNTY
Santa Barbara
Ventura
1
101
Pacific Ocean

Central California

Ventura County

It's little wonder that Ventura County has become a port of call for urban dropouts who pine for safe, sane, and smogless suburbs. Vacationers, tired of battling the Southern California throngs, have also begun pointing their flip-flops toward the 42 miles of coastline located here.

Once rural and primarily agricultural—the Oxnard Plain, which dominates the eastern part of the county, is one of the most fertile areas in the nation—Ventura County began growing in the 1960s at the point where Highway 101 (Ventura Freeway) meets Highway 1 (Pacific Coast Highway), near the cities of Oxnard and Ventura. Despite rapid growth, these cities retain more of a small-town feel than those on the coast of Los Angeles County. In fact, the Santa Monica Mountains, which lie between the two counties, cut them off from each other sociologically as well as geographically. To our way of thinking, the Central Coast begins here.

The beaches of Ventura County illustrate the yin and yang of oceanfront geography. Some of the beaches, such as *(continued on page 236)*

Coastal Ventura County's Climate

Oxnard Averages

	Daily High Temp. (°F)	Daily Low Temp. (°F)	Rainfall (inches)
January	66	44	3.6
February	67	43	3.0
March	67	45	2.2
April	68	47	1.2
May	69	51	0.1
June	72	54	0
July	75	57	0
August	76	58	0.1
September	76	56	0.3
October	75	52	0.2
November	71	47	1.8
December	67	44	2.0
Yearly Average	**71**	**50**	**14.5**

Source: National Weather Service data, National Oceanographic and Atmospheric Administration.

Ventura County

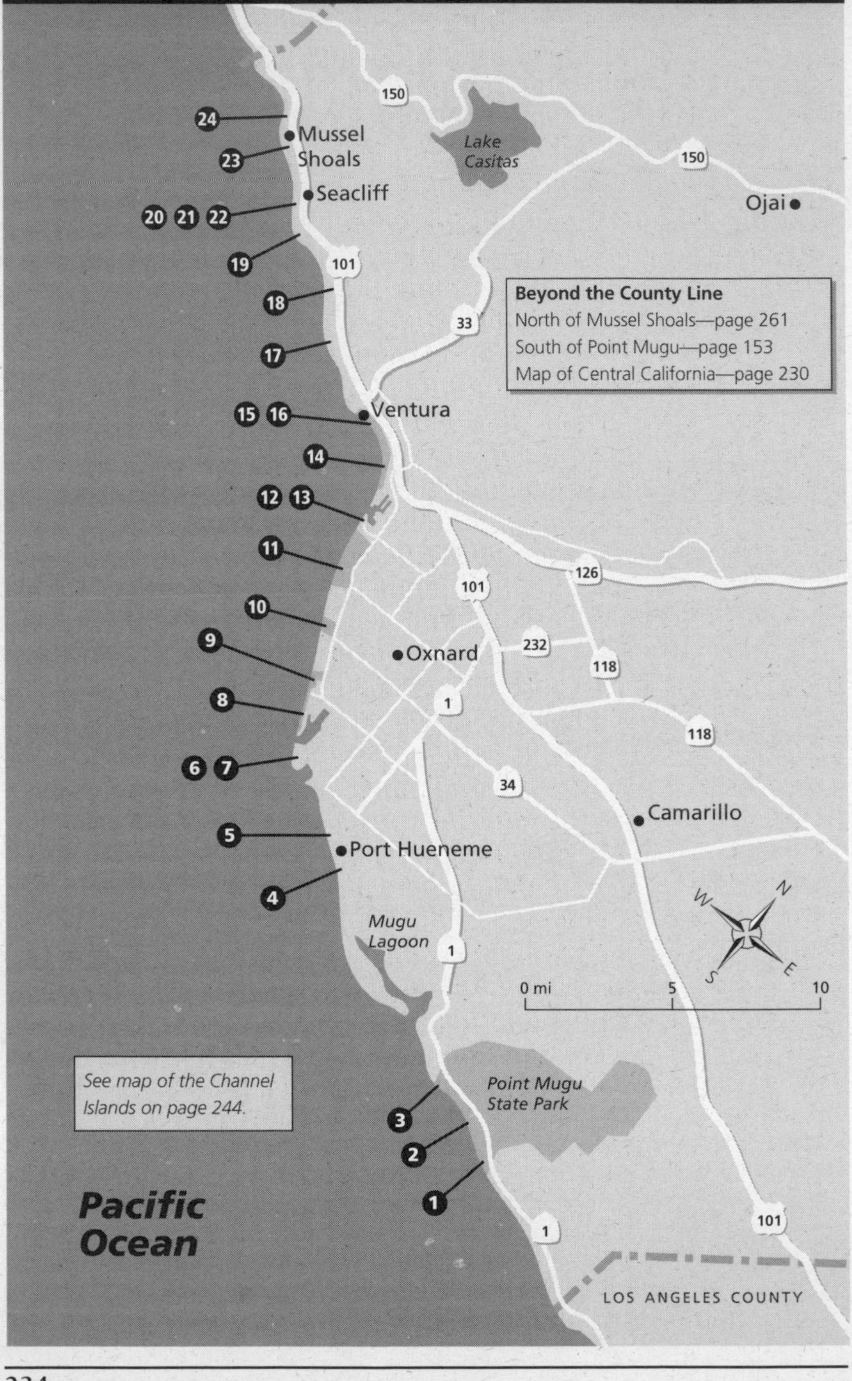

Ventura County Beaches

Map of Central California—page 230

(continued from page 233) Oxnard State Beach, Mandalay County Park, McGrath State Beach, and San Buenaventura State Beach, are as wide and inviting as any you'll find in California. Others, especially those fronting the small sea-walled communities at the north end of the county, are seemingly down to their last dozen grains of sand.

All are worth a peek, for different reasons. Even the thinnest ones, like Rincon Point and Oil Piers, offer the heart-stopping spectacle of bronzed surfers braving the jagged shore. If you're a beachcomber who thinks you've seen it all, head to Point Mugu, near the southern tip of the county, where you'll find a lagoon, bird sanctuary, monolith, beach, and missile testing ground. We also direct your attention toward the horizon, where the Channel Islands—a chain of eight pearly isles that have been called America's Galápagos—lie approximately 20 miles offshore. They constitute one of our most precious national parks and marine sanctuaries and beckon intrepid beach explorers.

Key to the Symbols

Bike path · Camping · Food and drink · Hiking · Nude

Pier · RVs allowed · Surfing · Volleyball

Crowd Rating

sweet solitude . . . moderate crowds . . . wall-to-wall

Overall Rating

① don't bother . . . ② ③ worth a visit . . . ④ ⑤ beach heaven

Point Mugu State Park

Location: Five miles northwest of the Los Angeles County line and 20 miles southeast of Ventura, on Highway 1.

Just inside Ventura County's southern border lie two of the newer "official" coastal access points in the state—Staircase Beach and County Line Beach. Adventurous beachgoers can park in dirt lots off the Pacific Coast Highway and walk down stairs to an isolated but beautifully rugged beach at both points. There, they'll find no phone, no facilities, and no lifeguards—nothing but rugged splendor and good, consistent surf that has been drawing devoted board bums (especially in winter) since the 1950s.

The next three beach-access points are more clearly marked and more popular. All fall under the auspices of Point Mugu State Park. Heading north, the first two—**Sycamore Cove Beach** and **Thornhill Broome Beach**—are augmented by popular and scenic campgrounds. The beach is just one facet of their appeal. The 14,980 acres embraced by Point Mugu State Park provide the lure of excellent hiking trails, most notably in Sycamore Canyon, which serves as a popular hikers' hookup to the Santa Monica Mountains. Here, majestic sycamores reach 80 feet, and deer and coyotes

Point Mugu Beach

Location: Seven miles southeast of Port Hueneme along the Pacific Coast Highway.

Parking: $6 entrance fee per vehicle or limited free roadside parking.

Hours: 9 AM to sunset.

Facilities: None.

Contact: For beach information, contact the Angeles District of the California Department of Parks and Recreation at (818) 880-0350.

See number 3 on page 234.

Sycamore Cove Beach

Location: Along Pacific Coast Highway, six miles north of the Los Angeles County line.

Parking: $6 entrance fee per vehicle.

Hours: 9 AM to sunset.

Facilities: Lifeguards, rest rooms, showers, picnic tables, and barbecue grills. There are 55 campsites for tents and RVs. Fees are $14 to $16 per night. For camping reservations, call Destinet at (800) 444-7275.

Contact: For beach information, contact the Angeles District of the California Department of Parks and Recreation at (818) 880-0350.

See number 1 on page 234.

Thornhill Broome Beach

Location: Along the Pacific Coast Highway, seven-and-a-half miles north of the Los Angeles County line.

Parking: $6 entrance fee per vehicle.

Hours: 9 AM to sunset.

Facilities: Lifeguards, rest rooms, showers, picnic tables, and barbecue grills. There are 102 campsites for tents and RVs. Fees are $7 to $9 per night. For camping reservations, call Destinet at (800) 444-7275.

Contact: For beach information, contact the Angeles District of the California Department of Parks and Recreation at (818) 880-0350.

See number 2 on page 234.

make appearances on some of the trails. Among the trails are the nine-mile Sycamore Canyon Loop and the three-mile Scenic Trail, which leads to stunning ocean overlooks.

The beaches at Sycamore Cove and Thornhill Broome are big with surfers and the campgrounds popular with families. The setting at Sycamore Canyon—a sandy, crescent-shaped beach with an amazing backdrop of cool, shady sycamores running up into the folded foothills—cannot be topped.

Point Mugu Beach has three attractions of its own—two natural, one man-made. There's Point Mugu itself, a mountainous, jutting headland that looms like a miniature Morro Rock, and Point Mugu Lagoon, an estuary and wildlife sanctuary. At 1,800 acres, it's the largest lagoon between San Diego and Morro Bay. The huge, white beach nestled between these two areas is within sight of the U.S. Navy's Pacific Missile Test Center. Nothing brings a beach bum back to reality more quickly than a billboard-sized sign that reads: "Danger: Live Fire." Still, the setting is one of our favorites in the Malibu/Ventura area.

For More Information

Contact Angeles District, California Department of Parks and Recreation, 1925 La Virgenes Road, Calabasas, CA 91302; (818) 880-0350. To reserve campsites, call Destinet at (800) 444-PARK.

Port Hueneme

Location: Adjacent to Oxnard, lying due southwest along Highway 1. Port Hueneme Beach Park, at the end of Port Hueneme Road, is the main beach in town.
Population: 21,000
Area Code: 805 **Zip Code:** 93041

The name is pronounced "Why-nuh-mee," as if the town is inquiring after its own identity. Being uprange from the largest missile testing ground on the West Coast, one can't blame the locals for asking questions. Within the town limits, approaching from the south on Highway 1, farmlands abound. Scientific and uniform, they sit row upon row, miles of green stubs with migrant workers bending and stooping under picked loads. A heavy industrial presence is also evident, with Kaiser Aluminum and a paper mill spewing smoke out their stacks.

Port Hueneme is packed with quiet, symmetrical neighborhoods where homes and apartment complexes are laid out not unlike the rows of crops that lead up to them. This anonymous uniformity is explained by the military presence in Port Hueneme. The U.S. Navy's missile range is to the south and the Navy's Construction Battalion Center owns the sea lion's share of the coastal access around the town center. Strewn among this hodgepodge are some fine beaches that manage, like the town residents, to quietly live out a natural and not-unpleasant existence.

Beaches

The first legitimate beach inside the town limits is **Ormond Beach**, which is located quite a ways off the beaten track. To get there, take Highway 1 to Hueneme Road. You'll pass by acres of farmlands, eventually making a left on Perkins Road, which leads to the beach via a corridor of warehouses and industrial plants. Park at the cul-de-sac and catch a whiff of the

 Map of Ventura County beaches—page 234

paper mills. The beach itself is healthy, with a full dune structure and not much human visitation. Though it offers a fascinating visual panoply, it's understandable why few come here except to sit in their car on their lunch hour and drink beer from brown bags.

At the west end of Surfside Drive is **Port Hueneme Beach Park**, site of an excellent beach and a handsome, 1,240-foot pier. Parking is self-pay, and the pier is open 24 hours a day, with cutting tables and sinks provided so you can filet all the sea bass you catch. The sand is grayish brown, wide, and dotted with volleyball nets, barbecue rings, and picnic tables. The beach ends at the south jetty of the naval complex.

On the north end of the navy's land lies **Silver Strand Beach**, the most intriguing of Port Hueneme's beaches. To find it requires making a circuitous route around the naval base: north on Ventura Road, left on Channel Islands Boulevard, left on Victoria Avenue, and left again on Ocean Drive to the Sawtelle Avenue access. It's a free, city-run beach with lifeguards in the summer. A shipwreck, the S.S. *La Jenelle*, forms a fishing jetty at the south end of the beach. Be careful when casting from here, though; it's slippery, and the surf can get rough.

Ormond Beach

2

Location: In Port Hueneme, at the end of Perkins Road off Hueneme Road.
Parking: Free parking lot.
Hours: Open 24 hours.
Facilities: None.
Contact: For beach information, contact the Oxnard Department of Parks and Facilities at (805) 385-7950.

See number 4 on page 234.

Port Hueneme Beach Park
(a.k.a. Hueneme Beach)

3

Location: In Port Hueneme, at the end of Surfside Drive
Parking: Metered parking lot.
Hours: Sunrise to 10 PM.
Facilities: Lifeguards, rest rooms, showers, picnic tables, and fire rings.
Contact: For beach information, contact Port Hueneme Recreation and Community Services at (805) 986-6555.

See number 5 on page 234.

For More Information

Contact the Port Hueneme Chamber of Commerce, 220 North Market Street, Port Hueneme, CA 93041; (805) 488-6993. Or try the Greater Oxnard and Harbors Tourism Bureau, 711 South A Street, Oxnard, CA 93030; (805) 385-7545.

Silver Strand Beach

3

Location: In Port Hueneme, along Ocean Drive at Sawtelle Avenue.
Parking: Free parking lot.
Hours: Open 24 hours.
Facilities: Lifeguards and rest rooms.
Contact: For beach information, contact the Oxnard Department of Parks and Facilities at (805) 385-7950.

See number 6 on page 234.

Oxnard

Location: 60 miles northwest of Los Angeles, 30 miles southeast of Santa Barbara, along Route 1 and Highway 101. Harbor Boulevard runs along much of Oxnard's seven miles of beaches. The main beaches are Oxnard State Beach and McGrath State Beach.
Population: 150,000
Area Code: 805 **Zip Code:** 93030

If a city were really serious about becoming a financial hub, a vacation mecca, and a site for the America's Cup competition, it would name itself something—*anything*—other than Oxnard. But Oxnard is quite intent on realizing these ambitious goals. Blessed by a beautiful setting, comfortable year-round climate, large and scenic harbor, strong prevailing winds, and wide, big-duned beaches, Oxnard is headed for bigger things.

Oxnard did not derive its name from the mighty ox. It was named for the mighty Henry Oxnard, a mogul whose sugar-beet empire was located hereabouts. With a population of 150,000, Oxnard is a medium-sized city with small-town ambience. It's situated in the middle of the fertile Oxnard Plain, with fields of crops as far as the eye can see. This agricultural delta was created by the once-mighty Santa Clara River (whose mouth has been reduced to a thin trickle by agricultural withdrawals). The river was damned, the delta became a plain, and the plain gave way to the multicolored fields that run to the east as far as the Santa Monica Mountains. Oxnard calls itself the Strawberry Capital of the World. California supplies 80 percent of the world's strawberries, and Oxnard celebrates with a Strawberry Festival every May. Other crops—such as lemons, corn, and broccoli—are grown here, too. Trucks and trains can be seen hauling off Oxnard's bounty around the clock to supermarkets the world over.

But Oxnard's "lower 40" is also filled with new middle-class housing and bank buildings—the things one associates with an up-and-comer. According to Chamber of Commerce-generated literature, Oxnard is "the fastest growing area in the state." It is a sentiment offered without irony, as though this were great news being delivered by a Peloponnesian runner from Olympus. Oxnard wears its recent growth as well as can be expected. Signs of it are obvious along Highway 1 on the outskirts of town, a suburbia of predictable sterility. But the beach areas, accessed via Harbor Boulevard, are low-key to the point of isolation. The beaches are so beautiful and healthy in Oxnard, it's surprising that they haven't been exploited like those down south. But we're not complaining.

Perhaps this is due to the fact that Oxnard caters primarily to a boating crowd. The scenic harbor and surrounding area are given over to biking and hiking trails, picnic tables, tennis courts, playgrounds, and a safe, secluded harbor beach. The entire coastline is situated at the proper angle to receive wind and water currents so vital to a rising water-sports capital. Channel Islands Harbor was dredged into existence in 1965 and modeled after a New England seaport, with 2,000 boat slips and a restaurant row.

It's obvious why Oxnard and neighboring Ventura are growing so quickly and how this incongruous overlap of suburbia and farmland came into being. The city is located 60 miles north of Los Angeles, where the Ventura Freeway meets the ocean, making it the next logical urban area for Angelinos to plunder. Actually, it is well along on its voyage of discovery, as the majority of boats docked at the harbor are owned by folks from L.A. You can almost hear Dan Loggins singing, "Please come to Oxnard in the springtime...."

Beaches

As if to reinforce the uniqueness of the coast in these parts, the 50-mile stretch from Ox-

 Map of Ventura County beaches—page 234

nard State Beach north to Gaviota State Park (above Santa Barbara) has been given its own name—the Channel Coast—a reference to the windswept Channel Islands, which are 20 miles offshore and visible on clear days.

The best way to access the public beaches of Oxnard is via Harbor Boulevard. Starting from the south, **Hollywood Beach** is a quiet city beach at the corner of La Brea Street and Ocean Drive, with volleyball nets and lifeguards on duty in summer. There's a little swimming beach near the harbor, locally known as **Channel Islands Harbor Beach**. A park runs around the inner flank of the harbor, offering grassy picnic sites and bike paths.

North of Hollywood Beach, also off Harbor Boulevard, is **Oxnard State Beach**, a great day-use facility for families and large groups. The park comprises 62 acres of athletic fields, picnic tables, barbecue pits, pedestrian and bike paths, and a trail system that leads over dunes to a stretch of sand so wide it will take your breath away. The surrounding residential area, Oxnard Shores, strikes a perfect balance between nature and human habitations, with low-lying architecture divided by canals, not unlike those in Venice Beach. Nonetheless, it's oddly devoid of human presence, as if a neutron bomb had gone off, leading us to wonder if these might be second homes for Los Angelinos.

Just north of Oxnard State Beach is **Mandalay County Park**. More of the same sandy masterpiece, it's a 104-acre facility that ends abruptly at the Southern California Edison Power Plant. The dunes are so healthy here that they stretch over to the eastern side of Harbor Boulevard like vine-covered beasts.

Channel Islands Harbor Beach

Location: In Oxnard, at San Nicholas and Ocean Streets.

Parking: Free street parking.

Hours: Open 24 hours.

Facilities: Lifeguards and rest rooms.

Contact: For beach information, contact the Oxnard Department of Parks and Facilities at (805) 385-7950.

See number 7 on page 234.

Hollywood Beach

Location: In Oxnard, at 501 Ocean Drive.

Parking: Free parking lot.

Hours: Open 24 hours.

Facilities: Lifeguards, rest rooms, and showers.

Contact: For beach information, contact the Oxnard Department of Parks and Facilities at (805) 385-7950.

See number 8 on page 234.

Mandalay County Park

Location: In Oxnard, along Mandalay Beach Road at Fifth Street.

Parking: Free parking lot.

Hours: At the time this book went to press, Ventura County was embroiled in a dispute with the city of Oxnard over plans to develop Mandalay County Park with a restaurant and recreational facilities. When these plans were met with citizen protest, the county closed the park, and the situation awaits resolution.

Facilities: None.

Contact: For beach information, contact the Ventura County Department of Parks and Recreation at (805) 654-3951.

See number 10 on page 234.

Then there's the most precious of Oxnard's treasures, **McGrath State Beach**. This hidden jewel is one of the most appealing of the state's coastal parks. McGrath is located between the city of Oxnard and the Santa Clara River bed, just south of Ventura. McGrath offers 174 wind-protected and shaded campsites, a visitor center, nature trails, a river estuary, dunes the size of small mountains, and two miles of wide, windswept beaches. Since the ocean currents are particularly strong here and the waves break on a deep, sloping shoreline, swimming is not recommended (though a lifeguard is on duty during the summer). This beach is best utilized for walking or surf casting, and the park is a living lab of natural wonders.

The dune structure at McGrath is among the healthiest left in Southern California. They are nonetheless fragile and should be traversed only on designated paths. Dunes occur where there is a sufficient source of sand moved around by ocean currents and winds. They are held in place by plants growing on them. These plants are easily broken or dislodged by any and all human disturbances: feet, mountain bikes, mopeds, Jeeps, and all-terrain vehicles.

The northern 160 acres of McGrath comprise the Santa Clara Estuary Natural Preserve, which was set aside to protect the habitat of the California least tern and the Belding's Savannah sparrow. A half-mile, self-guided trail accesses a portion of the preserve, offering glimpses of the freshwater and saltwater plants and animals that intermingle in this precious ecosystem. The murky water is a rich nursery of nutrients. Shrimp feed on plankton, fish eat the shrimp, and shorebirds devour the fish. All the while the next generation spends its formative months in this protected, nurturing habitat. If you want to camp at McGrath, be advised that reservations fill up in a hurry (especially in summer), and stays are limited to one week.

Bunking Down

There are less costly places to stay in Oxnard than the **Crown Sterling Resort** (2101 Mandalay Beach Road, 984-2500, $$$) but none that are so close to the beach. The Crown Sterling (formerly the Mandalay Beach Resort) is directly on Mandalay County Park, but this is just one reason among many to stay here. It goes beyond Oxnard's wildest dreams of luxury

McGrath State Beach

5

Location: In Oxnard, off Harbor Boulevard, one mile north of Mandalay County Park.

Parking: $5 entrance fee per vehicle.

Hours: 8 AM to 8 PM.

Facilities: Lifeguards, rest rooms, showers, picnic tables, and barbecue grills. There are 174 campsites for tents and RVs. Fees are $14 to $16 per night. For camping reservations, call Destinet at (800) 444-7275.

Contact: For beach information, contact McGrath State Beach at (805) 654-4744.

See number 11 on page 234.

Oxnard State Beach

4

Location: In Oxnard, on Harbor Boulevard between Beach Way and Falkirk Avenue.

Parking: $5 entrance fee per vehicle.

Hours: 8 AM to 8 PM.

Facilities: Lifeguards, rest rooms, picnic area, and barbecue grills.

Contact: For beach information, contact the Oxnard Department of Parks and Facilities at (805) 385-7950.

See number 9 on page 234.

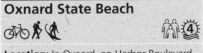

without a budget-smashing price tag. It is constructed along the lines of a Spanish estate, with grottoes, fountains, gardens, and waterfalls popping up at every turn. Getting lost on the way to your room is actually a pleasant experience. Buried among all the carefully manicured acreage is the largest free-form swimming pool in Southern California and two tennis courts. They also throw in a full, cooked breakfast in the Surf Room each morning.

A harborside version of Crown Sterling's oceanfront comfort can be found at the **Casa Sirena Resort** (3605 Peninsula Road, 985-6311, $$), a three-story, 275-room hotel and resort. Tennis courts, an exercise room, and patios and balconies overlooking the marina are a few of the amenities found here. There's also quite a good restaurant, the Lobster Trap, on the premises (see below).

Coastal Cuisine

The best way to check out Oxnard's showpiece, the Channel Islands Harbor, is from a restaurant window, especially toward sundown when the sailboats are returning to port. The **Lobster Trap** (3605 Peninsula Road, 985-6361, $$) is a waterside restaurant located on the extensive grounds of the Casa Sirena Resort. Established in 1969, the Lobster Trap flies in live Maine lobsters almost daily. Even more appealing are the local seafood specialties, like scalone and cioppino. The former is a puréed mixture of scallops and abalone, formed into a pancake and lightly sautéed.

For More Information

Contact the Greater Oxnard and Harbors Tourism Bureau, 711 South A Street, Oxnard, CA 93030; (805) 385-7545.

Channel Islands

Location: Eight islands located 14 miles off the coast of Ventura.

A string of eight pearl-like clusters that dot the horizon off California's Central Coast, the Channel Islands are part of the same geological chain that formed Santa Catalina Island. Like Catalina, each of the Channel Islands has its own unique ecosystem kept in changeless isolation by protective ocean boundaries. Five of the islands (Anacapa, Santa Cruz, Santa Rosa, San Miguel, and Santa Barbara) and the nautical mile that surrounds each (125,000 acres of submerged marine habitat) make up Channel Islands National Park. The other three islands (San Nicolas, San Clemente, and Santa Cruz) are off-limits to visitors.

The five isles that are accessible to the public are not nearly as accommodating as their Catalina cousin—at least not in the conventional sense. It takes careful planning to reach them. Visitors must arrange transportation to and from the islands (see below), and they must have a burning desire to rough it at primitive campsites and on rugged trails. The islands, with the possible exception of Anacapa, do not lend themselves to day-trips or quick look-sees. They require hearty souls (not to mention soles), as they can be harsh, windswept, and forbidding places. On the other hand, a visit to any of them will reward you with memories to last a lifetime.

The Channel Islands were originally inhabited by the Chumash tribe (*Chumash* means "island people"), who ventured off-island in their sturdy *tomols* (canoes) to trade with other tribes on the mainland and harvest the rich marine life in the waters of the Santa Barbara Channel.

In 1542, Europeans began to arrive. The Spanish explorer Juan Rodríguez Cabrillo came first, choosing to winter on San Miguel, where he eventually died—the result of a fall from a steep incline. (He was allegedly buried on San

Miguel, but his grave has never been discovered.) By the early 1800s the Chumash were packed off to missions on the mainland, and Europeans used the islands for hunting, grazing sheep and cattle, and growing grapes for California's earliest wines. The Channel Islands have since served as defense installations, as well as living labs for scientific inquiries of the Darwinian kind. The islands were declared part of the National Park System in 1980.

Because each of the islands offers unique treasures, and the logistics for reaching each island differs, the five are described individually below. Some general information, however, applies to all of them. First, the headquarters for Channel Islands National Park is on the harborfront in Ventura. Even if you don't plan to visit the islands, a trip to the headquarters is worthwhile. The museum offers an excellent exhibit detailing the rich panoply of life to be found offshore. You can also grab useful literature in the museum and adjoining shop. The best time to visit the Channel Islands is from March to July, though they're open to visitation year-round.

Although you can arrange transportation to the island with any licensed pilot, most people choose to book passage at Island Packers, next door to park headquarters. Because they have regularly scheduled departures to and from each of the five islands and are well-versed in the ways of the land, Island Packers has a sort of benign monopoly on the concession. Fares vary for travel to each island, as do schedules and trip duration.

If you go to the trouble of traveling for up to four hours one-way on a boat, you'll probably want to stay overnight. The only place to stay on the islands is in your own tent, and camping requires a permit from the National Park Service. Permits are free of charge and can be reserved in advance through park headquarters. (We suggest reserving from six months to a year before you plan to visit.) You also need to bring fresh water, because there are no facilities (except for latrines) on the islands. A park ranger is on site in case of emergencies.

Anacapa Island—Anacapa is the best choice for a day-trip. Perhaps you could use it to gauge how well you'll be able to manage an overnight stay in such surroundings. Actually three small islands in one, Anacapa is five miles long but covers only a single square mile of land area. East Anacapa is 11 miles from Ventura and the passage takes 75 minutes ($48 for adults, $30 for kids). Boats dock at Landing Cove, and the first hike a visitor takes here is straight up—154 steps to the top of the bluff, where the land levels out. From here, you can visit the Anacapa Island Lighthouse, which overlooks a rocky hangout of a healthy California sea lion population. You can also take the Loop Trail, a

Channel Islands

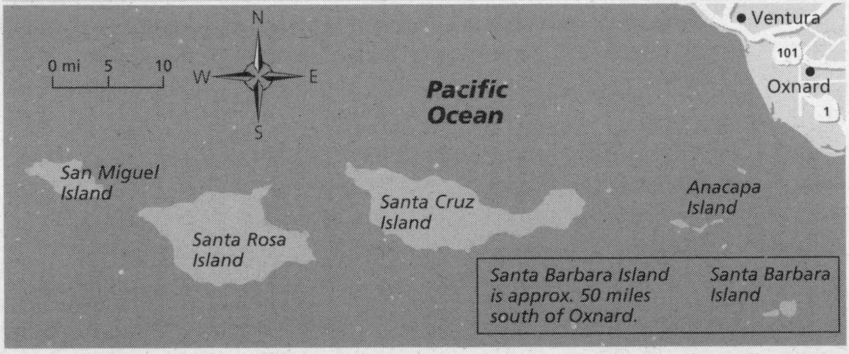

daunting 1.5-mile hike around the island whose highlights include sea caves, sea cliffs, and incredible bluff-top views. The terrain is rocky and the vegetation sparse on Anacapa—there are no trees—and the winds can be fierce. There are no sandy beaches, either, but on calm days you can swim at Landing Cove and dive at Cathedral Cove along the north shore. There are six tent sites on East Anacapa, with stays of up to 14 days permitted. West Anacapa, the largest and westernmost of the three islets, is off-limits, being the primary nesting spot for the brown pelican. Middle Anacapa has a landing spot at East Fish Camp.

Santa Cruz—This is the largest of the Channel Islands. (Twenty-four miles long, it occupies 96 square miles of land.) Santa Cruz is also the most varied in terrain and the most blessed with sandy beaches among its 77 miles of shoreline. It's home to more than 600 plant species and 140 bird species. However, visitation is limited. The western 90 percent is owned by the Nature Conservancy, a few scattered property owners, and the Santa Cruz Island Preserve. To land on the island you need to obtain permits from any or all of the above. Camping is not allowed here. For more information, contact:

- Island Packers, 1867 Spinnaker Drive, Ventura, CA 93001; (805) 642-1393.
- Nature Conservancy, Santa Cruz Island Project, 213 Stearns Wharf, Santa Barbara, CA 93101; (805) 962-9111.
- Santa Cruz Island Preserve, P.O. Box 23259, Santa Barbara, CA 93121; (805) 962-9111.

Santa Rosa—The second largest of the Channel Islands (15 miles long, 10 miles wide, occupying 53,000 acres), Santa Rosa is the best bet for overnight stays. It's got great hiking trails, mountains, canyons, the largest marsh on the islands, and a varied shoreline with sandy beaches on which harbor seals breed. Birdwatchers, kayakers, hikers, photographers, beachcombers, and rare-animal spotters—the Channel Island fox and spotted skunk are endemic to Santa Rosa—all love this island. There are only 10 campsites, so reserve a sight at least one year in advance. Boat trips take 3.5 hours one-way ($80 for adults, $70 for kids).

San Miguel—The farthest island from the mainland, San Miguel might be the most fascinating of the bunch. It is certainly the most primitive. The middle of the five islands in terms of size (eight miles long, five miles wide), at times it is whipped by ferocious winds that sculpt the sand into natural monoliths, a form of mineral sand-casting known as "caliche forests." A 15-mile hiking trail cuts through a raw landscape rounded by the wind from the beach at the landing all the way to Point Bennett at the western tip. En route, you can spot seals and sea lions on the beach, rare birds, and ground vegetation. Historians visit the island for its 500 archeological sites and the possibility of stumbling over Cabrillo's skeleton. A day-use boat leaves Ventura daily ($60 round-trip), but nine round-trip hours in a boat for a couple rough hours of beachcombing seems...barmy, mate. For campers, the boat fare is greater ($90 for adults, $80 for kids).

Santa Barbara—The smallest of the Channel Islands (640 acres) lies the farthest south, necessitating another long boat ride (3.5 hours each way, $75 for adults and $65 for kids). A visit to Santa Barbara Island almost demands an overnight stay to take advantage of the 5.5 miles of hiking trails. It's a particularly rewarding perch for bird-watchers, while snorkelers are often joined by playful seals. There are no shade trees on the island, and only eight primitive campsites.

For More Information

Contact Channel Islands National Park, 1901 Spinnaker Drive, Ventura, CA 93001; (805) 658-5700.

Ventura

Location: Ventura is located 65 miles northwest of Los Angeles and 25 miles southeast of Santa Barbara via Highway 101 (Ventura Freeway), which runs through the heart of town. Harbor Boulevard parallels the ocean and harbor. The main beaches in town are San Buenaventura State Beach and Seaside Park.
Population: 95,000
Area Code: 805 **Zip Code:** 93001

The full, legal, incorporated name of Ventura is San Buenaventura—a title officially bestowed in 1866—which is Spanish for "city of good fortune." Indeed, Ventura does possess the good fortune of not being anywhere near Los Angeles, from which it is separated by the Santa Monica Mountains and a one-hour freeway ride (assuming there are no traffic delays—ha!). It is also lucky not to be Oxnard, a larger nearby city that absorbs more of the migratory influx from Los Angeles. Ventura is separated from Oxnard by the dry bed of the Santa Clara River, and in some ways, the two towns bear a family resemblance—they are twin peas in the fertile pod of Ventura County, both of which have beautiful, uncrowded beaches and breezy harbor areas. However, as far as history, charm, and personality are concerned, Ventura shines beside its poorer relation.

The name San Buenaventura derives from the Catholic mission established here in 1782 by Father Junipero Serra. The original mission, chapel, and grounds have all been beautifully restored and maintained, as has the downtown Old Historic District that surrounds it. The San Buenaventura Mission (211 East Main Street, 643-4318) is open daily from 10 AM to 5 PM for tours. The entire town has internalized the lesson that historic preservation is a key to self-preservation. Other historic buildings open for touring include a pair of adobes, the Ortega Adobe (215 West Main Street, 648-5823) and the Olivas Adobe (4200 Olivas Park Drive, 644-4346). The Ortega Adobe is typical of the adobes that were found along Main Street in the 1800s, and from here, in 1897, the "Pioneer Ortega Chili" business was launched. The Olivas Adobe is a two-story adobe hacienda that was built around 1849 and is run today as a historical park by the city.

Next door to the San Buenaventura Mission is the Albinger Archaeological Museum, which houses artifacts spanning 3,500 years and five native cultures: Native American, Spanish, Mexican, Chinese, and American. Drop by San Buenaventura City Hall (501 North Poli Street, 654-7837) or the Ventura County Historical Museum (100 East Main Street, 653-0323) to pick up a walking tour guidebook of these and other historic attractions. City Hall, built in 1914 of simulated white marble, is an impressive piece of architecture in its own right. Even Ventura's post office is worth a look. Located three blocks away from City Hall on Santa Clara Street, the post office's interior houses a fascinating mural painted by WPA artist Gordon Grant, who spent most of 1936 and 1937 working on this tribute to the heroism of the common laborer and farmer.

Certainly, Ventura offers enough in the way of history, archeology, and architecture to keep anybody busy for a few days. But there's more for the educated browser as well: bookstores—eight of them in a two-block radius! Among them is the cooperative Book Mall of Ventura (424 Main Street, 641-2665), a 15-dealer bonanza of used, rare, and out-of-print books. Main Street Ventura is also stocked with art and antique stores, as well as a disproportionate number of thrift shops. In two blocks we counted half a dozen of them, which is bound to please that intrepid soul in search of the perfect bowling shirt. Then there's downtown Ventura's abundance of coffeehouses. Ventura is a real coffeehouse kind of town. They can be found all along California and Main Streets.

 Map of Ventura County beaches—page 234

Our nose for a good pun and a great cup of coffee led us to the Daily Grind (615 East Main Street, 641-1679) for a morning perk-me-up.

You get the picture. In all respects, Ventura operates at a more civilized and leisurely pace than the Southern California norm. You begin to sense a real break between the Southern and Central California sensibility, insofar as life along the coast is concerned. Ventura has got aspects of both: the compulsive physicality and cutting-edge cultural preoccupations of the Southland, and the less-harried and somewhat provincial outlook of the Central Coast. It was on the streets of Ventura, for instance, that we saw our first cowboy, a strapping fellow swathed in denim and crowned with a cowboy hat who politely asked us for spare change. Ventura admittedly faces growth problems, as more and more Angelinos flee their crisis-ridden city, opting to commute from or retire to Ventura County. Much of the growth has been absorbed by Oxnard, which has swelled like a goiter along the Highway 101 corridor. This buffer has thus far tempered the impact of Los Angelization upon Ventura. Its streets are still clean. The air of relaxation is palpable. The air itself is more breathable. You don't have to keep your guard up quite so reflexively.

If downtown Ventura is the heart of its history and culture, the Ventura Pier and Promenade is its recreational centerpiece. During weekends craftsmen and T-shirt and food vendors peddle their wares, and in-line skaters and cyclists pedal their wheels. The wide concrete promenade offers ample room to maneuver and extends for a good distance—up past Surfer's Point—with benches placed at intervals for restful contemplation of the ocean. At 1,200 feet, the Ventura Pier is the longest wooden pier in California. It dates back to 1872, when San Buenaventura was a busy harbor into which steamships would come and

Dirty Water

The beach report in Ventura County is cloudy, and we're not referring to the weather. The Ventura County chapter of the Surfrider Foundation—one of the largest in the state, with 700 members—reported in 1993 that 20 out of 20 beach locations tested showed unhealthy levels of bacteria. The usual suspects contributed to the murky water: untreated or inadequately treated wastewater from overworked municipal sewage plants, urban runoff from city storm drains and suburban lawns, and insecticides from agricultural operations.

In addition, the county has a problem with offshore oil platforms that emit air pollutants, which are blown inland and affect air quality. Despite the fact that their Chevron- and UNOCAL-owned platforms are given girls' names like Grace, Gail, Gilda, and Gina, they're not the kind of ladies you'd like to bring home to mother, collectively churning out 100 tons of nitrous oxides per year. Not to be outdone are the Edison generating plants at Mandalay and Ormond Beaches in Oxnard, which annually contribute 3,000 tons of pollutants. The end result: despite a paradisiacal location that inspired the 18th-century explorer Juan Cabrillo to refer to Ventura County as the "land of everlasting summers," Ventura County ranked in the Top 10 in the nation for ozone. Ozone is terrific in the stratosphere, where it belongs, but at ground level it's a pollutant created when oxides of nitrogen react with hydrocarbons in the presence of sunlight. In other words, you don't want to be breathing it.

go bearing cargoes of lumber, oil, and farm products. Between the pier and the harbor lies sandy San Buenaventura State Beach. Just north of the harbor, at the end of Seaward Avenue, is a bustling little neighborhood with a classic "California beach town" feel to it. On the east end of Ventura's oceanfront is Ventura Harbor, which comes with the obligatory "seaside village" of shops and restaurants, although this one is refreshingly Spanish in character, with red-piped-roof, mission-style architecture providing a sharp contrast to the clichéd New England fishing village motif commonly found elsewhere on the coast. Island Packers (1867 Spinnaker Drive, 642-1393), the authorized concessionaire to Channel Islands National Park (see the entry on page 243), is located on the harbor's south peninsula. Call or write ahead to book half-day or full-day excursions to the deserted islands.

Ventura's beachfront parks attract all kinds of folks. On a summer Sunday we saw a gaggle of surf punks cussing like they had Tourette's syndrome; a family wheezing past on a tandem bike, with the kids urging their huffing and puffing head of household to pedal faster; a counterculture minstrel curled up at the base of a tree, strumming a guitar; and elderly couples serenely surveying the ocean from park benches. It was a nice cross section of humanity enjoying a day at the beach.

Beaches

The city of Ventura has some fine beaches within its borders, from Ventura Harbor up to the county fairgrounds at the north end. South of Ventura Pier at the midsection of the city's beachfront area is **San Buenaventura State Beach**. It's a formidable two-mile beach, possessing good width and even a bit of dune structure. There's plenty of parking available, in lots and on the street. Crowds don't seem to be a problem. On a gorgeous summer weekend, even with a hefty contingent of bikers on hand for a charity road race, plenty of spaces were available. This long beach is good for swimming and sunbathing.

North of the pier, **Promenade Park** runs along a narrow, rocky, and highly eroded oceanfront. In fact, the most inviting feature of this park is the promenade itself, which connects the pier with Surfer's Point. Located at the end of California Street ("C Street," to the locals) at Seaside Wilderness Park, **Surfer's Point** is a 24-acre area of marshes and sand dunes at the mouth of the Ventura River. The point gets wrapped with winter swells from the north, with a healthy helping of distant storm-generated "juice" pushing the surf up to 20 feet on the outside break—not for neophytes or the faint of heart. Inshore waters, between California Street and the fairgrounds, are kinder and gentler. Even George Bush could master the waves here—after paying his respects to the Ronald Reagan Presidential Library up in Simi Valley first, of course.

There are also small beaches on the peninsulas immediately north and south of Ventura Harbor. Protected by jetties, **Marina Cove Beach** (a.k.a. Peninsula Beach) is considered the safest in the area for kiddies, including the added incentives of a child's play area and big picnic lawn. **Marina Park**, on the north side

Marina Cove Beach

3

Location: In Ventura, at the west end of Spinnaker Drive.

Parking: Free lot and street parking.

Hours: Open 24 hours.

Facilities: Rest rooms.

Contact: For beach information, contact the Ventura City Department of Parks and Recreation at (805) 652-4594.

See number 12 on page 234.

of the harbor, is another playland of boat docks, volleyball and basketball courts, and picnic sites.

Bunking Down

The place to stay in Ventura for the beach-obsessed is the **Holiday Inn Beach Resort** (450 East Harbor Boulevard, 648-7731, $$). This 10-story tower offers the best views of and closest proximity to the beach. Located near Ventura Pier and Highway 101, you couldn't ask for a better location, and the rooms take full advantage of this with balconies overlooking the water. It's a high-rise hotel, but the prices are fairly low ($79 to $89), especially compared with what you'd shell out for similar digs on the beach in Los Angeles County.

Only a modest notch down in location—and maybe a modest step up in amenities—is the **Doubletree Hotel** (2055 Harbor Boulevard, 643-6000, $$). It is located only a block away from the south end of San Buenaventura State Beach in a neighborhood removed from the downtown bustle. The rooms are spacious and well appointed, and a huge pool and Jacuzzi are the attractive centerpiece of the interior courtyard. The Doubletree is one of those high-end corporate fortresses that prides itself on attending to detail, and just about any need or whim can be met on the premises, from a stiff drink at C.J. Nelson's, the ground-floor lounge and nightclub, to a Southwestern-style dinner at the Gallery Restaurant.

Marina Park

3

Location: In Ventura, at the south end of Pierpont Boulevard.

Parking: Free parking lot.

Hours: Open 24 hours.

Facilities: Rest rooms and picnic tables.

Contact: For beach information, contact the Ventura City Department of Parks and Recreation at (805) 652-4594.

See number 13 on page 234.

Promenade Park

3

Location: In Ventura, from Ventura Pier west to Surfer's Point.

Parking: Free parking lot.

Hours: Open 24 hours.

Facilities: Rest rooms and picnic tables.

Contact: For beach information, contact the Ventura City Department of Parks and Recreation at (805) 652-4594.

See number 15 on page 234.

San Buenaventura State Beach

4

Location: In Ventura, along San Pedro Street at Pierpont Boulevard.

Parking: $5 entrance fee per vehicle in a lot, and metered street parking.

Hours: Open 24 hours.

Facilities: Lifeguards, rest rooms, showers, picnic areas, and fire pits.

Contact: For beach information, contact the Sector Office for the Channel Coast District of the California Department of Parks and Recreation at (805) 654-4610.

See number 14 on page 234.

Surfer's Point

3

Location: In Ventura, at Seaside Park, by the end of Figueroa Street.

Parking: Free parking lot.

Hours: Open 24 hours.

Facilities: Rest rooms and showers.

Contact: For beach information, contact the Ventura City Department of Parks and Recreation at (805) 652-4594.

See number 16 on page 234.

Talking Trash at the Beach

You just never know what might wash up on a California beach. But with our help, now you will. Setting aside a day for cleaning the beach was an idea pioneered in Oregon in 1984 and adopted by California in 1985. Traditionally the beach cleanup day is held on a Saturday in September or October. Now some counties are doing it monthly.

Here is a random sampling of some of the more offbeat items that have been collected by maintenance workers and volunteer beach cleanup crews in recent years. We'd say everything but the kitchen sink has washed ashore—but several of those have turned up, as well.

aluminum outdoor lighting grate
an "E.T." hand
angel-food cake pan
athletic supporters
baby bathtub
baby pacifiers
baggie of marijuana
bed springs
birth-control pills
bottom half of a set of false teeth
bowling ball
boxing glove
bungee cord
Bugs Bunny suit
camera
car parts
car windshield
cement park bench
cherry picker
Chicago Bulls cap
Christmas tree
couches
dead mouse in plastic bag
dead sheep
empty spools of cable
eyeglasses
family portrait
15-foot pipe
$50 bill
fireworks debris
fishing rods
Ford tractor
Frisbee
Grateful Dead concert tickets
Gucci watch
hypodermic needle
"I Love a Clean San Diego" bumper sticker
Jehovah's Witness booklets (a 10-pound bag)
kitchen sink
La-Z-Boy recliner
life-sized inflatable doll
loaded gun
logs the size of telephone poles
mail sack, undelivered
milk jugs
miniature Bible
motorcycle
New Age prism
one white patent leather shoe
plastic squid
propane tank
prosthetic foot
purse with credit cards and identification
radio
shopping carts
silk lei
soggy screenplay
soiled diapers
stove
surfboard
television set
tin of chewing tobacco
toaster
20-gallon oil drum
tweezers
two lottery tickets (both winners)
typewriter
vial of mystery liquid labeled "Love Potion"
washboard
washing machine
water heaters
xylophone

 Map of Ventura County beaches—page 234

Some statistics on the annual cleanup of California's beaches:

Year	Volunteers	Pounds of trash
1995	30,000	265,000 (133 tons)
1994	40,000	565,000 (283 tons)
1993	50,000	513,000 (257 tons)
1992	39,000	381,000 (191 tons)
1991	22,000	111,000 (56 tons)

The most prevalent items of trash picked up on the beach, from most to least common, based on a tabulation of data cards submitted after the 1992 cleanup:

1. cigarette butts
2. paper pieces
3. foam plastic pieces (Styrofoam)
4. plastic pieces
5. plastic bags and wrappers
6. plastic caps and lids
7. plastic straws
8. metal bottle caps
9. foam cups
10. glass bottles
11. plastic cups and utensils

California beach cleanups are organized by the California Coastal Commission and are sponsored by Pepsi, Lucky Supermarkets, and Southern California Edison. If you want to help, contact your county's Department of Parks and Recreation for more information. Or contact the California Coastal Commission, Adopt-A-Beach Program, 45 Fremont Street, Suite 2000, San Francisco, CA 94105; (415) 904-5200.

Another respectable choice is the venerable **Pierpont Inn** (550 San Jon Road, 643-6144, $$), set on seven beautifully landscaped acres atop a bluff overlooking Pierpont Bay. Built in 1908 and operated by the same family since 1928, the Pierpont Inn has an east and west wing, plus the Bluff House, an eight-room building perched on the bluff directly overlooking the ocean. The rooms include working fireplaces for those nights when the cold westerly winds blow off the ocean. The grounds are thick with flowers, and a path runs down the hill and under the freeway to the beach. A local landmark, the Pierpont attracts a faithful clientele.

Finally, if you're traveling on a budget, the **Vagabond Inn** (756 East Thompson Boulevard, 648-5371, $) is clean, comfortable, and sufficiently close to the action to have a footbridge to the beach and pier.

Coastal Cuisine

Let us again direct your attention to the **Pierpont Inn** (550 San Jon Road, 643-6144, $$$), this time for fine ocean-view dining. They serve good steaks, filet mignon, lamb chops, and so forth, but the bevy of fresh seafood items is not to be missed. If it's really, really fresh seafood you want, though—so fresh it hasn't even been cooked—step up to **Sushi Marina** (120 South California Street, 643-5200, $$). It's the swingingest sushi bar this side of Hermosa Beach. When we ate there it stayed packed till its 10 PM closing time with a young crowd of raw-fish addicts. Sushi Marina serves some of the finest and freshest sushi we've ever had. The sushi dinner consists of six pieces each of California and tuna roll, plus half a dozen assorted sushi items, including such exotic ones as bonito. If you're dragging a nonconvert with you, Sushi Marina has plenty of cooked selections, including teriyaki and sukiyaki.

For lunch you might try **Franky's Place** (456 East Main Street, 648-6282, $), especially if you're poling around Ventura's Old Historic District. The booths are separated by pieces of sculpture set on pedestals, and the red-brick walls are covered with original oil paintings. The quality of the food matches that of the art—and it's healthy, to boot. Serving natural foods with a vegetarian emphasis, Franky's offers pita and croissant sandwiches, heaping salads, and a great bowl of homemade soup.

Night Moves

Away from Southern California, with only rare exceptions, the term "nightlife" generally connotes something on the order of a grunion run. Yet while downtown Ventura is certainly no Sunset Boulevard in the party-down department, it's not entirely bereft of good times after dark. The restored **Ventura Theater** (26 South Chestnut Street, 648-1936) books a steady stream of nationally known acts. The varied likes of John Prine, Etta James, Eric Burdon, and Willie Nelson were advertised when we passed through town in early '96.

On the bar/club scene, we were pointed to a number of places, which we dutifully checked out. Our first stop was **Bombay Bar & Grill** (143 South California Street, 643-4404), the fanciest of the clubs in town. At the door was posted a portly bouncer squeezed into a tight-fitting tuxedo. The well-heeled crowd inside looked to be having fun, but we opted against paying a $6 cover charge to hear a mildly entertaining reggae band. If the music is to your liking, however, this looks to be a fun, civilized place to pass an evening.

More to our taste was the action at the **Metro Bay Club** (317 East Main Street, 653-2582), which attracts what was described to us as a "younger crowd." (Translation: a crowd in its early to mid-20s, plus never-say-die hipsters like us who try to fit in with them.) The Gen X-ers dance the night away in a club above a record store. Alas, it was so popular that we couldn't even get inside. The club was full to capacity, and the line of those waiting to climb aboard stretched down the block. It was '70s night at the Metro. The deejay played the era's music, and the crowd danced nostalgically to records that were popular when they were in Pampers. It seemed like an innocuous good time, and we would have happily caught Saturday Night Fever along with them, but an hour-long wait to get in was more than we could bear. At the same address, incidentally, is **Club Soda** (317 East Main Street, 652-0100), a party palace of long-standing.

An amiable longhair on line offered an alternative. A rock-and-roll band was playing at another place a few miles away, headed out of town. We decided instead to cut our losses and check out what was happening back at **C.J. Nelson's Sports Bar** in our hotel, the Doubletree. The answer was "not much." An earnest-looking foursome was performing fiercely inappropriate hard-rock arrangements of songs like "I Want to Hold Your Hand" to a small crowd who had ambled down from their rooms for a nightcap. A Japanese couple looked confused. We, on the other hand, had heard and seen it all before, so we called it an evening.

Some nights the party gods are with you, and some nights they're not.

For More Information

Contact the Ventura Visitors and Convention Bureau, 89-C South California Street, Ventura, CA 93001; (805) 648-2075.

Emma Wood State Beach

Location: Three miles north of Ventura off Highway 101. Take the State Beaches exit (if northbound) and the Seacliff exit (southbound).

We couldn't tell you who Emma Wood was. Nor could the parks' free handout literature or their rangers. Regardless, old Emma was so beloved that she had a nice state beach named after her. It's located north of Ventura, just before the turnoff for Old Rincon Highway. **Emma Wood** has sites for tents or RVs that are directly on the beach. The southern section of the park-designated Ventura River Group Camp has four group sites for tent campers that can accommodate up to 30 persons each, plus an RV group site and a few primitive hiker/biker sites. Got all that? If you plan on coming, especially during the warmer months, a prior reservation through Destinet (800-444-PARK) is an absolute necessity.

There's not much beach here, and what little there is virtually disappears at high tide. Still, the place is often full because rarely does one get to sleep this close to the ocean. Plus, there's good surfing, swimming, and fishing to be had good here. Anglers cast for perch, bass, cabezon, and corbina. At low tide, kids and amateur biologists study the ample marine life in the many tidepools. Bird-watchers find grebes, cormorants, curlews, willets, sandpipers, pelicans, and even a few songbirds and red-tailed hawks in the marsh at the southwest end of the beach. The Highway 101 overpass provides a uniquely legal opportunity to act like a hobo by camping beneath its cement and steel canopy. This is the only state campground we've ever seen that has a highway for a roof.

Emma Wood State Beach

Location: Along the Pacific Coast Highway, three miles north of Ventura.

Parking: $5 entrance fee per vehicle.

Hours: 8 AM to 11 PM.

Facilities: Lifeguards, rest rooms, showers, picnic tables, and barbecue grills. There are 61 campsites for tents and RVs. Fees are $10 to $12 per night. For camping reservations, call Destinet at (800) 444-7275. The southern portion of the park is designated the Ventura River Group Camp. At this site, there are four 30-person group campsites and several hiker/biker sites. Fees are $45 to $75 per night for the group sites and $3 for the hiker/biker sites. For camping reservations, call Destinet at (800) 444-7275.

Contact: For beach information, contact Emma Wood State Beach at (805) 654-4610.

See number 17 on page 234.

For More Information

Contact Emma Wood State Beach, 901 San Pedro Street, Ventura, CA 93001; (805) 654-4610.

Solimar Beach

Location: Five miles north of Ventura, off Highway 101.
Population: 250
Area Code: 805 **Zip Code:** 93001

At the south end of this tiny community, two miles north of Emma Wood State Beach along Rincon Parkway (a.k.a. Old Pacific Coast Highway), glimpses of the "old California" can be seen. Empty cars line the shoulder of the highway beside a mile-long seawall, their occupants atop surfboards in the water. There's no day-use fee, nor is there an official coastal access, because at the north end of the seawall lies the private "beach colony" of **Solimar Beach**. The not-so-pacific ocean waters beat relentlessly against the seawall and the thinning beach, leading one to suspect that this is an inevitably doomed stretch of road—not unlike the brief patch of Old Pacific Coast Highway south of here that now rests in the big drink. Meanwhile, surfers paddle happily out to Solimar Reef, about 300 yards offshore, which provides a six-foot swell in winter.

Solimar Beach

Location: Five miles north of Ventura in the community of Solimar, along the Rincon Parkway (Old Pacific Coast Highway).
Parking: Free roadside parking.
Hours: Sunrise to sunset.
Facilities: None.
Contact: This is a private community; no contact number is available.

See number 18 on page 234.

Faria Beach

Location: Seven miles northwest of Ventura, along Highway 101.
Population: 250
Area Code: 805 **Zip Code:** 93001

This minute town just north of Solimar Beach on Rincon Parkway (Old Pacific Coast Highway) consists of a string of residences facing the hungry ocean. The ocean's waves break directly onto the cement wall upon which the homes sit. Most of these houses look fairly new and underused, serving only to block public access to what little beach exists at low tide.

Nonetheless, **Faria Beach County Park** offers 42 campsites above the boulders that line a thin but pretty beach. Surfers come to try their luck off Pitas Point. They make the strenuous hike up to the point with their boards. The "outside" break is for experienced hands, the "inside" for learners. Two cautionary notes—there are no lifeguards on duty, and a sign warns: "Any mussels gathered may be poisonous." (The latter is no doubt due to sewage runoff from residential development.)

For More Information

Contact Faria Beach County Park, c/o Ventura County Parks, 800 South Victoria Avenue, Ventura, CA 93009; (805) 654-3951.

Faria Beach County Park

Location: At Pitas Point in the community of Faria Beach, along the Rincon Parkway (Old Pacific Coast Highway).

Parking: $2 entrance fee per vehicle.

Hours: Sunrise to sunset.

Facilities: Rest rooms, showers, picnic tables, and fire pits. There are 42 campsites for tents and RVs. Fees are $9 to $16 per night. For camping reservations, call the Ventura County Department of Parks and Recreation at (805) 654-3951.

Contact: For beach information, contact the Ventura County Department of Parks and Recreation at (805) 654-3951.

See number 19 on page 234.

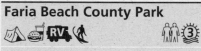

Seacliff

Location: Nine miles northwest of Ventura, off Highway 101.
Population: 250
Area Code: 805 **Zip Code:** 93001

Rincon Highway passes through Seacliff, yet another private "beach colony." The saving grace of Seacliff is **Hobson County Park**. It has a small campground and picnic facilities. Beach erosion is severe here, and the park actually closes during heavy storms. The surfing is good at Seacliff, but it's a half-mile swim out to Seacliff Reef. Between Seacliff and Faria, **Rincon Parkway North** serves as a linear campground for RVers, who can pull over for the night for a modest charge. Picnic tables and pit toilets are provided, and a sandy ribbon of beach runs alongside the parkway and seawall.

For More Information

Contact Hobson County Park, c/o Ventura County Parks, 800 South Victoria Avenue, Ventura, CA 93009; (805) 654-3951.

Hobson County Park

RV 3

Location: At the southern end of the community of Seacliff, along the Rincon Parkway (Old Pacific Coast Highway).
Parking: $2 entrance fee per vehicle.
Hours: Sunrise to sunset.
Facilities: Rest rooms, picnic tables, and fire pits. There are 31 campsites for tents and RVs. Fees are $9 to $16 per night. For reservations, call the Ventura County Department of Parks and Recreation at (805) 654-3951.
Contact: For beach information, contact the Ventura County Department of Parks and Recreation at (805) 654-3951.

See number 21 on page 234.

Rincon Parkway North

RV 2

Location: Between the communities of Faria Beach and Seacliff along the Rincon Parkway (Old Pacific Coast Highway).
Parking: Free roadside parking.
Hours: Open 24 hours.
Facilities: Rest rooms and picnic tables. There are 112 roadside campsites for RVs. The fee is $10 per night. No camping reservations are accepted.
Contact: For beach information, contact the Ventura County Department of Parks and Recreation at (805) 654-3951.

See number 20 on page 234.

Oil Piers Beach

Location: 10 miles northwest of Ventura, off Highway 101.

Among the more fascinating and eerie spectacles along the California coast are these four tentacles, the privately owned piers of the oil companies whose platforms you see on the offshore horizon. The longest pier leads to a man-made island, gussied up like a tropical paradise to disguise the oil-drilling pumps. Who's zooming who?

The stretches of beach south and north of the largest pier provide some of the best surfing in California. (In fact, that's the only action these beaches attract.) It's something of a rite of passage to surf in the shadows of such industrial might. For those curious to catch a glimpse of this spectacle, park alongside Rincon Parkway (Old Pacific Coast Highway) and poke your nose over the crest of the hill.

Oil Piers Beach

Location: At the northern end of the community of Seacliff, along the Rincon Parkway (Old Pacific Coast Highway).

Parking: Free roadside parking.

Hours: Sunrise to sunset.

Facilities: None.

Contact: This is private property; no contact number is available.

See number 22 on page 234.

Nollan v. California Coastal Commission

James Nollan, a Ventura County landowner, made national headlines in 1987 by taking his property-rights case to the U.S. Supreme Court—and winning. The verdict in the case of Nollan v. California Coastal Commission was seen as a victory for developers and property owners, and as a setback for the commission by restricting one of its key strategies for providing greater coastal access to the public.

The site that ignited the legal imbroglio was a 3,600-square-foot beachfront lot in Faria Beach, in rural northern Ventura County. On it was a tiny, decrepit beach cottage owned by James and Marilyn Nollan. In 1982, the couple applied for permits to raze and replace it with a two-story beach bungalow. The California Coastal Commission (CCC), empowered to grant or deny permits for development along the ocean, then routinely demanded public easements of landowners. In exchange for a permit, the CCC required the Nollans to grant a right of public access along a lateral strip of beach between the high-tide line and a seawall on their property. The area in question was 10 feet wide and extended along the length of their property. The CCC wanted to make it easier for the public to pass between a public beach located a quarter mile north of the Nollans' property and another that lay one-third mile south.

Under California law, the public owns the shoreline up to but not above the mean high-tide line. That is to say, you can legally walk along the part of the beach that is always or occasionally inundated by waves, but not above it. The dry-sand part of the beach can be privately owned, and crossing it without prior permission is an act of trespass, if the landowner is so inclined. The CCC, in *(continued on next page)*

Nollan v. California Coastal Commission *(continued)*

accordance with its mission to protect the state's coastline "as a natural resource belonging to all people," had for years and with uncontested success been imposing public-access dedication requirements upon permit-seeking property owners as a means of increasing public access to the beaches. Such conditions had been imposed upon 1,817 property owners through the end of 1984. Then came Nollan.

In the Ventura County Superior Court, the Nollans challenged the CCC-issued development permit with the contested condition. After the Nollans won their case, the CCC appealed. The California State Court of Appeal reversed the earlier decision, holding in favor of the CCC. Supported by the conservative Pacific Legal Foundation, the Nollans appealed to the U.S. Supreme Court, arguing that under the terms of the Fifth Amendment of the U.S. Constitution the CCC's demands for an easement constituted an unwarranted "taking" of private property. The clause in question comes at the end of the Fifth Amendment: "... nor shall private property be taken for public use without just compensation."

On June 26, 1987, in the last ruling handed down in the 1986–87 term, the Supreme Court held in favor of the Nollans. By a vote of 5–4, with Justice Antonin Scalia writing the majority opinion, the court ruled that granting public access to private property without compensation must be tied to a specific, justifiable public purpose. A condition placed on development, such as a grant of public easement, fails to pass the test of constitutionality if it "utterly fails to further the end advanced as the justification for the prohibition," said Scalia. In simpler language, if the CCC "wants an easement across the Nollans' property, it must pay for it."

The decision was a pivotal one in the area of private-property rights, pursued with vigor by the Rehnquist court with Justice Scalia at the forefront. The dissenting justices mustered strong arguments of their own, but the tilt of the conservative court opposes government limitations on private property development. The decision forced the CCC to rein in and reconsider their methods—which, in the long run, may have been more commendable in principle than constitutional in reality.

In the intervening years, the Nollan case has turned out to have a less severe impact on government regulation than some had initially feared. Even the CCC tried to put a positive spin on the Supreme Court verdict, with its executive director claiming that "we're pleased the courts explicitly upheld the right of local and state governments to require public access and dedication as long as they can show a direct relationship between the project and the conditions."

As for the Nollans, it was all more a matter of principle than practice. They had been allowing people to cross their property for years and said they would continue to do so, even after the court decision. "As long as the people are not obnoxious, we would give them permission to walk back and forth," said Mr. Nollan.

Case closed.

 Map of Ventura County beaches—page 234

Mussel Shoals

Location: 11 miles northwest of Ventura, off Highway 101.
Population: 250
Area Code: 805 **Zip Code:** 93001

Unlike the residential "colonies" to the south, Mussel Shoals is an actual town that sits on either side of the Pacific Coast Highway between Oil Piers Beach and the Santa Barbara County line. It's a likable setting, with the surf literally rumbling the earth below one's feet. Abandoned segments of Old Pacific Coast Highway can be seen here, affording a ghostly glimpse of what lies ahead for coastal planners.

Beaches

North of **Mussel Shoals Beach** lies La Conchita Point, where the surf breaks close to the pier and onshore rocks. Needless to say, this one is for fearless experts only. The sight of someone taking a wave here is breathtaking for those of delicate temperament. North of the point is **La Conchita Beach**, which can be reached off the Highway 101 shoulder via a riprap revetment, but it's not worth the trouble.

Bunking Down

For those who relish out-of-the-way overnight destinations, Mussel Shoals offers a pleasant inn located on the rocks right above the ocean. The name of this surfside haven is the **Cliff House** (6602 West Pacific Coast Highway, 652-1381, $$), and the rates are reasonable for romantic getaways and a little on the high side for surfers on safari. Crash here and get lulled to sleep by the sea.

La Conchita Beach

Location: Along Highway 101 at La Conchita Point, above the community of Mussel Shoals.
Parking: Limited free street parking.
Hours: Sunrise to sunset.
Facilities: None.
Contact: For beach information, contact the Ventura County Department of Parks and Recreation (805) 654-3951.

See number 24 on page 234.

Mussel Shoals Beach

Location: At the end of Ocean Boulevard in the community of Mussel Shoals, 11 miles northwest of Ventura.
Parking: Limited free street parking.
Hours: Sunrise to sunset.
Facilities: None
Contact: For beach information, contact the Ventura County Department of Parks and Recreation at (805) 654-3951.

See number 23 on page 234.

Where's the Beach?

In the 1980s, scientists Orrin Pilkey and Wallace Kauffman co-authored a book entitled *The Beaches Are Moving*. Pilkey is a renowned marine geologist and the director of the Center for the Study of Developed Shorelines at Duke University. He is something of a thorn in the side of developers and the U.S. Army Corps of Engineers, whose various projects have contributed significantly to the degradation of beaches and coastlines all over America. Were Pilkey to revise *The Beaches Are Moving* today, he might have to retitle it *The Beaches Are Disappearing*. If he were writing about coastal Ventura and Santa Barbara Counties, he could call it *The Beaches Have Disappeared*.

The problem of severe beach erosion has alarmed state and county officials. The beaches along Highway 101 between Ventura and Santa Barbara have become badly eroded, and not just in front of homeowners' property but at state and county parklands, too. At Hobson County Park, nine miles north of Ventura, the sea comes right up to the campground, where at one time it was buffered by a wide expanse of white, sandy beach. The problem of intensive erosion is also felt at Mussel Shoals, Solimar, Rincon, and Faria Beaches.

It's a mostly a man-made and partly a natural disaster. From the human side, the damming of streams and rivers has interrupted the supply of sand and sediment that replenishes the shoreline, especially during the high-flow winter storm season. Development along the coast—harbors, military bases, homes, and attendant beach-hardening structures such as jetties, seawalls, and breakwaters—has altered the southerly, longshore flow of sand, carrying it off the coast where it is forever lost in submarine canyons and depressions. Finally, nature itself goes through periodic cycles of enhanced storminess and erosion. Current evidence supports the idea that we are in a period of global warming, which may cause the sea level to rise and inundate low-lying areas. That, too, might well have a human-engineered component to it, if by industrial and consumer release of "greenhouse gases" into the atmosphere we are contributing to a rise in global temperatures.

In any case, as we wandered along the narrow, rocky strips between ocean and seawall at places like Rincon Beach, we found ourselves wondering, "Where's the beach?"

 Map of Ventura County beaches—page 234

Santa Barbara County

If you could put all the best beach ingredients into a pot (sand, sun, surf, seclusion, and scenery, plus decent food and oceanfront lodging), you'd have Santa Barbara County. Even factoring in such negatives as offshore oil platforms, this county has been graced with an abundance of coastline to glow and crow about. With the exceptions of ranchland around Point Conception and Vandenberg Air Force Base, Santa Barbara County is remarkably accommodating where the land meets the sea. The city of Santa Barbara is, in terms of geography, scenery, and climate, as close to being perfect as any city we've encountered. If we could afford it, we might even move there to loll in the sun and play volleyball on the beach for the rest of our days.

The county begins in the appealingly low-key town of Carpinteria, which boasts the "world's safest beach," and ends at Guadalupe, a speck of a burg that provides access to the tallest sand dunes on the West Coast. In between these extremes you'll find a 100-mile *(continued on page 264)*

Coastal Santa Barbara County's Climate

Santa Barbara Averages

	Daily High Temp. (°F)	Daily Low Temp. (°F)	Rainfall (inches)
January	65	43	4.3
February	66	44	3.7
March	67	46	2.5
April	69	48	1.5
May	70	51	0.3
June	73	54	0.1
July	76	57	0
August	77	59	0
September	77	57	0.2
October	75	53	0.3
November	71	47	2.1
December	67	43	2.7
Yearly Average	**71**	**50**	**17.7**

Source: National Weather Service data, National Oceanographic and Atmospheric Administration.

Santa Barbara County

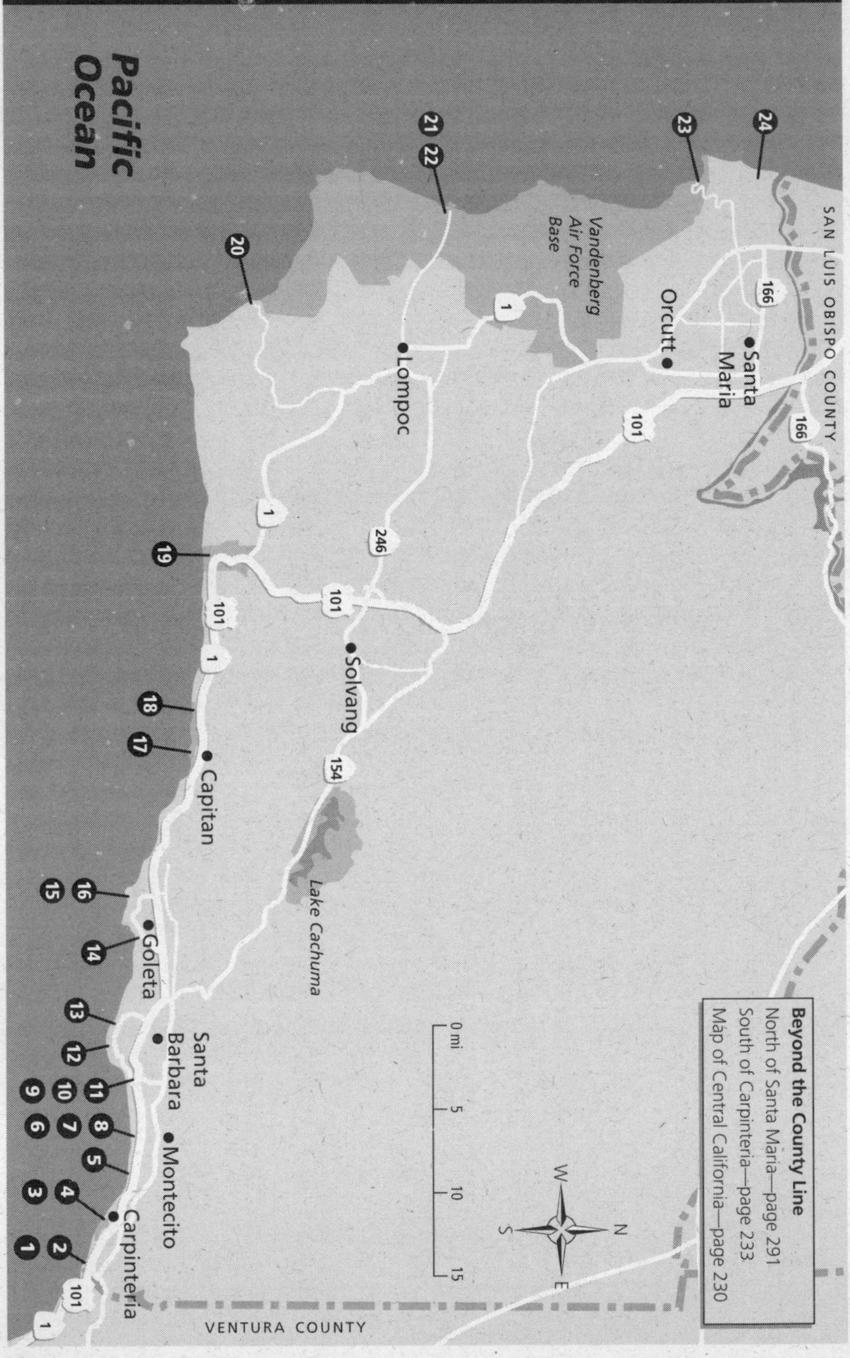

Santa Barbara County Beaches

Map of Central California—page 230

(continued from page 261) slice of heaven on earth that encompasses the urban amenities of Santa Barbara and the timeless isolation of Point Sal State Beach, not to mention a holy trinity of state beaches in the middle of the county—El Capitan, Rèfugio, and Gaviota—that are worth their weight in golden sand.

Key to the Symbols

Bike path Camping Food and drink Hiking Nude

Pier RVs allowed Surfing Volleyball

Crowd Rating

sweet solitude . . . moderate crowds . . . wall-to-wall

Overall Rating

1 don't bother . . . 3 worth a visit . . . 5 beach heaven

Rincon Point and Rincon Beach County Park

Location: Straddling the Ventura/Santa Barbara County line, Rincon Point can be reached via the Bates Road exit off Highway 101.

This is one of the best surfing spots in California, though it's not the easiest place to find. Because of the presence of beach-hogging private homes in the area, much of this coastline is inaccessible to all but the most intrepid beach bums. However, there is one dependable access point to this bounty of beaches—**Rincon Beach County Park**, a Santa Barbara County–run facility with an overlook, picnic tables, and free access to the beach via a winding wooden stairwell that descends the cliff face. Swimmers take the plunge to the north of the stairwell bottom (a sign designates that 220 yards of beach has been set aside for swimmers only).

But the real show begins 500 yards south of the stairwell at **Rincon Point**, a surfer's El Dorado. Just inside Ventura County—and also accessible via Rincon Point Parkway off Highway 101—Rincon has, we were told, "a classic right point break." It is also one of the best winter surf areas in the world because the seasonal swells provide "a flawless shape." The southernmost area is the most popular, attracting up to 100 surfers during peak season. Sometimes the surf is so tough that the problem isn't riding the waves but paddling out to them.

South of Rincon Point are a second and third point, like benign aftershocks from a surfing earthquake. They aren't as crowded as Rincon and have the added feature of tidepools to explore if the waves aren't breaking. As you stroll south, the bluffs of the county park give way to wide open vistas, from which you can see La Conchita Beach to the south, and Highway 101 and the Southern Pacific rail line to the east. The cobblestone beach is pretty to look at but not much fun for wading or swimming. Its isolation is yet another reason it's a surfer's wet dream.

As if to express their feelings about the homes that have made beach access difficult at this revered spot, surfers have covered the seawall in graffiti. Most of it is scatological; none of it is printable.

For More Information

Contact the Santa Barbara County Department of Parks and Recreation, 105 Anapamu Street, Santa Barbara, CA 93101; (805) 568-2460.

Rincon Beach County Park

Location: South of Carpinteria, take Bates Road off Highway 101 to the park.
Parking: Free parking lot.
Hours: 8 AM to sunset.
Facilities: Rest rooms and picnic area.
Contact: For beach information, contact the Santa Barbara County Department of Parks and Recreation at (805) 568-2460.

See number 2 on page 262.

Rincon Point

Location: Straddles the Ventura County line, along Highway 101 at Rincon Parkway (Old Pacific Coast Highway).
Parking: Limited free roadside parking.
Hours: Sunrise to sunset.
Facilities: None.
Contact: This is a private community; no contact number is available.

See number 1 on page 262.

Carpinteria

Location: 12 miles southeast of Santa Barbara, off Highway 101. Carpinteria State Beach is the main beach in this small town.
Population: 14,500
Area Code: 805 **Zip Code:** 93013

Many a coastal civic group has proclaimed its sandy land grant to be the "world's safest beach," but Carpinteria just might be the first beach to have been so ordained. Way back in 1602, Spanish explorers described it as *cosa segura de buen gente*, or "the safest beach on the coast." Nestled against the Santa Ynez Mountains on a fertile plain, Carpinteria is a small town with big assets: beautiful, uncluttered beach; a pleasing Mediterranean climate; and a commanding view of the Channel Islands. The slope of the beach is gentle, with no sudden dropoffs or riptides, making for worry-free swimming.

The original inhabitants of the Carpinteria Valley were Chumash Indians, who plundered the area's extensive tar pits for pitch to seal their canoes. Their canoe-building enterprise was, in fact, appropriated by the Spanish conquistadors who referred to it, mistakenly, as a "carpentry shop"—thus, the name of the town. Carpinteria literally sits atop a huge pool of the Chumash's black gold. Beneath the fertile soil in the valley lies a thick layer of tar, and below that, a sea of oil. Much of the industry around Carpinteria is related to petroleum production—seven oil platforms are visible offshore, and many more can be found north in the rich Santa Barbara Channel—although agriculture is pursued with equal gusto.

To a vacationer's eye, Carpinteria has the appeal of a quiet town with rural, slowpoke ways and excellent, naturally protected beaches. Some might even argue, with some justification, that Carpinteria is the last true undiscovered beach town in California. However, it is in the process of being discovered, and an upscale real-estate market is emerging. This feeds into the further privatizing of the shoreline, which is evident in the 12-mile stretch from Carpinteria to Santa Barbara. Much of the shoreline above Carpinteria is privately accessed via "gated communities" (an oxymoron?). One place, Padero, seems inordinately smitten with self-importance. Its surrounding walls and trees are peppered with "Absolutely No Trespassing" signs and coils of razor-edged barbed wire top their castle walls.

One note of consolation: it seems that Padero, et al., are walled in on both sides. What glimpses we could catch of their shore revealed a lot of riprap and precious little beach. The town of Carpinteria itself, though, is unpretentious, laid-back, and lovely.

Beaches

A "bathing beach" located where Linden Avenue ends at the water, **Carpinteria City Beach** is safe because an offshore reef acts as a natural breakwater, preventing rip currents from forming. It's a free beach, but you'll have to park on the surrounding streets. Some of the tar bubbling beneath the ocean floor (60 feet below the surface) seeps into the water and ends up on the bottoms of human feet, thus explaining the ubiquitous packets of "Tar Off" seen around town. Not to worry; it's part of a natural process, not an oil spill.

The more popular beach is **Carpinteria State Beach**, a 50-acre park with a one-mile-long sandy beach, large dunes, healthy tidepools, and 262 made-in-the-shade campsites. An interpretive display on the Chumash Indians is on the premises. To the south are a series of surfing spots—Holly, Tar Pits, Jelly

Bowl—used by locals but rarely worth the trouble to anyone else.

Bunking Down

Most overnight visitors to Carpinteria camp in the state park. The town also gets its share of day-users at the city beach on summer weekends. Motels are few and scattered, but their number will no doubt increase as word gets out about this charming town. As it is, no motel sits beside or near the beach, though you can make yourself comfortable several blocks away at the **Best Western Carpinteria Inn** (4558 Carpinteria Avenue, 684-0473, $$). Rates are not cheap ($100 to $130 in season), but very few accommodations in the Santa Barbara area are.

Coastal Cuisine

The usual assortment of low-key Ma and Pa pizza huts, cafés, and delis are available within walking distance of Carpinteria City Beach. For anything more ambitious, head to Santa Barbara, 10 minutes north, which is one of California's culinary capitals.

For More Information

Contact the Carpinteria Valley Chamber of Commerce, 5320 Carpinteria Avenue, Carpinteria, CA 93013; (805) 684-5479.

Carpinteria City Beach

Location: In Carpinteria, at the end of Linden Avenue.
Parking: Metered parking lot.
Hours: Sunrise to 11 PM.
Facilities: Lifeguards.
Contact: For beach information, contact Carpinteria Community Services at (805) 684-5405, ext. 449.

See number 4 on page 262.

Carpinteria State Beach

Location: In Carpinteria, at the end of Palm Avenue.
Parking: $5 entrance fee per vehicle.
Hours: Sunrise to sunset.
Facilities: Lifeguards, rest rooms, showers, picnic area, and fire pits. There are 262 tent and RV campsites, with hookups. Fees are $14 to $23 per night. For camping reservations, call Destinet at (800) 444 7275.
Contact: For beach information, contact Carpinteria State Beach at (805) 684-2811.

See number 3 on page 262.

Summerland

Location: Six miles east of downtown Santa Barbara. Take the Summerland exit off Highway 101. Summerland's lone beach can be found at Lookout County Park.
Population: 1,800
Area Code: 805 **Zip Code:** 93067

The seaside village of Summerland is a blink-and-you'll-miss-it community located a cat's whisker east of Montecito. What a great name: wouldn't we all like to live in a figurative heaven-on-earth called Summerland, where everyone is on permanent vacation and the sun's always shining? In terms of size, Summerland is to Montecito what Montecito is to Santa Barbara. In a word, tiny. But it's got a pair of nice bed-and-breakfast inns, a good restaurant, a few antique shops and a county-owned beach worth visiting if you're passing through.

Beaches

Lookout County Park offers the option of picnicking on the wooded bluff top above or playing on the sandy beach below. It is one of the more isolated beaches on the Santa Barbara coast, and is the only public beach of any consequence along the stretch of highway between Carpinteria and Santa Barbara. Lifeguards are on duty on summer weekends only.

Bunking Down

There are two good choices. The **Inn on Summer Hill** (2520 Lillie Avenue, 969-9998, $$$$) is a hotel/inn offering ocean views, a full breakfast, canopy beds, and English country decor. The **Summerland Inn** (2161 Ortega Hill Road, 969-5225, $$) has fewer amenities than its competitor, but its comfortable rooms go for about half the price. It's a great deal, almost a bargain, on this pricey part of the coast.

Coastal Cuisine

Quaint and casual, the **Big Yellow House** (108 Pierpont Avenue, 969-4140, $$) is comfortably situated in a 110-year-old Victorian mansion, offering home-style meals (steak, seafood, and pasta) and appetizing ocean views.

For More Information

Contact the Santa Barbara Conference and Visitors Bureau, P.O. Box 299, Santa Barbara, CA 93102; (805) 965-3021. Or drop by their information stand at 1330 State Street in Santa Barbara.

Lookout County Park

Location: In Summerland, six miles east of Santa Barbara, at the end of Lookout Park Road.
Parking: Free parking lot.
Hours: 8 AM to sunset.
Facilities: Lifeguards, rest rooms, picnic area, and fire pits.
Contact: For beach information, contact the Santa Barbara County Department of Parks and Recreation at (805) 568-2460.

See number 5 on page 262.

Montecito

Location: Three miles east of downtown Santa Barbara, 85 miles north of Los Angeles. Traveling along Highway 101, take the Olive Mill Road exit, which deposits you in the heart of the village. Channel Drive runs alongside Butterfly Beach, the little village's central beach.
Population: 9,100
Area Code: 805 **Zip Code:** 93108

The main reason to come to the upscale village of Montecito is to stay at one of its several splendid hotel-resorts. From beachside beauties like the Four Seasons Biltmore Santa Barbara and the Miramar to the San Ysidro Ranch in the steep hills, the bywords here are money and luxury. If, to the outside world, Santa Barbara is a bastion of good living brimming with comfort and money, then Montecito is an even more exclusive enclave. Olive Mill Road is Montecito's Rodeo Drive, lined with expensive shops that bear inscrutable names like "Angel" and "Object." On the real-estate market, you can't touch a decent piece of property here for under $400,000. Unspectacular homes costing a cool million are not unusual, and $4 or $5 million for a house and lot with a view doesn't raise an eyebrow.

Lately the town has had a population explosion. At one time a minor coda appended to Santa Barbara's seaside symphony, it is now a full fledged fugue in its own right. Currently, the population is listed at 9,100. You can gauge the community's wealth not only by its inflated real-estate prices but by such everyday things as the cost of gas at the pump ($2 a gallon for "full serve"), the presence of a Starbucks Coffee (the first we'd seen since Los Angeles), and the lost-pet ad we saw affixed to local telephone poles. Instead of a mangy mutt or tomcat, the heartbroken owner was looking for an exotic, and no doubt expensive, red-billed parrot that had flown the coop.

Beaches

To be honest, **Butterfly Beach** really isn't much of a beach. It has eroded so much that the ocean laps at the retaining wall at high tide. At low tide, there's a bit of beach to walk upon, but you can't help but feel that they're fighting a losing battle with nature here. The entirety of Butterfly Beach sits in front of the Santa Barbara Biltmore. Another beach close by, **Miramar Beach**, is accessible from and named after the Miramar Resort Hotel. Trails lead to **Hammonds Beach**, a public beach that lies between them. These two beaches are mainly enjoyed by guests of the Miramar or locals who want to escape the crowds in Santa Barbara. Both are fine beaches that lie off the beaten path. (The Miramar Resort itself luxuriates in 500 feet of prime, uncrowded ocean frontage.)

To get to Miramar and Hammonds Beaches, take Eucalyptus Lane to a small parking area at its end. Your own two feet will take over from there. Incidentally, bicycling is a great way to get out and see the Montecito/Santa Barbara beachfront. A bike path extends from the grounds of the Santa Barbara Biltmore hotel to the harbor area just north of Stearns Wharf,

Butterfly Beach

Location: In Montecito, at Butterfly Lane and Channel Drive, in front of the Four Seasons Biltmore Santa Barbara.
Parking: Free street parking.
Hours: 8 AM to sunset.
Facilities: None.
Contact: For beach information, contact the Four Seasons Biltmore Santa Barbara at (805) 969-2261.

See number 8 on page 262.

a distance of about four miles. Most of the hotels stock bikes for the use of their guests. Alternatively, you can pick one up at Beach Rentals (8 West Cabrillo Boulevard, Santa Barbara, 963-2524), across from Stearns Wharf.

Bunking Down

You'll find the area's most upper-crust hotels and resort properties in Montecito. For those seeking repose at the beach, the **Four Seasons Biltmore Santa Barbara** (1260 Channel Drive, 969-2261, $$$$) ranks at the top of the list. It is a property so posh and well established that it publishes its own folio-sized, book-length history. All you need to know is that the premises teem with orange trees and fragrant botanical gardens, and the rooms are palatial and comfortable. Graceful arches and brick walkways connect the villalike buildings. The grounds are covered with Monterey cypress, blue gums, and parlor palms. The Four Seasons Biltmore feels like a world unto itself—which, in a sense, it is, being situated directly on Butterfly Beach in Montecito, with traffic and any sense of proximity to in-town bustle completely absent. While there's admittedly not much of a beach left here, East Beach in Santa Barbara is just a short car or bike ride away.

At the Biltmore, guests can rent 12-speed mountain bikes for $3 a day. Other amenities include a fully equipped fitness center, a heated 50-meter outdoor pool and Jacuzzi, and two on-site restaurants. Formerly the Santa Barbara Biltmore, it was taken over by the Four Season chain in 1987, which gave it an $18.7 million facelift. You won't lack for cosseting here—and won't ever want to leave.

Up the road apiece, a few miles into the mountains off San Ysidro Road, is the legendary **San Ysidro Ranch** (900 San Ysidro Lane, 969-5046, $$$$). It is a 540-acre resort ranch whose chief claims to fame are that Vivien Leigh and Laurence Olivier were married on the grounds and that JFK and Jackie honeymooned here. These events are preserved in framed clippings hung in the lobby area. Rest and relaxation without pomp or pretense is the philosophy here. The rooms are in bungalows strewn around the sprawling estate. Some have their own Jacuzzi on a private deck. Nothing comes cheaply here: room rates range from $195 to $730 per night, and add-ons can be costly as well. The minibar charges, for instance, are outrageously jacked up: $4 for popcorn, $2.50 for a 10-ounce Coke, and so on.

The ranch has its own stables, and guests can opt for any kind of horse ride, from a trail ride into the mountains to a "meditation walk" around the grounds. On the latter, you close your eyes, bliss out, and let your equine bodhisattva lead you on a journey to the center of the mind. The ranch also offers spa ser-

Hammonds Beach

Location: In Montecito. Park at the end of Eucalyptus Lane; a trail leads to the beach.
Parking: Free parking lot.
Hours: 8 AM to sunset.
Facilities: None.
Contact: For beach information, contact the Santa Barbara County Department of Parks and Recreation at (805) 568-2460.

See number 7 on page 262.

Miramar Beach

Location: In Montecito, in front of the Miramar Resort Hotel at 1555 South Jamison Lane.
Parking: Limited free street parking.
Hours: 8 AM to sunset.
Facilities: None.
Contact: For beach information, contact the Santa Barbara County Department of Parks and Recreation at (805) 568-2460.

See number 6 on page 262.

vices, such as massage, aromatherapy, and skin treatments. A menu of these, ranging from an hour-long massage to a full two-day schedule of indulgent therapies, will set you back anywhere from $60 to $975.

Pets are welcomed and, somewhat ridiculously, pampered to the max. The "privileged pet" program includes peanut-butter canine cookies at check-in, VIP gifts upon arrival (rawhide chews, squeaky toys, personalized bowl), the pet's name hung on a wood-burned sign outside the cottage, doggie turn-down service, and Perrier for pets. Sound a bit excessive? It did to us, too. But maybe not to Pokey, Smoke, Chloe, Rexford, Fresca, and Sprite—some of the pooches whose names were entered in the pet guest register at the front desk. If money is no object and you're at home in an environment where nature's splendor outstrips manmade amenities—and especially if you're traveling with a pet accustomed to *la dolce vita*—then by all means saddle up and visit the San Ysidro Ranch.

Finally, we must mention the **Miramar Resort Hotel** (1555 South Jamison Lane, 969-2203, $$$$) and the **Montecito Inn** (1295 Coast Village Road, 969-7854, $$$$). The Miramar claims the technical distinction of being the only hotel on the beach in the area. That is to say, there's not even a street to cross to get to the sand. The hotel offers lodgers a choice of rooms, cottages, and bungalows at about 25 different price points, from $70 to $440. Closer to town, the Montecito Inn has some rich show-biz history attached to it. Charlie Chaplin and (though brochures don't mention him) the scandalized Fatty Arbuckle established the Montecito Inn in 1928. Its 53 rooms are decorated in French provincial style, while the lobby is a lake of Italian marble. The inn is three blocks from the beach. Chaplin's Little Tramp couldn't have afforded to stay here, but if you're solvent to the tune of $130 to $245 a night, they'll roll out the welcome mat.

Coastal Cuisine

All the best dining in Montecito is in the hotels. The **Stonehouse at the San Ysidro Ranch** (900 San Ysidro Lane, 969-5046, $$$) is well-nigh incredible. Many of the herbs and vegetables used are organically grown on the premises. The menu will help you "rediscover the great foods of America," as the dining room's motto proclaims. Appealing entrées include salmon roasted on a Chardonnay oak-barrel plank. For once, vegetarian dishes are as delectable as they are healthy, such as baked eggplant, Portobello mushrooms, and goat cheese with tomato linguine and asparagus. Such creativity led one Los Angeles food critic to proclaim the Stonehouse "almost certainly the best restaurant in all of food-conscious Santa Barbara County," and *Condé Naste Traveler* has proclaimed it one of America's 50 best restaurants.

The Four Seasons Biltmore has its own fine on-premises dining rooms as well: **La Marina Restaurant** (1260 Channel Drive, 969-2261, $$$$) specializes in gourmet continental and California cuisine, while the more casual **Patio Restaurant** ($$$) serves a decadent Sunday brunch spread from its glass-enclosed atrium.

Night Life

The Biltmore has a nice, civilized lounge with a pianist. If you want anything more from your evening than the sounds of a well-groomed gent tickling the ivories amid the clinking of cocktail glasses, you'll have to head into downtown Santa Barbara, where you'll find enough nightlife to last till sunrise.

For More Information

Contact the Santa Barbara Conference and Visitors Bureau, P.O. Box 299, Santa Barbara, CA 93102; (805) 965-3021. Or drop by their information stand at 1330 State Street in Santa Barbara.

Santa Barbara

Location: 92 miles northwest of Los Angeles, it can be reached via exits off Highway 101. State Street runs through the heart of town, ending near Stearns Wharf. Cabrillo Boulevard runs parallel to the beach. East Beach and West Beach form the main beach strand in Santa Barbara.
Population: 87,100
Area Code: 805 **Zip Codes:** 93101, 93103

If you were to feed all the variables that govern quality of life into a computer, Santa Barbara might just top the list. All it takes is a day or two's exposure to the beaches, the mountains, the teeming greenery, the Spanish architecture, and the relaxed ebb and flow of life to become convinced that this is America's most perfect setting for a city. This is true despite the very real problems (see sidebar, "The Other Side of Paradise") that have beset the community over the years. From whatever your perspective, Santa Barbara is a living postcard.

The reasons for Santa Barbara's blessed fortunes are many, and geography is not the least of them. Santa Barbara is encircled by the Santa Ynez Mountains, which act as a cradle to the city, staving off the winds that blow down from the north. Twenty miles offshore, the Channel Islands intercept the Pacific swells, protecting the coastline. Santa Barbara is the only city in California that faces due south, running along a figurative ledge that divides the Central and Southern California coasts. The climate is moderate year-round: comfortably cool in summer, never too cool in winter, shirt-sleeve weather almost every day. Located between Los Angeles (92 miles southwest) and San Francisco (332 miles north), Santa Barbara embodies elements of those polarized extremes without suffering the extreme urban angst common to both.

The people who live here are activist-aesthetes who have made a mission of keeping their city clean, green, and out of the hands of those who'd turn it into an urban Disneyland at the drop of a bank loan. Consequently, there's always some kind of battle being waged—city-hall caucuses and grassroots crusades aimed at saving parks and heading off the latest nefarious development proposal. Nonetheless, Santa Barbara is a supremely restful city, especially for two beachcombers burned out from months of rambling around the lion's den of Southern California.

Many residents made their money elsewhere, relocating here in their golden years. Santa Barbara exists in relatively easy harmony with its environment. Tourism is the closet thing to an industry, and even that is spurned in its more ostentatious manifestations. One of the great local controversies of the mid-1980s centered around the construction of a 360-room luxury motel, the Red Lion Resort, across from East Beach. The man behind the project was Fess Parker, the TV actor who played Davey Crockett. As a real-estate mogul, Fess undertook a very different kind of trailblazing—clearing acreage along the ocean for a sprawling lodge that hogs the best beachfront view to the eternal consternation of the local populace.

This is a city whose blocks are filled with museums, galleries, theaters, libraries, bookstores, and historic buildings. Public consensus ensures a progressive stand on such matters as controlled growth and habitat preservation. Following a devastating 1925 earthquake, the city council established an architectural board of review that drafted a design code. Consequently, Santa Barbara was rebuilt in the appealing Mediterranean style—low buildings, vanilla stucco exteriors, red-pipe roofing, arcades and walkways, wrought-iron railings, and flower and shrub-filled gardens—that reflect the city's 200-year Spanish and Mexican heritage.

 Map of Santa Barbara County beaches—page 262

The most visible example of this style is the Mission Santa Barbara (2201 Laguna Street, 682-4713), established in 1786. Dubbed the "Queen of the Missions," it sits on a knoll overlooking the town. At close range, it almost appears two-dimensional, like a Hollywood movie set. The grassy square before it is a greener green and the sky on a clear day a bluer blue than your most vivid Kodachrome fantasy. The graceful Spanish Colonial facade is dressed in pink and white tones; behind it rise twin bell towers. The grounds include a museum and flower garden. Of the 21 Franciscan missions established throughout California, only Mission Santa Barbara remains active as a parish church.

Continuing into the hills along Mission Canyon Boulevard, you'll come upon the Santa Barbara Botanical Garden (1212 Mission Canyon Road, 682-4726) and the Santa Barbara Museum of Natural History (2559 Puesta del Sol Road, 682-4711). The botanical garden encompasses 65 acres and 1,000 species of native California trees, flowers, shrubs, grasses, and annuals. The grounds are divided into environmental biomes (canyon, desert, arroyo, meadow, and woodland), each with its own trails. This lovely park plunges visitors back into pre-European, precondominium California. Inside the redwood grove, everything is stilled to a profound, cathedral-like silence beneath its huge boughs. The natural history museum offers geology and biology exhibits: a 33-foot model of a giant Pacific squid, a planetarium, a replica of a Chumash priest doing the "Seaweed Dance" (variations of which are performed nightly at the rock clubs down on State Street), and much more. Founded in 1916, it's impossible to miss: just look for the place with the 72-foot whale skeleton out front. *(continued on page 276)*

The Other Side of Paradise

Santa Barbara is a wonderful city. Seldom will you find such varied beauty—mountains, beaches, vineyards, hot springs—in such proximity, and with a perfect climate to top it all off. But the city, for all its magnificence, isn't enclosed inside a glass bubble. It is subject to the myriad stresses and strains that bear upon latter-day American cities—mainly economic pressures that lead to environmental and human cataclysms. It has fought many issues with the sort of diligent conscientiousness one wishes every community in America would someday muster. Nonetheless, this earthly paradise has seen its share of troubles. It has had more than its share, in fact, which seems unfortunate considering how hard its citizens (particularly the "gray panthers," scrappy AARP-ers with tons of fight left in 'em) have involved themselves in various battles. Here's a rundown of what's gone wrong in this lovely land of plenty:

• **Fire**—On June 27, 1990, an arsonist set a fire on the brushy western outskirts of Santa Barbara that consumed 4,900 acres, destroyed hundreds of homes, caused $238 million worth of damage, and killed one person. The belt of blackened, scorched earth extended from the hills and down the canyons toward the ocean, racing through neighborhoods in northern Santa Barbara and Goleta. In the aftermath of the fire, tourism slumped by 10 percent at the height of the season. Would-be visitors, particularly Europeans, believed from TV coverage that Santa Barbara had burned to the ground, including its hotels and restaurants.

(continued on next page)

The Other Side of Paradise *(continued)*

• **Drought**—In the 1970s, Santa Barbara elected not to tie into water supplies imported from the Sierras via the State Water Project, fearing that more water would mean more unwanted development. In the 1990s, it paid a heavy price for its well-intended self-reliance. As California entered its fourth year of drought in March 1990, with the dry summer season still to come, the city found one of its reservoirs empty and another only one-quarter full. The crisis forced the city to impose severe water conservation measures. Lawn watering was banned, and the city's green parks and gardens turned a dry, dead brown (just in time for the Painted Desert fire, described above). A tiered pricing system for water consumption was introduced; excessive usage was punished with rates 30 times higher than normal.

One Montecito resident, a corporate raider by profession (how perfect), paid no heed to the restrictions or the realities behind them as he selfishly continued inundating his considerable acreage, consuming 10 million gallons in a year—equal to what a family of four would typically use in 30 years—until his water access was cut off. "There seems to be a feeling that a rich man shouldn't be able to buy water from anyone," he huffed. Of course, he was all wet.

There was, finally, a happy ending to the water shortage (for the time being). The drought was officially declared over following the protracted rainstorms of early 1995 and the city has since lifted its stringent conservation measures.

• **Freeways and malls**—For years, Santa Barbara had stubbornly defied progress by refusing to do anything about Highway 101, which cuts through the center of town. Supposedly a freeway, it was in reality just another overtrafficked thoroughfare interrupted by stoplights. By 1989, traffic was so nightmarish that the city was forced to consider elevating the freeway above the fray. At the same time, residents hotly debated the construction of a downtown shopping mall.

Santa Barbara is by temperament mall-resistant, wanting to avoid the same mistakes that have led to the mauling (pun intended) of Southern California. It spent millions of dollars and convened nine civic commissions to study the downtown mall and freeway projects. When approval for both finally came, one native Santa Barbaran—a business consultant, amazingly enough—lamented, "You've seen the last gasps of what was a charming, small-town mentality."

The implementation of these projects was in some ways a comedy of errors. By the time Santa Barbara finally okayed the Highway 101 project, the state had temporarily run out of funds to pay for it. Likewise, the city dragged its heels on the mall project, losing commitments from several key department stores. All's well that ends, however. Freeway snarls are a thing of the past, and the downtown mall is not *that* egregious. (In terms of shopping opportunities, the mall is probably an improvement over the estimated 80 mom-and-pop shops it replaced.) But the projects did cause fallout, traumatizing and dividing the community for years.

 Map of Santa Barbara County beaches—page 262

• **Homelessness**—Thanks to its temperate year-round climate, Santa Barbara attracts a sizable population of homeless people. They congregate in clumps beneath the palm trees by the beach, tilting quart bottles and gazing benignly at the passing parade. But their presence, all political correctness aside, does blight the area. One group we saw had a dog as its mascot that was better dressed than they were. It wore a GI infantryman's hat, a tie-died T-shirt, and a knotted gypsy kerchief.

The hue and cry over Santa Barbara's homeless has been going on for many years. It reached a crescendo in August 1986, when an ordinance banning overnight sleeping in public was challenged by the late activist Mitch Snyder, who threatened to bring thousands of homeless to the streets of Santa Barbara in protest. The seven-year-old ordinance was amended by the city council to permit the homeless to sleep in vacant lots and parked cars—a move hailed as an act of "reasonableness and courage" by Snyder, who subsequently called off the march.

• **Offshore drilling**—The biggest bane of all in Santa Barbara is the presence of offshore oil-drilling rigs that have periodically polluted its beaches with oil and made visual pollution a constant feature on the horizon. Santa Barbara made national news and galvanized the environmental movement with a spectacular 1969 episode at an offshore drilling rig that sent 75,000 barrels (3.75 million gallons) of crude oil washing ashore. The spill befouled 150 miles of shoreline. Seabirds and marine mammals were covered with the goo, and their dead and dying bodies washed ashore on ruined beaches, providing gruesome footage to TV watchers who suddenly understood why an environmental counterbalance to the careless excesses of corporate America was necessary. As a result of the spill, fishers in the Santa Barbara Channel lost 50 percent of their trawling grounds, and some were driven out of business while waiting for settlements that were slow in coming.

Even when they're functioning properly, oil platforms produce high levels of pollution—the equivalent of 7,000 cars driving 50 miles a day. The oil industry is no stranger to Santa Barbara's coastline. The first oil rig, in fact, went up in 1896, offshore of Summerland. Bigger platforms were erected in the 1940s and 1950s. By the late 1980s, the 1969 spill was all but forgotten, and the number of offshore drilling platforms had risen to 23, with 11 more proposed. Then came the Exxon Valdez incident in 1989, and the debate over offshore drilling was rekindled for a while. Fortunately, the offshore oil rigs are beginning to come down as they reach the end of their useful life. Four of the 23 rigs in the Santa Barbara Channel are being dismantled and will be off the horizon by August 1996. Gradually, others will come down as well.

There is a proverbial silver lining to the oil-stained cloud. Migrating sea lions love and live on the oil platforms, whose solid surfaces provide habitat for mussels and meals for the hungry lions.

(continued from page 273)

Downtown, we recommend a walking tour of Santa Barbara's "Red Tile District." Visitors can view some 20 buildings of historical and architectural interest in a 12-block stroll. (For a map and guide, drop by the tourist information center at the foot of Santa Barbara Street, where it meets Cabrillo Avenue near East Beach.) One of the downtown "must-visits" is El Presidio de Santa Barbara State Historic Park (123 East Canon Perdid Street, 966-9729). Built in 1782, this was the northernmost of four military fortresses constructed by the Spanish along the coast. Two sections of the original Presidio quadrangle have survived earthquakes and are preserved today as a park that forms the heart of Santa Barbara's El Pueblo Viejo Historic District.

Santa Barbara boasts arts-and-crafts galleries, plus a smattering of theater, symphony, and ballet. It's also got a lot to offer college kids and lower-rung culture vultures like ourselves. The heart of Santa Barbara—as far as shops, restaurants, and nightlife are concerned—is State Street, from Los Olivos Street down to Stearns Wharf, the oldest operating wharf on the West Coast. State Street has its share of faux pool halls, dive bars, and tattoo parlors (e.g., "Rat-a-Tattoo"), but for the most part it is in tune with the real-life needs of its collegiate, retiree, and tourist patrons. Recreationally, there's tennis, golf, polo, yachting, and hiking in the hills. Some of the most competitive volleyball in the state is played on the sand courts of East Beach. Within the county's borders are 20 U.S. Forest Service, California State Park, and Santa Barbara County Park campgrounds. (Write to the Santa Barbara Conference and Visitors Bureau for a complete campsite directory.)

Last of all we'll mention the courthouse. If Mission Santa Barbara is the religious symbol of the community, then the Santa Barbara County Courthouse (1100 Anacapa Street, 962-6464) is the most impressive secular landmark in town. Built in an elaborate Spanish-Moorish style and occupying a full city block, it looks more like a palace than a courthouse. This turreted, muraled, chandeliered, hand-carved, tiled, terra-cotta'd, and stenciled treasure must be toured to be believed. It would indeed be honor to pay a traffic ticket here. The crowning touch is the clock tower ("El Maridor"), atop which is an observation deck that offers a sweeping 360-degree panorama of Santa Barbara. Pondering the city from this vantage point, one cannot help but reflect on the perfect yin-yang of the setting: mountains and ocean, warm sun and cool breezes, college kids and golden oldies, Spanish Colonial architecture and contemporary Americana.

Beaches

Santa Barbara's south-facing beach runs in a long arc along Cabrillo Boulevard. Its 2.5 miles are divided by Stearns Wharf into the plainly named **East Beach** and **West Beach**. These are calm-water beaches whose inland fringe is lined with huge, towering palms that list ever so slightly landward. There's ample parking to be found in huge lots, but for a breezy, bracing, nonmechanized tour we recommend the bike path that snakes along the beach zone. The beaches are sandy and broad, kept free of litter and well-patrolled by lifeguards. Everyone lopes or cruises the bike path at an unhur-

Arroyo Burro Beach County Park (a.k.a. Hendry Beach)

Location: Two miles west of Santa Barbara, off Cliff Drive.

Parking: Free parking lot.

Hours: 8 AM to sunset.

Facilities: Lifeguards, rest rooms, picnic area, and fire pits.

Contact: For beach information, contact the Santa Barbara County Department of Parks and Recreation at (805) 568-2460.

See number 13 on page 262.

ried pace, buried under a Walkman or smiling as if in a beatific trance. Down at East Beach there's more sand volleyball courts in one place, we'd venture, than anywhere else in California (except maybe Manhattan Beach). It's also the site of Cabrillo Pavilion, a recreational center, bathhouse, and architectural landmark dating from 1925.

Some locals will cop an attitude and disparage these big, wide, breezy beaches as being "too touristy," but there's enough beach here for everybody. On the down side, offshore oil rigs strike a dissonant aesthetic note. Santa Barbara has done its best to battle the oil rigs, but the county has little say about what goes on at sea beyond the three-mile limit. And so they grudgingly abide an industry they really don't want in their watery front yard. Landward of the bike path is a landscaped, grassy ribbon known as Palm Park. It serves as the site of a Sunday-afternoon crafts bazaar. It's an appealing green complete with picnic tables and a lawn that's trimmed, weedless, and more comfortable than shag carpeting. Ask the homeless who while away the hours sitting in the midday sun.

At the far end of West Beach, around the 1,000-slip harbor and breakwater that protects it, the coast gets hillier, and smallish beaches

East Beach

Location: In Santa Barbara, along East Cabrillo Boulevard, between Ninos Drive and State Street.

Parking: Metered lot and street parking.

Hours: Open 24 hours.

Facilities: Lifeguards, rest rooms, showers, picnic area, and barbecue grills.

Contact: For beach information, contact the Santa Barbara City Department of Parks and Recreation at (805) 564-5418.

See number 9 on page 262.

Leadbetter Beach

Location: In Santa Barbara, on Shoreline Drive, north of the Santa Barbara Harbor.

Parking: Metered parking lot.

Hours: Open 24 hours.

Facilities: Lifeguards, rest rooms, picnic area, and fire pits.

Contact: For beach information, contact the Santa Barbara City Department of Parks and Recreation at (805) 564-5418.

See number 11 on page 262.

Mesa Lane Beach (a.k.a. 1,000 Steps Beach)

Location: In Santa Barbara. Park at the end of Mesa Lane; a stairwell leads to the beach.

Parking: Free street parking.

Hours: Open 24 hours.

Facilities: None.

Contact: For beach information, contact the Santa Barbara City Department of Parks and Recreation at (805) 564-5418.

See number 12 on page 262.

West Beach

Location: In Santa Barbara, at the foot of State Street at Stearns Wharf.

Parking: Metered lot and street parking.

Hours: Open 24 hours.

Facilities: Lifeguards and rest rooms.

Contact: For beach information, contact the Santa Barbara City Department of Parks and Recreation at (805) 564-5418.

See number 10 on page 262.

are tucked into coves at stream mouths. **Leadbetter Beach** is located off Shoreline Drive, adjacent to Santa Barbara Harbor, and is a good board and windsurfing beach. It also makes a swell spot to pass the time watching boats sail in and out of the harbor. West of Leadbetter Beach, off Shoreline Drive at the end of Mesa Lane is **Mesa Lane Beach**, a kind of locals-only spot, which maintains a comfortable distance from the hubbub of downtown Santa Barbara.

Two miles west of Leadbetter Beach lies **Arroyo Burro Beach**, a secluded county park beneath the cliffs at the edge of a mesa. Arroyo Burro—that's Spanish for "Are you a burro?" (only kidding)—lies at the mouth of Arroyo Burro Creek. It's a pretty spot, and a pretty popular one, complete with a picnic area, a surprisingly good restaurant, and a sandy, crescent-shaped beach.

Bunking Down

At Fess Parker's **Red Lion Resort** (633 East Cabrillo Boulevard, 93103, 564-4333, $$$$), stucco walls meet red-tiled roofs, and the beach is literally steps away from the spacious, rambling grounds. You won't lack for things to do here, with a heated pool, whirlpool, sauna, shuffleboard and basketball courts, and putting green on the grounds. The convenient beach access is the most inviting amenity of all. There is no lodging closer to the sandy shore in Santa Barbara. And you don't have to wear a coonskin cap when you check in.

The **Santa Barbara Inn** (901 East Cabrillo Boulevard, 93103, 966-2285, $$$) is another good choice within sight of the beach. Located east of the downtown bustle, it's quiet at the Santa Barbara Inn. Rooms are spacious and comfortable, and you're only a crosswalk away from East Beach by Cabrillo Pavilion. The three-story hotel has a sundeck, pool, and whirlpool, plus a pricey but highly rated on-site French restaurant, **Citronelle** (963-0111, $$$$).

The third in our triumvirate of by-the-beach favorites is the **Harbor View Inn** (28 West Cabrillo Boulevard, 93101, 963-0780, $$$). The inn overlooks Stearns Wharf and has its own glass-enclosed pool and second-floor sundeck. Designed in the mission style, it offers a very civilized continental breakfast and evening wine and cheese. The grounds are gorgeous and the price range liberal: $85 to $135 to stay in the older west wing, $150 to $215 in the deluxe east wing. Whatever you pay, keep in mind that you're right by the beach, the wharf, and the action along State Street.

A good distance away but well worth mentioning is the **El Encanto Hotel and Garden Villas** (1900 Lasuen Road, 93103, 687-5000, $$$). Nestled in the foothills overlooking Santa Barbara, El Encanto is a European-style inn brimming with informal elegance; it's worth the drive up the mountain. At night, the town below glimmers like a distant field of flickering candles. Spread out on the grounds of El Encanto are the garden villas. The rooms and suites inside are each furnished differently, ranging from cozy to *magnifique* (and priced accordingly: $120 to $380). A large pool and Japanese koi pond are set among a thick, junglelike tangle of flowers and shrubs. A touch of class graces every aspect of El Encanto, where a casually California ambience tempers the European formality to a glow as rosy as a Pacific sunset.

Between the mountain tops and ocean's edge are some less expensive motels where one can lay in for under $100 a night. That is about the bottom-line limit in Santa Barbara; it's an expensive town. Our choice for the budget-minded, because of its location (a half-block from the beach, across from City Park) and brand name, is the **Travelodge Santa Barbara Beach** (22 Castillo Street, 93101, 965-8527, $$).

Coastal Cuisine

Every chef worth his salt mill wants to open a restaurant in Santa Barbara, which explains why there are somewhere in the neighbor-

 Map of Santa Barbara County beaches—page 262

hood of 400 of them. They publish brochures, flyers, and entire magazines about dining in Santa Barbara. Yet restaurants come and go on this highly competitive scene, which has lately been whittled down by the recession and supply exceeding demand. The competition is ultimately too keen to allow everyone to make a go of it.

One solid survivor of the food wars is **Downey's** (1305 State Street, 966-5006, $$$$). Quality will always win out, and chef proprietor John Downey's philosophy of serving fine dishes made with fresh ingredients and no corner-cutting has served him well. It's a small restaurant, with about a dozen tables. Specializing in "sophisticated California cuisine," it has been judged by the Zagat Survey to be among the top 25 restaurants in California. Dinner here is meant to be an unhurried experience, lingered over and savored. Appetizers of note included fresh deep-sea Santa Barbara mussels, served on the half shell in a tomato vinaigrette. Entrée items run the gamut from fresh catches, such as an extraordinary grilled Hawaiian escolar (a deep-sea dweller that occasionally turns up in tuna-fishers' nets), to sliced breast of duck, marinated and grilled to a pinkish turn. Santa Barbara County wines are spotlighted on the wine list.

On the fresh-fish front, the **Original Enterprise Fish Co.** (225 State Street, 962-3313, $$$) offers an array of chalkboard specials that change daily. The selection can range from local sea bass and lobster to Idaho rainbow trout and catfish, all grilled gently over mesquite and served in a cavernous old building with brick walls and exposed steel beams. Everything is cooked with a flourish over the grill in the center. The Original Enterprise Fish Co. is within casting distance of Stearns Wharf in the funky section of Santa Barbara known as Old Town. Over on the wharf itself, the **Harbor Restaurant** (210 Stearns Wharf, 963-3311, $$), specializes in oak-grilled fish and seafood and offers the best ocean view in town.

Joe's Café (536 State Street, 966-4638, $) merits commendation for very different reasons. If you can appreciate an old-time saloon with padded booths, checkered tablecloths, and a long bar where food and drink are served in generous quantities, you'll love Joe's. Serving supper since 1928, it is Santa Barbara's oldest restaurant. Their matchbook motto says it all: "Proud to be local and proud of our past." Mounted deer and moose heads look down on hungry diners awaiting the arrival of heaping, home-cooked blue-plate specials. More than once have we enjoyed their solid, stick-to-the-ribs grub: hot open faced roast beef sandwiches, brisket of beef, combination seafood plates, and more. Take our clichéd advice, and "Eat at Joe's."

A strong Mexican influence pervades Santa Barbara, and State, Haley, and Milpas Streets are lined with Mexican cantinas and eateries. Have at it, amigos, and may the best burrito win. The annotated listing above, incidentally, doesn't begin to do justice to the culinary possibilities in this cultured pearl of a town. Write the Santa Barbara Conference and Visitors Bureau for a more detailed listing or check local newspaper vending boxes for detailed dining guides.

Night Moves

State Street in downtown Santa Barbara is a veritable Whitman's Sampler of fun after dark. Just meander by all the bars and clubs emitting decibels into the night and listen for something that catches your fancy. The entire street is a nonstop block party. Nobody seems to give a hoot about how loud the hoopla gets, and this laissez-faire attitude is a welcome change from the usual opprobrium. We started off one evening listening to an unintentionally entertaining metal band that was blaring at **Alex's** (633 State Street, 966-0032). Beside us, at the bar, the head of a Hispanic man who'd had too much to drink repeatedly drooped until it hit the counter with a whimper, not a bang, just as the group reached the climactic riff in a clubfooted song about "media lies." Though the band was as wretched as a microwaved 7-Eleven burrito, the cold Sierra Pale Ale sure hit the spot. Alex's books different acts nearly every night of the week, so support local music and check it out.

The supply of suds and sounds along State Street is endless. On a single night we heard a folk trio at the **King's Tavern** (532 1/2 State Street, 963-9163), reggae at the **Calypso Bar & Grill** (514 State Street, 966-1388), alternative at **Revival** (18 East Ortega Street, 730-7383), an eclectic mix at the **Beach Shack** (500 Anacapa Street, 966-1634), a well-stocked CD jukebox at **O'Malley's** (523 State Street, 564-8904), and pure hip-hop/rap debauchery at **Safari** (634 State Street, 564-4362).

At O'Malley's, our jukebox money went for tunes by Elvis Costello, Blues Traveler, the Doors, and Crash Test Dummies (to give you some idea where our musical taste lies).

The real action that night, though, was a block away at Safari. We paid the cover and walked in on a debauched mob scene that looked like a caricature of an MTV dance party. Safari on a Tuesday night was as wanton as any weekend blowout we have witnessed in four summers of coastal travel. The music was ear-splitting, but not as loud as the laughter and screaming from the dance floor and bar area. Dry ice was sprayed into the crowd, giving the room the aura of a rock video. The music—1960s rock and soul blending into 1970s disco melding into the uncut hump-beat of 1990s rap and dance music—goosed the horde into shedding its inhibitions. Everything else going on in Santa Barbara that night was milk and cookies by comparison.

At some point during your nighttime wanderings you should angle out onto Stearns Wharf. This three-block wooden pier, built in 1872, widens into an over-the-water parking lot for all the people who have come to shop and dine at its restaurants. The best-known place on the wharf is the Harbor (see "Coastal Cuisine"). Upstairs, they dispense drinks and entertainment. The Harbor was once described to us as a "one-night romance kind of place" by a bellhop who appeared to be in the know. Indeed, we later saw him off in a corner, deep in negotiations for a one-night romance. As for us, we were approached by a deranged woman who accused us of being "fake preppies," insulted our clothes, refused to believe we weren't locals, asked for identification to prove otherwise, tried to swallow one of our driver's licenses, threatened not to return it, then made it abundantly clear she was available for the evening. One more story for (and from) the road.

For More Information

Contact the Santa Barbara Conference and Visitors Bureau, P.O. Box 299, Santa Barbara, CA 93102; (805) 965-3021. Or drop by the Visitors Bureau Information Stand at 1330 State Street, which is open every day except Sunday.

Partly Animals: Nightlife on the Sober Side

Back in the old days, it wasn't always this way. Now, however, since one of us no longer drinks and the other imbibes sparingly, we closely scrutinize the choices of nonalcoholic beverages at the beach. We're happy to report that a person's night moves need not be stymied just because they don't drink their body weight in draft beer for kicks.

In the past, if you chose not to drink, you'd have to settle for club soda with lime (if you were lucky) or flat ginger ale. Those days are gone, thank God (and perhaps thanks to the 12-Step Movement). The best part of the new sobriety is that you always get home okay. Moreover, you're able to function the next day while your fellow pub crawlers are shaking off a cruel hangover. Of course, the downside of sobriety is that you grow bored with the bar scene in less than an hour, realizing you aren't nearly as clever as the alligator mouths yapping a mile a minute on all sides.

The original nonalcoholic beers on the market were bad enough to make one ponder tipping the bottle again. But now, a batch of high-quality nonalkie brews have hit the bartop. They are not just palatable but quite tasty and refreshing. They're even less filling: 50 calories for a 12-ounce nonalcoholic beer vs. 250 for the same amount of "real" beer.

Naturally, the Europeans make the best near-beers. In the interests of journalistic integrity, we tried them all—several times. Here are our favorites, in descending order:

1. Kaliber (made by Guinness)
2. Clausthaler (Beck's)
3. Buckler (Heineken)
4. Sharp's (Miller; only if it's real cold.)
5. Old Milwaukee's NA
6. Coors Cutter
7. O'Doul's (Budweiser; the least appealing, ordered only when there was no other choice.)

Note to bartenders: Get smart and start stocking lots of nonalcoholic beer. It is a gold mine, because you can charge the same usurious prices charged for fortified beverages, but you don't have to pay alcohol taxes or fear you'll be sued for serving one beer too many to some bartly who tried to drive his car through a wall

Goleta

Location: Eight miles northwest of Santa Barbara. From Highway 101, turn south on Ward Memorial Boulevard. Drive to Sand Spit Road, turn left, and follow the road to the beach.
Population: 78,000
Area Code: 805 **Zip Code:** 93116

Goleta is an example of what we refer to as the "evil twin theory." For every lovely town that reins in development and maintains a high standard of living, there is another lurking nearby that lets such principles fall by the wayside. Santa Barbara's flip side is Goleta, a next-door neighbor nearly equal in size that doesn't attract a fraction of its neighbor's publicity. It functions as a repository for those things Santa Barbara wishes to keep outside its city limits—mainly the University of California-Santa Barbara, the Santa Barbara Airport, and people who don't earn six-figure salaries.

This is no knock on higher education, you see. UC-Santa Barbara is a fine school that turns out a lot of engineers, physicists, and surfers. But such is the nature of Goleta that the university located here nominally chooses to align itself with a city eight miles away. In terms of population, Goleta is 90 percent as large as Santa Barbara. But, in contrast to Santa Barbara's international reputation, Goleta is all but unknown to the outside world. It is essentially a seaside student ghetto. Its streets are dusty, its storefronts are generic, and the town has an overall look of plainness, pavement, and blight. The university is unquestionably the main attraction. The student body studies and lives here, and some of them surf at the base of the bluffs along which the school is situated. But for the most part they head into Santa Barbara to have fun. You should take their cue.

Goleta Beach County Park

Location: In Goleta, at 5990 Sand Spit Road.
Parking: Free parking lot.
Hours: 8 AM to sunset.
Facilities: Lifeguards, rest rooms, picnic area, and fire pits.
Contact: For beach information, contact the Santa Barbara County Department of Parks and Recreation at (805) 568-2460.

See number 14 on page 262.

Beaches

A terrific county park beach provides an oasis of escape from the strip-mall blues of Goleta. **Goleta Beach County Park** is a great spot in a gorgeous setting. Parking is free, and people come to picnic (tables, hibachis, and open-air shelters are provided), play volleyball, toss horseshoes, and frolic in the water. The 29-acre park includes a long, thin pier; a wide sandy beach; and more green acres than Hooterville. All in all, it's a very pleasant surprise.

Bunking Down

Your choices are pretty much the standard brand-name chain motels. Should you stay at the **Best Western South Coast Inn** (5620 Calle Real, 967-3200, $$) or the **Holiday Inn** (5650 Calle Real, 964-6241, $$)? Or perhaps **Motel 6** (5897 Calle Real, 964-3596, $)? Decisions, decisions...

Coastal Cuisine

Goleta Beach County Park has its own neat little restaurant, the **Beachside Bar Café** (5905 Sand Spit Road, 964-7881, $$). It overlooks the water, and serves fresh catches like local sea bass and ahi, plus everything from sandwiches to salmon *en papillote*.

For More Information

Contact the Goleta Valley Chamber of Commerce, 5730 Hollister Avenue, Goleta, CA 93117; (805) 967-4618.

Isla Vista

Location: Immediately west of Goleta, it can be accessed via Highway 101. Isla Vista Beach is the main beach in the vicinity, and Del Playa Drive runs parallel to it.
Population: 20,400
Area Code: 805 **Zip Code:** 93117

Isla Vista backs right up against Goleta, and indeed the two are so inseparable that everything we said under "Goleta" suffices to cover Isla Vista as well in all categories—except beaches, of which Isla Vista has more and better options. Both Isla Vista and Goleta share campuses of the University of California Santa Barbara. The main campus is at Goleta Point, in Goleta; the west campus is in Isla Vista, at Coal Oil Point. The town and its several beaches lie between the two points.

Beaches

For about 2.5 miles, between Goleta Point and Coal Oil Point, the coast runs on a near-perfect east-west axis. Sand beaches are located beneath the bluffs, beginning with **Isla Vista Beach**, accessible via stairways located at several street ends. A grassy bluff-top park, Sea Lookout Park, overlooks the beach. Here you can lounge, read, or gaze seaward from the ocean-facing wooden platforms. You can access another beach, though not without difficulty, at the university-owned **Coal Oil Point Natural Reserve.** The reserve mostly comprises protected coastal wetlands, though the beach below the frontal dunes is available to the public. Surfers call it Devereaux's (that's the name of the slough). Both of these Isla Vista beaches are enjoyed by surfers who relish the fact they don't have to fight crowds to get super rides.

For More Information

Contact the Goleta Valley Chamber of Commerce, 5730 Hollister Avenue, Goleta, CA 93117; (805) 967-4618.

Coal Oil Point Natural Reserve

Location: In Isla Vista, at the end of Storke Road, on the campus of the University of California at Santa Barbara.
Parking: Park in Isla Vista and walk across the campus or reserve a campus parking permit by calling the Natural Reserve System Office at (805) 893-4127.
Hours: Open 24 hours.
Facilities: None.
Contact: For beach information, visit the Natural Reserve System Office, Marine Science Institute (Trailer 342), University of California at Santa Barbara, or call (805) 893-8000.

See number 16 on page 262.

Isla Vista Beach

Location: In Isla Vista, at the south end of Del Playa Drive.
Parking: Free street parking.
Hours: 8 AM to sunset.
Facilities: Picnic tables.
Contact: For beach information, contact the Isla Vista Recreation and Parks Department at (805) 968 2017.

See number 15 on page 262.

El Capitan State Beach

Location: 24 miles northwest of Santa Barbara, via the State Beach exit off Highway 101.

North of Goleta, private ranchland dominates the terrain on both sides of Highway 101. This prohibits any viable beach access, unless you savor the idea of being mauled by a steer as you lope with your beach towel toward a stunning headland. Take time out instead to notice how your surroundings change as you proceed north. The distant peaks are higher, more jagged. The land is open, with rolling pasture between the ocean and mountains. The air even seems more breathable, and the winds blow with greater force. Road signs warn of "Gusty Winds."

Between Santa Barbara and Point Conception, the coastline runs east to west, and the beaches face due south. This keeps northern swells at bay, and anything else unpleasant is fended off by the Channel Islands. Ocean swimming is ideal here, and three of California's most appealing state beaches—El Capitan, Refugio, and Gaviota—can be found in a row along a 13-mile stretch.

The first of these is **El Capitan State Beach**. To get here, you'll pass beneath the Highway 101 overpass and through a lovely grove of sycamore and oak trees, ending at a sizable campground. Nature-lovers will enjoy exploring the many facets of this 133-acre park, including sea cliffs, tidepools, meadows, marine terraces, and canyonlands. A central stairwell cuts along the bluff to the beach below. It's a healthy strand with teeming tidepools. Swimming is safe, and good surfing is possible on winter swells. Surf-casting catches include perch, bass, and halibut. A trail for bicyclists and hikers runs along the bluff-top for 2.5 miles north to Refugio State Beach. A camp store is on the grounds, just in case you forgot sunscreen, potato chips, or "Tar Off" packets. There's also a boat launch ($5 per boat).

El Capitan State Beach was named for Jose Francisco de Ortega, the Spanish captain who scouted for the Portola expedition of 1769. Part of Ortega's old rancho serves as El Capitan Ranch Park, a privately owned campground in a canyon on the other side of the highway. Incidentally, the old Reagan Ranch is buried in the hills behind El Capitan.

El Capitan State Beach

RV 5

Location: Off Highway 101, 24 miles west of Santa Barbara.

Parking: $5 entrance fee per vehicle.

Hours: 8 AM to sunset.

Facilities: Lifeguards, rest rooms, showers, picnic tables, and fire pits. There are 140 tent and RV campsites. Fees are $14 to $16 per night. For camping reservations, call Destinet at (800) 444-7275.

Contact: For beach information, contact the regional park headquarters at Gaviota State Park at (805) 968-3294.

See number 17 on page 262.

For More Information

Contact the Channel Coast District Office, California Department of Parks and Recreation, 1933 Cliff Drive, Suite 27, Santa Barbara, CA 93101; (805) 899-1400.

Refugio State Beach

Location: 27 miles northwest of Santa Barbara, off Highway 101.

More than anything else, **Refugio State Beach** is a scaled-down version of El Capitan State Beach. Located three miles north of El Capitan, it offers 85 tent campsites and a slightly rockier shoreline, with rich tidepools, a 1.5-mile-long beach, and a beautiful view of the Channel Islands from the bluff above the campground. Refugio has an added botanical distinction: enormous banana palm trees line Refugio Creek to the east, lending the land a tropical feel that is rare this far north. In recent years, cliff erosion has threatened the sacred palms, 20 of which have been replanted farther inland. On one visit, we saw a knot of surfers getting some good long rides up at the western end of the beach. We also saw people swimming in the freshwater lagoon formed where Refugio Creek enters the ocean.

The name of the park comes from Spanish explorer Jose Francisco de Ortega's once extensive rancho, La Nuestra Señora del Refugio ("Our Lady of Refuge"). From this refuge, Ortega traded with pirates and smugglers until a band of French buccaneers came ashore, looted his mansion, and then burned it down. In the 1930s, a chap named Nelson Rutherford opened a campground here. He built a house that still stands and granted public access to a mineral spring on the beach. When his private campground became too much for him to handle, he sold it to the state in 1950.

Refugio State Beach

Location: Off Highway 101, 27 miles west of Santa Barbara.

Parking: $5 entrance fee per vehicle.

Hours: 8 AM to sunset.

Facilities: Lifeguards, rest rooms, showers, picnic tables, and fire pits. There are 85 tent and RV campsites. Fees are $14 to $16 per night. For camping reservations, call Destinet at (800) 444-7275.

Contact: For beach information, contact the regional park headquarters at Gaviota State Park at (805) 968-3294.

See number 18 on page 262.

For More Information

Contact the Channel Coast District Office, California Department of Parks and Recreation, 1933 Cliff Drive, Suite 27, Santa Barbara, CA 93101; (805) 899-1400.

Gaviota State Park

Location: 33 miles west of Santa Barbara, off Highway 101.

Gaviota State Park lies six miles up the road from Refugio State Beach. It provides the last user-friendly access to the coast until Pismo Beach, 60 miles north. It's also the last viable glimpse of the Southern California coast before the elemental rawness of the Central Coast takes over on the far side of Point Conception. The park derives its name from the Spanish word for seagull. It is here that Portola's gang came ashore and shot a seagull. (Don't get any ideas of your own.)

Gaviota offers full camping facilities (including showers and rest rooms), isolation without danger, natural wonders, 5.5 miles of coastline, and easy access to the beach. The setting of this large and varied park is as unusual as it is beautiful. The rusting hulk of an ancient railroad overpass towers majestically over the beachhead, spanning two sheer walls of rock. Near the water, 54 campsites are available, 36 of which have RV hookups. Located where Gaviota Creek empties into the ocean, the beach here is great for fishing, swimming, and beachcombing.

A fishing pier offers a three-ton hoist used to launch or haul power boats from the water. Away from the ocean, Gaviota's 2,700 acres provide extensive hiking possibilities among the hills to the east. Hikers and backpackers can make their way to hot springs (body temperature) that are just within the boundaries of Los Padres National Forest. An 11-mile trail crests at Gaviota Peak, a 2,458-foot promontory from which intrepid climbers can collect breathtaking coastline views as a reward for having made their way to the top.

East of the main entrance to Gaviota State Park, a pair of turnouts have trails leading to clothing-optional cove beaches. Proceeding up the coast on Highway 101, buff-beach fans should keep an eye out for signed turnouts to San Onofre and Vista del Mar Beaches, both of which lie on state-park property.

Gaviota State Park

RV 5

Location: Off Highway 101, 33 miles west of Santa Barbara.
Parking: $5 entrance fee per vehicle.
Hours: 8 AM to sunset.
Facilities: Lifeguards, rest rooms, showers, picnic tables, and fire pits. There are 54 tent and RV campsites. Fees are $12 to $14 per night. For camping reservations, call Destinet at (800) 444-7275.
Contact: For beach information, contact Gaviota State Park at (805) 968-3294.

See number 19 on page 262.

For More Information

Contact the Channel Coast District Office, California Department of Parks and Recreation, 1933 Cliff Drive, Suite 27, Santa Barbara, CA 93101; (805) 899-1400.

Jalama Beach County Park

Location: 55 miles west of Santa Barbara. Take Highway 1 to Jalama Beach Road and proceed west for 10 miles to the park.

The beach at **Jalama Beach County Park** is small (a half mile long, at most), but the campground is fairly large and set among 28 acres.

> **Jalama Beach County Park**
>
> **Location:** From Lompoc, drive five miles on Highway 1, then turn west onto Jalama Beach Road. Follow Jalama Beach Road for 10 miles till it ends at the beach.
>
> **Parking:** $3.50 entrance fee per vehicle.
>
> **Hours:** Open 24 hours.
>
> **Facilities:** Rest rooms, picnic tables, and fire pits. There are 120 campsites for tents and RVs. Fees are $13 to $16 per night. Camping reservations are not accepted.
>
> **Contact:** For beach information, contact Jalama Beach County Park at (805) 736-6316.
>
> **See number 20 on page 262.**

Jalama draws anglers, surfers, and hikers. Surfers love Jalama Beach in the summer and often trek south to Point Conception in search of a perfect wave. Surfing experts warn to be careful here, since "help is a long ways off."

If you just want the thrill of beach hiking, you're in heaven. A mile north is Vandenberg Air Force Base (watch for missile fragments while beachcombing), and five miles south is Point Conception. The trail to Point Conception retraces the route of Juan Bautista de Anza, who brought 250 colonists from Mexico through here in 1775–76 (they ended up founding San Francisco). The only safe time to walk this trail is at low tide. The beach trail starts out wide but thins and disappears at times, necessitating a walk along seawalls and railroad tracks. Just before reaching the point you will come upon Point Conception Coast Guard Lighthouse, which is as inhospitable as the ranches next door. Keep on trucking, as they say.

For More Information

Contact Jalama Beach County Park, 300 Goodwin Road, Santa Maria, CA 93455; (805) 736-6316.

Point Conception

Location: 50 miles northwest of Santa Barbara, a five-mile hike from Jalama Beach.

Traveling north from Santa Barbara County's three state-beach jewels—El Capitan, Refugio, and Gaviota—you have a choice. You can continue hugging a relatively inaccessible shoreline via Highway 1, or you can hit the freeway (Highway 101), which cuts an inland swath.

If you choose the Pacific Coast Highway, you will be rewarded with Point Conception, a formidable jut of land that signals the geographical end of Southern California. There is no direct access to Point Conception, due to the fact that private ranches swallow the Point Conception headland. These ranches—Bixby and Hollister, by name—are notoriously nasty to intruders, so be forewarned: we will not provide bail money should you be arrested with our book in hand. Still, getting to Point Conception is worth the difficult trek. As long as you stay below the high-tide line, you are within your legal right to walk to Point Conception via the beach. The best place to gain access is by hiking five miles south from Jalama Beach County Park (see the entry above).

Lompoc

Location: 25 miles south of the San Luis Obispo County line in northwestern Santa Barbara County, off Highway 1.
Population: 37,600
Area Code: 805 **Zip Code:** 93436

If you're up for another adventure after Point Conception, head out to **Ocean Beach County Park**. To find it, follow Highway 1 through the sweet-smelling, flower-filled fields of Lompoc (pronounced *lomPOKE*). Highway 246 (Ocean Park Road) cuts west from the town center, leading through Vandenberg Air Force Base. The road becomes curvier and bumpier with each of its 10 miles, finally giving out in a parking lot. Stop, look, and listen. Rusted railroad cars sit on an abandoned piece of track. The wind whistles through the sandy fields. You are officially in the middle of nowhere.

Ocean Beach County Park comprises 28 acres, embracing a broad, sandy beach and a lagoon at the mouth of the Santa Ynez River. The river mouth serves as a fragile riparian habitat for the California brown pelican and the least tern. A half-mile dirt path leads under the Southern Pacific Railroad trestle to a beach with healthy-sized sand dunes.

Vandenberg Air Force Base Fishing Access is the hard-core angler's El Dorado. Its beaches are reached out of a tiny blip on the mapmaker's radar called Surf, located at the mouth of the Santa Ynez River. Vandenberg offers limited access (50 people per day, weekends only) to an eight-mile stretch of coast from the Santa Ynez River to Purisima Point. No swimming or surfing is allowed—only fishing.

For More Information

To obtain an access permit, contact the Game Warden, Vandenberg Air Force Base, Building 6335, or call (805) 866-6804. Don't even think about sneaking onto the property.

Ocean Beach County Park

3

Location: At the mouth of the Santa Ynez River in Surf. From Highway 1 in Lompoc, turn west onto Ocean Park Road (Highway 246) and continue for 10 miles to the community of Surf.
Parking: Free parking lot.
Hours: 8 AM to sunset.
Facilities: Rest rooms, picnic tables, and fire pits.
Contact: For beach information, contact the Santa Barbara County Department of Parks and Recreation at (805) 568-2460.

See number 22 on page 262.

Vandenberg Air Force Base Fishing Access

2

Location: To access this beach, pass through Vandenberg Air Force Base, off Highway 1. Access is granted by reservation only. To obtain a free weekend fishing-access pass, contact the Vandenberg Air Force Base Game Warden at (805) 734-8232, ext. 51275. You will need a valid driver's license and a California fishing license; a limited number of passes are issued.
Parking: Free parking lot.
Hours: Saturday and Sunday only, from sunrise to sunset.
Facilities: None.
Contact: For beach information, contact the Vandenberg Air Force Base Game Warden at (805) 734-8232, ext. 51275.

See number 21 on page 262.

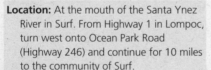

Point Sal State Beach

Location: Eight miles west of Guadalupe, off Highway 1.

Another spot for the lonesome traveler in northern Santa Barbara County is **Point Sal State Beach**, a free, day-use-only beach that takes nerves of steel to find. To get to this windswept, two-mile stretch of coastal wilderness, take unpaved Brown Road (just south of Guadalupe) to Point Sal Road. The latter is an 8.6-mile route to the coast that is occasionally untraversable, especially in winter.

Point Sal is a good surf-fishing spot and, during the winter migration, a great whale-watching point. Because the beach lies south of Point Sal, it is protected from the northwesterly winds that buffet the sand-dune ranges to the south. In other words, you don't have to hike the beach at a 45-degree angle. Still, swimming is hazardous in these treacherous waters, and surfing even more so.

The head of a excellent hiking trail can be found in Point Sal. This vertigo-inducing five-mile trail can be treacherous, too, as it tiptoes along the tops of bluffs a hundred precipitous feet above the water. Down below, you can spot seals and sea lions on the rocks and hear them barking above the roar of the surf.

Point Sal State Beach

Location: From Highway 1 in Guadalupe, turn west onto Point Sal Road and proceed for 8.6 miles to the beach.

Parking: Free parking lot.

Hours: 8 AM to sunset.

Facilities: None.

Contact: For beach information, contact the Channel Coast District of the California Department of Parks and Recreation at (805) 899-1400.

See number 23 on page 262.

For More Information

Contact the Channel Coast District Office, California Department of Parks and Recreation, 1933 Cliff Drive, Suite 27, Santa Barbara, CA 93101; (805) 899-1400.

Guadalupe-Nipomo Dunes Preserve

Location: Eight miles west of Guadalupe, via Highway 166.

North of Lompoc, sand dunes rise along the coast like bare white mountains for 20 miles. They reach their highest peaks west of the ramshackle town of Guadalupe, and the highway doesn't go anywhere near them. To access them, you must take Main Street (Highway 166) eight miles out of Guadalupe to its end at the beach, in what was formerly Rancho Guadalupe Park. Along the way, Main Street passes the town cemetery, a few rugged fields, and an open range where cows graze oblivious to the gusty winds, chilly temperatures, and sand.

Sand is everywhere. Sand blows over the road, obscuring it in places. Sand covers the parking lot. Sand forms a buffer between you and the beach. Sand gets in your eyes. This area—the first of three dune fields that make up a range of sand mountains known collectively as **Nipomo**

Dunes—is owned and protected by the Nature Conservancy, which provides trail information and interpretive brochures. Meditative strolls can be taken among the dunes at various points from here to Pismo Beach. Somewhere among all that sand you can find Mussel Rock, the highest dune on the West Coast. It is all sand, not rock, and stands 450 feet tall, give or take a few shifting grains. An arduous, ankle-sinking two-mile hike is required if you wish to see the biggest sand pile in the West. That might be your only recreation, because the ocean at the Guadalupe entrance to Nipomo Dunes is too rough for immersion. We saw no surfers, no swimmers, no picnickers, no fishers, and no lifeguards—nothing but sand, sand, sand. Enough to make Lawrence of Arabia feel at home.

In addition to the Guadalupe entrance off Route 166, the Nature Conservancy maintains a second access point to the dunes and several hiking trails at Oso Flaco Lake. Four miles north of Guadalupe on Highway 1, turn left on Oso Flaco Lake Road and drive about four miles to the preserve. Parking costs $4, and the Nature Conservancy provides a map of the area at the entrance kiosk. A boardwalk through Nipomo Dunes leads the 1.5 miles to the beach. Another trail, a seven-mile round-trip, winds along the shore of this pristine lake, which provides habitat for ducks, herons, and pelicans. Oso Flaco derives its name from the Spanish for "skinny bear," which is exactly what Portola's men killed here in 1769. There are no bears left, but there is a particularly secluded spot with a musical name, Hidden Willow Valley, where willows grow between the dunes. Bring a canteen and wear a hat.

This coastal preserve is one of the most unique in California, and because it's in the right hands, we can all sleep better. The entire Nipomo Dunes area has a history as fascinating as its terrain. These sands have been shifting for 20,000 years, embracing and covering any and all attempts at human habitation. As recently as the 1930s, the dunes were home to the "Dunites," a ragtag army of artists, hermits, nudists, and writers who inhabited shacks among the ephemeral sands and published their own *Dune Forum* magazine. The area indeed lends itself to solitary artistic activity, and after an hour or so of hopping about shifting ground cover, one is put in mind of Kobo Abe's disturbing but brilliant novel *Woman in the Dunes*. Reading that book is as close as we'd like to come to living among all this golden sand, as glorious as it is to look upon.

Guadalupe-Nipomo Dunes Preserve

Location: Eight miles west of Guadalupe, via Main Street (Highway 166).

Parking: Free parking lot.

Hours: By reservation only.

Facilities: Rest rooms.

Contact: For tour reservations, contact the Nature Conservancy between 9 AM and noon on Monday or Thursday at (805) 541-8735.

See number 24 on page 262.

For More Information

To learn more about the Nature Conservancy–run beach accesses and docent-led walks, call (805) 541-8735 between 9 AM and noon Monday and Thursday. Or contact the San Luis Obispo branch office of the Nature Conservancy, P.O. Box 15810, San Luis Obispo, CA 93406; (805) 546-8378.

San Luis Obispo County

One of the great joys of beach travel is to discover a stretch of coastline that has everything going for it *and* has been largely bypassed by thundering herds of tourists. Such is the case with the Central Coast in general, and San Luis Obispo County in particular.

This county begins at the remarkable Nipomo Dunes and ends just north of San Simeon's Hearst Castle—a human attempt to compete with the splendors of nature—at the welcome mat of magnificent Big Sur. The county takes its tenor from the town of San Luis Obispo, a scaled down version of Santa Barbara set in an agricultural valley. From this jumping-off point, a visitor can easily access the county's extraordinary beaches.

Pismo Beach, at the southern border, comprises five coastal "cities," but is best known for the Pismo clam—which Euell Gibbons, in his beach survival guide *Stalking the Blue-Eyed Scallop*, called **(continued on page 294)**

Coastal San Luis Obispo County's Climate

Pismo Beach Averages

	Daily High Temp. (°F)	Daily Low Temp. (°F)	Rainfall (inches)
January	63	43	3.8
February	64	44	3.0
March	65	44	2.3
April	67	45	1.0
May	68	47	0.3
June	70	50	0
July	70	52	0
August	70	53	0
September	72	53	0.3
October	72	51	0.7
November	68	47	2.0
December	64	43	2.7
Yearly Average	**68**	**48**	**16.7**

Source: National Weather Service data, National Oceanographic and Atmospheric Administration.

San Luis Obispo County

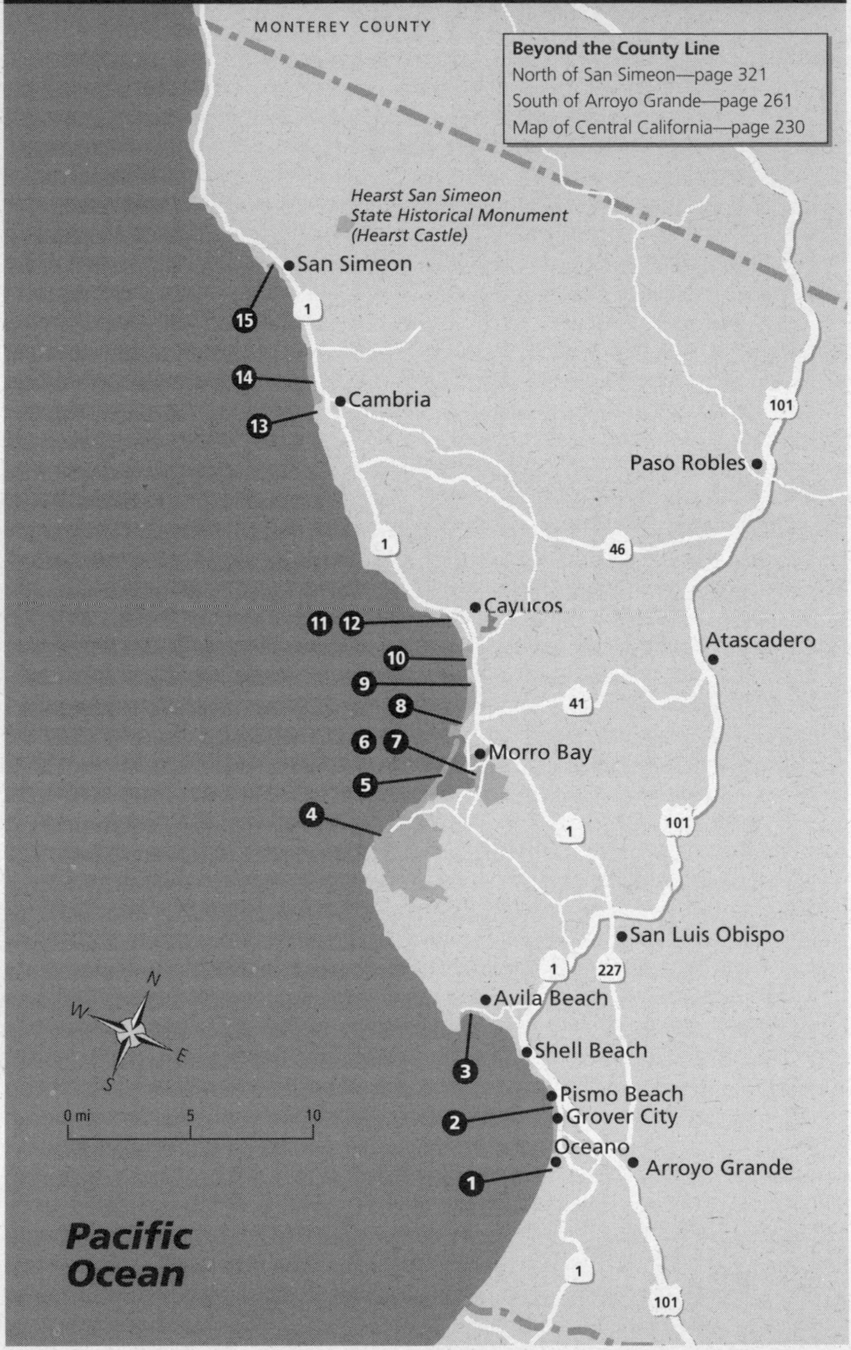

MONTEREY COUNTY
Beyond the County Line
North of San Simeon—page 321
South of Arroyo Grande—page 261
Map of Central California—page 230
Hearst San Simeon State Historical Monument (Hearst Castle)
San Simeon
Cambria
Paso Robles
Cayucos
Atascadero
Morro Bay
San Luis Obispo
Avila Beach
Shell Beach
Pismo Beach
Grover City
Oceano
Arroyo Grande
1
101
46
41
227
15
14
13
11
12
10
9
8
6
7
5
4
3
2
N
W
E
S
0 mi
5
10
Pacific Ocean

San Luis Obispo County Beaches

Map of Central California—page 230

(continued from page 291) "a clam refined to the absolute ultimate"—and its broad dune fields which are among the most extensive in the state. Pismo Beach is the only place in California where one can legally drive on the beach. Next door, the towns of Shell Beach and Avila Beach offer enticing, cliff-hugging views and great beaches. The visually arresting town of Morro Bay looks out on the marvelous monolith of Morro Rock, while Cambria's calling card is the romantic seclusion of Moonstone Beach.

Rolling hills and green valleys, clean air and comfortable temperatures, perfect sunsets and more than 30 inland wineries serve to complement San Luis Obispo's array of beaches. Come see for yourself.

Key to the Symbols

Bike path · Camping · Food and drink · Hiking · Nude

Pier · RVs allowed · Surfing · Volleyball

Crowd Rating

sweet solitude . . . moderate crowds . . . wall-to-wall

Overall Rating

1 2 3 4 5

don't bother . . . worth a visit . . . beach heaven

Arroyo Grande

Location: Five miles southeast of Pismo Beach, on Highway 101.
Population: 14,500
Area Code: 805 **Zip Code:** 93420

The 50-mile stretch of Highway 101 from Santa Barbara to Pismo Beach passes through some extraordinary interior scenery, from the flower fields of Lompoc Valley to the fire-scarred forest surrounding Guadalupe. Suddenly, in a swooping series of hairpin turns, the highway descends to the coastal plain again, heading back toward the beach with the precision of a heat-seeking missile. Before reaching the ocean, the highway passes by a crossroads called Arroyo Grande.

At this point, you have officially left Southern California and entered the Central Coast, an area that extends from here north to the border of San Francisco County. It is a radically different landscape from Santa Barbara on south. More Western than Californian, these inland towns are filled with less narcissistically body-conscious folks who go in for cowboy boots and motorbikes and whose homes aren't likely to be featured in *Architectural Digest*. Even the mountains that press against the towns are different, softer in tone and texture, less jagged and covered with gray-brown whiskers. Most of all, upon entering Arroyo Grande you're reminded that California is many states rolled into one.

Likewise, Pismo Beach is many towns rolled into one. They call this midcoast minimetropolis "the Five Cities." Following one another along Highway 101, the towns begin at Arroyo Grande, move on to Oceano, Grover City, and Pismo Beach proper, and end at Shell Beach. The manners and style seem to go up a notch with each "city," but each serves a prescribed role within the larger entity. Arroyo Grande is the primary business center and has, in recent years, been used as a backdrop for Hollywood film shoots. It has a pleasant hometown feel. The town center contains a few blocks of Victorian-era architecture, and its antique shops do a brisk business. Still, the best thing about Arroyo Grande is that it sends the Pacific Coast Highway shooting back toward the beaches and the Pismo Dunes.

Bunking Down

You'll notice soon enough that room rates drop once you round Point Conception and begin moving up the Central Coast. If you're laying over in Arroyo Grande, there's the attractive **Best Western Casa Grande Inn** (850 Oak Park Road, 481-7398, $) where rooms run $60 to $90. For that you get a pool, spa, gym, game room, breakfast, and a free drink—and you're only two miles from the beaches of Pismo Dunes (see the entry on page 296).

For More Information

Arroyo Grande Chamber of Commerce, 800 West Ranch Street, Arroyo Grande, CA 93420; (805) 489-1488.

Pismo Dunes State Vehicular Recreation Area

Location: From Grover City take Grand Avenue (or from Oceano take Pier Avenue) west till it ends at ramps that lead onto the beach.

Pismo Dunes is the only place left on the California coast where it is legal to drive on the beach. That's right. From Oso Flaco, at the north end of Nipomo Dunes, to Grover City—a distance of over four miles—cars are permitted on the beach. They call this the "Sand Highway." Its official name is Pismo Dunes State Vehicular Recreation Area, and it comprises 4,000 acres of sandy dunes and beaches. It can be accessed from Grover City and Oceano. The speed limit on the Sand Highway is 15 miles per hour, and you must drive in the hard-packed sand near the ocean's edge. Beginning at Post 2, in Oceano, all-terrain vehicles (ATVs) and off-highway vehicles (OHVs) are permitted on the dunes themselves, which stretch for almost a mile inland. (Cars are not permitted on the dunes.) ATVs and OHVs are those three-wheeled gizmos that look like big-wheeled riding lawn mowers. They pointlessly churn the sand so that red-faced dudes can brag they climbed a big dune, risking a rollover in the process.

These healthy dunes are among the Pismo Beach area's chief attractions. The tallest have no vegetation holding them in place, and thus drift with the winds. A few tire tracks here and there aren't going to matter much. Although the state maintains other off-road recreational areas, Pismo Dunes is the only one directly on the coast. Thus, a fleet of ATVs, OHVs, and "street legal" vehicles converges on the park during summer weekends. Be prepared. And look both ways before crossing the beach.

Beaches

The **Pismo Dunes** offer the southernmost beaches within the Five Cities, and they are among the most spectacular on the West Coast. You won't believe your eyes, especially when you're staring above your car's dashboard as you head directly for the ocean. Driving on the beach has a strange appeal, especially since it allows you to quickly cut away from the crowds and find a quieter stretch of sand that's more to your liking. Keep an eye on your car, though. Some people fall asleep while the high tide rolls in and.... Well, you can guess the rest. Also, be careful if you decide to go in the water, because there are no lifeguards.

Bunking Down

You can camp among the Pismo Dunes, but you are advised to make reservations well in advance. The sites are primitive—basically, wherever you throw down your tent—and the number of campers allowed here at any one time is limited to 500. You really don't need wheels to have fun. Plenty of excellent hiking trails traverse the dunes, the inland lagoons, and a fascinating array of terrain.

Pismo Dunes State Vehicular Recreation Area

Location: Access is via ramps at the end of Grand Avenue in Grover City and Pier Avenue in Oceano.

Parking: $4 entrance fee per vehicle.

Hours: 8 AM to 11 PM.

Facilities: Rest rooms. There are 500 tent campsites. The fee is $6 per night. For camping reservations, call Destinet at (800) 444-7275.

Contact: For beach information, contact Pismo Dunes State Vehicular Recreation Area at (805) 473-7230.

See number 1 on page 292.

Dune Struck

The sand dunes in the Nipomo and Pismo Beach area are the most extensive coastal dunes remaining in California. Healthy dunes are becoming a rarity not only in California but on the East Coast and Gulf Coast as well. There are many reasons for this decline. Some are natural and have to do with the way sand dunes are formed. At Pismo Dunes, for example, the material that forms these piles is washed into the ocean by rivers and creeks in the surrounding watershed. Deposits from this rich lode are carried by shore-paralleling ocean currents and then shaped into dunes by onshore winds.

The prevailing winds here push sand particles into wavy crests that run north-south. The slope is gentle on the windward (west) side, while the leeward (east) side is steep. As they are blown over the crest of the dune from west to east, sand particles cause the high crests to collapse, sliding leeward in what are called "slip-face" slopes.

The most stable dunes are those with vegetative cover—wildflowers, shrubs, and grasses that hold the sand in place by breaking the force of the prevailing winds. They are less prone to massive shifting than the glacial sands to the south. In Pismo Dunes, the holdfast vegetation on the smaller, more stable dunes includes arroyo willow, California sagebrush, sand verbena, and bush lupine, as well as a nonnative, European beach grass that was introduced 20 years ago to help stabilize the dunes and has since thrived.

This is where humans can make a difference. Most coastal vegetation is fragile, and must survive in a harsh environment of desiccating wind, hot sun, and deep water table. These plants can be easily dislodged if disturbed by contact with visitors' feet or wheels. Once the tops of the vegetative cover have been severed, the extensive root systems that hold the sand in place die off and the dune becomes the dancing partner of the next big blow.

The key to keeping dunes in place is to leave them undisturbed. That is, do not blaze trails among the vegetation, and stick to areas that have already been traveled. Maybe we're weird, but we've always wondered what kind of person could enjoy trampling vegetation while scooting around dunes atop a sputtering, gas guzzling grownup's tricycle.

On dunes like those at Pismo Beach, the biggest piles of sand are those that won't support vegetable cover. It is these places where all-terrain vehicles should be used (but not abused). Anyone caught churning through dune grasses deserves to be chopped up and fed to the Pismo clams.

You can pitch a tent at several more campgrounds in the area, too: the 64-site Oceano Memorial County Park (on Pier Avenue in Oceano), and the two camps at Pismo State Beach (see the Pismo Beach entry on page 299).

For More Information

Contact the Pismo Dunes State Vehicular Recreation Area, 576 Camino Mercado, Arroyo Grande, CA 93420; (805) 473-7230. Ask for a copy of the *Pismo Dunes Forum*.

Pismo Beach, Oceano, Grover City, and Shell Beach

Location: 90 miles north of Santa Barbara, along Highway 101 and Highway 1. Pismo Beach and surrounding towns in the "Five Cities" area boast 23 miles of beaches and extensive inland dune fields. Much of it falls under the province of Pismo State Beach, which runs from the Santa Barbara County line to the foot of Wilmar Avenue in Pismo Beach.
Population: 8,000
Area Code: 805 **Zip Code:** 93449

Pismo Beach is the heart and soul of the "Five Cities" (the other four are Arroyo Grande, Oceano, Grover City, and Shell Beach), and it's the living embodiment of the area mascot, the Pismo clam. Both the town and the clam are humble but majestic souls that have had good times and battled through bad to reemerge with renewed spirit and bright prospects for the future. Visitors are greeted by a spaceship-like sculpture of the Pismo clam at the Price Street exit off Highway 101. It is not for nothing that the Pismo is the town's pride and joy—it's one of the largest and most delicious clams on the West Coast. In fact, it's too tasty for its own good. In mid-1980s, the beleaguered bivalve found itself on the brink of extinction. For five years a law forbade any clamming of the Pismo, in order to allow them to replenish.

Other than the temporary loss of its clam, Pismo Beach has been blessed with natural gifts—the dunes to the south; the wide, hard-packed sand beaches in town; a perfect year-round climate; and unsurpassable vistas from jagged headlands that spread north into Shell Beach. The biggest problem it has faced is its image as a down-on-its-heels honky-tonk town. Take Shell Beach. This wealthier community ostensibly changed its name to get a separate post office (though it retains the same zip code and falls within the city limits). According to a Pismo businessman, however, it really wanted to distance itself from modest Pismo Beach.

A Shell Beach businesswoman theorized that what's keeping Pismo from becoming a major vacation destination is its lack of an upscale shopping district. "Oh, you can buy things there," she rejoined, "but...." Her "but" hung in the air, its silent aftermath implying that there's no Neiman-Marcus or New England seaport-themed shopping village in Pismo Beach. Maybe because shopping remains such a low priority for us, we're unable to grasp how a lack of boutiques is a drawback. One of our rules of thumb is the less bilking of tourists, the better the beach town. By that yardstick, Pismo Beach is perfect.

Our own theory about the town's image problem has nothing to do with shopping. It's the name. "Pismo" doesn't exactly roll off the tongue with a musical fanfare. But the name comes legitimately with the territory. As it turns out, *pismo* is a Chumash Indian word meaning "blobs of tar that wash up on beach." By the time the Spanish arrived, the Chumash had inhabited the area for 9,000 years. The Spanish had no problem with the name because for them *pismo* meant "a place to fish." Thanks to this semantic convergence, the town has a name as unique as Oxnard's.

Right now, Pismo Beach has little to do with either tarry blobs or upscale shopping, but a lot to do with sand, surf, and beach. Happily, the town has begun to address its image problem by focusing on its many natural blessings. The folks who flock here in the summer from the sweltering valleys aren't complaining. When the temperatures reaches 120 degrees inland, Pismo might as well be named Paradise. The hotter it gets in the valleys, the cooler it is in Pismo. The inland heat draws moist air

 Map of San Luis Obispo County beaches—page 292

off the ocean, bathing Pismo Beach in marine fog. This makes for endlessly varying cloud patterns and beautiful sunsets. Who wouldn't love such a setting, whatever the name?

Beaches

Pismo State Beach is a vast and lengthy stretch of sand with access points covering 23 miles of coast and four of the "Five Cities." The state beach operates two campgrounds, Oceano and North Beach. Coastal access points can be found in Oceano and Grover City, with several others in Pismo Beach and Shell Beach. Cars are allowed on the beach to the south (see the Pismo Dunes entry on page 296), making it California's answer to Daytona Beach, Florida, without the bathing beauties. Thankfully, the shoreline in Pismo Beach and Shell Beach are pedestrian-only, with plenty of room for swimming, tanning, fishing, and surfing. The latter has grown so popular in recent years that an annual tournament is now held in Pismo. Clam-digging in Pismo is rewarding once again (see sidebar, "Clamming for Pismos").

Pismo State Beach

Location: In Pismo Beach, from the Santa Barbara County line to Wilmar Avenue.

Parking: Free lot and street parking

Hours: Sunrise to sunset.

Facilities: Rest rooms, showers, picnic tables, and fire pits. There are 82 tent and RV campsites at the Oceano Campground, and the North Beach Campground offers 103 tent and RV campsites. Fees are $14 to $16 per night at both campgrounds. For camping reservations, call Destinet at (800) 444-7275.

Contact: For beach information, contact Pismo State Beach at (805) 489-1869.

See number 2 on page 292.

At the center of it all is the Pismo Beach Pier, a 1,250-foot structure at the end of Pomeroy Avenue that is perfect for surf casting and surfer-watching. The south side of the pier is one of the best surf spots in the county. The sea cliffs become more pronounced toward Shell Beach, where separate coves have been given appropriately cute names—Turtle Beach, Pirates Cove, and an elusive nude beach to the north whose whereabouts escaped us. Several overlooks are located on the bluff tops along Seacliff Drive, and four of them have been designated city parks: Margo Dodd, Ocean, Memory, and Spyglass. Stairwells from the first two, on the southern edge of Shell Beach, lead down to small, secluded cove beaches.

On a final note, we've lifted this pertinent quotation from (of all places) a Pismo Beach Chamber of Commerce brochure. It is by that legendary beach bum, Lord Byron:

There is rapture by the lonely shore,
There is society, where none intrudes,
By the deep sea, and music in its roar:
I love not man the less, but Nature more.

Bunking Down

Pismo State Beach has two campgrounds, Oceano and North Beach. You can't get a view much better than this, though you're competing with sand grains, stiff winds, and fellow campers who enjoy driving loud vehicles off the road.

In town, accommodations run the spectrum from seedy cheapies to semi-elegant luxury hotels. Most of the latter are available in Shell Beach. The best thing about Pismo Beach's lack of upscale cache is that room prices are kept within reason ($65 to $110 in season). You'll pay and receive a little more in Shell Beach.

The top-of-the-line is the **Cliffs at Shell Beach** (2757 Shell Beach Road, 773-5000, $$$). It is a five-story cliff-top resort that offers luxury without excess. They let the setting—100 feet above the sea stacks on Turtle Beach—speak for itself. The various on-premises amenities (large heated outdoor pool, sauna, well-groomed grounds and gardens, café and restaurant) complete the experience. The beach access here is via a stairwell along the cliff face.

The finest spot in Pismo Beach proper is the **Best Western Shore Cliff Lodge** (2555 Price Street, 773-4671, $$), a well-tended hotel set on stunning grounds. It comes with a heated pool. Not surprisingly, these two lodges also have two of the best restaurants in town attached to them.

Flanking the main beach in Pismo are two more motels worth considering. The **Sandcastle Inn** (100 Stimson Avenue, 773-2422, $$$) is directly on the beach and within easy walking distance of the pier. The rooms at the Sandcastle, a hotel condominium, are plush and come with balconies, and a continental breakfast is provided. The **Sea Crest Motel** (2241 Price Street, 773-4698, $$) is the best of the budget places. It's on the north side of Pismo, overlooking a cliff. A steep wooden stairwell leads to the sand. Also on the grounds are a number of jagged promontories upon which one can repose while contemplating the sun as it slips into the rough and tumble ocean.

Coastal Cuisine

It used to be that in the Esperanto of road hunger, "Pismo" meant "mediocre." The plain cloth from which Pismo was cut once yielded burger huts, taco stands, a chowder house, and sit-down seafood joints whose special of the day was fish-and-chips.

That is no longer true. Two excellent dining spots are now serving fine fare from panoramic, cliff-top dining rooms. The **Shore Cliff Restaurant** (2555 Price Street, 773-4671, $$), in the Best Western Shore Cliff Lodge, serves good, fresh seafood dishes in a glassed-in dining room that takes in a sweeping view of the ocean from its perch. Order the calamari piccata or the fresh catch of the day. They have the best clam chowder in town. It's not the typical thick, floury stew but more of a soup that lets the good taste of Pismo's finest shine through.

The best fine dining in town is at the **Sea Cliffs Restaurant** (2757 Shell Beach Road, 773-3555, $$) in the Cliffs at Shell Beach resort. At one time the in-house spot here was called Pismo Joe's, but the casual flavor was strangely inappropriate to the complex. Without much fanfare, the Sea Cliffs Restaurant chefs cook up some of the tastiest seafood on the Central Coast. Most of the seafood dishes are cooked on a mesquite grill. Lest we forget, you are now entering Wine Country. Several excellent wineries are within an hour's drive; ask your server for recommendations.

Night Moves

The daytime is really the right time in Pismo Beach. The social life centers around the pier and surrounding streets. At night, we've seen cars and pickup trucks circling the parking lot in an endless, desultory wagon train. It's the old small-town, life-in-the-slow-lane cruising scene. In the bars a few blocks farther along, you're likely to spot the occasional grizzled biker sporting his colors on a leather jacket (e.g., "The Condors from Bakersfield, CA."). The liveliest night spot in Pismo is **Harry's Cocktail Lounge** (690 Cypress Street, 773-1010). It has horseshoes for door handles and features live music on weekends, mostly country-and-western bands. For something a little more collegiate, head to Avila Beach or San Luis Obispo. One place worth mentioning is the **Great American Melodrama & Vaudeville** (Highway 1, Oceano, 489-2499). Admittedly corny, it provides a unique opportunity to entertain the whole family with live drama (e.g., *Sleeping Beauty*, *Ballad of Bayou Betty*) for a reasonable charge.

For More Information

Contact the Pismo Beach Convention & Visitors Bureau, 581 Dolliver Street, Pismo Beach, CA 93449; (805) 773-4382.

Clamming for Pismos

No less an authority than Euell Gibbons honored the Pismo clam (*Tivela stultorum*). In his 1964 beachcomber's bible, *Stalking the Blue-Eyed Scallop*, he wrote, "At the first bite I became a full-fledged convert to the Cult of Pismophagists, and I knew why Californians come year after year to do battle with the waves in order to get a bag of Pismos. It is just a clam, but a clam refined to the absolute ultimate."

Since the time Mr. Gibbons wrote that, the Pismos were almost eliminated, due to overclamming and shortsighted greed. Even then, he'd heard tales: "There are stories of local farmers gathering these clams by the wagon load by opening furrows across the beach at ebb tide with horse-drawn plows. Some…were sold on the market, but many a wagon load went back to the farms to fatten the pigs and chickens.… To hear of the way this vast wealth of clams was squandered is enough to make one weep."

But then, so is the taste of a Pismo clam. Its flavor, plenitude, and size—it is one of the largest clams in the world—are what made it so popular. After a total ban on Pismo clamming in the mid-1980s, they have begun to return. The Pismo clam requires a rock-free sand beach and constant exposure to ocean waves. The beaches from Oceano to Morro Bay are ideal for this, with their pure sand and gradually sloping shoreline.

Pismo clams reach a size of five inches in length and weigh about a pound at maturity, after four to seven years. A seven-incher is at least 15 years old. Some have lived to the age of 20 and weighed as much as five pounds. They are found in one to three feet of water at low tide, burrowing about a half-foot beneath the hard, wet sand. To find them requires probing every few inches of the ocean floor with a clam fork, one with a 4.5-inch clamming gauge. If a clam smaller than 4.5 inches is taken, it should be replaced with its shell opening toward the horizon.

The fun of Pismo clamming is that you have to spend your time knee deep in water. This means you get slapped around by the waves, too. "Ordinary clam digging might be poor sport," wrote Mr. Gibbons, "but this seeking the Pismo in the surf was wildly exhilarating. Not that the clams fight back. They don't need to. The clams merely lie quietly…and let the waves above do their fighting."

There is a limit on the number of Pismo clams you can take, which changes with the season. You also need a license from the California Department of Fish and Game to clam here. Some spots along the Central Coast are off-limits entirely to Pismo clamming (including Montana de Oro State Park, the Morro Bay strand, and, in Pismo Beach, north of Grand Avenue for a half mile). You must check environmental factors, too. In July 1994, the town of Pismo Beach spent $25,000 to test offshore waters for bacteria that had begun showing up in local shellfish.

For more information, write to the California Department of Fish and Game at P.O. Box 944209, Sacramento, CA 94233-2090, or call (916) 653-6420.

Avila Beach

Location: Five miles north of Pismo Beach, via the Avila Beach Drive exit off of Highway 101.
Population: 1,500
Area Code: 805 **Zip Code:** 93424

Around the corner from Shell Beach, on the other side of San Luis Obispo Bay, is Avila Beach. It is the Central Coast's sun-and-fun capital for college kids. Small and unpretentious, the town is built around Avila State Beach. This beach is heavily used by well-endowed student bodies from California Polytechnic State University in San Luis Obispo, the county seat 11 miles east. Locals lovingly refer to the young women as "Poly Dollies."

Avila Beach's status as a day-use haven is obvious from the absence of motels and the surplus of beautiful women. (Is this a prerequisite for enrollment at Cal Poly?) The weather is consistently sunny, and San Luis Obispans come here to work on their tans. They pull their towels up to the seawall, oil themselves, and bask. A troop of shirtless, red-baked guys in knee-length pants patrols the sidewalk above, peering over the seawall now and again. You can't really blame them (or us). Avila Beach was our last glimpse of bikini-clad California girls as we trekked northward. *Sigh...*

Besides the Poly Dollies, the second most exciting thing in Avila Beach is its new coastal hiking trail, a 10-miler from Avila to Montana de Oro State Park. This land had been off-limits for years. It is owned by Pacific Gas and Electric, which finally opened its Diablo Canyon nuclear facility in 1986 after years of litigation and engineering snafus. The Diablo Canyon Plant, like the one down in San Onofre, is located on an earthquake fault. As a concession to the public (for jeopardizing its very existence?), PG&E has paid for a hiking trail through part of the land. Called the Pecho Coast Trail, it can be accessed in Port San Luis, off Harford Drive. Along the trail you can see the Port San Luis Lighthouse (ca. 1890), known as the "Victorian Lady" to locals. The Nature Conservancy leads hikes twice a week to the lighthouse, with reservations required (541-8735). One noteworthy part of the trail is an oak grove dedicated to Pat Stebbins, a California Coastal Commission director who died in 1990 after years of advocacy for public use of beaches. We salute her memory. May her work live on forever!

The town of Avila Beach has a relaxed college-town air. Hutlike shops sell basic fare and bars are filled with friendly mayhem. The setting almost assures that this casual ambience will be retained. Just to the north are two workingman's piers (one for commercial fishing, the other owned by Union Oil) and Diablo Canyon. Up on the highest hill in town are a number of yellow oil tanks that won't be making way for resort development anytime soon.

Beaches

To get to Avila Beach from either Shell Beach or Highway 101, take Avila Beach Drive. It is the only road in and out—a circuitous rural stretch that requires your full attention. The collegians call it "Bust Road," because the cops

Avila State Beach

Location: In Avila Beach, along Front Street between San Rafael Street and Harford Drive.
Parking: Free street parking.
Hours: Sunrise to sunset.
Facilities: Lifeguards, rest rooms, and showers.
Contact: For beach information, contact the San Luis Obispo Port Authority at (805) 595-5400.

See number 3 on page 292.

lie in wait along the shoulder after the bars close. **Avila State Beach** is a mile-long beach with public facilities, a lifeguard stand, and a fishing pier. When stocked with well-oiled bodies from nearby Cal Poly, it looks like a scene from a '60s beach flick, with better (read: smaller) swimsuits.

Somewhere to the south, among the bluffs toward Shell Beach, over rocks and around coves, is an alleged nude beach. Theoretically it is populated by a tribe of Poly Dolly Amazons who want to take beach bums hostage and steal their book advances. (Well, that was our fantasy.) About a half mile to the north, between Port San Luis Pier and the Union Oil Pier is a sandy beach, accessed via Harford Drive.

Bunking Down

The only motel in direct view of the beach is the **Surfside Motel and Apartments** (256 Front Street, 595-2300, $$), a generic but clean and affordable ($55 to $85 in summer, $45 to $75 in winter) spot with 32 rooms and 10 suites. Most of the rooms come with kitchens.

Away from the ocean, among the woods along Avila Beach Drive, is a place that all weary travelers should be fortunate enough to stumble upon once in a lifetime. **Sycamore Mineral Springs Resort** (1215 Avila Beach Drive, San Luis Obispo, CA 93405, 595-7302) is many things—a gourmet restaurant (see the Gardens of Avila below), a place to stay, a botanical haven, and a spiritual way station. But it is primarily a mineral-spring spa and has been since 1897. Here, for a reasonable fee ($35 to $55), one can receive a professional massage and unlimited access to the natural hot springs. The friendly staff instantly makes you feel comfortable, and an hour later you will be too relaxed to get back in the car. This may mean staying overnight and eating dinner, neither of which is a punishing experience. In fact, they have a package deal called "Rub, Tub & Grub" that combines all of the above. The rooms are situated up in the woods, and each comes with its own mineral spa in a redwood tub. Eight hours of this and you could start your own religion.

Coastal Cuisine

The **Gardens of Avila** (1215 Avila Beach Drive, 595-7365, $$$) is located at the lush Sycamore Mineral Springs Resort. The eclectic menu ranges all over the globe, but fresh local seafood is the best bet, as it comes straight off the pier at Port San Luis. The **Olde Port Inn Restaurant** (Port San Luis Pier, 595-2515, $$$) serves fish straight from the boats, too. Literally, you get the catch of the day. The owner is named Leonard Cohen (presumably no relation to the poet/singer). Cohen started the California Cio-Pinot Cook-off, an annual cioppino and Pinot Noir contest that benefits local charities. Just ask for the latest award-winner and you can't lose.

Night Moves

Your best bet is **Mr. Rick's Beach Bar and Night Club** (480 Front Street, 595-9500). The late afternoon happy hour (5 PM to 7 PM) attracts a relaxed brood of collegians who swap tall tales and sway to the sounds of a decent jukebox. Live music begins most nights at 9 PM; expect a mix of rock, blues, and reggae.

For More Information

Pismo Beach Area Convention & Visitors Bureau, 581 Dolliver Street, Pismo Beach, CA 93449; (805) 773-4382.

San Luis Obispo

Location: 10 miles northeast of Pismo Beach, along Highway 101. San Luis Obispo isn't a beach town, but it is the county seat and hub of San Luis Obispo County and its nearby coastal communities.
Population: 43,000
Area Code: 805 **Zip Code:** 93401

Like Santa Barbara, San Luis Obispo is the sort of town you don't just want to visit—you want to live there. The natural setting—in a valley 2,000 feet below the Santa Lucia Mountains, bisected by a small river—blends perfectly with the culture and cuisine to produce a place as comfortable as a cashmere sweater.

Although it is not located directly on the beach, San Luis Obispo (pronounced *LOOiss* and called "SLO" for short) is a jumping-off point for numerous Central Coast getaways, including Pismo Beach, Avila Beach, Morro Bay, Cambria, and San Simeon. It is also a worthy destination in and of itself, with excellent amenities, history, scenery, and arts. They've got their own symphony and opera company, chorales, a Mozart Festival, theater companies, and arts and crafts galleries.

That's just the half of it. San Luis Obispo has an indefinable quality that transforms it from an otherwise pleasant crossroads into a real honey of a place. Perhaps it's the presence of California Polytechnic State University, with its hip, eco-minded student body of 11,000. In a college town, the continuous stream of fresh blood and new ideas guarantees that things won't get stale. There are also the surrounding agricultural valleys, which once earned SLO a reputation as a cow town. These days the massive greenbelt seems downright magical, contributing to the healthy bustle of the town. Every Thursday, a farmers market sets up on Higuera Street, and the entire town attends. One can only hope that San Luis Obispo—located roughly halfway between Los Angeles and San Francisco—will continue to preserve the natural treasures that make it so unique.

Once the heart of Mission San Luis Obispo de Tolosa, the town has deep historical roots. The mission was the first in California to use red-tiled roofs as fireproofing against Native Americans' flaming arrows. The mission's church has been restored (782 Monterey Street, 543-6850), and the nearby San Luis Obispo County Historical Museum (696 Monterey Street, 543-0638) contains Native American and early settlement artifacts. Much of the rest of the town's architecture dates from the Victorian period. Careful planning and refurbishing has kept growth within tasteful bounds.

Walking is the best way to see the local history and architecture. Two suggested hikes provide a larger perspective on this setting. The first is a 1.5-mile round-trip trek up to Bishop Peak, which provides views of the town and the valley. The second is a one-mile walk through Poly Canyon on the university campus. Park across from the Fisher Science Building on Perimeter Road and enjoy roaming among the wildflowers.

Another kind of touring is rewarding for those folks who, to paraphrase the sage words of the late Orson Welles' commercial pitch, buy no wine before its time. Forty wineries and vineyards are located in San Luis Obispo County. The best known of the bunch are Clairborne & Churchill (860 "E" Capitola Way, 544-4066), Edna Valley Vineyard (2585 Biddle Rand Road, 544-9594), and Corbett Canyon Vineyard (2195 Corbett Canyon Road, 544-5800). All three are in the greater San Luis Obispo city limits. To find the rest, pick up a brochure, complete with map, at any area restaurant or motel.

Bunking Down

You may not look out upon sand and surf, but you will get a nice view in San Luis Obispo, no matter where you stay. For romantic getaways, there are three excellent, slightly quirky places to consider. The **Madonna Inn** (100 Madonna Road, 543-3000, $$) is the best known for the simple reason there's no other place like it in California (or in the country, for that matter). Every one of its 109 rooms is decorated in a different style, and the architecture of the lodge itself is part Elizabethan, part gingerbread, part Victorian, part.... You get the idea. It's unabashedly eccentric, and the grounds are fun to stroll.

Equally delightful is the **Garden Street Inn Bed & Breakfast** (1212 Garden Street, 545-9802, $$). Built in 1887 on land once owned by the mission, the Garden Street Inn is a Italianate Queen Anne–style house that's historic without being musty. It's also right in the center of the downtown historic area. Finally, there's the **Apple Farm Inn** (2015 Monterey Street, 544-2040, $$$), which re-creates Victorian times with country classic stylings, an attached mill house and a restaurant that serves things like chicken and dumplings. Pass the peach pie, parson.

For budget-minded families, the **Vagabond Inn** (210 Madonna Road, 544-4710, $) offers a continental breakfast and the unique offer of "Kids under 19 stay free." Kids under *19*?

Coastal Cuisine

Pete's Southside Café (1815 Osos Street, Railroad Square, 549-8133, $$) has the right pedigree. It began as a small café in Avila Beach. Now it's thriving as a fine diner. But they still feature their hallmark Caribbean and Latin-American entrées. Their paella wins "best of" awards almost every year. **Simply Shrimp** (570 Higuera Street, 542-0237, $$) is the name of the place, but they actually serve a wide range of salads and seafood, including fish Veracruz.

Night Moves

Nightlife in SLO is anything but slow. It's a town full of college bars, with the laughter and manners one associates with that species ringing out of every doorfront after dark. The most popular place in town, **Tortilla Flats** (1051 Nipomo Street, 544-7575), extracts a cover charge to lure people inside for taped disco music. Here, you'll see valley cowboys trying to connect with Poly Dollies in a setting not designed for easy traffic flow-through. (It is a restaurant by day.) Prepare to have your buns squeezed.

More to our liking was **Brubeck's** (726 Higuera Street, 541-8688), which has a civilized upstairs bar with lots of mirrors allowing patrons to check out one another. More appealingly raunchy is the downstairs **Cellar**, where the college crowd screams and shouts around a great jukebox. In between conversation they scribble graffiti on the walls. (It's encouraged.) There's no standing on ceremony here. Just shout out what you want; usually one word ("draft") will suffice. We were told of a place that was popular with the thirty-something crowd. But what kind of fun can you have at the beach if you hang out with people our age? Give us arrested adolescents a hangout like the Cellar anytime!

The best live music venue is the **SLO Brewing Company** (1119 Garden Street, 543-1843). Grab a brew and, to quote Elvis Presley, if you can't find a partner grab a wooden chair.

For More Information

Contact the San Luis Obispo Chamber of Commerce, 1039 Chorro Street, San Luis Obispo, CA 93401; (805) 543-1323.

Map of San Luis Obispo County beaches—page 292

Montana de Oro State Park

Location: Three miles south of San Luis Obispo on Highway 101, take the Los Osos/Baywood Park exit and drive 12 miles west on Los Osos Valley Road, which becomes Pecho Valley Road. Follow Pecho Valley to the park entrance.

Just south of Morro Bay, near the small bayside towns of Los Osos and Baywood Park, **Montana de Oro State Park** spreads out across an immense swath of land. It faces the ocean for 3.5 miles, from the Morro Sand Spit south. Spanish explorers named the area "mountain of gold" because of the golden poppies that cover its hills and terraces. Monarch butterflies nest in the eucalyptus from October through March, adding to the gilded appearance. Today, this 8,400-acre wilderness park is one of the great treasures of California's state-park system. Montana de Oro's acreage encompasses sand dunes, jagged cliffs, coves, caves, and reefs, with 50 miles of trails for hiking, biking, and horseback riding. These trails traverse the inland canyons and mountains, as well as the shoreline. On a clear day, from the 1,845-foot summit of the Valencia Peak Trail, one can see 90 miles of coastline. People also come to fish, scuba dive, and tidepool along the rocky shore.

Montana de Oro State Park

Location: Three miles south of San Luis Obispo. From Highway 101, take the Los Osos/Baywood Park exit, and drive 12 miles west on Los Osos Valley Road, which becomes Pecho Valley Road. Continue to the park entrance.

Parking: Free parking lots.

Hours: Sunrise to sunset.

Facilities: Rest rooms, picnic tables, and barbecue grills. There are 50 campsites for tents. Fees are $7 to $9 per night. For camping reservations, call Destinet at (800) 444-7275.

Contact: For beach information, contact Montana de Oro State Park at (805) 528-0513.

See number 4 on page 292.

Montana de Oro is a primitive park, with only 50 unimproved campsites and minimal facilities. That is precisely what keeps it pristine, despite increasing visitation as word gets around. The road through the park plunges deep into forested foothills. The beaches are as wild as an unbroken colt, choked with rocky outcroppings and sea caves and pounded by a frothy, roiling surf. The coarse salt-and-pepper sand is not conducive to sunbathing, but the park and its coastline are ruggedly beautiful. Indefatigable surfers sometimes hike through the woods to the small beach at Hazard Canyon, where dangerous surf awaits. The best beach is the sandy crescent at Spooner's Cove (named for the rancher and dairyman who was the former landowner), where there's a primitive campground. The only other campground in the park is a special area for equestrian campers, which must be reserved in advance. One deterrent to heavy visitation is that there is no potable water inside the park.

For More Information

Contact Montana de Oro State Park, Los Osos, CA 93402; (805) 528-0513.

Morro Bay

Location: Morro Bay is nearly equidistant from Los Angeles (220 miles) and San Francisco (230 miles). For a more local orientation, it lies 30 miles south of San Simeon and 20 miles north of Pismo Beach, off Highway 1. The Embarcadero runs along Morro Bay's waterfront. The main beach is the south section of Morro Strand State Beach.

Population: 10,000

Area Code: 805 **Zip Code:** 93442

Morro Rock is an enormous monolith, the remnant of an active volcano, that sits just offshore from the town of Morro Bay. It is the pet rock of the Central Coast and the "Gibraltar of the Pacific," and it dominates the landscape in these parts the way a full moon fills the night sky. It is inescapable, commanding, awesome. The rock is so much an icon that its likeness appears on anything having to do with Morro Bay, from postcards and tourist brochures to ashtrays and motel-room trash baskets. The ubiquitous Portuguese explorer Juan Cabrillo dubbed the rock El Morro ("domed turban"), when he sailed into Estero Bay in 1542.

From a distance, it looks like a bare, brown geodesic dome. It is one of seven volcanic peaks, known as the Seven Sisters, that run in a nearly straight line from San Luis Obispo to Morro Bay. Morro Rock is the most northwesterly of these intrusive plugs. Because it is located offshore, it stands in bold relief and is the most spectacular to behold. It rises 578 feet above sea level and weighs 20 million tons. Dating from the early Miocene period and estimated to be between 22 and 26 million years old, it is part of a chain of submerged plugs and volcanic peaks collectively identified as the Morro Rock-Islay Hill complex.

Black Mountain, another of the Seven Sisters, rises close by in Morro Bay State Park. A paved road leads to Black Mountain Lookout, which, at 865 feet, is the highest point in the park. From here you are treated to a sweeping view of the coast. With its many different lithologies arrayed in a hodgepodge, this part of the Central Coast has been referred to as a "geological mulligan stew," and it does offer a lot of tasty geology to observe.

Morro Rock is composed of hard igneous rock that has outlasted the more resistant metamorphic rock of the Franciscan formation into which it intrudes. It looms above the landscape surrounding it, standing undaunted after millions of years. The only real threat to its well-being is the hand of man. Between 1891 and 1963, quarrying operations robbed Morro Rock of its sharp peak and some of its elevation. The volcanic rock and talus quarried off the rock were used to build breakwaters here and at Avila Beach, and to construct a causeway linking Morro Rock with the mainland. (It formerly stood 1,000 feet offshore.) After all that, it was discovered that Morro's lava rock doesn't hold up to constant pounding by the sea. Moreover, quarrying was beginning to affect the fragile Morro Rock ecosystem. Nesting grounds for the rare and endangered peregrine falcon were being destroyed—as was the rock itself. By the time local residents demanded a halt to quarrying, more than a million tons of rock had been hauled away. Morro Rock was designated a State Historical Landmark and a Peregrine Falcon Reserve in 1968. These days you can drive up to its base and even halfway around it. Climbing the rock itself was banned in 1973, in deference to the birds.

The Morro Bay Power Station is another massive feature on the landscape. Its three 450-foot-tall smokestacks are located directly across the road from Morro Rock, but you won't see them pictured on any postcards or promotional brochures for Morro Bay. They resemble enormous filter-tipped cigarettes, make a noise not unlike the drone in the film *Eraserhead*, and warm the nearby water by a few degrees. Between San Diego and Morro Bay we'd seen two nuclear power stations built on fault lines and now a power plant sited by one of the most wondrous natural features on the coast. When will they ever learn?

Its smokestacks aside, Morro Bay is an utterly charming community of 10,000 friendly souls. People come to this less harried part of the coast to lay back and watch Morro Rock. When not meditating on the rock, you can pursue other activities here, the most popular being deep-sea fishing. With a sizable sport and commercial fishing fleet operating out of the breezy harbor, Morro Bay has the authentic flavor of a fishing village with minimal tourist trappings. A number of outfitters operate along the Embarcadero, Morro Bay's waterfront avenue. Virg's Fish'n (1215 Embarcadero, 772-1222) reels in the most anglers. It bustles like the floor of the stock exchange. Folks are constantly coming and going, booking trips and consulting the experts. Half-day fishing trips cost $22; a full day runs $32. When the albacore are running, eager anglers flock to Morro Bay, and fishing fever takes over the town.

Every day, the commercial fleet sails in with fresh catches of salmon, albacore, ling cod, Pacific snapper, Alaskan halibut, and thresher shark. Morro Bay is one of the five largest estuaries in California and a biologically rich habitat. Visitors can partake of its bounty by boarding a water taxi from Virg's to the Morro Sand Spit, the four-mile peninsula that separates Morro Bay from the ocean. The 100-yard crossing will deposit you on a sand bank. It can be a mite uncomfortable on the spit "if the wind's blowin' like snot," according to our plainspoken skipper, so dress as you would for a tornado. Once on the spit, you can hike, dig for clams, surf cast, or bird-watch.

Still more soul-satisfying, nature-oriented activity can be found at Morro Bay State Park, attached to the southeastern end of town. It's a multiple-use recreation area with everything from campsites and hiking trails to a resort and (boo, who needs it?) an 18-hole golf course. A museum of natural history contains dioramas on nature, wildlife, and the area's early Chumash Indian inhabitants. The marsh, located where Los Osos Creek enters Morro Bay, is home to 250 species of birds. The park is the site of a six-acre eucalyptus grove that serves as a rookery for great blue herons, which nest in the treetops from January to August. You can rent a canoe and paddle the quiet waters of the estuary or row out to the spit.

The Embarcadero runs for about a mile from Morro Rock to Morro Bay State Park. It is a highly walkable mile, passing bait-and-tackle shops and fish-and-chip stands (serving *local* fish, they emphasize). At the corner of Morro Bay Boulevard and Market Street is the Centennial Stairway. This impressive redwood staircase descends to Fisherman's Memorial, a small harborside park with a monster 7,000-pound anchor as its centerpiece. The town's pride and joy is its Giant Chessboard, an outdoor game board whose dimensions are straight out of *Alice in Wonderland*. The redwood chessmen stand three feet tall and weigh 18 to 20 pounds each. If you would care to make reservations to play, call 772-6278.

Morro Bay has been trying to pursue a slow-growth policy in the face of strong developmental pressure. As people flee Southern California with bulging retirement accounts and golden parachutes, keeping a lid on growth has proven difficult. The issue isn't just the usual desire to preserve an unhurried way of life and an unspoiled landscape. Water, or the lack of it, is the real limiting factor. Officials are concerned that overuse of dwindling water resources could cause underground aquifers to draw in salty seawater, ruining local water tables. Meanwhile, migrating Southern Californians have been steadily pricing Central Valley residents out of Morro Bay's housing market. In the late 1980s, housing prices jumped 40 percent in one year. With their deep pockets, the Southlanders have

 Map of San Luis Obispo County beaches—page 292

simply outbid all other comers. Given the markets they're used to, they are paying prices that feel like bargains.

Morro Rock itself gazes benignly on the human activity at its base. It will still be standing long after the last fish-and-chip shop has closed its doors. More than most communities, Morro Bay takes a philosophical cue from this monolith, endeavoring to safeguard its essential qualities as a quiet, serene locale. The town refers to itself as a place "where the sun spends the winter." No matter what season, the view from Morro Bay is a fine one when the setting sun drops into the ocean. As the sun falls, look over at Morro Rock, which takes on a bewitching range of hues and auroras. One evening around twilight, we spied a small violet cloud hovering around the top of Morro Rock like a halo. Exquisite, yes.

Beaches

If you love the beach, bay, and ocean, you will find Morro Bay an ideal place to drop anchor. The smaller "north" section of Morro Strand State Beach lies three miles north of town, off Highway 1 (see the Cayucos entry on page 312). The "south" section, formerly known as Atascadero State Beach, offers a 104-site campground. Sand is one thing they have plenty of along the Central Coast, so the beach here is wide and runs for nearly two miles. RVers jam the campground, but the lack of shade might make **Morro Strand State Beach South** a

Bayshore Bluffs Park

Location: In Morro Bay, at the west end of Bayshore Drive.

Parking: Free parking lot.

Hours: Sunrise to sunset.

Facilities: Picnic tables.

Contact: For beach information, contact the Morro Bay Harbor Department at (805) 772-6254.

See number 6 on page 292.

Morro Bay State Park

Location: From Morro Bay, take Highway 1 one mile south to South Bay Boulevard and turn south. Follow South Bay Boulevard to the fork, bear right onto State Park Road, and continue into the park. Or follow Main Street south from downtown Morro Bay until it becomes State Park Road and continue into the park.

Parking: $6 entrance fee per vehicle.

Hours: Sunrise to sunset.

Facilities: Rest rooms, showers, picnic tables, and barbecue grills. There are 115 tent and RV campsites. Fees are $14 to $16 per night. For camping reservations, call Destinet at (800) 444-7275.

Contact: For beach information, contact Morro Bay State Park at (805) 772-2560.

See number 7 on page 292.

Morro Dunes Natural Area

Location: Access is via water taxi from the Embarcadero in Morro Bay or from the south via a four-wheel drive from Pecho Valley Road (see directions to Montana de Oro State Park on page 292).

Parking: Metered street parking in downtown Morro Bay; from there, you must take a water taxi to the preserve.

Hours: Sunrise to sunset.

Facilities: None.

Contact: For beach information, contact Morro Bay State Park at (805) 772-2560.

See number 5 on page 292.

little tough on tenters, who are better advised to check out Montana de Oro State Park (see the entry on page 306). Morro Strand is an inviting day-use beach. Large waves roll lazily toward the shore for a good distance, making for long rides. You can do everything on the beaches of Morro Strand but dig for clams, which is prohibited.

At the base of **Morro Rock** itself is a small, crescent-shaped beach that sits behind the breakwater. Sun worshippers head here. Spray flies off the top of the breakwater as waves thunder against it, but the water on the protected beach behind it is as calm as a rippled lake. Our advice: enjoy the beach, but leave the breakwater alone. If you're tempted to scale the rocks for the view from the top, think twice about it. We hoisted ourselves up the breakwater's slippery, wet staircase of boulders. As we neared the top there was a longer-than-usual pause between waves, and then we saw a monster cresting high above us. In the eerie seconds before we were washed down the wall of rock to the ground by the breaking wave, we said our prayers. The gods were with us that day; we only got soaked, not severed on the rocks. Wetter than a pair of sea otters but otherwise unhurt, we changed into dry clothes and swore off breakwaters.

The sand spit that extends north like an arm ends with a fist-shaped protrusion that nearly chokes the narrow neck of the bay. It runs for four long miles and can be reached via water taxi (boarded at the Embarcadero in downtown Morro Bay) or by four-wheel drive from the south, where it joins the mainland at Montana de Oro State Park. The spit is formally known as the **Morro Dunes Natural Area**. The dunes on the spit are well formed, reaching 85 feet in height. As a coda to all the big beaches in Morro Bay, there's a tiny town park on Bayshore Drive, off the south end of Main Street. **Bayshore Bluffs Park** abuts **Morro Bay State Park**; a stairway and graded path lead from the bluff-top picnic area to the beach.

Morro Rock and Beach

Location: On the north side of Morro Bay, at the end of Coleman Drive.
Parking: Free parking lot.
Hours: Sunrise to sunset.
Facilities: Lifeguards and rest rooms.
Contact: For beach information, contact the Morro Bay Harbor Department at (805) 772-6254.

See number 8 on page 292.

Morro Strand State Beach (South unit)

Location: Three miles north of Morro Bay off Highway 1, between Yerba Buena Avenue and Atascadero Road.
Parking: Free parking lot.
Hours: Sunrise to sunset.
Facilities: Rest rooms, picnic tables, and fire grills. There are 104 tent and RV campsites. Fees are $14 to $16 per night. For camping reservations, call Destinet at (800) 444-7275.
Contact: For beach information, contact the Morro Strand State Beach at (805) 772-8812.

See number 9 on page 292.

Bunking Down

Located halfway between Los Angeles and San Francisco, Morro Bay is an ideal rendezvous point for residents of the two metropolises. The town is equipped with accommodations in all price ranges, from modest park-at-your-door motels to more resort-oriented facilities. The golden mean in Morro Bay would be someplace like the **Best Western Tradewinds** (225 Beach Street, 772-7376, $$), which is the closest lodging to Morro Rock itself and only one short block from the waterfront.

The hotel of first choice has to be the **Inn at Morro Bay** (19 Country Club Road, 772-5651, $$$). Located just inside Morro Bay State Park, the inn is set some distance back from the modest bustle of the Embarcadero. A luxury resort with a romantic atmosphere, its 100 guest rooms feature cathedral ceilings, gas fireplaces, country French decor, and outdoor decks overlooking the bay. At night, while you're out dining, the housekeeping staff sneaks in like tooth fairies and turns down the bed, placing roses and chocolates on the pillow and leaving a small bottle of cognac and snifters on the bedstand. The suite-sized rooms are filled with heavy, hand carved furniture, and the brass-fixtured bathrooms come with a complimentary assortment of French soap. As lavish as it sounds, the Inn at Morro Bay has a cozy, country inn-style atmosphere, all for between $100 and $200 a night.

Another fine choice is the **Embarcadero Inn** (456 Embarcadero, 772-2700, $$), located on the bay at the south end of town. The rooms are large, and the furniture cushiony. There are VCRs in the room and films at the front desk. Most rooms have a gas fireplace and an outdoor balcony, and the inn has a pair of indoor saunas. With its slate-colored, weathered-wood exterior, the Embarcadero Inn is the most distinguished-looking lodge on the waterfront.

The town of Morro Bay is outfitted with a number of plainer but perfectly comfortable and inexpensive motels. The **Harbor House Inn** (1095 Main Street, 772-2711, $) and **El Morro Lodge** (1206 Main Street, 772-5633, $) are both attractive, nicely maintained properties within walking distance of the waterfront.

Coastal Cuisine

Improvements are steadily being made along the waterfront as fading mom-and-pop joints inevitably give way to something more contemporary and, frankly, nicer. (The charm of a generic basket of deep-fried fish-and-chips only goes so far.) The talk of the town on our most recent visit was the **Cannery** (235 Main Street, 772-4426, $$), a huge new franchise restaurant that aims to bring 24-hour eats to sleepy little Morro Bay. Is it an idea whose time has come or pure Southlander folly? Only time will tell.

You'll find such successful recent arrivals as the **Otter Rock Café** (885 Embarcadero, 772-1420, $), a high-quality fast-food spot where you order at the window and carry your food to tables that look out over the water. At Otter Rock, baskets of fried seafood (fish, squid, oysters, scallops) and chips are served for prices that run in the $6 to $7 range.

Old reliables on the scene include the **Harbor Hut** (1205 Embarcadero, 772-2255, $$$) and the **Great American Fish Co.** (1185 Embarcadero, 772-4407, $$$). Both are operated by the same longtime residents and serve freshly caught seafood. The Harbor Hut was the first restaurant on the waterfront in Morro Bay. It opened in 1948, serving chili and chowder in a small Quonset hut. Today it's a prosperous local institution where oysters are fixed a half-dozen different ways. Daily catches from snapper to swordfish are fried, broiled, steamed, or sautéed, and combination surf-and-turf platters will assuage hearty appetites. Also on the bay is **Bob's Seafood** (833 Embarcadero, 772-8473, $$). Bob posts a full menu of fried and broiled seafood and serves breakfast till noon. Seafood entrées are served charbroiled, grilled, sautéed, poached, or Cajun style.

Moving upscale and away from the beach, the Inn at Morro Bay has its own dining room, the **Blue Heron Restaurant** (19 Country Club Drive, 772-5651, $$$), which serves Cal-nouvelle cuisine with a subtle French flair. You can count on fresh ingredients, superb preparation, a respectable wine list, excellent service, and a spectacular view of the bay. The house specialty, Pasta El Encanto, was named after the inn's sister operation in Santa Barbara. The dish consists of spinach and egg linguine, combined with shellfish in a creamy lobster bisque.

Fish fans can indulge their yen for sushi at **Harada Japanese Restaurant and Sushi Bar** (830 Embarcadero, 772-1410, $$$). The must-stop place for breakfast is **Carla's Country Kitchen** (213 Beach Street, 772-9051, $), which serves knockout scrambled-egg dishes.

Night Moves

If you're hankering for a good dinner or a good time after dinner, go to **Rose's Landing Restaurant and Cocktail Lounge** (725 Embarcadero, 772-4441), a steak-and-seafood restaurant on the water that delivers live entertainment from Wednesday through Sunday in the summer.

For More Information

Contact the Morro Bay Chamber of Commerce, 895 Napa Avenue, Suite A-1, P.O. Box 876, Morro Bay, CA 93442; (805) 772-4467.

Cayucos

Location: 15 miles south of Cambria, off Highway 1. Ocean Avenue is the main drag through town, and Cayucos State Beach is the center of action.
Population: 2,950
Area Code: 805 **Zip Code:** 93430

Cayucos is tucked into the head of a V-shaped cove formed where Cayucos Creek empties into the ocean. The hamlet, which has a population of fewer than 3,000, is an anomaly on the Central Coast. It doesn't look like it could give a hoot about tourism. It has the feel of an Old West town—which, in fact, it is. Its saloons look like real Old West saloons, because they are. No enormous infusions of cash have been pumped into Cayucos to restore, refurbish, revive, revise, beautify, or falsify it. There's one wide central street (Ocean Avenue), with angle-in parking on both sides. Antique and gift shops predominate. The auto-repair garage on the north side of town has been here since 1932, which qualifies as ancient history on the West Coast. An enormous mobile-home park is nearby. People come here to fish, decide they like the place, and stick around for a while.

The Cayucos Pier, an old, planked affair that's got all kinds of personality, has been around since 1875. Vendors push carts around the beachfront, selling such things as "chorros" (long, greasy fried Mexican pastries rolled in sugar mm, mm, bad). In Cayucos, hot dogs and hamburgers outsell nouvelle cuisine. A juxtaposition of signs by the pier speaks volumes about the town. One by the town library announces the hours it is open: a mere two days a week, seven hours each day. Next to it is a sign for a sporting-goods store, whose wares include "tackle, bait, amo [sic], scuba gear." (Maybe if they kept their library open a little longer, the locals wouldn't make such blatant spelling errors.)

Cayucos Beach

Location: In Cayucos; access is via nine stairwells along Pacific Avenue, between 1st and 22nd Streets.
Parking: Free street parking.
Hours: Sunrise to sunset.
Facilities: None.
Contact: For beach information, contact the San Luis Obispo County Department of Parks and Facilities at (805) 781-5930.

See number 11 on page 292.

Cayucos looks out over the placid waters of Estero Bay onto magisterial Morro Rock, some five miles away. The little town lies in the proverbial shadow of Morro Rock and, hence, largely gets overlooked by those passing through the area. The Hearst Mansion brings crowds to San Simeon, Morro Rock attracts tourists to Morro Bay, and romantic bluff-top B&Bs draw couples to Cambria. However, nothing but empty ranchland and the town of Harmony (population 12) fills the 15 miles between Cayucos and Cambria. Cayucos is not a vacation destination per se, but if you want to experience a California beach town that has largely been left untouched, do drop in. In the words of a local who escaped a rat-race life on the East Coast decades ago, "What we offer is peace and serenity from the stresses of big-city life."

Beaches

Cayucos State Beach gets good waves and looks to be popular with boogie boarders, whom we've seen get pitched into forceful forward rolls by sizable breakers. Anglers are in their glory on the 940-foot Cayucos Pier, which is surrounded by bait-and-tackle shops and is lit at night. South of the state beach is **Cayucos Beach**, which can be accessed via nine stairwells along a 22-block stretch of Pacific Avenue. At its southern end Cayucos Beach gives way to the north section of **Morro Strand State Beach**. This is the smaller, less developed section of the park—the one without a campground (for information on the south unit of Morro Strand State Beach, see the entry on page 310).

Bunking Down

Most of the places here seem designed to meet the uncomplicated demands of those who have come to Cayucos to fish. Hence, kitchenettes are included with most rooms, so you can cook your catch. A couple of motels south of the town center rise above the no-frills standard. The most inviting of these is the **Beachwalker Inn** (501 South Ocean Avenue, 995-2133, $$), which is only a block from the beach. But don't come to Cayucos expecting to find pools, fireplaces, afternoon wine and cheese, and decanters of sherry.

Coastal Cuisine

For seafood, try **Sea Shanty** (296 South Ocean Avenue, 995-3272, $), which posts daily fresh-fish specials and is open seven days a week.

For More Information

Contact the Cayucos Chamber of Commerce, 80 North Ocean Avenue, P.O. Box 141, Cayucos, CA 93430; (805) 995-1200.

Cayucos State Beach

Location: In Cayucos, at Ocean Drive and Cayucos Road.

Parking: Free lot and street parking.

Hours: Sunrise to sunset.

Facilities: Rest rooms, picnic tables, and barbecue grills.

Contact: For beach information, contact the San Luis Obispo County Department of Parks and Facilities at (805) 781-5930.

See number 12 on page 292.

Morro Strand State Beach (North unit)

Location: In Cayucos, at Studio Drive and 24th Street.

Parking: Free parking lot.

Hours: Sunrise to sunset.

Facilities: Rest rooms and picnic tables.

Contact: For beach information, contact the Morro Strand State Beach at (805) 772-8812.

See number 10 on page 292.

Cambria

Location: Cambria is located on either side of Highway 1, halfway between San Francisco and Los Angeles, which are each 230 miles away. Moonstone Beach Road runs along Cambria's beautiful Moonstone Beach.
Population: 5,400
Area Code: 805 **Zip Code:** 93428

If there's a prettier setting for a beach in all of California than Cambria, we have yet to find it. Lying between Cayucos and San Simeon, Cambria is a shy princess knocking at the back door of the Hearst Castle. Its motto says it all: "Where the pines meet the sea." A century ago, Cambria was a thriving community of 7,000 souls who worked at whaling, mining, and farming. Today, its residents number fewer than that, hovering just above 5,000, and there's little more going on than agriculture, arts and crafts, and a modest tourist trade. Those who visit here are mostly the spillover from San Simeon, plus enlightened travelers who can tell a genuinely quaint village from a contrived imitation. Part of the attraction of Cambria is its seclusion, its wildness, and they work to keep it that way. "Most of the residents have a slow-growth policy," explained a local innkeeper. "Some would call it a no-growth policy."

Many of the more recent arrivals are retiring creative sorts—artists, writers, and craftspeople—who have given Cambria something of the flavor of Laguna Beach, without the hectic pace of Southern California. The town is divided by Highway 1 into East and West villages. East Village is older, with many of its historic homes dating from the days when Cambria was known as "Slabtown," after the rough-hewn boards from which they were built. West Village has been constructed somewhat in the image of the tourist town of Solvang, with a Danish look to it. East Village has all the shops and galleries, and it's the place to go to while away the hours on a foggy morning as you're waiting for the sun to break through.

West Village is where the beaches are. To get there, disengage from Highway 1 at Moonstone Beach Road. Immediately, you're in another world. You can see the steep, plunging mountains of Big Sur to the northwest, set against a backdrop of flower- and grass-filled meadows. A string of cozy B&B-style motel/inns lines the landward side of Moonstone Beach Road. The preeminent feature in this landscape is the grassy, wildflower-strewn mesa that overlooks the beach. Trails crisscross the area right to the bluff edges, and people stroll at all hours. Take your pick—early morning, midafternoon, at ruddy sunset, or by the light of the silvery moon. The scenery is always beautiful, and the variegated light plays on the panorama, revealing its many subtle facets.

Indeed, Cambria is the perfect spot for beach and nature lovers who aren't compelled to engage in frantic aerobic activities involving special equipment and sportswear. All you need in Cambria are walking shorts, a light sweater, tennis shoes, and maybe a camera—leave the rest to nature. It is hard to take a bad picture here. So come with your binoculars, tripod, and significant other, and prepare to savor some of the most breathtaking sunsets and scenery on the California coast.

Cambria is the sort of town that vigilantly eschews aesthetic breeches in the armor of good taste. While we were there, the townsfolk were up in arms about the impending arrival of a McDonald's. Reaction to this unwanted intrusion filled the front page of the local newspaper, spilling over into editorials and letters. One outraged local expressed the majority opinion: "The notion that something so insidious as a McDonald's chain restaurant may come to Cambria fills me with shock, anger, disgust, and disappointment." Don't let this minor blight discourage you from coming to Cambria, however.

Weather-wise, summer months are foggy —not the best time to visit the Central Coast, unless you're coming to escape the interior heat. September through October are usually picture-perfect: mild and clear, without blustery winds and choking fog. By the way, if you don't want to be pegged as a tourist, pronounce the town name "*CAMbria*", with a short "a" and the accent on the first syllable, as in "Camelot."

Beaches

Moonstone Beach runs for two miles until it tags up with San Simeon State Beach to the north. The coastline is rugged, with gnarled driftwood limbs and tangled mats of seaweed that have washed ashore. You can access Moonstone Beach at Leffingwell Landing, a quarter mile west of Moonstone Beach Drive's southern intersection with Highway 1. Moonstone Beach takes its name from the polished jade, agate, and quartz pebbles that collect in mounds here. On certain parts of the beach there is no sand, just heaps of these pea-sized stones.

A bluff-top trail wanders above Moonstone Beach, extending from end to end. At some points eroded, localized indentations in the coastline have brought the ocean precariously close to the roadside. Waves rise in perfect form, then crash mightily on the rocks, sweeping over the stony shoreline. Surfers congregate up toward a point at the beach's south end. Everyone else just walks and watches. Who could ask for anything more?

Moonstone Beach

Location: In Cambria, along Moonstone Beach Drive, between Leffingwell Landing and Highway 1.

Parking: Free parking lot.

Hours: Sunrise to sunset.

Facilities: Rest rooms and picnic tables.

Contact: For beach information, contact the Cambria Chamber of Commerce at (805) 927-3624.

See number 13 on page 292.

Bunking Down

Cambria is the most romantic coast hideaway this side of Mendocino, and Moonstone Beach is the site of the choicest accommodations. All are set in proximity to one another, and the decor, prices, and quality are fairly uniform among them. Nearly all advertise "Pool * Fireplace * HBO" on their outdoor signs. And all are well maintained, quiet, and comfortable. Having stayed there twice, we're partial to the **Sea Otter Inn** (6656 Moonstone Beach Drive, 927-5888, $$), which has gas fireplaces in all rooms, a heated pool, and TVs with VCRs and films for rent at the desk.

The **Best Western Fireside Inn** (6700 Moonstone Beach Drive, 927-8661, $$) may be the most affordable; it certainly has the most units, and they are modern and well kept. Others that earn high marks and offer similar amenities include the **Fog Catcher Inn** (6400 Moonstone Beach Drive, 927-1400, $$) and the **Sand Pebbles Inn** (6252 Moonstone Beach Drive, 927-5600, $$). The latter, with its country English decor, canopy beds, and tea room where continental breakfast is served, might just be the most inviting of all. However, you can't go wrong staying anywhere on Moonstone Beach Drive.

Coastal Cuisine

Let's hope Ronald McDonald's worldwide burger factory doesn't make it in Cambria. You can do your part by dining at the plentiful selection of nonfranchised restaurants around town, both in East Village and out by Moonstone Beach. As one local denizen put it, "We've already got Main Street Grill. Who needs McDonald's?"

Our own favorite of long-standing is the **Brambles Dinner House** (4005 Burton Drive, 927-4716, $$$). It is so named because of the bramble bushes that run riot throughout the property, growing right up to the restaurant's windows. The Brambles is an old-fashioned English dinner house. The walls are decorated with different patterns of china. Heavy red drapes hang in the windows, and the lights are turned down low. The house specialties run to surf-and-turf items prepared with a subtle Greek flair. For dessert, they serve a rich, diet-busting cheesecake, as well as various flavors of ice cream frothed to a milkshake's consistency with liqueurs. We tried chocolate ice cream laced with amaretto, a concoction so tasty we were guiltily driven to hike off the calories on the trail overlooking Moonstone Beach.

Another East Village favorite is **Robin's** (4286 Bridge Street, 927 5007, $$), a gourmet vegetarian restaurant serving ethnic dishes prepared with locally grown organic produce.

Out on Moonstone Beach, the **Sea Chest Restaurant** (6216 Moonstone Beach Drive, 927-4514, $$$) does a raging business serving generous portions of Alaskan crab legs, among other things, to crowds that happily pile in to break bread and crab legs in good company. The **Moonstone Beach Bar and Grill** (6550 Moonstone Beach Drive, 927-3859, $$$), formerly the Moonraker, serves a variety of fare, but the best bet is the ever-popular seafood pasta.

Night Moves

Go to the **Moonstone Beach Bar and Grill** (6550 Moonstone Beach Drive, 927-3859) if you're thirsty for a nightcap. In general, though, like most villages on this wild and scenic stretch of coastline, more noise is made by ocean waves than human beings after 10 PM. Knock off early and save your strength for a beach hike before breakfast.

For More Information

Contact the Cambria Chamber of Commerce, 767 Main Street, Cambria, CA 93428; (805) 927-3624.

San Simeon

Location: 42 miles north of San Luis Obispo on Highway 1. The main attraction in this minuscule village is Hearst Castle. Yet William R. Hearst Memorial State Beach, right off Highway 1 along San Simeon Road, is not to be overlooked.
Population: 250
Area Code: 805 **Zip Code:** 93452

Its owner christened it La Cuesta Encantada ("The Enchanted Hill"). The world knows it better as Hearst Castle. The state park system formally refers to it as Hearst San Simeon State Historical Monument. Whatever you want to call it, the 165-room palace overlooking the ocean from the Santa Lucia mountains is the Central Coast's gilded centerpiece. It's as simple as this: no visit to the area is complete without a tour of Hearst Castle.

San Simeon is castle country. Everything else—sun, sand, sea, and the mountains that roll down to it—takes a backseat to the incomprehensible enormity of Hearst Castle. The midcoast mountaintop hideaway was built by newspaper magnate William Randolph Hearst as a "carefully planned, deliberate attempt to create a shrine of beauty." One million people visit San Simeon every year, making it California's top state-run tourist attraction.

Hearst was one of America's wealthiest men when he commissioned work on the castle, portrayed as the tomblike "Xanadu" in Orson Welles' classic film *Citizen Kane*, the fictionalized biography of a newspaper tycoon who bears a striking resemblance to Hearst. Born in 1863, Hearst was the sole heir to the nation's third largest fortune. His father, George Hearst, made his millions speculating in gold and silver mines, including the Comstock Lode. The elder Hearst turned his attention to real estate in the 1860s, gobbling up ranchland at 65 cents an acre. By acquiring adjoining land grants in the San Simeon area, he amassed a spread of 275,000 acres. In the later years of the century, the family often embarked on summer retreats to San Simeon, living in a tent pitched on top of a 1,600-foot mountain they called Camp Hill.

William Randolph Hearst decided to build his dream castle on this site. He had not done badly for himself, thanks to his father's largesse. Hearst was given the *San Francisco Examiner* on his 24th birthday, and he went on to inherit the $11 million family fortune. He oversaw a vast media empire that grew to include 30 newspapers, 15 magazines, 6 radio stations, and several film companies. History primarily remembers Hearst as a yellow journalist whose papers' hysterical reportage helped start a war and elect a president.

His private passion for art collecting was greater even than his public passion for journalism and politicking. Hearst reportedly spent $1 million a year on artwork alone for 50 consecutive years. He intended his castle to be a Louvre-like repository for his priceless collection of Mediterranean Gothic and Renaissance paintings, tapestries, and antique ceilings. Work was undertaken on the buildings and gardens in 1919. Hearst enlisted Julia Morgan, a renowned Berkeley-trained architect, to work for and with him. She agreed to devote two weekends a month to the Hearst manse, a project that kept her occupied for 20 years.

In assembling his playground of privilege, Hearst indulged every whim and desire that could be conceived, given virtually boundless economic resources. The crowning glory of the hilltop estate is La Casa Grande, the 115-room main house (it has a staggering 31 bathrooms). It also includes the gargantuan Refectory and Assembly Room, each filled with priceless art and artifacts, two libraries, and a movie theater. There's no place like home, especially when home is surrounded by 123 acres of exotic gardens, plus a line of 100-foot Mexican fan palms. Three guest houses—Casa del Mar, Casa del Sol, and Casa del Monte—adjoin the big house, as do huge indoor and outdoor swimming pools. Hearst, an animal fancier, made a virtual nature preserve of his estate, importing 90 species from around the world and allowing them to roam the hills and fields. To this day, zebra and Barbara sheep, remnants of this bestiary, wander the grounds.

There is no end of jaw-dropping facts about the castle and tales about the celebrity aristocracy who were Hearst's constant guests during the gilded age of the 1920s and 1930s. Artifacts on display include Greek and Roman temple relics, 2,000-year-old sarcophagi, *millefleur* tapestries from the north of France, a Spanish castle ceiling (shipped overseas in 100 crates and reassembled at San Simeon). You even hear of a storage room filled with fur coats, provided as a courtesy for female guests wary of catching a shiver in the cool mountain air after stepping out of the 345,000-gallon heated outdoor pool.

America is fascinated with "the Big Money" (to borrow a John Dos Passos book title), and that is what keeps the tourist buses chugging

Touring Hearst Castle

Four completely different daytime tours are offered of Hearst Castle, and, in the spring and fall, evening tours are available. All tours involve about a half mile of walking and between 150 and 400 steps. Here's a quick overview of each tour:

- **Tour 1:** This is the General Tour, recommended for first-time visitors. It covers the ground floor of the main building, one of the guest houses, the pools, and part of the gardens.
- **Tour 2:** On the Private Quarters Tour, visitors explore the upper floors of the main building, two suites, library, kitchen and pantry, and both pools.
- **Tour 3:** The North Wing Tour consists of two floors of guest suites, a top-floor suite, one of the guest houses, both pools, and a short film.
- **Tour 4:** The Garden Tour guides you through—surprise, surprise—Hearst's gardens, as well as a guest house, the wine cellar, and both pools. The main building is not entered. This tour is offered only from April through October.
- **Tour 5:** The Evening Tour provides a nighttime glimpse of the castle on Fridays and Saturdays, from March through May and September through December, as well as every night during some holiday periods, such as Easter and Christmas. The tour includes highlights from Tours 1, 2, and 4.

For reservations, call Destinet at (800) 444-4445 or (800) 444-7275, or visit a local Destinet outlet. Tickets may also be purchased at the Hearst Castle ticket office, open daily from 8 AM to 4 PM. Reservations can be made up to 8 weeks in advance for individuals and 12 weeks in advance for groups. Reservations for wheelchair-accessible tours can be made directly with Hearst Castle by calling (805) 927-2020 at least 10 days in advance.

up the mountain day in and day out. Though we don't have a king and queen, we do have a palace, and its name is San Simeon. Seven years after Hearst's death in 1951, the estate was turned over to the state of California by his heirs in exchange for $56 million in tax breaks. Today, tours run like clockwork from 8:20 AM to 3:00 PM (later in summer) every day of the year but Christmas, Thanksgiving, and New Year's Day. Tickets cost $14 per tour for adults, $8 for children 6 to 12. (Night tours cost a little more and last a little longer.) Tickets can be purchased at the Hearst Castle ticket office (open 8 AM to 4 PM) or reserved up to eight weeks in advance by calling (800) 444-4445 or (800) 444-7275. For more information, write or call San Simeon State Park, 750 Hearst Castle Road, San Simeon, CA 93452; (805) 927-2020.

Each tour lasts just under two hours and involves a fair amount of walking and gawking. Visitors are shepherded around the grounds by smiling guides who remind you not to step off the indoor-outdoor carpet runners that keep tourist hoof prints off the priceless marble, tile, and wood floors. A word to the wise: castle tours might be a little boring for fidgety young kids and lowbrow adults. However, we'd recommend it without hesitation to travelers possessing any level of interest in art, architecture, and (of course) lifestyles of the rich and famous. Incidentally, the Hearst Corporation endures as a vast media empire, controlling newspapers, magazines, and book-publishing houses—not to mention 80,000 acres of land surrounding Hearst Castle.

Beaches

Although the Hearst Castle eclipses everything around it, two public beaches in San Simeon give you something else to do when you're in the area. **San Simeon State Beach** is located between Santa Rosa and San Simeon creeks, abutting queenly Cambria to the south. If you've come a-castling but would rather camp than put up at a motel or inn, the park offers 187 campsites and a day-use beach. Surfing is

San Simeon State Beach

Location: At the north end of Cambria, along San Simeon Creek Road off Highway 1.

Parking: Free parking lot.

Hours: Sunrise to sunset.

Facilities: Rest rooms, showers, and picnic tables. There are 134 tent and RV sites at the San Simeon Creek Campground. Fees are $14 to $16 per night. There are 53 tent and RV sites at the Washburn Campground. Fees are $7 to $9 per night. For camping reservations, call Destinet at (800) 444-7275.

Contact: For beach information, contact Hearst Castle at (805) 927-2068.

See number 14 on page 292.

William R. Hearst Memorial State Beach

Location: In San Simeon, along San Simeon Road, west of Highway 1.

Parking: $3 to $4 entrance fee per vehicle.

Hours: Sunrise to sunset.

Facilities: Rest rooms, picnic tables, and fire pits.

Contact: For beach information, contact Hearst Castle at (805) 927-2068.

See number 15 on page 292.

hit or miss and swimming is for polar bears, but the diving is usually swell.

William R. Hearst Memorial State Beach lies at the foot of the Hearst property. The grounds include picnic tables and a small, tree-shaded beach. San Simeon Point protects Hearst Beach from the ocean's onslaught, but the real attraction is a 1,000-foot fishing pier, where anglers cast for snapper and rockfish or charter boats for deep-sea fishing.

From this vantage point you'll be in the old, often bypassed village of San Simeon. Formerly a whaling village, it is now just a small cluster of buildings on a short spur road off Highway 1. There's not much more here than an old schoolhouse and the oldest store in the state, Sebastian's General Store, which smells of coffee and fresh produce.

Bunking Down

The first motel in the area was the **San Simeon Lodge** (9520 Castillo Drive, 927-4601, $). Built in 1958, the year in which the state acquired the Hearst Castle, it offers serviceable accommodations and reasonable, family-friendly prices. A whole strip of motels has grown up alongside the year-round industry of castle touring. At the moment, Best Western seems to have a lock on the market with two of the better properties to be found in the area. The **Best Western Cavalier Inn & Restaurant** (9415 Hearst Drive, 927-4688, $$) is the only oceanfront motel in San Simeon, boasting 900 feet of coastline, plus fireplaces, balconies, and other upscale amenities more common to Cambria than San Simeon. The **Best Western Green Tree Inn** (9450 Castillo Drive, 927-4691, $$) is a tad cheaper and a bit more recreational, offering an indoor pool and spa, plus tennis courts.

The **California Seacoast Lodge** (9215 Hearst Drive, 927-3878, $$) puts a bit of Cambria's B&B-style amenities (country English decor, fireplaces, canopied beds) close to the Hearst Castle. For the budget-minded, a clean new **Motel 6** (9070 Castillo Drive, 927-8691, $) offers economy and convenience.

Coastal Cuisine

Because they feed more than a million mouths a year, the restaurateurs of San Simeon share a common philosophy toward the hungry tourists: herd 'em in, fill 'em up, and move 'em out. They arrive by the busload for an hour of carbohydrate loading before touring the house that Hearst built. One restaurant manager bragged to us about her restaurant's ability to feed literally thousands a day. The secret is to cajole them into eating from serve-yourself buffet troughs. "Don't even let 'em see a menu," she told us. "They might get ideas."

The **San Simeon Restaurant** (9520 Castillo Drive, 927-4604, $$), which adjoins the San Simeon Lodge, has been around the longest and has the art of mass feeding down to a science. Legend has it that Hearst himself ate here on occasion, back when it was the only restaurant in town. One must heave open a veritable castle door to get inside. The dining room is filled with San Simeon memorabilia. The house specialty is prime rib, which suits this meat-and-potatoes crowd fine.

At the other extreme is **Europa** (9240 Castillo Drive, 927-3087, $$), which would have better suited Hearst's kingly ambitions. In any case, this internationally flavored menu of beef, pasta, and fish specials is an attractive option if you're suffering from the all-you-can-eat blues.

Night Moves

William Randolph Hearst is dead, and after dark so is San Simeon. One viable choice is an evening tour of **Hearst Castle** (see sidebar, "Touring Hearst Castle").

For More Information

Contact the San Simeon Chamber of Commerce, 9511 Hearst Drive, P.O. Box 1, San Simeon, CA 93452; (805) 927-3500.

Monterey County

The coastline of Monterey County has inspired epic poems, novels, photographs, paintings, spiritual retreats, and nature cults—not to mention the ardent environmental activism that keeps its centerpiece, Big Sur, in a state of a perpetual inspiration. On a personal level, Monterey County has never failed to reduce us beach bums to an awed silence.

Millions of people pass through Monterey County on the Pacific Coast Highway each year. Driving along Big Sur and around the 17 Mile Drive is sort of a vacationer's rite of passage. The experience is not unlike riding through the Louvre on a motorbike, with one masterpiece after another coming into view, varying enough in geologic shape and size to keep things consistently breathtaking. The cove beaches of southern Big Sur spill into the raw contours of the Ventana Wilderness, the exquisite beauty of Andrew Molera State Park and Point Lobos, the blinding white sand beach at Carmel, the calming stands of pine in Pacific Grove, *(continued on page 324)*

Coastal Monterey County's Climate

Carmel Averages

	Daily High Temp. (°F)	Daily Low Temp. (°F)	Rainfall (inches)
January	60	43	4.1
February	62	44	2.6
March	62	44	2.6
April	63	45	1.7
May	64	48	0.4
June	67	50	0.2
July	67	51	0
August	69	52	0.1
September	72	52	0.3
October	72	51	0.7
November	66	47	2.4
December	63	43	3.2
Yearly Average	**65**	**48**	**18.3**

Source: National Weather Service data, National Oceanographic and Atmospheric Administration.

Monterey County

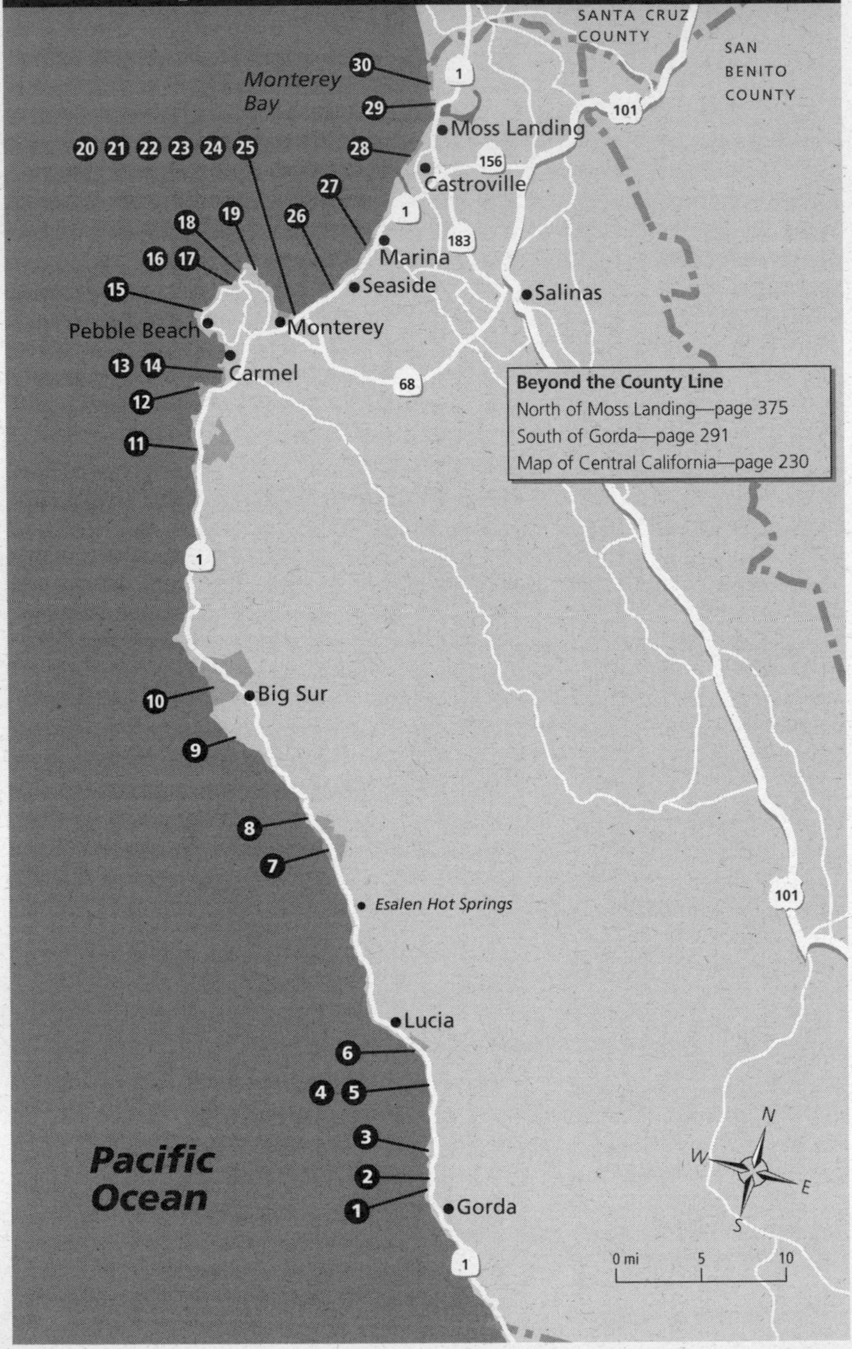
SANTA CRUZ COUNTY
SAN BENITO COUNTY
Monterey Bay
Moss Landing
Castroville
Marina
Seaside
Salinas
Monterey
Pebble Beach
Carmel
Big Sur
Esalen Hot Springs
Lucia
Gorda
Pacific Ocean
1
101
156
183
68
1 2 3 4 5 6 7 8 9 10 11 12 13 14 15 16 17 18 19 20 21 22 23 24 25 26 27 28 29 30
Beyond the County Line
North of Moss Landing—page 375
South of Gorda—page 291
Map of Central California—page 230
N
E
S
W
0 mi
5
10

Monterey County Beaches

Map of Central California—page 230

(continued from page 321) the rich underwater life off Monterey, and the fertile pastures and farmlands of Moss Landing and Castroville.

Although the delight of much of the county is purely visual (look, but don't touch), a number of jewel-like parklands can be found where land meets sea—in particular, Andrew Molera State Park and Point Lobos State Reserve. Don't just whiz through Monterey County like every other harried tourist. Stop and smell the roses...and the artichokes.

Key to the Symbols

Bike path · Camping · Food and drink · Hiking · Nude

Pier · RVs allowed · Surfing · Volleyball

Crowd Rating

sweet solitude . . . moderate crowds . . . wall-to-wall

Overall Rating

1 don't bother . . . 3 worth a visit . . . 5 beach heaven

Big Sur

Location: The coastal region of Big Sur stretches from San Simeon (in San Luis Obispo County) to the Carmel River (in Monterey County), a distance of 89.7 miles, along Highway 1. There is an actual community called Big Sur, which occupies a four-mile stretch roughly 65 miles north of San Simeon. Infrequent beach-access points dot the Big Sur coast. The more noteworthy among them are Pfeiffer Beach and Andrew Molera State Park, at the northern end of Big Sur.

Population: 1,300

Area Code: 408 **Zip Code:** 93920

Big Sur has inspired more verbiage than a dozen Norton anthologies. Poetry, prose, proclamations, postcards—you name it, and it has been written about Big Sur, one of the last great untamed, unregulated wilderness areas in the lower 48 states.

Maybe it's the jagged rocks in the water. Or the crashing waves flinging cataracts of foam in the air. Or the portentous fog that hangs over land and sea. Or the enticing mystery of nature at its most inhospitable—a raw ocean backed by the Santa Lucia Mountains and Los Padres National Forest. "Harsh and lovely," wrote local novelist Lillian Bos Ross, "held fast to their ancient loneliness by a sheer drop of 5,000 feet by a shoreless sea." Whatever it is, one is never at a loss for words when describing Big Sur. Yet in the final reckoning, most attempts to describe it are inadequate.

Still, some noble efforts have been made. Robinson Jeffers wrote his most heroic verse while living here. Novelist Richard Brautigan also mythologized the area, as did noted photographers Edward Weston and Ansel Adams, their visual record of Big Sur gracing many a coffee table. Nouveau salon painters continue the tradition of freeze-framing Big Sur, their efforts filling many a trendy gallery on the California coast.

Despite its obvious magnetism for artists and writers, it was not until itinerant savant and Brooklyn native Henry Miller moved to Big Sur in 1944 that the region gained widespread notice. The same man who sparked obscenity trials with his erotica turned to watercolors here. About his new Canaan, he wrote: "At dawn its majesty is almost painful to behold. That same prehistoric look. The look of always. Nature smiling at herself in the mirror of eternity."

Another writer, Jack Kerouac, came to Big Sur seeking solitude, briefly encamping here in 1960 to escape the wages of fame, which hounded him like a pack of baying beatniks. He lit out for a shack in a Big Sur canyon and managed to capture a piece of it in his novel *Big Sur*. "Big elbows of rock rising everywhere, sea caves within, seas plollicking all around inside them crashing out foams, the boom and pound on the sand, the sand dipping quick (no Malibu Beach here). Yet you turn and see the pleasant woods winging upcreek like a picture in Vermont. But you look up into the sky, bend way back, my God you're standing directly under that aerial bridge with its thin white line running from rock to rock and witless cars racing across it like dreams! From rock to rock! All the way down the raging coast!"

Enough of artistic inquiry. A few geographic facts are in order to distinguish Big Sur the place from Big Sur the state of mind. Big Sur stretches, roughly, from the San Luis Obispo County line to the Carmel River, just above Point Lobos, a distance of 90 miles. It extends to the east beyond Ventana Wilderness. All told, it covers 300 square miles (192,000 acres). The population of the region has hovered around 1,000 for decades, a stability attributable to the high price of available land, the scarcity of water, and the near impossibility of getting new structures approved under strict local ordinances. (The number of residents is now a whopping 1,300.) The largest part of coastal

Big Sur—the part that most visitors see along the cliff-hugging Pacific Coast Highway—is privately owned. The town of Big Sur is not really a town but a sparsely settled strand of inns, restaurants, and residences, most of which are hidden on backcountry ridges. "No Trespassing" and "No Beach Access" are familiar signs here, because the locals are hermits who don't want to be bothered.

The name Big Sur derives from a rare meeting of English and Spanish. "Sur" is taken from El Pais Grande del Sur, which means "the big country to the south." The name was bestowed by the Spanish at Carmel Mission in the late 1700s, denoting the impassable region along the coast. But many moons before the missions were built, the Esalen Indians inhabited the region. Their villages along the Big Sur Val-

Living with Big Sur

Other than glimpses gleaned from Henry Miller's later writings and curt chats with "hippie types" who camp here, we've never sated our fascination with, and fantasies about, what life in Big Sur must be like year-round. Maybe we're would-be utopians, longing for a community of 1,300 enlightened souls evenly spaced out along 90 miles of precipitous ridges and rugged shores. But, with habitations out of sight of the road, chance encounters with Big Sur residents are pretty much limited to head-on collisions on Highway 1.

That is, until we encountered a loquacious local at a Big Sur restaurant one evening. She was our "server," and when we told her of our longtime curiosity, she gladly entertained and enlightened us with tales of her 12 years of life here. Articulate, witty, self-effacing and yet self-assured, she was not averse to telling all, in the best sense. (Since Big Sur is a community where everybody knows their neighbor's business, we'll call her Angela to protect her identity.)

Angela came here from Pittsburgh, after getting a degree in social work that led to some unsatisfying success as a counselor for troubled souls. Deciding her long blonde hair and gentle spirit were not suited to life as resident counselor at a state prison, she came to Big Sur, where she has resided ever since. She has lived in many homes, hopping from one precious rental unit to another as they became available, and camping in a tent when they do not. Angela even had the ultimate Big Sur experience of living in Henry Miller's former digs on Partington Ridge, a mystical place now in disarray but which still attracts scores of rude interlopers. She is, in short, immersed in this seemingly invisible community, a gregarious soul living among hermits. She takes painting lessons from an elderly woman who serves as a sort of guru and wanders into the hills with her easel like Van Gogh at Arles. "So much comes up when you put oil on canvas," she says. "Who needs a psychiatrist?"

She also takes on "body work"—nutrition, health, hygiene, and massage. She grows herbs and English lavender, from which she makes medicinal potions. She is attractive and ageless. In Big Sur, no one agonizes over the issue of age as we do in the real world. Wrinkles betoken wisdom. What people do care about here is privacy. And though it's not apparent to the naked eye, our server insisted that things

 Map of Monterey County beaches—page 322

ley date back 3,000 years. They discovered an abundance of earthly delights at their disposal—plenty of fish and meat, as well as hot springs. Then the Spanish came to convert the contented Esalen to Christianity. The tribes died off soon thereafter. Today, one of the tribes' sacred springs is the centerpiece of the Esalen Institute, a spiritual organization blazing new trails in self-awareness.

The first-time visitor to Big Sur will take the Pacific Coast Highway in and out. For all intents and purposes, this is the only road through here. Though a few back roads exist, only one—the sometimes inaccessible Nacimiento-Fergusson Road—actually pierces the mountains, connecting with Highway 101, which lies 30 miles east. Other roads in the area are little more than dirt tracks, barely large

are changing in changeless Big Sur. Upon one of the back ridges, 25 new homes have been built where there was just one when she first arrived. Rumors have flown about Rush Limbaugh or Robin Williams or Ted Turner buying property. Then there are the stragglers and scavengers who think nothing of poking around someone's land looking for intrigue or the ghost of Henry Miller.

"As much as I love him, Henry Miller is long gone," Angela said. She also bemoaned the high property taxes reflected in her monthly rent, which force her to work three shifts at the restaurant to afford shelter. Then there's the summertime traffic snarl of tourists who take the spectacular drive along the Pacific Coast Highway and stop in for touristy souvenir baubles and burgers and whatnot.

Worst of all, the owner of the house where Angela lives—he's an organic agronomist in San Francisco—was threatening to kick her out of the apartment, allegedly to start a five-year agriculture experiment along "her" unblemished ridge. She'd been there five years herself, and "this was the first year the roof hasn't leaked," she says, exasperated but not embittered.

She'll be okay, she insists. She has enough hooks in the community to keep a roof over her head. She can always go back to the tent life. "That was okay when I was young, but...."

It doesn't seem fair, though we've seen it everywhere at the beach. People like our server, who have the lowest impact on the coastal environment, are the renters. They're the ones who intuitively know that life is temporary, so why try to own everything, mark off boundaries, make ever more money, rearrange nature to please some anal acquisitive bug that is never pleased anyway?

It's different here than it is in other free-spirited places. This is Big Sur. Invisible to the eye but nourishing to the spirit. Still, there are times even here when life becomes more disquieting than quiet.

As for those who own real estate in Big Sur in these uncertain times, we humbly issue this request: Don't sell off the land. The rest of the world is a motel lobby. Predictable. Bland. Big Sur is heaven.

enough for one car and best suited for four-wheel-drive vehicles.

The 90-mile passage through Big Sur on Highway 1 is as legendary as it is exhilarating. As a driving experience, it is unsurpassed. In 1966, Lady Bird Johnson proclaimed it the nation's first Scenic Highway. Today more cars and RVs lumber through here than through Yosemite National Park each year. Like a naturally occurring roller coaster, Highway 1 varies in elevation from 20 to 1,200 feet, in width from 18 to 24 feet, and in scenic splendor from "Oh, wow!" to "Harry, don't get too close!" Various points of interest along the road are designated not by address but by milepost from the south or north boundary. For example, "Milepost 28S/63N" means that you are 28 miles from the northern boundary and 63 miles from the southern boundary.

Before embarking on this epic drive, take a few precautions. Fill the gas tank. Make sure the tires and brakes are in good shape. Drive from north to south, if possible—the most breathtaking views are seen that way. Let the passengers do all the ogling. If you want a closer look, 300 turnouts have been carved into the roadside for that purpose. En route, the constantly changing landscape will captivate and enrapture you. It's the natural world's version of "Can you top this?" At points, the road might even nauseate you. Bring crackers, soda, and Dramamine, in case of car sickness. Some places, particularly a handful of beaches, are worth a side trip off Highway 1.

Strap yourself in and enjoy the ride of a lifetime.

Beaches

Because we've organized this guidebook moving from south to north, the wonders of Big Sur will be described in that direction. (Both north and south mileposts are provided in the practical beach information below, however.) It will help to carry a map of Big Sur with you. One can be found in *El Sur Grande*, a newspaper-style guide that identifies all pertinent landmarks. Pick up a free copy while you're in the area or contact the Big Sur Chamber of Commerce (address below) to have one mailed to you.

Some of the easiest coastal access in Big Sur can be found along a four-mile marine terrace at the south end, between Willow and Wild Cattle Creeks. **Willow Creek Picnic Area** and **Jade Cove** offer a scenic overview

Andrew Molera State Park

Location: In Big Sur, at Milepost 21.4S/68.3N on Highway 1.

Parking: $4 entrance fee per vehicle.

Hours: Sunrise to sunset.

Facilities: Rest rooms, picnic tables, and fire pits. There are 60 primitive campsites for tents. The fee is $3 per person, per night. No camping reservations.

Contact: For beach information, contact Big Sur Station, an information service of California State Parks, the U.S. Forest Service, and CalTrans, at (408) 667-2315.

See number 10 on page 322.

Garrapata State Park

Location: At the north end of Big Sur, next to turnouts 13 and 14 along Highway 1.

Parking: Free roadside turnouts.

Hours: Sunrise to sunset.

Facilities: None.

Contact: For beach information, contact Big Sur Station, an information service of California State Parks, the U.S. Forest Service, and CalTrans, at (408) 667-2315.

See number 11 on page 322.

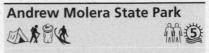

of the region's geologic treasures. Willow Creek is primarily a spot for a quick lunch—though an access leads to a rocky cove beach—while Jade Cove is worth a longer pause. At the Jade Cove access, you scale a stepladder over a fence and hike across a field of wildflowers to a dirt path that leads, via stumbling and sliding steps, down to a rocky beach. Visitors can scan the rocks and pebbles on shore for the mineral jade, specifically nephrite jade ("the stone of heaven"). Anything below the high-tide line is up for grabs, and some people make off with handsome hauls. As is always the case with a golden goose, though, people will pluck all the eggs. That is, amateur rock hounds and gallery-bound artists have picked so much of the nephrite, according to state authorities, that

Jade Cove

Location: In Big Sur, at Milepost 59.8S/29.9N on Highway 1.
Parking: Free parking lot.
Hours: Sunrise to sunset.
Facilities: None.
Contact: For beach information, contact Big Sur Station, an information service of California State Parks, the U.S. Forest Service, and CalTrans, at (408) 667-2315.
See number **2** on page 322.

Kirk Creek Campground

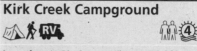

Location: In Big Sur, at Milepost 54.0S/35.7N on Highway 1.
Parking: Free parking lot.
Hours: Sunrise to sunset.
Facilities: Rest rooms, picnic tables, and fire pits. There are 33 tent and RV campsites. The fee is $15 per night. No camping reservations.
Contact: For beach information, contact Big Sur Station, an information service of California State Parks, the U.S. Forest Service, and CalTrans, at (408) 667-2315.
See number **5** on page 322.

Julia Pfeiffer Burns State Park

Location: In Big Sur, at Milepost 37.0S/52.7N on Highway 1. Note: There are beach overlooks but no beach access in this park.
Parking: $6 entrance fee per vehicle.
Hours: Sunrise to sunset.
Facilities: Rest rooms and picnic tables. There are two environmental campsites for tents. The fee is $16 per night. For camping reservations, call Destinet at (800) 444-7275.
Contact: For beach information, contact Big Sur Station, an information service of California State Parks, the U.S. Forest Service, and CalTrans, at (408) 667-2315.
See number **7** on page 322.

Limekiln State Park

Location: In Big Sur, at Milepost 52.1S/37.6N on Highway 1.
Parking: $6 entrance fee per vehicle.
Hours: 8 AM to 8 PM.
Facilities: Rest rooms, picnic tables, and fire pits. There are 43 tent and RV campsites. Fees are $19 to $21 per night. For camping reservations, call Destinet at (800) 444-7275.
Contact: For beach information, contact Limekiln State Park at (408) 625-4419.
See number **6** on page 322.

the Lands Commission is considering stepping in to monitor the activity. In 1971, divers took a 9,000-pound jade boulder worth $180,000. You can understand the temptation.

A half mile north of Jade Cove is **Sand Dollar Picnic Area and Beach**, consisting of tree-shaded picnic tables and a cove that can be reached by hiking across a field. The beach here got stripped of its sand during severe storms in January 1995. Natural processes may replenish it over time. A similar setting exists at the **Mill Creek Picnic Area**, although the beach is a bit rockier and the trail leading to it steeper. Forest Service campgrounds can be found at Plaskett Creek and Kirk Creek. Plaskett Creek Campground is a 43-siter located on the east side of Highway 1, nestled against the Santa Lucia Mountains nine miles south of the little town of Lucia. **Kirk Creek Campground** sits on the bluffs overlooking the ocean, four miles

Mill Creek Picnic Area

4

Location: In Big Sur, at Milepost 54.5S/35.2N on Highway 1.

Parking: Free parking lot.

Hours: Sunrise to sunset.

Facilities: Rest rooms, picnic tables, and fire pits.

Contact: For beach information, contact Big Sur Station, an information service of California State Parks, the U.S. Forest Service, and CalTrans, at (408) 667-2315.

See number 4 on page 322.

Partington Cove

4

Location: In Big Sur, at Milepost 35.2S/54.5N on Highway 1.

Parking: Free limited roadside parking.

Hours: Sunrise to sunset.

Facilities: None.

Contact: For beach information, contact Big Sur Station, an information service of California State Parks, the U.S. Forest Service, and CalTrans, at (408) 667-2315.

See number 8 on page 322.

Pfeiffer Beach

5

Location: From Highway 1 in Big Sur, turn west onto Sycamore Canyon Road (Milepost 27.1S/63.2N) and continue two miles to the beach.

Parking: Free parking lot.

Hours: Sunrise to sunset.

Facilities: None.

Contact: For beach information, contact Big Sur Station, an information service of California State Parks, the U.S. Forest Service, and CalTrans, at (408) 667-2315.

See number 9 on page 322.

Sand Dollar Picnic Area and Beach

4

Location: In Big Sur, at Milepost 59.3S/30.4N on Highway 1.

Parking: Free parking lot.

Hours: Sunrise to sunset.

Facilities: Rest rooms, picnic tables, and fire pits. Across Highway 1 is the entrance to Plaskett Creek Campground. There are 43 tent and RV campsites. The fee is $15 per night. No camping reservations.

Contact: For beach information, contact Big Sur Station, an information service of California State Parks, the U.S. Forest Service, and CalTrans, at (408) 667-2315.

See number 3 on page 322.

south of Lucia. Trails lead down to the water and up into Ventana Wilderness. Two miles north of Kirk Creek is the state park system's newest acquisition, **Limekiln State Park**. Formerly a private campground, it was acquired by the state and opened for business in the summer of 1995. Campsites are scattered in the redwoods and by the beach at the mouth of Limekiln Creek, so-called for the remnants of historic lime kilns found in the area.

After a dozen or so miles of hairpin turns, you come upon **Julia Pfeiffer Burns State Park**. A 3,580-acre day-use park whose chief scenic attraction is Waterfall Cove, it is arguably the most spectacular spot on the Big Sur coast. To find it requires a short hike along McWay Creek, which ends up plummeting 50 feet to the beach below. It is the only place on the California coast where a waterfall empties directly into the ocean. Major photo op here, and a lovely cove beach, to boot. Divers submerge with joy into the 1,680-acre underwater reserve. Two environmental campsites are available, requiring a half-mile hike out to a bluff overlooking the ocean.

Willow Creek Picnic Area

Location: In Big Sur, at Milepost 61.5S/28.2N on Highway 1

Parking: Free parking lot.

Hours: Sunrise to sunset.

Facilities: Rest rooms, picnic tables, and fire pits.

Contact: For beach information, contact Big Sur Station, an information service of California State Parks, the U.S. Forest Service, and CalTrans, at (408) 667-2315.

See number 1 on page 322.

Partington Cove is the site of a 110-foot tunnel burrowed into the rock in the 1880s by pirates, who stashed their booty here. Later, it served as a landing point for the early settlers and as a place for Prohibition-era bootleggers to bring liquor to shore. There is no official beach access at Partington Cove, but visitors can scout out a steep path to the small beach. It is marked by an iron gate and black mailbox on the ocean side of the highway, 1.8 miles north of Julia Pfeiffer Burns State Park.

Two miles up the road is the Coast Gallery (Milepost 33S/52N, 667-2301), where local artists exhibit their work. Housed in two enormous redwood barrels (each probably 100 feet wide), the gallery is a favorite stopping place for bus tours. Passengers pile out and plow through the art collection—some good, some bad, and some touristy (bronze sea otters, silver seagulls). What makes the Coast Gallery special is its extensive collection of original Henry Miller lithographs and watercolors. Miller devotees should also visit the Henry Miller Memorial Library, a few hundred yards up the road (see sidebar, "Henry Miller Memorial Library"). A bookshop and a café are attached to the gallery.

The first of Big Sur's truly great beaches lies five miles farther up the road. A poorly marked turnoff, Sycamore Canyon Road (Milepost 27.1S/63.2N), leads down to **Pfeiffer Beach**. The narrow two-mile dirt road takes you past inhabited Sycamore Canyon. Makeshift homes list among the trees like pine cones, testaments to the rough life still to be found in the wilderness (and a cautionary note to those who fantasize life here as an easy paradise). From the parking lot, a quarter-mile path leads through cypress trees to the beach. Miracle of miracles, Pfeiffer Beach is a wide sandy beach, bashed by waves that rush through sea caves and arches to the shore in foamy torrents. A strong undertow discourages swimming. No camping or fires are allowed, either.

Another mile on yields Pfeiffer-Big Sur State Park, a splendid 821-acre retreat along the east side of Highway 1, at the foot of the Santa Lucia Mountains along the Big Sur River Gorge. Set among redwoods, oaks, and meadows, the park beckons campers (offering 217 developed sites along the pristine Big Sur River at $14 a night) and hikers (there are half a dozen trails in the park, ranging from 0.3 to 4 miles). There's also an inn (see below). Some of the ancient, stately trees here predate the signing of the Magna Carta. Others, long dead, lie like toppled Greek columns in backwood groves. One of the more memorable hiking trails leads to lovely Pfeiffer Falls. The Pfeiffers, whose names adorn so much around here, were the first European immigrants to permanently settle here, arriving in 1869.

Five miles north, at **Andrew Molera State Park**, Big Sur's second greatest beach can be found. Molera allows public access to the ocean along a portion of Big Sur that is otherwise mostly held by the El Sur Cattle Ranch, which restricts public access with barbed-wire fences and nasty signs. (Subliminal message: boycott beef.) The largest state park in Big Sur, its 4,800 acres feature scenic trails through former pastureland and alongside the Big Sur River, an area particularly rich with bird life. The beach at Andrew Molera is one of the few strollable sand strips in Big Sur. Still, it's rock-backed and pounded by rough surf that sucks much of the sand out to sea and makes for hazardous swimming. A 60-site tent-only campground lies right above the ocean. Campers must pack in all gear on the half-mile trek from the parking lot, but it is not an arduous hike. The campground is a big, grassy common area; there's a formal limit of 350 campers per night, but they try not to turn anyone away.

Trails in the park allow for riverside, lagoonside, meadow, headland and bluff-top hikes. A private horse stable rents out the steeds for guided tours along what they call the "most spectacular ride in America." For reservations and information on horseback riding, call Molera Trail Rides, 625-8664.

Andrew Molera State Park was named for the grandson of Juan Bautista Roger Cooper, the original owner of the ranch that encompasses Molera Point. It is speculated that Cooper used his "Ranch of the South" to import goods without paying the high customs in Monterey. Beyond that, Molera was a legitimate dairy man, famous for his Monterey Jack cheese.

Five miles north of Andrew Molera, the Point Sur Light Station shines a beacon on coastal history and continues to warn oceangoing vessels of the treacherous waters off Point Sur. Built in 1889 on a volcanic rock 361 feet above the pounding surf, Point Sur is the only functioning lighthouse on the California coast with all of its original buildings intact. The Stanton Center in Monterey displays its original Fresnel lens (it could be seen 23 miles out to sea); today, the U.S. Coast Guard manages the station's automated light function and fog signal. Guided tours of the lighthouse, which is on the National Register of Historic Places, are given by docents on weekends. For information, call 625-4419.

Closer to the northern boundary of Big Sur—5.4 miles above Point Sur, to be exact—Highway 1 crosses Bixby Creek Bridge, one of the West Coast's most photogenic spans. This concrete arch, a true engineering marvel, is 700 feet long and towers 260 feet above the creek. It was the longest bridge of its kind in the world when built in 1932. Back when the local sea otter population had almost dwindled to zero, it is believed that the sole surviving male—the one from whom all others are now descended—lived as part of a colony in the waters beneath Bixby Creek Bridge.

Six more miles brings yet another spectacular Big Sur parkland that screams out at passersby who think they've seen it all. **Garrapata State Park** lays claim to over four miles of coastline among its 2,879 acres. The trails that lead down to the rugged beaches wind through several different kinds of coastal vegetation, including cactus and redwood groves. Garrapata (which means "tick" in Spanish) is

 Map of Monterey County beaches—page 322

Henry Miller Memorial Library

Could there be a more perfect setting than Big Sur for a literary legacy as exuberant as Henry Miller's? For years, even after Miller left Big Sur to live in semiseclusion in Pacific Palisades, his good friend Emil White created and ran the Henry Miller Memorial Library out of his Graves Canyon home, where the library still lives today—a glimpse of green serenity along a dusty curve in the Pacific Coast Highway. White's archive consisted of his personal collection of Miller's books, mementos, and watercolors. A charming raconteur, White was also a factotum and screener of Miller's endless army of admirers, with a weakness for nubile flesh even more pronounced than ol' Henry's. In some ways, White's congeniality made him the unofficial greeter for the entire Big Sur community.

When White died in 1989 (Miller died in 1980), the Henry Miller Memorial Library limped along under the loose reins of kindred spirits, but none had much administrative skill or plans to expand the Miller legacy. Then, in 1994, Magnun Toren arrived to offer a steadying hand to this endeavor. He cordially maintains the idyllic setting for the time being. He has also expanded White's original collection and is in the process of amassing a definitive archive of Miller's myriad works. The library is now owned and operated by the Big Sur Land Trust (see "Big Sur Land Trust" on page 337).

Too many literary shrines are as stiff as the writer's cadaver; a painful shuffling of feet ensues while a wooden tour guide recites vital statistics as you stroll by the writer's roped-off pen and pencil set. There's no such formality here. The Henry Miller Memorial Library is a sort of "serve yourself" kind of place, the spirit of which is found in a "Notice to Visitors" that Miller wrote and posted on his own door. A facsimile of Miller's note sits outside the Miller library, gently offering such words of wisdom as, "When you come, be so kind as to check your neuroses and psychoses at the gate. Gossip may be exchanged during the wee hours of the morning when the gremlins have left.... Let us do our best even if it gets us nowhere. In the midst of darkness there is light."

The Henry Miller Memorial Library is located at Milepost 29.7S/61.3N. It is open from 11 AM to 5 PM daily from May to October, and it's open on weekends only the rest of the year. There is no charge to enter, and a small gift store and bookshop are on the premises. For more information, contact the Henry Miller Memorial Library, Highway One, Big Sur, CA 93920; (408) 667-2347.

not for everyone, however, as the rough trails don't lend themselves to quick jaunts. The park trails are worth every step, offering spectacular views of the ocean, cavorting sea otters, and tidepools. Parking and day-use access to the park is free, but it is primitive. You pull your car over at either Turnout 13 (west side) or Turnout 14 (east side). The unmarked paths from Turnout 13 lead out to Sobranes Point and up to Whale Peak—a prime whale-watching promontory. As if to confirm our suspicions about the sort of hearty souls who'd seek this place out, the beach at Garrapata has a big reputation among the clothing-optional set.

Esalen Institute

The Esalen sulfur springs, a sacred spot to the original Native American inhabitants of Big Sur, are now home to the Esalen Institute, an outfit that offers workshops in "human potentialities." Their weekend and five-day retreats emphasize philosophy, religion, physical, and behavioral sciences. Many activities center around the hot waters themselves, which explains why they are off-limits to the public except from the God-forsaken hours of 1 AM until 3 AM (yes, that's 1 o'clock in the morning!). Not only are you limited to soaking your buns in the water at that hour, there's a $10 charge for the privilege (unless, of course, you're a guest at the institute). Additional fees are charged for access to the massage staff, who are among the world's best. Call well ahead of time to make a reservation.

Esalen is located at Milepost 41S/50N in Big Sur. To receive a catalog of programs offered by the Esalen Institute, call (408) 667-3000. To make reservations for the hot springs, call (408) 667-3047.

Finally, the northernmost visitable spot on the Big Sur coast is Point Lobos State Reserve, a locale so extraordinary it warrants its own write-up (see the entry on page 338).

Bunking Down

A complaint we've often heard about Big Sur is that it's hard to get a foot in the door, so to speak. That is, people who don't want to rough it by camping but still want to check out Big Sur are intimidated by the prospect of staying here. Fear not—there are plenty of places to stay. They've just been mandated into near invisibility. Built off the road, they blend into the landscape so well that if you speed through on the Pacific Coast Highway, you'll miss them. Do not look for glowing green "Holiday Inn" signs jacked a hundred feet in the air. There are no brand-name motel chains to be found between San Simeon and Carmel. Accommodations run the gamut from primitive campsites to award-winning luxury lodges. There are 10 campgrounds in the region, most on national forest or state park land. We've discussed six of them above, all of which are set along or close to the ocean. Reserve all accommodations in Big Sur, campsites included, in advance. The best month to visit, everyone seems to agree, is October.

For those who don't want to camp but still want to give nature a great big bear hug in the morning, the 62-unit **Big Sur Lodge** (Milepost 26.0S/63.7N, P.O. Box 190, 667-2171, $$) is the answer. It's actually a number of semiprivate cottages—duplexes, triplexes, and larger—scattered among the trees in Pfeiffer-Big Sur State Park. Clean and comfortable, the rooms come with fireplaces, and some have kitchens. There's even a heated swimming pool, a comfortable place to soak among the cool air and redwoods. In-season rates are reasonable ($89 to $159), and they drop lower still after September.

Anywhere else but in Big Sur, the **Glen Oaks Motel** (Milepost 66N/25S, 667-2105, $$) would be your typical No-Tell Motel. Its typicality makes it stand out here. Actually, it's a clean "post adobe" not unlike any other roadside mom-and-pop motel with 15 rooms. Speaking of mom, we had a tough time convincing the congenial matron to honor our reservation for a room with two beds here. But she eventually solved the problem with some last-minute room-shuffling. The two guys who pulled in after us weren't so lucky. They decided to make do with one bed, vowing to maintain "a discreet and dignified distance."

Later, we saw one of them dragging a chaise lounge into the room. No credit cards are accepted; bring plenty of cash.

Then there's Ventana, a resort that exists on a whole other plane entirely. Do you want a honeymoon you'll never forget, or simply an unexcelled retreat from everything, including the usual romantic resort affectations? If the answer is "yes," then the **Ventana Big Sur Country Inn Resort** (Milepost 62.7N/28.3S, 667-2331, $$$$) is your window on the wilderness and one of the finest resting spots anywhere. Everything is arranged to enhance the embrace of solitude, from the exposed wood architecture to the fireplaces in the rooms, the meditative grounds strung out across two heaven-focused ridge tops, the serenade of birds, the almost noiseless leaping of deer through the underbrush. At check-in, guests are issued a white, hooded terrycloth robe by a fellow who is as calm as a Zen master. After a day spent wandering around in your robe, you'll feel like a little bit like Gary Snyder. No wonder the motto here is "Nourish your spirit." (Follow your bliss, while you're at it!)

Further nourishing can be had at Ventana's health club, sauna, and library. An extensive array of massage services will cleanse away all worldly dust within you. Twelve masseuses are available, each with his or her own special expertise. One advertised being "certified in Postural Integration Deep Tissue work," while another promised to "sculpt your body using a blend of techniques from deep tissue to subtle cranial work and energy balancing." (Decisions, decisions!) Needless distractions are kept at a minimum, which explains the ambivalence toward kids as guests. In the words of the innkeepers: "Ventana was designed and is operated as a retreat for adults. We do not have any activities for children and therefore we do not encourage people to bring them here.... Many people have come here for a few days expressly to get away from their own children." Ah, if only all resorts purporting to be "escapes" were so enlightened—and honest.

If you want company, a continental breakfast and afternoon wine-and-cheese buffet are served in the library and lobby. It's a spread of delights the likes of which you won't encounter anywhere else, including the best granola we've ever tasted. Relative to the peerless amenities and priceless peace and quiet, room rates at Ventana are reasonable beyond any Zen master's expectations. (They range from $200 to $400 a night; there are 60 units in 12 buildings.) What is the sound of two beach bums smiling?

The newest arrival in Big Sur, and new arrivals are a glacial occurrence out here, is the **Post Ranch Inn** (P.O. Box 291, 667-2200, $$$$). It opened for business in the spring of 1992—the first new resort to grace the Big Sur coast in more than two decades. The 30 cabins are spread out among the redwoods along a ridge overlooking the ocean; some are designated "ocean houses," others "tree houses," for obvious reasons. Take your pick—wood or water?—and come prepared to pay handsomely for this splendid hermitage ($255 to $495 per night—ouch!).

Coastal Cuisine

No pre-prandial stroll can top the 10 minute walk from the Ventana Inn to the **Ventana Restaurant** (667-2331, $$$$). Lit by small shoe-level bulbs, the path crosses a woodland and ascends a ridge top with moon and stars above and wild game loping into the brush at ground level. The restaurant setting extends this sense of natural communion. Its understated elegance is conveyed in the lovely varnished wood and exposed beam interior. The dining room is surrounded by windows (*ventana* means "window" in Spanish) that look out on the 800-acre spread and is staffed by folks who seem positively clairvoyant about your needs. An 18-page wine list offers rare and interesting California vintages, plus well-chosen and affordable ones, including a custom Ventana label Chardonnay and Riesling. Chef David Daniels' ever-changing menu is kept to a manageable size, offering artfully prepared appetizers and main courses. We supped contentedly on petit filet mignon with a fresh corn pudding sauce and grilled rainbow trout with fresh spinach and new potatoes. And we slept contentedly afterward. In fact, we paused on the pathway back to the inn to lay on our backs and look up at the night sky, with the moon shining brightly. Pure magic.

At **Nepenthe** (Milepost 62.2N/28.8S, 667-2345, $$), the Ambrosiaburgers roll out of the kitchen like beer barrels in Milwaukee. They're essentially large hamburgers served with steak fries; Jack Kerouac referred to them as "Heavenburgers" in his overlooked novel *Big Sur*. While they won't win any major culinary awards, people come to Nepenthe (it means "no sorrow" in Greek) for more than the food. They come for the heavenly view, overlooking the ocean from 808 dazzling feet above sea level. Originally an adobe and redwood house built by a student of Frank Lloyd Wright and bought as a wedding gift for Rita Hayworth by Orson Welles, Nepenthe has been run as a restaurant by the same family since 1949.

Across the street from the Glen Oaks Motel (see "Bunking Down") is the **Glen Oaks Restaurant** (667-2623, $$$), a surprisingly nice dining spot, with fresh seafood and pasta dishes in a rustic setting. Two other old reliables are **Deetjen's Big Sur Inn** (Milepost 60.8N/30.2S, 667-2377, $$$) and the **River Inn** (Milepost 66.5N/24.5S, 667-2700, $$$). Deetjen's is the more offbeat of the two, with a shrine to Robinson Jeffers taking up one entire corner. The Norwegian-style complex includes a 14-room inn and a restaurant that serves breakfast and dinner. The River Inn lies in the Big Sur Valley, where the Big Sur River discharges into the ocean. If you're driving from north to south, plan for an early-morning chowdown at the River Inn. Try the trout and eggs, as one of us did many years ago during an unforgettable sojourn in the cool blue light of morning. The River Inn also includes an 18-unit motel, gas station, gift shop, and grocery store.

Night Moves

Nepenthe (Milepost 62.2N/28.8S, 667-2345) is as close to a public meeting spot as there is in this notoriously hermitic community. People nurse their drinks on the art-bedecked patio, warm their hands over a fire, and enjoy the views of the ocean and artwork, including a driftwood angel sculpture and eerie mosaic that are, like the restaurant, total originals.

As Kerouac poetically stated it in *Big Sur*, "There's the laughter of the loon in the shadow of the moon." In other words, stay where you are and savor the sounds of nature.

For More Information

Contact the Big Sur Chamber of Commerce, P.O. Box 87, Big Sur, CA 93920; (408) 667-2100. Or call Big Sur Station, an information service, at (408) 667-2315. For information on National Forest holdings, which encompass two million acres in five counties, contact Los Padres National Forest, 6144 Calle Real, Goleta, CA 93117; (805) 683-6711. For specific information on Ventana Wilderness, the 150,000-acre unit within the Los Padres National Forest system that includes the Big Sur coast and Santa Lucia Mountains, contact Monterey Ranger District Office, U.S. Forest Service, 406 South Mildred Avenue, King City, CA 93930; (408) 385-5434. A detailed topo map of Ventana Wilderness and a broader map of the entire Los Padres National Forest, including developed and undeveloped campgrounds and maintained and primitive hiking trails, are available for $3 each. Make checks payable to "USFS—Monterey Ranger District."

 Map of Monterey County beaches—page 322

Big Sur Land Trust

The future of Big Sur is a topic so hot that the locals have been burning up over it for the last two decades. At present, Big Sur is an untamed wilderness—geographically and politically. The majority of the coastal lands are in private hands, while the interior mostly falls under federal and state jurisdiction. Despite efforts to have Big Sur declared a National Seashore—and thus, theoretically, protected in perpetuity—it is not presently controlled by any governmental body.

Flying directly in the face of those who say Big Sur should be federally maintained, the Big Sur Land Trust (BSLT) was founded in 1978, with the goal of "retaining the land in its natural state." The Land Trust has devised various creative ways by which locals can donate their land without shafting their next of kin—e.g., Conservation Easement, Charitable Remainder Trust, and Life Estate. To date, more than 8,000 acres of the Big Sur coast and the Monterey Peninsula have been protected by the Land Trust.

The Land Trust's success notwithstanding, arguments on both sides of the issue carry merit. The locals don't want Big Sur to become another playland like Yosemite and Yellowstone, overrun with tourists and RVs. They also don't want to be told what to do in their backyard by outsiders, even by well-known ones like Robert Redford and the late Ansel Adams, both of whom led battles on Capitol Hill to annex Big Sur in the 1980s. As a show of good faith, they've adopted the stringent guidelines of the California Coastal Commission to ensure that no desecration of the land takes place. Still, the signs are there—"For Sale" signs on plots of land in southern Big Sur—and the potential for exploitation exists with the selling of land from generation to generation.

Although we agree in spirit with the local folks, one sentence in the Land Trust's glossy brochure gave us pause: "BSLT works in partnership with private landowners, assisting them in finding appropriate solutions for their particular land-use problems." Whether the Land Trust has any control over the mood of private landowners is still very much in question. A 1993 case pitted the hermitic whims of the local residents against the Land Trust itself. In 1987, BSLT bought some property with the agreement that the regional park district would buy the land from them, to be used for an "open-space preserve." This 1,340 acre preserve, in Mill Creek Canyon, would include hiking trails and a full-time ranger. But the snippy locals had a bizarre hissy fit that still has things tied up in bureaucratic knots.

"Why disturb what's perfect?" snipped one local resident (herself a recent arrival). "Private property is a worthwhile idea in this area."

Giving money to a cause that assists private landholders seems somewhat dubious to us. But it's a measure of how special Big Sur is that we'd pony up some dough to the Land Trust if we had any, our quibbles notwithstanding. For more information, contact the Big Sur Land Trust, P.O. Box 221864, Carmel, CA 93922; (408) 625-5523.

Point Lobos State Reserve

Location: Three miles south of Carmel on Highway 1 at Riley Ranch Road.

A rugged, primeval headland jutting out into fierce seas south of Carmel, **Point Lobos State Reserve** is billed as the "crown jewel of the California State Park system," a claim that's hard to dispute. The name derives from a much longer Spanish appellation that translates as "point of the sea wolves." In the 1700s and 1800s, it variously served as a livestock pasture, abalone cannery, whaling station, and shipping point for coal mined nearby. At one point, developers planned to subdivide it as Point Lobos City. Its purchase by a farsighted owner, A. M. Allan, forestalled such a fate. In 1933 Point Lobos was acquired by the Save the Redwoods League and donated to California to maintain as a parkland. Today it is jointly run by the state and the Point Lobos Natural History Association, whose volunteers lead nature walks and staff the reserve's information station. Trailers and campers are prohibited, as is any kind of camping. The reserve is open from 9 AM to 6 PM daily, and closes later in summer. Plan to arrive early, as the reserve has a "carrying capacity" of 450 people, and latecomers have to wait to gain entrance.

The reserve occupies 554 land acres and 750 submerged acres. With the addition of the latter in 1960, Point Lobos became the first underwater reserve in the nation. Roads take you only so far into the park, which is fine, since Point Lobos begs to be explored on foot. Pick up a detailed map at the entrance station outlining 14 possible hikes. The Cypress Grove Trail, an 0.8-mile loop, leads to the granite cliffs overlooking Pinnacle Cove and passes through one of two remaining natural stands of Monterey cypress in the world. (The reserve was originally established to protect these gnarled wonders.) Skittering ground squirrels, fields of yellow Lizard Tails and apricot-colored Sticky Monkey Flowers, and offshore rocks acrawl with sea lions and harbor seals are but a few of the sights to enjoy in this wild place.

Hikers who wish to traipse the perimeter should allow at least three hours to cover the six-mile trek from Bird Island to Granite Point. Beaches are tucked into several coves along the eastern side of the point's southern flank. Imagine our surprise to turn a corner on Bird Island Trail and catch sight of China Cove Beach, 100 feet below down a long staircase, looking like an emerald-green, icy counterpart to Tahiti. At the mouth of Gibson Creek, where the Bird Island and South Plateau Trails run out, you'll find Gibson Beach. It's separated from China Cove by Pelican Point, and is another swell spot for launching a dive or braving a swim in frigid waters. Both can be reached via wooden staircases. The one-mile South Shore Trail yields its own bounty of rocky, shell-strewn beaches between Sea Lion Point and the Bird Island parking area, including Hidden Beach, Weston Beach, and Sand Hill Cove. Just be careful while wandering out on the rocks and keep a mindful eye on the always unpredictable sea.

For More Information

Contact Point Lobos State Reserve, P.O. Box 62, Carmel, CA 93923; (408) 624-4909.

Point Lobos State Reserve

Location: South of Carmel, along Riley Ranch Road, off Highway 1.

Parking: $6 entrance fee per vehicle.

Hours: 9 AM to 6 PM PST (8 AM to 5 PM PDT)

Facilities: Rest rooms.

Contact: For beach information, contact Point Lobos State Reserve at (408) 624-4909.

See number 12 on page 322.

Carmel

Location: Carmel is situated off Highway 1 along Carmel Bay, between Monterey and Big Sur. It lies 130 miles south of San Francisco and 350 miles north of Los Angeles. Ocean Avenue is the main route through town, leading from Highway 1 to Carmel City Beach.
Population: 4,500
Area Code: 408 **Zip Code:** 93921

Among small American towns, Carmel is a celebrity. It can't travel to New York to appear on *The Late Show With David Letterman*, but in every other respect it fits the bill. Carmel is well known for being well known. It is a de rigueur stop on California bus-tour decathlons. Carmel's fame went into orbit when its most famous resident, Clint Eastwood, served a two-year term as mayor in the late 1980s. As is usually the case with a celebrity, strangers are drawn to it, desiring to bask in Carmel's limelight, as if proximity might confer some mysterious luster upon them as well.

Given its popular perception as a see-and-be-seen kind of place, Carmel can get mighty crowded. Cars gridlock the streets of this peninsular village and buses hog-tie it, discharging an endless cargo of sightseers who clog the sidewalks. Attracted by its air of sophistication, foreigners descend on Carmel in droves, chattering in heavily accented English or their own native tongues. However, the universal truth that binds all visitors is that beyond a visit to an established historical landmark such as the Carmel Mission no one can really figure out what there is to do in Carmel. Most visitors amble desultorily up and down Ocean Avenue, munch on sweets, pose for pictures in front of rocks and trees, duck into quaint shoppes to ogle overpriced goods, and pause thrice daily for meals.

So why all the fuss? For starters, Carmel is a gorgeous village, blessed with a natural setting that could turn any gutter-mouthed Dirty Harry into a beatific babbler like native son Robinson Jeffers. Carmelites refer to their community as "a village in a forest"—and that brief description neglects to mention the roiling ocean that crashes on the sugar-white sand of cypress-dotted Carmel City Beach. Nowhere in the world is the margin where land and sea meet as spectacular as it is in Monterey County from Carmel south through Point Lobos and Big Sur. That isn't just the lofty rhetoric of two itinerant beach bums; it comes close to being a verifiable truth. Moreover, the residents of Carmel are well educated, arts-savvy, and genuinely appreciative of their natural bounty.

So what's the problem? As bucolic as it may seem, the village of Carmel is swimming in contradictions. The election of "Mayor Clint" back in 1988 only let some of the most obvious ones out of the closet. Issues constantly being debated in this contentious community boil down to development vs. preservation, old (stodgy) vs. young (progressive), tourists vs. natives, and arts vs. sports. The last of these refers to what we perceive as an undeclared war between painters and golfers for the soul of Carmel, and the outcome will determine whether its future will be visionary or banal.

From a visitor's standpoint, this can lead to mixed messages. They want you, but they don't want you. Or, put another way, they don't want you but they do need you. Carmel derives 60 percent of its operating revenue from tourism, while homeowners—mostly retirees—provide a meager 11 percent. Many Carmelites frankly and publicly disdain the locustlike invasions that overrun their streets. Yet tourism is a necessary evil in Carmel, so they've made a deal with the devil in the interest of keeping the money flowing. This grudging tolerance can be seen in a cartoon that graced the front cover of a shopping guide (ca. 1987) published by the Carmel

Mayor Clint

Things had gotten out of hand in Carmel. Folks had grown weary of the way matters were being handled. Why, a developer might wait 10 years to get a building permit. The old guard and the new arrivals had squared off and were at each other's throats. There was a lot of grumbling, differences of opinion—plenty of talk about change, but no action. Cleaning up this mess was a job that called for the biggest, toughest gunslinger on the Monterey Peninsula—none other than Clint Eastwood.

In 1986, Eastwood—Carmel's most famous celebrity resident—ran for and won the position of mayor, garnering 75 percent of the vote. (A typical headline in the world press: "Dirty Harry Wins Election!") He held the post for a single two-year term. To some, his tenure was a raging success. To others, it was a big bother, given all the tourists who suddenly descended on Carmel to catch a glimpse of its movie-star mayor. For two years they trampled the flower beds in front of city hall and knocked down curbside trees with their cumbersome Winnebagos. "We don't want the kind of people that a movie draws," crowed one irate citizen.

Eastwood's mayoral stint did engender some political opposition as well. One group that kept tabs on his pro-development agenda was informally referred to as the "Get Clint Cult." Was he a good mayor? Depends on who you ask. Many who wanted to see Carmel act with more dispatch on matters of growth and development were pleased to have him cut through the red tape. But there were dissenters, such as the Carmel resident who wrote the following for the *San Jose Mercury News* late in Eastwood's term: "Though he is mayor, he is seldom seen by most Carmel residents and business people except at monthly city council meetings. His assistant

Business Association. On it, a Carmel native is shown squashing a tourist with a boulder dropped from a balcony, while his wife screams, "Damn it, Claude, we need a FEW tourists!"

Inside, the guide goes on to state: "You'll find no boardwalks here, no bikini-clad bathers wandering about the town munching hot dogs, and not a semblance of a neon sign anywhere." You'll also find scant parking, few sidewalks, and no lights on any street except Ocean Avenue, the main drag. Traffic coming into town is pure hell, backing up to Highway 1 as testy motorists inch their way along, engines and tempers overheating. Buses are not allowed past a certain point, so they wheeze down a side street to a special bus-berthing spot, discharging their blinking passengers into the brilliant sunlight to hoof it about hilly Carmel. Wheezing themselves after a few paces, this army of day-trippers marches obediently into the business district, only to discover that the principal diversion in this faux country village is shopping. Ocean Avenue is a miracle mile of bakeries, bistros, galleries, and gift shops where you can score anything from gold chains to goat cheese.

The setup appears to go something like this: they want you to breeze into Carmel in the morning, while away the day dropping loot on gifts, antiques, and meals, and then blow out of town before night falls. If you haven't taken the hint, Carmel rolls up the sidewalks after dark. Off of Ocean Avenue you'll find few streetlights to guide your steps, and the signs identifying street names are almost deliberately small, as if

handles all his phone calls and generally refers problems to other city officials.... No one else as mayor would be allowed such a privilege. No one could escape severe criticism for such an obvious distortion of the normal give-and-take between the mayor and his electorate. Especially in such a small town."

Still, celebrity politicos make good copy. Those monthly city hall meetings became major tourist photo ops. Between all the neck-craning moms, pops, and paparazzi, the city had to move them to a large public hall. Eastwood fired back at his enemies in his weekly column for the *Carmel Pine Cone*. He referred to his opponents as "wolves and coyotes...pack animals that tear their victims apart." He refused to grant a variance to a resident who wanted to enlarge his home. The same person, a former councilmember, had once given Eastwood trouble over design plans for a building he wanted to construct downtown. A letter-writer charged that at council meetings Eastwood "uses his gavel like a gun" to silence opposing views. One of his first acts as mayor was to replace four officials of the seven-member city planning commission with his own appointees. It was their "unfriendly" actions in denying him permission to build a retail-office complex next to Hog's Breath, his downtown Carmel restaurant, that drove him to run for mayor in the first place.

Now that the dust has cleared, Carmel doesn't appear to have changed all that radically. It's more business-friendly, to be sure, but to the outward eye of the occasional visitor it's no big deal. Having tasted political power, one wonders if Eastwood won't run for office again, this time at a higher level. How does President Dirty Harry sound to you?

to confound and frustrate outsiders. Despite the tug of war between pro-growth, slow-growth, and no-growth factions, Carmel zealously guards its privacy while its denizens espouse a political outlook that comes closer to Libertarianism than either of the mainstream political parties. One of the town newspapers, *Freedom of Speech*, sprinkles its antigovernment, Clinton-bashing cartoons and editorials with articles reprinted from such beacons of democracy as *Soldier of Fortune* magazine. Beneath a masthead of red, white, and blue, articles decrying all levels of government (federal, state, local) with barely concealed hysteria bordering on the paranoid mix uneasily with news of the latest arts festivals and updates on "wine events." It's cranky, crackpot stuff and all too revealing of the community mind-set.

The denizens of Carmel are wealthy. They strongly defend their right to acquire and preserve without interference and regulations (except for those they impose on others). They have essentially burned their bridges to the outside world, leaving a narrow footpath into the village accessible only to those bearing the passport of a credit card and/or ready cash. Though such an outlook may seem peevish and elitist, even we cannot argue with the results (though we'd quibble with the philosophy). They have tended their community well, keeping vulgar commercialism at arm's length. For that, you'll have to head up the peninsula, to Monterey or Seaside. Having viewed the entire coastline at close range, we'll concede that in certain cases enlightened despotism may be preferable to the unregulated rule of market forces. You see, they simply want Carmel to remain a pleasant seaside village. *Theirs*.

To that end, Carmel has been buttressing itself against growth and development since day one. Carmel got its start in 1906 as a seaside colony populated by artists and academics who had been displaced by the San Francisco's Great Earthquake. The village attracted a literary elite that included Jack London, Upton Sinclair, Sinclair Lewis, and Robinson Jeffers. Artists came as well. All were enchanted by the refreshing climate, gossamer sunlight, pine-forested hills, rugged cliffs, and powdered-sugar beaches of the Monterey Peninsula. From the beginning, the citizens of Carmel banded together to ensure that their way of life would be preserved. Restrictive zoning ordinances passed in the 1920s outlawed things that have become commonplace everywhere else, like tall buildings and neon signs. In 1929, Carmel wrote its guiding philosophy into the city charter: "The city of Carmel-by-the-Sea is...predominantly a residential city, wherein business and commerce are...subordinated to its residential character." Words alone are not enough to ensure such an outcome, so the town requires a permit for just about everything, from cutting down a bush to filming a movie scene. The result is governmental gridlock where nothing is granted, nothing gets done, and therefore nothing much changes.

Consequently, Carmel has the look—although crowds deny it the feel—of a rural English village. The same determined spirit not to yield to unchecked growth has remained viable throughout the century, although the composition of the town has shifted from artists to retirees. This is a polite way of saying that Carmel is evolving into a community that reveres golf tournaments more than Bach festivals. Still, there is a continuity between generations in that both resist the forces of change. Today, village preservation is pursued with an even greater twinge of fanaticism, since so much more can go wrong in the slipshod modern world. There are no street numbers in Carmel, for instance. No numbers means no addresses and, therefore, no mail delivery. The atavistic Carmelites must personally collect their mail at the local post office. When a small movement to number the houses of Carmel surfaced, an outspoken local newspaper and barometer of community opinion headlined its disparaging editorial, "What, a Subway Next?" When such issues arise, the battle cry becomes, "Save Carmel from Santa Cruz-itis!"

Carmel is a village of roughly 5,000 well-to-do souls—one-tenth the size of Santa Cruz—tucked into the lower left-hand corner of the Monterey Peninsula. It occupies exactly one square mile. The town starts at the top of a hill, where Ocean Avenue intersects Highway 1, and plunges steeply toward the ocean. It is along Ocean Avenue, as well as a block or two off the streets it crosses, that most of Carmel's upscale shops can be found. Inns and bed-and-breakfasts materialize closer to the water. Ocean Avenue gives out by Carmel City Beach, but the steep gradient continues down a hillock of pure white sand to the water's edge. Because traffic tends to snarl, particularly on weekends in season, you're best advised to park on the outskirts and walk into town. Be further advised that the retail shops in Carmel are not for the faint of pocketbook. Most of the older mom-and-pop shops have been squeezed out by places that can deal with $20,000 monthly rents for commercial space. A retailer must sell a hell of a lot of cashmere sweaters or pastel wall hangings to make ends meet, and you can believe that the cost of doing business in Carmel is passed along to the consumer.

Amid all this upscale merchandise, the old Carmel Mission remains an eminently worthwhile place for travelers to stop, rest, and refocus. Its full name is the Basilica of Mission San Carlos Borrodeo Del Rio Carmelo (cha cha cha). Constructed from 1793 to 1797, it was the

 Map of Monterey County beaches—page 322

personal favorite of the nine missions founded by Father Junipero Serra throughout California. The ambitious padre is, in fact, buried here. Architecturally, the mission is notable for its large, arcaded quadrangle, but there are also attractive gardens, informative exhibits, and a museum on the premises. A small donation is suggested. It is well worth it for the peace to be found inside the mission walls.

Carmel is indisputably a beautiful place, nestled among stands of pine and cypress against the ocean's indigo backdrop. It is a smogless village whose only drawback may be that too many people want to share in its natural bounty. For the lucky visitor who comes to stay for a few days or a week, Carmel makes a relaxing place to recharge the batteries in splendid surroundings. Day-trippers with harried itineraries will catch only a fleeting glimpse of what makes Carmel special. Natives condescendingly abide the influx of outsiders while trying to control their numbers and minimize the impact on Carmel's all-important quality of life. The question is, how do you moderate the crowds without creating bad feelings and severing the economic jugular that allows the town to endure in its visitor-subsidized prosperity? They're debating that very question day by day, issue by issue, with great caution in Carmel.

Beaches

A wide crescent between forested points, **Carmel City Beach** is among the most stunning settings for a beach on any coast, in any part of the world. The first glimpse of this shoreline is unforgettable. As it nears the water, Ocean Avenue slopes sharply downhill, ending at a sandy circle with a Monterey cypress in the center. A heart-stopping plunge down steep-sloped dunes leads to the ocean. Carmel City Beach will mesmerize you with the clarity of the air and vivid brightness of the light; the impregnable points of land that jut out on either side, framing the beachfront; the wind-sculpted cypress trees perched atop the dunes, their agonized contortions a testament to adaptive fortitude; the inscrutable metallic blue of the churning sea; and, finally, the resounding cymbal crash of huge, unforgiving waves.

It is a rough beach to swim on, but a beautiful one to look at. The beach forms a sandy amphitheater upon which people sit and watch the sun set, listen to the crashing breakers, and enjoy a breathtaking tableau of sun, sea, sky, and cypress. Beachgoers spread out towels and blankets and sun themselves on windless indentations on the high dunes. Had we been plopped here unawares, we might have believed ourselves to be on a beach along the Côte d'Azur. We heard more French accents

Carmel City Beach

5

Location: In Carmel, at the end of Ocean Avenue.

Parking: Metered street parking.

Hours: Sunrise to 10 PM.

Facilities: Rest rooms, picnic tables, and fire rings.

Contact: For beach information, contact the Carmel Department of Forests, Parks and Beaches at (408) 624-3543

See number 14 on page 322.

Carmel River State Beach

2

Location: One mile south of Carmel off Highway 1, along Scenic Road at Carmel Street.

Parking: Free parking lot.

Hours: Sunrise to sunset.

Facilities: Rest rooms.

Contact: For beach information, contact the Monterey District of the California Department of Parks and Recreation at (408) 649-2836.

See number 13 on page 322.

than English. If you're up for a walk, Scenic Road runs parallel to the ocean, affording bluff-top views and occasional access to the beach via staircases. The southernmost of these leads to **Carmel River State Beach**, a 100-acre sanctuary located on both sides of the mouth of the Carmel River. (More beach can be accessed south of here, off Ribera Road and Highway 1.) As the surf is hazardous and unpredictable, swimming is discouraged. Divers, however, enjoy exploring the offshore Carmel Bay Ecological Reserve. The Monterey pines and cypress are, incidentally, found nowhere else in the world.

Bunking Down

La Playa Hotel (Camino Real at Eighth Avenue, P.O. Box 900, 624-6476, $$$) easily makes our short list of best places to stay at the beach in California. It is a comfy, sun-dappled paradise by the sea. Located on a quiet side street, with the hotel on one side and roomy bungalows on the other, La Playa sprawls across some of the choicest commercial real estate in Carmel. Purple bougainvillea crawl across the rooftops. The gardens outside the bungalows are a riot of flowers and greenery. An interior courtyard, fragrant with floral scents, encloses a pool. Carmel's amazing beach is a few short blocks away. In the style of the finest lodging places, La Playa creates the feel of a serene world-within-a-world that immediately relaxes visitors and drains away cares. The slapping of waves on the shore is audible from the open windows of the cottages. We stayed at a guest cottage named Log Haven, a two-story wooden house with a pair of sizable bedrooms, a high-ceilinged living room with a fireplace and hardwood floors, a fully equipped kitchen, an upstairs sitting room, and lots of storage alcoves. The guest cottages run quite a bit more than rooms at the hotel, but offer enough room to accommodate several couples or a large family with no problem.

Another well-tended inn is the **Colonial Terrace Inn** (San Antonio and 13th Avenue, P.O. Box 1375, 624-2741, $$). It's as close as any hotel gets to the beach in Carmel. The inn's seven buildings are decorated with heritage furnishings in the colonial style, and no two are alike. All rooms have gas fireplaces, some look out on the ocean, the gardens are beautiful, and a complimentary continental breakfast is served each morning.

Several enticingly low-key inns can be found in the heart of Carmel, along Ocean Avenue near the beach. Nestled amid the oaks and pines of old Carmel, **Lobos Lodge** (Monte Verde at Ocean Avenue, P.O. Box L-1, 624-3874, $$) is rustic on the outside and modern on the inside. Each of the 29 units is decorated differently, and all have fireplaces and patios. Some of Carmel's heart-of-the-village inns verge on the cutesy, such as the **Lamp Lighter Inn** (Camino Real and Ocean Avenue, P.O. Box 604, 624-7372, $$), which is straight out of fairy-tale land. Its nine cottages have names like "Hansel and Gretel" and the "Blue Bird Room" and are painted to resemble gingerbread houses. The owner extends the fantasy by talking about the elves that play in the garden and referring to her associate as an "elf's helper." We were not certain she was playing with a full deck, but the Lamp Lighter Inn seems charming enough, and they also handle rentals at the four-room **Blue Pacific Inn**, located nearby in a garden setting. A note for those seeking to travel economically: room rates drop substantially during weekdays in winter.

South of Carmel, high on a hill overlooking the ocean, is the **Highlands Inn** (Highway 1, P.O. Box 1700, 624-3801, $$$$). The inn is a historic property, built in 1916, renovated and modernized in recent years. It is a smooth-running, first-class resort popular with honeymooners (1,000 weddings are performed here annually) and anyone looking for a great escape in the rural highlands overlooking the

 Map of Monterey County beaches—page 322

ocean along the Central Coast. The view of the Pacific from the inn's "Grand Lodge" is splendid; it's as if you're on the bow of a ship suspended over the ocean. Each room is outfitted with a fireplace and vista deck. You will pay dearly for such pampering: rooms start at $265 a night and top off close to $700. Yes, it's a sharp upward climb to the Highlands Inn, both for the car and the pocketbook, but worth it if both are running smoothly.

Coastal Cuisine

We're partial to a couple of restaurants outlying the village of Carmel proper. Both are run by the same ambitious owner, a chap named Tony Tollner (who's also readying a third restaurant in the area). **Rio Grill** (Rio Road and Highway 1, 625-5436, $$$) is an extremely popular Southwestern-themed restaurant located in the Crossroads Shopping Center, a mile or so outside the village where the land begins dropping to the Carmel Valley floor. Caricatures by celebrity folk artist George Rodrigue—a relocated Cajun painter whose trendy "blue dog" is a recurring motif—fill the walls of the bar and lobby area. A jar of crayons on each table encourages adults to doodle and scrawl on paper tablecloths before the food arrives. And what food! Most entrées are grilled or cooked in a wood-burning oven. Selections range from hearty fare like rabbit, duck, chicken, and ribs to daily seafood specials. Tollner's other restaurant, Tarpy's Roadhouse, is worth visiting as well (see the Monterey entry on page 356).

We'd be neglectful if we didn't mention the culinary houses of worship co-owned and operated by Carmel's most famous citizen, Clint Eastwood. By now, all the world knows about **Hog's Breath** (San Carlos Street and Fifth Avenue, 625-1044, $$), the restaurant and saloon that is an in-town landmark. If you didn't know about Eastwood's involvement, the menu would quickly tip you off. Selections include the Dirty Harry Burger, the Sudden Impact (Polish sausage, Monterey Jack, and jalapeños on a French roll), the Eiger Sandwich (roast beef), and the For a Few Dollars More steak dinner. (Hey, why not "Magnum Forcemeat"?) Tourists crowd in during the daytime and crane their necks in the unlikely hope of glimpsing Clint. What the crowds don't know is that the restaurant was shut down for a spell in 1988 owing to health-code violations "too numerous to list," according to Monterey County health inspectors. The kitchen was described as "filthy," suggesting there was some veracity in the naming of the Dirty Harry Burger. In defense of Hog's Breath, the kitchen's sanitation problems were in part due to bureaucratic delays in granting permits for renovation and enlargement. It was the owners' eight-year wait for permits that inspired Eastwood to run for mayor of Carmel. The restaurant has long since cleaned up its act, so cross Eastwood's named off the list of "Unforgiven." Eastwood has also acquired the **Mission Ranch** (26270 Dolores Street, 625-9040, $$$), a historic property on the Carmel River. The house specialties are stick-to-the-ribs ranch food. The menu is heavy on steaks—barbecue, prime rib—though you'll find a few catch-of-the-day specials as well. The prime rib comes in either a regular or "ranch" cut, the latter suggested for Paul Bunyan type appetites only.

Inside the village area, Carmel is the site of pricey, intimate restaurants hidden on side streets—places like **Creme Caramel** (San Carlos Avenue and Seventh Street, 624-0444, $$$$) and **Sans Souci** (Lincoln Street between Fifth and Sixth Avenues, 624-6220, $$$$). Both are long-established restaurants serving gourmet French cuisine in a cozy, romantic setting. Another restaurant of long-standing, this one with a strong seafood emphasis, is **Flaherty's Seafood Grill** (Dolores Street and Sixth Avenue, 625-1500, $$$). At Flaherty's the fish and shellfish come right off of local boats or are flown in fresh from the East Coast.

Worthy new arrivals on Carmel's culinary scene include the **Rain Forest Grill** (Su Vecino

Court, off Lincoln Street between Fifth and Sixth Avenues, 626-8837, $$$) and the **Grill On Ocean Avenue** (Ocean Avenue between Dolores and Lincoln Streets, 624-2569, $$$). The former brings Brazilian cuisine, with its sauces of lime, coconut, and hot pepper, to Carmel. The latter offers an eclectic array of creative dishes—French and California cuisine with Japanese grace notes—bringing yet another unique range of flavors to the discriminating palettes of Carmel. Finally, if you're looking for a good meal for a reasonable tab, check out the **Clam Box** (Mission Street and Fifth Avenue, 624-8597, $$). They don't stand on ceremony, but they do dole out memorable dishes like Rainbow Trout Meunière and Prawns Newburg—not to mention the namesake clam preparations—for what qualifies as rock-bottom prices in upscale Carmel. Eat here and you might have enough shekels left over to wander around to Hog's Breath for a nightcap. Read on.

Night Moves

While wandering the darkened streets of Carmel in search of **Hog's Breath** one foggy night, we ran into a wizened old soul looking like the ghost of Ernest Hemingway. We asked for directions and he instructed us to follow him. "I've lived here 30 years, and I still get lost," he said. We trailed the kindly codger as he winded his way through back streets and alley ways. All the while he kept up a steady stream of chatter, muttering about Eastwood's restaurant-cum-watering hole, which he variously referred to as "Hog's Butt" and "Clam Breath." We followed him through a rear entrance into the courtyard of Hog's Breath. Without turning around or breaking stride he bade us farewell for the night and exited through the front door.

There is virtually no other nighttime activity in the village of Carmel than the quiet boozing going on at Hog's Breath. They close around 1 AM, a little earlier or later depending on the crowd. We planted ourselves on the outdoor patio, where giant tree trunks gnarl their way out of the ground. The restaurant's interior is more intimate, with tables set off in alcoves for romantic tête-à-têtes. After a civilized drink or two, we groped our way back through the dark and fog to our inn, recalling the words of our self-appointed sage and sherpa: "The nightlife around here is strictly for the newly wed and nearly dead."

For More Information

Contact the Carmel Business Association, San Carlos Avenue between Fifth and Sixth Avenues, P.O. Box 4444, Carmel, CA 93921; (408) 624-2522.

Pebble Beach

Location: Three miles north of Carmel, along the 17 Mile Drive. Five separate gates provide access to the drive. The entrance fee is $6.50 per car.
Population: 4,300
Area Code: 408 **Zip Code:** 93953

We're not overly fond of Pebble Beach and the excessive privatization of its splendid coastline, so we'll be painlessly brief in our opprobrium. Pebble Beach is known for its two resorts (the Pebble Beach Lodge and the Inn at Spanish Bay), its five golf courses (notably the Pebble Beach Golf Links), and the 17 Mile Drive (see sidebar, "The 17 Mile Drive: A Must to Avoid"). The origins of Pebble Beach as a resort date back to 1887, with the construction of the grand Del Monte Hotel and a private scenic drive that circled the property. In 1915, the grandnephew of telegraph inventor Samuel Morse oversaw a full-tilt series of "improvements" to the property, including the construction of the Lodge at Pebble Beach, the laying out of the Pebble Beach Golf Links, and the paving of the 17 Mile Drive. Millionaires built seaside mansions on the property; the owner of one marble-faced palace went so far as to heat her private beach with underground pipes. In 1946, Bing Crosby began crooning a new tune as the impresario of an annual pro-am tournament played here that bore his name. (These days it's called the AT&T-Pebble Beach National Pro-Am Golf Championship.) In 1979, the whole shebang was sold to 20th-Century Fox. Now the Japanese own it. One of the new Nipponese owners was forced to issue a public apology after acting arrogantly. Since when has this been a departure from the norm in Pebble Beach?

Set along the western side of the Monterey Peninsula in the heart of the Del Monte Forest, Pebble Beach is private and restricted, accessible only through five pay-to-enter gates along the 17 Mile Drive. If you've won the lottery or made a killing in the market, perhaps you can afford to stay at the Lodge at Pebble Beach ($250 to $495 per night) or swing a set of clubs on its famed golf course ($225 for 12 holes) or dine at one of its fine restaurants (four-course prix-fixe dinner with wine, $60 per person). If

The 17 Mile Drive: A Must to Avoid

Chances are if you're coming to the Monterey Peninsula, the 17 Mile Drive is penciled in on your itinerary. Almost everyone succumbs, believing the hype that it is a "not-to-be-missed scenic drive through pine forests and groves of Monterey cypress and along a coastline of singular beauty."

From our perspective, you are wasting your time and money if you take the 17 Mile Drive. It would be a time-consuming bore if it were free, but the greedheads who live in Pebble Beach charge $6.50 for the dubious privilege of driving through their "private community." This is highway robbery, and we mean that literally. The money is not funneled into state or county coffers, nor does it benefit some worthy environmental cause. Instead, it goes to the Pebble Beach Company, now owned by a Japanese investment firm headquartered in Tokyo.

To add to the bottomless greed of it all, the brochure we were handed at the gate turned out to be a retail catalog for pricey golf wear from the *(continued on next page)*

The 17 Mile Drive: A Must to Avoid *(continued)*

Pebble Beach Lodge. Year after year, the 17 Mile Drive remains a large draw, recommended as one of the top attractions on the Monterey Peninsula. The scenery is not nearly as striking as the hundreds of miles of public highways along California's coastline that can be driven for free. The drive through Big Sur, 90 miles of non-golf-coursed coastal wonder, puts the 17 Mile Drive to shame and doesn't cost a penny.

When informed of our beach-book venture, the crabby, Walter Brennan–like gatekeeper barked: "If you quote from anything in the brochure, you've got to ask permission." Here's a quote from the brochure that says it all: "Fulfill your shopping desires by choosing from the ultimate in golf and tennis gear, jewelry, women's designer fashions, art, gift items, and more." We did not ask permission. Furthermore, we urge you to steer clear of Pebble Beach and stick to those parts of the coast that are, as they should be, free to all.

In fact, we'll save you the entrance fee into 17 Mile Drive, which you can apply toward the cost of buying this book for a friend or relative. Climb in the car with us as we pay the $6.50, drive through the gate, and see the sights. First, you pass miles of what looks like any well-to-do suburban neighborhood in America, trailing fuming buses and a line of other hoodwinked motorists looking for the overrated sights. Along a stretch where the road hugs the coastline, they've erected signs pointing to alleged photo ops like the "Restless Sea" and "Point Joe," which are just your average waves-slapping-rocks routine and nothing out of the ordinary for the Central Coast. But because the Pebble Beach Company has given them names and numbers and charged money to drive past them, people believe they're experiencing something unique and worthwhile. Or maybe they don't, judging from some of the comments we overheard.

Eventually, you pass the Pebble Beach Golf Links, a wondrous man-made study in the fine art of turning an elemental coastal forest into a denuded plain of overfertilized, close-cropped grass. We cruised onward. The sights were getting more sightless by the minute: earth-moving equipment, average-looking homes, charred trees. Even the "Lone Cypress"—the signature attraction of the 17 Mile Drive, and the pride and joy of Pebble Beach (it's part of their corporate logo)—is down on its heels, having become ridden with termites. It seems that vandals tried to burn the tree 12 years ago—proving there's no crime so perverse that someone won't eventually think to attempt it in California—and now termites have invaded the tree's weakened, charred, ocean-facing side. Not to worry! The Pebble Beach Company is nursing a replacement Lone Cypress in a secluded spot.

After a while, we couldn't wait to exit. We had a parting taunt ready for the gatekeeper, but a sign said "Do Not Stop At Gate" on the way out, presumably sparing the hired hands a chewing out from hotheaded tourists now $6.50, two hours, and one gallon of gas poorer.

two of you share a high-end room, the cost of an overnight stay, a game of golf, and a meal would total $1,065 plus tax and gratuities. On the positive side, they will refund the cost of passing through the 17 Mile Drive toll gate if you're laying in at one of the lodges. That brings the pretax total of your one-night, one-meal, one-game stay down to $1,058.50 per couple.

Beaches

Believe it or not, there are actually some public beaches around Spanish Bay. No doubt they are a grudging concession from the developers exacted by the California Coastal Commission in exchange for permit approvals. From the junction of Asilomar Boulevard and Sunset Drive in Pacific Grove, a biking and hiking path called the Spanish Bay Recreation Trail leads through the forest behind the Inn at Spanish Bay, joining up with the 17 Mile Drive and its procession of small cove beaches a short distance later. It also intersects a boardwalk that leads from the hotel lobby over the dunes and out to **North** and **South Moss Beach**, where you can sun yourself without spending a fortune (or a night). The best surfing is found at **Spanish Bay**—"a half-mile of smooth beach surf," according to our bard of the longboard, Bank Wright—which frugal surfers get to by hiking from Asilomar State Beach. One of Pebble Beach's more notable cove beaches is **Fanshell Beach**, a north-

Fanshell Beach

2

Location: In Pebble Beach, along Signal Hill Road at the 17 Mile Drive.

Parking: Free parking lot (after paying $6.50 to enter the 17 Mile Drive).

Hours: Entrance booths onto the 17 Mile Drive are closed to nonresidents of Pebble Beach and nonguests of its lodges at times of day that vary by season. Call for hours.

Facilities: None.

Contact: For beach information, contact the Pebble Beach Company at (408) 649-8500.

See number 15 on page 322.

Moss Beach

3

Location: In Pebble Beach, north of Point Joe along Spanish Bay Road, which is accessible via both ends of the 17 Mile Drive.

Parking: Free parking lot (after paying $6.50 to enter the 17 Mile Drive).

Hours: Entrance booths onto the 17 Mile Drive are closed to nonresidents of Pebble Beach and nonguests of its lodges at times of day that vary by season. Call for hours.

Facilities: None.

Contact: For beach information, contact the Pebble Beach Company at (408) 649-8500.

See number 16 on page 322.

Spanish Bay

3

Location: In Pebble Beach, behind the Inn at Spanish Bay, along the Spanish Bay Recreation Trail.

Parking: Free parking lot (after paying $6.50 to enter 17 Mile Drive).

Hours: Entrance booths onto the 17 Mile Drive are closed to nonresidents of Pebble Beach and nonguests of its lodges at times of day that vary by season. Call for hours.

Facilities: None.

Contact: For beach information, contact the Pebble Beach Company at (408) 649-8500.

See number 17 on page 322.

facing sugar-textured sand beach located at Signal Road and 17 Mile Drive.

Bunking Down

Your choices are the **Lodge at Pebble Beach** (17 Mile Drive, 624-3811, $$$$) or the new kid on the block, the **Inn at Spanish Bay** (2700 17 Mile Drive, 647-7500, $$$$). In neither place will you lack for comfort. Each has a private beach, golf courses, tennis, pools, bikes, horses, health club, hiking trails, restaurants, stores, picnic tables, patios, balconies, and fireplaces. In addition the Lodge at Pebble Beach has a post office and bank. Are we leaving anything out? The Inn at Spanish Bay is described as the more "casual" of the two, which means you get a bit of a break on the room rate: $245 to $350 a night for a double room at the Inn at Spanish Bay vs. $295 to $450 at the Lodge at Pebble Beach. A top of the line suite at the latter goes for a whopping—brace yourself—$1,800 a night.

Coastal Cuisine

The celebrated restaurants at the Pebble Beach resorts are **Club XIX** (Lodge at Pebble Beach, 624-3811, $$$$) and the **Bay Club** (Inn at Spanish Bay, 647-7500, $$$$). Club XIX serves a French country menu, while the Bay Club tends toward Northern Italian. Both are quite good, and both so expensive that (as the cliché goes) if you have to ask how much it is, you probably shouldn't be here. Club XIX is especially *mahvelous.* Dinner for two will cost around $90, exclusive of beverage, tax, and tip.

For More Information

Contact the Pebble Beach Company, 2700 17 Mile Drive, Pebble Beach, CA 93953; (408) 649-8500.

Pacific Grove

Location: Adjacent to Monterey, Pacific Coast can be reached off Highway 1 from the south by taking the Highway 68 East exit and from the north via Del Monte Boulevard. Lighthouse Avenue is the main street through town, while Palm and Ocean View Boulevards run along the waterfront. The west-facing Asilomar State Beach is the principal beach in the area.
Population: 16,500
Area Code: 408 **Zip Code:** 93950

Pacific Grove is the shy but beautiful daughter of the Monterey Peninsula. Hidden by trees and cooled by steady winds off Monterey Bay, this modest seaside village of 16,000 is a place that values a sensible regimen of spiritual nourishment, moderate exercise, fresh food, and lots of beauty rest. She's not a bit covetous of her peninsular siblings' popularity. Pacific Grove is content to let Carmel, Pebble Beach, and Monterey deal with the vulgarities of fame.

This attitude comes with the territory. More hometown than boomtown, Pacific Grove has led a quiet, ascetic life since her birth in 1875 as a "Christian seaside resort." The original 100 acres of pine-, oak-, and cypress-covered wilderness that make up the central grid of the town were marked off by the Methodist Episcopal Church for use as a camp-meeting retreat. The first camp meeting was held on August 8, 1875, and the lots were sold in 30- by 60-foot increments—large enough to accommodate a substantial tent. But a crowd of 450 worshippers turned out, more than had been anticipated, and in the ensuing years still more arrived. When summer rolled around, Pacific Grove became a virtual tent city. At summer's end, the wooden frames were left

 Map of Monterey County beaches—page 322

standing while the tents were unfurled and stored in Chautauqua Hall, a utilitarian wood structure built in 1879 for the "presentation of moral attractions."

With this many people seeking it out for solace, Pacific Grove could not remain a simple religious retreat for long. In 1889, a permanent, year-round population of 1,300 incorporated a square-mile area of woodlands, and the town was created. The tents disappeared, replaced by tiny board-and-batten cottages, some built directly on the old frames. Larger Victorian dwellings were also built. These homes, along with the original churches, Chautauqua Hall and the Point Pinos Lighthouse, still stand in Pacific Grove as unpretentious reminders of a quiet past.

This is not to imply that Pacific Grove is a spinster living among dusty hymn books and faded memories. On the contrary, her original homes are in good repair and constant use as residences, inns, and offices—and their rising real estate value has begun pricing this "last hometown" almost out of the reach of the middle-class folks that have always been its mainstay. Most of the homes have plaques on the front door that identify the original owner and the year of its construction. In terms of area, Pacific Grove embraces a choice corner of the wild Monterey Peninsula. You enter the town through a forest, and by the time you reach the seaside retreat you might as well have stepped back a century in time.

A full day can be spent hiking around Pacific Grove, admiring her restorations and resilience. An especially rewarding experience is the Pacific Grove Historic Walking Tour, an entertaining packet dispensed by the Chamber of Commerce from their neat little office at Forest and Central Avenues. They've devised it as a scavenger hunt, and to make sure you've taken it in, they include a step-by-step quiz. You're supposed to answer each question before moving on to the next site. For example, "What is interesting about the two squid in their bottles?" and "What animal serves to show wind direction at the peak of their roof?" Your efforts will be rewarded with a patch and a thorough knowledge of Victorian-era California trivia.

The most informative tour-stop is the Pacific Grove Museum of Natural History (165 Forest Avenue, 648-3116). Founded in 1881, it's one of the best of its size in the country. It's also free of charge, though you'll be moved to give a donation. In two floors of gallery space, every facet of Monterey County's rich natural history is showcased. This includes insects, rodents, birds (400 species), fish, reptiles, rocks, fossils, Native Americana, and the town's evocative symbol, the monarch butterfly (*Danaus plexippus*).

A more appropriate mascot could not be found for Pacific Grove, which, when it gets the slightest bit of boosterism, bills itself as "Butterfly Town, U.S.A." Every year, thousands of orange-and-black monarchs migrate to the pine groves nearby. They arrive on November 1st and leave by March 1st. On dull winter days, they hang in thick clusters from the trees, but on warm, sunny days they swoop all over town. The city protects these fluttering critters, imposing fines of up to $1,000 for "molesting butterflies." This same ordinance asks citizens to "protect the butterflies in every way possible from serious harm and possible extinction by brutal and heartless people." If you don't want to be assaulted by a mob of angry matrons wielding antique butter churns, then you'd better leave the sweet little things be.

On the other hand, you may never see a monarch butterfly. They're gone by summer and are sometimes undetectable in winter. Their wings fold inward, so that only their neutral-colored undersides are visible. The distinctive, lovely markings are seen only by those with the patience to look closely. The same is true of Pacific Grove. The closer you look at it, the more of its charming detail and coloring will be revealed.

Beaches

For so understated a town, Pacific Grove is actually quite large in terms of area. While the old historic neighborhoods can be pleasantly strolled in an afternoon, the ruggedly beautiful shoreline goes on for miles, especially in and around Asilomar State Beach. The beaches beg to be explored on bicycle. In fact, Pacific Grove is a peninsula within a peninsula. The terrain out here is relatively flat, the roads less traveled by cars, and the neighborhoods safer than in Monterey. The Pacific Grove Bicycle Trail solves all your beachcombing problems. It starts at the south near Spanish Bay, cuts through Asilomar, Point Pinos, and Lover's Point, and then hooks up with the more heavily trafficked Monterey Bay Recreational Trail near the Monterey Bay Aquarium. The best place to rent wheels is Adventures by the Sea (372-1807), located directly on the beach at Lover's Point, just off the bike trail. (They also rent kayaks, diving gear, and so forth for those who want to brave the bay.) From there, one can continue north, through Monterey and up to Seaside—quite a haul, though it gets progressively less meditative with each passing mile.

Back at Spanish Bay, one comes face to face with the enmity that other Monterey Peninsula residents feel toward their Pebble Beach neighbors. This was once the most exquisite cove beach in the area, a favorite with locals, surfers, artists, and photographers. Now, it's the backdrop for a luxury resort (the Inn at Spanish Bay and its adjoining golf course, the Links at Spanish Bay), which, after years of heated legal dickering, was finally approved by the local zoning board. They must have been out of their sand bunkers! To make it worse, the beach at Spanish Bay is private. Why don't they just complete the deal by building a crocodile-infested moat around the compound? Ansel Adams, whose gallery is located in Pebble Beach, would be appalled.

There is a way to circumvent this privacy. Take the hiking trail at nearby Asilomar State Beach that leads, via a wooden boardwalk, to

Asilomar State Beach

Location: In Pacific Grove, along Sunset Drive between Asilomar and Jewel Avenues.

Parking: Free street parking.

Hours: Sunrise to sunset.

Facilities: Rest rooms and showers.

Contact: For beach information, contact Asilomar State Beach at (408) 372-4076.

See number 18 on page 322.

Lover's Point

Location: In Pacific Grove, along Ocean View Boulevard at 17th Street.

Parking: Free parking lot.

Hours: Sunrise to 10 PM.

Facilities: Rest rooms, picnic tables, and barbecue grills.

Contact: For beach information, contact the Pacific Grove Parks Department at (408) 648-3130.

See number 19 on page 322.

Shoreline Park

Location: In Monterey, along Ocean View Boulevard between Lovers Point and Point Cabrillo.

Parking: Free street parking.

Hours: 6 AM to 10 PM.

Facilities: None.

Contact: For beach information, contact the Monterey Parks Department at (408) 648-3860.

See number 20 on page 322.

the Inn at Spanish Bay's parking lot. Continue walking, pausing long enough to thumb your nose at the resort. You will soon hook up with the Coastal Bluff Hiking Trail, which leads to Point Joe, the most scenic spot on the overly hyped 17 Mile Drive. You will be standing on the beach itself—not viewing it from some coerced overlook—and you will have saved $6.50, the tariff to enter the 17 Mile Drive by car. The view? Imagine Ansel Adams' finest photograph.

Located off Sunset Drive (Highway 68) and Asilomar Avenue, **Asilomar State Beach** is a meditative mix of rocky headlands, tide pools, and cove beaches. The beach is a half mile of sand backed by healthy grass-covered dune fields that stretch for hundreds of yards toward the Asilomar Conference Grounds. It's popular with surfers, divers, and sunbathers. Parking and day use are free at Asilomar State Beach.

The bike trail courses around the rocky headlands at Point Pinos and the Pacific Grove Shoreline Marine Refuge, a feast for the eyes. The beaches here are more for browsing than swimming, with many rich tidepools but sand and pebbles too coarse for bare feet. Pretend you're a seagull soaring above this buffet, which is probably what all those birders sitting in their cars with binoculars are doing. The waves create a teeming stew of fish, shells, kelp fronds, sea grapes, starfish, and sea grass. These are the same tidepools that inspired John Steinbeck and his hero Doc Ricketts in the novel *Cannery Row*. (Steinbeck: "It is a fabulous place: when the tide is in, a wave-churned basin, creamy with foam...but when the tide goes out the little water world becomes quiet and lovely, fantastic with hurrying, fighting, feeding, breeding animals.") His grandparents had a house nearby, now a modest John Steinbeck Memorial Museum (222 Central Avenue, 373-6976).

Speaking of literary inspiration, Robert Louis Stevenson spent many ecstatic hours in Pacific Grove, too. He sat out at Point Pinos—the entrance to Monterey Bay—perhaps staring longingly toward Tahiti. The Point Pinos Lighthouse, built in 1855, is the oldest light station in continuous service on the West Coast, guiding navigators through these sometimes rugged waters. The building, lenses, and prisms are all original, and they can be viewed by the public on Saturdays and Sundays, between 1 PM and 4 PM. (For information, call the lighthouse at 648-3116.)

Although surfers love Asilomar State Beach in the winter—when waves reach heights of eight feet—the heaviest bombers come to Point Pinos. Between Point Pinos and Lover's Point is an area known as "Boneyards," where the surf breaks perilously close to the rocky headlands. At high tide, do-or-die surfers consider this spot a must. Families gravitate to **Lover's Point**, a large, grassy area with volleyball courts, a baby's swimming pool, snack bar, rest rooms, and sandy beaches. The surf here is nowhere near as rough as that at Point Pinos. The entire area is lined with grassy parks set on bluff tops above the shore, along which runs the Monterey Peninsula Pedestrian Trail, a paved pathway for walkers and cyclists. This linear bayfront green passes and encompasses a series of small parks set back from the bay—including Berwick Park, Greenwood Park, and Andy Jacobsen Park. Collectively, the parks are known as **Shoreline Park** and offer access to pebbly pocket beaches here and there via short, sloping trails. Benches provide strollers with ample rest stops and offer further proof that Pacific Grove may indeed be the Monterey Peninsula's last real hometown. Finally, this same area—from Asilomar to Lover's Point—is a great promontory from which to watch whales migrate in the winter.

Also in the immediate area is a golfing opportunity par excellence, one of the few we wholeheartedly endorse at the beach. Pacific Grove Municipal Golf Course (77 Asilomar Boulevard, 648-3117) is a pleasant, low-key alternative to Pebble Beach's overpriced "links." It's a truly a public course with the same stunning scenery. The fairway of the 16th hole, for example, runs alongside the Point Pinos Lighthouse. The greens fees are reasonable ($24 for 18 holes, as opposed to $225 at Pebble Beach), the staff friendly, and the manners decidedly casual.

Bunking Down

The **Asilomar Conference Center** (800 Asilomar Avenue, 372-8016, $$) might just be the best bargain on the Monterey Peninsula. Don't let the name put you off. A conference at Asilomar is as likely to be a quiet family retreat as a meeting of corporate eager beavers spouting sales figures and studying pie charts. Founded in 1913 by the YWCA as the premier "chautauqua" in California, the Asilomar Conference Center is now run on a nonprofit basis by the California State Park System. The original 11 buildings (all National Historical Landmarks) were designed by Julia Morgan, the San Francisco architect responsible for Hearst Castle at San Simeon. They're spread out among 105 acres of Monterey pines and cypress, with wooden walkways leading across the dunes to the state beach. Facing due west, Asilomar is treated to stunning sunsets, and its 28 woodsy lodges have appealingly rustic names like "Willow Inn" and "Oak Knoll." Though conference facilities are available, guests need not be part of a group to come here. A full breakfast, served cafeteria-style in a large hall, comes with the room. It's like being back at camp.

The rest of the town's accommodations are similarly neat, trim, low-key and/or historic, making Pacific Grove the ideal place to stay if you're laying over on the peninsula. Options range from small motels like the **Larchwood Inn** (next to Asilomar at 740 Crocker Avenue, 373-1114, $$) to the **Lighthouse Lodge and Suites** (1249 Lighthouse Avenue, 655-2111, $$). The latter is set among the shady acres close to Point Pinos Lighthouse, virtually guaranteeing a quiet vacation.

Pacific Grove is probably best known as a happy hunting ground for bed-and-breakfast inns, original Victorian homes that have been lovingly converted into lodgings. Several excellent ones include the **Green Gables Inn** (104 Fifth Street, 375-2095, $$) and the **Gosby House** (643 Lighthouse Avenue, 375-1287, $$). The Green Gables is situated on a quiet cove, while the Gosby House is "in the neighborhood," on the town's main thoroughfare. Both provide ideal escapes from modern civilization, offering more privacy than the average B&B amid trappings of quaint Victorian splendor that the old queen herself would definitely have approved. The Gosby House has been an inn since it was built in 1887, its earliest guests having been pilgrims to the camp meetings. It has a quiet garden and courtyard, and the 22 rooms (7 with private entrances) are filled with period furnishings, artwork, stuffed bears, and McGuffey's Readers. Both inns are very reasonably priced ($85 to $130) for what you get.

Coastal Cuisine

The Monterey Peninsula is now marketing itself, in a low-key way, as the "Provence of California," and indeed a revised approach to cuisine is developing around the abundant fresh local produce and seafood. It's little wonder when 80 percent of the world's broccoli and strawberries are grown in the vicinity, as are large percentages of artichokes, grapes, lettuce, and ranch-raised game. **Fandango** (223 17th Street, 372-3456, $$$) is the first of several restaurants to add to your dinner wish list. Run by the ever-pleasant (and present) Pierre Bain, Fandango resembles a villa in the south of France. It's as real as the owner, who comes from a family restaurant tradition dating back 250 years in the Basque region. Prior to opening Fandango with his wife, Bain was at Club 19 in Pebble Beach.

The experience of eating here is top of the line, the menu prices eminently fair and affordable. As an appetizer, the Veloute Bongo Bongo

 Map of Monterey County beaches—page 322

Paella Fandango

Here's a recipe for Paella Fandango, one of the signature dishes served at Fandango in Pacific Grove. Fandango is among our favorite restaurants on the entire California coast. Chef Pierre Bain's recipe for this classic Spanish dish is relatively easy to prepare and delicious beyond belief. In Bain's own words, "If you follow the recipe, it turns out perfectly every time." Al buon gusto!

1/2 cup olive oil
1 large onion, chopped
2 cloves garlic, chopped
2 large tomatoes, diced
1 each red and yellow bell pepper, cut in strips
2 cups uncooked white rice
8 cups chicken broth
3 tablespoons fresh parsley, chopped
2 large pinches saffron threads
2 chicken breasts (cut into 4–5 pieces each)
1/2 pound chorizo sausage, cut into 1/2-inch slices
1/2 pound scallops
1/2 pound shrimp, peeled with tails intact
1/2 pound calamari
8–10 little neck clams
8–10 mussels
1 cup peas, fresh or frozen
salt, pepper, cayenne

In a skillet, heat olive oil and add onion, garlic, tomatoes, and bell peppers. Sauté until limp. Add white rice and chicken broth, and bring to a boil. Add the parsley and saffron and cook for 20 minutes at a simmer. Add the remaining ingredients and cook until done, about 20 to 40 minutes. Season to taste with salt, pepper, and cayenne, and serve. (Note: green pepper can be substituted for red and/or yellow.) Serves 8.

is hard to top. It's a thick, hearty soup made from fresh spinach, oysters, and cognac. The house specialty is Paella Fandango (see sidebar, "Paella Fandango"), a veritable fishing boat of goodies, including littleneck clams, scallops, calamari, shrimp, mussels, chicken, and much more. Other specialties include rack of lamb Provençal, Basque-style lamb shank, and mesquite-grilled salmon and swordfish.

The locals' favorite seafood venue is the **Fishwife at Asilomar Beach** (1196 Sunset Drive, 375-7107, $$). The freshest catches are served with a Caribbean flavor that consistently wins "Best Seafood" awards for the entire peninsula. The house specialties are Snapper Cancun (seasoned with achiote and topped with salsa brava), Prawns Belize, Calamari Abalone-Style, fish chowder, and Key lime pie. The setting is casual, the prices are right, and the line is out the door. The Fishwife is so successful that a second one has opened in Seaside (Fishwife Seafood Café, 789 Trinity Avenue, 394-2027), the nondescript oceanfront town grafted onto the flanks of Monterey.

Another longtime favorite is the **Tinnery** (631 Ocean View Boulevard, 646-1040, $$), located right on the water at Lover's Point. It's not exactly gourmet cuisine but by Pacific Grove's standards it's affordable family dining. The Tinnery is staffed by friendly, wholesome locals, and the dining room has a peerless bay view. At sunset, you can watch fishing boats returning to Monterey, and on clear days you can see as far as Moss Landing and Santa Cruz, way on the other side of the bay. After you're as stuffed as a halibut, take an after-dinner stroll along Lover's Point before retiring to your room at the inn.

Another longtime resident of the Pacific Grove dining scene is the **Old Bath House** (620 Ocean View Boulevard, 375-5195, $$$$), a pricey place that does unusual things with seafood and game dishes. House specialties include such too-delicious-to-be-true items as lobster cakes and hot pecan ice cream fritters.

Night Moves

Your stroll along Lover's Point (originally, Lovers of Jesus Point) should suffice for nightlife in Pacific Grove. More by silent agreement than by local ordinance—though it was "dry" until 1972—Pacific Grove has no bars. Nor will you find pool halls, nightclubs, discos, or beer joints here. About all you can do is quaff a drink to tepid lounge music at the **Tinnery** and the **Old Bath House** (see above). For anything more lively than this, head over to Monterey. In the ascetic spirit of Pacific Grove, we chose to pass up an evening of square-dancing at Crocker Hall in the Asilomar Conference Center. It just seemed too darned wild.

For More Information

Pacific Grove Chamber of Commerce, Central and Forest Avenues, P.O. Box 167, Pacific Grove, CA 93950; (408) 373-3304.

Monterey

Location: Along the south end of Monterey Bay, at the tip of Monterey Peninsula along Highway 1. Del Monte Boulevard runs along the waterfront, becoming Lighthouse Avenue as it makes a northwesterly turn toward Pacific Grove. Monterey has few sand beaches. The main waterfront attractions are Fisherman's Wharf and the Monterey Bay Aquarium.
Population: 32,000
Area Code: 408 **Zip Code:** 93940

If the Monterey Peninsula were a baseball team, Carmel would lead off and play second base, Pebble Beach would be the overpaid designated hitter, and Pacific Grove would be the utility infielder who exerts a stabilizing influence on the bench. Monterey would be the cleanup hitter, because that's exactly what it does. It cleans up after the tourists. This is no accident. By design, Monterey draws the tourist hordes who roam the streets, starving, hysterical, clad in goofy clothing, looking for an angry fix of clam chowder.

Nothing is wrong with tourism. It gives people something to do two weeks a year and helps keep our temperamental economy afloat. It is also a "clean industry," for the most part, having a relatively minimal impact on the environment. Monterey's rich history, the restoration of the canneries, and the magnificent Monterey Bay Aquarium (see sidebar, "Monterey Bay Aquarium") are all part of the attraction. Unlike many tourist traps, Monterey actually has something to offer other than shopping and eating.

Still, in years past, a visit here always gave us the nagging and inescapable feeling that Monterey was more of a trap than it needed to be. Thankfully, on our most recent pass through town we discovered the city has been changing for the better. An excursion to Monterey today is worthwhile, particularly when it's combined with side trips to Big Sur and other peninsular communities.

That said, it is not exactly easy to find your way around the town of Monterey. Oh sure, it's the biggest town on Monterey Peninsula, but the layout of its streets and the web of exits that lead into it are confusing. Spread out around the curve of a harbor and groping inland, Monterey is a nicely contoured combination of the old and the really old. The center of the latter is historic Old Town, which can be toured with a decent pair of sneakers and a

Monterey National Marine Sanctuary

Monterey Bay is the centerpiece of the largest protected marine area in the United States. Encompassing one-fourth of California's coastline, the Monterey National Marine Sanctuary stretches from the waters off San Simeon at the southern end of Big Sur to the Golden Gate Bridge in San Francisco (with a 71-square-mile "raw sewage exemption zone" off San Francisco). In all, 5,312 square nautical miles—1.5 times the size of the largest national park in America—are protected from offshore oil and gas development, ocean dumping, subsea mining, agricultural runoff, and untreated sewage disposal. Although it would seem a good idea to protect all of our coastlines from the above encroachments, it's downright imperative in order to protect the rich ecosystem of Monterey Bay, which is:

- the permanent or seasonal home to 27 species of sea mammals, including endangered whales and threatened sea otters;
- home to 345 species of fish, most of California's species of algae, and among the world's richest assemblage of invertebrate life; and
- the nesting area or sanctuary to 94 species of seabirds, some endangered.

We learned about the bay's rich, teeming assemblage of invertebrates one night. After an obligatory swing through Monterey's clubs and bars, we returned to our car, which was parked along Cannery Row's waterfront. There, in the water just offshore, we spied a veritable navy of fishing vessels. Pitch dark though it was on shore, it was bright as day on the bay. A circle of boats with powerful, mounted klieg lights eerily illuminated the surface of the water. They were fishing for squid, and this technique—using light to throw off their prey's biological clocks—brings the squid to the surface in search of food. Instead, it's gotcha—one more unsuspecting squid snagged by the net, soon to be a fried calamari strip on Fisherman's Wharf.

The Monterey National Marine Sanctuary is a center for international research on marine life and marine ecology, encompassing 11 research institutions. Its driving purpose is to monitor all forces affecting the marine area, including effluent from ships and land, development, and recreational uses, as well as monitoring the populations of aquatic species. Monterey Bay became the center of this sanctuary in 1992, when the federal government, after a 15-year fight, designated it as such. At present, the sanctuary is managed by the National Oceanic and Atmospheric Administration (NOAA), but in the future, the management of the sanctuary may be transferred to a joint public-private venture.

Canning Cannery Row

One path of history that you should avoid in Monterey is the one that leads through Cannery Row. Its past is indeed fascinating, but you will not find a genuine legacy here. With the shining exception of the Monterey Bay Aquarium, you will find a monument to bad taste and Reagan-era consumerism that somehow refuses to die. You will find a degraded shopping zone that trades on the name of John Steinbeck so shamelessly as to sicken anyone who has read this great writer's work. You will find money-grubbing Jesus freaks using proselytizing techniques that would even embarrass Jim Bakker. You will find anything and everything but a tribute to the hardworking blue-collar spirit of yesteryear.

Originally, Cannery Row was a line of packhouses where sardines were weighed, sorted, counted, and canned by guys and dolls who never dreamed that what they were doing to make ends meet would be glamorized decades later. The first canneries were built in the 1890s. By the late 1940s, they were completely shut down, because the bay and ocean were overfished and polluted. This was the place Steinbeck wrote about in his novel of the same name. Published in 1945, *Cannery Row* caught Monterey at the peak of those canning days, when 4,000 workers canned 237,000 tons of sardines in a year. Steinbeck saw Cannery Row as "a poem, a stink, a grating noise, a quality of light, a tone, a habit, a nostalgia, a dream. Cannery Row is the gathered and scattered, tin and iron and rust and splintered wood, chipped pavement and weedy lots and junk heaps."

This is not what exists along Cannery Row today. The shops here, many of which bear either Steinbeck's name or a lame pun based on one of his books' titles, are less interesting than any you will find at an amusement park, unless your taste in history runs to "old-fashioned" creamy fudge, jelly beans, and taffy. The "olde" arcade—one of the faithfully restored structures—has the depressingly musty feel of a financial failure limping along while in Chapter 11. This was epitomized by a scene we witnessed there that could have taken place at the sleaziest state fair sideshow.

Manning one of the booths was a gap-toothed, long-haired dude who was chatting with an equally disreputable-looking buddy. He spotted a mother and her young progeny coming his way, assumed a loony expression and an inauthentic smile, and pitched an uninspired spiel intended to entice mom, who had probably already paid upward of $200 to stay at a nearby hotel, to shell out more money to have their kids' likenesses emblazoned on a T-shirt or a magazine cover, one of which was a mock porno rag. More terrified than intrigued, the clucking mom herded her brood away from the affront, guiding them toward a pie vendor.

Steinbeck expressed it best toward the end of his life, when he returned to see what had become of the Monterey he knew. "They fish for tourists now," he said forlornly.

map. This section of Monterey has been taken over by the California State Park System (in conjunction with the Monterey History and Art Association), which does these sorts of things right. They've laid out an excellent self-guided walking tour, called "the Path of History," which allows you to explore the meticulously restored adobes, chapels, theaters, and pubs that make Monterey "the most historic city in California."

Monterey has several histories rolled into one. Founded in 1542 by Juan Cabrillo, it has been the capital of California on three separate occasions. It has also served as an international trading center, a whaling mecca, a giant industrial sardine cannery, and, finally, the place where the state of California was born. This historic event transpired at the Constitutional Convention of 1849, held in the still standing Colton Hall. Soon after, gold was discovered up north. San Francisco swiftly became the preeminent city in California, leaving Monterey to ponder its past. The best place to begin a tour of the wonderful remnants of Old Town—and to pick up all the available free literature—is at the Monterey State Historic Park Visitor Center (5 Custom House Plaza, 649-7118). Stop here to get acclimated, then start walking.

On the Path of History you'll see the original Custom House, where all imported goods were brought ashore and inspected before permission was granted to unload. Many a sea captain averted this procedure by off-loading on one of the islands south of Carmel, returning later to pick up the untaxed cargo. Also on the path is the state's first theater, still producing live drama when not serving ale and food under the name Jack Swan's Tavern. Other highlights include the Pacific House (an 1847 military storehouse, now an excellent museum of California history), the state's first kiln-fired brick house, the old whaling station, and the Robert Louis Stevenson House. Built in 1847, the Stevenson House is where the author lived when he was courting Fanny Osbourne, a married woman who vacationed here. Civil War buffs can see the house where William Tecumseh Sherman lived from 1847 to 1849, back when he was a man about town (before he torched Georgia). Even the historic houses that are not official stops on the path have been commandeered for other functions—investment firms, real-estate offices, law offices, Mexican restaurants—leading one to turn an old cliché on its head: the more things stay the same, the more they change in Monterey.

One welcome addition to the waterfront that has rekindled interest in Monterey's history is the Stanton Center. This 18,000-square-foot structure is devoted to the rich maritime and European colonial history of the peninsula. Its centerpiece is the Maritime Museum of Monterey (5 Custom House Plaza, 373-2469). The museum focuses on the town's history as California's premier port, recreating life aboard a ship, inside the Custom House, and at a lighthouse. Original artifacts, vintage photographs, and excellent documentary footage are used to convey these settings. The treasure is a two-story, five-ton Fresnel lens that served as the beacon at Point Sur Light Station for 100 years. A modest admission fee is charged ($5 for adults, $2 for kids), but the seven exhibit areas are a good return on investment. Next to the center, in the outdoor plaza, a performance space stages historic skits for the kids. The entire area is a successful compromise between doing justice to history and meeting tourist needs—a balance that Monterey itself has needed to strike for years.

The Stanton Center and its environs have gone a long way toward improving downtown Monterey, which was drastically altered by all the corporate development wedged onto the waterfront in the 1980s. The log jam of growth reconfigured the old street grids into a maddening and confusing maze. Ironically enough, this corporate strangulation discouraged locals from frequenting the downtown area. In the words of one entrepreneur, the ill-planned growth "castrated the town, sapping the vitality out of Alvarado Street, where things were once hopping all the time." But now the downtown is coming back, even if the electrical current that kept Alvarado humming has been short-circuited by obstructive hotel complexes like the Doubletree.

To us, there's no mystery about it. We've seen it a hundred times, in nearly every American beach town. If a community plays to its strengths—ocean, sand, and sun—it will never lose. If it goes too far toward accommodating entrepreneurial greed, replacing genuine atmosphere with gold-plated fakery, it will eventually pay the price for lost authenticity with diminished interest.

Take the two best-known attractions in town...please. They are Fisherman's Wharf and Cannery Row. Situated on opposite sides of a Coast Guard facility and 10 minutes apart by foot, they are similar in appeal—twin strips of tourist flypaper around which buzzes an endless procession of dazed and confused humanity who unwittingly participate in a game of historical charades. In truth, both were once the haunts of working men, clanging machines, and ladies of the night. In short, they were raw places with a peculiar history all their own.

These days Fisherman's Wharf is easily the more appealing of the two areas, having been considerably spruced up in recent years. Originally built by slave labor as a safe harbor for cargo-laden schooners rounding the horn from the east, the old Fisherman's Wharf was the center of the West Coast whaling industry. Since the late 1800s, it has been the domain of a fleet of Sicilian fishermen whose efforts made Monterey the sardine capital of the world. The seafarers have erected a shrine at the mouth of the harbor in honor of Santa Rosalia, their patron saint. Most of the old-family Italians who settled here eventually made a fortune in real estate.

Cannery Row, on the other hand, is a dubious attraction in every way and, thankfully, the most excessive tourist bilking has begun to wane (see sidebar, "Canning Cannery Row"). You will, however, want to poke your nose into the Coast Guard facility. Sea lions can be observed from the Coast Guard Pier, basking in the sun on the breakwater. These lazy-looking, heavy-lidded beasts lounge around like overfed tourists on a motel-room bed. Appearances are deceptive, though. The breakwater here is just a resting place on their annual migrations between Mexico and Canada. Feeding them is forbidden; they must catch their own calamari.

Beaches

Visitors come to Monterey for many reasons, but beaches are not one of them. Better beaches lie elsewhere on the peninsula (see Pacific Grove and Carmel) and directly above it (see Seaside and Marina). Still, there is some coastal access to be gained, however meager. **Monterey State Beach** offers several access points. A narrow stretch of sand known as Windows on the Bay can be found north of Fisherman's Wharf # 2 (a municipal wharf built in 1926 for commercial fishing). Another unit lies a mile northeast, at the end of Sand Dunes

Del Monte Beach

Location: In Monterey, along Park Avenue at Del Monte Boulevard near Wharf #2.

Parking: Limited free street parking.

Hours: 6 AM to 10 PM.

Facilities: Rest rooms.

Contact: For beach information, contact the Monterey Parks Department at (408) 646-3860.

See number 24 on page 322.

Drive. This one is broader, sandier, and "dunier" than the first.

The surf along the beaches of Monterey is too cold and hazardous for swimming, and the wind blows nearly nonstop, so don't wear that wacky straw hat you bought on Cannery Row, unless you want to see it end up on the head of a sea lion at the Coast Guard Pier. Water receation rules on Monterey Bay. Scuba diving, deep-sea fishing, ocean kayaking, sailing, and windsurfing are all popular pastimes, and local merchants can set visitors up with equipment rentals and instruction. The best spots for diving are **Macabee Beach**, **San Carlos Beach Park** (accessible along Cannery Row) and Coast Guard Pier, where you can swim alongside the sea lions and admire the rich marine life of Monterey Bay.

The best place for kids to hit the water is at **Del Monte Beach** along a lake in El Estero Park, on the other side of Del Monte Boulevard from the ocean. Ducks and migrating birds come here, and canoes and kayaks can be rented. There's also a toddlers' wading pool and the aptly named Dennis the Menace Play Area, designed by Hank Ketcham, the creator

Macabee Beach

Location: In Monterey, along Prescott Avenue at Cannery Row.

Parking: Metered street parking

Hours: 6 AM to 10 PM.

Facilities: None.

Contact: For beach information, contact the Monterey Parks Department at (408) 646-3860.

See number 21 on page 322.

Monterey State Beach (Sand Dunes Drive unit)

Location: In Monterey, at the end of Sand Dunes Drive off Highway 1, just south of the Monterey Beach Hotel.

Parking: Free parking lot.

Hours: 9 AM to a half hour after sunset.

Facilities: Rest rooms.

Contact: For beach information, contact Marina State Beach, administrative headquarters for the north beaches of the Monterey District, at (408) 384-7695.

See number 25 on page 322.

Monterey State Beach ("Windows on the Bay" unit)

Location: In Monterey, on the north side of Wharf #2.

Parking: Limited free street parking.

Hours: 9 AM to a half hour after sunset.

Facilities: Rest rooms.

Contact: For beach information, contact Marina State Beach, administrative headquarters for the north beaches of the Monterey District, at (408) 384-7695.

See number 23 on page 322.

San Carlos Beach Park

Location: In Monterey, at the end of Reeside Avenue between Cannery Row and Coast Guard Pier.

Parking: Metered street parking.

Hours: 6 AM to 10 PM.

Facilities: None.

Contact: For beach information, contact the Monterey Parks Department at (408) 646-3860.

See number 22 on page 322.

Monterey Bay Aquarium

The Monterey Bay Aquarium opened in 1984 with the expressed goal of "expanding public interest and knowledge and concern for the marine life of Monterey Bay and the ocean environment." In just over a decade, they have more than achieved their goal. In fact, they are something of a yardstick by which environmental education ought to be measured. With fresh and regularly changing exhibits, tanks full of living specimens, video and film footage, and live presentations, the aquarium re-creates the rich underwater habitat of Monterey Bay right outside its back door. A relief map we'd seen at the Pacific Grove Museum of Natural History showed how the bay plunges 300 feet straight down into an underwater canyon that eventually reaches 8,400 feet in depth. This nutrient-rich canyon nourishes a wide variety of marine species, from which the aquarium draws its exhibits.

State-of-the-art does not mean virtual reality at Monterey Bay Aquarium. It means actual reality! That is, kids are allowed to watch real plants and animals do their things (everything from octopuses and sharks to sea slugs and barnacles). They have a kelp forest, a sandy shore, coastal stream, a reef, a bat-ray tank, and a touch pool (the underwater equivalent of a petting zoo). Outdoor presentations take the visitor into the surrounding waters for a fins-on experience in more ways than one.

Among the regular activities that visitors most enjoy is the daily feedings of sea otters (at 10:30 AM, 1:30 PM, and 3:30 PM). They are indeed irresistibly cute little critters. A sea otter, we learned, eats one-third of its weight in food every day (roughly the same fraction as the average Cannery Row tourist). Only 2,100 of these otters are left in California. Still, their numbers are increasing. The four who reside at the aquarium were rescued from poachers and now cavort here, to the immense delight and relief of all.

Although the price of admission isn't cheap (approximately $11 for adults, $8 for students, $5 for kids), the aquarium is endlessly rewarding, warranting at least a half-day's studious wandering. You'll want to return year after year, too. The best deal is to become a member of the Monterey Bay Aquarium, which allows an entire family unlimited admission for a year for about $57. There's also a great book and gift shop on the premises that is superior to any museum shop we've seen on any beach. As if that weren't enough, there's a decent restaurant, the Portola Café (648-4870, $$), on the premises, where you can dine on crab cakes, calamari, prawns, grilled fish—that is, if the sight of all those seafood delectables on a plate doesn't sicken you after having just admired them alive and well in their native habitat.

Located at the north end of Cannery Row in Monterey, the Monterey Bay Aquarium is open daily from 10 AM to 6 PM. For more information, contact the Monterey Bay Aquarium, 886 Cannery Row, Monterey, CA 93940; (408) 648-4888.

 Map of Monterey County beaches—page 322

of that famous comic strip. It features innovative equipment and a real train engine for first-hand exploration.

The Monterey Bay Recreational Trail, a five-mile shoreline bike path that takes in the Monterey waterfront between Pacific Grove and Seaside, is a great way to get a ground-level feel for the town and the bay. Try renting a two-wheeler at Bay Bikes, which has locations on Cannery Row in Monterey (640 Wave Street, 646-9090) and in downtown Carmel (Lincoln Street between Fifth and Sixth Streets, 625-2453).

Bunking Down

More than any other town on the peninsula, Monterey has welcomed large corporate hotels to set up shop. In fact, the Doubletree, Marriott, and Hyatt have been accused of undermining the town character. By far the best of the larger luxury hotels is the **Hotel Pacific** (300 Pacific Street, 373-5700, $$$$), which blends in nicely with its neighborhood and is located within easy walking distance of many attractions. Done up in peach tones, the Hotel Pacific has mastered the art of relaxed opulence. The architecture reflects the California mission style that is Monterey's architectural heritage. Even the layout is missionlike, with a series of discrete buildings constructed around four courtyards and linked with terra cotta–tiled pathways that pass beneath archways and beside adobe gardens. The accommodations feel less like a hotel room than a real, open living space. Floors are either hardwood or adobe tiled. The second-floor library, where the hotel serves continental breakfasts in the morning and wine and cheese in the afternoon, contains a better selection of true literature (as opposed to best-seller dreck) than we've ever seen at a hotel or inn. A outdoor hot tub is hidden off to the side on an upper-floor landing. The town of Monterey itself spreads out on all sides, begging to be strolled. Yes, you pay for such convenience and elegance ($160 to $220 per night). But the Hotel Pacific, unlike some of its high-priced neighbors, exudes warmth and personality. It is the only place we've stayed where, in addition to the standard Gideon's Bible, a copy of *The Teachings of Buddha* had been placed in the nightstand.

The most enjoyable B&B in town is the **Old Monterey Inn** (500 Martin Street, 375-8284, $$$$). Parental discretion is advised because this is a couples' getaway. Built as a private residence in 1929, it is set amid beautiful gardens of roses, begonias, ferns, and rhododendron and a forest of giant California live oaks. It is an English country cottage whose 10 unique rooms have been given evocative, offbeat names (such as "Serengeti" and "Tattershall"). The proprietors, Ann and Gene Swett, are delightful hosts who make you feel that this is not just their home (as it has been for 25 years) but yours. When we arrived, we asked, "Where's the office?" Gene paused, reflected, smiled, and threw his arms out as he generously announced, "There is no office here." We immediately loved the place. Room rates include an elaborate home-cooked breakfast and a nice spread of wine and cheese in the afternoon. The Swetts know the area intimately, and their inn has won numerous awards over the years. They definitely know how to "Swett" the details.

The best beachfront hotel—indeed, the only place to stay on a sand beach in Monterey—is the **Best Western Monterey Beach Hotel** (2600 Sand Dunes Drive, 394-3321, $$). It is a banquet-sized lodge nestled among the healthy dunes beside Monterey State Beach, a formidable stretch of sand that extends north of here. The hotel was built in 1969, before the California Coastal Commission began automatically nixing such projects. As such, it is an anomaly: a real beach hotel. It surely could not be built so close to the water in this day and age. Garden- and ocean-view rooms are available. ***(continued on page 366)***

Full Moon Over Monterey

It was not our day. Or, should we say, night.

We made the mistake of arriving on the Monterey Peninsula without hotel reservations. It was an honest oversight. An inadvertent keystroke made while computerizing our itinerary some months earlier erroneously indicated that we were staying at a fine hotel in Monterey on July 23rd when, in fact, our reservation was for July 25th. We showed up on the 23rd, and there was no room at the inn.

Every experience on the road, even the bad ones, are useful to us in some way. Long after the fact, the bad ones often turn out to be the most fun to write about. Besides, there are lessons to be learned from them. Perhaps you can benefit from our misfortune in this instance. The moral of the story is twofold: (1) do not show up in popular vacation destinations on summer weekends without confirmed reservations; and (2) double-check your itinerary for accuracy before leaving.

Our botched Saturday night went down like this:

A day of driving and drinking in the beauty of Big Sur had left us exhausted, and we were eagerly anticipating the turn of a key in a hotel room door and the opportunity to drop bags and collapse. Fatigue weighed heavy on us. Then we discovered that our intended hotel was sold out for that evening—and that this particular Saturday had been completely booked months in advance. In fact, hotels all across the peninsula were booked solid. In Pacific Grove, Carmel, and Monterey the "no vacancy" signs were glowing at every turn. Inquiries for advice on where to try next were met with words to the effect of "Go east, young men." East to Salinas, that is.

Salinas is a city 20 miles inland from Monterey. It is Steinbeck country, population 100,000, surprisingly clean and modern. But it is not at the beach, not where we wanted to be, not where we needed to be. That was okay, though. It was late, and beggars can't be choosers. Imagine our surprise to discover that even Salinas was booked solid. No room at the Comfort Inn. No room at fleabags with names like "El Sombrero." One vacancy at the Holiday Inn Express: a smoking room with only one bed for $105. No thanks; we weren't that desperate yet. We agreed that we would sleep sitting up in our car at Laguna Seca State Park before we would pay $105 to pass the night in Salinas. We continued checking one motel after another. Upscale, low-rent, chains, independents. We ducked into and out of a seedy property in obvious disrepair, reeking of Indian curry. All were full. Packs of cowboys—or, rather, guys in cowboy hats—were hollering "yee-haw" in parking lots.

What the hell? After an hour of chasing no-vacancy signs and peering into the lobbies of no-tell motels where we wouldn't even want our corpses interred, we conceded defeat and swung out of Salinas. By now we were cruising the endless broccoli fields of the Salinas Valley in a state of confused semiexhaustion as the day's final rays streaked the darkening night sky with a brilliant blaze of orange.

 Map of Monterey County beaches—page 322

We eventually negotiated a circuitous loop through the area. We had begun in Monterey, proceeded to Salinas, and then headed northwest to the Castroville/Watsonville area before returning in defeat to Monterey. This redundant trek added 100 pointless miles to our rented car's odometer. Here were the three main reasons we could not locate a room:

1. It was the height of the summer season in Monterey—the 10th most popular tourist destination in the state of California—on a Saturday that marked the first sunny weather in the area in weeks.
2. Salinas was hosting the 85th annual California Rodeo that very weekend.
3. Laguna Seca State Park was revving up for a car race that drew fans of fumes and noise from all over.

Tourists, cowboys, and racing aficionados alike were all pressing upon the peninsula at the same time. It was a rare confluence of attention, and we were just two more bodies added to the overflow.

We tried the city of Marina, where the recently decommissioned Fort Ord—which had housed and processed 60,000 troops when fully operative—was now a ghost town. The Travelodge, the Inn Cal—both large, both full. Grimly we drove south to Seaside, the town that sits like a boil on the ass of Monterey. There we found an entire strip of motels—good, bad, and ugly—most of them flashing "no vacancy" signs. The proprietor of one flyblown dive, chattering distractedly on a portable phone, said he'd heard there was one room left at another fleabag across the way. "Go, go!" he urged us. Alas, we moved too slowly. Some other sucker snapped it up.

However, good fortune smiled on us at last. The Bay Breeze Motel had one room left. One bed, $65. On any other night, we would have balked. At the time, it sounded like the answer to a prayer. The room was spartan but clean. It would do. We made haste to throw the mattress on the floor, instantly creating two beds out of one—and a certain backache for the sap who had to sleep on the box springs. We flipped for it. In no time we'd turned the motel room into a crash pad. It was like being in college again. We rested on our respective mattresses, heads reposing on thin, lifeless pillows as we reflected on and recovered from the automotive nightmare of the last several hours. This is the darker side of traveling, the part where it becomes no fun, where you pine for the comfort and safety of your bed back home.

The bay breezes blew some cooling air through the window. The same breeze also carried with it the sounds of a couple who were arguing in Spanish in the parking lot. Soon they were joined in disharmony by another squabbling couple. "You got a attitude problem," the male bellowed, vowing "I be taking care of that" in menacing tones.

What was going on here? We looked up into the cloudless night sky and saw a radiant full moon. Ah, that explains it, we realized. That explains it all.

(continued from page 363) Downtown Monterey is about two miles away. Waves crash with particular vigor here—all the better for lulling you to sleep at night.

Of course, there are scads more hotels and motels and inns all over Monterey. We've written about three of our favorites; if you would like a more extensive listing, contact the Chamber of Commerce and request a "Monterey Peninsula Hotel & Motel Guide."

Incidentally, a flock of budget motels can be found in the vicinity of Seaside, Sand City, and Marina, the low-end burghs that border Fort Ord northeast of Monterey. None are as inviting or as economical as they would have you believe. Mostly, they're a shabby row of generics held together by spackling compound that do business only as places fill up to capacity in the more desirable communities around the peninsula.

Coastal Cuisine

In years past, Monterey did not have a dining scene worthy of its history as an international trading center. Mostly, it was run-of-the-mill fried fish, calamari strips, and "world-famous clam chowder" so pasty and thick that a spoon would stand up in it.

That all-you-can-eat mentality has magically changed in recent years. The most telling sign of transformation can be witnessed on Old Fisherman's Wharf—that former dead zone for hunger pangs—where you can now get a decent, well-prepared meal. The dish of choice for tourists still seems to be that horrid chowder, served in round, hollowed-out hunks of Italian bread. We did quite well for ourselves, stumbling on **Liberty Fish Co.** (43 Fisherman's Wharf, 375-5468, $$), where the salmon smoking on the grill looked too good to pass up for lunch. It was excellent, perfectly singed and flavored, and served on a fresh salad. The marinated octopus salad looked good, too.

One step down the wharf is **Café Fina** (47 Fisherman's Wharf, 372-5200, $$), which is one step up in cuisine. The service surprised us with its quality, as did the house specialty, Pasta Fina, a healthy and hearty plateful of shrimp over linguine. Better still is **Domenico's** (50 Fisherman's Wharf, 372-3655, $$$), an Italian classic of long-standing. Seafood and pasta, often in combination, are the prime entrées. Grilled sea bass, Dungeness crab, Monterey Bay prawns—you really can't go wrong.

And that's only Fisherman's Wharf. In town, the cuisine has blossomed into a world-class act. The two most interesting we found—though there are many others—were **Fresh Cream** (99 Pacific Street, Heritage Harbor, 375-9798, $$$) and **Tarpy's Roadhouse** (2999 Highway 68, 647-1444, $$$). Fresh Cream serves French cuisine with a California touch (e.g., sautéed salmon on an artichoke purée), and it overlooks Monterey Bay, making it the most romantic dining spot in town.

Tarpy's Roadhouse serves up hearty American fare a few miles outside of town, on the road toward Salinas. This is a showpiece for Tony Tollner, a new breed of restaurateur who deserves considerable credit for elevating Monterey's dining scene. In keeping with the quasi-rural setting, the menu choices are "from the ranch" (rabbit, veal, duck, beef) and "from the sea" (scallops, prawns, salmon). The Dungeness crab cake and oak-grilled eggplant appetizers sent our taste buds soaring. Entrée-wise, they do things with rabbit that even magicians haven't thought of. The oak-grilled ribs are a house specialty, but you're safe ordering any of the tummy-filling items served here. The stone-house setting is as original as the eclectic multimedia art that lines the walls. The restaurant, incidentally, was named for Matt Tarpy, a local landowner from the 1800s who died protecting his property.

For old time's sake we always take one of our Monterey meals at **Gianni's Pizza** (725 Lighthouse Avenue, 649-1500, $). The best way to find this institution is to follow your nose a few blocks up the hill from the dining dregs of Cannery Row. Family-owned and -run since 1974, Gianni's smells of homemade pasta, rich sauce, and fresh, oven-baked goods. While waiting for your pizza, try the homemade garlic and cheese breadsticks—two or three of these will set you right! Gianni's is a family-style place in the very best sense.

Night Moves

Monterey will always hold a special place in the hearts of rock-and-roll fans. The first true rock festival took place here in 1967, later immortalized in the documentary *Monterey Pop*. Eric Burdon wrote a hit song about the event ("Monterey"), extolling the virtues of Flower Power two years before Woodstock. But the Monterey Pop Festival was a one-shot deal. It was the bastard son of the Monterey Jazz Festival, which is still held here each September at the Monterey Fairgrounds, a 24-acre field surrounded by oak trees. Blues fans gather for their own festival each June as well.

As for ongoing nightlife, Monterey holds the flickering candle for the entire peninsula. The easy-listening set can tap toes at several piano bars, the **Brasstree at the Doubletree Hotel** (2 Portola Plaza, 649-4511) being the most popular. (They offer "barking seal karaoke", feel free to investigate.) A little more lively is **McGarrett's** (Alvarado Street and Del Monte Boulevard, 646-9244), which has live reggae bands and a "beach party" every Friday.

The closing of Fort Ord—former home to thousands of young and restless weekend party animals—has toned down the wildest excesses of Monterey's club scene. The two most viable venues for live rock and roll are **Doc Ricketts' Lab** (95 Prescott Street, 649-4241) and **Planet Gemini** (625 Cannery Row, 373-1449). Doc Ricketts' is located in the bottom of what was once the marine-life collecting lab of Doc Ricketts himself, the main character in John Steinbeck's *Cannery Row*. Besides being one of the few Cannery Row structures that has a legitimate connection with Steinbeck's legacy, it's the only place around that features bands on a regular basis. The happy specimens who dance here nightly are a testament to the transformative power of live rock and roll.

In the spirit of the retro-'90s, we went to Planet Gemini to see an Eagles tribute band from Reno, Nevada. They were called Heartache Tonight (after one of the Eagles' songs), and they performed eerily accurate human-jukebox recreations of the Eagles' old hits, bloodlessly studied right down to the 10-gallon hats they wore and the buzzard skulls and Old West totems that littered the stage. Some months later, one of us saw the Eagles perform on their reunion tour, weaseling a review assignment from a newspaper that willingly forked over the $100 that a single ticket cost. The upshot is that we paid a measly $3 to see Heartache Tonight play the Eagles' songs better than the Eagles did themselves for $100.

Beyond all that, Planet Gemini is a club in search of an identity, raving to techno and hip hop one night and drooling to country line-dance music the next. Still, hope springs eternal for Monterey's nightlife. With part of Fort Ord having been converted into a branch of the state university system, the town should be happily hopping again.

For More Information

Contact the Monterey Peninsula Chamber of Commerce, 380 Alvarado Street, Monterey, CA 93940; (408) 649-3502.

Salinas

Location: 20 miles east of Monterey, on Route 68.
Population: 100,000
Area Code: 408 **Zip Code:** 93902

Though Salinas is not on the ocean, it makes a great day trip for visitors to the Monterey Peninsula, primarily because it is the hometown of John Steinbeck. The half-hour drive east on Route 68 cuts through wide agricultural tracts and enters this pleasantly cluttered "cow town" at the heart of fertile Salinas Valley. The setting of many of Steinbeck's novels—including *East of Eden* and *Tortilla Flat*—Salinas is an authentic slice of western life that has grown into a sizable city but has changed little in atmosphere from the days when the author lived here.

The best place to start is the Steinbeck Center Foundation (371 Main Street, 753-6411), where you'll find the authoritative collection of Steinbeckiana, exhibits on his life, and guides to walking and driving tours of town. Not far away is the John Steinbeck House (132 Central Avenue, 424-2735), the Victorian-era home dating from 1897 where Steinbeck was born (in 1902) and raised. In addition to the preserved shrine (entrance is free), a dandy little restaurant is located on the premises, but you should call for reservations. They have two seatings for lunch, at 11:45 AM and 1:15 PM. Serious Steinbeck scholars will want to visit the John Steinbeck Library (350 Lincoln Avenue, 758-7311), a full-fledged public library with the author's archives are housed in a separate wing. These include books, manuscripts, tapes, correspondence, clippings, and photographs. The library is open Monday through Saturday, and the archives are open by reservation only

To celebrate its native son, Salinas holds an annual Steinbeck Festival the first week in August that includes lectures, films, tours, panel discussions, and live dramatizations of his work. Another wildly popular event in Salinas is the California Rodeo, held the third week in July. One of the nation's largest and most celebrated, the rodeo packs the peninsula every year.

Finally, for lovers of roadside oddities, check out the sculpture on the lawn of the Salinas Community Center (940 North Main Street). Created by Claes Oldenberg and entitled *Hat in Three Stages of Landing*, it features three cowboy hats, each weighing 3,500 pounds.

For More Information

Contact the Salinas Chamber of Commerce, 119 East Alisal Street, P.O. Box 1170, Salinas, CA 93902; (408) 424-7611.

 Map of Monterey County beaches—page 322

Seaside and Sand City

Location: Two miles northeast of Monterey, along Highway 1.
Population: 31,000
Area Code: 408 **Zip Code:** 93955

The town of Seaside straddles the coast between Monterey and Fort Ord like a fat flea sucking blood from its unwilling host. Believe it or not, Seaside is actually as large as Monterey, in terms of population. In every other way, however, it is Monterey's inferior. The only reason a visitor would need to know about it is if you can't find lodging anywhere else on the Monterey Peninsula (see the sidebar "Full Moon Over Monterey" for a firsthand account of such a plight). Seaside is full of one-star motels and fast-food stands, looking like a Salvation Army warehouse for all the things that Monterey, Pacific Grove, and Carmel had no use for. Part of **Monterey State Beach** is in Seaside, just north of the Best Western Monterey Beach Hotel. It's part of the same wild and windy beach that extends down from Marina, and you can't argue with the price—it's free.

Sand City is a tiny community of 184 souls on a narrow strip of sand between Highway 1 and the ocean. It was here that a planned 136-room oceanfront hotel and conference center was shot down by the California Coastal Commission in 1991, much to the consternation of locals who'd hoped the hotel would aid their failing economy.

For More Information

Contact the Seaside Chamber of Commerce, 505 Broadway Avenue, Seaside, CA 93955; (408) 394-6501

Monterey State Beach
(Seaside unit)

Location: In Seaside, just north of the Monterey Beach Hotel off Highway 1.
Parking: Free parking lot.
Hours: 9 AM to a half hour after sunset.
Facilities: Rest rooms.
Contact: For beach information, contact Marina State Beach, administrative headquarters for the north beaches of the Monterey District, at (408) 384-7695.

See number 26 on page 322.

Marina and Fort Ord

Location: Four miles north of Monterey, on Highway 1. Marina State Beach is the largest beach in the area, including Monterey.
Population: 25,000
Area Code: 408 **Zip Code:** 93933

Like a smaller version of Camp Pendleton, Fort Ord lays claim to 28,500 acres of prime California coastland. Until 1993, when Defense Department budget cuts forced the phased closing of the base, the Army infantry training center was home to thousands of service personnel and their families. It also encompassed two golf courses, shopping centers, housing developments, and miles of beaches.

Obviously, the departure of so many folks has taken a toll on the local economy. But it was not nearly as bad as the pro-military forces projected. The slack has been picked up by courting tourism.

They still have a ways to go on this count. The towns of Seaside and Marina, between which Fort Ord is sandwiched, are pretty shoddy, as is the military installation itself. But the shooing away of the military has a potential happy ending. In fact, Monterey Peninsula, in the long run, might be better off. Already a new branch of the state university system, California State University, Monterey Bay, opened in the fall of 1995 on the site of a former army base. Also in the cards is the razing of an army housing area and its replacement with 350 new homes. Two 18-hole courses at Fort Ord now belong to the town of Seaside. As for the four miles of beaches that belonged to the military, they will become part of Fort Ord State Park. When it opens to the public—and the 885-acre park is projected to do so by 1998—it will be the largest of the 12 state beaches along Monterey Bay.

Marina State Beach

4

Location: Just north of Monterey, in the town of Marina, at the end of Reservation Road.
Parking: Free parking lot.
Hours: 8 AM to a half hour after sunset.
Facilities: Rest rooms.
Contact: For beach information, contact Marina State Beach at (408) 384-7695.

See number 27 on page 322.

Beaches

The best beach access at the moment is **Marina State Beach**. With the sand a golden brown, the dunes rising gently, and no jagged rocks along the shore, Marina State Beach is as close to the look of a Southern California beach as you'll find along Monterey Bay. If this shoreline is any indication, Fort Ord's beaches will be real show-stoppers when they are open to the public. During the summer, when temperatures hover around 100 degrees in the valleys and deserts to the east, Marina State Beach is packed with sunbathers. The surf here is too rough for swimming, and the wind whips ferociously at times, explaining the hang-glider ramp that sits atop a big brown whale of a dune at the beach's center. A 2,000-foot boardwalk leads across the dunes to the beach. It is a compelling place to stroll around and learn about dune vegetation, as accompanying charts explain the "good" (sand verbena, primrose, sagewort, lizard tail) and the "bad" (Hottentot fig, European dune grass) vegetation. Most of the stuff on the "bad" list consists of exotic species that were introduced for purposes of dune stabilization but overran the place, altering native ecosystems.

For More Information

Contact the Marina Chamber of Commerce, P.O. Box 425, Marina, CA 93933; (408) 384-9155.

Castroville

Location: 12 miles north of Monterey, where Route 1 crosses Routes 156 and 183.
Population: 4,500
Area Code: 408 **Zip Code:** 95012

Castroville lies a whisper to the west of the beach. It's not on the coast per se, but it's close enough to merit mention. Besides, we're fond of artichokes, and Castroville is the artichoke heart of America. This is farm country. "What we do here in Castroville is grow artichokes" is how a local Chamber of Commerce member plainly put it to us. The entire town marches to the beat of a different vegetable. They are completely devoted to the 'choke, which is a tasty if unusual plant. (Actually, it's a flower.) Looking something like a green pineapple, the artichoke's leaves are disengaged one by one and the edible part is scraped off with your teeth until you arrive at the delectable heart. Between Monterey and Half Moon Bay, we've enjoyed many a Castroville artichoke, dunking them in mayonnaise, butter, or vinaigrette as if they were green potato chips.

If you're in the area, you should stop and eat the artichokes. The main house of artichoke worship in these parts is the Giant Artichoke (11261 Merritt Street, $$, 633-3204). They do everything that can be done to an artichoke. They serve it fried with garlic mayonnaise, steamed with butter, boiled into artichoke soup, placed atop beef patties with Monterey Jack cheese (the Castroville Burger), and baked into quiches. The smart way to go if you're a true devotee is the Artichoke Sampler, which offers a little of everything. But don't pass up the seafood entrées as well: calamari, snapper, you name it.

The produce and seafood to be had in the area couldn't be fresher. We whiled away part of an afternoon at local produce stands, savoring the sights and smells of just-picked vegetables bulging in the bins. We felt healthier just looking at them. Of course, we purchased artichoke-decorated T-shirts. Every year, they have an Artichoke Festival. Posters scattered around town urged support for various candidates for the title of Artichoke Queen. Would you believe that Marilyn Monroe herself won the title of Artichoke Queen back in 1947?

For More Information

Contact the Castroville Chamber of Commerce, P.O. Box 744, Castroville, CA 95012; (408) 633-6545.

Moss Landing

Location: 15 miles north of Monterey, along U.S. 1. Three state beaches are strung closely together here.
Population: 500
Area Code: 408 **Zip Code:** 95039

There's not much to Moss Landing, a harborfront community in northernmost Monterey County that is quickly passed through, unless you're hunting for beaches. Three state beaches—Salinas River, Moss Landing, and Zmudowski—lie within striking distance. So does another prominent coastal feature: Elkhorn Slough. It is a long slough that stretches seven miles inland, harboring a variety of wildlife. Visitors can tour it via guided sea-kayaking trips and marine biologist-led pontoon-boat tours. You'll see harbor seals, sea otters, shore birds, and more. For additional information, contact Elkhorn Slough Safari (408-424-3939). Moss Landing also has a safe T-shaped harbor that's used by pleasure boaters.

Beaches

Just south of Moss Landing, beach mavens will find **Salinas River State Beach**. It is a haunting, windswept location that is fairly inhospitable unless you come dressed and prepared for it. A wooden walkway leads from the parking lot onto the beach. A sign warns "Swimming and Wading Unsafe," and the heavy chop on the water does look daunting. The beach is broad and sandy, with steep dunes. On one visit, we saw a few intrepid fishers braving gale-force winds while a sailboat offshore seemed on the verge of capsizing. All we saw on a return visit several years later was a shivering group of migrant workers and a dancing clump of college coeds. The former were drinking and the latter were

Salinas River State Beach

Location: One mile south of Moss Landing, at Portrero Road and Highway 1.
Parking: Free parking lot.
Hours: 8 AM to a half hour after sunset.
Facilities: Rest rooms.
Contact: For beach information, contact Marina State Beach, administrative headquarters for the north beaches of the Monterey District, at (408) 384-7695.

See number 28 on page 322.

Moss Landing State Beach

Location: North of Moss Landing Harbor in Moss Landing, at Jetty Road and Highway 1.
Parking: $3 entrance fee per vehicle.
Hours: 6:30 AM to a half hour after sunset.
Facilities: Rest rooms.
Contact: For beach information, contact Marina State Beach, administrative headquarters for the north beaches of the Monterey District, at (408) 384-7695.

See number 29 on page 322.

Zmudowski State Beach

Location: North of Moss Landing, at the end of Geiberson Road, which can be reached by following the signs to Zmudowski State Beach from Highway 1.
Parking: Free parking lot.
Hours: 8 AM to a half hour after sunset.
Facilities: Rest rooms.
Contact: For beach information, contact Marina State Beach, administrative headquarters for the north beaches of the Monterey District, at (408) 384-7695.

See number 30 on page 322.

grooving to boom-box music, both groups having found their own way to ward off the wind and chill. The 518-acre Salinas River Wildlife Refuge adjoins the beach to the south. Salinas River State Beach occupies a very rural setting, although the smokestacks of a nearby power plant are visible.

Next up is **Moss Landing State Beach**, which offers access to Elkhorn Slough, a tidal slough that rewards nature lovers with a close look at coastal wetlands. The beach itself is broad and windswept, the surf rough and dangerous, the view (onto power-plant smokestacks) not the best. But Elkhorn Slough is not to be missed. The entrance to **Zmudowski State Beach**, the last beach in the county, lies a few miles north of Moss Landing. Be forewarned: when you make the turnoff from Route 1, you're still a jump from the water. The road to Zmudowski skirts fields of artichokes and Brussels sprouts. On the beach a sign warns: "Danger: Intermittent Waves of Unusual Size and Force." That is in addition to the blasts of wind of unusual size and force. Zmudowski, like Moss Landing State Beach, is a good place for clamming and surfing. The only folks we saw on the beach, though, were a family trying to picnic while getting sandblasted silly. This one may not be worth the effort it takes to get there.

Coastal Cuisine

Even if you're bypassing the beaches, you must stop for a crab sandwich at **Bob's Crab** (Highway 1, 633-3127, $). Each year the orange trailer that houses this modest operation looks a little more flyblown, but the house specialty, a delicious crab-on-sourdough sandwich, tastes wonderful all the same. Bob gets his crabs fresh from Half Moon Bay and apportions the spread generously between two fat slices of bread. Accompanied by a jar of chilled apple juice, it makes a fine lunch for five bucks or so. Haul it out to the beach and have an impromptu picnic. We've done so on several occasions.

If you're looking for a sit-down meal, the **Moss Landing Café** (421 Moss Landing Road, 633-3355, $$) is a bargain and a boon to the area, which needs all the good restaurants it can get. Specialties include squid and eggs, crab cakes, and deep-fried artichokes. Finally, don't leave town without trying the oysters and prawns, served with homemade sauces, at the **Landing Oyster Bar** (413 Moss Landing Road, 633-5302, $$). Prices are fair, portions are large, and the ambience is local.

For More Information

Contact the Moss Landing Chamber of Commerce, P.O. Box 41, Moss Landing, CA 95039; (408) 633-4301.

Santa Cruz County

For beachy symbolism, you can't beat this fact: the first east-west road encountered in southern Santa Cruz County is called Beach Road, and it leads to Palm Beach. The beach due north of it is called Sunset Beach. In short, Santa Cruz County is something of a throwback to the beach-blanket bingo of Southern California (or vice versa). We started seeing things we hadn't seen much of since we were as far south as Malibu: jail-bait in bikinis, surf bars, a surfer's shrine and museum, seaside arcades, and people of all ages wearing anything from tentlike bathing suits to monokinis to nothing at all. (Note: There's lots of the last item, especially on the remote north county beaches.)

The shapes and sizes of the beaches vary as widely as the visitors—from tiny coves that only privileged handfuls know about to broad, sandy expanses where countless volleyball games are played while surfers cheerfully bob on the horizon. Santa Cruz, the city and the county, is the playpen of the populated burgs of the Santa Clara Valley, *(continued on page 378)*

Coastal Santa Cruz County's Climate

Santa Cruz Averages

	Daily High Temp. (°F)	Daily Low Temp. (°F)	Rainfall (inches)
January	60	38	6.5
February	62	40	4.8
March	64	41	3.8
April	67	42	2.5
May	71	45	0.5
June	74	48	0.2
July	75	51	0.2
August	75	51	0.1
September	77	50	0.4
October	74	47	1.2
November	66	42	3.6
December	61	39	5.2
Yearly Average	**69**	**45**	**29.0**

Source: National Weather Service data, National Oceanographic and Atmospheric Administration.

Santa Cruz County

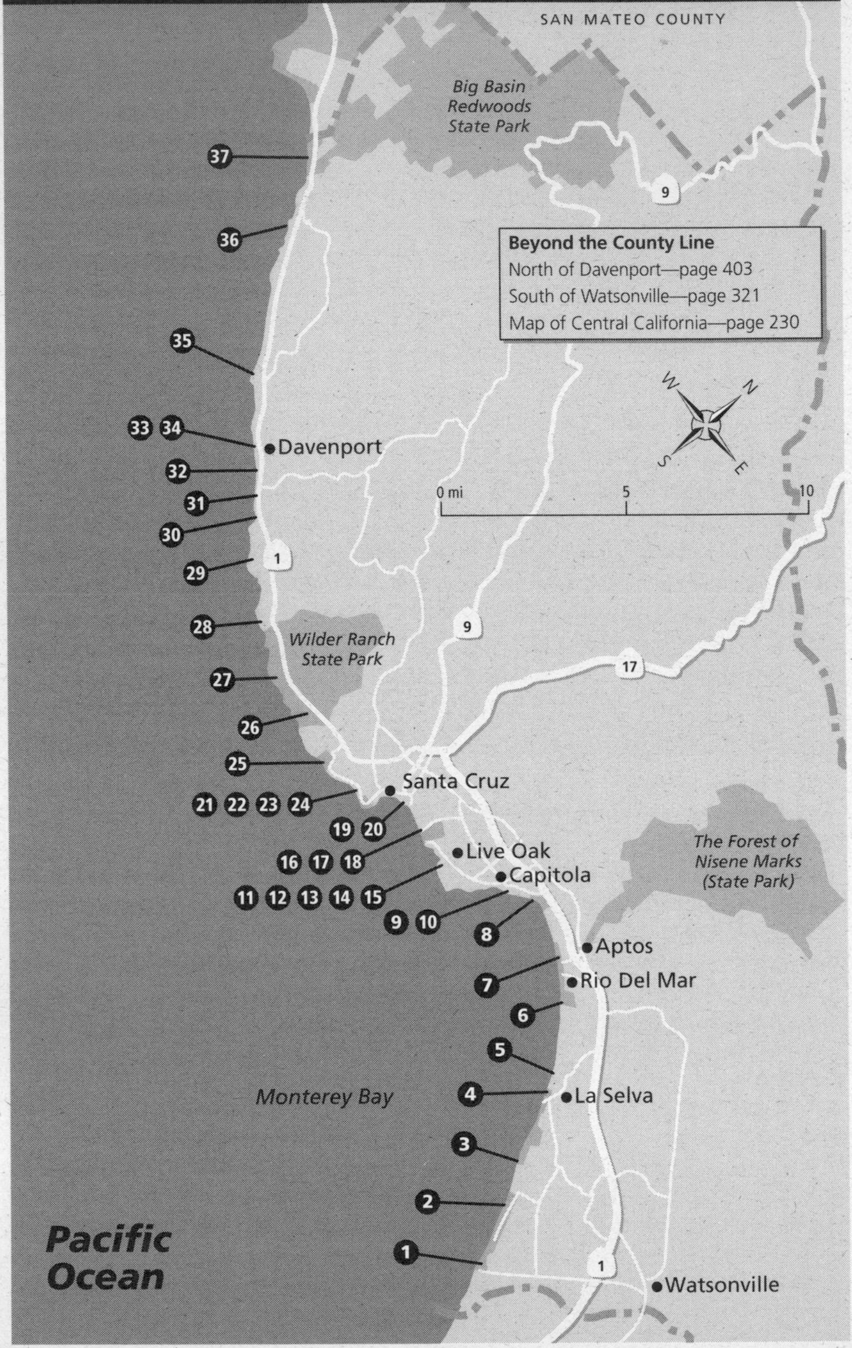

SAN MATEO COUNTY
Big Basin Redwoods State Park
Beyond the County Line
North of Davenport—page 403
South of Watsonville—page 321
Map of Central California—page 230
W N S E
0 mi 5 10
Davenport
Wilder Ranch State Park
Santa Cruz
Live Oak
Capitola
The Forest of Nisene Marks (State Park)
Aptos
Rio Del Mar
La Selva
Watsonville
Monterey Bay
Pacific Ocean
1 9 17
1 2 3 4 5 6 7 8 9 10 11 12 13 14 15 16 17 18 19 20 21 22 23 24 25 26 27 28 29 30 31 32 33 34 35 36 37

Santa Cruz County Beaches

Map of Central California—page 230

(continued from page 375) located up and over the Santa Cruz Mountains. Santa Cruz itself is one of the most liberated places on the planet, the urban equivalent of one of those mystery-spot attractions where gravity doesn't seem to behave quite the way it does everywhere else. Cut off from the rest of the world by geography, Santa Cruz has evolved a distinct character of its own—a product of social Darwinism at work, if you will. The ambience of the county's coastal communities varies from the upscale residential villages in the south to the wild and raucous playland of Santa Cruz to the vastness and isolation of the beaches that run north to the San Mateo County border.

Key to the Symbols

Bike path · Camping · Food and drink · Hiking · Nude

Pier · RVs allowed · Surfing · Volleyball

Crowd Rating

sweet solitude . . . moderate crowds . . . wall-to-wall

Overall Rating

1 don't bother . . . 3 worth a visit . . . 5 beach heaven

 Map of Santa Cruz County beaches—page 376

Sunset State Beach

Location: From Highway 1, near the Monterey County line, turn west on Beach Road and drive five miles to the beach.

Santa Cruz County is a wonderland of unspoiled beaches in jaw-droppingly-beautiful settings. Sometimes confined to coves, sometimes running for great distances along a regular shoreline, the beaches are pressed against staggering backdrops that include sheer cliff faces and steep, vegetated dunes.

The public beaches begin with **Palm Beach** (not to be confused with Florida's wealthy enclave for the rich infamous). It can be reached by taking the Beach Road turnoff from Highway 1 and traversing five miles of bumpy back roads that pass fertile farmland. Palm Beach is a unit of Sunset State Beach, located well off the beaten track and offering two completely different outdoor experiences separated by a whale of a sand dune. The first is a grove of eucalyptus trees whose limbs provide a fragrant canopy for a scattering of picnic tables. It is a calm, shaded environment protected from stiff and steady onshore winds by high, humpbacked dunes. Cross the dunes and a different story unfolds: warm sun, wide sandy beaches, and breakers rolling ashore in perfect sets, urged along by seemingly ceaseless breezes. Incidentally, Palm Beach borders the Pajaro River Bike Path, a nine-mile route that runs along the river separating Santa Cruz and Monterey counties.

Up the road lies the main entrance to **Sunset State Beach**. It has more facilities—paved parking lots, covered picnic tables, developed campsites. A cliff-hugging road zigzags down to the campground and, a little farther on, the beach. Cultivated fields border the park. Monstrous silver driftwood logs have washed ashore. Whether you're looking down at the beach from the vantage point of the bluffs, or up from the water's edge, Sunset State Beach offers breathtaking scenery. It's lifeguarded and popular, both with day visitors and overnight campers. The surf, alas, is hazardous, but that doesn't deter crowds from frolicking on the ample strand. Palm Beach to Sunset encompasses seven miles of beachfront.

For More Information

Contact Sunset State Beach, 201 Beach Road, Watsonville, CA 95077; (408) 724-1266.

Palm Beach
(a part of Sunset State Beach)

Location: In Watsonville, five miles west of Highway 1 via Beach Road.

Parking: \$3 entrance fee per vehicle.

Hours: 7 AM to a half hour after sunset.

Facilities: Rest rooms, picnic area, and fire pits.

Contact: For beach information, contact Sunset State Beach at (408) 724-1266.

See number 1 on page 376.

Sunset State Beach

Location: West of Watsonville, at the end of Sunset Beach Road, off Highway 1.

Parking: \$6 entrance fee per vehicle.

Hours: 7 AM to a half hour after sunset.

Facilities: Lifeguards, rest rooms, showers, picnic area, and fire pits. There are 90 tent and RV campsites. Fees are \$14 to \$16 per night. For camping reservations, call Destinet at (800) 444-7275.

Contact: For beach information, contact Sunset State Beach at (408) 724-1266.

See number 2 on page 376.

La Selva

Location: Manresa State Beach—both the main beach and the "Manresa Uplands" unit—are near La Selva, just south of Aptos. From San Andreas Road, turn onto Manresa Beach Road to get to the former and Sand Dollar Drive for the latter.

A little community that's as snug as the proverbial bug in a rug hides off the highway, tucked between a string of long, lonely state beaches in southern Santa Cruz County and the reappearance of civilization in Aptos. La Selva is a self-contained burg that boasts its own public library and surf shop. Handwritten signs urge you to slow down. You can't get to the beach directly from town, but a bluff-top park offers a spectacular coastal overlook. We watched four horse-and-riders gallop around free as the breeze on the wide, sandy (and private) expanse below. Above La Selva Beach is **Lundborgh Beach**, which lies in front of a very prominent train trestle. It is public, but you can get to it only by walking north from Manresa State Beach, being careful to stay on the public side of the mean high-tide line while crossing La Selva Beach, lest you rile the locals who own the property.

Manresa State Beach lies just south of La Selva Beach. It is a dual-access park. The **Manresa Uplands** unit offers walk-in tent camping in a scrub-and-shrub setting and beach access from a smallish parking lot. Stretch those calf muscles before sallying forth, because 170 steps lead down the stairs to the beach. Crumbly, light brown sandstone bluffs

Lundborgh Beach
(a.k.a. Trestle Beach)

Location: Reachable only by walking north from Manresa State Beach.
Parking: None.
Hours: Sunrise to sunset.
Facilities: None.
Contact: No contact number available.

See number 5 on page 376.

Manresa Uplands
(a part of Manresa State Beach)

Location: In La Selva, at the end of Manresa Beach Road, west of San Andreas Road.
Parking: $6 entrance fee per vehicle.
Hours: 7 AM to a half hour after sunset.
Facilities: Rest rooms, picnic areas, showers, and fire pits. There are 64 tent campsites. Fees are $14 to $16 per night. For camping reservations, call Destinet at (800) 444-7275.
Contact: For beach information, contact Manresa Uplands State Beach at (408) 761-1795.

See number 3 on page 376.

Manresa State Beach

Location: In La Selva, at the end of Sand Dollar Drive, off San Andreas Road.
Parking: $6 entrance fee per vehicle.
Hours: 7 AM to a half hour after sunset.
Facilities: Lifeguards and rest rooms.
Contact: For beach information, contact Manresa State Beach at (408) 724-3750.

See number 4 on page 376.

loom behind the beach, recalling the way the coast looks down south in San Clemente.

The main entrance to Manresa is more accessible—a mere 55 steps down to the beach—which may help justify the $6 per car day-use fee. We saw lots of folks surfing and sunbathing and giggling in the sand. Those of limited means park their vehicles by the side of the road and hike in to avoid the entrance fee.

For More Information

Contact Manresa State Beach, 205 Manresa Beach Road, La Selva, CA 95076; (408) 724-3750.

Aptos

Location: Eight miles south of Santa Cruz, along Highway 1. Rio Del Mar Boulevard runs from Highway 1 to Rio Del Mar Beach.
Population: 23,000
Area Code: 408 **Zip Code:** 95003

Bisected by Highway 1, Aptos is a study in contradictions. It's a charming, quiet village, and a bustling, harried town. It's a friendly place but one where people lose patience when something gets in their way. For example, shortly upon arriving in Aptos one stunning and slightly chilly July afternoon, we encountered: (1) a punky kid at **Rio Del Mar Beach**, humoring himself by boxing a plastic barrier meant to keep cars off the beach while his friends clapped and cheered; (2) a blasé and unhelpful clerk at the local post office who sold us a box but wouldn't give us a strip of tape to seal it; and (3) a typically impatient freeway flyer who leaned on his horn and flashed his headlights because we apparently interfered with his God-given right to exceed the speed limit. Proof positive of that old maxim that when too many people horn in on paradise, it ain't paradise anymore.

Nerves jangled by a brief foray into the part of Aptos that lies on the dry side of Highway 1—the part where you'll find all the strip malls—we rolled down the roller-coaster hill of Rio Del Mar and onto the beach. That part of Aptos is just what the doctor ordered—a

Rio Del Mar Beach
(a part of Seacliff State Beach)

Location: In Aptos, at the end of Rio Del Mar Boulevard.
Parking: $6 entrance fee per vehicle.
Hours: Sunrise to 10 PM.
Facilities: Rest rooms and showers.
Contact: For beach information, contact Seacliff State Beach at (408) 688-3222.

See number 6 on page 376.

Seacliff State Beach

Location: In Aptos, at the end of State Park Drive, off Highway 1.
Parking: $6 entrance fee per vehicle.
Hours: Sunrise to 10 PM.
Facilities: Lifeguards, rest rooms, showers, picnic area, and fire pits. There are 26 tent and RV campsites. Fees are $21 to $23 per night. For camping reservations, call Destinet at (800) 444-7275.
Contact: For beach information, contact Seacliff State Beach at (408) 688-3222.

See number 7 on page 376.

flat, open beach; pretty neighborhoods tucked into green, viney hills; and a handful of motels and restaurants within view of the water.

Beaches

Rio Del Mar Beach is a splendid beach that's so wide you'll work your calf muscles into oxygen deficit hauling across the deep, soft sand to the water's edge. You could walk from here down to the Monterey County line on a nearly continuous beach. Moving in the other direction, lying just a short, hikeable distance east of Rio Del Mar Beach, is **Seacliff State Beach**. This is the site of a real curiosity: the Palo Alto, an old World War I supply boat that never saw active duty and now serves as an addendum to a fishing pier. Towed here in 1929, it served as a kind of pleasure palace—dining, dancing, what have you—before going financially bust two years later and then literally busting up in a storm. Lashed to the end of the fishing pier, it's open to visitors, who can mount a few rusty steps onto its deck and toss a line into the water or just poke around. The park is heavily used by anglers, picnickers, and campers. Commercial facilities include a bait-and-tackle shop and snack bar boasting "homemade sandwiches." The beach is reached by a steep, winding road. It's got 26 campsites with full trailer hookups right by the water, and you'd better believe they are rarely vacant. A bike path links Rio Del Mar with Seacliff.

Bunking Down

Beach lovers flock to the **Rio Sands Motel** (116 Aptos Beach Drive, 688-3207, $$), which takes pride in being "100 steps to the beach." We didn't count, but give or take a few footfalls, that seems accurate. An unusually comfortable motel, the Rio Sands is set on a quiet side street. Some of the rooms are actually suites, with small kitchens, comfy bedrooms, and a separate living area with couch, TV, and balcony. An outdoor spa is nestled in a peaceful courtyard garden. All that for only $80 or so a night in season—a real bargain.

Coastal Cuisine

You can't get any closer to the beach than the **Café Rio** (131 Esplanade at Rio Del Mar, 688-8917, $$$), a modern-looking, wood-and-neon place that has good fresh seafood and is situated a stone's throw from the beach. For breakfast and lunch, the **Broken Egg** (7887 Soquel Drive, 688-4322, $) serves up omelettes, crepes, and "eggs in a basket." Then there's **Café Sparrow** (8042 Soquel Drive, 688-6238, $$$), a cozy continental hideaway that offers grilled chicken, lamb, and veal dishes and has a strong wine list.

Night Moves

Most night moves are made in the direction of Capitola and Santa Cruz. Aptos maintains more of a village atmosphere than its noisy neighbors. Still **Café Rio** (see above) does have a nice bar and a semblance of life after dark.

For More Information

Contact the Aptos Chamber of Commerce, 9099 Soquel Drive #12, Aptos, CA 95003; (408) 688-1467.

Capitola

Location: Three miles east of Santa Cruz via Highway 1. Capitola Avenue runs from Highway 1 into the village and ends near the beach. The Esplanade runs alongside Capitola City Beach, the most popular beach in the area.
Population: 10,450
Area Code: 408 **Zip Code:** 95010

If they can afford it, many who work in Santa Cruz prefer to live in Capitola, Aptos, or Soquel, the upscale villages that lie just southeast of town. These bonny seaside towns look like botanical gardens compared to the weeded-lot appearance of much of Santa Cruz. Capitola—or Capitola-by-the-Sea, as some prefer—is situated south of Highway 1 and east of 41st Avenue, a heavily trafficked road lined with shopping centers and gas stations. The easiest way to get to the heart of Capitola and its city beach is to take the Capitola Avenue exit off Highway 1 and proceed south until you start smelling suntan lotion.

Capitola is built around a broad, sandy cove. The Esplanade runs along the water, and Capitola Avenue parallels it for a few blocks. All the town's best shops, restaurants, and action can be found here. After a few laps around the shopping district, it becomes clear that Capitola is an upwardly mobile melange of coffee-drinking bookstore/artist types and Northern California beach bums and bunnies who have driven down for the day from UC-Santa Cruz, San Jose, and points inland. When we visited, the beaches and sidewalks of Capitola were crawling with more apple-cheeked, blond-haired beauties than we'd seen in hundreds of miles. Indeed, Capitola and Santa Cruz are the northernmost example of the classic California beach life.

There's only one snag when it comes to enjoying this hidden, cold-water Acapulco: the parking. "Going to Capitola today?" a Santa Cruz merchant asked with raised eyebrows. "Good luck finding a parking space." Get ready to drive in circles for half an hour and pounce when a car pulls away from a meter. If you're not up for playing musical parking spaces, there's miles of vacant state beaches running south to the Monterey county line.

Incidentally, there used to be a lot more beach lapping at Capitola's shores than there is today. That changed with the construction of jetties at the Santa Cruz Small Craft Harbor in 1985. Due to alterations in the littoral current, all of Capitola's beaches washed away that winter. Capitola City Beach was subsequently restored with trucked-in sand and protected by a jetty built south of Capitola Fishing Wharf. But that jetty itself has contributed to a domino effect, starving beaches beneath the Grand Avenue cliffs (south of the Capitola City Beach) and causing erosion and property loss. All of which goes to prove you'll never create anything but disaster by messing around with the natural order.

Capitola is a pretty village, with cute homes nestled into the hills and ravines along Soquel Creek. The town celebrated its 125th birthday in June 1994. Way back in 1869, Capitola was a campground retreat and then, in 1894, site of the Grand Capitola, a palatial resort hotel comparable in its heyday to San Diego's Hotel del Coronado. Financial troubles prompted the hotel to close its doors in 1929, and when a fire destroyed the building that December, some suspected arson. Today Capitola supports a modest tourist industry and entertains large numbers of Central Valley day-trippers fleeing the scorching summer heat. It's a great beach town in miniature, with a small, crescent-shaped beach, a modest 600-foot fishing wharf, and a lagoon near the mouth of Soquel Creek known as "Little Venice," where paddle boats are rented.

Beaches

Capitola City Beach, one of the loveliest beaches in a county blessed with an abundance of them, attracts students, families, locals, valley girls and guys, and more. The beach is about a quarter mile long and 100 yards at its widest point. At times every square foot is packed with sprawling, lounging bodies and volleyball players. The shopping area that surrounds it is full of stores that display trendy merchandise (designer swimwear, arts and crafts) and tend to the sweet tooths of the perambulating beach crowd. Occasionally the ocean water gets bacterially contaminated to unsafe levels by runoff from Soquel Creek, but this is not usually a problem in the dry summer season. Incidentally, Capitola also has an intermittently sandy beach, known as **Hooper Beach**, beside its fishing wharf.

Generally, Capitola City Beach is clean and safe. Folks even come out at night. Concrete benches line the Esplanade, and strollers come to breathe the salt air and meditate to the musical mantra of the sea's waxing and waning. One evening, out of the darkness, a man wearing only a pair of red Speedos and a shower cap bolted across the beach on a mission: a midnight swim. Disbelieving spectators shouted advice and encouragement to this would-be polar bear as he disappeared into the inky darkness where night and ocean meet: "Buddy, you're gonna freeze." "Go, go!" "Damn, he went in." He returned dripping wet but none the worse for wear, climbing into his van and turning on the heater while pondering the briny deep from which he'd just emerged.

A mile northeast of Capitola is **New Brighton State Beach**, reached via the Park Avenue exit off Highway 1. Signs point into a tree-shaded glen, beyond which lie high, grass-covered dunes and a flat, sandy beach. New Brighton, which faces due south, is spared the prevailing winds that mercilessly wrack other stretches of the Santa Cruz coast. This area was originally known as China Cove or China Beach, from a time in the late 1800s when Asian fishermen dragged the water with fishing nets. Tall beach grasses and thick, scrubby vegetation hold the steep dunes in place. At the foot of the dunes is a gravel road used by joggers, and hiking trails line the cliffs. New Brighton has a mile's worth of coastline, which is excellent for surf fishing and clamming, and 112 developed campsites set behind the dunes among stands of cypress and pine trees.

Capitola City Beach

4

Location: In Capitola, along the Esplanade.
Parking: Metered street parking.
Hours: Open 24 hours.
Facilities: Lifeguards and rest rooms.
Contact: For beach information, contact the Capitola Public Works Department at (408) 475-7300.

See number 9 on page 376.

Hooper Beach

2

Location: In Capitola, west of Capitola Fishing Wharf, at the foot of Wharf Road.
Parking: Metered street parking.
Hours: Open 24 hours.
Facilities: None.
Contact: For beach information, contact the Capitola Public Works Department at (408) 475-7300.

See number 10 on page 376.

Hooper Beach lies just west of the Capitola Wharf. It's a small, narrow beach in the best of years, located at the foot of a stairwell. In the summer of 1995, Hooper didn't build back up because of the high tides and pounding storms of the previous winter. Only time will tell if it returns.

Bunking Down

Capitola isn't exactly a teeming tourist mecca, but there are a few places to stay. Two are located side by side near the Capitola Fishing Wharf, overlooking the beach and bay. One of them, the **Capitola Venetian Hotel** (1500 Wharf Road, 476-6471, $$), has an interesting history. It's located next door to the Venetian Court, California's first condominium development. At the time of its construction in 1920, the word "condominium" didn't exist to describe the concept of individual ownership of apartment-style, stucco-and-tile cottages. Over the years, the Venetian Court and Hotel—located at mouth of Soquel Creek, an area known as "Little Venice"—have taken their share of direct hits during winter storms. Still, most owners seem determined to remain and rebuild, probably because you can't get any closer to the ocean or the heart of Capitola than this. Another place to stay on the bay is the **Harbor Lights Motel** (5000 Cliff Drive, 476-0505, $$), a 10-unit motel that provides balconies, deck chairs, and complete kitchens. And for those who don't mind parting with the beach for a while (not to mention a lot of bucks), the **Inn at Depot Hill** (250 Monterey Avenue, 462-3376, $$$$) is a sumptuous bed and breakfast just up the hill.

New Brighton State Beach

Location: In Capitola, at the end of Park Avenue, off Highway 1.

Parking: $6 entrance fee per vehicle.

Hours: Sunrise to 10 PM.

Facilities: Lifeguards, rest rooms, showers, picnic areas, and fire pits. There are 112 tent and RV campsites. Fees are $14 to $16 per night. For camping reservations, call Destinet at (800) 444-7275.

Contact: For beach information, contact New Brighton State Beach at (408) 475-4850.

See number 8 on page 376.

Coastal Cuisine

All conversations about dining in Capitola inevitably begin and end with **Shadowbrook** (1740 Wharf Road, 475-1511, $$$), a romantic dining spot that's been around since 1947. Set along Soquel Creek in a quiet, residential part of Capitola, Shadowbrook serves seafood, prime rib, and other tasty fare in an elegant yet comfortable setting. Getting there is half the fun. To reach the restaurant, you must park in a lot above it and then make the descent via a red cable car that's been a fixture since 1958. There are half a dozen different dining rooms, including the Wine Cellar and the garden-view Greenhouse.

And speaking of wine cellars, Shadowbrook has an extensive one—amazingly, they lost only a bottle or two in the '89 quake, thanks to prescient earthquake proofing only a year or so earlier—and serves some tasty liqueur-spiked coffee beverages.

Capitola is also home to a top quality seafood restaurant that's located on the second floor of the Crossroads Center shopping mall. It's called **Seafood Mama** (820 Bay Avenue, 476-5976, $$$), and their specialty is grilled fish—sea bass, monkfish, yellow-fin tuna. Order whatever's fresh that night, and you can't go wrong. The portions are generous, the prices fair, and you can watch them cook your entrée on a mesquite grill. The appetizers are good, too: crab cakes, raw oysters, sashimi. Yum.

Finally, if you're looking for a gourmet take-out repast, head for **Gayle's Bakery and Roticceria** (504 Bay Avenue, 462-1200, $). It's worth fighting the inevitable crowds to peruse their mind-blowing selection of sandwiches, salads, cheeses, deli meats, appetizers, and desserts.

Night Moves

At night, the area surrounding Capitola City Beach becomes a popular promenade. Several square blocks of Spanish-style stucco exteriors are bathed in cursive neon script. Couples stroll shoulder to shoulder with youths who wander between coffee shops, pizza parlors, and the beach. By 9 or 10 PM, several mild-mannered restaurants make a Clark Kent–style change-eover into nightclubs. Two old reliables are **Margaritaville** (321 Esplanade, 476-2263) and **Zelda's** (203 Esplanade, 475-4900). The former was the liveliest place we ducked into, having the decided plus of an outdoor deck overlooking the water. In fact, it gets so lively that occasional fights break out, much to the consternation of the locals. We happened to read an editorial on the subject in the weekly paper: "Margaritaville remains an asset to the community. But at what point does it become a detriment?" We're still scratching our heads over that one. Down the street is Zelda's, a restaurant that offers live entertainment once the kitchen shuts down. One night, we heard a local singer-guitarist have a go at some blues numbers with a fair amount of virtuosity and feeling. Just goes to prove you never know what you'll stumble onto at the beach.

For More Information

Contact the Capitola Chamber of Commerce, 621-B Capitola Avenue, Capitola, CA 95010; (408) 475-6522.

Santa Cruz

Location: Santa Cruz sits at the north end of Monterey Bay, facing the city of Monterey due south across the bay. It lies 80 miles south of San Francisco, reachable via the Ocean Street exit off Highway 1. The center of activity is the Santa Cruz Beach and Boardwalk (a.k.a. "Main Beach").
Population: 55,000
Area Code: 408 **Zip Code:** 95060

Santa Cruz, located north of just about anywhere that serves authentic burritos, is frequently compared with Southern California. Maybe it's the sandy, swimmable beaches that are as numerous and varied as those down in Laguna Beach and La Jolla. Or maybe it's the world-class volleyball scene at Cowell Beach, the nimble-fingered set going for it with a spiky determination that would do their L.A. cousins proud. Surfing, too—that religion of Southern California—is worshipped and even enshrined in Santa Cruz at the lighthouse above Steamer Lane. Then there's the party-hearty atmosphere, the free-for-all on the boardwalk, the endless sea of youthful faces, the happy kids, the zit-encrusted adolescents, the hormone-driven teens, and the youth-thirsty adults trying to stave off middle age. Come to think of it, Santa Cruz is Southern California with a little Jersey Shore thrown in for good (or bad) measure.

If Santa Cruz can be said to resemble any one town, it would be Santa Monica. Open-minded tolerance has led both to become sanctuaries for the downtrodden, those seeking alternative lifestyles, and the hopelessly confused. If Santa Cruz were a border town, the surrounding nations would be Woodstock, Lollapalooza, Altamont, Tijuana, Surf City, and Desolation Row. To add to the confusion, the

 Map of Santa Cruz County beaches—page 376

open-minded tolerance of the town's 1960s-bred leaders has been sorely tested by the latest wave of rebels (see sidebar, "Young and in the Way"). It's a puzzling and intriguing place—even the Coast Highway can't make up its mind what to do, boldly entering the city from the south and then becoming a confusing maze of turns and exits.

Suffice it to say that Santa Cruz—which means "sacred cross"—is many things. It's a patchwork of lifestyles, politics, land forms, and roads that converge to make up the largest seaside resort north of Santa Barbara. A base population of 55,000 is swelled on weekends by crowds from Silicon Valley, San Jose, and San Francisco.

From the start, the town was marked by mysterious events. The mission that was built here in 1791, Mission La Exaltacion de la Santa Cruz, vanished without a trace. It was located somewhere near the San Lorenzo River and was perhaps swallowed by it (to this day, the river is subject to destructive flooding). A replica of the mission has been built outside of town, but few go out of their way to see it.

That is just as well, because Santa Cruz turned away from spiritual matters in 1865, when the first public bathhouse was built on the beachfront. A boardwalk, dance hall, and casino were added, bolstered by a lucrative logging economy that transformed the quiet town into a resort. A roller coaster and carousel followed. The crowds began arriving when the railroad company feverishly promoted a "Suntan Special," which deposited visitors from San Francisco and San Jose on the main beach at Santa Cruz. This, in turn, inspired more railroad stations to be built up and down the coast, paralleling what is today Highway 1. The original roller coaster and carousel—the latter with beautiful mounts designed and painted by Charles Looff in 1911—are still in service, and many of the fine Victorian homes of the logging moguls are still standing.

Santa Cruz is built around the San Lorenzo River, which snake-dances through town before emptying in the ocean south of the main beach. On the sandy end of this watery axis, Santa Cruz is a beach resort. Over by the cliffs that lay upriver, Santa Cruz is more upscale and suburban. Everywhere else, the town is a hotbed of liberalism and laissez-faire lifestyles. New Age free-thinkers seem to hold sway here to a greater degree than any other community in America (save for Bolinas). We took a political/philosophical reading from two bumper stickers spied on different cars within minutes of each other: "Visualize Industrial Collapse" and "Never Drive Faster Than Your Angel Can Fly."

Still, for a supposedly peaceable haven, you don't always feel safe in Santa Cruz, especially after dark. It has an underside, as do most places where eccentricities are not only tolerated but encouraged. We picked up some unnerving snatches of conversation around town. Walking along Pacific Avenue, for instance, we caught up to a pair of bookish-looking guys talking a blue streak. It turned out that the subject was guns: "nine millimeter, they're good for, like, urban warfare." Okayyyy. Moving right along, we traipsed past a squadron of loiterers from another planet, affecting kind of a punky-hippie hybrid, a look that bespoke poverty and defiance. We always get panhandled within minutes of parking downtown.

All over, it's the same dreary look: tousled cataracts of hair spilling out from under wool caps; morguelike black clothes draped over hunched shoulders; wispy nature trails of facial hair; fish hooks, grommets, and other forms of "jewelry" piercing lips, nostrils, cheeks, and assorted other anatomical parts. One night, a petri dish of such specimens had gathered outside a club where the band was mangling a Jimi Hendrix song. It was, all too appropriately, "I Don't Live Today."

Down the street, a '60s acid casualty who was having a very bad hair day gave a running commentary on a young street musician's performance: "It's not that you can't play, man. You play pretty good. It's just that you're not utilizing your talent to any creative, original purpose." The fact that the lad was wearing a plastic clown's nose as he earnestly strummed away lent some credence to the hippie elder's critique.

The biggest liberal melting pot in this decidedly left-of-center burg is the University of California at Santa Cruz, a 2,000-acre campus northeast of town. Founded in 1965, the campus is set on a former cattle ranch now home to an arboretum of rare plants, groves of redwood trees, and packs of wild animals. The buildings are hidden among the trees, making it one of the best-concealed institutions of higher learning on the planet. The sports mascot is a banana slug, the campus restaurant is called The Whole Earth (serving "Thai-style Tofu and Veggies"), narrative evaluations are given instead of grades, and courses bear names like "The Pursuit of Truth in the Company of Friends" and "Female Masturbation." (Does the latter qualify as vocational training?) All levity aside, it is heartening to find a university that isn't just mass-producing business majors. Student-led tours are available (call 459-4008). To get to UCSC, take Highway 1 north to Bay Avenue, turn right, and follow the signs. And now, follow us to the beaches.

Beaches

Due to the winding San Lorenzo River and the boa-like bending of the roads, Santa Cruz has many beach-access points. Unfortunately, except for those on the western side of the San Lorenzo River—from Main Beach to Natural Bridges—they are not easy to get to. The access points are in residential areas, with limited parking. Appropriate stairwells and paths are marked, but you still have to find them.

Corcoran Lagoon Beach

Location: In Live Oak, along East Cliff Drive between 22nd and 23rd Avenues.

Parking: Limited free street parking.

Hours: 6 AM to 10 PM.

Facilities: Rest rooms.

Contact: For beach information, contact the Santa Cruz County Department of Parks, Open Space, and Cultural Services at (408) 462-8300.

See number 14 on page 376.

Cowell Beach

Location: In Santa Cruz, along Bay Street at West Cliff Drive, west of the Municipal Wharf.

Parking: Metered street and lot parking.

Hours: Open 24 hours.

Facilities: Lifeguards and rest rooms.

Contact: For beach information, contact the Santa Cruz Beach Lifeguard Station at (408) 429-3747.

See number 20 on page 376.

Its Beach

Location: This is a seasonal pocket beach in Santa Cruz reachable via the stairwells between Lighthouse Field State Beach and Natural Bridges State Beach along West Cliff Drive.

Parking: Metered street parking.

Hours: Open 24 hours.

Facilities: None.

Contact: For beach information, contact the Santa Cruz Department of Aquatic Services at (408) 429-3110.

See number 23 on page 376.

Only the initiated know the whereabouts of some of these coves, and each seems to be claimed by a different crowd.

A number of small, unnamed coves can be accessed via paths or stairs at the ends of avenues off East Cliff Drive between Capitola and the Santa Cruz Small Craft Harbor. The cove beaches located off the higher-numbered avenues lead up to Pleasure Point, and they're outposts for surfers and tidepoolers that disappear at high tide. Park on neighborhood streets and observe the rites of surfing from a cliff-top overlook at 41st Avenue, or walk down to the beach via a path at 35th and 38th Avenues. **Key Beach** is located off Opal Cliffs Drive, east of **Pleasure Point** near Capitola. To get to it means crossing private property and opening a locked gate with a key purchased on site from the owner. Needless to say, unless you're a surfer who really loves the waves at this spot, you probably won't be putting Key Beach on your itinerary.

Around the far side of Pleasure Point lies **Moran Lake Beach**, the next drape of sand. People come here mostly to sunbathe; it's a flat expanse protected from the wind by large

Key Beach

Location: In Live Oak, at Opal Cliffs Drive and 45th Avenue.

Parking: Limited free street parking

Hours: Sunrise to sunset.

Facilities: None.

Contact: No contact number available.

See number 11 on page 376.

Lincoln Beach
(a part of Twin Lakes State Beach)

Location: In Santa Cruz, at the ends of 12th, 13th, and 14th Avenues.

Parking: Limited free street parking.

Hours: 8 AM to 10 PM.

Facilities: Rest rooms.

Contact: For beach information, contact the Santa Cruz District of the California Department of Parks and Recreation at (408) 429-2850.

See number 16 on page 376.

Lighthouse Field State Beach

Location: In Santa Cruz, at Point Santa Cruz along West Cliff Drive.

Parking: Metered street parking.

Hours: Sunrise to sunset.

Facilities: Rest rooms, picnic tables, and fire pits.

Contact: For beach information, contact the Santa Cruz County Department of Parks, Open Space and Cultural Services at (408) 462-8300.

See number 22 on page 376.

Main Beach
(a.k.a. Santa Cruz Beach)

Location: In Santa Cruz, along Beach Street, east of the Municipal Wharf.

Parking: Metered lot and street parking.

Hours: Open 24 hours.

Facilities: Lifeguards and rest rooms.

Contact: For beach information, contact the Santa Cruz Department of Aquatic Services at (408) 429-3110.

See number 19 on map page 376.

rocks at either end. **Corcoran Lagoon** sits behind the beach that bears its name; tidepools can be found on its eastern side (accessible from a path to the beach near East Cliff Drive and East 21st Street). **Sunny Cove** draws the bodysurfers, and **Lincoln Beach** attracts contemplative types. Parking on the surrounding residential streets can be a problem, since much of it is by permit only. On the other side of Schwan Lagoon is **Twin Lakes State Beach**. This 86-acre park is alive with party people pumpin' their fists like this (to borrow a line from a George Clinton song). Twin Lakes is broken in half by the Santa Cruz Small Craft Harbor. The unit of Twin Lakes that lies on the far side of the yacht basin is called **Seabright Beach** (though sentimental locals prefer Castle Beach). The most popular pastimes at Seabright's mile-long strand are playing volleyball by day and building bonfires at twilight. Despite all the attractive options that lie east of the San Lorenzo River, you'll probably wind up on **Main Beach** if you're not a local. As the name suggests, it's the longest and widest strand in town, fronting the famed Boardwalk. Most of the town's beach-area accommoda-

Mitchell's Cove

Location: This is a seasonal pocket beach in Santa Cruz reachable via the stairwells between Lighthouse Field and Natural Bridges State Beaches along West Cliff Drive.

Parking: Metered street parking.

Hours: Open 24 hours.

Facilities: None.

Contact: For beach information, contact the Santa Cruz Department of Aquatic Services at (408) 429-3110.

See number 24 on page 376.

Moran Lake Beach

Location: In Live Oak, on East Cliff Drive at 26th Street.

Parking: Free parking lot.

Hours: 6 AM to 10 PM.

Facilities: Rest rooms.

Contact: For beach information, contact the Santa Cruz County Department of Parks, Open Space, and Cultural Services at (408) 462-8300.

See number 13 on page 376.

Natural Bridges State Beach

Location: In Santa Cruz, on Natural Bridges Drive at West Cliff Drive.

Parking: $6 entrance fee per vehicle.

Hours: 8 AM to sunset.

Facilities: Rest rooms and picnic area.

Contact: For beach information, contact Natural Bridges State Beach at (408) 423-4609.

See number 25 on page 376.

Pleasure Point Beach

Location: In Live Oak, at East Cliff Drive, between 35th and 38th Avenues.

Parking: Limited free street parking.

Hours: Sunrise to sunset.

Facilities: None.

Contact: For beach information, contact the Santa Cruz County Department of Parks, Open Space, and Cultural Services at (408) 462-8300.

See number 12 on page 376.

tions are arrayed close by. Touristy or not, Main Beach and the Boardwalk should be strolled and experienced.

The Boardwalk has been spruced up since the 1980s. Back then it looked like the setting for a Bruce Springsteen song about hard times on the Jersey shore. Today it's much improved. Neptune's Kingdom, a clean if generic arcade, is a recent addition. Parents can toss down schooners of beer upstairs while their progeny destroy galaxies on video games downstairs. A "historium" justifies the nautical motif with a few educational placards. Outside in the bright sun, beach bums have their pick of things to ride, eat, and play, including our old boardwalk favorite, Skee-Ball. (We copped some plastic skull rings this time out.)

The Sky Glider ski lift carried us high above the frivolity, providing an incredible panorama of the town, beach, and ocean. Caterpillar cars dipsy-doodle on the roller coaster next door, allowing total strangers to share moments of gleeful terror. A multitude of food stalls sell typical beach fare, and an equally large number of rides will help you lose it. One spinning capsule holds riders suspended upside down

Seabright Beach
(a.k.a. Castle Beach)

5

Location: In Santa Cruz, at the end of Seabright Avenue.
Parking: Metered street parking.
Hours: Open 24 hours.
Facilities: Lifeguards and rest rooms.
Contact: For beach information, contact the Santa Cruz Department of Aquatic Services at (408) 429-3110.

See number 18 on page 376.

Steamer Lane

5

Location: In Santa Cruz, at Lighthouse Point off West Cliff Drive.
Parking: Metered street parking.
Hours: Open 24 hours.
Facilities: None.
Contact: For beach information, contact the Santa Cruz Department of Aquatic Services at (408) 429-3110.

See number 21 on page 376.

Sunny Cove

2

Location: In Live Oak, at the end of Sunny Cove, off East Cliff Drive.
Parking: Limited free street parking.
Hours: 6 AM to 10 PM.
Facilities: None.
Contact: For beach information, contact the Santa Cruz County Department of Parks, Open Space, and Cultural Services at (408) 462-8300.

See number 15 on page 376.

Twin Lakes State Beach

4

Location: In Santa Cruz, on East Cliff Drive at 7th Avenue.
Parking: Metered lot and street parking.
Hours: 8 AM to 10 PM.
Facilities: Lifeguards, rest rooms, and fire rings.
Contact: For beach information, contact the Santa Cruz District of the California Department of Parks and Recreation at (408) 429-2850.

See number 17 on page 376.

at its apogee for several seconds, then flings them back to earth in a frightening blur. Do people really pay for this sort of torture? Apparently so, because an annual pass to the boardwalk rides costs $58.75. If you're buying by the ride, these stomach churners can add up—go for a day pass. In sum, Santa Cruz Beach is a classic boardwalk scene that from a distance—say, from Lighthouse Point—confers an airy, nostalgic quality upon the town.

If boardwalk revelry isn't your kids' idea of fun, two options remain. First, lengthy psychological testing. (What child doesn't love being suspended upside down a hundred feet above the ground?) Second, take the Santa Cruz Steam Train. It's a turn-of-the-century steam locomotive that leaves from the back of the boardwalk arcade and travels inland through the redwood forest near Felton, along the San Lorenzo River canyon. It stops at Roaring Camp, a former gold-mining area. It's a great half-day excursion. (Call 335-4484 for fares and schedules.)

At the north end of the oceanfront, on the other side of the municipal wharf, is **Cowell Beach**. Years ago, the Miss California pageant was held here but was canceled because (we think we heard this correctly) spectators pelted the contestants and each other with raw meat. Now, Cowell confines its contests to an annual volleyball tournament. Wimps need not apply; this is the domain of serious athletes. Some of the best surf that California has to offer can be found just north, across the slippery and deadly rocks at **Steamer Lane**. This is the name for the surfing spot off Lighthouse Point. Only the best and bravest surfers come here, because the swells reach mountainous heights and threaten to hurl their fearless riders against the base of the cliffs or fillet them on rocks that barely jut above the surface. Surfers who aren't in the water sit on the rocks, waiting their turn. Everyone else stands on the edge of an eroding cliff, watching nervously, taking photographs and creating an intimate community based on fear (or sadism). Waves slam against the shore, sending spray upward. Before the fence was erected, occasional onlookers were washed over the edge to their deaths. Yee-haw!

The state allocated funds to create **Lighthouse Field State Beach** to commemorate this legendary spot. An integral part of the 40-acre park—which stretches into the lands above the bluff—is the Mark Abbott Surfing Museum, located in the lighthouse. Like the California Surf Museum in Oceanside, this is an imperative stop. Lovingly displayed photographs adorn the walls—of people riding hollowed-out 16-foot longboards, of 19 surfers crammed inside a woodie—and videos and news clippings document the sport's rich history. The centerpiece is a shrine where the ashes of 18-year-old Mark Abbott are interred beneath a pile of rocks and shells. This young man challenged the sea and lost... but the war rages on in Steamer Lane. The book shop here has a great selection of surf and beach publications. (For more information, call 429-3429.) A small city-owned beach next door, **Its Beach**, is popular with dog owners, who are allowed to unleash their canines in the morning and evening. **Mitchell's Cove** is another cove that does the disappearing beach trick during winter months, when storms scrub the shore line of its sand. Most years, it reappears when fair weather builds the beaches back up.

Finally, if you're not yet beached out, follow West Cliff Drive north to **Natural Bridges State Beach**, named for the offshore stone formations that resemble—you guessed it—bridges. Though no lifeguards patrol the tiny beach, it's considered safe, and chaperoned tots wade giddily in the foaming waves at the Joseph M. Long Marine Laboratory and Aquarium, a working research facility with an aquarium full of sea urchins, sea sponges, abalone, anemones, and starfish. There's also a sea-lion-viewing perch, as well as the skeleton of a blue whale. It's a cheap way to educate the

 Map of Santa Cruz County beaches—page 376

kids and learn something yourself. (The laboratory is open Tuesday through Saturday from 1 PM to 4 PM; for information, call 459-4308.)

Bunking Down

The motel scene in Santa Cruz, like the scene around the boardwalk and arcade, has been improving of late. In the past, sobering stories were told about oceanfront motels here—tales of crime, degeneracy, noise, overcrowding of rooms, disgusting odors, and substance abuse. Our favorite story: a teenager sneaks out to get a soda one evening, leaving his grandmother in the room with the door unlocked. He lingers awhile on the boardwalk. When he returns, he finds a derelict passed out in bed next to his grandma, who has somehow slept through it all. Then, there was the "hippie" (they use that word around here a lot) who lived for a month inside a hotel elevator....

We've taken an informal inventory of the available hotels and motels near Main Beach, where rooms start as low as $40 in the dead of winter and get jacked up to $125 and more at places with letters missing from their signs. Some Santa Cruz innkeepers are reluctant to quote hard-and-fast prices, especially on busy summer weekends, when they charge whatever the market will bear.

The best-known hotel on the beach is the **Dream Inn** (175 West Cliff Drive, 426-4330, $$$$), a formidable high-rise overlooking Cowell Beach's vaunted volleyball pits. It really ought to be renamed the Dream On—rooms here are absurdly overpriced. Sorry, no hotel in Santa Cruz can justify charging $190 for a room that can be equaled by a **Holiday Inn Express** (600 Riverside Avenue, 458-9660, $$) that's only two blocks away and costs half the price, with a free breakfast thrown in. There's also a comfortable, full-scale **Holiday Inn** (611 Ocean Street, 426-7100, $$) near a footbridge that leads over the San Lorenzo River into the downtown area. The grounds are nicely maintained, a heated outdoor pool graces the premises, and you feel safe coming and going—no small consideration in Santa Cruz.

Coastal Cuisine

Santa Cruz has got a wide and varied dining scene—everything from fast food to New Age alternatives, from seafood restaurants on the wharf to sushi restaurants on the side streets. The Santa Cruz Municipal Wharf is the place to go for seafood with a view. Take your pick of about half-a-dozen sit-down restaurants with picture windows that face the ocean. One such place, a longtime wharf resident, is **Stagnaro Brothers** (Municipal Wharf, 423-2180, $$). A restaurant and a fish market, Stagnaro's motto is "Caught today, cooked today." You can eat your catch in a casual atmosphere or take it to go. The red clam chowder is a house specialty, a hearty concoction that really cuts the chill when a cold ocean breeze is blowing.

A neighboring establishment that serves a good meal is the **Miramar** (552 Municipal Wharf, 423-2666, $$). We had a fine lunch of sole meunière, salad, and fresh bread while watching monstrous winter waves threaten to pound the wharf to smithereens one January afternoon. It is a huge, bulky wharf extending 3,000 feet (more than half a mile) into the ocean. There's usually plenty of parking; you collect a ticket at the entrance gate and pay by the hour. Gazing out the restaurant windows while gale-force winds blew the rain sideways, we could see an ocean kayaker get tossed around in what looked less like recreation than reckless endangerment. Then came a run of big waves. Every time another giant struck the pier, it was like the sound of a bowling ball scattering a set of tenpins. Kee-blam! The wharf would jiggle and the overhead lights would sway. We found ourselves wondering how the pier could endure such abuse winter after winter. And yet the Santa Cruz Municipal Wharf has been standing on this spot since 1914.

Young and in the Way

Picture the scene: a bunch of gray, balding hippies sitting around agonizing about the problems of today's youth. Though this may sound like the plot to an ill-advised sequel to *The Big Chill*, it's really happening in Santa Cruz in the 1990s.

If you thought the youth-culture tidal wave that created grunge was a tough nut to crack, get a load of the teens on the loose here. They aren't spare-change artists (yet) or surf punks, like their big brothers were. They are, however, loud. They are angry, ugly, and bored. And they are everywhere, though they have no place to go. They are not allowed in the bars (too young). They are often refused service in the cafés (too scruffy). They are attracted to the rundown areas of beach communities such as Santa Cruz, where they can squat in quarters unfit for rental.

Youth-as-enemy should have a familiar ring in Santa Cruz, where the city council is made up of erstwhile hippies, socialists, and protesters who still wear the battle scars of their civil disobedience. Ponder the irony of aging hippies trying to bust the chops of today's youth. Underneath it all nothing has changed, really, except for the wardrobes. Thirty years ago it was long hair, tie-dyed T-shirts, headbands, patchouli, unkempt facial hair, bells, beads, and bangles. Now it's shaved heads, backward baseball caps, nasty jackboots, tattoos, pierced body parts, and soiled thrift-shop clothing. The favorite pastimes of today's punks consist of spray-painting angry slogans on walls—often one-word epithets like *bile*—and hanging out. Therein lies the rub. Santa Cruz is sick and tired of them hanging out.

Another waterfront restaurant is the **Crow's Nest** (2218 East Cliff Drive, 476-4560, $$), near Twin Lakes State Beach and the small craft harbor. They get their fish from the fleet next door, have easy access to the beach, and are family friendly with kids' menus and a treasure chest full of trinkets. Wednesdays they hold a clambake on the beach. A favorite eatery near the Boardwalk is the **Beach Street Café** (399 Beach Street, 426-7621, $), a good bet for breakfast or lunch. While basking in the friendly chatter, enjoy the framed collection of Maxfield Parrish prints, one of the largest in the U.S. Good coffee, great omelettes.

For killer Mexican food in an atmospheric setting, head over to **El Palomar** (1336 Pacific Garden Mall, 425-7575, $$), where you can choose from two eating areas. There's a fancy dining room with high-end Mexican seafood dishes. On the other side of the hall is a stand-up taco and booze bar where you can scarf down unbelievable snapper tacos. The staff hand-presses the soft corn tortillas before your very eyes from a mound of dough. It's a bustling room in which a terrific, quick meal can be made from several soft tacos and a Mexican beer or two.

Another Mexican favorite is **Rosie's Rosticeria** (495 Lake Avenue, 479-3536, $), located by the Yacht Harbor and very reasonably priced. For something completely different, try **Vasili's Greek Food & Barbeque** (1501 Mission Avenue, 458-9808, $$), where they serve a dynamite roasted chicken swimming in lemon, olive oil, and artichoke hearts. One of the strangest eateries of all in a town where the margins define the mainstream is **Mobo Sushi** (105 South River Street, 425-1700, $$$). It's a sushi restaurant where the filleting and assembly of raw fish is done by white boys. They're all

 Map of Santa Cruz County beaches—page 376

This issue hit home at Vertigo, a downtown café owned by Brian Friedman, an early thirty-something whose other business—an antiboutique called Anubis Warpus—dispenses tattoos, nipple rings, and other essentials. But it's Vertigo that made homeowners angry. They claim that ever since it opened in January 1994, petty crime and physical assaults in the neighborhood have increased. The youths allegedly pissed on lawns, sidewalks, and shrubbery, showing little respect for the mostly elderly residents. They dealt drugs. And they made lots of noise.

Entrepreneur Friedman was well aware of the problems and took steps to cooperate with the police. Prior to opening the café, he spent $55,000 improving what was a useless, decrepit property. When presented with residents' complaints, he posted a list of 36 undesirables permanently banned from Vertigo. He was trying to make a living and working with (and within) the law. But he can't solve society's problems, and, alas, Vertigo was closed down by the city council's ex-hippies.

Such problems are, of course, not unique or new to Santa Cruz. For decades, the town has been a repository for society's discards. But these youths, the old guard like to imply, are different. Nastier. More menacing. It stands to reason that with Vertigo closed, the kids have no place to hang out, and that they're even more pissed off than usual. The problem has not been solved, just pushed aside like the kids themselves. Maybe the real reason they are a problem is that they are thought of as "they," and not "us."

well trained, as reverential of their craft as the Japanese masters, and very creative. Consider these Mobo Maki Maki items: the Crop Burning (avocado, cucumber, shiitaki, cilantro, and spicy sauce) and the Pink Caddy (unagi, hamachi, sake, ebi, and spicy sauce).

Santa Cruz Coffee Roasting Co. (1330 Pacific Avenue, 459-0100, $) is a coffee bar in the true sense of the word. You order the kind of coffee you want, then they place a paper filter inside a Melita-style cone, spoon in fresh-ground coffee, and pour boiling water over the grounds. You stand waiting as your mug fills drop by drop. Additives include the usual cream and sugar, plus such healthy alternatives as soya milk and honey.

Another morning institution in Santa Cruz is the **Bagelry** (320 Cedar Street, 429-8049, $), where fresh, hot bagels are baked in such flavorful combinations as tomato herb pesto and oatmeal date. They've got all sorts of tasty spreads to go with them and, of course, good coffee. (Santa Cruz is like a microcosm of Seattle in that regard.)

The one place we're not so hot on, for reasons having nothing to do with food, is the **Ideal Fish Restaurant** (106 Beach Street, 423-5271, $$$). The owner has been a thorn in the side of public-beach access efforts in Santa Cruz. His 1991 lawsuit against the California Coastal Commission tied up needed improvements for two years. Now he has taken part of a public beach to build his own private deck and, in the words of the mayor of Santa Cruz, "made it difficult for a lot of merchants." Make it difficult for him by dining elsewhere.

Night Moves

Santa Cruz is a party town in the grand tradition. People dance to any type of music—live,

Map of Santa Cruz County beaches—page 376

taped, synthesized, loud, soft, garage, grunge, Glenn Miller. It doesn't matter. Clubs are scattered around town, catering to a cross section of nighthawks who range from local students to party animals from over the mountains.

The best clubs are the Crow's Nest and the Catalyst, two different means to the same approximate end. The **Crow's Nest** (see above) turns the second floor of its seafood restaurant into a happy danceteria, and after the plates are put away downstairs, they crank up the volume. Occasionally they feature live acts, but mostly it's decent taped music—we could hear James Brown's "I Feel Good" several blocks away—and the dance floor is jam-packed all night. It a thirty-something crowd, though not a somnolent one.

The **Catalyst** (1011 Pacific Avenue, 423-1336) is a former bowling alley transformed into a world-renowned venue for alternative music. More collegiate and liberalized, it's a cavernous clubhouse with two floors, several rooms, and bars everywhere you turn. All strata of society (and all ages) can be found at the Catalyst, which has a long and storied history dating back to hippiedom.

The oldest section of Santa Cruz, referred to as simply "downtown," is one of the few square street grids in the area. It's on the west side of the San Lorenzo River, occupying four long blocks along Pacific Avenue. Much of downtown was rebuilt or renovated after the 1989 earthquake, and it's now generally an okay place to stroll around. We're not going to overromanticize it, though; at times it has the unnerving aura of a war zone. We were warned not to walk the handful of blocks from our hotel over the river to the downtown mall after dark. Too dangerous. Lots of human time-bombs skulk around the riverfront. One morning, we stumbled upon a bum changing clothes under the eaves of our hotel, beside a sign that read "Panhandlers Are Not Welcome and Will Be Prosecuted." So it goes in Santa Cruz.

Downtown you will find good book shops, coffeehouses, and bars filled with locals. The **Poet & Patriot Irish Pub** (320 East Cedar Street, 426-8620) is a friendly den of local writers, artists, and dart throwers. A newer arrival is **99 Bottles of Beer on the Wall** (Walnut Street, 459-9999). True to its name, it offers 99 brands of beer.

For More Information

Contact the Santa Cruz Area Visitors Information Center, 701 Front Street, Santa Cruz, CA 95060; (408) 425-1234.

Wilder Ranch State Park and Four Mile Beach

Location: Two miles north of Santa Cruz on Highway 1.

Wilder Ranch is one of California's newest and most intriguing oceanfront parks. It opened in the early 1990s. For the 100 years prior to its acquisition by the state in 1974, the ranch was operated as a farm by the Wilder family. About 900 of the 3,578 acres are still under cultivation, with one-eighth of the nation's Brussels sprouts grown inside park boundaries. Twenty-two more acres have been set aside as a cultural preserve, and many of the original Wilder family buildings stand intact.

But it's the other 3,000 or so acres that are irresistibly attractive to beach bums. There are six beaches inside the state park. One way to get to them is to hike the Ohlone Bluff Trail, a majestic 20-minute stroll to the shore. The closest beach, Wilder Beach, is off-limits to the public because it's a preserve for the endangered snowy plover. The other beaches appear as separate coves below the bluff top, and the names are as appealing as the scenery: Fern Grotto Beach, Sand Plant Beach, Strawberry Beach, Three Mile Beach, and Four Mile Beach.

Logically enough, **Four Mile Beach** (the most popular) is four miles north of town. Keep an eye on the odometer, measuring the distance from where Highway 1 and Mission Street meet in Santa Cruz; then look for a rut-filled parking lot on the west side of the highway. A 10-minute walk across railroad tracks and a wetlands area leads to the beach. Clothed and unclothed beachcombers and surfers use Four Mile by day, and teen hell-raisers show up later (like vampires they only come out at night).

In addition to the Ohlone Bluff Trail, there are 28 miles of backcountry trails that wind through the inland hills, climaxing at a eucalyptus grove and offering spectacular views of Monterey Bay. These trails are popular with horseback riders and mountain bicyclists. No camping is allowed. Guided tours and hands-on demonstrations of ranch life are offered on the weekends; reservations are required.

For More Information

Contact the Wilder Ranch State Park, 1401 Old Coast Road, Santa Cruz, CA 95060; (408) 423-9703.

Four Mile Beach
(a part of Wilder Ranch State Park)

4

Location: Four miles north of Santa Cruz off Highway 1.
Parking: Free roadside parking.
Hours: 8 AM to sunset.
Facilities: Rest rooms.
Contact: For beach information, contact Wilder Ranch State Park at (408) 423-9703.

See number 27 on page 376.

Wilder Ranch State Park

5

Location: Two miles north of Santa Cruz off Highway 1.
Parking: $6 entrance fee per vehicle.
Hours: 8 AM to sunset.
Facilities: Rest rooms.
Contact: For beach information, contact Wilder Ranch State Park at (408) 423-9703.

See number 26 on page 376.

Red, White, and Blue Beach

Location: Five miles north of Santa Cruz on Highway 1.

Red, White, and Blue Beach is a private nude beach on the ocean side of Highway 1. (Keep an eye out for the mailbox with the patriotic color scheme.) A day-use fee is charged, and camping fees are $12 to $16 per night. As is the custom on all of California's nude beaches, you must be 21, married, or accompanied by your parents to be allowed onto the beach, where there are disrobing facilities and volleyball nets.

The beach is open from 10 AM to 6 PM in the summer and from 10 AM to 4 PM the rest of the year. Unless you're camping, you have to vamoose by closing time. The beach is a third-of-a-mile long; a warm, sunny day can draw a crowd of 500 or so, most of whom choose to exercise the no-clothing option.

For More Information

Contact Red, White, and Blue Beach, 5021 Old Coast Road, Santa Cruz, CA 95060; (408) 423-6332.

Red, White, and Blue Beach

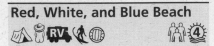

Location: Five miles north of Santa Cruz at Scaroni Road and Highway 1. Look for the red, white, and blue mailbox.

Parking: $7 entrance fee per person.

Hours: 10 AM to 6 PM (4 PM in winter).

Facilities: Rest rooms and fire pits. There are 29 tent and RV campsites. Fees are $12 to $16 per night.

Contact: For camping or beach information, contact Red, White, and Blue Beach at (408) 423-6332.

See number 28 on page 376.

Bonny Doon Beach

Location: Bonny Doon Beach is located nine miles north of Santa Cruz, at Milepost 27.6 on Highway 1. Yellowbank Beach is one mile south of Bonny Doon Beach, and Panther Beach lies another 0.3 miles farther south. Laguna Creek Beach is 1.7 miles south of Bonny Doon.

Over the next five miles, several cove jewels can be accessed along Highway 1, including **Laguna Creek**, **Yellowbank**, and **Panther**. Each requires pulling onto the shoulder of the road and then hiking up a bluff and down to the beach—often a steep scramble down a loosely consolidated berm or sea cliff. (One unlucky soul was killed in this area when the bluff he was standing on gave way during the 1989 earthquake.)

The best known of the lot is **Bonny Doon Beach**, which lies where Bonny Doon Road meets Highway 1. Way up in the hills is the little, bucolic settlement of Bonny Doon. From a gravel pullout, follow the rough trail straight up, then cross the railroad tracks. Soon you'll come upon an absolutely stunning beach that resembles a natural amphitheater, with cliffs on either side that keep the winds at bay. The remoteness of the site and the protection afforded sunbathers by the encircling cliffs have made Bonny Doon one of the premier nude beaches on the California coast. It is also one of the friendlier haunts of the bare-assed set, who congregate at the cove at the north end. The other beaches in this daisy chain are equally endowed with sheltering cliffs and desirable isolation. To make a visit worth your while, plan on staying an entire day by bringing food, drinks, and some good reading material (like this book).

A word of caution about the beaches of north Santa Cruz County. Their character tends to change after dark from a nude Dr. Jekyll to a drunk Mr. Hyde. Do not at any time come to them alone, day or night. These beaches hold some dark secrets. Nighttime is when young party animals from the Santa Clara Valley come to raise hell. They build bonfires on the beach, drink themselves senseless, and litter the sand with glass, garbage, and puke. As one high school student told a reporter for the *San Jose Mercury News*, "We party at Bonny Doon. You have to walk down a hill, and cops don't go down there. So you light a bonfire and drink until you can't walk. A lot of times people just spend the night; they're way too drunk to walk back up the hill." For years the authorities have tried to curb this kind of behavior. They've tried ticketing cars that park on the shoulders of Highway 1 at night. They've broken up many

Bonny Doon Beach

Location: About nine miles north of Santa Cruz at Bonny Doon Road and Highway 1.

Parking: Free parking lot.

Hours: 6 AM to 10 PM.

Facilities: None.

Contact: For beach information, contact the Santa Cruz County Department of Parks, Open Space, and Cultural Services at (408) 462-8300.

See number 31 on page 376.

Laguna Creek Beach

Location: About seven miles north of Santa Cruz at Laguna Creek Road and Highway 1.

Parking: Free roadside parking.

Hours: 6 AM to 10 PM.

Facilities: None.

Contact: For beach information, contact the Santa Cruz County Department of Parks, Open Space, and Cultural Services at (408) 462-8300.

See number 29 on page 376.

a beachside bacchanal (some of which have attracted a thousand kids). But there's only so much they can do; as the poet said, "Youth will have its fling."

The darker side of all this is fights, drunk driving, falls down cliff sides, drownings, and murders. Even during daylight hours we've seen some dubious-looking characters hanging around the north-county pullouts. Perhaps they're only latter-day Kerouacs, perhaps common thugs. Auto break-ins are another problem—don't leave valuables inside your car or trunk. Watch your step, watch the company you keep, and don't drink and drive. Enough kids have died or gotten hurt out here that the authorities and general public are unamused by alcohol-related lawbreaking, even if it is part of the perceived adolescent rites of passage.

For More Information

No address or phone number is available for information on Bonny Doon Beach.

Panther Beach

4

Location: About eight miles north of Santa Cruz off Highway 1.
Parking: Free roadside parking.
Hours: 6 AM to 10 PM.
Facilities: None.
Contact: For beach information, contact the Santa Cruz County Department of Parks, Open Space, and Cultural Services at (408) 462-8300.

See number 32 on page 376.

Yellowbank Beach

4

Location: About eight miles north of Santa Cruz off Highway 1.
Parking: Free roadside parking.
Hours: 6 AM to 10 PM.
Facilities: None.
Contact: For beach information, contact the Santa Cruz County Department of Parks, Open Space, and Cultural Services at (408) 462-8300.

See number 30 on page 376.

Davenport

Location: 12 miles north of Santa Cruz, along Highway 1.
Population: 300
Area Code: 408 **Zip Code:** 95017

For such a little place, Davenport has some worthwhile attractions. It is home to the Davenport New Cash Store, a one-of-a-kind restaurant, bakery, bed-and-breakfast inn, and art gallery. In winter and early spring, the town is one of the premier spots in Northern California to watch gray whales as they make their way between their feeding grounds in the Arctic and their breeding grounds in Mexican lagoons. It is also the site of a giant, Depression-era cement plant. The decayed pilings of a massive, 3,000-foot wharf, where the plant once loaded its product onto ships, list in the water. For beach fanatics, however, Davenport's main attraction is its trinity of divine beaches: Davenport Beach, Davenport Landing, and Scott Creek Beach.

Beaches

From the highway, it's just a short dash to the huge, wide expanse of sand at **Davenport Beach**. The healthy dune structure that backs the beach makes for a lulling walk along the water's edge, where the only threat to your serenity might be the occasional hang glider leaping from the cliff top above. Incidentally, a half mile south of town is Davenport Cove (a.k.a. Shark's Tooth Cove), a scantily visited beach mainly frequented by scantily attired (i.e., nude) beachgoers.

Davenport Landing Beach is accessed by the looped Davenport Landing Road, one mile north of town. You can park free along the roadside from 6 AM to 10 PM, but there's only room for about 20 cars. It's a lot easier to get to than Bonny Doon, as you take a short stroll down a gradually sloping embankment, revealing cliffs at either end of a scenic cove. On a perfect Thursday in late July, we had the beach to ourselves.

Arguably the loveliest of the three Davenport beaches is **Scott Creek Beach**, which is backed by wetlands on the eastern side of the highway and a sandy delta where the creek trickles into the Pacific. When we visited, surf casters were digging the scene with an anglers' lean (though no fishing is allowed in the creek itself). In addition to surf casters, windsurfers are drawn to Davenport Landing and Scott Creek. Again, you can park on the roadside from 6 AM until 10 PM.

Bunking Down

For a real North Coast getaway, book a room at the **New Davenport Bed & Breakfast Inn** (Highway 1 and Davenport Avenue, 425-1818, $$), which occupies rooms above the restaurant and behind the store.

Coastal Cuisine

The **Davenport New Cash Store** (Highway 1 and Davenport Avenue, 426-4122, $$$) is more than a casually bohemian gourmet eatery. It's a restaurant, pottery gallery, B&B inn, and bakery rolled into one. Breakfast and lunch are great, and dinner's sublime. The emphasis is on creative seafood and pasta dishes, as well as local wines.

For More Information

Contact the Santa Cruz County Conference & Visitors Council, 701 Front Street, Santa Cruz, CA 95060; (408) 425-1234.

Davenport Beach

Location: In Davenport, about 11 miles north of Santa Cruz off Highway 1.

Parking: Free roadside parking.

Hours: 6 AM to 10 PM.

Facilities: None.

Contact: For beach information, contact the Santa Cruz County Department of Parks, Open Space, and Cultural Services at (408) 462-8300.

See number 33 on page 376.

Davenport Landing Beach

Location: About 13 miles north of Santa Cruz off Highway 1.

Parking: Free roadside parking.

Hours: 6 AM to 10 PM.

Facilities: None.

Contact: For beach information, contact the Santa Cruz County Department of Parks, Open Space, and Cultural Services at (408) 462-8300.

See number 34 on page 376.

Scott Creek Beach

Location: About 14 miles north of Santa Cruz off Highway 1.

Parking: Free roadside parking.

Hours: 6 AM to 10 PM.

Facilities: None.

Contact: For beach information, contact the Santa Cruz County Department of Parks, Open Space, and Cultural Services at (408) 462-8300.

See number 35 on page 376.

Waddell Creek Beach

Location: 30 miles north of Santa Cruz and 1 mile south of the San Mateo County line, along Highway 1.

Located where a creek empties into the ocean, Waddell Creek Beach is bounded by a large state park that extends into the Santa Cruz Mountains, making an overnight stay in the campground an attractive proposition. The 18,000 acres of Big Basin Redwoods State Park include 80 miles of backcountry hiking trails, waterfalls, and tent-camping sites—145 at the base camp and more than 40 walk-in sites.

The beach at **Waddell Creek** is windy most of the time. While discouraging sunbathing, this makes it a favorite spot for windsurfers and hang gliders. A self-guided nature center offers insight on local flora and fauna (including a sobering note about the dwindling steelhead and rainbow-trout populations, which once spawned happily in Waddell Creek). Nonetheless, it's a good spot for rockfishing, with anglers landing perch, ling cod, and croaker. The pinnacle of fishing in these parts, however, is found at **Greyhound Rock Fishing Access**, not quite two miles south of Waddell Creek. Developed by the Department of Fish and Game, Greyhound Rock has a trail and stairwell that lead down to the beach.

For More Information

Contact Big Basin Redwoods State Park, 21600 Big Basin Way, Boulder Creek, CA 95006; (408) 338-8860.

Greyhound Rock Fishing Access

2

Location: About 28 miles north of Santa Cruz, at Swanton Road and Highway 1.
Parking: Free roadside parking.
Hours: 6 AM to 10 PM.
Facilities: Rest rooms.
Contact: For beach information, contact the Santa Cruz County Department of Parks, Open Space, and Cultural Services at (408) 462-8300.

See number 36 on page 376.

Waddell Creek Beach

4

Location: One mile south of the San Mateo County line, off Highway 1.
Parking: $3 entrance fee per vehicle.
Hours: 6 AM to sunset.
Facilities: Rest rooms.
Contact: For beach information, contact Big Basin Redwoods State Park at (408) 338-8860.

See number 37 on page 376.

San Mateo County

If Barbara Walters asked the Santa Cruz coast, "If you were a human being, what kind of human being would you be?" no doubt the response would be a mop-topped surfer, his slight edge tempered by a basically sunny disposition. If she turned her attention to the San Mateo Coast, a completely different creature would emerge: a grizzled veteran of the sea—maybe a retired navy captain or a steely-eyed fisherman—less comely and charming than his southern cousin, but possessed of a maturity and contemplative nature. He'd also be a bit harder to get to know.

The rocky shoals and heavy fogs in the southern end of this 55-mile shoreline have long put the fear of shipwrecks in sailors' hearts, and the steep, shifting terrain in the Devil's Slide area up north have tossed both a coastal railroad and a highway into the Pacific. Between these two ominous bookends lie the perfectly appealing towns of an area known as Coastside, comprising Half Moon Bay, Princeton, Moss Beach, *(continued on page 406)*

Coastal San Mateo County's Climate

Half Moon Bay Averages

	Daily High Temp. (°F)	Daily Low Temp. (°F)	Rainfall (inches)
January	58	43	5.3
February	59	44	3.7
March	58	44	3.5
April	60	44	2.1
May	61	47	0.6
June	63	50	0.3
July	64	51	0.1
August	65	52	0.2
September	67	52	0.4
October	66	49	1.6
November	63	46	3.0
December	59	44	4.4
Yearly Average	**62**	**47**	**25.2**

Source: National Weather Service data, National Oceanographic and Atmospheric Administration.

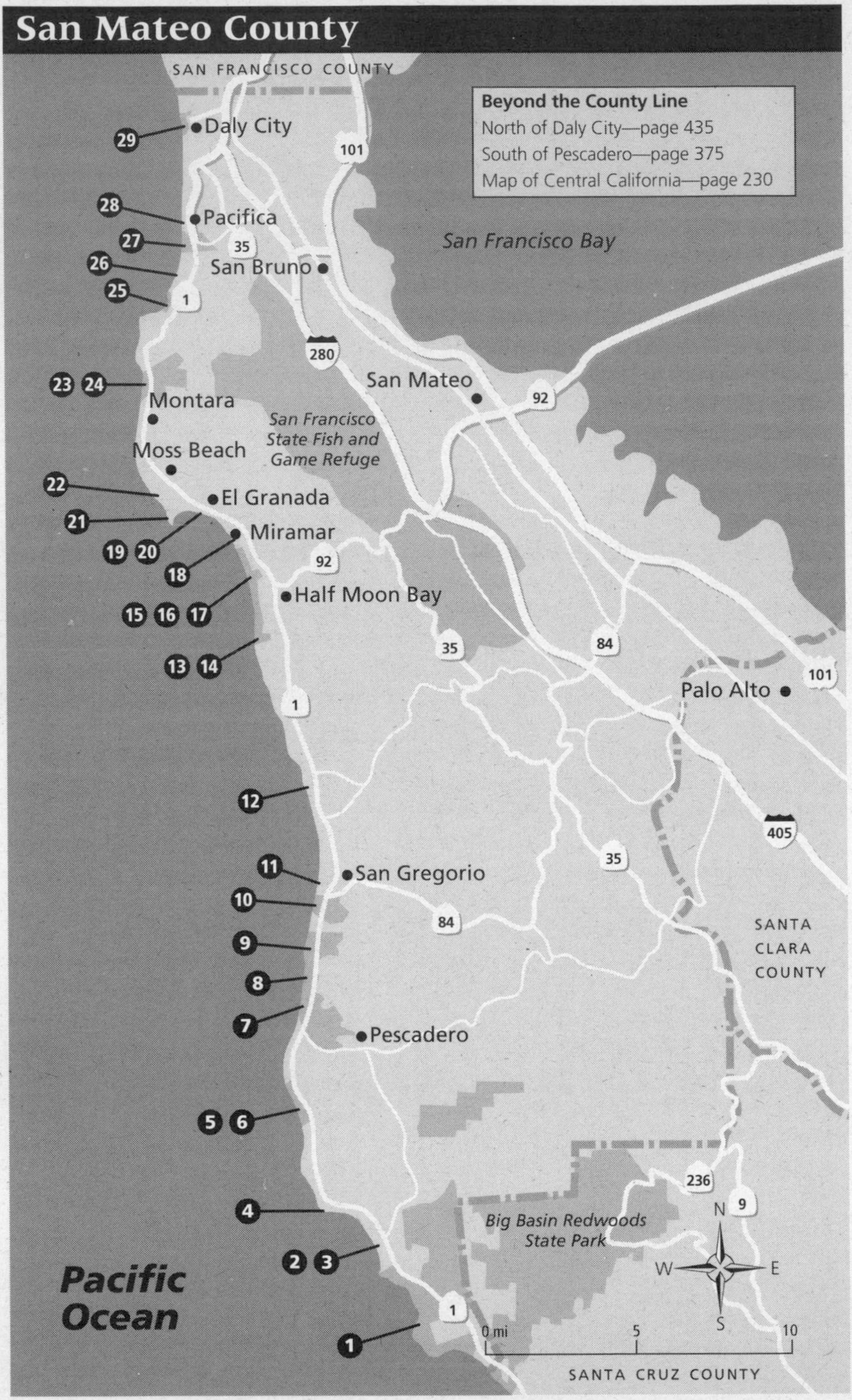
San Mateo County
SAN FRANCISCO COUNTY
Beyond the County Line
North of Daly City—page 435
South of Pescadero—page 375
Map of Central California—page 230
Daly City
Pacifica
San Bruno
San Francisco Bay
San Mateo
Montara
Moss Beach
San Francisco State Fish and Game Refuge
El Granada
Miramar
Half Moon Bay
Palo Alto
San Gregorio
Pescadero
SANTA CLARA COUNTY
Big Basin Redwoods State Park
Pacific Ocean
SANTA CRUZ COUNTY
0 mi
5
10
N
W
E
S
101
35
1
280
92
84
405
236
9
1
2
3
4
5
6
7
8
9
10
11
12
13
14
15
16
17
18
19
20
21
22
23
24
25
26
27
28
29

San Mateo County Beaches

Map of Central California—page 230

(continued from page 403) and others. There's also the wild isolation of Año Nuevo State Reserve and a string of state beaches—Bean Hollow, Pescadero, Pomponio, San Gregorio, and Montara. It is a land of grazing cattle and agriculture, especially green vegetables that love the cool fogs that frequently shroud the area.

With San Francisco to the north, San Jose and the Santa Clara Valley to the east, and Santa Cruz to the south, San Mateo County exists in a sort of urban-to-rural transition zone. Despite its proximity to populated areas, it is largely a land that time and developers have forgotten.

The beaches themselves are generally too cold and hazardous for swimming, and about the only beauties you'll see sunbathing here are northern elephant seals at Año Nuevo State Reserve. The blubbery darlings are the largest pinnipeds in this hemisphere, capable of reaching 16 feet in length. In addition to seal watching, San Mateo County offers such low-impact pastimes as tidepooling, strolling, fishing, camping, birding, and whale watching—not to mention ample opportunity for solitude on a raw and elemental shoreline.

Key to the Symbols

Bike path · Camping · Food and drink · Hiking · Nude

Pier · RVs allowed · Surfing · Volleyball

Crowd Rating

sweet solitude . . . moderate crowds . . . wall-to-wall

Overall Rating

1 don't bother . . . 2 . . . 3 worth a visit . . . 4 . . . 5 beach heaven

Año Nuevo State Reserve

Location: 55 miles south of San Francisco and 25 miles north of Santa Cruz, along Highway 1.

Año Nuevo is first and foremost a wildlife refuge. It is the mainland rookery of the northern elephant seal. Second, it is a park open to human visitation. The reserve's 4,000 acres include scrub-covered coastal hills and rocky intertidal beaches. The shoreline consists of sandy coves and rocky headlands, with one of California's last and largest surviving dune fields bordering the wildlife protection area. Visitors can hike to a place where they might spy seals playing on the beach or offshore chunks of rock. One elongated outcrop is particularly surreal, as several abandoned buildings stand on it. Both rocks and buildings are covered with seals and cormorants and stained with their droppings, giving the site the peculiar appearance of a Hollywood stage set that's been overtaken by wildlife.

The tang of the air, the crashing of the waves, and the barking of the seals make for an enchanting nature experience. From the parking lot past the entrance station, it's a hike of 0.4 mile to Cove Beach, 0.9 to the Wildlife Area Trailhead, and 1.6 to Point Año Nuevo. A round-trip walk to the wildlife observation area takes about two hours and is well worth the effort. A section of the park south of Cascade Creek is off-limits to visitors during seal breeding season (December 15 through March 31), though guided tours of small groups are conducted by volunteer naturalists at this time. These walking tours cover three miles and take two-and-a-half hours. Bight Beach is another seals-only playground by the sea. It lies between South and North Points, and is backed by a vast dune field covering 350 acres. Humans are allowed by permit only between April and November.

Whale and bird-watching, clam digging, and surf casting are other popular activities. In addition to the elephant seals, harbor seals, northern fur seals, sea lions, and otters make their home here for at least part of the year, and California gray whales pass by Point Año Nuevo during their winter migration. Año Nuevo's rocky, south-facing beach runs along a mile of curving coastline. Surfers have been known to catch a wave off the point, which breaks best in summer. The park is open daily from 8 AM until sunset. While you're here, one of the regulations asks visitors to stay at least 40 feet from the seals. No cheating!

For More Information

To hear prerecorded information about guided walks, call (415) 879-0227. For reservations, which can be made up to eight weeks in advance, contact Destinet at (800) 444-7525. For other information about the park, contact Año Nuevo State Reserve, c/o San Mateo Coast District, 95 Kelly Avenue, Half Moon Bay, CA 94019; (415) 879-0595.

Año Nuevo State Reserve
(Cove Beach & Bight Beach)

5

Location: Two miles northwest of the Santa Cruz County line, on New Years Creek Road west of Highway 1.

Parking: $4 entrance fee per vehicle.

Hours: 8 AM to 6 PM (April through September), 8 AM to 4 PM (October through November), guided walks only (December 15th through March 31st).

Facilities: Rest rooms. Guided walks through the reserve are offered during breeding season. Fee is $4 per person (plus parking fee). For reservations for Año Nuevo Elephant Seal Walks, call Destinet at (800) 444-7275.

Contact: For beach information, contact Año Nuevo State Reserve at (415) 879-2025.

See number 1 on page 404.

Gazos Creek Access and The Fist

Location: At the south end of Gazos Creek Bridge, on Highway 1, six miles north of the Santa Cruz County line.

Stairs lead to a lagoon and beach from a free parking lot by the **Gazos Creek** Bridge. The creek meanders into the sea here, and the beach is sandy and wide. Behind it rise the redwood canyons of Gazos, Whitehouse, and Cascade creeks, combined into an undeveloped 4,000-acre reserve. Between Año Nuevo and Gazos Creek is a beach locals frequent that won't show up on any maps. It's called **The Fist**, after the dead, gnarled tree trunk that's this hidden beach's most visible feature. The Fist has got a protected cove at the south end, tidepools and rocky ledges at the north end, and golden sand perfect for solitary strolling in between. The Pigeon Point Lighthouse is visible to the north. Located a mile south of Gazos Creek, it takes a 10-minute hike over the dunes to reach the Fist. If you need it badly enough, you'll find your way here.

For More Information

Contact the Bay Area District of the California Department of Parks and Recreation, (415) 330-6300.

The Fist

Location: Park one mile south of Gazos Creek along Highway 1 and walk over the dunes.

Parking: Limited free roadside parking.

Hours: 8 AM to sunset.

Facilities: None.

Contact: For beach information, contact the Bay Area District of the California Department of Parks and Recreation at (415) 330-6300.

See number 2 on page 404.

Gazos Creek Access

Location: Six miles north of the Santa Cruz County line, at the south end of Gazos Creek Bridge along Highway 1.

Parking: Free parking lot.

Hours: 8 AM to sunset.

Facilities: Rest rooms.

Contact: For beach information, contact the Bay Area District of the California Department of Parks and Recreation at (415) 330-6300.

See number 3 on page 404.

Pigeon Point

Location: 20 miles south of Half Moon Bay, turn west onto Pigeon Point Road from Highway 1, and continue to the beach.

There are parking turnoffs and beach access points all along Pigeon Point Road, which loops off and returns to Highway 1. The big attraction is the lighthouse at **Pigeon Point**, the second tallest structure of its kind in California. It operates as a hostelry where you can stay for a pittance out here on the wild edge of the San Mateo Coast.

The 115-foot-tall lighthouse has been guiding mariners since 1872. Because so many ships sank off the point—including the catastrophic 1853 breakup of a San Francisco–bound vessel carrying valuable cargo, and the subsequent wreck of the boat dispatched to salvage it—the lighthouse remains a vital navigational aid.

Tours of the lighthouse are given on Sundays only; call ahead for times and reservations. The Pigeon Point Lighthouse Hostel is housed in bungalows that formerly accommodated Coast Guard families. There are private rooms for couples and families, as well as dormitory-style bunkrooms for travelers out for a communal experience. Rooms cost under $30 a night (with discounts for American and International Youth Hostel members). A big hot tub overlooking the ocean is available for rental. South of the lighthouse, a trail leads to Gazos Creek Beach. There's good tidepooling in the vicinity of Pigeon Point.

For More Information

Contact the Pigeon Point Lighthouse Hostel, Pigeon Point Road, Pescadero, CA 94060; (415) 879-0633.

Pigeon Point

Location: 20 miles south of Half Moon Bay, at the end of Pigeon Point Road off Highway 1.

Parking: Free parking lot.

Hours: 7:30 AM to 9:30 PM.

Facilities: Rest rooms and showers. There's also a 52-bed hostel at Pigeon Point Lighthouse. The cost is $14 per person, per night ($11 for American Youth Hostel members). For reservations, call the Pigeon Point Lighthouse Hostel at (415) 879-0633.

Contact: For beach information, contact the Pigeon Point Lighthouse at (415) 879-0633.

See number 4 on page 404.

Pebble Beach and Bean Hollow State Beach

Location: 17 miles south of Half Moon Bay. The main entrance to Bean Hollow State Beach lies a half mile south of Pebble Beach, off Highway 1.

Pebble Beach is so named for the crop of smooth, rounded pebbles found at the surf's edge. Their origins are unclear, but one theory holds that this is the site of a former stream mouth whose pebbly remnants were bound up in the sandstone-conglomerate overlay in the recent geological past. In any case, you're encouraged to admire the pebbles but to leave them where they lie. The sandstone in this vicinity takes on a distinctive orange hue. Rare, lacelike formations called tafoni are carved into the coastal rocks. Offshore, the roiling surf whips up an oozy froth.

An instructional trail connects Pebble Beach with the main entrance to **Bean Hollow State Beach**, about a mile to the south. A helpful brochure, which can be picked up in boxes at either end of the trail, is keyed to numbered posts along the way, and the basic geology, ecology, and marine biology of the area is conveyed in easy-to-follow text. One of the more interesting facts we learned has to do with coastal bluff erosion. Where the sandstone is soft, cliffs can retreat as much as 22 feet per year. Living proof of this can be seen in the rerouting of the trail that's been necessitated in places by the shoreward retreat of the bluffs.

A shelf of rocks divides Bean Hollow into broad coves. The rocky surf is plagued with rip currents. Raw, elemental beach wilderness is the main feature at Bean Hollow. Come here to escape and meditate. It's mostly rocky surf, save for the small, sandy coves at Pebble Hollow and Arroyo de Frijoles Beach, located at the south end of Bean Hollow.

For More Information

Contact Bean Hollow State Park, Highway 1, Pescadero, CA 94060; (415) 879-2170.

Bean Hollow State Beach

Location: 17.5 miles south of Half Moon Bay off Highway 1.
Parking: Free parking lot.
Hours: 8 AM to sunset.
Facilities: Rest rooms and picnic tables.
Contact: For beach information, contact the Bay Area District of the California Department of Parks and Recreation at (415) 330-6300.

See number 5 on page 404.

Pebble Beach

Location: 17 miles south of Half Moon Bay off Highway 1.
Parking: Free parking lot.
Hours: 8 AM to sunset.
Facilities: Rest rooms and picnic tables.
Contact: For beach information, contact the Bay Area District of the California Department of Parks and Recreation at (415) 330-6300.

See number 6 on page 404.

Pescadero State Beach

Location: 14.5 miles south of Half Moon Bay, off Highway 1.

There are three beach-access points at **Pescadero**. The best is the northernmost lot, where a day-use fee is collected. The south one has a larger parking lot perched at bluff's edge, overlooking the raging sea. All three offer access to Pescadero State Beach Marsh Preserve, on the other side of the highway, where hiking trails wander through one of the most important freshwater/brackish coastal marshes in California. It is a critical resting place on the Pacific flyway. A bird checklist is available to visitors, and free ranger-led marsh walks begin at the lot just south of Pescadero Creek. Call (415) 879-2170 for a schedule.

The beaches of Pescadero capture the San Mateo Coast at its wildest: rough surf, rocky beach, nearly leveled headlands that people explore for close encounters with nature *in extremis*. Offshore, breakers violently pound rocky outcrops. It is so haunting and undeveloped out here that one roadside sign says it all: "Next Gas 35 Miles." Incidentally the community of Pescadero, a tiny hamlet located a short distance inland, is in the heart of a rural area renowned for its trout fishing—and Duarte's Tavern (202 Stage Road, 879-0464, $$), a former stagecoach-era saloon, where locals flock for seafood and gossip. (Oh, and remember to pronounce it *DOOarts*, or they'll know you're from out of town.)

For More Information

Contact Pescadero State Beach, Highway 1, Pescadero, CA 994060; (415) 879-2170.

Pescadero State Beach

Location: 14.5 miles south of Half Moon Bay along Highway 1.

Parking: $4 entrance fee per vehicle at north lot. Free parking at central and south lots.

Hours: 8 AM to sunset. Marsh walks are offered on Saturday at 10:30 AM and Sunday at 1 PM throughout the year. Meet at the parking lot on Highway 1 just south of Pescadero Creek, identified by a sign that says "Pescadero State Beach Marsh Preserve." No reservations needed.

Facilities: Rest rooms and picnic tables.

Contact: For beach information, contact Pescadero State Beach at (415) 879-2170.

See number 7 on page 404.

Pomponio State Beach

Location: 12 miles south of Half Moon Bay, off Highway 1.

Pomponio is the smallest of the trio of state beaches situated at creek mouths in the sparsely populated, bucolic midsection of San Mateo County. The semicircular beach is not quite as stunning as San Gregorio or as large as Pescadero, but neither is it as heavily visited. It follows the same general layout of a sandy creek-fed beach flanked by grassy bluffs. Pomponio takes its name from an Indian outlaw who lived in a nearby cave during Spanish rule. There's a half-dozen picnic tables and a small parking lot, and a modest day-use fee is assessed. What more can we tell you?

Actually, there's a bit more to the story. At its southern end, Pomponio is a clothing-optional beach. It's a bit hard to reach. If you're walking along the water line, this stretch is accessible from the parking lot only at low tide, lying 0.7 miles to the south. There are other ways in—walking up from Pescadero State Beach (same distance) or taking a trail down from the highway. Look for the trailhead, identified by wooden posts. This hideaway beach goes by the informal name **The Gulch**. Which brings up another point. Although there are formal coastal-access points, such as the state beaches, informal beach access exists everywhere in San Mateo County. Whether to avoid the state-beach charges or to escape the madding crowd (or both), people park their vehicles along shoulder pullouts on Highway 1. These are particularly plentiful between Pomponio and Pescadero state beaches.

For More Information

Contact Pomponio State Beach, Highway 1, Pescadero, CA 94060; (415) 879-2170.

The Gulch

Location: Between Pescadero and Pomponio State Beaches. Hike in via a trail from the highway (wooden posts mark the trailhead), or walk north from Pescadero or south from Pomponio.

Parking: Free roadside parking.

Hours: 8 AM to sunset.

Facilities: None.

Contact: For beach information, contact the Bay Area District of the California Department of Parks and Recreation at (415) 330-6300.

See number 8 on page 404.

Pomponio State Beach

Location: 12 miles south of Half Moon Bay along Highway 1.

Parking: $4 entrance fee per vehicle.

Hours: 8 AM to sunset.

Facilities: Rest rooms, picnic tables, and fire pits.

Contact: For beach information, contact the Bay Area District of the California Department of Parks and Recreation at (415) 330-6300.

See number 9 on page 404.

San Gregorio State Beach

Location: 10.5 miles south of Half Moon Bay, off Highway 1.

San Gregorio State Beach is a great spot for hiking. Scenic paths wander atop mustard-colored sandstone bluffs overlooking the ocean, and the beach itself is wonderfully wide at the mouth of the San Gregorio Creek. Away from the creek, it narrows dramatically in both directions, hemmed in by the ocean and the cliffs. The beaches of San Mateo County, and San Gregorio in particular, are amazing to behold. The topography is rugged, the ocean chilly and tempestuous. Solitary beach hiking is an inviting activity, though you are advised to keep an eye on tides and sleeper waves.

On one late July weekend afternoon, the broad apron of beach below the parking lot was packed with all kinds of folks: a church youth group playing blindfold games on the beach; families of every ethnic persuasion gathered around picnic baskets, college students basking in the sun; and little children charging madly about. There was, however, not a single soul braving the water.

The parking lot at San Gregorio has been paved and greatly enlarged in recent years, and you'll shell out four bucks for a day-use fee at a manned kiosk. Just up the hill, south of the bridge over San Gregorio Creek, people park on the shoulder and enter for free along paths that lead down to the beach. We, being ardent supporters of California State Parks, urge one and all to ante up their fair share and spare the crumbling bluffs their destructive footsteps.

For More Information

Contact San Gregorio State Beach, Highway 1, Pescadero, CA 94060; (415) 330-6300.

San Gregorio State Beach

Location: 10.5 miles south of Half Moon Bay along Highway 1.

Parking: $4 entrance fee per vehicle.

Hours: 8 AM to sunset.

Facilities: Rest rooms, picnic tables, and fire pits.

Contact: For beach information, contact the Bay Area District of the California Department of Parks and Recreation at (415) 330-6300.

See number 10 on page 404.

San Gregorio Private Beach and Martin's Beach

Location: San Gregorio Private Beach is located at the end of a dirt toll road 100 yards north of the intersection of Highways 1 and 84, near the crossroads community of San Gregorio. Martin's Beach lies six miles south of Half Moon Bay, at the end of Martin's Beach Road, off Highway 1.

These beaches are privately owned. One is for fishing, the other for disrobing. **Martin's Beach** is a private fishing cove; you pay a toll to enter the road and cast a line. There's an on-site store that's open in summer, plus rest rooms and picnic tables.

San Gregorio, not to be confused with the same-named state beach just south of it, is clothing optional. It's not just any old nude beach, though. San Gregorio Privates—er, we mean Private—Beach claims to be America's first nude sand patch, having first welcomed the genitally liberated back in 1960. Located below steep bluffs, San Gregorio offers an expansive stretch of scenic beauty. Yet it's not entirely a nudist's Shangri-la out here. In addition to true-blue au naturel aesthetes, some prurient opportunists get past the gates. Driftwood lean-tos referred to as (titter, titter) "sex condos" have been assembled on the beach. Still, there's plenty of beach to go around out here—two long, lonesome miles of it—leaving room enough for those who came for the sun, as well as those in search of more searing activity. Crowds numbering upward of 500 let it all hang out on summer weekends.

Some avoid the charges by parking along the roadside and making the treacherous hike down via trails. Such high-impact intrusions are no doubt responsible for accelerating erosion. Be a sport and enter where you ought to. As an option, you can hike north along the beach for half a mile from San Gregorio State Beach.

For More Information

Contact Martin's Beach, Martin's Beach Road, Half Moon Bay, CA 94019; (415) 712-8020. There is no phone number for San Gregorio Private Beach.

Martin's Beach

Location: Six miles south of Half Moon Bay, at the end of Martin's Beach Road, off Highway 1.
Parking: $4 entrance fee per vehicle.
Hours: 6 AM to 6 PM (later in summer).
Facilities: Rest rooms and picnic tables.
Contact: For beach information, contact Martin's Beach at (415) 712-8020.

See number 12 on page 404.

San Gregorio Private Beach

Location: At the end of a dirt toll road 100 yards north of the intersection of Highways 1 and 84.
Parking: $3 entrance fee.
Hours: 9 AM to 7 PM.
Facilities: Rest rooms.
Contact: There is no phone number for San Gregorio Private Beach.

See number 11 on page 404.

Half Moon Bay

Location: 28 miles south of San Francisco on Highway 1. Half Moon Bay can also be reached by taking Route 92 west till it ends at the coast. Half Moon Bay is the site of a series of beaches referred to as Half Moon Bay State Beaches, of which Francis Beach is the most popular and best equipped.
Population: 9,400
Area Code: 415 **Zip Code:** 94019

For a while, Half Moon Bay appeared to be growing rapidly, as suburban sprawl pushed south from San Francisco. Formerly a nub in the middle of the rural San Mateo Coast, where Route 1 meets Route 92, the quaint, seaside town served as an overflow valve for stressed-out urbanites fleeing the congested inland Bay Area. However, coastal zoning regulations, limitations in the sewer capacity and water supply, and the hassles of living here—that is, the hassles of commuting from here—have caused the influx to taper off in recent years. The final straw was the January 1995 collapse of Highway 1 in the area north of Half Moon Bay known as Devil's Slide, which stymied traffic trying to reach San Francisco via the most direct route. The mandated detour over Route 92, a road not designed to handle that volume of traffic, created traffic snarls and added hours to the commute.

Half Moon Bay is at the heart of an area known as Coastside—a string of towns strewn like seashells along the central San Mateo County coast. In addition to Half Moon Bay, Coastside comprises El Granada, Miramar, Princeton, Moss Beach, and Montara. The combined population of these and a few inland hamlets is 22,000. Much of the land along the foggy coast is used for agriculture. Artichokes, Brussels sprouts, pumpkins, and flowers are harvested at various times of year. Alongside the modest homes of agricultural workers have gone up Cape Cod–style shoreline developments, mining the cutesy fishing-village theme that's been done to death everywhere else. It's still relatively peaceful in the Coastside communities, but the tranquillity has been disturbed and the future is uncertain. Much depends on how accessible the area becomes as improvements to the primary arteries are made. Many who live here don't want to see it change much, and you can't blame them. Then there's the minority opinion: a Florida-based developer who wants to build an 81,000-square foot, glassed-in mall with an accompanying hotel at Pillar Point.

The oldest community in San Mateo County, Half Moon Bay has already been upscaled to a degree. Art galleries, trendy boutiques, and sophisticated eateries like Pasta Moon and the 2 Fools Café and Market have taken up residence on Main Street alongside the more homely San Mateo County Farm Supply and Cunha's Country Store. The August issue of a monthly local magazine ran a major article on the "Economic Effects of the Art and Pumpkin Festival"—an October event that is the city's principal claim to fame. This is small-town stuff, albeit with an increasingly wealthy population. Half Moon Bay is attractive to Bay Area weekenders, offering a selection of comfortable bed-and-breakfast inns, a few nice restaurants, some interesting boutiques, and plenty of the meditative calm that allow Type A city-dwellers to chill out. And we mean *chill out*.

Frequently buried beneath a ceiling of coastal overcast, Half Moon Bay has a gray, austere look. Heavy fogs can carry as much as a million gallons of water shoreward per hour. The weather is unvarying: highs in the 60s, lows in the 40s, year round. Emplaced in a natural setting of waves and sand backed by rolling brown hills and jutting headlands, the Coastside area is appealingly raw.

Map of San Mateo County beaches—page 404

Beaches

The Half Moon Bay State Beaches are a trio of bayside retreats with access points at Francis, Venice, and Dunes beaches. The six-mile Coastside Trail connects the three beaches, running along the marine terrace above the water. It's used by joggers, bicyclists, and hikers. An equestrian trail runs parallel to it. Horses can be rented by the hour at private stables in Half Moon Bay.

Francis Beach is the largest and most popular unit. It is reached by heading west along Kelly Avenue (off Highway 1) and then turning right on Balboa Boulevard to the gated entrance. On several visits, we saw cars backed up waiting to get in. A field of grassy short bluffs above the beach is studded with picnic tables. All the picnicking families and their victuals draw a mass of hungry shorebirds that squawk for handouts and forage through garbage cans in a scene resembling Alfred Hitchcock's *The Birds*. Wave erosion and human feet have carved gullylike paths down to the beach. From the sandy strand, it's another sharp drop down to where the waves wash

Dunes Beach
(a part of Half Moon Bay State Beach)

Location: In Half Moon Bay, at the end of Young Avenue off Highway 1, 1.5 miles north of the Highway 92 intersection.

Parking: $4 entrance fee per vehicle.

Hours: 8 AM to sunset.

Facilities: Rest rooms and picnic area.

Contact: For beach information, contact Half Moon Bay State Beach at (415) 726-8820.

See number 17 on page 404.

Cowell Ranch Beach
(a part of Half Moon Bay State Beach)

Location: 0.6 mile south of Pelican Point off Highway 1. A dirt road leads a half mile to a small parking lot. The beach is reached via a 133-step staircase.

Parking: Free, small parking lot. If full, park on shoulder of Highway 1 and walk down dirt road to parking lot and staircase.

Hours: 8 AM to sunset.

Facilities: Rest rooms.

Contact: For beach information, contact Half Moon Bay State Beach at (415) 726-8820.

See number 13 on page 404.

Francis Beach
(a part of Half Moon Bay State Beach)

Location: In Half Moon Bay, at the end of Kelly Avenue off Highway 1.

Parking: $4 entrance fee per vehicle.

Hours: 8 AM to sunset.

Facilities: Rest rooms, showers, picnic tables, and fire pits. There are 55 tent and RV campsites. Fees are $12 to $14 per night. There is also tent camping for groups up to 50 at Sweetwood Group Camp, a mile north of Francis State Beach. Fee is $75 per night per group site. For camping reservations, call Destinet at (800) 444-7275.

Contact: For beach information, contact Half Moon Bay State Beach at (415) 726-8820.

See number 15 on page 404.

up. The steep gradient indicates a strong backwash; this does not look to be a particularly safe beach for swimming. Water temperature rarely rises above 50 degrees, and hypothermia is almost guaranteed without a wet suit. Yet crowds descend on Francis Beach to camp, picnic, and play games.

If you want to beat the crowds at Francis, try the smaller **Venice Beach** and **Dunes Beach**. However, our feeling is if they're going to charge four bucks at the gate, the least they could do is pave the rutted road leading to the beach and the parking lots. Between Venice and Dunes is the Sweetwood Group Camp, a tent-only group campsite that can accommodate up to 50 persons and 12 vehicles.

Cowell Ranch Beach is a unit of Half Moon Bay State Beach three miles south of town that opened in 1995. There's still not much there, and getting to the beach requires a ride down a dirt road and a descent down a steep staircase. **Pelican Point Beach**, which lies about two miles south of the Highway 1 and Route 92 interchange in Half Moon Bay, has a bit more to offer. The private campground has 84 campsites for tents and RVs, as well as beach access.

Pelican Point Beach

3

Location: 2.25 miles south of the intersection of Highway 1 and Route 92, at the end of Miramontes Point Road. A dirt trail leads to the beach.

Parking: Free roadside parking.

Hours: Sunrise to sunset.

Facilities: Rest rooms, showers, and picnic tables. There are 84 tent and RV campsites at Pelican Point RV Park, a commercial campground near the coastal-access trail. Fees are $18 to $27 per night. For camping reservations, call Pelican Point RV Park at (415) 726-9100.

Contact: For beach information, contact Pelican Point RV Park at (415) 726-9100.

See number 14 on page 404.

Venice Beach
(a part of Half Moon Bay State Beach)

2

Location: In Half Moon Bay, at the end of Venice Boulevard off Highway 1, one mile north of the Highway 92 intersection.

Parking: $4 entrance fee per vehicle.

Hours: 8 AM to sunset.

Facilities: Rest rooms and picnic area.

Contact: For beach information, contact Half Moon Bay State Beach at (415) 726-8820.

See number 16 on page 404.

Bunking Down

The old Victorian buildings of Half Moon Bay have been preserved, and a few have been put to use as bed-and-breakfast inns. The most lavish of these is the **Mill Rose Inn** (615 Mill Street, 726-9794, $$$$), a pricey, overblown-but-romantic retreat in Half Moon Bay's Old Town district surrounded by an English country garden. Sherry is served in the evening and champagne accompanies breakfast. They pamper you to the nines here: robes, wine and cheese, tubs for two, outdoor spa in a white gazebo, and so on. Roses are everywhere. Honeymooners, take note. Another denizen of the B&B scene is the **Old Thyme Inn** (799 Main Street, 726-1616, $$), done in Queen Anne style with an herb garden and prices that, at $65-$135 per night, are very affordable. Half Moon Bay also has a couple of newer arrivals in the motel category, namely a **Ramada Ltd**.

(3020 Highway 1, 726-9700, $), a **Holiday Inn Express** (230 South Cabrillo Highway, 726-3400, $$), and the posh **Half Moon Bay Lodge Best Western** (2400 South Cabrillo Highway, 726-9000, $$$), which overlooks the Half Moon Bay Golf Links.

Coastal Cuisine

Since the restaurants of Half Moon Bay serve the discriminating palettes of many people who now live (or once lived) in San Francisco, there is a respectable dining scene here. Topping the list is **Pasta Moon** (315 Main Street, 726-5125, $$$), where linguine with scallops and other seafood-pasta combos are worth raving about, and **San Benito House** (356 Main Street, 726-3425, $$$), a turn-of-the-century inn and restaurant known for California cuisine in a French country setting. (Note: San Benito was the original name of the settlement at Half Moon Bay.) **Three Amigos** (200 South Cabrillo Highway, 726-6080, $$) will have you doing handstands and hat dances over its high-quality Mexican food. Gourmet take-out fare (or eat-in fare, if you prefer to chow down in the small dining room) can be found at the **2 Fools Café and Market** (408 Main Street, 712-1222, $$). Finally, the **Main Street Grill** (435 Main Street, 726-5300, $) serves the best home-cooked breakfast and lunch on the coast, from omelettes and sourdough French toast to burgers and microbrewed beers.

Night Moves

The **Half Moon Bay Inn** (401 Main Street, 726-5977), a dimly lit tavern smack dab in the center of town, is where the locals come to bend an elbow. If you're looking for something a little livelier or more upscale, head up the road to the **Miramar Beach Restaurant** (Mirada Road, Miramar, 726-9053) or the **Moss Beach Distillery** (Beach and Ocean Streets, Moss Beach, 728-5595), an atmospheric steak-and-seafood joint supposedly haunted by the ghost of the Blue Lady.

For More Information

Contact the Half Moon Bay/Coastside Chamber of Commerce, 520 Kelly Avenue, Half Moon Bay, CA 94019; (415) 726-8380.

Miramar

Location: Two miles north of Half Moon Bay, off Highway 1.
Population: 400
Area Code: 415 **Zip Code:** 94019

Miramar is more remarkable for what it used to be than what it is today. It was once the site of the Palace Miramar, a seaside resort hotel (ca. 1916) complete with an indoor saltwater plunge. During Prohibition, Miramar served as the drop-off point for bootleg liquor bought in Canada and shipped down to Half Moon Bay. Local rumrunners paddled out to meet the large ships and carry the hootch to shore under cover of darkness. The Miramar Beach Inn (ca. 1918) was designed and constructed as a Prohibition roadhouse and, it is rumored, bordello. These days, the same building does business as the Miramar Beach Restaurant, a rustic eatery and music club with great ocean views. Miramar itself is a sweet nothing of a town, a few residential streets running parallel to a beach that disappears rapidly as high tide approaches.

Beaches

Miramar Beach abuts the larger El Granada Beach (see next entry), which runs up to the breakwater at Pillar Point Harbor. That breakwater, built in 1959, has been responsible for massive erosion along the beaches that lay south of it. The breakwater interrupted the natural longshore transport of sand and focused greater wave energy on the beaches, resulting in accelerated sea-cliff erosion. Parts of Mirada Road have been foreshortened and destroyed, and the highly erodible cliffs have retreated an estimated 90 feet due to the harbor construction project. Life is a beach, unless you live downstream of a breakwater or jetty, in which case life is a shrinking beach. No fair. No fun.

Bunking Down

The **Cypress Inn** (407 Mirada Road, 726-6602, $$$) is a bright and contemporary bed-and-breakfast outfitted in Southwestern decor. The three-story, 12-room inn was built a literal stone's throw from the ocean in 1989, and every comfortable room has a gas fireplace, balcony, and view of Miramar Beach.

Coastal Cuisine

The **Miramar Beach Restaurant** (131 Mirada Road, 726-9053, $$$) has been revamped in the last half-dozen years. It's still got a sturdy, lived-in feel of dark wood and brass, but the menu has been expanded and updated. In addition to grilled steaks and seafood, you can order the likes of linguine with fresh cracked crab and bay shrimp, or salmon in puff pastry served on a bed of roasted red peppers, Tuscan beans, and shrimp ragout.

Night Moves

For a town that's just a blip on the coastal radar, Miramar boasts two night spots. The **Miramar Beach Restaurant** (131 Mirada Road, 762-9053) tends to book the remnants of San

Miramar Beach

Location: In Miramar Beach, at the end of Mirada Road, two miles north of Half Moon Bay off Highway 1.
Parking: Free street parking.
Hours: Half hour before sunrise to half hour after sunset.
Facilities: None.
Contact: For beach information, contact the Half Moon Bay Parks Department at (415) 726-8297.

See number 18 on page 404.

Francisco bands that stood the world on its ear in the '60s and are somehow scraping by in the '90s. During our trek through the area, former members of Moby Grape, the Doobie Brothers, and the Sons of Champlin were all booked. The other side of the musical coin is the **Bach Dancing and Dynamite Society** (Mirada Road, 726-4131), an oceanfront beach house whose owner and impresario, Peter Douglas, hosts 26 Sunday afternoon concerts a year—mainly jazz and the classics. You can bring your own wine and picnic on the deck while the band plays. Smokin'!

For More Information

Contact the Half Moon Bay/Coastside Chamber of Commerce, 520 Kelly Avenue, Half Moon Bay, CA 94019; (415) 726-8380.

El Granada

Location: Three miles north of Half Moon Bay, along Highway 1.
Population: 4,426
Area Code: 415 **Zip Code:** 94018

El Granada is a mostly residential town arrayed in semicircular roads located on the dry side of Highway 1. It's got just a touch of everything for the tourist: a nice, comfy inn that's a five-minute stroll from the beach (Harbor View Inn, 51 Avenue Alhambra, 726-2329, $$), a good continental bistro that's got live jazz and classical music on weekends (Café Classique, 726-9775, $$$), and **El Granada Beach**. The beach here is wide but the short bluffs behind it keep eroding when winter storms do their damage. The Pillar Point Harbor (see next entry) has brought increased commerce to Coastside, but it's made a mess of the beach next door. Still, water-sports enthusiasts—boogie boarders, ocean kayakers, and surfers—have fun just below the east breakwater, an area that is locally known as Surfers' Beach.

For More Information

Contact the Half Moon Bay/Coastside Chamber of Commerce, 520 Kelly Avenue, Half Moon Bay, CA 94019; (415) 726-8380.

El Granada Beach
(a.k.a. Surfers' Beach)

Location: Three miles north of Half Moon Bay on Highway 1, between Mirada Road and the East Breakwater at Pillar Point Harbor.

Parking: Metered lot parking at Pillar Point Harbor.

Hours: Half hour before sunrise to half hour after sunset.

Facilities: None.

Contact: For beach information, contact the Half Moon Bay Parks Department at (415) 726-8297.

See number 19 on page 404.

Princeton-by-the-Sea and Pillar Point

Location: Four miles north of Half Moon Bay, off Highway 1.
Population: 1,000
Area Code: 415 **Zip Code:** 94018

The cliffs of Pillar Point form a protective shield enfolding the development known as Pillar Point Harbor. The Army Corps of Engineers built two breakwaters in 1961, further protecting the harbor and allowing expansion to its present size of 369 berths. Surrounding the harbor is the community of Princeton-by-the-Sea, an unpretentious gathering of Cape Cod–type homes that were here long before the faux New England architectural theme became an overplayed cliché on the coast. It's a quiet town located on Harbor Road, which curves off and rejoins Highway 1. Pillar Point is a real working harbor whose 180-boat fishing fleet lands close to 10 million pounds of fish a year.

Not surprisingly, there are some terrific seafood restaurants in the area—probably the best grouping of them between San Francisco and Santa Cruz. Still, the harbor complex doesn't appear to be prospering the way its developers might have hoped. A huge, glassed-in harborfront retail complex, complete with cushy hotels and restaurants, never got beyond the planning stages because of the depressed economy. That's just as well—it's nice the way it is.

Beaches

Pillar Point made headlines in 1994 when a world-class surfer was killed while riding a 16-foot wave in an area called **Mavericks**. Thirty-six-year-old Mark Foo, one of the sport's great big-wave surfers, met his match two days before Christmas. He disappeared inside a wave, and his body was found floating at the mouth of the harbor a short while later. Mavericks lies beyond the cliffs along the north shore of Pillar Point, where huge swells from far-distant storms can create waves as high as 30 feet a few times each winter. Mavericks is not for the timid or inexperienced, but word is out—both about the size of waves when they're breaking,

Mavericks

Location: Southwest of Princeton-by-the-Sea, below the cliffs along the north shore of Pillar Point. Take West Point Road to the U.S. Air Force Radar Tracking Station and park in the lot by the marsh. A trail leads to the bluffs and beach.
Parking: Free parking lot.
Hours: Sunrise to sunset.
Facilities: None.
Contact: For beach information, contact the San Mateo County Harbormaster at (415) 726-5727.

See number 21 on page 404.

Pillar Point Harbor

Location: Four miles north of Half Moon Bay off Highway 1, along Capistrano Road.
Parking: Metered parking lot.
Hours: Sunrise to sunset.
Facilities: Rest rooms and picnic area.
Contact: For beach information, contact the San Mateo County Harbormaster at (415) 726-5727.

See number 20 on page 404.

and their lethal potential. Why not just stay onshore and look for whales instead? Pillar Point is a prime location for whale watching from December through March. Those are always more fun to spot than dead surfers.

Bunking Down

But for the west-facing coastline, the **Pillar Point Inn** (380 Capistrano Road, 728-7377, $$$) might have you convinced you're in Massachusetts rather than California. This stately gray Cape Codder has 11 rooms filled with feather beds and decor accenting the local history of the area.

Coastal Cuisine

This is really where Princeton scores high marks. Seafood makes a quick passage from fishing boats to restaurant kitchens in this area. For a heavenly fresh seafood dinner in comfortably funky surroundings, duck into **Barbara's Fishtrap** (281 Capistrano Road, 726-7049, $$). You may have to wait—it's-line-out-the-door popular, and they accept neither credit cards nor reservations—but the fried seafood is as good as good gets.

Another local institution is the **Shore Bird Restaurant** (390 Capistrano Road, 728-5541, $$$). The building is an exact replica of a house on Cape Cod, copied by the architect down to the minutest detail. Overlooking the harbor and surrounded by a garden and a white picket fence, the Shore Bird looks more like a prosperous sea captain's home than the area's most popular restaurant. The restaurant specializes in fresh fish served in its simplest and best form: broiled. The catch can range from salmon and sea bass to swordfish and shark. You really can't go wrong anywhere around the harbor. We made a good, simple midday meal of clam chowder and sourdough bread at **Ketch Joanne's** (25 Johnson Pier, Pillar Point Harbor, 728-5959, $$$), a complex that includes a bar/restaurant, fish market, and open-air seafood barbecue grill. As usual, the listing of fresh fish just goes on and on.

Night Moves

You can grab a beer at **Ketch Joanne's Harbor Bar** (17 Johnson Pier, Pillar Point Harbor, 728-5959), but for anything more animated than that you'll need to head up to Moss Beach or down to Miramar. Hey, see if you feel like partying after a hard day of hauling fish onto the deck of a wave-tossed boat.

For More Information

Contact the Half Moon Bay/Coastside Chamber of Commerce, 520 Kelly Avenue, Half Moon Bay, CA 94019; (415) 726-8380.

Moss Beach

Location: Six miles north of Half Moon Bay, off Highway 1.
Population: 3,000
Area Code: 415 **Zip Code:** 94038

Tucked off the highway, Moss Beach is another unprepossessing Coastside community that makes this stretch of San Mateo County so inviting. It's got a New England–village feel, but in a natural and not voguish way. Remnants of the little town's rumrunning history survive in the Moss Beach Distillery, a Prohibition-era roadhouse that's endured as a popular restaurant and landmark. The chief natural attraction of Moss Beach is the James V. Fitzgerald Marine Reserve, which runs for three miles below the bluffs between Montara and Pillar Points.

Beaches

We had a queasy feeling about the shoreline at Moss Beach, which is formally known as the **James V. Fitzgerald Marine Reserve**. We wanted to enter from the parking lot at the Moss Beach Distillery, but a sign announced the closure of the trail into the reserve. Crumbling cliffs, washed-out trails—same old story. We somehow made it down to the beach (later we found out there's easy access from the reserve's well-marked parking lot—follow the signs from Highway 1). It was a weird stretch of sand that smelled of seaweed and was covered with black gunk that looked like asphalt chunks. At low tide, the ocean pulls back to reveal acres of tidepools—the place's big draw—which you can investigate on your own or on one of the scheduled ranger-led walks. For information on times and places call the reserve at (415) 728-3584, and to make group reservations, call (415) 340-7208.

In the end, we discovered that Moss Beach does have its charms. When we explored a trail leading up one of the southern cliffs, we found ourselves in a large, eerie cypress forest—perfect for an impromptu game of hide-and seek. From there, we found a staircase leading down to a lovely, secluded beach. No complaints, honest.

James V. Fitzgerald Marine Reserve

Location: In Moss Beach, at the end of California Avenue six miles north of Half Moon Bay off Highway 1.
Parking: Free lot and street parking.
Hours: Sunrise to sunset.
Facilities: Rest rooms and picnic tables.
Contact: For information on ranger-led tidepool walks, contact James V. Fitzgerald Marine Reserve at (415) 728-3584.

See number 22 on page 404.

Bunking Down

The **Seal Cove Inn** (221 Cypress Avenue, 728-7325, $$$) is a recently constructed English manor house that overlooks the ocean in a setting of cypress and wildflowers. It's the kind of comfortably luxurious place to which people come to decompress from life in the city—you know, kick back, light a fire, read a book, and get sane again.

Coastal Cuisine

The **Moss Beach Distillery** (Beach Way and Ocean Boulevard, 728-5595, $$$) is celebrated for its great beachside location, its history, and its possession by ghosts. There's a long story that goes with this, centering around the legend of the Blue Lady, a married woman who died in a car wreck en route to meet her lounge-lizard boyfriend here 70 years ago. Now they both supposedly haunt the place—as does the lounge lizard's distraught wife, who leapt to her death upon learning of his infidelity. The distillery has parlayed this far-fetched bit of lore into a dinner/seance routine that sounds fishy (and we don't mean the menu items). On appointed nights, a "renowned psychic" summons the resident spirits and channels their messages in what sounds like the world's longest-running soap opera. The cost to attend is $75 per person—enough to cause us to drop dead on the spot and begin wandering the premises with all the other apparitions.

Beyond this amusing nonsense, the Moss Beach Distillery offers a superb coastal view and serves entrées (available in petite or regular portions) that run the gamut from pasta to steak to a host of fresh seafood specials. The prevailing culinary approach is uncomplicated but serviceable. And don't you just love the address: the intersection of Beach Way and Ocean Boulevard, evoking a figurative seaside paradise where we should all be so lucky to spend the rest of our days.

Night Moves

Again, the **Moss Beach Distillery** (see above) is the place to come for an afternoon libation or a late-evening nightcap. There is an outdoor patio with heat lamps, deck chairs, and heavy blankets. Order a drink, tuck yourself in, and watch the sunset—if you're lucky enough to catch one. If you eventually start seeing double, it will probably have nothing to do with ghosts.

For More Information

Contact the Half Moon Bay/Coastside Chamber of Commerce, 520 Kelly Avenue, Half Moon Bay, CA 94019; (415) 726-8380.

Montara

Location: Eight miles north of Half Moon Bay, off Highway 1.
Population: 2,500
Area Code: 415 **Zip Code:** 94037

As luck would have it, we spent our last day of beachcombing for this book on the beach at Montara. The gods were with us that August afternoon, because the sunset we witnessed was one for the ages—sort of a solar going-away prize for us, we figured. For about 10 wonderful minutes, people spontaneously dropped what they were doing—be it surfing at Montara State Beach or dining on surf-and-turf at the Chart House—to watch the last sublime rays before the sun dropped from sight. Oddly enough, the sky was cloudy except for a narrow clearing of blue just above the horizon. All of a sudden, a brilliant gold band of light appeared between the cloud bank and the ocean. The sun glowed a fiery red-orange as it made its brief but stunning sojourn, dipping behind the horizon with a final flicker 'n' twinkle that drew whoops and applause. It was, we offer with no irony, a religious experience. Ah, California.

Montara was originally conceived at the turn of the century as an artists' colony by a bohemian magazine publisher from San Francisco. However, his grand plans for a seaside community of creative types never took hold, and the artists were displaced by bootleggers. Today, Montara has reclaimed some of its intended character. It's another likable link in the Coastside chain—a nice place to visit or live. Unless, of course, you have to commute over Devil's Slide.

Beaches

Montara State Beach is the hippest beach in San Mateo County. That's not saying a lot, really. From Montara south to the Santa Cruz

 Map of San Mateo County beaches—page 404

County line, only 24,000 people live along the coast, and relatively few of them are self-consciously hip in the MTV sense of youthful, studied cool. Many pick artichokes and Brussels sprouts. Others make real-estate deals. Then there are the retirees. Montara, for some anomalous reason—probably having to do with proximity to Pacifica and San Francisco—draws a younger crowd. They play games on the beach—volleyball, Frisbee, paddleball—as if they believe themselves to be down in Capitola rather than knocking on the backdoor of Fogtown. Waves are good, if inconsistent. As Mr. T used to say, "It's cool."

Bunking Down

We stayed at the **Farallone Inn** (1410 Main Street, 728-8200, $$) back before it got its recent massive facelift. Suffice to say that it needed it, and now it's a modernized, refurbished wonder. All nine rooms have decks and Jacuzzis, yet there are still reminders of its 1908 heritage. The **Goose and Turrets** (835 George Street, 728-5451, $$) is a rambling house with a lot of character. You can walk to the beach or lie in the garden hammock, reading or just dreaming about the four-course breakfast that's served every morning. If you're living on a shoestring, you can board cheaply at **Montara Lighthouse Hostel** (Highway 1 at 16th Street, P.O. Box 737, 728-7177, $).

Montara State Beach

Location: In Montara, adjacent to the Chart House Restaurant at the intersection of Highway 1 and 2nd Street, eight miles north of Half Moon Bay.

Parking: Free parking lot.

Hours: 8 AM to sunset.

Facilities: Rest rooms.

Contact: For beach information, contact the Bay Area District of the California Department of Parks and Recreation at (415) 330-6300.

See number 23 on page 404.

Coastal Cuisine

Steve's Blue Pacific Restaurant (Seventh Street and Highway 1, 728-5209, $$) is the kind of place that locals like to keep to themselves and out-of-towners wouldn't think to visit without being tipped off. Well, consider yourself tipped. Barbecue is the specialty, and the smoked entrées—prime rib, baby-back ribs, beef bones—rule, dude. You can also order charbroiled salmon, halibut, and prawns. The **Foglifter** (8455 Highway 1, 728-7905, $$) is another locals' favorite whose rather ramshackle facade belies the cozy dining room and excellent seafood and Italian fare within. The local **Chart House** (8150 Highway 1, 728-7366, $$$) is a kind of landmark, overlooking and sharing a parking lot with Montara State Beach. It's pricey, basic franchised surf-and-turf stuff unworthy of a rave for any other reason than location. When Devil's Slide shuts down Highway 1, this is where the "Road Closed" signs go up.

For More Information

Contact the Half Moon Bay/Coastside Chamber of Commerce, 520 Kelly Avenue, Half Moon Bay, CA 94019; (415) 726-8380.

Gray Whale Cove State Beach

Location: Three miles south of Pacifica, off Highway 1 at Devil's Slide.

Strange as it sounds, the state of California is a partner of sorts in the nude-beach business. **Gray Whale Cove** (a.k.a. Devil's Slide) is privately managed on behalf of the state as a clothing-optional beach. There are rest rooms, pop machines, even a hot-dog stand. It's up to you, though, to bring the buns. (Ha ha!) By the way, the water here is indecently cold. The drill goes like this: you park on the east side of Highway 1, hike down to the small, 800-foot cove, pay your money, and let it all hang out.

For More Information

Contact Gray Whale Cove State Beach, Highway 1, Montara, CA 94037; (415) 728-5336.

Gray Whale Cove State Beach
(a.k.a. Devil's Slide)

Location: At Devil's Slide off Highway 1, three miles south of Pacifica and one mile north of Montara.

Parking: $5 entrance fee per person.

Hours: 8 AM to sunset.

Facilities: Rest rooms, picnic area, and fire pits.

Contact: For beach information, contact Gray Whale Cove State Beach at (415) 728-5336.

See number 24 on page 404.

Devil's Slide: A Hell of a Headache

Pretend you live in Montara and work in San Francisco. Or you live in San Francisco and want to visit the San Mateo Coast. Or you're a tourist traveling on Highway 1 in this vicinity. Regardless of your reasons, for much of 1995 you'd have been stymied. That is because Highway 1 negotiates a treacherous and unstable passage between Pacifica and Montara known as Devil's Slide. It has always been subject to short-term closures for various reasons, but during January 1995, in the midst of a considerable rainy spell, all hell broke loose. The road at Devil's Slide essentially slipped off its hinges.

A four-mile section of Highway 1 through Devil's Slide was immediately closed with no indication of when it might reopen. The closure created commuter havoc, necessitating an hour-long detour each way. Then the debate began. Repair the existing road? Blast a tunnel through the mountain? Build an inland bypass of Devil's Slide? Highway engineers and environmentalists have been locked in a pitched battle over Devil's Slide since the 1960s. CalTrans would like to pursue the inland option, cutting across McNee Ranch State Park, but the Sierra Club has filed suit to protect the parkland. Environmental groups instead want to see a tunnel put through the mountain that separates Montara and Pacifica. CalTrans says that would be a pro-

Pacifica

Location: 10 miles south of San Francisco, along Highway 1.
Population: 38,500
Area Code: 415 **Zip Code:** 94044

Pacifica is not just one small city but a conglomeration of nine separate townships and subdivisions that came together in 1957. For this reason, it is not your average municipality. There is no center of town, per se, and each area retains something of an independent personality. Pacifica's chief problem, as regards tourism, is that it lies in the long shadow of San Francisco. (Somehow, "If you are going to Pacifica/Be sure to wear some flowers in your hair" just doesn't have the same ring.)

No one in their right mind is going to make Pacifica a vacation destination with San Francisco's overwhelming plenitude of attractions so close at hand. And those from San Francisco and the East Bay who are looking for a weekend getaway simply pass through Pacifica—if they pass through at all—en route to the Half Moon Bay area. Add to that the fogbound look that shrouds Pacifica most of the summer, and you've got an image problem. Then there are the ever-present problems with Devil's Slide, the route that links Pacifica with the rest of San Mateo County.

That said, Pacifica does have a few things going for it: a couple of good surfing beaches, a restaurant-motel complex at Rockaway Beach, and a fishing pier at Sharp Park where striped bass are there for the taking. Fall and winter are particularly nice times to visit—it's generally sunny, with moderate temperatures.

Beaches

Pacifica has pinned its modest hopes of capturing a few of the tourist dollars that whiz

hibitively expensive and a geological gamble. Neither group can agree on the cost of either alternative, though figures between $70 and $110 million are tossed around. The environmentalists make compelling arguments against the bypass, saying that it would scar the landscape, silt the watershed, and subject drivers to dense, dangerous fogs much of the time. However, the San Mateo-coast business community views the Sierra Club and related groups as bleeding-heart obstructionists. They want the damn road blasted through now so that the area can return to business as usual. "We'd much rather have a safe road than another state park," groused a restaurant manager, echoing the prevailing sentiment.

In the midst of all the pointed fingers and raised voices, a 1,700-foot section of Highway 1 continued slipping and sliding toward the sea. The roadbed at Devil's Slide has dropped a total of 40 feet since the 1930s. The latest slippage baffled the experts, since it conforms to no prior patterns. Meanwhile, between 9,000 and 13,000 drivers per day had to take a hellish bumper-to-bumper detour around Devil's Slide. Though Highway 1 through Devil's Slide has reopened, a long-term solution still hasn't been made.

through town on **Rockaway Beach**. Here you'll find a complex of motels and restaurants that can't seem to decide if they're in or out of business. The Lighthouse Hotel, for instance, has been in and out, and is now back in. A couple of the restaurants appeared to us to be down for the count, or close to it. Nick's and the Moonraker, however, have been around for years and will no doubt weather the changeable economic tides. The physical tides are another matter—some of the biggest winter waves on the Central Coast roll ashore on the cocoa-colored sands of Rockaway Beach.

About a half mile south lies **Pacifica State Beach** (more commonly known as San Pedro Beach) whose light brown sand and calmer waters provide sharp contrast to Rockaway Beach; Pedro Point provides partial protection from another big, dangerous wave break. **Sharp Park State Beach** is a little over a mile north of Rockaway. Drainpipes poke the ocean at either end of the dark-sanded beach, their vile smell adding to the drab setting. A concrete pier that only an angler could love sits up at the north end. The lure at Sharp Park is fishing, both from the 1,020-foot Pacifica Pier and the beach. Catches include salmon and striped bass (in summer), plus rock bass, surf perch, and jacksmelt. Up at the north end of Pacifica, where Palmetto Avenue meets the Esplanade, is a staircase that leads down steep cliffs to **Esplanade Beach**. At the top is a gazebo that's ideal for sunset gazing; down

Esplanade Beach

3

Location: In Pacifica, on the Esplanade at Palmetto Avenue.

Parking: Free street parking.

Hours: Open 24 hours.

Facilities: None.

Contact: For beach information, contact Pacifica Parks, Beaches, and Recreation at (415) 738-7381.

See number 28 on page 404.

Pacifica State Beach
(a.k.a. San Pedro Beach)

2

Location: In Pacifica, between Crespi Drive and Linda Mar Boulevard on Highway 1.

Parking: Free street parking.

Hours: 8 AM to sunset.

Facilities: Rest rooms and showers.

Contact: For beach information, contact Pacifica Parks, Beaches, and Recreation at (415) 738-7381.

See number 25 on page 404.

Rockaway Beach

2

Location: In Pacifica, at the end of Rockaway Beach Avenue, off Highway 1.

Parking: Free parking lot.

Hours: Open 24 hours.

Facilities: None.

Contact: For beach information, contact Pacifica Parks, Beaches, and Recreation at (415) 738-7381.

See number 26 on page 404.

Sharp Park State Beach

2

Location: In Pacifica, along Santa Rosa Avenue at Beach Boulevard.

Parking: Free street parking.

Hours: Open 24 hours.

Facilities: Rest rooms.

Contact: For beach information, contact Pacifica Parks, Beaches, and Recreation at (415) 738-7381.

See number 27 on page 404.

below, plenty of beach on which to stroll or sunbathe.

Bunking Down

Built in 1985, the **Lighthouse Hotel** (105 Rockaway Beach Avenue, 355-6300, $$) is a perfectly serviceable, 92-unit motel that's a cut below luxe and a cut above a place to dump your bags. They could do more with it, but a certain tentativeness pervades Rockaway Beach. There's also a newish-looking Victorian-styled **Days Inn** (200 Rockaway Beach Avenue, 359-7700, $$) in the complex.

Coastal Cuisine

The **Moonraker** (105 Rockaway Beach Avenue, 355-6300, $$$) offers romantic dining tending toward elaborate seafood preparations in the $15-$20 range. It's been in business for three decades, but only assumed its present location at the Lighthouse Hotel a few years ago. Both the Moonraker and **Nick's** (100 Rockaway Beach Boulevard, 359-3900, $$$) take their fine-dining rep seriously, with a tuxedo-clad wait staff bustling about. Nick's serves three meals, seven days a week, with à-la-carte entrées ranging from about $11 to $19 ($3 extra for a full dinner).

Night Moves

In addition to being a restaurant, **Nick's** (see above) is a cocktails-and-dancing kind of place with live music on weekends.

For More Information

Contact the Pacifica Chamber of Commerce, 450 Dondee Way #2, Pacifica, CA 94044; (415) 355-4122.

Daly City

Location: Abutting the southern end of San Francisco. Route 35 (Skyline Boulevard) runs closest to the coast through Daly City. Thornton State Beach is the main public beach.
Population: 98,000
Area Code: 415 **Zip Code:** 94015

A backdoor suburb of San Francisco, Daly City offers unsightly evidence of the area's insatiable need for bedrooms. It was Daly City that inspired folksinger Malvina Reynolds to write "Tiny Boxes," her sarcastic retort to these suburban projects: "Tiny boxes, little boxes, and they're all made out of ticky-tack." Not much has changed since Reynolds' lampoon except more tiny boxes have gone up and a verse about cheesy condos could be added. Tightly packed together, running up and down the hillsides, they look like a plague of plastic Monopoly houses.

Daly City does have a broad, extensive beach. **Thornton State Beach** lies below steep coastal bluffs and is best accessed by walking down from Fort Funston or up from Mussel Rock City Park. A hiking trail follows the bluff top. People sometimes scramble down the cliffs to reach the sand. (Not recommended.) The main attraction on Thornton Beach is surf casting. As anyone who lives out here will tell you, the beach is all but useless for any other purpose during the summer months, which are foggy and cold. They do become more hospitable in the delayed, de-facto-summer season of September through November, when temperatures warm and the sun breaks free of its fog-induced funk. At press time, Thornton State Beach was in the process of being transferred from the state to the feds, with plans to make it part of Golden Gate National Recreation Area.

For More Information

Contact the Greater Daly City Chamber of Commerce, 244 92nd Street, Daly City, CA 94015; (415) 755-8526.

Thornton State Beach

Location: In Daly City, at the end of Thornton Beach Road.
Parking: Free parking lot.
Hours: Thornton State Beach was technically closed to the public as this book went to press. It is in the process of being transferred from the state to the Golden Gate National Recreation Area, pending repair of storm drains by CalTrans.
Facilities: Picnic tables.
Contact: For beach information, contact the Bay Area District of the California Department of Parks and Recreation at (415) 330-6300.

See number 29 on page 404.

Northern California Beaches

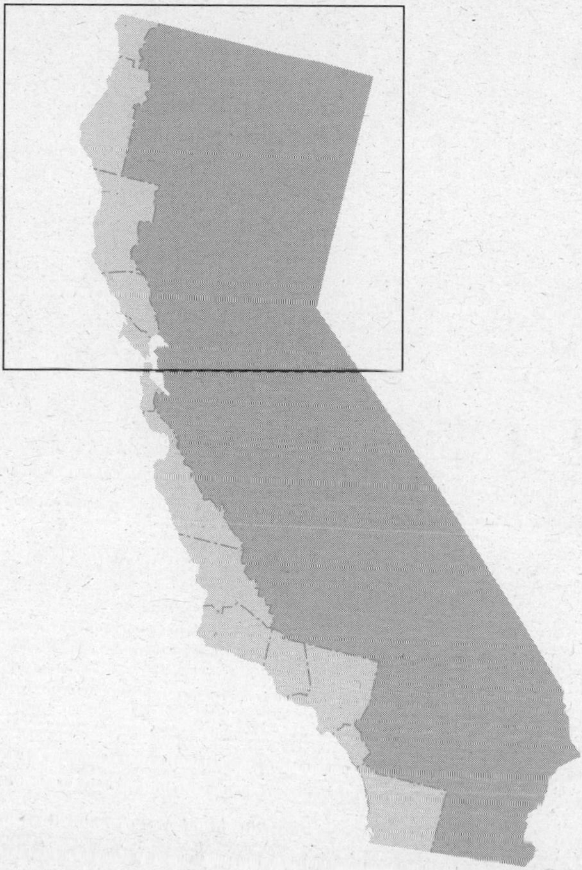

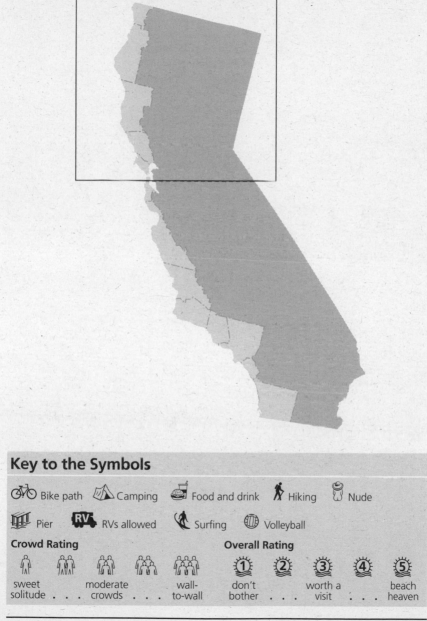

Key to the Symbols

Bike path · Camping · Food and drink · Hiking · Nude

Pier · RVs allowed · Surfing · Volleyball

Crowd Rating

sweet solitude . . . moderate crowds . . . wall-to-wall

Overall Rating

1 don't bother . . . 3 worth a visit . . . 5 beach heaven

Northern California

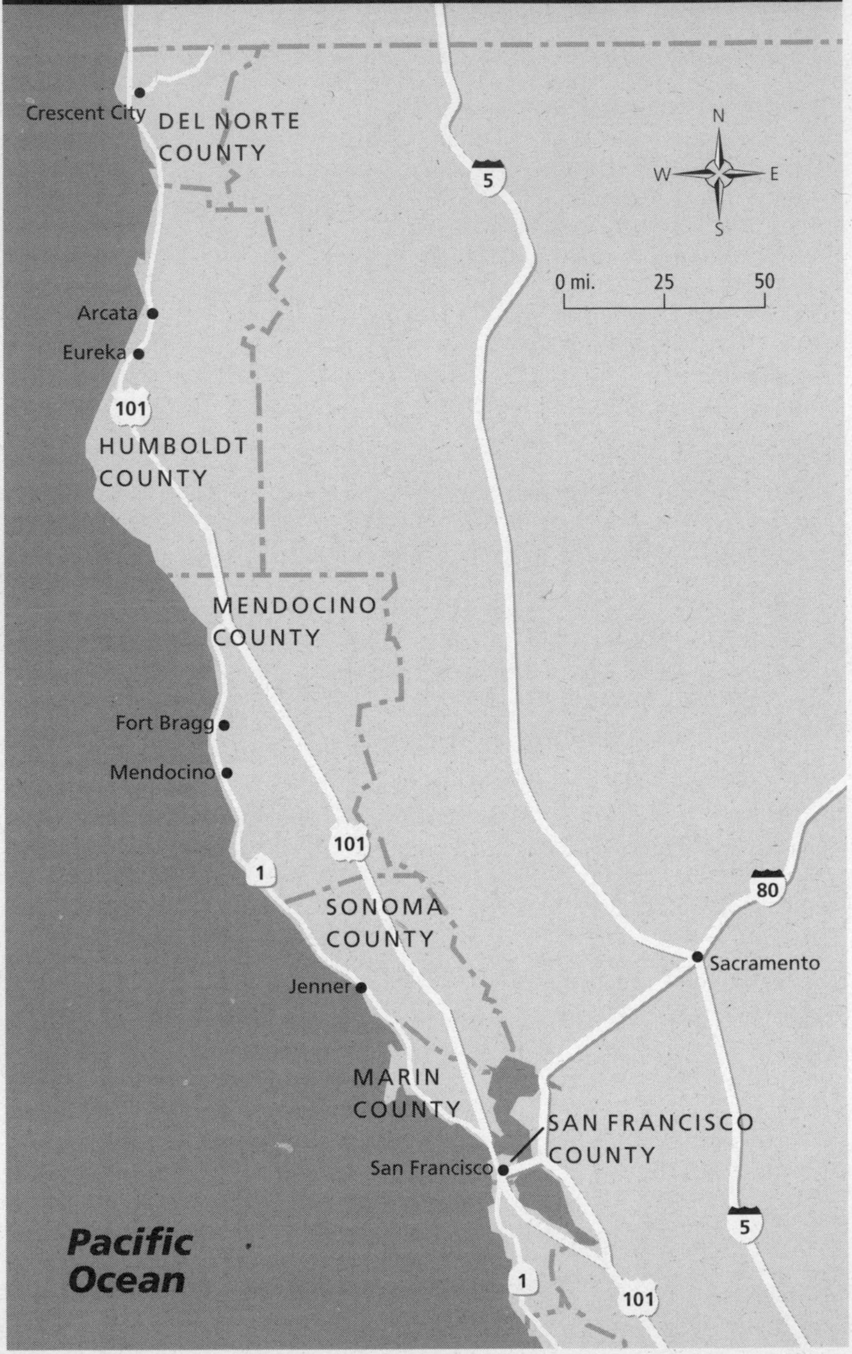
Crescent City
DEL NORTE
COUNTY
N
W
E
S
5
0 mi.
25
50
Arcata
Eureka
101
HUMBOLDT
COUNTY
MENDOCINO
COUNTY
Fort Bragg
Mendocino
101
1
80
SONOMA
COUNTY
Sacramento
Jenner
MARIN
COUNTY
SAN FRANCISCO
COUNTY
San Francisco
5
Pacific
Ocean
1
101

Northern California

San Francisco County

While one can easily leave their heart in this remarkable city-cum-county, we left our footprints in the sand. That's right. The city by the bay has an unheralded beachy side to its personality. The eight-mile stretch of ocean coastline from the San Mateo border to the Golden Gate Bridge is all public land, and much of it is fronted by sand.

An ocean beach in San Francisco, you say? No, not just an ocean beach, but *the* Ocean Beach, a four-mile strand that stretches from Daly City to an old resort landmark, the Cliff House. This beach seemingly has it all—sand dunes, sea walls (dressed up by WPA murals from the 1930s), walkways, promontories. So where are all the swimsuit-clad beachgoers? Oh, we forgot to mention that San Francisco's beaches don't see very many days of sunshine or wind-free warmth. Especially during the summer months, the shoreline fog is so thick you need a divining rod to find the water. And when you do, the frigid, tempestuous waves *(continued on page 438)*

Coastal San Francisco County's Climate

San Francisco Averages

	Daily High Temp. (°F)	Daily Low Temp. (°F)	Rainfall (inches)
January	56	42	4.5
February	59	48	2.8
March	60	49	2.6
April	61	49	1.5
May	63	51	0.4
June	64	53	0.2
July	64	53	0
August	65	54	0.1
September	69	56	0.2
October	68	55	1.1
November	63	52	2.5
December	57	47	3.5
Yearly Average	**63**	**51**	**19.4**

Source: National Weather Service data, National Oceanographic and Atmospheric Administration.

San Francisco County

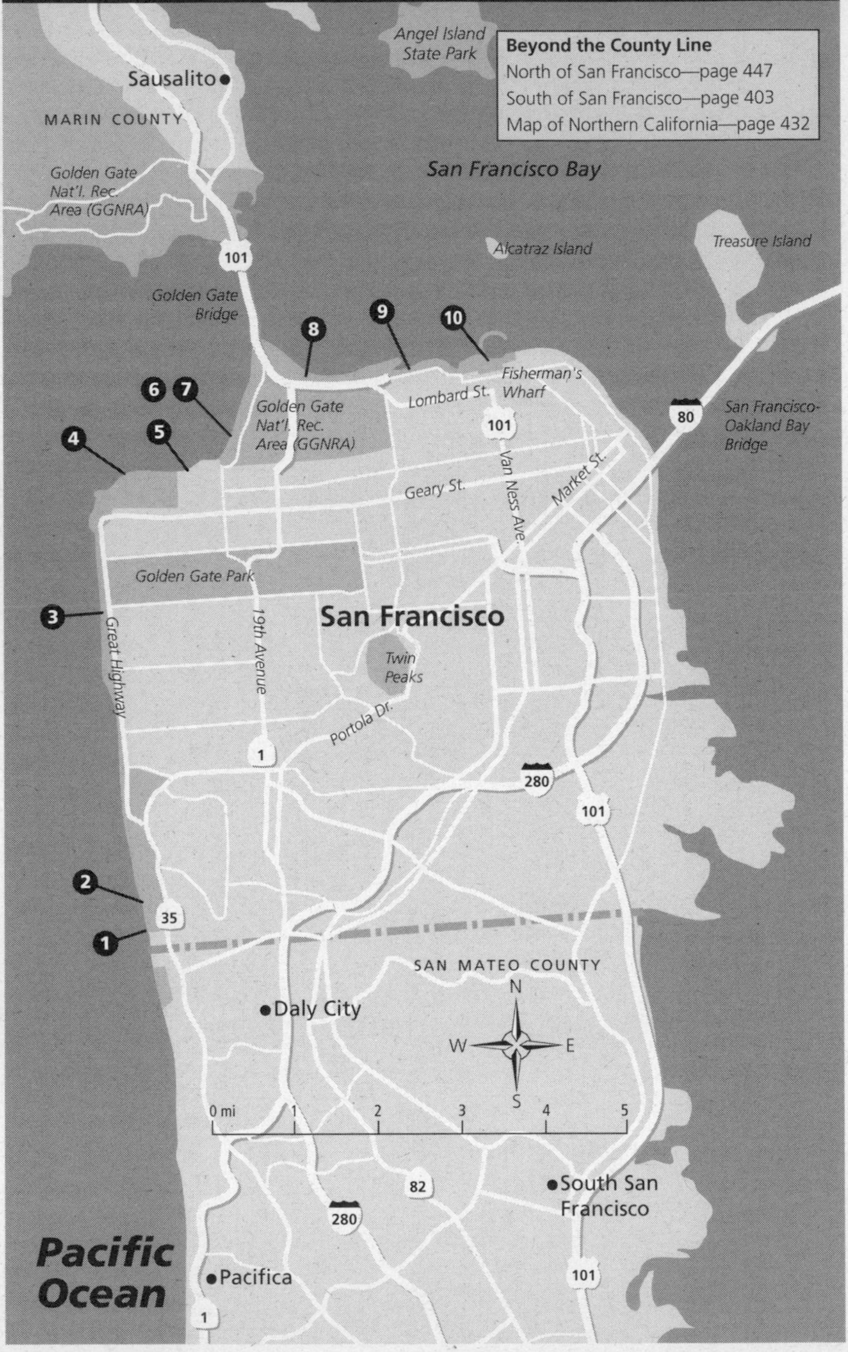
Beyond the County Line
North of San Francisco—page 447
South of San Francisco—page 403
Map of Northern California—page 432
Angel Island State Park
Sausalito
MARIN COUNTY
Golden Gate Nat'l. Rec. Area (GGNRA)
San Francisco Bay
Alcatraz Island
Treasure Island
101
Golden Gate Bridge
8
9
10
6
7
4
5
Fisherman's Wharf
Lombard St.
Golden Gate Nat'l. Rec. Area (GGNRA)
101
80
San Francisco-Oakland Bay Bridge
Market St.
Van Ness Ave.
Geary St.
Golden Gate Park
3
Great Highway
19th Avenue
San Francisco
Twin Peaks
Portola Dr.
1
280
101
2
35
1
SAN MATEO COUNTY
N
W
E
S
Daly City
0 mi
1
2
3
4
5
82
South San Francisco
280
Pacific Ocean
Pacifica
101
1

San Francisco County Beaches

Map of Northern California—page 432

(continued from page 435) roar their disapproval of swimming. It's fine for surfing, though.

No city in America is as blessed with awe-inspiring ocean vistas as San Francisco. The view from the Presidio's coastal trail north toward the Golden Gate Bridge and the Marin Headlands is one that everybody should lay eyes on during their lifetime. And there are indeed a couple of beaches—Baker Beach and China Beach—where one can sunbathe. They're located around the protective bend of Lands End.

In an old cartoon from a book about the Beat Generation, a beret-sporting swimmer with a goatee shouts toward shore, "Like help!" After a few days in this city, we knew exactly how he felt. We, like, needed all the, like, help we could, like, get to point ourselves back on the road, man.

Key to the Symbols

Bike path · Camping · Food and drink · Hiking · Nude

Pier · RVs allowed · Surfing · Volleyball

Crowd Rating

sweet solitude . . . moderate crowds . . . wall-to-wall

Overall Rating

1 don't bother . . . 3 worth a visit . . . 5 beach heaven

San Francisco

Location: At the northern tip of the San Francisco Bay Peninsula, bordered by the Pacific Ocean to the west and the San Francisco Bay to the north and east. San Francisco is the gateway to Northern California.
Population: 800,000
Area Code: 415 **Zip Code:** many

San Francisco really doesn't belong in this book. Coming to this magnificent city for its beaches is like going to Las Vegas for its libraries—no doubt they exist, but they hold a very low priority among visitors, and they're far from being the best example of their kind. The beaches of San Francisco just aren't where you'd want to spend a lot of vacation time. The water's cold, the surf rough, the wind stiff, the fog chilling. That said, it's also true that on one of those rare golden days when the sun is out and the wind has subsided to a mere whisper of a breeze, there's no more glorious place to be, especially at sunset.

But back to the original point. We would have preferred to bypass San Francisco and left this splendid city to the myriad travel books devoted exclusively to its charms. However, the city does have beaches, so we'll dutifully cover that aspect of its geography forthwith. Just don't expect anything more comprehensive than a quick overview of San Francisco's waterfront, because 400 miles of Northern California coastline remain ahead of us, and we must be moving on.

If you're coming here, especially if you plan to be on or near the beach, be sure to pack warm clothes. Just because it's summertime, don't think you can get away with wearing shorts and a T-shirt. In the words of Mark Twain, "The coldest winter I ever spent was a summer in San Francisco." Dress as you would for autumn in New England; wear long pants and keep a sweater tied around your neck. And if you venture westward in the winter, make sure you pack an umbrella—the rainy season typically extends from November to April.

Before we get to the beaches, we should say a few words about Fisherman's Wharf, that working dock turned tourist trap. It's overrun by disposable-camera-toting outsiders and shunned by locals. All the same, there's a few good reasons for dropping by (and an equal number for not sticking around too long). Come to stroll the bayside streets, dodging the low-rent vendors' plaints if possible. We're fond of the seafood take-out counters lined outside the wharfside restaurants. For a few bucks, you can grab a cup of crab, shrimp, lobster, or squid, topped with a tangy dollop of cocktail sauce and a squeeze of lemon. (The protein will fortify you for hiking around Nob Hill, Russian Hill, and all the other hills in this vertically inclined city when you tire of the waterfront.) If you're looking for a more substantial meal, there are several Italian-surnamed seafood restaurants in the area.

Shopping opportunities abound, although we must warn you that there is a distinct low-end aspect to the Fisherman's Wharf retail experience. Along Taylor Street, which runs right down to the wharf, we had unsettling flashbacks of Venice Beach in Southern California. Sidewalk peddlers hawk their wares, mostly T-shirts, sunglasses, and sweatshirts (the Unholy Trinity of street sales). Some of the stores and the characters aren't much to write home about, unless you're writing to say, "I thought San Francisco would be nicer than this." At the other end of the spectrum, visitors with a ready line of credit will want to explore the maze of shops and boutiques at the Cannery (a former Del Monte produce-packing plant) and Ghirardelli Square (a converted chocolate factory). East of Fisherman's Wharf is Pier 39, a teeming bazaar that draws a zombiefied crowd in whose brains some sort of chip must have been implanted that commands them to buy and browse, and buy and browse, and buy and

Map of San Francisco County beaches—page 436

browse some more. Fat, overfed sea lions bob about the green water, barking at tourists for handouts. The crowd-pleasing pinnipeds have mutated from intelligent, vigorously active creatures into slovenly pier bums, much like their human counterparts.

Other wharf-area attractions include ferry rides and tours of islands in the bay, which leave from Piers 41 and 43-1/2. The National Park Service conducts trips to Alcatraz (546-2805), the small, jutting island on which a grim-looking former federal penitentiary housed America's most hardened felons, including the Bird Man and Al Capone. If you go, be sure to rent one of the audiotape tours available at the park; narrated by former wardens and prisoners, it paints a realistic and compelling portrait of life on the Rock. Angel Island, a 760-acre island that actually lies within Marin County waters, serves as a more idyllic state park offering panoramic views of San Francisco from a trail that leads to the top of Mount Livermore (781 feet). Picnicking, tent camping, hiking, and biking can all be enjoyed on Angel Island (call 435-1915 for ferry schedules and fares), which is hardly a secret but still a wonderful escape. In addition to all this, ferries make frequent crossings to the bay-hugging, picturesque Marin communities of Sausalito, Tiburon, and Larkspur. Shifting direction around the eastern side of this boxy peninsula, the piers of the Embarcadero take over, offering deep-water berthing in one of the world's great natural harbors.

Highly recommended to all who want to tour the city by automobile is the 49-Mile Scenic Drive. You can begin at City Hall (Van Ness Avenue and McAllister Street) or at any other point en route. Just follow the blue-and-white seagull signs and allow plenty of time to eyeball San Francisco's scenic sights and heights. An annotated outline of the route can be picked up at the Visitor Information Center (Hallidie Plaza, at Powell and Market Streets), which is, in any event, a good place for a visitor to stock up on maps and tourist tips.

Beaches

Much of San Francisco's coastline—all of it, in fact, that is sandy and fronts the ocean—falls under the holdings of the Golden Gate National Recreation Area, the vast tri-county public park land that is managed by the National Park Service. This includes the eight-mile stretch from the San Mateo county line to Aquatic Park, east of Golden Gate Bridge. Half of that length, from the county line to Point Lobos, faces the ocean square on, running along a nearly perfect north-south axis. Coming up from the south, this area encompasses **Burton Memorial Beach** (which straddles San Mateo and San Francisco counties), **Fort Funston** (a

Aquatic Park

3

Location: In San Francisco, near the intersection of Polk and Beach Streets, just west of Fisherman's Wharf.

Parking: Metered lot and street parking.

Hours: Open 24 hours.

Facilities: Rest rooms.

Contact: For beach information, contact the Golden Gate National Recreation Area at (415) 556-0560.

See number 10 on page 436.

Baker Beach

4

Location: In San Francisco, at the west end of Gibson Road, near the southwest corner of the Presidio.

Parking: Free parking lot.

Hours: 6 AM to one hour after sunset.

Facilities: Rest rooms and picnic tables.

Contact: For beach information, contact the Golden Gate National Recreation Area at (415) 556-0560.

See number 6 on page 436.

popular launch site for hang gliders), and **Ocean Beach** (a long, flat stretch of beach paralleled by the Great Highway). People come to Ocean Beach to park and watch the sun set; to fish on the beach or surf the often sizable waves; and to jog, walk, and ride bikes along pathways that run on both sides of the Great Highway. Unspoiled, impressively empty, the beach is regrettably unsafe for swimming—too rough and too cold.

As you drive north, the road begins to rise, meeting a San Francisco landmark, the Cliff House. A jaw-dropping overview of Ocean Beach can be had from the deck of the Cliff House, looking south down the Great Highway to where the land rises and the road is forced to pull away from the coast.

Tourist buses choke the area around the Cliff House with gassy fumes. The tourists pile out to gawk at the bird- and seal-covered rocks offshore and browse in the shops, museums, and restaurants before moving on to the next stop. The Cliff House Visitor Information Center, run by the National Park Service, is a good place to get brochures, books, and maps covering the recreational opportunities of the Golden Gate National Recreation Area, from visiting forts to hiking ridge tops to primitive camping on the beach. Parking is available along Point Lobos Avenue, the Great

Burton Memorial Beach

Location: In San Francisco, south of Fort Funston at Skyline Boulevard (Highway 35), near the San Mateo County line.

Parking: Free parking lot.

Hours: 6 AM to one hour after sunset.

Facilities: None.

Contact: For beach information, contact the Golden Gate National Recreation Area at (415) 556-0560.

See number 1 on page 436.

China Beach

Location: In San Francisco, at the end of a steep path that begins at Seacliff Avenue and El Camino Del Mar.

Parking: Free limited street parking.

Hours: 6 AM to one hour after sunset.

Facilities: Lifeguard, rest rooms, showers, and picnic area.

Contact: For beach information, contact the Golden Gate National Recreation Area at (415) 556-0560.

See number 5 on page 436.

Crissy Field

Location: In San Francisco, along Mason Street in the northeast corner of the Presidio.

Parking: Free parking lot.

Hours: 6 AM to 10 PM.

Facilities: None.

Contact: For beach information, contact the Golden Gate National Recreation Area at (415) 556-0560.

See number 8 on page 436.

Fort Funston Beach

Location: In San Francisco, off Skyline Boulevard (Highway 35), one mile north of the San Mateo County line.

Parking: Free parking lot.

Hours: 6 AM to one hour after sunset.

Facilities: Rest rooms and picnic tables.

Contact: For beach information, contact the Golden Gate National Recreation Area at (415) 556-0560.

See number 2 on page 436.

Highway, and El Camino Del Mar. The remains of the Sutro Baths, a turn-of-the-century natatorium, lie below the sandstone bluffs. Trails crisscross the knobby area known as Lands End between the Cliff House and China Beach. It's a fascinating area to explore, with paths running down to the ocean, through tunnels, and up and over the bluffs. Great views of the open ocean and across the Golden Gate.

Around Lands End, the coastline runs east for a short distance before making a sharp turn north again to the foot of the Golden Gate Bridge. **China Beach** can be found tucked into the protected stretch of coastline, a small sandy cove that is, believe it or not, lifeguarded from April through October. China Beach lies below all the gorgeous stucco homes that line El Camino Del Mar. You park up there and make the steep descent, via a path or a paved service road (for handicapped parking only) to the beach.

In terms of size, however, China Beach has got nothing on **Baker Beach**, a 1.5-mile ribbon of sand that runs all the way up to the Golden Gate Bridge. Its vantage affords wonderful shots of the photogenic steel span and the Marin Headlands. Everyone we saw,

Lands End Beach

Location: In San Francisco. Turn north off Geary Boulevard onto Merrie Way, then park and follow Lands End Trail to the beach.

Parking: Free street parking.

Hours: 6 AM to one hour after sunset.

Facilities: None.

Contact: For beach information, contact the Golden Gate National Recreation Area at (415) 556-0560.

See number 4 on page 436.

North Baker Beach

Location: In San Francisco. Park at Baker Beach and walk north along the beach until you pass a "high tide" sign and the beach narrows.

Parking: Free parking lot at Baker Beach

Hours: 6 AM to one hour after sunset.

Facilities: None.

Contact: For beach information, contact the Golden Gate National Recreation Area at (415) 556-0560.

See number 7 on page 436.

Marina Green

Location: In the Marina District of San Francisco, along Marina Green Drive, 1.5 miles east of the Golden Gate Bridge.

Parking: Metered lot and street parking.

Hours: Open 24 hours.

Facilities: Rest rooms.

Contact: For beach information, contact the San Francisco Parks Department at (415) 666-7200.

See number 9 on page 436.

Ocean Beach

Location: In San Francisco, along the Great Highway, between the Cliff House and the San Francisco Zoo.

Parking: Free street parking.

Hours: 6 AM to 10 PM.

Facilities: Rest rooms.

Contact: For beach information, contact the Golden Gate National Recreation Area at (415) 556-0560.

See number 3 on page 436.

though, was otherwise engaged: figures sleeping on the beach, couples groping on the sand, picnickers at tables under the protected windbreaks of cypress groves, fishermen casting lines into the water. **North Baker Beach** sheds its inhibitions and becomes clothing optional. Should you happen to wander off in that direction, don't be surprised if you stumble onto a colony of beachgoers as naked as seals.

Rounding out the city's sandy shoreline are **Marina Green** (managed by the San Francisco Parks and Recreation Department) and **Aquatic Park** (a celebration of all things maritime), which lie east of the Golden Gate Bridge. Marina Green is a broad bayfront green space used by outdoor-minded San Franciscans as a place to do a little bit of everything: bicycling, jogging, walking, Frisbee-tossing, kite-flying, and,

Golden Gate National Recreation Area

This amazing park encompasses 74,000 acres (114 square miles) spread across three counties: San Mateo, San Francisco, and Marin. The Golden Gate National Recreation Area (GGNRA) is a veritable urban greenbelt that ensures this growing metropolitan area will never want for recreational lands in natural settings. In conjunction with the similar-sized holdings of the Point Reyes National Seashore up north, it puts San Francisco in the enviable position of having more dedicated parkland close at hand than any other major city in the United States. The citizens of San Francisco should be dancing in the street about this backyard windfall, established by an act of Congress in 1972.

Eight miles of San Francisco's ocean-facing coastline fall under the domain of the GGNRA, providing green space and beaches to urban dwellers. The 1,500-acre Presidio, until recently a military installation, has been added to the park. In Marin County, the GGNRA holdings are vast, running the length of the county in a band that follows Highway 1 and taking in everything from the Marin Headlands and Muir Woods to Stinson Beach, Olema Valley, and Tomales Bay. A 1,014-acre tract in San Mateo County, Sweeney Ridge, is a recent addition. GGNRA holdings include historic sites (Alcatraz Island, the Cliff House, various seacoast fortifications) and scenic treasures (redwood forests, mountains, bays, and beaches). Included within all this are 28 miles of shoreline and 100 miles of trails. In addition, the National Park Service conducts regular tours and educational events at sites throughout the system. These can range from guided hikes and bird-watching expeditions to hands-on seminars on how to go crabbing in the bay.

To learn about the park, contact the Golden Gate National Recreation Area, Fort Mason, Building 201, San Francisco, CA 94123; (415) 556-0560. Ask for a copy of the quarterly publication "Park Events." In addition to the park headquarters at Fort Mason, there are visitors centers at the Cliff House (556-8642), Fort Point (556-1593), the Marin Headlands (331-1540), and Muir Woods (388-2596). You can also call for information on Stinson Beach's weather (868-1922), Alcatraz Island boat transportation (546-2700), and the National Maritime Museum (556-3002).

offshore **Crissy Field**, windsurfing. It's San Francisco's latter-day equivalent of the traditional village green, serving as a gathering place for celebrations and rallies, not to mention being a good place to hang out on a nice day.

Aquatic Park lies between Marina Green and Fisherman's Wharf. It's protected by two piers and a breakwater. The 1,850-foot Municipal Pier is great for fishing. Onshore, there's the National Maritime Museum (556-2904), tourable ships, more green space, and a small sandy beach. (Don't base your vacation around the latter, though.) The square-rigger *Balclutha*, built in Glasgow in 1886 and docked at Hyde Street Pier (556-6435), can be toured for a fee. It is one of seven vessels belonging to the maritime museum, which also houses model ships and seafaring artifacts.

Bunking Down

You want to stay at the beach? We've got just the place for you. It ain't fancy, but it's clean and at the beach—and that's what this book is about. It's **Roberts-at-the-Beach Motel** (2828 Sloat Boulevard, 564-2610, $), where you're invited, logically enough, to "sleep by the sea." Roberts is a block off the Great Highway, near the San Francisco Zoo and Golden Gate Park.

Two blocks farther landward on the same street is a **Days Inn** (2600 Sloat Boulevard, 665-5440, $$), offering a modicum of brand-name dependability. Actually, we found our room and its furnishings quite comfortable, although the plastic-wrapped pastries and canteen of coffee by the front desk made a poor excuse for the promised continental breakfast.

Another find close to the beach—very close, in fact, to the Cliff House, Lands End, and the Presidio—is the **Seal Rock Inn** (545 Point Lobos Avenue, 752-8000, $$), an older hotel that makes up in location what it lacks in amenities.

Down by touristy Fisherman's Wharf, you'll find a wide range of places to stay. On the high end, there are humongous 500-room towers run by **Sheraton** (2500 Mason Street, 362-5500, $$$$) and **Hyatt** (555 North Point Street, 563-2218, $$$), as well as slightly less impressive (and less expensive) properties by **Holiday Inn** (1300 Columbia Avenue, 771-9000, $$), **Ramada Inn** (590 Bay Street, 885-4700, $$$), and **Howard Johnson's** (580 Beach Street, 775-3800, $$). You know what you're getting with those kinds of places—a guarantee of quality within a narrow standard of deviation. All are within three blocks of Fisherman's Wharf. (You'll pay dearly to stay near the wharf, but you'll pay dearly to stay anywhere else in San Francisco, too.)

Slightly outside the area, between Fisherman's Wharf and the Financial District, are four affiliated motor inns of late-model vintage that offer a real break on price and value ($78 a night, year-round). They're strung along busy Lombard Avenue, with the **Cow Hollow Motor Inn** (2190 Lombard Street, 921-5800, $$) close to Marina Green, and the **Lombard Motor Inn** (1475 Lombard Street, 441-6000, $$) close to Fisherman's Wharf. In between you'll find the **Coventry Motor Inn** (1901 Lombard Street, 567-1200, $$) and the **Chelsea Motor Inn** (2095 Lombard Street, 563-5600, $$).

If you're looking for more of a bed-and-breakfast experience, you might try the **Marina Inn** (3110 Octavia Street, 928-1000, $$), a 40-room hotel on the corner of Lombard, behind Fort Mason in the Marina District. Now if you want something really far out—so far out it's in the water—you can stay on a floating B&B. That's boat and breakfast, as you'll be staying on a yacht berthed at Pier 39. Prices run from $115 to $225 per night. Contact **Bayside Boat and Breakfast** (Pier 39, 444-5858, $$$).

Coastal Cuisine

San Francisco rightly enjoys a reputation as an epicurean paradise. There are more than 3,300 restaurants to be found in the City by the Bay.

Since breaking down a subject so large is well beyond the scope of this book, we've narrowed our commentary to restaurants in the vicinity of Fisherman's Wharf or out by Ocean Beach. Even there we've been selective.

Starting back by Sloat Boulevard and the Great Highway, there's a hole-in-the-wall restaurant that turns out the best ribs and barbecue this side of Oakland. **Leon's BBQ** (2800 Sloat Boulevard, 681-3071, $$), has got a real down-home neighborhood atmosphere to go with the hearty servings of ribs and 'Q. So come on in for some home-cooked chow and leave with an "I Porked Out at Leon's BBQ" bumper sticker. Noncarnivores will fare better at **Greens** (Building A in the Fort Mason complex, Marina Boulevard at Laguna Street, 771-6222, $$$), a stylish vegetarian restaurant run by Zen Buddhists (only in California!) with stunning waterfront views.

Up where Point Lobos Avenue meets the Great Highway sits a San Francisco institution, the **Cliff House** (1090 Point Lobos Avenue, 386-3330, $$$). Five different structures have occupied the same site since its conception in 1897. One of them burned down when a boatload of nitroglycerin crashed into the cliff on which it sits. The latest edifice is physically quite secure, though locals often sniff that its culinary reputation isn't as firmly grounded. Visitors, dazzled by the glorious views and the old San Francisco ambience, don't seem to care. The Cliff House is a multilevel complex with a popular bar and two completely different restaurants. Downstairs is more seafood oriented, with an art-deco interior. Upstairs you'll find a broader menu, with pasta, veal, and beef dishes available in addition to the inevitable seafood fare. The bar at the Cliff House, incidentally, has an extensive appetizer/deli-sandwich menu, if you just want to drop in for a drink and a snack.

The Fisherman's Wharf area has long served as a punching bag for food critics, who insult it directly when they don't ignore it entirely. This is a little unfair. Sure, the area in general is tacky, with a scuzzy commercial underside whose carnivalistic aura is more reminiscent of Times Square than a working wharf and fish market. But some of the restaurants of long standing do a good job of serving quality seafood. **A. Sabella's** (2766 Taylor, 771-6775, $$$), for instance, dates back to the 1920s, when Antone Sabella—whose father ran a retail market on Fisherman's Wharf—opened a restaurant on this spot. Sabella's is still run by Antone Sabella (albeit the founder's grandson). Fittingly, the menu's pièce de résistance is a dish named after the founder: Antone, a swordfish concoction baked in a beurre blanc, stuffed with deviled shrimp, and topped with parmesan cheese and white sauce. The crab legs (sautéed, fried, or Bordelaise) and crab cioppino (simmered with shrimp and shellfish in tomato sauce) also are excellent. Sabella's is tops in our book, both for the food and the view—three stories above the Fisherman's Wharf hubbub, with an unobstructed outlook on the bay.

Another good bet on the wharf is **Scoma's** (Pier 47, 771-4383, $$$). San Francisco's highest-grossing restaurant, it attracts the crowds for one reason (well, besides location): dependably fresh, well-prepared seafood. Scoma's signature dish is a little bit of culinary inspiration called Shellfish Sec, a symphony of seafood in a light wine sauce. The combination seafood cocktail (crabs and prawns), the Louis salad (pronounced *LOOee*), and the sautéed entrées are also highly recommended. Scoma's has its own fish-receiving station, complete with off-loading and processing operation that goes 16 hours a day. You can wander over and look at what might turn out to be your dinner being cleaned and filleted.

Elsewhere near the water, seafood fans flock to the **Pier 23 Cafe** (on the water, near the end of Lombard Street, 362-5125, $$), whose al fresco dining patio and lively atmosphere attracts a young, hip crowd on nice days. Other popular spots include **Scott's**

Seafood Grill, which has locations in the Marina District (2400 Lombard Street, 563-8988, $$$) and in the Financial District (3 Embarcadero Center, 981-0622, $$$), and **Café Pescatore** (2455 Mason Street, 561-1111, $$$), a small Italian seafood restaurant excelling in such creative concoctions as ravioli stuffed with minced scallops and covered with a tomato garlic cream sauce.

And before we leave the subject of seafood, we have to break our vow about not straying from the water's edge when it comes to reviewing restaurants. It's an ironic fact of life that when San Franciscans crave food with fins, they head inland. Four of the best fish joints in town: the venerable **Tadich Grill** (240 California Street, 391-1849, $$$), which claims to be California's oldest restaurant in continuous operation; its younger neighbor **Aqua** (252 California Street, 956-9662, $$$), a decidedly upscale and pricey Financial District favorite; the **Hayes Street Grill** (320 Hayes Street, 863-5545, $$$), a more casual Civic Center eatery; and the **Swan Oyster Depot** (1517 Polk Street, 673-1101, $$), where a friendly staff plunks down incredibly fresh, simply prepared seafood on its long lunch counter. Frankly, you'll find excellent and creative seafood dishes in nearly all of the better restaurants in town—culinarily speaking, this is a city in love with the denizens of the ocean (and lakes and rivers and bays). Finally, we can't exit San Francisco without saying a word about sourdough bread. The best to be had in the city is at **Boudin Sourdough Bakery & Café** (156 Jefferson Street, 928-1849, $), which brings us back to Fisherman's Wharf. There are also Boudin locations at Pier 39 and Ghirardelli Square.

Night Moves

San Francisco is often touted as the most cosmopolitan city in America, and it's certainly one of the most open minded. Contained within its borders is a little bit of Paris, Rome, Vienna, Sodom and Gomorrah. Everything from ballet to bondage bars can be located on its fog-shrouded streets after dark. You really don't need us to tell you where or how to have a good time in San Francisco, so we'll just offer a few stray observations before calling it a night.

The tavern at the **Cliff House** (1090 Point Lobos Avenue, 386-3330) is patronized and enjoyed even by famously tourist-wary San Franciscans (at least when they have out-of-town guests in tow). With its log-burning fireplace and "oh, wow" views, this is a must-visit place to drain a coffee mug or wine glass. Down at Fisherman's Wharf, **Lou's Pier 47** (300 Jefferson Street, 771-0377) presents live local rock and blues bands.

It's a yuppie world now, and reminders of this are evident in most every neighborhood, even in North Beach, that traditionally working-class, Italian neighborhood that was the old stomping ground of the Beat Generation. (By the way, North Beach used to mark the actual shoreline before landfill was used to extend the city by half a mile out to its present location at Fisherman's Wharf and the Embarcadero.) Today this landlocked beach is a grab bag of brass-encrusted cafés, coffeehouses, bars, and bookstores. If you'd like to trod in Kerouac's footsteps, try the following, which were beat-generation hangouts in the 1950s and still retain an air of authenticity: **Caffé Trieste** (609 Vallejo Street, 392-6739), **Mario's Bohemian Cigar Store** (566 Columbus Avenue, 362-0536), **Tosca Cafe** (242 Columbus Avenue, 391-1244), and **Vesuvio's** (255 Columbus Avenue, 362-3370). The last two establishments are nestled right by the famed **City Lights Bookstore** (261 Columbus Avenue, 362-8193).

For More Information

Contact the San Francisco Convention and Visitors Bureau, 201 Third Street, San Francisco, CA 94101; (415) 391-2000. Request a copy of *The San Francisco Book*, a comprehensive overview of where to stay and what to do, see, and eat in the city.

 Map of San Francisco County beaches—page 436

Marin County

By cartographic consensus, Marin County signals the beginning of Northern California, though people as far south as Monterey and beyond consider themselves Northern Californians, blithely ignoring the outsiders' penchant to divvy up the state into northern, central, and southern regions. Not wishing to provoke a turf war, we nonetheless think it's safe to point out that the leap over the Golden Gate Bridge signals a psychological and geographic break from the rest of the state.

Just as we were crossing that very span on one trip, Van Morrison's "Call Me Up in Dreamland" came on the car radio. Coincidence or fate? Either way, we couldn't argue with the sentiment, for Marin County signals the beginning of a particularly seductive dreamscape. From here to the Oregon border, the scenery changes around every mind-boggling bend in the road. How tempting it must have been over the years to turn these sentinels, the precious green Marin Headlands, into *(continued on page 450)*

Coastal Marin County's Climate

Point Reyes National Seashore Averages

	Daily High Temp. (°F)	Daily Low Temp. (°F)	Rainfall (inches)
January	57	38	5.3
February	59	40	4.5
March	59	41	3.5
April	60	43	2.1
May	61	45	0.6
June	63	50	0.2
July	64	51	0.1
August	65	51	0.2
September	67	51	0.4
October	66	47	1.6
November	63	41	3.0
December	58	38	4.9
Yearly Average	**62**	**45**	**26.4**

Source: National Weather Service data, National Oceanographic and Atmospheric Administration.

Marin County

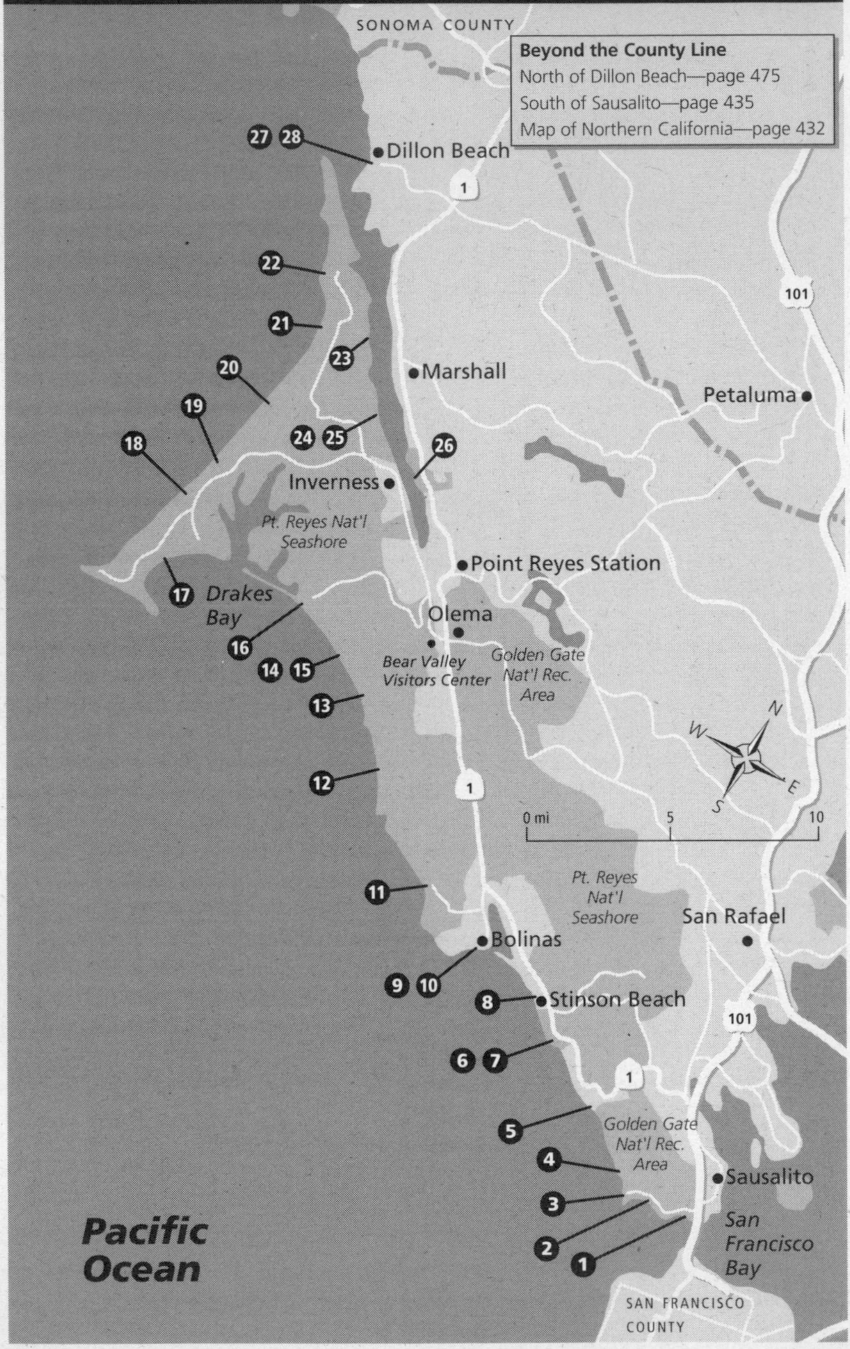
SONOMA COUNTY
Beyond the County Line
North of Dillon Beach—page 475
South of Sausalito—page 435
Map of Northern California—page 432
27 28
Dillon Beach
1
22
21
23
101
20
Marshall
Petaluma
19
24 25
26
18
Inverness
Pt. Reyes Nat'l Seashore
Point Reyes Station
17
Drakes Bay
Olema
16
Bear Valley Visitors Center
Golden Gate Nat'l Rec. Area
14 15
13
N
W
E
S
12
1
0 mi
5
10
11
Pt. Reyes Nat'l Seashore
San Rafael
Bolinas
9 10
8
Stinson Beach
101
6 7
1
5
Golden Gate Nat'l Rec. Area
4
Sausalito
3
San Francisco Bay
2
1
Pacific Ocean
SAN FRANCISCO COUNTY

Marin County Beaches

Map of Northern California—page 432

(continued from page 447) suburban enclaves for the rich. How extraordinary that they never were, and never will be. Perhaps most remarkable is that much of the headlands was once owned by the military. How they were persuaded to surrender them to the National Park Service is one of the miracles that can probably be answered only through extensive prayer and fasting.

Perhaps Marin's good fortune can be chalked up to a convergence of factors: the presence of the San Andreas Fault (which runs through the heart of Marin County), Mount Tamalpais (which forms a formidable, albeit lovely, barrier to easy access), and a tradition of environmentalism that goes back to the county's most celebrated citizen, John Muir. For whatever complex of reasons, Marin County has kept its shoreline in as pristine a condition as you'll ever find so close to a major American city.

As it is with any activity that requires some expenditure of effort, the rewards of making the difficult passage to these beaches are all the greater. What this does—as all true devotees of Marin County know full well—is to separate flighty tourists from real travelers. This, in turn, keeps things relatively quiet for the hearty souls who live in windswept west Marin. While most San Franciscans in search of fun in the sun converge on Stinson Beach, the real spirit of place can be found on the Point Reyes Peninsula—truly a land that stands apart from the rest of the continent.

Key to the Symbols

Bike path · Camping · Food and drink · Hiking · Nude

Pier · RVs allowed · Surfing · Volleyball

Crowd Rating

sweet solitude . . . moderate crowds . . . wall-to-wall

Overall Rating

1 don't bother . . . 3 worth a visit . . . 5 beach heaven

Marin Headlands

Location: Take the Alexander Road exit off Highway 101 north of the Golden Gate Bridge to Conzelman Road, which traverses the Marin Headlands.

The Marin Headlands unit of the Golden Gate National Recreation Area (GGNRA) stares down San Francisco from the north side of the Golden Gate Bridge. It used to be U.S. Army land, and the remnants of forts and batteries dot the terrain. For purposes of this book, we'll provide a brief perusal of the beaches, beginning with Kirby Cove (near the foot of the bridge), proceeding west to Point Bonita, then heading northwest to Muir Beach.

The best way to get a handle on the headland's scenic heights is to follow Conzelman Road. To get onto it, cross the Golden Gate Bridge into Marin County on Highway 101, take the Alexander Avenue exit, then make a left turn into GGNRA territory, where you'll pick up Conzelman Road. It is a twisty, windy, sometimes one-way corkscrew that works its way out to Point Bonita Lighthouse, providing some incredible vistas en route.

Kirby Cove is half a mile from where you pick up Conzelman Road. Marin County's geographical counterpart to San Francisco's Baker Beach, it's identifiable by a locked gate in front of a dirt road leading to the beach. There's a narrow, quarter-mile beach and a cave that people like to explore. They also tend to get naked out here, which is pretty much the case with most of the GGNRA beaches. The park service looks the other way, so to speak, unless they get complaints.

There are some fairly difficult-to-find beaches in the vicinity of **Bonita Cove**, which is broken by rocky points into pocket beaches. They are notable for their composition, being products of wave-pulverized pillow lava. The more inaccessible, the better, is how nude

Bonita Cove

3

Location: Take the Alexander Road exit off Highway 101 north of the Golden Gate Bridge to Conzelman Road. Bonita Cove is at the southwest tip of the Marin Headlands, which can be reached via a hiking trail from Battery Alexander.

Parking: Free parking lot.

Hours: Open 24 hours.

Facilities: None.

Contact: For beach information, contact the Marin Headlands unit of the Golden Gate National Recreation Area at (415) 331-1540.

See number 2 on page 448.

Kirby Cove

3

Location: Take the Alexander Road exit off Highway 101 north of the Golden Gate Bridge to Conzelman Road in the Marin Headlands.

Parking: Free parking lot.

Hours: Open 24 hours.

Facilities: Rest rooms, picnic tables, and fire pits. There is a limited number of walk-in campsites, for tents only. There is no fee, but a permit from the National Park Service is required. No camping reservations.

Contact: For beach information, contact the Marin Headlands unit of the Golden Gate National Recreation Area at (415) 331-1540.

See number 1 on page 448.

beach aficionados look at it, and all three beaches are frequented by those who like to recreate au naturel.

Moving on, **Rodeo Beach** is the most accessible beach in the headlands, but it's just a pebbly cove. A picnic area sits above it. Behind it lies Rodeo Lagoon, which is encircled by hiking trails. The headlands' prolific mix of bird life can best be studied here. There's also a beach at **Tennessee Cove** and a pond with yet more bird life. Getting there requires a two-mile hike from the Tennessee Valley parking area.

The next accessible stretch of sand is Muir Beach (see next entry). There's plenty more to do in the Marin Headlands—camping, hiking, horseback riding, visiting seacoast fortifications—than this brief synopsis can even begin to touch on. The tri-county Golden Gate National Recreation Area is the largest urban park in the world and deserving of a full-length travel guide in its own right.

For More Information

Contact the Golden Gate National Recreation Area, Fort Mason, Building 201, San Francisco, CA 94123; (415) 556-0560. For specific queries about the Marin Headlands, call (415) 331-1540.

Rodeo Beach

Location: Take the Alexander Road exit off Highway 101 north of the Golden Gate Bridge to Bunker Road. Rodeo Beach is at the end of Bunker Road.

Parking: Free parking lot.

Hours: Open 24 hours.

Facilities: Rest rooms and picnic area.

Contact: For beach information, contact the Marin Headlands unit of the Golden Gate National Recreation Area at (415) 331-1540.

See number 3 on page 448.

Tennessee Cove

Location: From Highway 1 in Mill Valley, turn west on Tennessee Valley Road and proceed till it ends. A trail from the parking lot leads to the beach.

Parking: Free parking lot.

Hours: Open 24 hours.

Facilities: None.

Contact: For beach information, contact the Marin Headlands unit of the Golden Gate National Recreation Area at (415) 331-1540.

See number 4 on page 448.

Muir Beach

Location: The entrance to Muir Beach is at the intersection of Highway 1 and Pacific Way.

Not only did he have a stand of redwoods dubbed after him, but pioneering environmentalist John Muir rated a beauty of a beach to bear his name. Signs along Highway 1 point to **Muir Beach**, which is located within the Golden Gate National Recreation Area and linked to various other Marin Headlands units via the 35-mile Coastal Trail. To reach the beach from the parking lot, visitors must cross a rocky field and pass over a bridge that spans a small lagoon (the more adventuresome opt for a makeshift series of boards and stepping stones instead).

Framed by a creek and dense, green woods, Muir Beach provides a striking setting even when the elements are inhospitable. Frequently windy and draped in fog, Muir Beach does have its serene days—especially during Indian Summer, when things warm up. The iffy weather, by the way, hasn't stopped the area from being unofficially partitioned into clothed and clothing-optional beaches. The former is what you walk to from the parking lot. The latter is reached by walking north up the main public beach, across a lagoon and over a rock pile.

Coastal Cuisine

Muir Beach is the site of one of Marin County's most unique dining and lodging establishments, the **Pelican Inn** (10 Pacific Way, Muir Beach, CA 94965, 415-383-6000, $$$). As authentic-looking as any place in the Cotswolds, the large, Tudor-style building houses a pub and restaurant on the ground floor and seven small guest rooms upstairs. Rooms are snug and appointed with quaint British touches. The pub, as the throng of locals can attest, is just the sort of place you'd want to knock back a pint of Guinness or a warming glass of port on a chilly day. The food is good, hearty pub fare: bangers and mash (sausage and potatoes), fish-and-chips, and the like. The Pelican also serves a popular Sunday brunch, and there's a lovely patio out back for al fresco dining on balmy days.

For More Information

Contact the Golden Gate National Recreation Area, Marin Headlands Visitor Center, Building 948, Fort Cronkite, Sausalito, CA 94965; (415) 331-1540.

Muir Beach

Location: At Pacific Way and Highway 1, in the community of Muir Beach.

Parking: Free parking lot.

Hours: 9 AM to 10 PM (summer); closing hours vary between 7 PM and 9 PM the rest of year.

Facilities: Rest rooms, picnic tables, and fire pits.

Contact: For beach information, contact the Stinson Beach ranger station at (415) 868-0942.

See number 5 on page 448.

Steep Ravine Beach

Location: Two miles south of Stinson Beach, off Highway 1. From the roadside parking turnouts, it is a mile-long hike to the beach.

Steep Ravine Beach

Location: Two miles south of Stinson Beach off Highway 1.

Parking: Free limited roadside parking.

Hours: 7 AM to 10 PM (summer); closing hours vary between 6 PM and 9 PM the rest of year.

Facilities: Rest rooms, picnic tables, and fire pits. There are six tent campsites. Fees are $7 to $11 per night. There are 10 cabins for rent at $30 per night. For reservations, call Destinet at (800) 444-7275.

Contact: For beach information, contact Mount Tamalpais State Park at (415) 388-2070.

See number 6 on page 448.

At **Steep Ravine Beach**, you can experience a sensation unique on the California coast: tiptoeing into the water at low tide to sit in warm springs that percolate through the ocean floor. Visitors can tent camp or stay in one of 10 rustic cabins here, with prior reservations. To book one of the cabins or primitive campsites, call Destinet at 800-444-7275.

Steep Ravine is a little more foreboding if you're day-tripping—a wild, rocky, sandless beach that necessitates a steep, mile-long hike off Highway 1. (You better believe they don't call it Steep Ravine for nothing.) To reach the oceanfront look for dirt pullouts and a road with a locked gate, two miles south of Stinson Beach. If you're camping, you can drive part of the way there. If not, you must park along Highway 1 and hoof it.

For More Information

Contact Mount Tamalpais State Park, Mill Valley, CA 94941; (415) 388-2070.

Red Rock Beach

Location: Parking turnouts for Red Rock Beach are two miles south of Stinson Beach, on Highway 1 near Milepost 11.

Red Rock Beach has been touted as the coast's friendliest and most popular nude beach. That's friendly as in, "C'mon down, take your clothes off, and stay awhile." We stumbled upon it by accident many years ago, while researching an earlier book. It's located about a mile-and-a-half south of Stinson Beach and is identified by a dirt parking lot by the side of Highway 1. Fairly sizable though it is, we found the lot full, with the overflow lining both sides of the road. There are no signs, nor is the beach visible from the road. We saw a trail leading down, so we took it. Imagine our surprise to round a corner at the bottom and find ourselves face to face with a beach full of naked bodies. The packed crowd was evidently having fun in their liberated state of undress. Lots of them were flinging Frisbees. There were more people here, in fact, than at the public beach we'd just left. Maybe next time we'll join them. As far as the beach goes, it's a fine, quarter-mile cove situated on state-park property, though no one bothers the skinny-dippers (or vice versa). The path to the beach is fairly steep and takes about 15 minutes to walk each way. If you wear nothing else, wear shoes.

For More Information

Contact Mount Tamalpais State Park, Mill Valley, CA 94941; (415) 388-2070.

Red Rock Beach

Location: 1.5 miles south of Stinson Beach off Highway 1, near Milepost 11. Trail leads to beach from roadside turnout.

Parking: Free limited roadside parking.

Hours: 7 AM to 10 PM (summer); closing hours vary between 6 PM and 9 PM the rest of year.

Facilities: None.

Contact: For beach information, contact Mount Tamalpais State Park at (415) 388-2070.

See number 7 on page 448.

Stinson Beach

Location: 20 miles north of San Francisco, along Highway 1.
Population: 2,000
Area Code: 415 **Zip Code:** 94970

Stinson Beach is where San Francisco heads when it wants to enjoy a day at the beach. Stinson is a flat, sandy three-mile break in the action between the Marin Headlands and the sea cliffs of Bolinas. Big crowds turn out on weekends when the sun is shining and the air is calm, especially in the months between summer's foggy chill and winter's stormy surliness. There's a bargain aspect to Stinson Beach that no doubt adds to its popularity. It is part of the Golden Gate National Recreation Area, administered by the National Park Service. Unlike the state beaches, which charge entrance fees of up to $6, Stinson is absolutely free.

The beach and the small town that surrounds it are nestled at the base of Mount Tamalpais in a storybook setting. You must earn your passage to this sandy wonderland, and the price to be paid is carsickness. (Has anybody tried those acupressure wristbands that claim to ward off motion sickness? Do they really work?) To get here most easily, follow Highway 1, which disengages from Highway 101 near Mill Valley. The road follows the curves and contours of Mount Tam, passing south of Muir Woods. The horseshoe curves will make you queasy. On any given turn you may encounter a snorting Greyhound AmeriCruiser or a house-sized RV with its wheels in your lane, so drive carefully. It's all worth it for the panoramic views along the cliff edges, from which more ocean is visible than anywhere outside of a window seat on an airplane. You could occupy yourself hiking and sightseeing around Mount Tamalpais, Muir Woods, and the surrounding parklands of the Golden Gate National Recreation Area without ever making it down to Stinson. (But being sea-loving creatures, we never succumb to such inland charms for long.)

A long descent eventually leads into the small town of Stinson Beach, which has one or two of everything for day-trippers and passers-through: grocery store, gas station, antique shop, bookstore, surf shop, restaurants, and a couple of small roadside motels. With a rise of mountains to provide a dramatic backdrop, pure Marin County air to breathe, and a wide white-sand beach to play on, Stinson Beach is well worth the curves nature throws in your path to get there.

Beaches

We've seen **Stinson Beach** in all kinds of weather, when it was forbiddingly gray and deserted, and when was been packed with a young crowd enjoying the sun and even kicking around the water a little. On such days, the crowds swell to as much as 15,000 folks and traffic backs up on Highway 1. Still, the enormous parking lots appear capable of taking on all comers. Stinson is a great spot for surfing, hence the presence of one of the North Coast's best surf shops, Live Water Surf Shop

Stinson Beach

Location: Along Highway 1, 20 miles north of San Francisco.
Parking: Free parking lot.
Hours: 9 AM to 10 PM (summer); closing hours vary between 7 PM and 9 PM the rest of year.
Facilities: Lifeguards, rest rooms, picnic area, and fire pits.
Contact: For beach information, contact the Stinson Beach ranger station at (415) 868-0942.

See number 8 on page 448.

(3450 Highway 1, 868-0333), which rents and sells wet suits and boards of all kinds. Winter and fall are optimum for surfing, although we've seen some monster waves breaking in summer, too.

Bunking Down

Casa del Mar (37 Belvedere Avenue, 868-2124, $$$) is the inn of first choice in the vicinity. The site of a former terraced garden maintained by the University of California School of Landscape Architecture, the Casa is a five-room bed-and-breakfast set in the hills behind the beach. Works of art, both natural and man-made, are celebrated in this airy, Mediterranean-style villa. Trails lead out the backdoor and up Mount Tam. Another overnight alternative is the **Ocean Court Motel** (18 Arenal Avenue, 868-0212, $$), which rents rooms and suites by the day, week, or month.

Coastal Cuisine

The **Parkside Café and Snack Bar** (43 Arenal Avenue, 868-1272, $-$$) is a friend to snacking surfers and serious eaters alike. The café serves three meals a day, with dinners tending toward traditional Italian fare. The snack bar's hamburgers have been warming the bellies of beach bums for going on 50 years. The **Stinson Beach Grill** (3465 Highway 1, 868-2002, $$) is the place to go for that West Marin County staple, barbecue oysters, as well as pasta and seafood. Another casual Stinson Beach restaurant, the **Sand Dollar** (3458 Highway 1, 868-0434, $$), serves fresh local seafood. What's more, you've got a choice of sitting outside on the patio or inside by the fireplace.

Night Moves

The **Sand Dollar** (see above) has the town's only full bar and, therefore, its only nightlife. The beach itself, incidentally, remains open till 10 PM in summer. Since there are fire pits and picnic tables aplenty, maybe this is the place to party. You and your friends could always attempt a huddled, flannel-clad, North Coast version of a '60s-style, Southern California beach flick.

For More Information

Contact the West Marin County Chamber of Commerce, 11431 Highway 1, Suite 15, P.O. Box 1045, Point Reyes Station, CA 94956; (415) 663-9232.

Bolinas

Location: 25 miles north of San Francisco, on the southern tip of the Point Reyes Peninsula. Follow Highway 1 over the Golden Gate Bridge. Four miles north of Stinson Beach, make a left on an unmarked road. This is Olema-Bolinas Road, though the road sign identifying this as the way to Bolinas never stays up for very long.
Population: 2,500
Area Code: 415 **Zip Code:** 94294

If Bolinas had a town motto, it would be something along the order of "Go away." The locals-only mentality espoused by Southern California surfers hasn't got a thing on the anti-outsider bias practiced by Bolinians. They really don't want the world to beat a path to their door, and while they're not openly mean about it, they're just not, well, openly hospitable. There's the issue of the road sign, for instance. To get to Bolinas, you must turn off Highway 1 onto Olema-Bolinas Road, just north of Bolinas Lagoon. If you don't know what you're looking for, you won't know where to turn. Not only is there no directional marker pointing to this coastal hamlet, but the very road sign identifying Olema-Bolinas Road is often missing, a tradition that started in the late 1960s and continues to this day. Between 1970 and 1990, hard-core Bolinas isolationists stole off with 36 road signs (must be quite an interesting collection somewhere).

So listen up: To get to Bolinas, with or without signs, turn west off Highway 1 where the roads fork at the lagoon, approximately five miles south of Olema and four miles north of Stinson Beach. (If this page is missing from the book, you'll know some Bolinian got to it before you did.)

If you somehow make it to town, you'll think you've stumbled into a '60s time warp. The denizens of Bolinas looks like the survivors of a caravan of Merry Prankster buses that fled the Haight-Ashbury in the late '60s to burrow and lick their wounds in more natural settings. Remnants of this lost clan populate the rugged coast from Marin County to the Oregon state line. Bolinas, being closest to their spawning ground, San Francisco, is one of their strongholds.

Hallmarks of the Haight-Ashbury mentality are everywhere: a multicolored, cabalistic rendering of the sun painted in the street, bearing the legend "Super Solstice to All"; a bakery/café that prides itself on being the area's "only all-organic flour bakery" and is staffed by what looks like—and might well be—former members of the Diggers (the free-food cooperative that fed indigent hippies in the Haight); a funky local library that hosts a reggae dance on Monday nights; and a fleet of vehicles so ragged and rusty it's a miracle their engines turn over. It's all part of the eccentric appeal of a community that hasn't gone for the corporate land-grab and cutesy boutiquing that have stripped too much of the coast of its natural look and heritage. Peevish though they may be, the natives of Bolinas are easily understood and forgiven. (By us, at least, being sons of the '60s ourselves.) There's not much for an outsider to do in Bolinas, particularly the kind of well-heeled tourist who's looking to dump the wife at a trendy gallery or outlet mall while he shoots 18 holes of golf and drinks imported beer with his buddies.

Still, if you're even mildly curious, Bolinas is worth the side trip off Highway 1. One incentive is the Point Reyes Bird Observatory, located atop Bolinas Mesa. While you're in town, be sure to stop at the Bolinas Bay Bakery & Café and pick up some picnic supplies—sandwiches, salads, wholesome organic goodies—to take with you out on Point Reyes National Seashore, where you'll be not only welcomed but expected.

Beaches

You can drive out to **Bolinas Beach** by following Olema-Bolinas Road to Wharf Street, which ends in a concrete ramp by a pile of riprap that holds a section of the eroding spit in place. If you do come out here, make sure you're proficient at making three-point turns, because there is no turnaround at the end of Wharf Road. (One suspects this is just one more built-in excuse to discourage visitation.) The south-facing beach looks across Bolinas Lagoon, a nature preserve for migratory waterfowl, towards Stinson Beach. Bolinas Beach ends at a jetty, becoming precipitously narrow on the other side, where waves lap at the base of the bluffs.

Facing the ocean more directly is **Agate Beach**, whose principal attraction is its access to Duxbury Reef, a mass of offshore rock where marine and intertidal life can be observed. It can be reached by taking Elm Road till it ends and then descending the stairway to the beach. Soon it will be evident that the forces of nature are doing more damage to the Bolinas-dwellers than any feared tourist influx. The sea cliffs upon which Bolinas rests are composed not of sandstone but mudstone, a much more erosive material. Geologist Gary Griggs describes the Bolinas sea cliffs as "one continuous plane of landslides." You'd think this would make those Bolinians more circumspect—and therefore less protective of their real estate. As the Youngbloods sang, "C'mon, people now, smile on your brother."

Bunking Down

For all its isolation, Bolinas has a surprising number of inns and guest houses, including **One Fifty-five Pine** (Box 62, 868-2721, $$), a beach cottage overlooking the ocean, and the **Blue Heron Inn** (11 Wharf Street, 868-1102, $$), a small Victorian cottage located over a restaurant, lounge, and espresso bar in the center of town. The two guest rooms at **Thomas' White House Inn** (118 Kale Road, 868-0279, $$) also have a funky charm and dynamite coastal views.

Coastal Cuisine

The aforementioned **Bolinas Bay Bakery & Café** (20 Wharf Street, 868-0211, $$) takes pains to make things the healthy way, using organic flour and greens, and stressing vegetarian preparations. Their salads are great: curried tuna, tofu, and eggplant in Asian barbecue sauce, raspberry poppyseed cole slaw...you get the idea. Baked goods include loaves of "Stems and Seeds" bread (a nine-grain, three-seeded whole wheat, but, alas, no cannabis), sun-dried

Agate Beach

2

Location: In Bolinas, at the end of Elm Road.
Parking: Free parking lot.
Hours: Open 24 hours.
Facilities: None.
Contact: For beach information, contact Bolinas Beach Utility District at (415) 868-1224.

See number 10 on page 448.

Bolinas Beach

3

Location: 4.5 miles north of Stinson Beach, turn from Highway 1 onto Olema-Bolinas Road and follow through Bolinas. Turn onto Wharf Road and follow to beach.
Parking: Free street parking.
Hours: Open 24 hours.
Facilities: None.
Contact: For beach information, contact Bolinas Beach Utility District at (415) 868-1224.

See number 9 on page 448.

tomato and Parmesan sourdough bread, and poppyseed custard cake. They're not doctrinaire vegans, either. You can order a hamburger (made from Bolinas-raised, natural ground beef, natch) or smoked baby-back ribs (the pig, too, had a natural upbringing). They also make great pizzas, pastas, soups, and a pesto croissant stuffed with spinach, walnuts, and six cheeses. Never in our experience has healthy eating seemed so decadent.

Night Moves

Smiley's Schooner Saloon (41 Wharf Road, 868-1311) jumps to the beat of live bands on weekends, many of them survivors of the golden age of the San Francisco scene. You may hear the likes of New Riders of the Purple Sage, Commander Cody, Maria Muldaur, or Barry Melton—surely you remember the wiry-haired ex-guitarist for Country Joe and the Fish? Incidentally, Smiley's also runs a little hotel with guest rooms up the hill from the saloon.

For More Information

Contact the West Marin County Chamber of Commerce, 11431 Highway 1, Suite 15, P.O. Box 1045, Point Reyes Station, CA 94956; (415) 663-9232.

Point Reyes National Seashore

Location: Off Highway 1 in Olema, at Sir Francis Drake Boulevard or Limantour Road.
Population: None
Area Code: 415 **Zip Code:** 94956

The wilderness area known as Point Reyes is a geological island in time. It is an island arc that hitched a ride across the Pacific Ocean and slammed into the North American plate, becoming part of the great state of California many millions of years before it was so named. The tectonic fun and games continue to this day, as the Pacific and North American plates engage in the geological equivalent of sumo wrestling. Sooner or later, immense pressure builds along the fault line and the plates slip past each other—an adjustment known as an earthquake. During the famous San Francisco quake of 1906—whose epicenter was in the nearby town of Olema—land along the Point Reyes Peninsula moved 16 feet in 45 seconds. Even when the San Andreas Fault isn't throwing one of its seismic temper tantrums, it propels the hook-shaped peninsula northwesterly at an average rate of two inches per year. (No wonder the park service has made "A Land in Motion" Point Reyes' official slogan.)

All this continental drift has helped create California's most unique coastal landmass, one of only seven National Seashores in the United States and the only one on the West Coast. Point Reyes is, in essence, a world apart.

Besides being separated from the rest of California by the San Andreas Fault—which, in this area, runs from Bolinas Lagoon to Tomales Bay—the Inverness Ridge on the western side of the fault line helps create a distinctive climate zone. East of this ridge, the weather is the same as it is in the mainland valleys. West of this ridge, toward the Pacific Ocean, the land is frequently blanketed in thick, blinding fog, pelted with rains of biblical intensity, and blasted by stiff, chilling winds that blow as high as 100 miles per hour out by the lighthouse at land's end. It's as if nature were trying to scare human beings away, screaming, "You've got all that other land to play with, but this is mine, mine, mine!" (In fact, at least one lighthouse keeper has been driven mad by the relentless winds.)

 Map of Marin County beaches—page 448

By now you're probably wondering why in the world you'd ever be tempted to visit such a forbidding place, but Point Reyes remains a land of great natural beauty, abundant flora and fauna, and rich history. Before venturing onto the peninsula, stop in Olema at the Bear Valley Visitors Center, the main entrance to the National Seashore off Highway 1. Maps and advice are freely dispensed, and the well-stocked bookshop includes numerous titles about Point Reyes. For an informed, thorough overview we recommend *Point Reyes: A Guide to the Trails, Roads, Beaches, Campgrounds, Lakes, Trees, Flowers, and Rocks of Point Reyes National Seashore* by Dorothy L. Whitnah (Wilderness Press, 1985).

There are other visitors centers close to the beaches at Drakes Bay and at Point Reyes Lighthouse, but Bear Valley is the best place to get your bearings (all three centers are open 9 AM to 5 PM weekdays, 8 AM to 5 PM weekends; call 415-663-1092). Point Reyes is foremost a hiker's paradise, crisscrossed with 140 miles of trails. To whet your appetite, try the 0.7-mile Earthquake Trail, which traverses the San Andreas fault line outside the Bear Valley Visitors Center. A reconstructed Miwok Indian village is also located on the premises.

On a clear day, the drive from Bear Valley out to the beaches of Point Reyes is as scenic as any in the state. Around every bend in the road, a new and fascinating wrinkle in the land seems to materialize. Forests give way to meadows, which yield in turn to dunes and marshes. Hawks soar above the hills and fields, looking for a rustling in the grass that signals a fat mouse. Herons stand like ghostly sentinels in the wetlands. Deer and elk bound nervously out of the shadows. Dairy cows and beef cattle graze stiffly in the buffeting winds. The only signs of human habitation on the peninsula, in fact, are at these still-operating dairy farms, the remnants of the private landholders left from 1962, when the area was declared a National Seashore. This is the Wild West in its wildest state.

The history of the area is the real thing, too. That is, Point Reyes is the *real* New England. That distinction was bestowed in 1579 by none other than Francis Drake (not yet a "Sir"), who beached his ship, *The Golden Hinde*, on the southern coast of Point Reyes in order to make repairs and gather supplies before heading back to England with a load of Spanish plunder. Here, he met a peaceful tribe of hunters and gatherers called the Miwok, who'd made this their homeland for centuries. The cliffs above the coast vaguely resemble Dover, causing a homesick Drake to dub his find Nova Albion (or New England). He claimed the land in the name of Queen Elizabeth, and asserted his rights by leaving behind "a plate of brasse, fast nailed to a great and firme post."

But that's about as far as the English influence went, because the Spanish were next up to the Pacific plate. And in 1603, they swung for the fences, naming the land mass La Punta de Los Reyes, after the Feast of the Three Kings, and pressing the Miwok into forced labor in the missions farther inland. (If Native Americans ever decided to hit up Spain for reparations, they'd have a very strong case by our calculations.) After California became a state in 1850, the large land grants were divvied into several ranches—hence, the herds of cattle frolicking about.

Everyone who lives within 200 miles of Point Reyes seems to have their own secret spot staked out. We couldn't possibly do justice to the enormity of nature's choices open to visitors. So, we will keep our commentary as closely tied to the beaches as possible and hope that intrepid travelers will ferret out the other goodies that lie inland (creeks, hills, forests, pools, mountain trails). Suffice it to say, with 74,000 acres of pristine wilderness at your disposal, there's enough here for everyone.

On a sad note, the largest fire in 65 years charred 12,000 acres on Point Reyes and destroyed 40 homes in Inverness in the fall of 1995. Roughly a fifth of the park turned into a tinderbox when an illegal campfire set by four teenagers accidentally erupted into a raging wildfire on October 3rd. The Vision Fire, as it came to be known, closed the park for two weeks. It took a firefighting team of 2,000 to bring the blaze under control.

Beaches

Beachcombers may find it rough going, but those who like it wild and woolly will be in their glory on this rugged peninsula. There are 30 miles of coastline to be found out here. All are wilderness beaches—hazardous places for swimming, but wonderful for hiking, sunning, and seeking solitude. The beaches can be reached from three park entrance points: Mesa Road (out of the town of Bolinas, off the unsigned Olema-Bolinas Road); Limantour Road (a turnoff from Highway 1 near Olema); and Sir Francis Drake Boulevard (which meets Highway 1 south of Point Reyes Station and passes through Inverness).

The best and safest beaches are on the southern half of Point Reyes, sheltered by the protective hook of the peninsula. The arm that extends back toward mainland California—officially known as Point Reyes—acts as a sort of windbreak and jetty and explains why Drake chose to land here, rather than along the wild shore to the north. The quickest access to the southern beaches is via Limantour Road, a lovely route that winds through the nifty little

Abbotts Lagoon

Location: From Highway 1 in Point Reyes Station, turn west onto Sir Francis Drake Highway. Bear right onto Pierce Point Road at fork approximately 2.5 miles north of Inverness. Continue for three miles on Pierce Point Road to Abbotts Lagoon parking lot. A two-mile trail leads to the beach.

Parking: Free parking lot.

Hours: Open 24 hours.

Facilities: Rest rooms.

Contact: For beach information, contact Point Reyes National Seashore at (415) 663-1092.

See number 20 on page 448.

Drakes Beach

Location: From Highway 1 in Point Reyes Station, turn west onto Sir Francis Drake Highway. Proceed for 15.5 miles to turnoff for Drakes Beach and follow signs to beach.

Parking: Free parking lot.

Hours: Open 24 hours.

Facilities: Rest rooms, showers, picnic tables, and fire rings.

Contact: For beach information, contact Point Reyes National Seashore at (415) 663-1092.

See number 17 on page 448.

Kehoe Beach

Location: From Highway 1 in Point Reyes Station, turn west onto Sir Francis Drake Highway. Bear right onto Pierce Point Road at fork approximately 2.5 miles north of Inverness. Continue for five miles on Pierce Point Road to Kehoe Beach parking lot. A half-mile trail leads to the beach.

Parking: Free parking lot.

Hours: Open 24 hours.

Facilities: Rest rooms.

Contact: For beach information, contact Point Reyes National Seashore at (415) 663-1092.

See number 21 on page 448.

town of Inverness and passes the American Youth Hostel before coming to a dead end at Limantour Beach.

For beachgoers who are disinclined to hike, **Limantour Beach** will more than suffice, as it offers good swimming in calm waters and picnicking without tornado gusts. In the 1950s, a Carmel-type commercial development (Drakes Beach Estates) was on the drawing board until distressed conservationists intervened to save Limantour, arguably the peninsula's most idyllic spot. Limantour Spit protects the rich and

Kelham Beach

Location: A 4.8-mile hike from the Bear Valley Visitors Center, via Bear Valley Trail, on Point Reyes Peninsula.

Parking: Free parking lots at the Bear Valley Visitors Center and other park locations.

Hours: Open 24 hours.

Facilities: Picnic table.

Contact: For beach information, contact Point Reyes National Seashore at (415) 663-1092.

See number 13 on page 448.

Limantour Beach

Location: From Highway 1 in Olema, take Bear Valley Road for one mile to Limantour Road. Follow till it ends at Limantour Beach.

Parking: Free parking lot.

Hours: Open 24 hours.

Facilities: Rest rooms.

Contact: For beach information, contact Point Reyes National Seashore at (415) 663-1092.

See number 16 on page 448.

Marshall Beach

Location: From Highway 1 in Point Reyes Station, turn west onto Sir Francis Drake Highway. Bear right onto Pierce Point Road at fork approximately 2.5 miles north of Inverness. Continue for 1.5 miles to L Ranch Road, just past entrance to Tomales Bay State Park. Turn right and drive for 2.5 miles to the end of L Ranch Road. A 1.5-mile trail leads to the beach.

Parking: Free parking lot.

Hours: Open 24 hours.

Facilities: Rest rooms.

Contact: For beach information, contact Point Reyes National Seashore at (415) 663-1092.

See number 23 on page 448.

McClures Beach

Location: From Highway 1 in Point Reyes Station, turn west onto Sir Francis Drake Highway. Bear right onto Pierce Point Road at fork approximately 2.5 miles north of Inverness. Continue for nine miles to the end of Pierce Point Road. A half-mile trail leads to the beach.

Parking: Free parking lot.

Hours: Open 24 hours.

Facilities: Rest rooms.

Contact: For beach information, contact Point Reyes National Seashore at (415) 663-1092.

See number 22 on page 448.

varied Estero de Limantour, and inland trails skirt its shoreline. Bring the binoculars for whale watching and bird-watching (350 species of shorebirds and waterfowl have been counted).

More beaches are strung along south of Limantour, but they are accessible only by park trails. The first of these wilderness beaches is **Santa Maria Beach**, where the primitive but

Palomarin Beach

Location: 4.5 miles north of Stinson Beach, turn from Highway 1 onto Olema-Bolinas Road and follow for 1.75 miles. Turn right onto Mesa Road and continue for 4.5 miles until road ends. Park in gravel lot and hike to beach from Palomarin Trailhead.
Parking: Free parking lot.
Hours: Open 24 hours.
Facilities: None.
Contact: For beach information, contact Point Reyes National Seashore at (415) 663-1092.

See number 11 on page 448.

Point Reyes Beach North

Location: From Highway 1 in Point Reyes Station, turn west onto Sir Francis Drake Highway. Proceed for 13 miles to turnoff for North Beach and follow signs to beach.
Parking: Free parking lot.
Hours: Open 24 hours.
Facilities: Rest rooms.
Contact: For beach information, contact Point Reyes National Seashore at (415) 663-1092.

See number 19 on page 448.

Point Reyes Beach South

Location: From Highway 1 in Point Reyes Station, turn west onto Sir Francis Drake Highway. Proceed for 16 miles to turnoff for South Beach and follow signs to beach.
Parking: Free parking lot.
Hours: Open 24 hours.
Facilities: Rest rooms.
Contact: For beach information, contact Point Reyes National Seashore at (415) 663-1092.

See number 18 on page 448.

Santa Maria Beach

Location: Hike for nine miles from the Bear Valley Visitors Center, via Bear Valley Trail, or for 2.5 miles from Point Reyes Hostel, via the Coast Trail, on Point Reyes Peninsula.
Parking: Free parking lot at the Bear Valley Visitors Center and other park locations.
Hours: Open 24 hours.
Facilities: Rest rooms, picnic tables, and fire grills. There are 14 campsites for tents only. There is no fee, but a camping permit must be obtained at the Bear Valley Visitors Center. For camping reservations, call Point Reyes National Seashore at (415) 663-1092.
Contact: For beach information, contact Point Reyes National Seashore at (415) 663-1092.

See number 15 on page 448.

popular Coast Camp lies behind a sandy ridge. To get there, one can either walk 1.5 miles south along the beach from Limantour, or hike for 2.5 miles over dunes and past marshes

Sculptured Beach

Location: Sculptured Beach is reachable only at low tide by walking east along the beach from Santa Maria Beach (see next entry). Consult tide tables.

Parking: Free parking lots at the Bear Valley Visitors Center and other park locations.

Hours: Open 24 hours.

Facilities: None.

Contact: For beach information, contact Point Reyes National Seashore at (415) 663-1092.

See number 14 on page 448.

Wildcat Beach

Location: Part of Point Reyes National Seashore and reachable by hikes of approximately five miles in length from trailheads at Palomarin, Five Brooks, and Bear Valley. Consult a park map for details.

Parking: Free parking lots at Palomarin, Five Brooks, and Bear Valley Visitors Center.

Hours: Open 24 hours.

Facilities: Rest rooms and picnic tables. There are 12 campsites for tents and four group sites for up to 25 people each. There is no fee, but a permit must be obtained at the Bear Valley Visitors Center. For reservations, call Point Reyes National Seashore at (415) 663-1092.

Contact: For beach information, contact Point Reyes National Seashore at (415) 663-1092.

See number 12 on page 448.

along the Coast Trail from its trailhead at the American Youth Hostel. (The Coast Trail, incidentally, stretches for 16 miles, from the hostel down to the Palomarin parking area, near the Point Reyes Bird Observatory.)

Sculptured Beach lies 1.3 miles south of Santa Maria, off the Coast Trail. It is more of a visual delight than a swimming hole, with sea caves, sea stacks, and crumbling ocher cliffs providing a rugged setting. (Be careful not to get stranded against the cliffs by a rising tide!) Those who like to live dangerously can proceed around a rubbly point at low tide to another cove, the aptly named Secret Beach.

Back on the Coast Trail, **Kelham Beach** lies 2.3 miles south of Sculptured Beach, around Point Resistance. Continue another 0.7 miles, and you can crawl through a sea tunnel at Arch Rock (but only at low tide). A beloved backpackers' mecca, Wildcat Camp, lies 3.5 miles farther down the trail. Actually, a shorter hike to Wildcat Camp can be had by departing from the Five Brooks Parking Area, five miles south of Olema on Highway 1. The camp sits 5.7 miles west of Five Brooks, via Stewart Trail (as opposed to 10.5 miles via the Coast Trail from the American Youth Hostel). Wildcat Camp occupies a grassy meadow near a small stream. **Wildcat Beach** is close by at the end of a short spur trail, and it's another cliff-backed wilderness wonder.

There's one more named beach on the southern flank of Point Reyes National Seashore. **Palomarin Beach** lies west of the Palomarin parking area, just above Bolinas, off Mesa Road. This parking area also serves as the southern trailhead for the Coast Trail; Wildcat Camp lies 5.5 miles north; Coast Camp, 13.2 miles north. Got all that? If not, pick up a Point Reyes trail map at the Bear Valley Visitors Center. Palomarin Beach is narrow (a minus) and isolated (a plus), and leashed dogs are permitted.

The most popular beach on Point Reyes is **Drakes Beach**, which, though located on its southern half, is accessed via an entirely different route than its Limantour Beach neighbor. Back in Inverness, you hop on the Sir Francis Drake Highway (a.k.a. Sir Francis Drake Boulevard), and 18 miles later you are at the Kenneth C. Patrick Visitors Center, a well-appointed facility ideal for families. Easy hikes are available through three different beach habitats—shore, lagoon, and bluff. The beaches and dunes are postcard perfect. Heck, you can even swim here sometimes.

The second most popular spot on the peninsula is just around the bend from Drakes Beach, where Sir Francis Drake Boulevard dead-ends at the lighthouse. It's a great, if somewhat overvisited, spot for viewing migrating whales and birds, especially at Sea Lion Overlook. The trek to Point Reyes Lighthouse, which was built in 1870, requires 300 steps down (which, obviously, means 300 steps back up). It is not for everyone, especially those with heart conditions. A great alternative to the lighthouse is Chimney Rock, which lies at the very end of Point Reyes' hook. A visit involves a 1.5-mile trek but it's worth every step for the solitude. In the winter, over 20,000 gray whales have been counted passing this checkpoint. Just don't let the idyllic panoramic view fool you. In the teeming waters just below the rocks lie the carcasses of countless ships that have wrecked in the smothering fog, the second thickest in America (Cape Disappointment, up the coast in Washington, owns the "thickest" title).

The beaches to the north of the lighthouse are the hidden treasures of Point Reyes National Seashore. However, be aware that these beaches can be formidable terrain, whipped by winds and waves and fog, like something out of a Shakespearean tragedy. The water is subject to severe undertow and sneaker waves (the kind that hit when you least expect it). And the bluffs are subject to erosion. Be careful when trekking along here, and before setting out, check the tide tables to make sure you won't be trapped by high tide. The only lifeguards are the tule elk, who'll probably laugh demonically like creatures from *Far Side* cartoons.

Even with that warning, we recommend visiting the northern beaches. The closest ones to the lighthouse simply are called **Point Reyes Beach, North and South**, which are accessible at two spots several miles apart on Sir Francis Drake Boulevard. Together, they present a 10-mile beach that is oceanfront real estate in its purest form. When the weather cooperates, the area is a paradise for walkers, photographers, artists, and picnickers—but always an inferno for swimmers and surfers.

We leave you with a few more beaches on the north shore. Frankly, the best swimming in this region is not in the ocean, but on the beaches of Tomales Bay. The water there is warmer and (very important) much safer. (See the Tomales Bay State Park entry on page 468.) Out on the ocean beaches—well, we'll turn the mike over to the National Park Service at this point. The posted warning at the trailhead leading to Kehoe Beach just about says it all: "The 19-mile northwestern shore of Point Reyes National Seashore is unsafe for swimming, surfing, or wading. Do not enter the water. This warning applies to all beaches from Tomales Point south to the Point Reyes Headland, including McClures Beach, Kehoe Beach, **Abbotts Lagoon** Beach, North Beach, and South Beach. Cold water, rough surf, and loose footing make hazardous swimming conditions, but there are more serious dangers. Rip currents, sharks, and sneaker waves are constant threats."

Another panel adds that fatal attacks by great white sharks were reported in five different years between 1960 and 1977. (Can anyone hum the theme from *Jaws*?) Don't say you haven't been warned. But, speaking of mandibles, hiking out to these beaches provides a jaw-dropping glimpse of nature in the raw. The path to **Kehoe Beach** is 0.6 miles, revealing a world of mountainous dunes, towering bluffs, intensely variegated vegetation, and (if you're lucky) baby-blue skies dotted by silver-lined clouds like you've never seen in your life. Some of the locals prefer Kehoe because you can bring dogs out here (they're prohibited elsewhere), but the beaches and the walks out to them are magnificent all along this leg of the peninsula.

Kehoe Beach has a counterpart due east across Inverness Ridge on Tomales Bay. **Marshall Beach** is the only publicly accessible bay beach within Point Reyes National Seashore. But, it's a bit hard to get to, requiring a four-mile drive off Sir Francis Drake Highway and a somewhat dreary 1.5-mile hike from the parking lot. It's probably worth the trouble only if you want to save the $5 entrance fee at Tomales Bay State Park, where you can drive your car right to Hearts Desire Beach.

Near the parking lot at the end of Pierce Point Road, a half-mile trail leads to **McClures Beach**. Here is more of the Pacific at its most elemental. At low tide, tidepools beckon to explorers, along with beautiful water-sculpted driftwood. (A beach to the north, toward Tomales Point, is unofficially known as Driftwood Beach.) Again, be careful while walking the beaches. To be on the safe side, stay away from the water's edge, and don't even think about swimming. If the threat of razor-sharp teeth and sleeper waves doesn't deter you, keep in mind that the average water temperature is a bone-numbing 55 degrees.

Bunking Down

One of the nation's most splendid hostels is located seven miles from Bear Valley park headquarters, on Limantour Road. The **Point Reyes Hostel** (P.O. Box 247, 663-8811, $) has 44 beds, wood stoves, and complete kitchens. A modest fee of $10 per night is charged. Reservations can be made by mail, but are usually recommended only for groups. Other accommodations of various stripes are readily available just outside the National Seashore (see the Olema, Point Reyes Station, and Inverness entries on pages 469, 471, and 472 respectively).

Coastal Cuisine

You can grab a snack at **Drakes Beach Café** (Drakes Beach Visitors Center, 669-1297, $), which is open Friday through Tuesday, 11:30 AM to 4 PM, "weather permitting." In other words, don't bet the ranch that it will be open. Your only other option is to leave the park. There are restaurants and grocery stores in the surrounding communities.

For More Information

Contact the Point Reyes National Seashore, Bear Valley Road, Point Reyes, CA 94956; (415) 663-1092.

Tomales Bay State Park

Location: On either side of Tomales Bay, north of Inverness and Point Reyes Station.

Tomales Bay State Park consists of 1,840 acres adjoining the National Seashore on the Point Reyes Peninsula. This super state park sits east of Inverness Ridge along Tomales Bay, which provides safe beaches with calm currents and water that can reach 80 degrees by summer's end. Clamming at low tide (limit of 50, with a fishing license) and surf casting (no license needed) are popular activities. The most visited of the sheltered, warm-water wonders along Tomales Bay is **Hearts Desire Beach**. It is flanked by Indian Beach and Pelican Beach, which lie north and south, respectively, via half-mile trails. Farther down is **Shell Beach,** a locally popular destination that can be reached by a four-mile hike from Hearts Desire or a half-mile walk from a nearby parking lot. The Jepson Trail is a 6.5-mile stunner that cuts through one of the few remaining virgin stands of Bishop pine.

On the other side of Tomales Bay, along Highway 1 between Point Reyes Station and Marshall, is the Millerton Point unit of the state park. You'll find a west-facing bay beach here, **Alan Sieroty Beach**, as well as a picnic area.

Alan Sieroty Beach

Location: At Millerton Point on the eastern shore of Tomales Bay, 4.5 miles north of Point Reyes Station off Highway 1.

Parking: Free parking lot.

Hours: 8 AM to sunset.

Facilities: Rest rooms, picnic tables, and fire grills.

Contact: For beach information, contact Tomales Bay State Park at (415) 669-1140.

See number 26 on page 448.

Hearts Desire Beach
(Tomales Bay State Park)

Location: From Highway 1 in Point Reyes Station, turn west onto Sir Francis Drake Highway. Bear right onto Pierce Point Road at fork approximately 2.5 miles north of Inverness. Continue for one mile to entrance to Tomales Bay State Park.

Parking: $5 entrance fee per vehicle.

Hours: 8 AM to sunset.

Facilities: Rest rooms, picnic tables, and fire grills. There are 20 campsites for tents. Fees are $12 to $14 per night. No camping reservations.

Contact: For beach information, contact Tomales Bay State Park at (415) 669-1140.

See number 24 on page 448.

For More Information

Contact Tomales Bay State Park, Star Route, Inverness, CA 94937; (415) 669-1140.

Shell Beach

Location: Hike south along Tomales Bay via Johnstone Trail for four miles from Hearts Desire Beach (see above entry), or park at the end of Camino del Mar, off Sir Francis Drake Highway, and follow half-mile trail to beach.

Parking: $5 entrance fee per vehicle at Tomales Bay State Park. Free parking lot at the end of Camino del Mar.

Hours: 8 AM to sunset.

Facilities: None.

Contact: For beach information, contact Tomales Bay State Park at (415) 669-1140.

See number 25 on page 448.

The Communities Along Tomales Bay

Man does not live by beach alone. (Okay, nor do women.) This is especially true on the Point Reyes Peninsula, where 30 wild miles of coastline fall under the province of the National Park Service. Because of this protected status, if you're determined to stay at the beach, it will have to be at either Wildcat Camp or Coast Camp—primitive park campgrounds near the beach that are reachable only by backpacking in. If you want to explore Point Reyes but backpacking isn't your style, there are places to stay, eat, drink, and be merry in the communities just south and along both sides of Tomales Bay, the narrow, linear indention that rests atop the San Andreas Fault. For this reason, we have included write-ups on Olema, Point Reyes Station, Inverness, Marshall, and Dillon Beach, which follow.

Olema

Location: 29 miles north of San Francisco on Highway 1.
Population: 125
Area Code: 415 **Zip Code:** 94950

Olema was bigger in the 1870s than it is in the 1990s. But while it's hardly a bustling metropolis today, it does serve as a major West Marin crossroads (where Highway 1 meets Sir Francis Drake Boulevard) and gateway to Point Reyes National Seashore. The Bear Valley Visitors Center lies just one-third mile west of town. The word *olema* means "coyote" in the language of the native Miwok Indians. The area attracted some counterculture types in the 1960s, including members of the Youngbloods, who recorded a musical retort to country singer Merle Haggard's hippie-baiting "Okie from Muskogee," which they entitled "Hippie from Olema." This little town, incidentally, is located at the epicenter of the Great San Francisco earthquake of 1906, when the ground jumped 16 feet laterally in less than a minute. (A fashion/jewelry store in town bravely attests to this legacy by calling itself "The Epicenter.") Plate tectonics and the earth's shifting priorities might have something to do with why there hasn't been a population boom out here, all of which serves to keep Olema pleasantly low key.

Bunking Down

The **Olema Inn** (10,000 Sir Francis Drake Boulevard, 663-9559, $$) has been around since 1876, standing proud at the crossroads. It's a pretty three-room inn with a garden setting and a pleasant ground-floor restaurant. It merits a literary footnote, too, having been a favorite with Jack London and John Steinbeck. Nearby stands another commendable bed-and-breakfast inn, **Roundstone Farm** (9,940 Sir Francis Drake Boulevard, 663-1020, $$), which occupies a 10-acre horse ranch in the hills overlooking the Olema Valley and Tomales Bay. In terms of age, it's at the opposite extreme of the Olema Inn, having been designed and built in 1987 as a five-room B&B, complete with solar heating and skylights. Another recent addition to the local lodging scene, the **Point Reyes Seashore Lodge** (10,021 Highway 1, 663-9000, $$$), provides weary travelers with a host of modern conveniences such as whirlpool baths and wet bars.

A Horse Is a Horse—Unless It's From Marin County

The residents of Point Reyes move to the beat of the proverbial different drummer. We were told by one of the first people we met that West Marin County was "different" from East Marin County—or anywhere else, for that matter. We didn't quite understand how, until we came across a certain news story in the local weekly.

The headline read "Community Rallies to Save Hurt Horse." How nice, we thought, a quiet country town is deeply concerned about a fallen plow mare. Then we read a little further. The horse was not a plow mare but a purebred equestrian jumper. When something spooked the horse in an open field, she sustained the kind of leg injury that usually signals a trip to the glue factory. However, the paper reported that an "animal communicator" was called in from Inverness. Through "conversations" with the fallen filly, the expert concluded that she had a "very positive attitude about her recovery and was determined to walk again." This gave the horse's owner the courage to hang in there with her steed. Another expert was brought in to administer acupuncture and herbal salves. A third healer strode out of the wings to work in massage. We never did learn if the plucky filly recovered, but, whatever the outcome, the tail, er, tale speaks volumes about life in West Marin.

Coastal Cuisine

The restaurant at the quaint and inviting **Olema Inn** (10,000 Sir Francis Drake Boulevard, 663-9559, $$$) has a Cal-Mediterranean slant (e.g., calamari with cilantro pesto) and a fine wine list. Tomales Bay oysters, Petaluma duck, and vegetarian dishes are other menu staples. **Jerry's Farm House** (Highway 1, 663-1264, $$) is a basic all-American steak, chicken, and seafood kind of place, perfect for families.

For More Information

Contact the West Marin County Chamber of Commerce, 11431 Highway 1, Suite 15, P.O. Box 1045, Point Reyes Station, CA 94956; (415) 663-9232.

Point Reyes Station

Location: 33 miles northwest of San Francisco. Cross the Golden Gate Bridge and drive 9 miles north on Highway 101. Take the Sir Francisco Drake Boulevard exit and proceed west for 21.5 miles. Turn right onto Highway 1 and travel 2.5 miles to Point Reyes Station.
Population: 400
Area Code: 415 **Zip Code:** 94956

Point Reyes Station lies along Highway 1 (which itself lies along the San Andreas Fault, geology fans). As you enter from the south, the road makes a sharp left turn, taking you past a few blocks of stores. This is the raison d'être of Point Reyes Station, the center for provisioning on the peninsula. Here the New West meets the Old West for a showdown on Main Street, whose three-block shopping district sets art galleries cheek-by-jowl with a saddle shop and a feed store. Times have changed. The former outnumber the latter by about six to one. Still, when the noon whistle blows in Point Reyes Station, it's not a whistle at all that marks the time, but a mechanized "moo."

Point Reyes Station makes a convenient, centralized point of entry into the National Seashore. Accordingly, it's got a smattering of bed-and-breakfast inns, some good restaurants, and even a hint of after-hours activity.

Bunking Down

You can let someone else do your booking for you by calling **Inns of Marin** (663-2000), a referral-and-reservation lodging service for the West Marin area. You will no doubt want to stay in a bed-and-breakfast out here. In fact, you have little choice in the matter; the rural landscape practically mandates the B&B experience. We had a fine stay at **Thirty-Nine Cypress** (39 Cypress, 663-1709, $$), a single-story redwood home that overlooks pastures, marshlands, and the fringes of Inverness Ridge. The **Holly Tree Inn** (3 Silverhills Road, 663-1554, $$) is a four-roomer located near park headquarters on a 19-acre estate overlooking Tomales Bay.

Coastal Cuisine

The **Station House Café** (11180 Main Street, 663-1515, $$) is one of the few gourmet restaurants along this stretch of the coast. It's warm, comfortable, and unpretentious on the inside, offering live music on Sunday afternoons and piped-in jazz the rest of the time. But the real virtuosity is to be found in the kitchen. For starters, try some oysters. They couldn't be fresher, having been raised close by on Tomales Bay. They're served several different ways: broiled in garlic and butter; barbecued and slathered with a tasty sauce; and served raw with a spicy cocktail sauce. The entrées run from steak, raised organically on a North Coast ranch, to vegetarian plates. Seafood dishes include salmon broiled with a saffron cream sauce and halibut cooked to a delicate turn and served with a yellow-pepper vinaigrette. Such accompaniments as a sweet-tasting, pureed beet ginger tart round out the very attractively presented dinner items. You're urged to save room for dessert. The lemon pot de crème, for instance, delivers a nice grace note after a seafood entrée. The service is friendly and attentive, and the clientele—as is so often the case in West Marin County—offers an interesting study in ruggedly eccentric individualism. In other words, the joint's got character, as well as great food. The Station House is open seven days and serves three meals.

Night Moves

When the sun is hanging low in the sky, Point Reyes Station resembles the backdrop from the old *Gunsmoke* series. Rather than draw a six-gun and start plugging varmints, head to the **Western Saloon** (Main Street, 663-1661), a local institution. It's got the obligatory long wooden bar with a brass rail and a gunmetal-gray cash box, and every now and again (or so we were told) someone gets real drunk and rides a horse into the Western. Pool tables, pinball games, and an eclectic jukebox provide other diversions. A bumper sticker above the cash box reminds you that "Nobody's Ugly After 2 AM." They wouldn't add our proffered McDonald's gift certificate to the collection of grubstake pinned to the wall, but the Western is otherwise a very hospitable place.

Then there's the **Station House Café** (see above), which is the most civilized place to hoist a few and has live weekend jazz to boot.

A newer arrival is the **Café Reyes Roastery & Pub** (Main Street, 663-8368), which has live entertainment on weekends. (Jesse Colin Young leading mug-swinging sing-alongs of "Get Together"?) Actually, it pains us to report when we were in town that a "rave" of sorts had become a weekly happening. Seems one of the rangers at the National Seashore owns a bunch of dance records and spins them on Sunday night. (He may be gone by now, for all we know, reassigned to New York City.) From the street we could hear maniacal dance beats breaking the silence and reflexively headed in the other direction. That is the sort of thing people come to Point Reyes to escape, us included.

For More Information

Contact the West Marin County Chamber of Commerce, 11431 Highway 1, Suite 15, P.O. Box 1045, Point Reyes Station, CA 94956; (415) 663-9232.

Inverness

Location: 35 miles north of San Francisco on the west side of Tomales Bay, along Sir Francis Drake Boulevard above Point Reyes Station.
Population: 600
Area Code: 415 **Zip Code:** 94937

In the words of a local innkeeper, "Inverness runs at two speeds: dead slow and stop. Usually, it's the latter." Slow or no, Inverness provides a convenient and idyllic bayside base for exploring the Point Reyes peninsula.

Bunking Down

The **Golden Hinde Inn and Marina** (12939 Sir Francis Drake Boulevard, 669-1389, $$) offers innlike comforts (continental breakfast, some fireplaces) in a motel setting (comfortable rooms, TVs, showers) directly on Tomales Bay. The adjacent marina serves as a boat launch and berthing spot. Rates are very reasonable ($55 to $125), and some units have kitchens, which might come in handy if you happen to catch your own dinner.

On the bed-and-breakfast front, there's the venerable **Blackthorne Inn** (266 Vallejo Avenue, 663-8621, $$$), which has been called a carpenter's fantasy because of its ornate, multilevel construction from redwood, cedar, and Douglas fir milled right on site. In addition to its architectural charms, the inn has a 2,500-square-foot sundeck, a hot tub, and a glassed-in, upper-story room, dubbed the Eagle's Nest. Nearby, **Manka's Inverness Lodge** (Argyle Street, 669-1034, $$$) proffers eight cozy guest rooms and two one-bedroom cabins in a secluded, woodsy setting.

To find out about other inns scattered around Inverness and surrounding communities, contact **Inns of Point Reyes** (P.O. Box 145, Inverness, CA 94937; 485-2649); you can also request hiking and day-trip guides.

Coastal Cuisine

Because the median income of Inverness is relatively high and many of the townsfolk are restaurant-going retirees, the local dining choices are varied and of good quality. They run the culinary gamut from Cal-nouvelle to Czech. At **Barnaby's by the Bay** (12938 Drake Boulevard, 669-1114, $$), the restaurant at the Golden Hinde Inn, there's always plenty of freshly harvested mussels and oysters on hand. You'll also find applewood-smoked ribs, chicken, and fish (including crab cioppino). **Vladimir's Czechoslovakian Restaurant** (12785 Drake Boulevard, 669-1021, $$) is interesting because of the man whose name it bears. A self-proclaimed "mechanical genius" and "extremely hard worker," Vladimir Nevl is an expatriate who skied his way to freedom in 1948 after the Communist takeover. He came to Inverness, where he opened his eatery in 1960. Every entrée proudly bears his name: Vladimir's Garlic Lamb Shank, Vladimir's Beef Tongue, etc., etc. Another Czech-inspired restaurant is **Manka's Inverness Lodge & Restaurant** (30 Callendar Way, 669-1034, $$$). Located on the site of a former hunting lodge in the hills above the bay, the small, rural-chic restaurant is very well regarded even by snobby San Francisco food critics, and specializes in game dishes (e.g., rabbit-walnut sausage, pan-seared elk loin) and local seafood.

For More Information

Contact the West Marin County Chamber of Commerce, 11431 Highway 1, Suite 15, P.O. Box 1045, Point Reyes Station, CA 94956; (415) 663-9232.

Marshall

Location: On the eastern shore of Tomales Bay, along Highway 1 north of Point Reyes Station.
Population: 500
Area Code: 415 **Zip Code:** 94940

Marshall is a blink-and-you-miss-it town along the eastern shore of Tomales Bay. The local specialty in West Marin County is barbecued oysters and more than half the state's commercial shellfish farms are in Marshall. The oysters typically come in two varieties: Hog Island (more freshwater than saline, mild flavored, best raw on the half shell) and Johnson's (saltier, better suited to roasting and slathering with barbecue sauce). Either way, you're in bivalve heaven.

Coastal Cuisine

Oysters are served in restaurants all over the county, but no one does 'em better than **Tony's Seafood Place** (18863 Highway 1, 663-1107, $$). One gray afternoon we sat out on the deck and waited for our oysters while watching a guy standing over a charcoal brazier, basting the bubbling bivalves with a sweet-spicy barbecue sauce.

For More Information

Contact the West Marin County Chamber of Commerce, 11431 Highway 1, Suite 15, P.O. Box 1045, Point Reyes Station, CA 94956; (415) 663-9232.

Dillon Beach

Location: At the north end of Tomales Bay, just south of the Sonoma County line.
Population: 100
Area Code: 707 **Zip Code:** 94929

Dillon Beach is the northernmost beach in Marin County. A subdivision of second homes and vacation rentals sprawls upon the hills overlooking the tip of Point Reyes. The big draw is Lawson's Landing, a private campground at the mouth of Tomales Bay where you can rent boats and dig for clams, and Lawson's Resort, a private day-use beach facing the ocean where you can surf cast, tidepool, or poke-pole. "Poke-poling" is not as obscene as it sounds; it involves taking a 14-foot-long bamboo pole fitted with a hook and leader, and sticking it under the crevice of rocks at low tide in order to catch eel, cabezon, and so forth. Lawson's Resort also handles home and cottage rentals. At **Lawson's Landing**, open-meadow camping is available. They also run a barge over to the sand bar at low tides (approximately 7 to 10 days per month) so you can dig for giant clams. Barge rides are $3 per adult, $2 per child.

For More Information

Contact Lawson's Resort, 1 Beach Avenue, Dillon Beach, CA 94929; (707) 878-2204. Or contact Lawson's Landing, 137 Marine View Drive, Dillon Beach, CA 94929; (707) 878-2443.

Dillon Beach (Lawson's Resort)

Location: At Beach Avenue in Dillon Beach, off Highway 1 near the Sonoma County line.
Parking: $5 entrance fee per vehicle.
Hours: 8 AM to 6 PM (7 PM on weekends).
Facilities: Rest rooms and picnic tables.
Contact: For beach information, contact Lawson's Resort at (707) 878-2204.

See number 28 on page 448.

Lawson's Landing

Location: At the end of Marine View Drive, five miles west of Tomales and south of Dillon Beach off Highway 1.
Parking: $5 entrance fee per vehicle.
Hours: 7 AM to sunset.
Facilities: Rest rooms, showers, picnic tables, and fire rings. There are open-meadow tent and RV campsites. The fee is $11 per night. For camping reservations, call Lawson's Landing at (707) 878-2443.
Contact: For beach information, contact Lawson's Landing at (707) 878-2443.

See number 27 on page 448.

Sonoma County

In Sonoma County, they refer to the Pacific Coast Highway as Dramamine Drive, which offers a clue to the lay of the land: over, under, sideways, down. Add to that the sparse human population, and you have a travel experience not unlike exploring the Scottish highlands or a slow-motion replay of Big Sur. In this part of Northern California, you drive through a series of winding bends in the road—including some screeching hairpin turns—and after 10 miles of awe-inspiring vistas of rocky headlands and vast ocean you come upon a town. Actually, the town is likely to be a series of well-hidden structures and ramshackle tackle huts that cling like barnacles to the rocks above the roaring Pacific or along the banks of a clear, cool river.

In other words, the concept of the beach resort has to be modified in Sonoma County—in all of Northern California, for that matter. Fishing villages, for the most part, include Bodega Bay and *(continued on page 478)*

Coastal Sonoma County's Climate

Fort Ross Averages

	Daily High Temp. (°F)	Daily Low Temp. (°F)	Rainfall (inches)
January	56	40	6.0
February	58	42	5.1
March	58	42	4.0
April	59	42	4.0
May	61	44	0.7
June	64	47	0.2
July	65	48	0.1
August	66	49	0.2
September	67	48	0.4
October	65	46	1.8
November	57	41	3.4
December	57	41	5.5
Yearly Average	**61**	**44**	**29.9**

Source: National Weather Service data, National Oceanographic and Atmospheric Administration.

Sonoma County

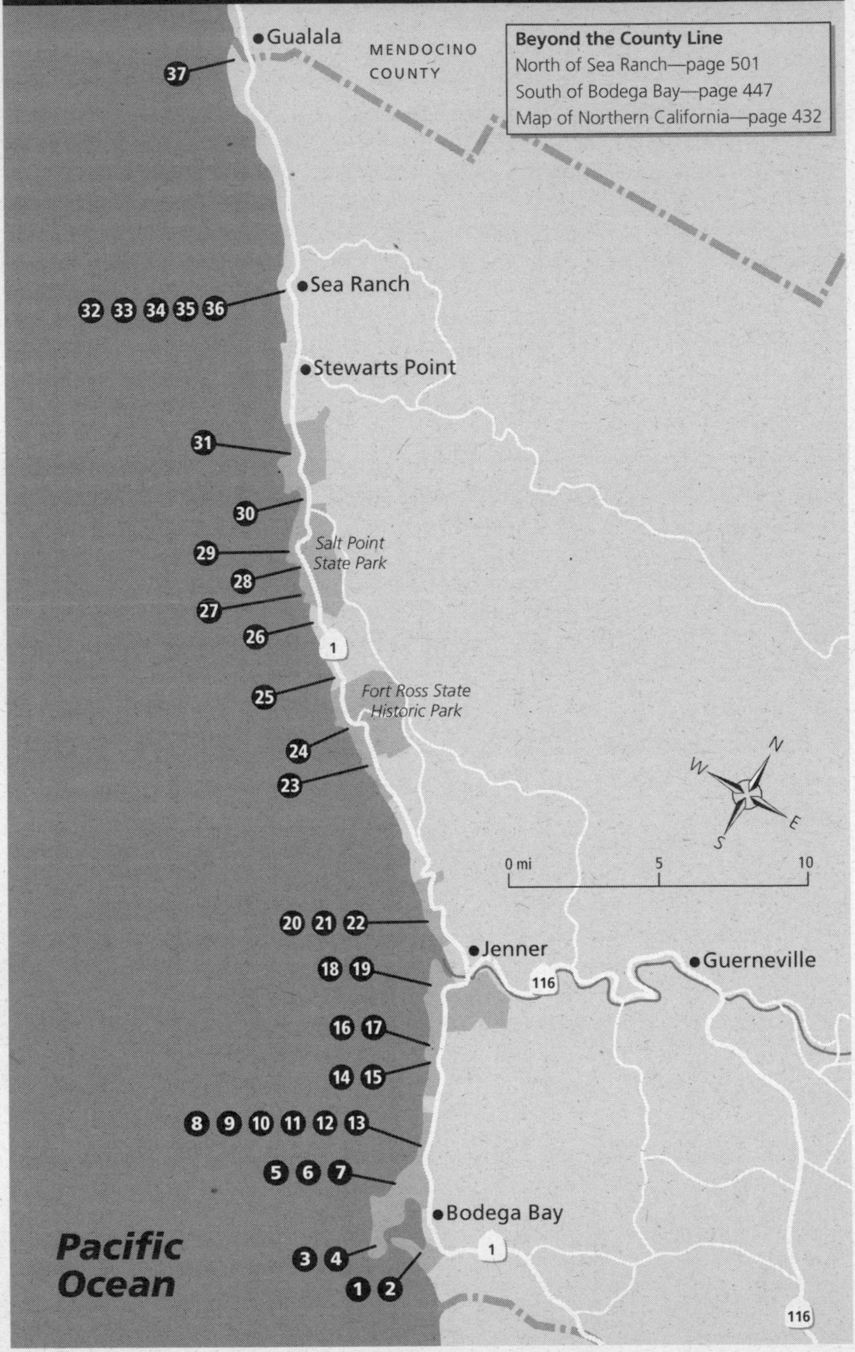

Gualala
MENDOCINO COUNTY
Beyond the County Line
North of Sea Ranch—page 501
South of Bodega Bay—page 447
Map of Northern California—page 432
37
Sea Ranch
32 33 34 35 36
Stewarts Point
31
30
Salt Point State Park
29
28
27
26
1
25
Fort Ross State Historic Park
24
23
N
W
E
S
0 mi
5
10
20 21 22
Jenner
Guerneville
18 19
116
16 17
14 15
8 9 10 11 12 13
5 6 7
Bodega Bay
Pacific Ocean
3 4
1
1 2
116

Sonoma County Beaches

Map of Northern California—page 432

(continued from page 475) Jenner—both former logging and fur-trading centers that fell into blissful sleepiness in the early years of the century when the trees and otters went thataway. Slowly these outposts have reawakened as retreats and fishing holes—perfect tonics for the tortured nerves of the urban dwellers who make regular pilgrimages here.

This is not to say that Sonoma County has no beaches. On the contrary, the southern third of the county is one large state beach—a 16-mile series of coves collectively known as Sonoma County State Beaches. They're excellent for fishing and tidepooling, but not for swimming or even wading; an unexpected wave can knock you off your feet and a rip current will finish the job. No lifeguards are posted at any of the county's beaches, so watch your step wherever you comb (see sidebar, "Sonoma Coast Safety Check").

The evil twin of this state-beach enclave is Sea Ranch, a private beach colony that owns the northern third of the county coast. Accesses are provided to some of the cove beaches along Sea Ranch—not, incidentally, obtained without litigation—but the overall feeling is that no welcome mat has been rolled out for you. Our philosophy is, with so much beach to go around, who needs 'em anyway? The middle third of the Sonoma Coast is neither fish nor fowl—that is, it's not owned by the state nor has it fallen into private hands. Instead, the beaches remain in the purview of the scattered hamlets clinging to the headlands.

Key to the Symbols

Bike path · Camping · Food and drink · Hiking · Nude

Pier · RVs allowed · Surfing · Volleyball

Crowd Rating

sweet solitude . . . moderate crowds . . . wall-to-wall

Overall Rating

1 don't bother . . . 3 worth a visit . . . 5 beach heaven

Bodega Bay

Location: 40 miles north of San Francisco, along Highway 1.
Population: 900
Area Code: 707 **Zip Code:** 94923

After bypassing the Point Reyes Peninsula, Highway 1 rejoins the coast at Bodega Bay, Sonoma County's busiest harbor and pleasure port. So many fishing boats use Bodega Bay that several large marinas are kept active, and the main boat launching ramp is six lanes wide.

The harbor could not have been planned any better than the way Mother Nature drew it up. Bodega Head is a slug-shaped headland that protects the harbor from the west. The sand spit known as Doran Beach Regional Park provides a sort of tonsil in the harbor's throat, protecting it from the south.

Bodega Bay Harbor hasn't always been a smooth-sailing operation. The inner bay, near the warehouses and docks, has had a recurrent problem with silting. A deep-water dredge was performed in 1943, creating a channel that could service a large fishing fleet. By the 1950s, Bodega Bay was processing 1,000,000 pounds of fish, 900,000 pounds of crab, and 400,000 pounds of albacore a year. Now it primarily serves as a port for recreational and smaller-scale commercial fishing, as its fortunes have waned in tandem with the dwindling world fishing catch. Still, they do their best to share what's left. Deep-sea fishing boats are vomited oceanward past Doran Beach's tonsils, and no resident salmon or rock cod is safe, especially in the waters off Tomales Point.

Bodega takes its name from a Spanish word meaning "resting place." Our idea of rest in Bodega Bay was to let others do the fishing while we ate and lay around on the beaches. Of course, this was before we learned that Bodega Bay was the setting for Alfred Hitchcock's terrifying film *The Birds*. (In fact, you can still visit the schoolhouse immortalized in the movie.) Despite a sudden wariness about our feathery friends, we ventured out to the lovely shoreline, roaming by foot rather than boat.

All visits, of course, should begin at the wharf, a beehive of boating activity where you can charter a fishing boat or simply order a seafood dinner at one of the restaurants that continually receive fresh catches. Both Bodega Bay Sportfishing (875-3344) and Jaws (875-3495) offer boat rentals and guides.

Beaches

Doran Beach Regional Park can be reached via Doran Park Road, the turnoff by the Best Western Bodega Bay. Continue past the hotel and you'll find yourself driving alongside the bay and encountering a couple of different areas to park and play. The best of these is the Cypress area. It's a picturesque setting, with plenty of small craft at anchor, bobbing on the bright blue water. Doran is a county-owned beach at which a $3 day-use fee is collected. It features an extensive bayside campground. There are also places to picnic, clean fish, and launch boats. **Westside Regional Park**,

Bodega Head

Location: From Highway 1 in Bodega Bay, turn west onto Bay Flat Road and follow to Westside Road. Bodega Head is at the end of Westside Road.
Parking: Free parking lot.
Hours: 8 AM to one hour after sunset.
Facilities: Rest rooms.
Contact: For beach information, contact the Russian River District Office of the California Department of Parks and Recreation at (707) 865-2391.

See number 4 on page 476.

another county-run facility, is located on the inner, harbor-facing side of **Bodega Head**. It's got much the same menu of amenities: boat launch, picnic tables, campsites, sand beach.

A web of coastal trails crisscrosses Bodega Head. The longest leads through thick dunes to South Salmon Creek Beach (see next entry). A shorter trail leads east across Bodega Head to **Campbell Cove**, a harbor beach with a boardwalk leading to an observation deck overlooking a small lagoon known as "Hole in the Head." Another trail leads to the top of the headland, providing stunning views of the ocean, bay, harbor, and migrating whales. The aquatic mammals pass south mostly in December and January and return north primarily in March and April. Trails lead down the bluffs to small, scenic coves. Winter waves and weather can be ferocious, so be advised. The University of California operates its Marine Biological Research Lab on Bodega Head. It is open to the public for tours on Fridays only from 2 PM to 4 PM; call 875-2211 for information.

Campbell Cove

Location: Along the western mouth of Bodega Bay Harbor, off East Shore Road.

Parking: $2 entrance fee per vehicle.

Hours: 8 AM to one hour after sunset.

Facilities: Rest rooms and picnic tables.

Contact: For beach information, contact the Russian River District Office of the California Department of Parks and Recreation at (707) 865-2391.

See number 2 on page 476.

Doran Beach Regional Park

Location: In Bodega Bay, at the end of Doran Park Road off Highway 1.

Parking: $3 entrance fee per vehicle.

Hours: Sunrise to sunset.

Facilities: Rest rooms, showers, picnic tables, and fire pits. There are 108 tent and RV campsites. The fee is $14 per night. No camping reservations.

Contact: For beach information, contact the Sonoma County Parks Department at (707) 875-3540.

See number 1 on page 476.

Bunking Down

The nicest motel in Bodega Bay is the **Best Western Bodega Bay Lodge** (Highway 1, 875-3525, $$). Each of the 78 large rooms has a balcony overlooking the bay and Doran Beach. Amenities include pool, spa, sauna, gym, and fireplace. A free breakfast comes with the room, and dinner can be had on premises at the Ocean Club. A newer, slightly more upscale hostelry is the **Inn at the Tides** (800 Highway 1, 875-2751, $$), which offers the same peerless water views and a restaurant, the Bayview Room.

Westside Regional Park

Location: From Highway 1 in Bodega Bay, turn west onto Bay Flat Road and follow to Westside Road. The park entrance is on Westside Road, along the western shore of Bodega Bay Harbor.

Parking: $3 entrance fee per vehicle.

Hours: Sunrise to sunset.

Facilities: Rest rooms and picnic tables. There are 47 tent and RV campsites. The fee is $14 per night. No camping reservations

Contact: For beach information, contact the Sonoma County Parks Department at (707) 875-3540.

See number 3 on page 476.

Sonoma Coast Safety Check

If you want to enjoy a healthy relationship with the ocean on the rugged North Coast, you have to treat it with respect. At the Albion River Inn—which lies farther north, in Mendocino County—we came upon the following guidelines for doing just that. They seem so sensible and appropriate to all of Northern California that we've included them here, in abbreviated form, for your safety:

- The ocean is not a large lake or a bubbling creek. It's rough, powerful, and frigid.
- When you're down below a bluff, you can't be seen or heard from above. Children, in particular, should not be allowed to climb down alone.
- Always consult tide tables if you plan to hike along the beach.
- Bluff and headland trails are cut into erodible, soft rock. Before descending any trail, study the terrain and waves from above. Pay special heed to the force and size of incoming waves.
- Do not turn your back on the ocean.
- If you're hit by a large, unexpected wave, don't panic, and don't try to save anything other than yourself (i.e., drop your camera, backpack, or paintbrush).
- Don't go beachcombing or exploring cliff tops alone.
- Beware of poison oak, which thrives all over the North Coast.

Coastal Cuisine

You won't get seafood any fresher than a restaurant on the docks where the fishing boats come in. **Lucas Wharf** (595 Highway 1, 875-3522, $$) is in the thick of things, serving a decent, if unspectacular, seafood spread. The **Tides Seafood Restaurant** (835 Highway 1, 875-3652, $$$) serves freshly caught seafood at prices that seem a little jacked up ($12.50 to $18.95) given the location and basic nature of preparations (grilled, sautéed, deep fried). Other parts of the menu affect a French Creole accent, which seems a tad pretentious for a California fishing village. It's the kind of place that refers to potatoes and rice as the "starch of the day." C'mon, now—drop the phony accent and the prices and hustle that grilled halibut out *pronto*. Breakfast at the Tides is terrific. We recommend the Hangtown Fry, a piled high plate of plump fried oysters with eggs, bacon, hash browns, and toast.

For More Information

Contact the Bodega Bay Chamber of Commerce, 555 Highway 1, Bodega Bay, CA 94923; (707) 875-3422. For information on Westside and Doran Beach Regional Parks, contact the Sonoma County Parks Department, 2300 County Center Drive, Room 120 A, Santa Rosa, CA 95403; (707) 875-3540.

Bodega Dunes State Beach and South Salmon Creek Beach

Location: A half mile north of Bodega Bay, off Highway 1.

Bodega Dunes is one of the last remaining dune fields in California. The sandy wonders have been preserved in a park that includes a 98-site campground where campers can pitch tents or park RVs beneath a canopy of pines and firs. Enormous dunes, covered with a thick profusion of swaying grasses, protect the campground from offshore winds. A zigzagging wooden walkway leads over the dunes to **South Salmon Creek Beach**, which runs for roughly three miles, from the mouth of Salmon Creek to Mussel Point on Bodega Head.

All sorts of compelling reasons are offered against swimming here, including a strong backwash, rip currents, and sleeper waves. The camping is as good as it gets at the beach—but leave the swimsuit at home; the average water temperature on the Sonoma coast beaches is between 48 and 52 degrees. If you don't die of hypothermia or get gnawed to bits by a great white, you might get filleted on the rocks into *tekka maki* by an oversize wave. So what can you do on a beach like this? Put on a hooded sweatshirt, walk along the shoreline, and "visualize world peace" (to borrow the text of a bumper sticker we saw in the parking lot). We did our bit for global harmony, incidentally, by giving a va-

Bodega Dunes

Location: A half mile north of Bodega Bay off Highway 1.
Parking: $5 entrance fee per vehicle.
Hours: 8 AM to one hour after sunset.
Facilities: Rest rooms, showers, picnic tables, and fire pits. There are 98 tent and RV campsites. Fees are $12 to $14 per night. For camping reservations, call Destinet at (800) 444-7275.
Contact: For beach information, contact Bodega Dunes Campground at (707) 875-3483.

See number 5 on page 476.

North Salmon Creek Beach

Location: Two miles north of Bodega Bay off Highway 1, above the north bank of Salmon Creek.
Parking: Free parking lot.
Hours: 8 AM to one hour after sunset.
Facilities: Rest rooms.
Contact: For beach information, contact the Russian River District Office of the California Department of Parks and Recreation at (707) 865-2391.

See number 7 on page 476.

South Salmon Creek Beach

Location: 1.5 miles north of Bodega Bay, along Highway 1 at Salmon Creek. South Salmon Creek Beach extends from the creek mouth to Mussel Point.
Parking: Free parking lot.
Hours: 8 AM to one hour after sunset.
Facilities: Rest rooms.
Contact: For beach information, contact the Russian River District Office of the California Department of Parks and Recreation at (707) 865-2391.

See number 6 on page 476.

cationing German family a ride from the beach back to their campsite. They left us a car full of sand in return.

Recently, the park began a dune restoration project at South Salmon Creek Beach. After being denuded of their native vegetation, studded with ecosystem-altering exotic plants, and generally abused by foolish humans for a century, the dunes are being restored to pristine condition as much as possible. The project has involved reshaping the dunes, reintroducing native flora, and laying down boardwalks to minimize damage from human traipsing. A good idea and money well spent; the results speak for themselves.

For More Information

Contact Sonoma Coast State Beaches, Salmon Creek Lagoon, Bodega Bay, CA 94923; (707) 875-3483 or the Russian River District Department of Parks and Recreation, P.O. Box 123, Duncan Mills, CA 95430; (707) 865-2391.

Sonoma Coast State Beaches

Location: North of Jenner, along a 16-mile stretch of Highway 1.

You've heard of ghost towns. Well, Sonoma is a ghost county. Travelers who are sick of crowds, development, and predictable vacations will find the Sonoma coast appealing, but the beaches here can be a bit, well, ghostly. They exist, to be sure, but these lonely and wild stretches of sand are as pleasurable to ponder from a bluff top as they are to wander down and see up close and personal.

Collectively known as the Sonoma Coast State Beaches, the 16-mile stretch from Bodega Bay to just north of Jenner offers over 5,000 acres of public land, 1,000 acres of which are dunes and the rest coastal bluffs, with nearly 30 separate units overseen by the state park staff. Here's a list of the beach units, moving from south to north:

- Bodega Bay
- Campbell Cove
- Bodega Dunes Campground
- South Salmon Creek Beach
- North Salmon Creek Beach
- Miwok Beach
- Coleman Beach
- Arched Rock Beach
- Marshall Gulch
- Carmet Beach
- Schoolhouse Beach
- Portuguese Beach
- Gleason's Beach
- Duncan's Cove
- Rock Point
- Duncan's Landing
- Pacific View
- Wright's Beach
- Furlong Gulch
- Shell Beach
- Blind Beach
- Goat Rock Beach
- Russian Gulch

That's an average of one beach-access point every two-thirds of a mile. To get to each of them requires a hike of varying length and an often harrowing descent to the beach. We've taken a gander at several over the years, but have by no means made the trek out to all of them. (What, do we look crazy?) Several, such as Rock Point, aren't beaches at all, but headlands overlooking the ocean. Then there's the Willow Creek Unit, which isn't even on the ocean, lying upstream of Willow Creek and several miles from the coast. It's confusing, we admit. We're not sure we've got this Sonoma Coast State Beaches business completely nailed down ourselves, but this accounting is as

Map of Sonoma County beaches—page 476

comprehensive as any official listing we've seen (and some of them contradict each other). Ah, sweet mystery—that's the beauty of a wilderness coastline, wouldn't you agree?

To reduce this laundry list to a manageable size, we'll focus on some of the units that are more heavily used and have facilities. From the south, the first of the beach accesses is **Bodega Dunes** (see the entry on page 482), one of two coast campgrounds. The second can be found at **Wright's Beach**, six miles farther north. There are fewer campsites here than at Bodega Dunes, but they're smack on the beach.

Shell Beach is favored by beachcombers, tidepoolers, and anglers. We walked out to this one for a good, close look. It's a straight, drivewaylike shot off Highway 1 to the parking lot at Shell Beach. You can descend the steep, partially paved path to the beach, or wander over the bluff tops to Goat Rock Beach via the Kortum Trail, a 2.6-mile hike. There's lots of cormorants in the area; apparently, these dark, long-necked birds like hanging out here. But beware. One sign reads: "The surf at this beach has caused the death of many people who were simply walking the shoreline." Those

Arched Rock Beach

Location: 3.25 miles north of Bodega Bay off Highway 1. A trail leads to the beach.
Parking: Free parking lot.
Hours: 8 AM to one hour after sunset.
Facilities: None.
Contact: For beach information, contact the Russian River District Office of the California Department of Parks and Recreation at (707) 865-2391.

See number 10 on page 476.

Carmet Beach

Location: 3.75 miles north of Bodega Bay off Highway 1. A steep trail leads to the beach.
Parking: Free parking lot.
Hours: 8 AM to one hour after sunset.
Facilities: None.
Contact: For beach information, contact the Russian River District Office of the California Department of Parks and Recreation at (707) 865-2391.

See number 11 on page 476.

Blind Beach

Location: On Goat Rock Road, off Highway 1 near the mouth of the Russian River south of Jenner.
Parking: Free parking lot.
Hours: 8 AM to one hour after sunset.
Facilities: Rest rooms.
Contact: For beach information, contact the Russian River District Office of the California Department of Parks and Recreation at (707) 865-2391.

See number 18 on page 476.

Coleman Beach

Location: Three miles north of Bodega Bay off Highway 1. A steep trail leads to the beach.
Parking: Free parking lot.
Hours: 8 AM to one hour after sunset.
Facilities: None.
Contact: For beach information, contact the Russian River District Office of the California Department of Parks and Recreation at (707) 865-2391.

See number 9 on page 476.

pesky sneaker waves again. But wait, there's more: "The cliffs along this coast have caused many deaths." Gulp. It's a pretty spot, nonetheless. Just keep an eye on the cliffs, the water, and your footing.

Portuguese Beach is good for rock fishing and surf casting. Picnic tables await your dining pleasure at Rock Point, Goat Rock, Russian Gulch, and Wright's Beach. Hit Bodega Head for whale watching. **Duncan's Landing** is the place to go if you fancy drowning. Otherwise known as Death Rock, it's the single most dangerous spot on California's deadliest stretch of coastline—the 16 miles between Bodega Head and Russian Gulch.

Just south of the Russian River mouth you'll find **Goat Rock Beach**. Turn off Highway 1 onto Goat Rock Road, which kicks you coastward to the headlands on the south bank of the Russian River, opposite Jenner. As the name implies, goats used to graze on the massive offshore rock that overlooks the hard black sand of the beach. Now Goat Rock is inhabited by harbor seals and sea birds, and is off-limits to humans—and goats, for that matter. The best time to visit the beach is from March

Duncan's Landing

1

Location: Five miles north of Bodega Bay, off Highway 1. This is the most dangerous spot along the Sonoma Coast, in terms of number of drownings.

Parking: Free parking lot.

Hours: 8 AM to one hour after sunset.

Facilities: None.

Contact: For beach information, contact the Russian River District Office of the California Department of Parks and Recreation at (707) 865-2391.

See number 15 on page 476.

Gleason Beach

2

Location: 4.75 miles north of Bodega Bay off Highway 1. A trail leads to the beach.

Parking: Free parking lot.

Hours: 8 AM to one hour after sunset.

Facilities: None.

Contact: For beach information, contact the Russian River District Office of the California Department of Parks and Recreation at (707) 865-2391.

See number 14 on page 476.

Goat Rock Beach

4

Location: South of Jenner, at the end of Goat Rock Road, off Highway 1 near the mouth of the Russian River.

Parking: $5 entrance fee per vehicle.

Hours: 8 AM to one hour after sunset.

Facilities: Rest rooms, picnic tables, and fire pits.

Contact: For beach information, contact the Russian River District Office of the California Department of Parks and Recreation at (707) 865-2391.

See number 19 on page 476.

Miwok Beach

2

Location: 2.5 miles north of Bodega Bay off Highway 1. A trail leads to the beach.

Parking: Free parking lot.

Hours: 8 AM to one hour after sunset.

Facilities: None.

Contact: For beach information, contact the Russian River District Office of the California Department of Parks and Recreation at (707) 865-2391.

See number 8 on page 476.

to August, when the waves are less menacing and the seals are mating. Goat Rock Beach, incidentally, is a great place to collect driftwood. In fact, you're encouraged to help yourself and haul it away.

The other Sonoma Coast Beach accesses are more for surf casters and meditative types. Sure, they're marvelous to look at and fully deserving of the melodic names bestowed upon them. But after slipping and sliding down long, steep paths to get at several of them, we're more inclined to pull the car over and enjoy them from a safe distance.

For More Information

Contact Sonoma Coast State Beaches, Salmon Creek Lagoon, Bodega Bay, CA 94923; (707) 875-3483. Or contact the Russian River District Department of Parks and Recreation, P.O. Box 123, Duncan Mills, CA 95430; (707) 865-2391.

Portuguese Beach

3

Location: 4.25 miles north of Bodega Bay off Highway 1. A trail leads to the beach.

Parking: Free parking lot.

Hours: 8 AM to one hour after sunset.

Facilities: Rest rooms.

Contact: For beach information, contact the Russian River District Office of the California Department of Parks and Recreation at (707) 865-2391.

See number 13 on page 476.

Schoolhouse Beach

2

Location: Four miles north of Bodega Bay off Highway 1. A steep trail leads to the beach.

Parking: Free parking lot.

Hours: 8 AM to one hour after sunset.

Facilities: None.

Contact: For beach information, contact the Russian River District Office of the California Department of Parks and Recreation at (707) 865-2391.

See number 12 on page 476.

Shell Beach

4

Location: Seven miles north of Bodega Bay off Highway 1.

Parking: Free parking lot.

Hours: 8 AM to one hour after sunset.

Facilities: Rest rooms.

Contact: For beach information, contact the Russian River District Office of the California Department of Parks and Recreation at (707) 865-2391.

See number 17 on page 476.

Wright's Beach

RV 3

Location: Six miles north of Bodega Bay off Highway 1.

Parking: $5 entrance fee per vehicle.

Hours: 8 AM to one hour after sunset.

Facilities: Rest rooms, picnic tables, and fire pits. There are 30 tent and RV campsites. Fees are $17 to $19 per night. For camping reservations, call Destinet at (800) 444-7275.

Contact: For beach information, contact the Russian River District Office of the California Department of Parks and Recreation at (707) 865-2391.

See number 16 on page 476.

Jenner

Location: 70 miles north of San Francisco, along Highway 1.
Population: 300
Area Code: 707 **Zip Code:** 95450

Human beings take a backseat to nature in the hamlet of Jenner. The physical setting on the mouth of the Russian River is nothing short of regal, and the town is suitably humble, bravely clinging to the cliffs along the riverside and the curves of Highway 1. Just south of town, vista points offer an opportunity to watch this undammed and undeveloped California river roll westward into the Pacific. Pull over and enjoy. The area is rich in history as well as scenic beauty. Russian fur trappers originally named the river Slavyanka, meaning "Russian girl," but that proved too much of a mouthful so Americans renamed it the Russian River.

Later settlers used this stretch of Highway 1, which was carved into the jagged cliff tops in 1874–75, as a logging trail. Hacked redwoods were floated down the Russian River toward the sea, where they were loaded onto boats and wagons. If you'd like to learn more about this era, the Jenner Visitor Center (Highway 1, 875-3483) delves into Sonoma Coast history in greater detail.

North of town, you ascend the Jenner Grade, one of the most dramatic and scenic stretches of highway on the coast, rivaling even Big Sur for vertigo-inducing thrills and chills as you negotiate a series of steeply graded switchbacks. Do we need to add "Fasten your safety belt"? If you'd like to set a spell before tackling this driving challenge, Jenner and its environs offer a handful of fine restaurants and inns that burrow off the highway.

Beaches

The state owns much of the coastal land north of the Russian River mouth. Several beaches

North Jenner Beaches

Location: A series of steep coastal-access trails lead from Highway 1 to the beach along a two-mile stretch between Jenner and Russian Gulch.
Parking: Free roadside turnouts.
Hours: 8 AM to one hour after sunset.
Facilities: None.
Contact: For beach information, contact the Russian River District Office of the California Department of Parks and Recreation at (707) 865-2391.

See number 20 on page 476.

Russian Gulch

Location: 2.5 miles north of Jenner off Highway 1. A trail leads to the beach.
Parking: Free parking lot.
Hours: 8 AM to one hour after sunset.
Facilities: Rest rooms.
Contact: For beach information, contact the Russian River District Office of the California Department of Parks and Recreation at (707) 865-2391.

See number 21 on page 476.

Vista Point

Location: Four miles north of Jenner, at Meyers Grade Road and Highway 1.
Parking: Free parking lot.
Hours: 8 AM to one hour after sunset.
Facilities: Rest rooms and picnic tables.
Contact: For beach information, contact the Russian River District Office of the California Department of Parks and Recreation at (707) 865-2391.

See number 22 on page 476.

Navigating the North Coast

We hate to sound like a couple of old biddies, but driving the North Coast of California is not like driving the Oldsmobile to church on Sunday morning. It requires a focused mind and a steady pair of hands to see you safely through.

Beginning just north of Bodega Bay, Highway 1 hugs the rugged, rolling contours of the coastal cliffs, sending vehicles soaring skyward, twisting around hairpin turns and edging precariously toward the sides of cliffs (with seaward drops of hundreds of feet and no protective guardrails). If the topography doesn't unnerve you, Highway 1 might set roaming beasties or fully laden lumber trucks in your path. Indeed, this section of the Coast Highway is even more treacherous and difficult to drive than the legendary Big Sur. Not to say that it doesn't have its rewards, mainly in the form of unobstructed views of wild, pristine coastline perhaps unrivaled anywhere in the world.

Unless God is your copilot, though, you might want to ponder the following driving tips. We picked them up from local sources and through personal experience on our many forays up and down the coast.

- As this two-lane road is the only north-south route on the coast, Highway 1 bears a fair amount of traffic. Don't get involved in a test of wills or a drag race with those driving too fast or slow for your liking. Pull off the highway onto one of the many turnouts and overlooks that have been carved into the roadside to let hotfoots streak by, or wait patiently for slowpokes to do so.
- State law prohibits holding up more than five vehicles in a row (although the act of stopping a pokey vehicle to ticket the driver for this infraction would seem to stymie progress even more). If you've got a convoy trailing you, be a sport and pull over to the side to let 'em by.

between Jenner and Russian Gulch, collectively known as the **North Jenner Beaches**, are reachable by steep trails down eroding bluffs. **Russian Gulch** itself, a unit of the Sonoma Coast State Beaches, is covered under that heading in the previous entry. **Vista Point** is a relatively new overlook, picnic spot, and beach-access point located four miles north of Jenner, where Meyers Grade Road meets Highway 1.

Bunking Down

Sea Coast Hide-A-Ways (21350 Highway 1, 847-3278) is the biggest vacation-home rental agency in town. All their rentals are clean and comfortably furnished, with full kitchens. Many travelers opt for **River's End** (Highway 1, 865-2484, $$), a many-splendored operation: excellent restaurant, boat-rental agency, general store, bar, campground, and lodge. The remodeled cabins at River's End hug the cliffs and offer stupendous views of the ocean. Another restaurant/lodge operation is **Murphy's Jenner by the Sea** (Highway 1, 865-2377, $$). You can choose between bed-and-breakfast-style rooms and suites at River House (on the Russian River) or Longfellow's Landing (by a creek). In addition, Murphy's has a cabin that sleeps eight, and they handle private home rentals.

- Don't try to pass anyone. There's a firm double-yellow line plastered on most of this road and straightaways are scarcer than gull's teeth.
- Stay alert at night and in the frequent fog. Keep an eye out for wildlife—especially deer—and cattle.
- Turn on your headlights in the fog, using normal (not high) beams. This not only helps you see, but also allows oncoming traffic to see you.
- Watch out for the many bicyclists sharing the road. This requires extra caution from drivers because so little shoulder room (if any) exists. In other words, there's no margin for error. One tiny mistake can mean somebody's life.

This brings up another aside. As much as we admire this physically challenging and eco-friendly mode of transportation, we can't quite grasp the pleasure of bicycling the Coast Highway. Riding side by side with cars and campers, cyclists huff and puff while fighting stiff winds and steep grades on heavily laden mountain bikes. Indeed, in some ways, bicyclists are the biggest hazard a driver faces here. The experience of rounding an uphill hairpin curve to find a horde of latex-clad pedal-pushers in your lane is enough to rattle the best driver's nerves. Maybe a bike lane could be tacked onto the Coast Highway (we'd vote for that!), but until that unlikely day, be careful out there—drivers and riders alike.

Our concern is motivated by a personal loss. Last year, a friend died cycling the Pacific Coast Highway in Northern California. He was attempting to bike from Seattle to San Francisco and was hit from behind by a car whose driver did not even see him. Though he wore a helmet, he never knew what hit him. R.I.P., Tom Sinclair.

Coastal Cuisine

River's End (Highway 1, 865-2484, $$$) is one of the premier restaurants on the Northern California coast. In addition to the restaurant they run an on-premises cooking school. The fare tends to hearty game dishes—rabbit, duck, quail, venison—and seafood, all prepared with Germanic flair, assembled with local ingredients, and pungently flavorful. (We can heartily recommend their coconut-covered prawns and plump Pacific oysters.) A splendid meal is all but guaranteed, but you must make reservations well in advance. The view of the ocean from the restaurant and the deck that encircles it is sublime.

Jenner's other restaurant of note is **Murphy's Jenner by the Sea** (Highway 1, 865-2377, $$$), which offers seafood, vegetarian, and beef dishes; a full bar graced by a stone fireplace; and, on weekends, live jazz, classical, and New Age music.

For More Information

Contact the Sonoma County Convention and Visitors Bureau, 5000 Roberts Lake Road, Suite A, Rohnert Park, CA 94928; (707) 566-8100.

Fort Ross

Location: 11 miles north of Jenner, on Highway 1.

The most historic site in the area is Fort Ross, a 1,160-acre Russian stronghold 11 miles north of Jenner. (Not to worry, Joint Chiefs: Fort Ross was abandoned by the Russians in 1841.) The original Russian settlers came to the California coast searching for new sources of fur (mainly sea otters) and food for the enrichment of the Tsarist Russian empire. They landed in Bodega Bay in 1809 and held all the coastal land from there to this site, building the fort in 1812 out of local redwood. Eighty Native Americans (Aleuts) and 25 Russian fur trappers kept the Spanish at bay—actually, at ocean—while the job was completed. Fort Rossiya was also a base for growing wheat to supply Russian colonies in Alaska. The Russians, unlike the Spanish, did not try to suppress Native American culture or subjugate the natives. Instead, they intermarried with the local tribe (the Kashaya Pomo) and traded extensively with them. Even today, the largest collection of Pomo artifacts is stored in a museum in St. Petersburg, Russia.

Fort Ross has been faithfully preserved. Restored and reconstructed buildings include barracks, a stockade, a Russian Orthodox

We Brake for Cows

Highway 1 through Sonoma County is cow country. The critters are all over the darn place, wandering aimlessly like a herd of acid-dosed Woodstock pilgrims trying to find the freeway shoulder they parked their van on. During one passage through coastal Sonoma, we were coming around a mountain when we suddenly had to screech to a halt. A big black cow was standing in our lane, staring us down like a Bergmanesque apparition of death. Pea-soup fog was draped around the beast's neck like a shawl, rendering her all but invisible. We skidded to a stop inches from her steaming nostrils. The cow slowly, carefully appraised the situation, then lumbered over to let us pass. Moove, she seemed to say. We pulled around the bovine obstruction and continued on our journey. Had an RV come rumbling around the bend at that moment, Sonoma would have been either one head of cattle poorer, or the world, one beach book lighter.

On a recent visit we counted no fewer than nine bossies in the road. A clump of three clung to an inside curve, barely off the shoulder, pressed against the cliffs. Others nonchalantly clomped across the road. It was a vertical plunge of hundreds of feet to the ocean, and a sheer wall of rock rose high above the road. How did the cows get there? How would they get back to wherever they came from? (Seems like a case for *The X-Files* if you ask us.) They pose a clear danger to unwary motorists, particularly the show-offish stooge trying to prove how well his new sports car can handle the curves, just like on the commercials. If it were foggy, a sap like that would be history. We had to wonder how many cars have tumbled over the cliffs in Sonoma County, with Elsie's face their last conscious memory.

chapel, blockhouses, and the commandant's residence. An on-site museum is open daily from 10 AM to 4:30 PM (19005 Highway 1, 847-3286). A "Living History Day" is held on the last Saturday in July, to re-create a typical day at the fort in 1836. (Bring your own Stoli?)

Beaches

Just beyond Fort Ross's front gate, beachgoers will find **Fort Ross Cove**, a small beach frequented by shell collectors, and a nearby garden filled with exotic plants is a popular picnicking spot. An underwater park for divers, designated **Fort Ross Reef**, sits offshore. Three miles south is Fort Ross Reef Campground. Trails from the campground lead to coves and beaches in the area, including the beach at Fort Ross.

Bunking Down

If you want to stay overnight but not inside a tent, the **Fort Ross Lodge** (20705 Highway 1, 847-3333, $$) offers accommodations with ocean views, fireplaces, and coastal access in a wide range of prices.

For More Information

Contact Fort Ross State Historic Park, 19005 Highway 1, Sea Ranch, CA 95497; (707) 847-3286.

Fort Ross Cove

3

Location: 11 miles north of Jenner off Highway 1, inside Fort Ross State Historic Park.
Parking: $5 entrance fee per vehicle.
Hours: 10 AM to 4:30 PM.
Facilities: Rest rooms and picnic tables.
Contact: For beach information, contact Fort Ross State Historic Park at (707) 847-3286.

See number 24 on page 476.

Fort Ross Reef

RV 2

Location: Eight miles north of Jenner off Highway 1.
Parking: $2 entrance fee per vehicle.
Hours: 8 AM to one hour after sunset.
Facilities: Rest rooms, picnic tables, and fire grills. There are 20 tent and RV campsites. The fee is $10 per night. No camping reservations.
Contact: For beach information, contact Fort Ross State Historic Park at (707) 847-3286.

See number 23 on page 476.

Timber Cove

Location: 12 miles north of Jenner, along Highway 1.

Bunking Down

Timber Cove is the site of a couple of unrelated and dissimilar operations. One is a luxury lodge and restaurant, the **Timber Cove Inn** (21780 Highway 1, Jenner, CA 95450; 707-847-3231, $$$), at which you'll pay between $85 and $350 a night. The other is the **Timber Cove Campground and Boat Landing** (21350 Highway 1, 847-3278). Your choice—splurge or save?—but if you're coming to the campground, bring a tent or RV. At the inn, just bring your work-weary self and a credit card; they'll take it from there. If you want to cut down on the cost of a stay at the Timber Cove Inn, book a nonocean-view room. The on-site restaurant is as lavish and upscale as the inn, with a French-Continental menu that's on the expensive side. Both inn and campground are situated on cliffs overlooking the spectacular coast. At the campground, you will find all things boat- and fishing-related—rentals, launches, licenses, tackle shop. At the inn, you may be shocked to discover a 72-foot obelisk by the late sculptor Benjamin Bufano, entitled *The Expanding Universe*. Ponder that while you're watching the whales go by; a major moment of clarity couldn't be far behind.

For More Information

Contact the Timber Cove Campground and Boat Landing, 21350 Highway 1, Jenner, CA 95450; (707) 847-3278.

Timber Cove

Location: 12 miles north of Jenner off Highway 1.

Parking: $6 entrance fee per person.

Hours: 8 AM to sunset.

Facilities: Rest rooms, showers, picnic tables, and fire pits. There are 40 tent and RV campsites, with hookups. Fees are $17 to $19 per night. For camping reservations, contact Timber Cove Campground at (707) 847-3278.

Contact: For beach information, contact Timber Cove Campground and Boat Landing at (707) 847-3278.

See number 25 on page 476.

Stillwater Cove Regional Park

Location: 16 miles north of Jenner, off Highway 1.

Four miles north of Fort Ross is the lovely **Stillwater Cove Regional Park**, a county-run facility that is often passed without a second look by tourists hellbent on making Mendocino before nightfall. It's more popular with locals, who are given discounts on the day-use and camping fees. The appeal is obvious. A looped hiking trail leads along Stockoff Creek, through a small forest, and down to a cove frequented by abalone divers.

Bunking Down

Near the park is an unusual place to stay: **Stillwater Cove Ranch** (22555 Highway 1, Jenner, CA 95450; 707-847-3227, $). It's a find in that coastal accommodations in Sonoma County are few and far between, and rarely are they priced so reasonably. Actually, the place is not so much a ranch as an assortment of rustic rooms and cabins. The ocean is right across the highway, making this a good spot for fishing, whale watching, hiking—and making runs in either direction to enjoy the uncommonly good restaurants between the towns of Jenner and Gualala. Good thing, too: they don't serve meals at Stillwater Cove Ranch, and all but a handful of rooms lack cooking facilities.

For More Information

Contact Stillwater Cove Park, 2300 County Center Drive, Building A (Suite 120), Santa Rosa, CA 95403; (707) 847-3245.

Stillwater Cove Regional Park

Location: 16 miles north of Jenner off Highway 1.

Parking: $3 entrance fee per vehicle.

Hours: Sunrise to sunset.

Facilities: Rest rooms, showers, picnic tables, and fire grills. There are 23 tent and RV campsites. Fees is $14 per night. No camping reservations.

Contact: For beach information, contact Stillwater Cove Regional Park at (707) 847-3245.

See number 26 on page 476.

Salt Point State Park

Location: 18 miles north of Jenner, on Highway 1.

This is another heaven-sent state park, the perfect way station on the North Coast for those who want a bit of everything. Among its 5,970 acres, the park has six miles of rugged shoreline with dozens of hard-sand cove beaches, as well as hiking trails that head inland and reach elevations of 1,000 feet in the foothills. There are both coastal (Gerstle Cove) and upland (Woodside) campgrounds. The former is situated by the Gerstle Cove Underwater Reserve, a diving and tidepooling spot with 30 improved sites. The latter is a bit farther removed, offering 109 improved sites, 20 tent-only, and 10 hiker/cyclist sites.

The most rewarding hike is to **Stump Beach**, a two-miler that leads along the bluff tops to a lovely cove beach that derives its name from the driftwood that washes up here, much of it the residue of a dying logging industry. Nearby is **Gerstle Cove**, an ecological preserve that serves as a whale-watching site December through April. Two more beaches—**Fisk Mill Cove** and **North Horseshoe Cove**—lie off Highway 1, one and two miles north (respectively) of Stump Beach. Fisk Mill has facilities, and an entry fee is charged. North Horseshoe Cove costs nothing, and nothing is provided—except, of course, an exceptionally scenic beach.

From April to June, the 300-acre Kruse Rhododendron State Reserve, located a mile inland from Salt Point State Park, is ablaze with the multicolored rhododendron. These showy shrubs were planted to replace a forest of firs that was destroyed by fire. The reserve is also

Fisk Mill Cove
(a part of Salt Point State Park)

4

Location: 20 miles north of Jenner, off Highway 1.
Parking: $5 entrance fee per vehicle.
Hours: Half hour before sunrise to half hour after sunset.
Facilities: Rest rooms, picnic tables, and fire pits.
Contact: For beach information, contact Salt Point State Park at (707) 847-3221.

See number 30 on page 476.

Gerstle Cove
(a part of Salt Point State Park)

RV 5

Location: 18 miles north of Jenner, off Highway 1.
Parking: $5 entrance fee per vehicle.
Hours: Half hour before sunrise to half hour after sunset.
Facilities: Rest rooms, picnic tables, and fire grills. There are 30 campsites at Gerstle Cove for tents and RVs. There are also 79 campsites at Woodside for tents and RVs, 20 walk-in sites for tents, and 10 hiker/biker sites for tents. Fees are $3 to $14 per night. There is one group campground for up to 10 vehicles. The fee is $120 per night. For camping reservations, call Destinet at (800) 444-7275.
Contact: For beach information, contact Salt Point State Park at (707) 847-3221.

See number 28 on page 476.

noteworthy for its extensive system of hiking trails covered with foliage ranging from rhododendrons to redwoods.

North Horseshoe Cove
(a part of Salt Point State Park)

Location: 21 miles north of Jenner, off Highway 1.

Parking: Free parking lot.

Hours: Half hour before sunrise to half hour after sunset.

Facilities: None.

Contact: For beach information, contact Salt Point State Park at (707) 847-3221.

See number 31 on page 476.

Ocean Cove

Location: 17 miles north of Jenner, off Highway 1.

Parking: $5 entrance fee per vehicle.

Hours: 7 AM to 7 PM.

Facilities: Rest rooms, showers, picnic tables, and fire pits. There are 116 tent and RV campsites. The fee is $12 per night. For camping reservations, call Ocean Cove Campground at (707) 847-3422.

Contact: For beach information, contact Ocean Cove General Store and Campground at (707) 847-3422.

See number 27 on page 476.

Bunking Down

A mile south of Salt Point State Park is **Salt Point Lodge** (23255 Highway 1, 847-3234, $), a contemporary motel with reasonable rates, a broad grassy lawn, playground equipment, a sundeck, a sauna, and a hot tub. The management also runs a small restaurant serving three meals a day. Across the road is **Ocean Cove** (Highway 1, 847-3422), a private beach and bluff where you can camp, fish, and dive for abalone.

For More Information

Contact Salt Point State Park, 25050 Highway 1, Jenner, CA 95459; (707) 847-3221.

Stump Beach
(a part of Salt Point State Park)

Location: 19 miles north of Jenner, off Highway 1.

Parking: Free parking lot.

Hours: Half hour before sunrise to half hour after sunset.

Facilities: Rest rooms, picnic tables, and fire pits.

Contact: For beach information, contact Salt Point State Park at (707) 847-3221.

See number 29 on page 476.

Bobbing for Abalone

Swathed in a shell of mother-of-pearl, endowed with a delectable taste, the abalone is one of the most prized denizens of the deep along the California shoreline. Abalone belong to the mollusk clan, a large phylum that includes more than 100,000 species of invertebrate critters, such as squid, clams, oysters, mussels, snails, and octopi. The abalone is one of the largest mollusks, ranging from four to ten inches in width.

There are more than 100 species of abalone worldwide, eight of which dwell along California's coast, though the term "dwell" could be interchanged with "dwindle" because they've been hunted to near extinction. They live on rocks in shallow water along rugged shorelines, clinging tenaciously to their perches and feeding on algae. The couch potatoes of the sea-life set, abalone are so stationary that they're often covered with other organisms. In order to wrest them from their resting places one needs a pry bar—a miniature crowbar available in bait-and-tackle shops.

Humans have long valued abalone for its tasty meat (which is actually its visceral mass, or muscle) and its beautiful oval shell, but we're not the only ones who dig these crazy mollusks. Sea otters—who eat one-third of their body weight daily—also relish abalone. Once they've pried the shell loose, they smash them open on the rocks and scoop out their bounty.

The North Coast is one place where abalone are relatively plentiful, and bagging a few is a regular rite of vacation passage for some intrepid souls. But one must be prepared for the battle before climbing into Neptune's bathtub, as the water along the Sonoma coast is cold and the surf can be brutal. Here are a few pointers for abalone hounds:

- Wear a wet suit. The water temperature ranges from 48 to 52 degrees most of the time.
- Have a valid fishing license in plain view on your person, preferably in a clear, waterproof pouch.
- Use a seven-inch measuring bar to make sure the abalone shell is of legal size. Return anything smaller.
- Use a proper pry bar. Improper tools can break the shell and kill the abalone immediately.
- Never wade or dive alone.
- Wait for a good minus tide (-1.0 foot or better).
- Beware of sleeper waves—waves of unusual force that rise suddenly.
- Check rocky kelp beds first. This is where abalone are most often found.
- Take only your legal limit of four. Wardens will bust you good and proper if you get greedy, and it won't do much for your karma, either.

Stewarts Point

Location: Six miles north of Salt Point State Park, on Highway 1.

Two roadside curiosities converge at the historic site of Stewarts Point, overlooking Fisherman's Bay. One is Stewarts Point Store, a nifty general emporium on Highway 1 that's truly a relic from a bygone era. From the mid-19th to the early 20th century, so-called doghole schooners turned this rugged shore into a busy port town that serviced the logging trade. The only trustworthy way to haul the timber from the north woods was by sea, with the cargo being loaded primarily via cables tied from the bluffs to the anchored ships. Most of the lumber ended up in San Francisco, where the redwood was incorporated into Victorian homes while the Douglas fir was used for schooners. The doghole schooners were so named because they had to be nimble enough to anchor in bays that were just big enough, as the sailors used to say, "for a dog to turn around in."

The store and an abandoned stagecoach-stop hotel are all that remain from these colorful times. As you pass the turnoff to Tin Barn Road, look to the east for the second curiosity. You'll spy Odiyan, a Tibetan Buddhist monastery, as anomalous as the Russian Orthodox chapel at Fort Ross. It's not open to the public.

For More Information

Contact the Stewarts Point Store, 3200 Highway 1, Sea Ranch, CA 95497; (707) 785-2406.

Sea Ranch

Location: 24 miles north of Jenner, along Highway 1.
Population: 1,300
Area Code: 707 **Zip Code:** 95497

The last 10 miles of coastline in Sonoma County belongs lock, stock, and barrel to a private development known as Sea Ranch. It's a planned, 5,500-acre community for the second-home wealthy. Originally meant to be an exclusive haven, Sea Ranch met stiff resistance from the California Coastal Commission and environmental groups who objected to the land grab. (At one time, Sea Ranch was part of a 17,500-acre Mexican land grant, Rancho de Herman, and a former sheep ranch). The developers finally compromised and allowed seven coastal-access footpaths, spaced every two

Black Point Beach
(a part of Sea Ranch)

Location: Park in the roadside lot off Highway 1 just north of Sea Ranch Lodge at Milepost 50.8. Hike the public-access trail to the beach.
Parking: $3 entrance fee per vehicle.
Hours: Sunrise to sunset.
Facilities: None.
Contact: For beach information, contact Gualala Point Regional Park at (707) 785-2377.

See number 32 on page 476.

Pebble Beach
(a part of Sea Ranch)

Location: Park in the roadside lot off Highway 1 near Milepost 52.3. Hike the public-access trail to the beach.
Parking: $3 entrance fee per vehicle.
Hours: Sunrise to sunset.
Facilities: None.
Contact: For beach information, contact Gualala Point Regional Park at (707) 785-2377.

See number 33 on page 476.

Shell Beach
(a part of Sea Ranch)

Location: Park in the roadside lot off Highway 1 near Milepost 55.2. Hike the public-access trail to the beach.
Parking: $3 entrance fee per vehicle.
Hours: Sunrise to sunset.
Facilities: None.
Contact: For beach information, contact Gualala Point Regional Park at (707) 785-2377.

See number 35 on page 476.

Stengel Beach
(a part of Sea Ranch)

Location: Park in the roadside lot off Highway 1 near Milepost 54.0. Hike the public-access trail to the beach.
Parking: $3 entrance fee per vehicle.
Hours: Sunrise to sunset.
Facilities: None.
Contact: For beach information, contact Gualala Point Regional Park at (707) 785-2377.

See number 34 on page 476.

miles through their 10-mile oceanfront property. Each trail is about a quarter-mile long and leads to a cove beach, but a stringent set of rules governing would-be hikers just about kills whatever fun you might have had on the way.

In all fairness, we have to admit that Sea Ranch does boast one of the top golf courses in California, and the complex has won awards for its environmentally sensitive architecture and planning. But all of the houses—wood-shingled and built low to the ground, blending in with the pines and fir trees—look drearily similar in the cold light of day. In truth, Sea Ranch struck us as devoid of life as the surface of the moon.

Walk-On Beach
(a part of Sea Ranch)

Location: Park in the roadside lot off Highway 1 and Leeward Spur Road, near Milepost 52.3. Hike the public-access trail to the beach.

Parking: $3 entrance fee per vehicle.

Hours: Sunrise to sunset.

Facilities: None.

Contact: For beach information, contact Gualala Point Regional Park at (707) 785-2377.

See number 36 on page 476.

Beaches

The cove beaches here include, from south to north, **Black Point Beach**, **Pebble Beach**, **Stengel Beach**, **Shell Beach**, and **Walk-On Beach**. They are all pretty much the same, and the short trails that access them are heavily regulated. We walked to the end of three Sea Ranch trails before throwing in the beach towel. There are no facilities save for portable rest rooms at the trailheads, and should you stray off course, the parking gremlins will get you (i.e., if you don't have a parking permit, you could find your car shod with the dreaded Denver Boot).

Bunking Down

Some of the houses at Sea Ranch can be rented, or you can lay in at the **Sea Ranch Lodge** (Box 44, 785-2371, $$$).

For More Information

Public access to beaches at Sea Ranch is administered by Gualala Point Regional Park. Contact the park at (707) 785-2377.

Gualala Point Regional Park

Location: 1 mile south of the Mendocino County line, off Highway 1.

The 125-acre **Gualala Point Regional Park** is officially in Sonoma County, even though it looks across the river at Gualala, which is in Mendocino County. Gualala Point shares a fence with the adjacent Sea Ranch, which deeded the land for the park. Every 50 yards or so, you are reminded of this fact by signs warning against trespassing on private property. But the view north toward the river mouth, the ocean, and the town of Gualala is rewarding. Tuck your $3 entrance fee into the self-pay box and, before setting out for the beach, peruse the visitors center's collection of relics from the days when Gualala was a logging port. A trail leads to Gualala Point, which offers even more spectacular views of the rocky coastline. A campground, with a selection of developed and primitive sites for the outdoors inclined, lies on the other side of Highway 1, along the Gualala River.

Gualala Point Regional Park

Location: One mile south of the Mendocino County line off Highway 1.
Parking: $3 entrance fee per vehicle.
Hours: Sunrise to sunset.
Facilities: Rest rooms, showers, picnic tables, and fire pits. There are 26 tent and RV campsites. Fees are $14 for improved sites, $3 for primitive sites. No camping reservations.
Contact: For beach information, contact Gualala Point Regional Park at (707) 785-2377.

See number 37 on page 476.

For More Information

Contact Gualala Point Regional Park, (707) 785-2377.

Mendocino County

Mendocino is seemingly several counties in one. Its 130 miles of coastline extend from the unpretentious town of Gualala to the southern end of what is justifiably known as the Lost Coast. In between these borders are some of the state's most appealingly romantic retreats. Then there's Fort Bragg, the county seat and a hardworking center of commerce.

Southern Mendocino County reprises the splendid isolation of Sonoma County. The two regions are, in fact, often lumped together under the nickname "Mendonoma." Low-key and perfectly appealing towns—Gualala, Anchor Bay, Point Arena, and Elk—appear every 10 scenic miles or so, each with its own quiet charm. At Albion, north of where Highway 128 funnels into Highway 1, the tone becomes more upscale. Albion, Little River, and Mendocino are bonafide "destinations," to borrow a travel-industry term that signals good food, fine lodging, wine, views, shopping, art, attractions, recreation, and culture. Far-northern *(continued on page 504)*

Coastal Mendocino County's Climate

Fort Bragg Averages

	Daily High Temp. (°F)	Daily Low Temp. (°F)	Rainfall (inches)
January	55	40	7.8
February	57	41	5.9
March	57	41	5.1
April	59	43	3.1
May	61	46	1.0
June	63	48	0.4
July	64	49	0.1
August	64	50	0.4
September	65	50	0.7
October	63	47	2.7
November	60	44	5.4
December	56	41	6.8
Yearly Average	**60**	**45**	**39.4**

Source: National Weather Service data, National Oceanographic and Atmospheric Administration.

Mendocino County

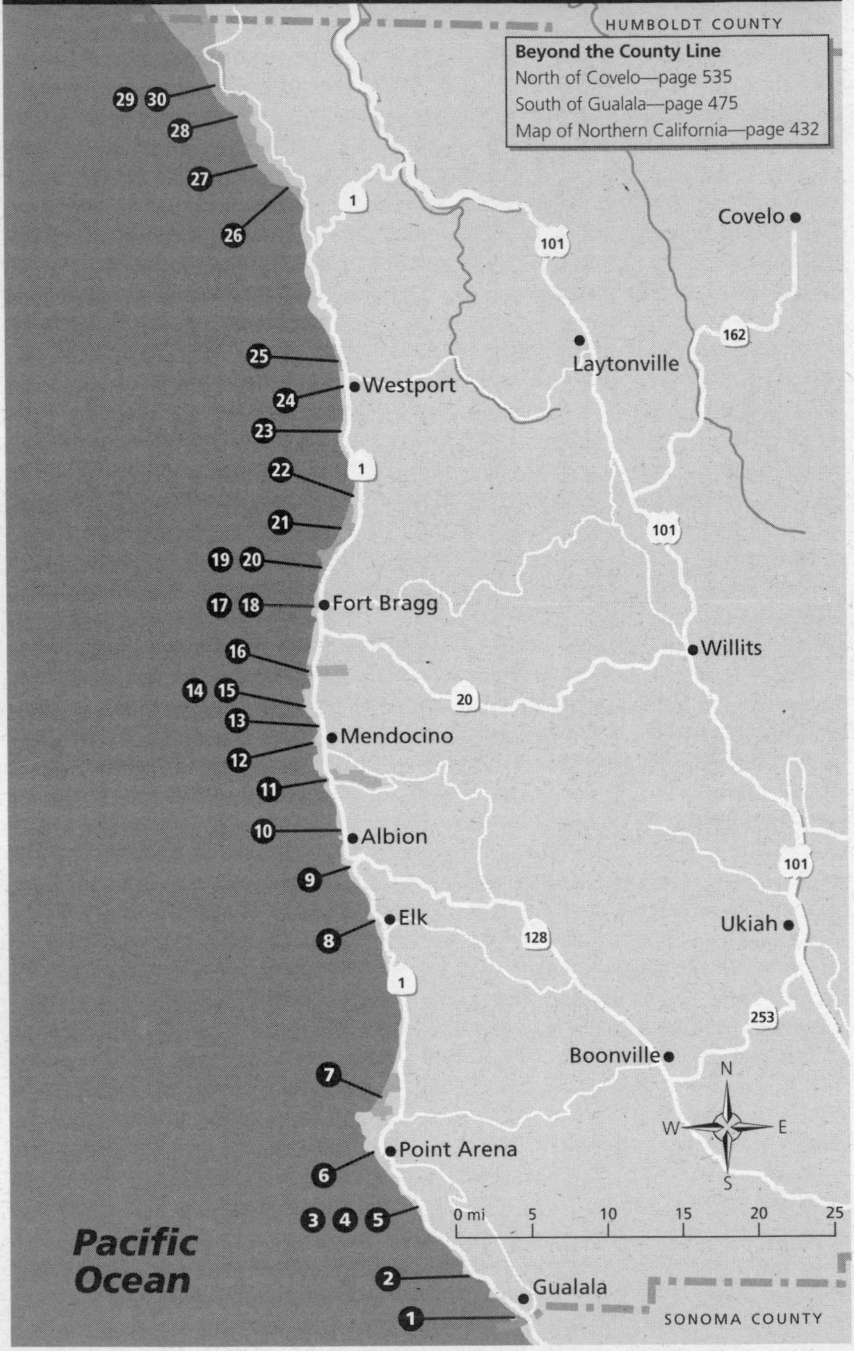

HUMBOLDT COUNTY
Beyond the County Line
North of Covelo—page 535
South of Gualala—page 475
Map of Northern California—page 432
Covelo
Laytonville
Westport
Fort Bragg
Willits
Mendocino
Albion
Elk
Ukiah
Boonville
Point Arena
Gualala
SONOMA COUNTY
Pacific Ocean
0 mi 5 10 15 20 25
N
W
E
S
1
101
162
20
128
253
29 30
28
27
26
25
24
23
22
21
19 20
17 18
16
14 15
13
12
11
10
9
8
7
6
3 4 5
2
1

Mendocino County Beaches

Map of Northern California—page 432

(continued from page 501) Mendocino County has no cultural appeal whatsoever, because most of it is pristine wilderness—which in itself is quite a sufficient raison d'être.

The beaches are as varied and fascinating as the towns. As usual, the state of California has been kind to the coast, preserving exceptional locales such as Manchester State Beach, Van Damme State Park, Mendocino Headlands State Park, Jug Handle State Reserve, MacKerricher State Park, Westport-Union Landing State Beach, and Sinkyone Wilderness State Park. The flip side of Mendocino County's romantic allure is the palette of possibilities it affords those who love to play outdoors. These include canoeing and kayaking on the ocean and the rivers that empty into it; hiking, biking, and diving; and, finally, openly offering prayers to the gods for having created this glorious county.

Key to the Symbols

Bike path Camping Food and drink Hiking Nude

Pier RVs allowed Surfing Volleyball

Crowd Rating

sweet solitude . . . moderate crowds . . . wall-to-wall

Overall Rating

1 2 3 4 5

don't bother . . . worth a visit . . . beach heaven

Gualala and Anchor Bay

Location: One mile north of the Sonoma County line on Highway 1. Anchor Bay is four miles north of Gualala on Highway 1.
Population: 600
Area Code: 707 **Zip Code:** 95445

Gualala (properly pronounced *WAHlahlah*) is a town without airs. The stuffy manners observed next door at Sea Ranch are of no use here; in fact, they're as out of place as a sombrero on an Eskimo. The only birdies Gualalans shoot have wings, and the carts they tend to ride are manufactured by Harley-Davidson.

Gualala has the wide-open feel of the Old West, to which it bears a legitimate connection. Gualala was once a thriving mill town, but once the forests were depleted, it fell to other means of making a living, including fishing for salmon and trout. The Gualala River runs parallel to the ocean for two miles here, creating the oddest sort of beachfront (makes sense that *gualala* is an Indian word meaning "where waters meet"). You double your viewing pleasure, but it's hard to figure out what you're peering at—or how to get down to have a closer look.

The source of Gualala's Old West flavor is the town's centerpiece, the Gualala Hotel. This flaking, rusting, creaking structure sits on Highway 1 exhibiting the rakish charm of a frontier saloon. It has operated as a triple-threat bar, inn, and restaurant since before the Great Earthquake of 1906 hit San Francisco. (We found ourselves wondering how this ramshackle old place survived that destructive temblor.) Entering Gualala, one feels compelled to hitch the car to the post out front, hop the dusty wooden steps, and say, Stetson in hand, "I'd be much obliged iff'n you'd direct me to the nearest livery, stranger." Because Gualala is more of a sloppy, let-it-all-hang-out kind of place than its neighbors, the town has witnessed a steady influx of growth, as evidenced by the countless "Land For Sale" signs dotting the countryside. Though all the new business no doubt boosts the local economy, it can only mean that sweet, antiquarian Gualala will eventually turn trendy, especially when the inevitable occurs—i.e., that the Gualala Hotel succumbs to old age.

One sign of the new wave can be found diagonally across the street from the venerable hotel. It's a slick new inn (opened in August 1994) that boasts urbanite-friendly amenities like cable TV but also obscures the view of the Gualala River. (For shame, for shame.) Be that as it may, Gualala has so many more natural charms that one need only do what the native Gualalans do. That is, shrug your shoulders and go on about your business.

Beaches

Gualala's beaches start below the Mendocino County line, a mile south of town, with Gualala Point Regional Park, which shares a fence with Sea Ranch (see the entry on page 498 in Sonoma County). In Gualala itself, the **Gualala River** forms a broad lagoon, making it difficult to get to the sand spit that fronts the Pacific. One way around this is to take to the water in a kayak and paddle back and forth between the river and ocean. Darn, left yours at home? Try Gualala Kayak Rental (39175 Highway 1, 884-4705).

The nearest and best access to the beach is actually in tiny Anchor Bay (pop. 175), four miles north of Gualala on Highway 1. A small rocky cove, Collins Landing, is on the property of the Serenisea Lodge; access requires permission. **Fish Rock Beach** can be reached via Anchor Bay Campground (P.O. Box 1529, Gualala, 884-4222). Fish Rock is a nearly mile-long sand beach and campground complex comprising 66 sites on a tall bluff shaded by redwoods. A modest day-use fee is charged to gain access.

Bunking Down

If you're in an adventurous, devil-may-care mood, the **Gualala Hotel** (Highway 1, 884-3441, $) is a relatively inexpensive blast from the past. The place desperately pines for a coat of paint, but as one guest wrote in the ledger, "Nostalgia is good for the soul." When we arrived, no one was at the front desk, a weather-beaten table. A hand-lettered sign advised us to "Register for rooms with the bartender." We did just that, negotiating our tariff with a curt but efficient hostess at the bar. The digs aren't grand here—a clean room with shared baths and a ceiling so high you couldn't touch it with the aid of a trampoline—but the comforting cloak of history more than makes up for any lack of luxury. By contrast, what experience could you have at the slick, modern inn across the road that could possibly rival the slice-of-old-time-life you'd enjoy at the Gualala Hotel for less than half the price?

Farther up Highway 1 the tariff and comforts increase considerably at **St. Orres** (36601 Highway 1, 884-3303, $$). This inn is an architectural wonder that offers an incomparably meditative North Coast experience on its 42 acres of rolling woods and gardens. St. Orres was designed by owners Eric and Ted Black, and built on the foundation of the old Seaside Hotel. The Blacks capture the flavor of the earliest Russian settlers with rustic and somewhat exotic elegance. The inn was constructed from 100-year-old timber. The eight European-style rooms have double beds and shared baths, some with views of the forest, some of the ocean. Just beyond the hotel are 12 hand-crafted cottages of varying size and levels of amenities.

The **Old Milano Hotel** (38300 Highway 1, 884-3256, $$) is an atmospheric North Coast lodge (ca. 1905) located directly above the ocean on a bluff top. The Milano has nine guest quarters, all well tended and intimate, including a lovely cottage and a real railroad caboose. Also on the ocean—and actually laying claim to their own cove beach and tidepools—are the **Serenisea Ocean Cabins** (36100 Highway 1, 884-3836. $$). Officially in Anchor Bay, these 22 cabins bring you closer to the beach than any lodge in the area at rates that run

Fish Rock Beach

Location: Four miles north of Gualala at Anchor Bay Campground, off Highway 1.
Parking: $1 entrance fee per vehicle, plus $1 per person.
Hours: 7 AM to 7 PM.
Facilities: Rest rooms, picnic tables, and fireplaces. There are 66 tent and RV campsites, with hookups. Fees are $21 to $23 per night. For camping reservations, contact Anchor Bay Campground at (707) 884-4222.
Contact: For beach information, contact Anchor Bay Campground at (707) 884-4222.

See number 2 on page 502.

Gualala River

Location: Just north of the Sonoma County line, along the north bank of the Gualala River, follow dirt access roads off Highway 1.
Parking: Free parking lot.
Hours: Open 24 hours.
Facilities: None.
Contact: For beach information, contact Gualala Kayak Rental at (707) 884-4705.

See number 1 on page 502.

from $70 to $170. Anchor Bay is also home to one of the state's most luxurious bed-and-breakfasts, the **Whale Watch Inn** (35100 Highway 1, 884-3667, $$$). Admittedly they stretch the B&B concept a bit by including two-person whirlpool baths, breakfast in bed, condo units, golf, and tennis. But the setting is magnificent, and trails lead down to a private beach.

Coastal Cuisine

St. Orres must have been the patron saint of good taste. The **St. Orres Restaurant** (36601 Highway 1, 884-3335, $$$) offers one of the finest and most distinctive dining experiences on the California coast. Set inside a cathedral-like dining room, it is part of a structure suggestive of the area's Russian roots. You won't believe your eyes when you pass the onion domes of St. Orres—Moscow on the Pacific?—located on a bluff along the east side of Highway 1. The food is exceptionally well prepared and competently served. A meal starts with homemade garlic bread and the soup of the day. Entrées might include steelhead and salmon, or such game items as a stuffed wild-boar chop or juicy rabbit. The kitchen utilizes fresh ingredients from on-premises gardens, as well as local produce farms and ranches. In addition to the à-la-carte selections, St. Orres offers a nightly three-course, prix-fixe special. This place is wildly popular, so you'll have to make your reservations well in advance.

The restaurant at the **Gualala Hotel** (Highway 1, 884-4840, $) is the class act of that operation. Old and endowed with a weathered dignity, the dining room dishes up healthy North Coast cuisine such as rigatoni with white beans and tomatoes, as well as heartier fare like chicken and game dishes. If we had to prioritize what to do on the premises of the Gualala Hotel, we'd eat, drink, and sleep in that order.

Night Moves

If you're headed to Gualala for a romantic getaway, you don't need any advice from us. But if you want to bathe in the sloppy friendliness of a hard-drinking saloon, welcome to the **Gualala Hotel** (Highway 1, 884-4840). The scene that greeted us one Saturday night was, no doubt, typical of what has been going on here for a century (after all, this was a favorite haunt of writer Jack London): four members of a motorcycle club stand at the bar, laughing uproariously over a novelty-store item called "Spotted Owl Helper." (In case you haven't noticed, folks in logging country aren't overly fond of this particular feathered friend.) Two more bikers quietly play Pac-Man. A tanned young man with impossibly blond tresses and an earring regales his aging yuppie companions with tales of his acting career down in L.A. He claims to have landed a bit part in a series slated to air opposite *Seinfeld* (talk about a guaranteed ticket to oblivion). Three enormous women in glowing polyester slacks perch on consecutive bar stools and discuss ostrich racing, smoking to beat the Surgeon General. An elderly man sits alone at a corner table, nursing a beer and harboring a grudge. The jukebox plays "Suzie Q" by Creedence Clearwater Revival (the long version).

The heads of moose, deer, and bear adorn the walls, as do various large fish. Photographs document the expeditions that led to these game trophies. One picture shows a dead fish being offered a Hamm's Beer. Another shows a man hanging upside down from a fish scale.

We hung around the bar for a while, then called it a night, since we faced a long drive south the next day. We shouldn't have bothered; the noise and laughter kept us up till the wee hours. For our money, the bar at the Gualala Hotel just might be the wildest hangout between San Francisco and the Oregon border.

For More Information

Contact the Fort Bragg-Mendocino Coast Chamber of Commerce, 332 N. Main Street, P.O. Box 1141, Fort Bragg, CA 95437; (707) 961-6300.

Point Arena

Location: 19 miles north of Gualala, on Highway 1.
Population: 526
Area Code: 707 **Zip Code:** 95468

Officially, Point Arena is a city, the only incorporated one in Mendonoma. But this sleepy burg feels more like Mayberry-by-the-Sea, with its collection of quaint homes, old-time theater, and Main Street–type businesses. Aside from its small-town charm, Point Arena has been blessed with more than its share of coastside delights—a six-mile stretch of both sandy and rocky cove beaches and a scenic, historic lighthouse.

When it was incorporated in 1908, Point Arena could rightly be called a city. The busiest port on the North Coast, it was a rollicking place with saloons, cathouses, banks, and shoot-outs on the main drag. Schooners steamed up from San Francisco daily, and off-duty loggers came out of the woods to make this their Sin City. Some old buildings have survived (Victorian homes, the town theater), but many were destroyed in the 1906 earthquake. The original wharf was obliterated by storms in 1983, and a brand-new Point Arena Pier has since been built on Arena Cove.

The most interesting remnant of the area's history is Point Arena Lighthouse (admission is $2.50 for adults, 50 cents for kids). It's set on the end of a windswept headland, two miles out on Lighthouse Road. The drive to the lighthouse is one of the most amazing on the North Coast, passing through pastureland that ends abruptly at the lip of the raging Pacific. The lighthouse, a blinding white monolith, is pinned against a blue backdrop. Built in 1870, the lighthouse used a powerful Fresnel lens, which is still installed but no longer operable. To see this remarkable piece of engineering requires a six-story ascent (145 steps), but it's worth every huff and puff. The view is spectacular, and the guides are friendly and informative. Some of the tourists, on the other hand, are a pain in the ass, including one whiny woman who nearly shoved us down the circular metallic stairs in her haste to get by.

For more lengthy ruminations on coastal ecology and maritime history, don't miss the excellent museum housed in the Fog Signal Building next door. The lighthouse and museum's setting is timeless enough to have been used as the backdrop for the Mel Gibson movie *Forever Young*, a romantic weeper about a cryogenically preserved World War II bomber pilot seeking his long-lost, lighthouse-dwelling love. Yeah, right.

Beaches

The most accessible beaches in the area are, from south to north, **Schooner Gulch Beach**, **Bowling Ball Beach**, and **Moat Creek Beach**. Schooner Gulch embraces 70 acres of headlands and a short trail that leads to tidepools and a driftwood-covered beach. Bowling Ball is a great beachcombing spot, dotted by black, rounded stones (hence the name), but you must park on the highway shoulder to get to it. ("Park facing south only on Highway 1" reads the warning sign.) At low tide, you can walk south to Schooner Gulch. Moat Creek, better known as "Whiskey Shoals" to the surfers who come here, provides access to Ross Beach. You park in a dirt lot and follow a trail down the cliff. Just north of Point Arena Lighthouse, off Miner Hole Road, you can park near the south bank of the Garcia River, a steelhead fisherman's favorite that's also the wintertime home of tundra swans. From here a path leads to sandy beach at the river's mouth.

Flanking the Point Arena Pier is **Arena Cove Beach**. Some of the best waves on California's North Coast can be found here, but because of the razor-sharp offshore reef this spot's strictly

 Map of Mendocino County beaches—page 502

for experts. Diving for abalone and chartered sportfishing expeditions are big here as well.

Bunking Down

Ever wanted to spend the night with Mel Gibson? Well, you can't. But you can rent a romantic cottage at the lighthouse where he made a movie. At the **Point Arena Lighthouse** (P.O. Box 674, 882-2777, $$), three homes on the property are available as vacation rentals, the proceeds going to the nonprofit lighthouse preservation society. Each has 1,400 square feet of space, three bedrooms, two baths, a kitchen, a fireplace, and a TV. Okay, so you'll have to bring your own sheets, pillow cases, and towels, and the cottages could use a coat of paint. But for $90 to $120 a night in an unbeatable setting, it seems like a steal.

Less adventurous, but perhaps more comfortable, is the **Wharf Master's Inn** (785 Port Road, P.O. Box 674, 882-3171, $$$), which overlooks the pier at Arena Cove. Three separate structures provide surprisingly lush amenities (Jacuzzi, private deck, Victorian appointments), given the spartan fisherman's setting below.

Coastal Cuisine

It's not exactly a gourmet's getaway, but there is a pleasant restaurant beside the Point Arena Pier. The Galley at Arena Cove (882-2189, $$)

Arena Cove Beach

(3)

Location: In Point Arena, at the end of Port Road, off Highway 1.
Parking: Free parking lot.
Hours: Open 24 hours.
Facilities: Rest rooms.
Contact: For beach information, contact Arena Cove Pier at (707) 882-2583.

See number 6 on page 502.

Moat Creek Beach

(2)

Location: 2.5 miles south of Point Arena off Highway 1.
Parking: Free parking lot.
Hours: Open 24 hours.
Facilities: None.
Contact: For beach information, contact the Mendocino Coast Division of the California Department of Parks and Recreation at (707) 937-5804.

See number 5 on page 502.

Bowling Ball Beach

(1)

Location: Follow Bowling Ball Beach trail, which begins in the parking lot at Highway 1 and Schooner Gulch Road.
Parking: Free roadside parking.
Hours: Open 24 hours.
Facilities: None.
Contact: For beach information, contact the Mendocino Coast Division of the California Department of Parks and Recreation at (707) 937-5804.

See number 4 on page 502.

Schooner Gulch Beach

(4)

Location: 3.5 miles south of Point Arena at Highway 1 and Schooner Gulch Road. Trails lead over the bluffs to the beach.
Parking: Free roadside parking.
Hours: Open 24 hours.
Facilities: None.
Contact: For beach information, contact the Mendocino Coast Division of the California Department of Parks and Recreation at (707) 937-5804.

See number 3 on page 502.

is made airy and light by its spacious, second-floor setting. The seafood is taken straight from the adjoining fisherman's pier—which is, incidentally, the only boat-launch facility between Bodega Bay and Fort Bragg.

For More Information

Contact the Fort Bragg-Mendocino Coast Chamber of Commerce, 332 North Main Street, P.O. Box 1141, Fort Bragg, CA 95437; (707) 961-6300.

Manchester State Beach

Location: One mile north of Point Arena Lighthouse, off Alder Creek Road.

Manchester State Beach lies at the point where two creeks and the San Andreas Fault decide to make a break for the sea. The 1,400-acre preserve offers five miles of broad, mocha-colored sand backed by dunes matted with thick grass and wildflowers. Manchester provides good steelhead fishing in the winter, and some of the best surf casting in Mendocino County all year long.

Perhaps the most notable thing about the beach is that it looks like a graveyard for driftwood. The whitened logs are the skeletons of dead trees that have washed onto the beach like soldiers killed in a maritime invasion. Picnickers and sunbathers use the logs as windbreaks. They come in handy, especially in summer when stiff winds make for harsh beachcombing. One brave kid we saw was playing catch with the ocean, tossing his plastic ball out to sea and then having it returned by the waves.

Part of the thrill is the drive out to Manchester. Three roads provide access to the beachfront; all day-use is free of charge. On the way out, you pass an AT&T relay station that seems either abandoned or staffed by robots, but is, in fact, the trans-Pacific link for undersea phone service to Hawaii and the Far East. The old cable was replaced in 1989 by a fiber-optic job, allowing the Aloha State the dubious benefits of pay TV. The park's Kinney Road entrance leads to a campground offering 48 primitive sites ($7 to $9 a night) that are snapped up quickly. Fishermen and bird-watchers, in particular, like to stay here. The beach is a 15-minute walk from the camp.

In addition to wintering swans, pelicans, godwits, killdeer, and surf scoters (a type of sea duck) await to delight birders in this area. Other beach accesses lie at the ends of Alder Creek and Stoneboro Roads. The latter is typi-

Manchester State Beach

Location: From south to north, Stoneboro, Kinney, and Alder Creek Beach Roads lead to different sections of Manchester State Beach, which lies north of Point Arena off Highway 1.

Parking: Free parking lots.

Hours: Open 24 hours.

Facilities: Rest rooms, picnic tables, and fireplaces. There are 48 tent and RV campsites off Kinney Road near the beach. Fees are $7 to $9 per night. For camping reservations, call Destinet at (800) 444-7275. There is also a commercial campground, Manchester Beach KOA, adjacent to Manchester State Beach. There are 73 tent and RV campsites, with hookups. Fees are $26 to $32 per night. For camping reservations, call Manchester Beach KOA at (707) 882-2375.

Contact: For beach information, contact the Mendocino Coast Division of the California Department of Parks and Recreation at (707) 937-5804.

See number 7 on page 502.

cal of what is meant by beach access on this hardy stretch of the coast. From the highway, you drive 1.6 miles through cow pastures, park in a dirt lot, and hike through the humpbacked dunes to the sea. Incidentally, a vista point at Mallo Pass Creek (four miles north of Manchester) affords a magnificent panorama of the ocean, as well as the forests and creek canyons to the east and north. Bring the camera.

For More Information

Contact Mendocino Coast State Parks, c/o Russian Gulch State Park, Highway 1, P.O. Box 440, Mendocino, CA 95460; (707) 937-5804.

Elk

Location: 20 miles north of Point Arena, off Highway 1. A small cove beach lies at the mouth of Greenwood Creek.
Population: 200
Area Code: 707 **Zip Code:** 95432

Elk used to be known as Greenwood in the boomtown days of logging and fishing. The lumber business closed down around these parts in 1932, and nowadays Elk is awash in bed-and-breakfast inns, with nature being explored rather than exploited. The town may seem out of the way but is easy to reach, as Route 128 meets Highway 1 just five miles north of here.

Beaches

The appeal of Elk is obvious at **Greenwood Creek State Beach**, just north of town. It is a 47-acre park with a sandy, mile-long cove beach, sea stacks, and cliffs. Park free in the lot across from Elk Store and hike the quarter-mile along a headland to the beach. Once a redwood mill flourished here, and the surviving mill office was recently converted into a visitors center (call 877-3458 for more information). The cove beach at Greenwood Creek offers all sorts of activities: driftwood collecting, ocean kayaking, steelheading, wildlife observation, picnicking, walking the beach, or just staring at the sea.

Greenwood Creek State Beach

(4)

Location: In Elk, at the mouth of Greenwood Creek off Highway 1.
Parking: Free parking lot.
Hours: Open 24 hours.
Facilities: Rest rooms, picnic tables, and fire rings.
Contact: For beach information, contact the Mendocino Coast Division of the California Department of Parks and Recreation at (707) 937-5804.

See number 8 on page 502.

Navarro River Beach Access

(3)

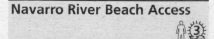

Location: Two miles south of Albion off Highway 1, turn west on Navarro Bluff Road.
Parking: Free parking lot.
Hours: Open 24 hours.
Facilities: Rest rooms. There are 12 primitive campsites for tents. The fee is $5 per night. No camping reservations.
Contact: For beach information, contact the Mendocino Coast Division of the California Department of Parks and Recreation at (707) 937-5804.

See number 9 on page 502.

North of Elk is **Navarro River Beach Access**, where yet another of the North Coast's pristine waterways empties into the ocean... almost. Like the scene in Gualala, the river here runs parallel to the ocean for a long way, providing double the beach pleasure. But the Navarro stops just shy of the Pacific, either defying the laws of nature or making a lie of Pete Townshend's song, "The Sea Refuses No River." Primitive camping is permitted; a row of open sites along the bluff is available to intrepid tenters. The fishing in the river and from the shore is good, but the wind can be ferocious. The drive to the beach along Navarro Bluff Road is a curious one. Rickety, abandoned homes line the roadway, including a forlorn, boarded-up hotel called Navarro-by-the-Sea.

Bunking Down

By our count, you've got your choice of five bed-and-breakfasts in tiny Elk. One of the best is the **Elk Cove Inn** (6300 Highway 1, 877-3321, $$). Lying just north of Greenwood Creek, this collection of romantic cottages is one of the few North Coast B&Bs that offers direct beach access; just take a set of stairs down to the water's edge. Another fine oceanfront lodge is the **Sandpiper House Inn** (5520 Highway 1, 877-3587, $$). Built in 1916, the Sandpiper offers a secluded beach, lovely gardens and grounds, and a view that'll knock your socks off. The palatial **Harbor House Inn** (5600 Highway 1, 877-9997, $$$) is a replica of the California timber industry's exhibit hall at the 1915 Panama-Pacific International Exposition. The six guest rooms and four cottages are luxuriously appointed and command wonderful views of the coast and gardens. The prices are steep, but breakfast and dinner at the inn's fabulous restaurant are included.

Coastal Cuisine

The café at the **Greenwood Pier Inn** (5928 Highway 1, 877-9997, $$) serves healthy California garden cuisine. The inn itself, a playful, 11-room, cliff-clinging wonder, is worth a visit as well. Two tables a night are set aside at the well-regarded **Harbor House** (5600 Highway 1, 877-3203, $$$) for nonguests of the inn. They serve a $26 prix-fixe menu; advance reservations are essential. At the other end of the scale, the **Roadhouse Café** (6061 Highway 1, 877-3285, $) serves all the usual staples for breakfast and lunch, plus a few more imaginative dishes (e.g., omelettes packed with goat cheese, red peppers, and garlic) that put them a cut above the usual home-cookin' joint.

Night Moves

For a relaxed, end-of-day drink, if not an entire meal, try Bridget Dolan's Irish pub inside yet another of Elk's B&Bs, the **Griffin House at Greenwood Cove** (5910 Highway 1, 877-3422, $$).

For More Information

Contact the Fort Bragg-Mendocino Coast Chamber Commerce, 332 North Main Street, P.O. Box 1141, Fort Bragg, CA 95437; (707) 961-6300.

Albion

Location: 10 miles south of Mendocino, on Highway 1. Beach access available at the mouth of the Albion River, an area known as Albion Flat.
Population: 400
Area Code: 707 **Zip Code:** 95410

Perhaps because one of Northern California's rare east-west roads (Route 128) meets Highway 1 just south of here, Albion has a more grown-up feel than its pleasant but snail-like neighbors to the south. We mean grown-up in the sense of being overseen by an enlightened community. This is our delicately worded way of saying that we rejoiced at being able to begin the day with a decent cup of coffee and a current daily newspaper.

Yes, there's more to distract the city-bred from Albion north to Fort Bragg. More than that, one gets the feeling that the local citizens have a firm grip on what will become of their towns—the quality of its life, the sustainment of local economies, and so forth. These are places where big-city dwellers feel more comfortable. The lodging and dining tariff rises accordingly—but not that much higher, and the full North Coast experience is worth every buck.

Albion has a storied past that only reinforces its adulthood. Portuguese, Spanish, Russian, and English sailors took turns plying the coastal waters here in the 1600s. Many versions of how the town came to be called Albion are told, but the most frequent is that Francis Drake briefly moored here after naming California "New Albion" (Anglophiles will remember that Albion is one of England's historic nicknames), annexing it in the name of good Queen Bess. It's the same tale they spin at Point Reyes, leading us to suspect that the philandering Drake said that to all the girls. In 1850, after a crew from San Francisco arrived to salvage a wrecked trading vessel, the city slickers got a hankering for the region's redwood-draped shores. Fresh from their Gold Rush feeding frenzy, they soon turned Albion into a logging center, with a large wharf and sawmill. The latter was capable of manufacturing 4,000 feet of wood a day. Then shipping bowed out to railroads, which bowed out to trucks, and the last log was milled here in 1928.

Fishing followed as the new boom industry, but when catches dwindled along the North Coast, Albion turned to tourism. Two of the earliest tourists were John Dillinger and Pretty Boy Floyd, both of whom hid out in this quiet village. In the late '60s, Albion became an early home of renegades of a different stripe—dropouts from the counterculture, who also erected a beachhead up in Mendocino.

The setting could not be more ideal for getaways. The highway winds through redwoods, then rounds the crest of a rugged headland, crossing a majestic steel-and-wood trestle over the beautiful Albion River, emptying into the ocean alongside a scenic harbor and quiet village. Above this backdrop—with waves crashing on the jagged sea stacks—the sound of a foghorn fills the air every thirty seconds, 24 hours a day, 7 days a week, 365 days a year. Instead of being bothersome, as you might think at first, the foghorn insinuates itself into your stay here. After a while, you are lulled into a state of perfect, uncomplaining complacency.

Beaches

At the mouth of the Albion River, in the shadows of the spectacular cliff-spanning bridge, a sandy river-mouth beach known as **Albion Flat** provides easy access to the ocean. It's mainly for fishermen and boaters who cast off from the nearby boat dock. Canoe rentals are also available here. The beach is not for swimming, but surf-casting and rock-fishing opportunities are plentiful. Nearby, Albion River Campground (P.O. Box 217, 937-0606, $) offers tent and RV camping. Full-hookup RV camping can be had at **Schooner's Landing** (P.O. Box 218, 937-5707, $), east of Albion Flat. The latter operation offers all sorts of diversions: hiking, picnicking, boat launching, and swimming.

Bunking Down

One of the North Coast's true jewels is the **Albion River Inn** (3790 Highway 1, 937-1919, $$$), which can be seen from the road as Highway 1 passes north over Albion River Bridge. The view of the ocean and Albion Cove from these 20 New England–style, cliff-top cottages is spectacular. The rooms are cozy, the foghorn sings its deep-throated lullaby, and the 10 acres of gardens and grounds offer ample opportunities for strolling and daydreaming. You are guaranteed to regenerate from any of the stresses that brought you here.

Coastal Cuisine

If you don't stay in one of the cottages, you should at least eat at the restaurant at the **Albion River Inn** (3790 Highway 1, 937-1919, $$$), a truly remarkable place where the food matches the view. The restaurant predates the inn (which was launched in 1982), and is part of the original complex that opened in 1916. Its founder, Carl Larsen, built a smithy out of wood salvaged from the *Girlie Mahoney*, an ill-fated steamer than happened to be carrying 400,000 feet of lumber aboard when she went down in the cove. The haul eventually spawned a general store and a restaurant (how's that for recycling?) that quickly became a North Coast staple. It was the Harbor Lights in the 1950s, the Windjammer in the 1960s, the Blacksmith Inn in the 1970s. Now the Albion River Inn, the restaurant is nestled inside Larsen's lovingly renovated original structure.

Always a great family dining spot, the Albion River Inn has emerged as one of the finest gourmet eateries in Northern California. The menu changes daily to reflect what's freshest in the local seafood and produce markets. The Pacific Rim Bouillabaisse, for example, bathes Aqua Gem clams, mussels, rock shrimp, and other deep-sea delights in a lemon grass, tomato, and fennel broth. A scrumptious sea-bass dish we tried was sautéed with artichoke hearts and Madeira wine. Snuggled into a rocky pocket atop a cliff, the restaurant is staffed by friendly, sharp-witted locals, and the extensive wine list features the products of fine local vineyards, many accessible via Route 128. The Albion River Inn offers a taste of the good life at a fair price—a feast for the eyes, stomach, and soul.

Albion Flat

RV 4

Location: 10 miles south of Mendocino on Highway 1, at the mouth of the Albion River.

Parking: $5 per person.

Hours: 6 AM to 5 PM.

Facilities: Rest rooms, picnic area, showers, and fire pits. There are 90 campsites at Albion River Campground for tents and trailers, with hookups. The fee is $15 per night. For reservations, contact Albion River Campground at (707) 936-0606.

Contact: For beach information, contact the Albion River Campground and Fishing Village at (707) 937-0606.

See number 10 on page 502.

Night Moves

There's a small bar at the **Albion River Inn and Restaurant** (3790 Highway 1, 937-1919). Barring that, Mendocino lies 10 miles up the road. We made do with the foghorn's serenade and the view over the cliffs from the inn.

For More Information

Contact the Fort Bragg-Mendocino Coast Chamber of Commerce, 332 North Main Street, P.O. Box 1141, Fort Bragg, CA 95437; (707) 961-6300.

Rubes With a View

You can always tell when the wrong sort of city slickers come to the North Coast. They're the ones who talk too loud and wear purple designer polo shirts and loud pullovers advertising the tourist attraction where they spent their vacation last year. All the while, they so desperately try to manifest the self-importance of young, upwardly mobile sorts who have made their money too quickly in some dubious profession in which nothing useful is produced.

One night, we had the pleasure of dining at a restaurant with the most stunning view of the Pacific Ocean on the North Coast. We had the additional pleasure of being seated at a table close to a window that looked out to where a river flows into the ocean at a rocky cove. It was just before sundown, and the sky was bathed in a heavenly orange-pink glow that would render most people quiet and grateful for the view.

Next to us, at the best table in the house, sat a couple who were neither quiet nor grateful. The man ran his mouth at a volume that was just loud enough to interrupt our peaceful thoughts, and the woman nodded and giggled goofily—his wife, we thought at first, then quickly realized he was cheating on his wife. He spent his dinner hour at this coveted perch boisterously recounting the dirty jokes his colleagues had told him on the golf course that afternoon. ("And then she got down on all fours and he tore all her clothes off in the kitchen, and..."). After those witticisms were exhausted, he gamely charged on to jokes he'd heard at work the previous week.

From there, the conversation moved on to the usual list of suspects—O.J., Roseanne, Michael Jackson, Madonna. "I don't care how many animals she's screwed!" he angrily huffed at one point, to which his companion nodded assent. Then he embarked on tales of last winter's ski expeditions and a deconstruction of his golfing game. "Did you know that 70 percent of your stroke is from your hips? So it's an inefficient use of energy.... I feel I should be kicking more, but it doesn't really do much good for your stroke...."

In between each mindless volley of chitchat and coarse laughter, there was conspicuous silence, as they stared vacuously at their wine glasses. Joke, story, giggles, then empty silence. Meanwhile, the sun was going down and the unfolding scene was one we'd like to think will greet us in heaven after our lifetime of good works.

At the same time, another couple was seated at a table by the window. He was a burly guy wearing a New York Giants T-shirt, sunglasses dangling suggestively down the front on a designer cord (sunglasses at night?). His gal pal wore a pink sweatshirt that said "BEVERLY HILLS CALIFORNIA." They loudly ordered martinis and began guzzling and...he let out a belch. Lovely.

These two couples obviously came all the way up here from some stressed-out urban center. They spent $200 for a room, another $100 for a meal. They are sitting at the best tables in the nicest restaurant on the North Coast. It is sundown on a perfect day. The music is playing softly. And they are missing it. They are missing it all.

Mendocino and Little River

Location: Mendocino lies 180 miles north of San Francisco. From San Francisco, take Highway 101 north. Just above Cloverdale, pick up Highway 128, which proceeds in a northwesterly direction to the coast for 60 miles, joining Highway 1 near Albion. Mendocino lies 10 miles north. It is an area in which headlands are more accessible than beaches, but there is a sandy beach accessible on the south bank of the Big River.
Population: 10,000
Area Code: 707 **Zip Code:** 95460

The communities of Mendocino and Fort Bragg are about 10 miles apart. They form a sort of North Coast yin and yang, based on their respective appeals. The rap goes something like this: Mendocino is artsy-craftsy, while Fort Bragg is working-class. Mendocino is boutiques; Fort Bragg is hard goods. Mendocino is secluded bed-and-breakfast inns; Fort Bragg is roadside motels. Mendocino is Café Beaujolais; Fort Bragg is Taco Bell. Mendocino is couples; Fort Bragg is families. You get the idea.

This has been the situation for years, though of late there's been a symbiosis between these two seeming opposites as they grow together in discernible ways. Still, change comes slowly to this section of the coast. The locals scrutinize every permit application as if adding a few more units to a B&B was tantamount to erecting Trump Tower in the pristine wilderness. (Seriously, we've been told you must meet 44 terms and conditions in order to get a zoning or use permit up here.) You've got to love their attitude, simply because it works. No one puts up a fight or monitors growth and development like these unreconstructed north-woods liberals. Essentially, a few more inns have materialized on the highway between Mendocino and Little River in the past half-dozen years. The good news for travelers is that prices appear to have dropped a mite lately, reflecting economic realities (i.e., people don't have as much disposable income as they did in the 1980s).

To get a proper handle on Mendocino, it helps to think of it as a kind of impressionistic painting. Perspective is the key. Observed at close range, the town appears to be a pleasant rural outpost of scattered wood-frame houses and postcard-quaint inns. As one pulls back to observe the big picture, though, Mendocino reveals itself to be a town with a vision. And to grasp that vision, one has to understand the people who live here.

Mendocino's roots date back to the mid-1800s, when California's first redwood mill was built on the banks of the Big River. This slow-moving river empties into the ocean beneath the steep headlands on which Mendocino was founded. The community enjoyed nearly a century of prosperity as a lumber town, followed by decades of decline in the wake of the sawmills' closing. In the 1950s, it was discovered by artists and dropouts drawn from the burgeoning cities, especially San Francisco. Rising apartment rents and the stodgy middle-class conformity of the postwar era drove more sensitive souls into the countryside to seek sanctuary. To those who were searching for another way to live—closer to nature, in an environment more conducive to contemplation—Mendocino exerted a magnetic pull. The old, abandoned wood houses came cheaply, the rugged Northern California coast was quiet and rarely visited, and the natural beauty of Mendocino's coast and forest lands provided a constant source of inspiration.

With the founding of the Mendocino Arts Council in 1959, the character and mission of the community became official, and art remains

 Map of Mendocino County beaches—page 502

a rallying point for the loose-knit denizens of this town. In the 1960s, the area became a refuge for counterculture types who found the increasingly grimy and crime-ridden streets of Haight-Ashbury too congested for their liking. The Sir Douglas Quintet had a Top Forty hit in 1969 with a song entitled "Mendocino," which put this little North Coast speck on the map (at least in the eyes of the counterculture). Its chorus perfectly caught the stoned, soulful tenor of the times: "Mendocino, Mendocino, where life's such a groove you'll blow your mind in the morning."

Amazingly, things haven't changed so very drastically since those halcyon days. Mendocino remains a place where a life of reflection can be lived on relatively modest means. Artists can scrape by without selling out, musicians and film people come to find seclusion, and lesser cultural aspirants can, at the very least, manage to keep a roof over their head. For instance, we spied a run-down pickup truck by the side of the road, whose owner advertised his wares in juvenile hand-lettering on the side panels: "Firewood and Donkey Dung." There's also a downside to this sylvan scene. Mendocino is still getting invaded by San Franciscans. Yet instead of solitude-seeking Sixties transcendentalists, it's lately been infested by homeless and often drug-addled derelicts. They collect their welfare checks and mill around like sewer rats. "Ex-cons, street crap from Union Square" is how one disgusted innkeeper referred to the pests, who can be seen ambling aimlessly about the streets of the village center. The rate of welfare in Mendocino County is now 20 percent, so the area is not without problems, its natural bounty notwithstanding.

Size-wise, Mendocino is home to about 1,000 people in town and 9,000 out in the woods. In Fort Bragg, the number of townies and woodsies is 6,000 and 6,000. One thing both communities share is clean air. The National Clean Air Monitoring station is located in Mendocino County. After passing over thousands of miles of open ocean, the air is the freshest you'll ever breathe, and the nation's standard for clean air is measured by that sampled in Mendocino. That in itself makes the place an appealing destination. The sunsets are yellow and gold, not brown as they are in more sooty locales.

There's more good news: wildlife is making a comeback in the area. Salmon are returning to some of the local rivers. Ospreys, red-tailed hawks, and peregrine falcons have been sighted in increased numbers. Habitat protection is paying dividends. It feels good to pass along some positive news in the environmental realm for a change.

Like much of the remote North Coast, you have to really want to be in Mendocino to make it worth the drive over winding roads, trailing RVs driven by slow-moving tourists unused to the curves. Then there's the weather. Mendocino is frequently shrouded in fog and, in winter, heavy rains. These coast fogs don't creep in on little cat's feet, either (to borrow an image from Robert Frost); they clop in on heavy cattle hooves.

Somehow, this is part of Mendocino's allure as a romantic hideaway. The cool, gray days of summer provide a good excuse to stay inside a cozy room and light a fire. The phrase is overused, but Mendocino truly is the place to go to get away from it all. The town makes a convenient base for exploring the wineries of Mendocino and Sonoma Counties during the day. The high points in the calendar year are the Annual Summer Fair and the Mendocino Music Festival, but you can always be sure there's always something art-worthy going on in town. Outdoors enthusiasts also find plenty to do, including hiking, canoeing, fishing, and diving for abalone. There are miles of beaches and parklands in and around Mendocino begging to be explored on foot. But the best thing about Mendocino is that you really don't have to do anything at all.

Beaches

Yes, there are beaches way up here, especially north of Mendocino at places like MacKerricher State Park, where they run for mile after unbroken mile. In Mendocino per se, the beach is less accessible and remarkable than the headlands and parklands that back up to them. **Mendocino Headlands State Park** runs north from the banks of the Big River. Narrow, linear headlands extend out from the mainland like serpents' tongues. Trails skirt the bluffs, and you can peer over the side to the beaches at their bases, way down below. Be careful, though. The Mendocino Headlands remain a work in progress, a symphony of rock carved by the relentless crescendo of waves. A wide, sandy beach exists on the south bank of the Big River. However, we'd recommend finding

Mendocino Headlands State Park

Location: On the headlands overlooking the ocean in the town of Mendocino.

Parking: Free parking lots.

Hours: Open 24 hours.

Facilities: Rest rooms.

Contact: For beach information, contact the Mendocino Coast Division of the California Department of Parks and Recreation at (707) 937-5804.

See number 12 on page 502.

Russian Gulch State Park

Location: Two miles north of Mendocino off Highway 1, at the mouth of Russian Gulch Creek.

Parking: $5 entrance fee per vehicle.

Hours: Open 24 hours.

Facilities: Rest rooms, showers, picnic tables, and fire pits. There are 30 tent and RV campsites. Fees are $12 to $14 per night. There is also a group site for up to 40 campers (no RVs allowed). The fee is $60 per night. For camping reservations, call Destinet at (800) 444-7275.

Contact: For beach information, contact the Mendocino Coast Division of the California Department of Parks and Recreation at (707) 937-5804.

See number 13 on page 502.

Van Damme State Park

Location: In Little River, three miles south of Mendocino, off Highway 1.

Parking: $5 entrance fee per vehicle to enter state park on inland side of Highway 1. The day-use lot on the beach side of the highway is free.

Hours: Open 24 hours.

Facilities: Rest rooms, showers, picnic area, and fire rings. There are 74 tent and RV campsites and 10 hike-in sites for tents only. Fees are $3 per night for the hike-in sites, and $12 to $14 per night for the developed sites. There is also a group site for up to 50 campers. The fee is $75 per night. For camping reservations, call Destinet at (800) 444-7275.

Contact: For beach information, contact the Mendocino Coast Division of the California Department of Parks and Recreation at (707) 937-5804.

See number 11 on page 502.

Canoeing the Big

The longest unspoiled estuary in Northern California is the Big River, which spills into the Pacific Ocean just south of Mendocino. Its pristine riverine marshes, canyons, and streambeds are vital to the regional ecosystem. The river's first eight miles are tidal and, thus, subject to the ebb and flow of the ocean. The constant infusion of saline water into this section renders it a sanctuary for ducks, seals, ospreys, and countless smaller critters on the food chain.

We were told there were two beaches somewhere along this eight-mile stretch. In the interest of journalistic integrity, we decided to strike out for them. The fact that one was called Dead Man's Beach did not deter us, perhaps because the other one was named Lilly's Beach. What kind of harm could a Lilly do? But in order to explore the Big River, one needs a canoe. Speedboats and Jet Skis are banned (thank God), as is development of the river banks, damming its flow, or turning the mouth into a harbor—all common occurrences up this way. For our fearless trip into the unknown, we procured an outrigger at Catch-a-Canoe & Bicycles, Too!, whose redwood and fiberglass craft are designed by a local artisan named Robert Cummings. The outriggers can be steered by foot controls and will not flip over. They also cut through the water at great speed with minimal effort. All in all, it seemed like the perfect conveyance for two road-weary beach bums.

Okay, we'd like to report that we found Dead Man's Beach and lived to tell about it. Hey, we'd have settled for Lilly's Beach. We found neither. Actually, we never got that far, turning back after four miles. (The old knees aren't what they used to be.) But we did experience that rarest of pleasures in this day and age: a clean, life-filled river, tall trees on both banks, nesting birds, frolicking seals, blue skies, and total silence from anything made by man. That was enough for us.

Catch-a-Canoe also rents and sells canoes, kayaks, and mountain bikes equipped with shocks for riding the wilderness trails in Jackson National Forest or Van Damme State Park. They provide bike racks and maps if you want to take your rentals farther up or down the coast.

For more information, contact Catch-a-Canoe & Bicycles, Too!, Highway 1 and Comptche-Ukiah Road, P.O. Box 487, Mendocino, CA 95460; (707) 937-0273.

a place to perch high up on the fissured headlands, where you can stare out to sea and, in season, look for whales.

Three miles south of Mendocino in Little River (pop. 412) is **Van Damme State Park**. This 2,100-acre park spreads inland for four miles from its small, sandy beach. Located at the mouth of the Little River, this beach is considered the best abalone-diving spot on the North Coast. Inland, Van Damme encompasses a sword-fern canyon and a forest of stunted conifers. Van Damme's 10 miles of hiking trails and cool, shaded, 84-site campground make it a popular place, especially during the relatively warm, dry months from May through September.

Two miles north of Mendocino is **Russian Gulch State Park**, which is home to serene redwood groves and an open beach where Russian Gulch Creek runs into the ocean. A big attraction is Devil's Punchbowl, a blowhole that's 100 feet long and 60 feet deep. The force of incoming waves funneling through this collapsed sea cave creates geysers and noisy explosions. Another natural wonder is a 36-foot waterfall. Thirty choice campsites are situated along the creek inside a canyon forested with second-growth redwoods, as well as firs, hemlocks, oaks, and laurels. Again, as demand is far greater than supply, reservations are necessary. Skin diving and rock fishing are the main activities pursued on the beaches at Van Damme and Russian Gulch.

Bunking Down

On the inn scene, the trend in Mendocino is away from cloned Victoriana and toward more contemporary, original, and nature-oriented presentations. The B&B craze is over, for the most part, and only the strong will survive from here on out. Because of economic conditions, people simply are not traveling and spending as freely as they used to. Business has been down all over the coast in recent years, with a painfully low 50-percent occupancy rate being whispered among innkeepers. (Still, the coast campgrounds are full every night in season. It's the economy, stupid!)

The secret to survival in the bed-and-breakfast business these days is quality. People want the vacation experience to be immediate and intense. "People want to be plushed," said one hotelier.

You can certainly get plushed at the **Stanford Inn by the Sea** (Highway 1 at Comptche-Ukiah Road, 937-5615, $$$$). Set high on a hillside overlooking the ocean, it strikes a perfect balance between a four-star hotel and a cozy B&B. Rooms are spacious and decorated with unfinished, knotty-pine walls, four-poster beds, and wood-burning fireplaces. A decanter of burgundy from a nearby winery is provided, as are confections from the local chocolatier. Logs are stacked by the hearth, along with instructions on how to build a fire.

In the morning, guests load up trays in the lobby with pastry, juice, coffee, and tea. After breakfast, they can enjoy the greenhouse-enclosed pool and sauna, or check out the organic garden and greenhouse (Big River Nurseries) on the premises. At the foot of a gravel drive leading down to the river's edge is another of owner Jeff Stanford's businesses: Catch-a-Canoe & Bicycles, Too! (937-0273), where you can rent canoes, kayaks, and outriggers to paddle upriver or out to sea.

The **Joshua Grindle Inn** (44800 Little Lake Road, 937-4143, $$$) is a two-story captain's house situated a short walk from the village. The grounds are a riot of flowers and shrubbery. Rooms are quite comfortable, whether in the main house or the rustic buildings out back. A full hot breakfast is served each morning.

Just south of Mendocino in the town of Little River, the **Stevenswood Lodge** (8211 Highway 1, 937-2810, $$$) impresses with its gleaming, polished hardwood floors, and air of newness. Individual rooms are outfitted in light woods with natural finishes, and named for the 19th-century founders of the town. A Japanese poi garden offers a peaceful setting out back. Deer and other forest critters wander to the edge of the property. The operative philosophy at the lodge is to bring the outdoors inside via windows and skylights that capture the streaming rays.

Breakfast is home cooked and tremendous: baked muffins the size of catcher's mitts, eggs Benedict, bowls of fruit salad. Another plus is the fact that owner Robert Zimmer's brother runs an art gallery in Mendocino. The spillover from the gallery winds up on the lodge's walls, in the halls, in the rooms, even in a small, on-site showroom—all very attractive, all for sale. "No paintings of the surf, no giant yellow waves smashing the shore, no goddamned surrealism," Zimmer emphasizes.

 Map of Mendocino County beaches—page 502

Coastal Cuisine

Café Beaujolais (961 Ukiah Street, 937-5614, $$$), a restaurant with a world-class reputation, is located in the heart of Mendocino. The English country-cottage decor creates a casually elegant environment, from the hardwood floors and floral print wallpaper to the subtle background music. The café has its own bakery, which turns out extraordinary breads such as Red Seal rye, Mendocino sourdough (made from white and rye flours), and—the killer—nine-grain Australian sunflower-seed bread. Among the many stellar entrées is oven-steamed sturgeon with a sauce of garlic, lemon, tomato, olive oil, and herbs. Café Beaujolais also serves meat and game "from animals raised humanely in a free-range environment," as the kitchen asserts. There's a good selection of local wines, and they do neat things with coffee, too. All in all, Café Beaujolais, which serves dinner nightly and brunch on weekends, offers a top-notch North Coast dining experience.

The owners of **955 Ukiah** (955 Ukiah Street, 937-1955, $$$) have built their restaurant into something special through hard work and vision. The accent is Continental, the culinary offerings pure poetry, bearing up the elaborate menu descriptions. The salmon, for instance, is poached in a "mirror-like bouillon," while the free-range chicken is "serenely captivated by a sauce of wild mushrooms." You, too, will be serenely captivated by the food and ambience at 955 Ukiah.

Night Moves

In the informed opinion of a local innkeeper, the **Heritage House** (5200 Highway 1, 937-5885) still mixes the best drinks on the coast. They also have one of the best views of the sea, not to mention fine food and lodgings on a 37-acre spread. Heritage House is located in Little River, a few miles south of **Mendocino.** **MacCallum House** (Albion Street, 937-5763), a century-old Victorian mansion that does double duty as a classy restaurant and B&B, has a small but sociable bar in a parlor to the left of the main hall. It's called the **Grey Whale Bar & Café**, and if you don't feel up to the culinary extravaganza across the hall, you can opt for the bar's menu of burgers and pub grub.

Finally, if you feel up for something wilder than an after-dinner drink, make for the Caspar Inn, four miles north of Mendocino (see the entry on page 523).

For More Information

Contact the Fort Bragg-Mendocino Coast Chamber of Commerce, 332 North Main Street, P.O. Box 1141, Fort Bragg, CA 95437; (707) 961-6300.

Caspar

Location: Four miles north of Mendocino, west of Highway 1 on Caspar Lake Little Road. Caspar is the site of Caspar State Beach and Caspar Headlands State Reserve.
Population: 20
Area Code: 707 **Zip Code:** 95437

Caspar is a friendly ghost of a town, located far enough west of Highway 1 to escape most of its bustle. During its lumber-milling heyday, Caspar was a bustling town of 500; the first on the coast, in fact, to get electricity. Now it's little more than a dot on the map off the main road, though it's got a viable artistic community and is home to several galleries. Beyond that, little Caspar also scores big on two counts: beaches and nightlife. Read on.

Beaches

The state has acquired several acres of the crumbling, fissured **Caspar Headlands State Reserve**, intermingled with private property. (A housing development sits close by.) The headlands, located logically enough at the end of Headlands Drive, can be visited only with an entry permit, obtainable at the State Park District Office at Russian Gulch State Park. Is it worth the trouble? Probably not, since the impressive headlands at nearby Mendocino are open to all without red tape. **Caspar State Beach** sits at the head of a long, bottleneck-shaped bay where Doyle and Caspar Creeks empty into the Pacific. Bookended by low bluffs, it's a sandy beach accessible from Point Cabrillo Road (also known as Old Highway 1).

Caspar Headlands State Reserve

4

Location: Five miles north of Mendocino, turn west from Highway 1 onto South Caspar Drive, and then turn onto Headlands Drive and follow to reserve.
Parking: Free roadside parking.
Hours: Open 24 hours.
Facilities: None.
Contact: For beach information, contact the Mendocino Coast Division of the California Department of Parks and Recreation at (707) 937-5804.

See number 14 on page 502.

Caspar State Beach

RV 3

Location: In Caspar, at Point Cabrillo Road (Old Highway 1) at mouth of Doyle Creek, across from Caspar Beach RV Park.
Parking: Free parking lot.
Hours: Open 24 hours.
Facilities: None on the beach. There are 100 tent and RV campsites, with hookups, at Caspar Beach RV Park, a commercial campground across the road. Facilities include rest rooms, showers, picnic tables, and barbecue grills. Fees are $15 to $22 per night. For camping reservations, call Caspar Beach RV Park at (707) 964-3306.
Contact: For beach information, contact the Mendocino Coast Division of the California Department of Parks and Recreation at (707) 937-5804.

See number 15 on page 502.

Bunking Down

If you want to bunk down in Caspar, camping is the best (and maybe only) option. **Caspar Beach RV Park** (14401 Point Cabrillo Road, 964-3306, $) features 100 sites (56 with full hookups) and ocean frontage in a wooded, creekside setting. It's also got everything a camper might need: camp store, showers, Laundromat, and playground.

Coastal Cuisine

There's a small café, **Oscars at Caspar** (Caspar Road, 964-0602, $), beside the venerable Caspar Inn (see below). At Caspar's the accent is on fresh, healthy food for eat-in or take out.

Night Moves

This is where Caspar really shines. The **Caspar Inn** (Caspar Road, 964-5565) is one of the last true vestiges of the '60s. A night here is what hanging around the funky clubs and ballrooms of San Francisco in its counterculture prime might have been like. The inn books live bands, true hair-to-the-waist anachronisms that like to boogie; recently, we were blown away by a band called Clan Dyken. What a pleasant surprise to find out that live, original rock and roll still lives in nooks and crannies like the Caspar Inn.

It is a scene that's almost impossible to describe. The friendly crowd really gets into dancing. We had to back up a few paces when a floor full of eager gyraters began encroaching on our turf with their frantic footwork. Clan Dyken had 'em on their feet for hours with original songs that could have passed muster with Jefferson Airplane and some other figurehead San Francisco Scene bands. The crowd lost itself in dancing, from the Hispanic fellow who assayed some rather formal-looking flamenco steps to the hirsute dude who was practically dancing sideways, shaking his mane as he grew ever more consumed by the music. If you have trouble finding the Caspar Inn, just look for the place that's got cars parked on the street out front in both directions.

For More Information

Contact the Fort Bragg-Mendocino Coast Chamber of Commerce, 332 North Main Street, P.O. Box 1141, Fort Bragg, CA 95437; (707) 961-6300.

Jug Handle State Reserve

Location: Between Caspar and Fort Bragg, off Highway 1.

Now we know how mountain climbers feel when they get within reach of a legendary peak. Here at this 769-acre park, we ventured onto the farthest point of a fingerlike headland, striding cautiously toward the inviting horizon of Caribbean-blue ocean water and jagged, reddish-brown sea stacks. It became a test of nerves to venture all the way out. We wobbled onto our knees and crept forward, shivering as it became clear, with the wind whipping us, that if we weren't careful, we could fall over the side and get smashed to bits.

Jug Handle State Reserve gets our vote for most exciting beach promontory on the North Coast. Several of these slivers of land poke way out into the ocean, and we hereby warn you to prepare yourself for a sudden bout of vertigo. In addition to these remarkable bluff tops, the reserve offers a 2.5-mile nature trail that leads up an ecological staircase of marine terraces through 500,000 years of geological history. The lowest (youngest) of the five terraces bears the full brunt of the ocean waves. The next one is covered in sea grass and wildflowers, the third one supports a pygmy forest, and the fourth and fifth ones have taller, more mature forests. You can't imagine the majesty of Jug Handle State Reserve. It simply must be seen!

Bunking Down

If you want to make an overnight stay of it, the small but pleasant **Jug Handle Beach Country Bed & Breakfast Inn** (32980 Gibney Lane, Fort Bragg, CA 95437; 707-964-1415, $$) is within viewing distance of these coastal headlands. The inn was built in 1883 and is far enough away from the bustle of Fort Bragg to make for a quiet getaway.

For More Information

Contact Mendocino Coast State Parks, c/o Russian Gulch State Park, Highway 1, P.O. Box 440, Mendocino, CA 95460; (707) 937-5804.

Jug Handle State Reserve

Location: 1.5 miles north of Caspar, off Highway 1.

Parking: Free parking lot.

Hours: Open 24 hours.

Facilities: Rest rooms and picnic tables.

Contact: For beach information, contact the Mendocino Coast Division of the California Department of Parks and Recreation at (707) 937-5804.

See number 16 on page 502.

Fort Bragg

Location: 10 miles north of Mendocino on Highway 1. The best beach in the area—and in all of Mendocino County, for that matter—is MacKerricher State Park, with access points that begin in town and continue to the main park unit three miles north.
Population: 7,000
Area Code: 707 **Zip Code:** 95437

"I'm fond of saying that Fort Bragg is poised on the verge of greatness," contends Colette Bailey, who runs the venerable Grey Whale Inn. At her suggestion the prior evening, we joined her for an early-morning walk along an abandoned log-haul road that runs along the ocean north toward MacKerricher State Beach. It was 7 AM, and she was keeping an Olympic pace while offering a running commentary on Fort Bragg. En route, we passed dozens of like-minded walkers out for their morning jaunt by the sea. They're here each day like clockwork. We labored to keep up with her, waddling like the friendly pack of ducks whose path we had crossed earlier.

Colette may have a point about Fort Bragg's bid for better days. Unlike many boutiqued-to-death coastal destinations, Fort Bragg has the feeling of a real working community. In fact, the town is defined by the delicate balance that's struck between its two largest industries, timber and tourism. The big employer in these parts is the lumber giant Georgia Pacific, but they've fallen on hard times, downsizing in recent years. At this point, the two industries are neck in neck in terms of revenue generated. As far as which provides more tax money to the municipal coffers, tourism is way ahead, with the bed tax in large part funding it. There are many more guest rooms in Fort Bragg than Mendocino, and these are geared at travelers across the spectrum—not just couples, but families and those traveling on business. It's also becoming a popular place for retirees to settle. They're moving in and building big homes, infusing much-needed cash into the local economy.

Revitalization is under way not just in economic terms but aesthetically as well. Artists who have been priced out of Mendocino have moved to Fort Bragg, and the town has been receptive to their arrival. A Center for the Arts has opened, providing regular doses of culture and cheap studio rents for the army of artisans who are replacing the lumberjacks. The arts come to the people on "First Friday," a monthly tour of local galleries and studios. (Call 961-0360 for details.)

The appeal of the area is easy to understand. Fort Bragg isn't completely dominated by hermitic, offbeat types as is Mendocino. It's just a working town that's mending its nets and looking to rebound. Fort Bragg has the largest port between San Francisco and Eureka, and is the largest coastal city along that same stretch.

For anyone who lives in the mountains and valleys to the east or along the coast in either direction, Fort Bragg is a vital service center. Hey, harbor seals and abalone are nice, but neither can tune an engine nor perform an appendectomy. Thus Fort Bragg has given itself over to the role of supply center and employer for the county. With that comes the good (cheaper prices on rooms and meals), the bad (slipshod commerce, strip malls), and the ugly (Georgia Pacific's timber mill, which hogs much of the beachfront and belches steam and smoke on one and all).

Money has been pumped into the town and its various attractions, bed-and-breakfast inns and antique shops have boomed in recent years, and an influx of new immigrants has added a likable ethnic mix to this once close-minded meat-and-potatoes town.

One cultural event we passed up—but only because we were farther up the road when it took place—was Cow Chip Bingo. Here's how it works. A local football field is divided into 500 squares. Contestants lay claim to squares for $5 apiece. Three cows are turned loose onto the field to graze and (you guessed it) make cow pies. The owner of the square first plopped in wins $500, second $1,000 and third $1,500. Unless one is intimate beyond imagination with the excretory habits of cows, our guess is it's a game of chance, not strategy.

Though referred to as "historic" Fort Bragg in all the tourist literature, the town's history can be summed up in two sentences. A fort was established here in 1857 to keep the nearby Indians in check and was closed seven years later. Timbering and railroads arrived in 1885, and have been leading industries ever since. From this, they've managed to create a 28-stop walking tour of historic sites (mostly restored Victorian homes and inns). To visitors, the biggest attraction is the Skunk Train, an authentic re-creation of the logging railroad that ran from Fort Bragg to Willits, 40 miles inland. The train consists of observation cars hauled by a diesel logging locomotive. It makes several round-trips to Willits and Northspur (the midway point) daily. Your best bet is the three-hour round trip to Northspur, which runs along the Noyo River through redwood forests and mountains. The Skunk Train Depot is located at the foot of Laurel Street. (Call 964-6371 for information; round-trip fares to Northspur cost $18.50 for adults, $9 for kids.)

Finally, a parting comment on the North Coast weather, which applies to Fort Bragg, Mendocino, and surrounding coastal destinations. You can always tell how hot it is inland by how heavy the fog is on the coast. When they're sweating in Sacramento, they're putting on sweaters in Mendocino. The inland heat creates a temperature differential that sucks cool, moist air off the ocean, bathing the northern coastal counties in fog. It almost never rains in the summer, but overcast is common. It generally burns off by midday, but gray skies can linger for weeks.

Fort Bragg and its environs receive their warmest weather in September and October, when the mercury can climb to 80 degrees. The months of December through February are the height of the rainy season. Because the coast environment is so strongly influenced and moderated by the ocean, temperature extremes in either direction are rare. They may get a frost or two each winter and a dusting of snow every half-dozen years, but that's the worst of it. Autumn is really the ideal time to come, because of the Indian summer weather: clear and warm.

Beaches

The state park system provides access to the best beaches in the vicinity: Jug Handle State Reserve (two miles south) and at MacKerricher State Park (three miles north); see the entries on pages 524 and 529, respectively. The **Pudding Creek Beach** access to MacKerricher State Park is the closest to a classic sand beach that Fort Bragg has to offer. Here, Pudding Creek trickles into the ocean and a small dirt parking lot allows limited (and free) entry. You must walk under a condemned train trestle, but the mountain of sand is as inviting as one of Ulysses' sirens. The waves break invitingly, too, but a sign warns of "Recurring Rip Currents." No lifeguards are on duty.

One creek-mouth north is **Virgin Creek Beach**, a wide, sandy beach that draws local crowds. An unmarked pulloff by the side of the road is your only clue about this one. Both Pudding Creek and Virgin Creek beaches lie along the eight-mile log-haul road now used by joggers, walkers, and bicyclists. Elsewhere in Fort Bragg, the beach pickings are as slim as a Georgia Pacific toothpick. The lumber company, incidentally, guards its beachfront property with the ferocity of pit bulls, surrounding it with fencing, barbed wire, and "No Trespassing" signs (not realizing the irony that no one in his or her right mind would want to trespass). More ironic, however, is that this pro-America company patrols its compound with foreign-made trucks. It was Georgia Pacific, remember, who waved the American flag while lobbying to cut first-growth timber. All you need to know about Georgia Pacific's love of country is what can be seen with your own two eyes: a rusted, burned-out wasteland. The public beach next to this property, **Glass Beach**, is a mess, too, suffering from proximity to the lumber mill, although it is bounded by a marsh on the other side. Allegedly, you can scavenge for wave-polished pebbles and glass bits at Glass Beach, but it looked none too inviting.

The west end of the **Noyo Harbor** (accessed via Noyo Harbor Drive, next to the bridge off Highway 1) is home to a tiny cove beach bordered by rock jetties that hold open the river's mouth. It's quite a setting, though mostly for viewing. The Pacific waves break loudly

Glass Beach

1

Location: In Fort Bragg, at the end of Elm Street.
Parking: Free street parking.
Hours: Open 24 hours
Facilities: None.
Contact: For beach information, contact the Fort Bragg-Mendocino Coast Chamber of Commerce at (800) 726-2780.

See number 18 on page 502.

Noyo Harbor

1

Location: In Fort Bragg, at the end of Noyo Harbor Drive at the mouth of the Noyo River, off Highway 1.
Parking: Free parking lot.
Hours: Open 24 hours.
Facilities: Rest rooms and showers.
Contact: For beach information, contact Noyo Harbor Pier at (707) 964-0167.

See number 17 on page 502.

Pudding Creek Beach
(a part of MacKerricher State Park)

3

Location: On the north side of Fort Bragg, at the end of Pudding Creek Road, off Highway 1.
Parking: Free parking lot.
Hours: Open 24 hours.
Facilities: None.
Contact: For beach information, contact the Mendocino Coast Division of the California Department of Parks and Recreation at (707) 937-5804.

See number 19 on page 502.

Virgin Creek Beach
(a part of MacKerricher State Park)

4

Location: On the north side of Fort Bragg, along Highway 1 at the mouth of Virgin Creek.
Parking: Free parking lot.
Hours: Open 24 hours.
Facilities: None.
Contact: For beach information, contact the Mendocino Coast Division of the California Department of Parks and Recreation at (707) 937-5804.

See number 20 on page 502.

against the jetties, and the bridge span arches dramatically in the background. Be careful on the jetties if you choose to fish from them, as they are slick.

Bunking Down

It's true that rooms are cheaper and more plentiful in Fort Bragg than in the coastal towns to the south, but you get what you pay for. That is, for a few dollars more, you can have a total North Coast experience in Mendocino, Little River, Albion, and Elk. Still, a fair number of nice and new Fort Bragg motels provide the sort of dependably simple ambience and comfort many road-weary travelers crave. (We'll be the first to admit that it sometimes requires more social energy to enjoy the charms of bed-and-breakfasts than we possess.) In that regard, the **Best Western Vista Manor Lodge** (1100 North Main Street, 964-4776, $$) and the **Quality Inn Seabird Lodge** (191 South Street, 964-4731, $$) are your best bets.

The **Grey Whale Inn** (615 North Main Street, 964-0640, $$) was the first bed-and-breakfast in Fort Bragg, and has been a North Coast landmark for years. The handsome, four-story building used to be the general hospital for the area, once boasting 36 beds. With such a background, it's no surprise that the inn is very wheelchair accessible, with wide ramps running throughout. The rooms are large, impeccably decorated, and immaculately maintained. Walls are paneled with broad redwood planks. Beds are covered with homey quilts. There's a game room downstairs with a pool table and a television. Each morning, a mouth-watering breakfast is served, including such goodies as a breakfast strudel of spinach and sun-dried tomatoes layered in a custard of bread and eggs. Croissants, fresh fruit salad, yogurt, granola, a special blend of coffee, and cinnamon-flavored hot tea round out the meal. The Grey Whale offers 14 rooms, ranging from what owner Colette Bailey describes as "French country simplicity" to suites (with fireplaces and refrigerators) and penthouses. Recently, a woman who was born here when it was a hospital returned to spend her wedding night at the Grey Whale.

The closest lodge to the beach access at Pudding Creek is the **Pudding Creek Inn** (700 North Main Street, 964-9529, $$), a well-heeled little Victorian manor that offers a full buffet breakfast and an enclosed garden court.

Coastal Cuisine

An influx of foreign immigrants has given Fort Bragg a much-needed shot of diversity in the food department. The most interesting new-comer, and one of the great finds on the Mendocino coast, is **Viraporn's Thai Café** (500 South Main Street, 964-7931, $). It's owned and operated by a native of the Phrae province in northern Thailand. She prepares every dish using fresh, authentic ingredients. Her chicken lemon-grass soup and Pad Thai will rescue you from all those burgers you've eaten elsewhere in Fort Bragg. Viraporn's also offers East African cuisine (on Mondays and Tuesdays only), prepared by a native of Kenya. How many places within a thousand miles can make that claim?

Ye olde Fort Bragg–style chowdown can still be had at **Round Man's Smoke House** (137 Laurel Street, 964-5954, $), which offers the North Coast's best smoked salmon, albacore, and cod, as well as salmon and turkey jerky. Sample tastings are encouraged. For breakfast and lunch, you can't go wrong with **Schat's Bakery and Café** (360 North Franklin Street, 964-1929, $). If you want fish, go where they reel 'em in. Overlooking busy Noyo Harbor is the **Cliff House** (1011 South Main Street, 961-0255, $$), where they dish out fresh local seafood on four dining levels.

Less touristy and more local in flavor is **The Wharf** (780 North Harbor Drive, 964-4283, $$), which is perched over the water beneath the Noyo River Bridge, among the ramshackle flotsam of the fishing trade. The nautical bustle

 Map of Mendocino County beaches—page 502

and sea breezes will transport you to a proverbial Treasure Island of the tummy on the back of a freshly grilled salmon steak.

Night Moves

The **North Coast Brewing Company** (444 North Main Street, 964-2739) is a friendly pub that has been winning awards every year for its home-brewed ales and stouts. Try the Scrimshaw Pilsner, Red Seal Ale, and Old No. 38 Stout. The pub grub is good, too, including smoked fish and stump-sized burgers that would sate the hungriest lumberjack's appetite.

For More Information

Contact the Fort Bragg-Mendocino Coast Chamber of Commerce, 332 North Main Street, Fort Bragg, CA 95437; (707) 961-6300.

MacKerricher State Park

Location: Three miles north of Fort Bragg, off Highway 1.

Mendocino County hugs the coast for 130 miles, much of it an inaccessible stretch of sea cliffs and tiny pocket beaches. **MacKerricher State Park**, however, is a North Coast anomaly, offering a broad, mostly sandy beach that runs for eight uninterrupted miles. MacKerricher's lengthy expanse and shoreline equestrian trail are ideal for horseback riding. Horses can be rented just outside the park at Ricochet Ridge Ranch (707-764-PONY). Bicyclists, joggers, and walkers make use of the old logging road that runs through the park. Anglers find good fishing around the headlands and in Lake Cleone. You can do just about everything but swim in the 50-degree water.

For a scenic stroll, a boardwalk leads out from the main parking lot of the state park to Laguna Point. "This is what we're known for," boasted a proud ranger. Laguna Point is indeed a stunning promontory from which to view migrating whales and harbor seals. At low tide, the tidepools are chock full of life, but at high tide, the Pacific waves pound the point with profound fury. We watched in amazement as the lush and beautiful marine vegetation just rolled with the ceaseless punches.

Elsewhere on the premises is Lake Cleone, a 15-acre freshwater lake stocked with trout. It's a popular duck haven, too. The sand on the beach itself is large-grained and blackish in color. The hard-packed granules make for great bike riding. The beach runs unbroken from Pudding Creek to Ten Mile River, with accesses at the end of Ward Avenue and Mill Creek Drive in Fort Bragg.

For More Information

Contact Mendocino Coast State Parks, c/o Russian Gulch State Park, Highway 1, P.O. Box 440, Mendocino, CA 95460; (707) 937-5804.

MacKerricher State Park

Location: Three miles north of Fort Bragg on Highway 1.

Parking: Free parking lot.

Hours: Open 24 hours.

Facilities: Rest rooms, showers, picnic areas, and fire grills. There are 153 tent and RV campsites. Fees are $13 to $14 per night. For camping reservations, call Destinet at (800) 444-7275.

Contact: For beach information, contact the Mendocino Coast Division of the California Department of Parks and Recreation at (707) 937-5804.

See number 21 on page 502.

Westport

Location: 15 miles north of Fort Bragg, along Highway 1. Several beaches can be found in this area, the best of them being Chadbourne Gulch.
Population: 327
Area Code: 707 **Zip Code:** 95488

North of Fort Bragg, Highway 1 continues along the coast before pulling away to join Highway 101 at Leggett. Along this stretch lies a quartet of accessible beaches clustered in the vicinity of a one-horse town called Westport.

Beaches

Starting from the south, **Seaside Creek Beach** is located at the mouth of Seaside Creek. Parking is by the side of the road. Offshore sea stacks are visible, and driftwood lines the sandy beach. **Chadbourne Gulch** is the keeper—a mile-long, sandy beach that's good for sunning, surfing, and surf casting. There's lots of beach to wander, though not much room for cars, which must park on the highway shoulder. At high tide, the beach becomes none too wide itself. These creek-mouth beaches of northern Mendocino County are very fisherman friendly, being good places for netting smelt, catching steelhead, and foraging for abalone.

The next two are prime North Coast camping spots. **Wages Creek Beach** is a privately run campground with sites along the creek overlooking the ocean. Located a half mile north of Westport, it primarily draws RV nomads and anglers. **Westport-Union Landing State Beach**, three miles north of Westport, offers bluff-top camping at seven campgrounds along its two-mile ocean frontage. Trails and stairs lead to a primarily rocky beach; the sandy, quarter-mile-long beach that begins at the mouth of DeHaven Creek on the park's south end is known as Pete's Beach. Westport-Union Landing can be a raw spot indeed in winter, when stormy weather and rough seas pound the bluff bases, sending wave spray soaring 50 feet in the air, all the way up to campground level. Divers, tidepoolers, and surf casters especially seem to enjoy this primitive, sea-swept environment.

Chadbourne Gulch

3

Location: Two miles south of Westport on Highway 1.
Parking: Limited free roadside parking.
Hours: Open 24 hours.
Facilities: None.
Contact: For beach information, contact the Mendocino Coast Division of the California Department of Parks and Recreation at (707) 937-5804.

See number 23 on page 502.

Seaside Creek Beach

4

Location: One mile north of the mouth of Ten Mile River on Highway 1.
Parking: Free roadside parking.
Hours: Open 24 hours.
Facilities: None.
Contact: For beach information, contact the Mendocino Coast Division of the California Department of Parks and Recreation at (707) 937-5804.

See number 22 on page 502.

Bunking Down

If camping sounds a little austere but being near this wild and rocky coast holds some appeal, you can always opt for comfort and proximity to nature by staying at one of the bed-and-breakfast inns scattered about the area. This part of the coast is uncrowded and unhurried. If you're serious about getting away, you couldn't do better than Westport. Our picks: **Howard Creek Ranch** (40501 Highway 1, 964-6725, $$) and **DeHaven Valley Farm Country Inn and Restaurant** (39247 Highway 1, 961-1660, $$), both of which are located on the highway and offer oceans and mountains for a backdrop. With ten and eight rooms respectively, these are the largest inns in Westport; others are smaller but just as charming.

For More Information

Contact the Fort Bragg-Mendocino Coast Chamber of Commerce, 332 North Main Street, P.O. Box 1141, Fort Bragg, CA 95437; (707) 961-6300.

Wages Creek Beach

Location: 17 miles north of Fort Bragg, off Highway 1 in Westport.

Parking: $10 entrance fee per vehicle.

Hours: 10 AM to 5 PM.

Facilities: Rest rooms, showers, picnic tables, and fire rings. There are 175 tent and RV campsites. The fee is $17 per night. For camping reservations, call Wages Creek Beach Campground at (707) 964-2964.

Contact: For beach information, contact Wages Creek Beach Campground at (707) 964-2964.

See number 24 on page 502.

Westport-Union Landing State Beach

Location: Three miles north of Westport, off Highway 1.

Parking: Free parking lot.

Hours: Open 24 hours.

Facilities: Rest rooms, picnic tables, and fire pits. There are 100 tent and RV campsites. Fees are $7 to $9 per night. No camping reservations.

Contact: For beach information, contact the Mendocino Coast Division of the California Department of Parks and Recreation at (707) 937-5804.

See number 25 on page 502.

Sinkyone Wilderness State Park

Location: Northwest corner of Mendocino County. Three miles north of Rockport on Highway 1, pick up County Road 431 and continue six miles to Usal Campground. Access to the north end of the park is gained from the Humboldt County town of Redway. Pick up Briceland Road, which leads to a visitors center and campgrounds at Needle Rock 36 miles away. Be advised that roads within the park are only seasonally passable to most vehicles.

Here's a new one on us: a park you can't get to. At least some of the time, that is. Two roads lead into Sinkyone: one from Rockport in Mendocino County, one from Redway in Humboldt County. Both are steep, winding, and difficult to negotiate under the best of circumstances—and flat-out impassable when the rains are heavy. RVs and trailers are out of the question all the time. Cars and pickups will work from March to October. Four-wheel drives are best for getting around the rugged terrain of an area that's colloquially known as the Lost Coast.

So what's the attraction? Try 7,300 acres of deep coastal wilderness that even Highway 1 fails to penetrate. Ten primitive, hike-in campgrounds, and one where you can park your

Bear Harbor Beach
(a part of Sinkyone Wilderness State Park)

Location: Take the Redway exit off Highway 101 north of Garberville in Humboldt County, and turn west on Briceland Road. Proceed for approximately 28 miles to Orchard Camp in Sinkyone Wilderness State Park. Park and hike south along the Lost Coast Trail for 0.4 mile to the beach.

Parking: Free parking lot.

Hours: Open 24 hours.

Facilities: None. There are three campsites for tents at Bear Harbor. There are also three tent sites apiece at Railroad Camp and Orchard Camp, both close by. The fee is $9 per night. No camping reservations.

Contact: For beach information, contact Sinkyone Wilderness State Park at (707) 986-7711.

See number 28 on page 502.

Jones Beach
(a part of Sinkyone Wilderness State Park)

Location: Take the Redway exit off Highway 101 north of Garberville in Humboldt County, and turn west on Briceland Road. Proceed for approximately 25 miles to Jones Beach Camp. Park and hike along the Jones Beach Trail for 0.3 mile to the beach.

Parking: Free parking lot.

Hours: Open 24 hours.

Facilities: None. There are three campsites for tents at Jones Beach Camp. The fee is $9 per night. No camping reservations.

Contact: For beach information, contact Sinkyone Wilderness State Park at (707) 986-7711.

See number 30 on page 502.

car. The 22.1-mile Lost Coast Trail, which zigs and zags along the coastline, sometimes at sea level and other times atop ridges at elevations of 800 feet.

The steep mountains rise to heights of 1,800 feet and support a diverse array of plants, from second-growth coast redwoods and California laurels to grasslands, meadows, and shrubs. The region was heavily logged for a century—from 1888 to 1986, the last owner being Georgia Pacific. Now the land is recovering and reverting to a wild state. It's hard to believe in the midst of this now-empty country that Georgia Pacific and its forerunners created bustling company towns at Wheeler and Usal, which were burned by the lumber company in 1969 to eliminate liability problems from leaving the old buildings standing. Prior to the timberfest, this land was the home of the Sinkyone Indians, and the story of their subjugation is another sordid chapter in the history of the abuse of native populations.

Today, the old ranches and lumber camps are abandoned and overgrown. Except for a small visitors center at Needle Rock House, a former rancher's home, Sinkyone Wilderness State Park has little more than trails and gravel roads running through it. Camping is first come, first served, and you must bring your own water and firewood. The most interesting campground is at Bear Harbor Cove, site of a former dog-hole port where lumber was

Little Jackass Creek Beach
(a part of Sinkyone Wilderness State Park)

Location: Three miles north of Rockport, turn off Highway 1 onto Usal Road (County Route 431). Follow for six miles to Usal Campground. Park and hike north along the Lost Coast Trail for 7.5 miles to Little Jackass Creek Camp.

Parking: Free parking lot at Usal Campground.

Hours: Open 24 hours.

Facilities: None. There are four campsites for tents. The fee is $3 per night. No camping reservations.

Contact: For beach information, contact Sinkyone Wilderness State Park at (707) 986-7711.

See number 27 on page 502.

Needle Rock Beach
(a part of Sinkyone Wilderness State Park)

Location: Take the Redway exit off Highway 101 north of Garberville in Humboldt County, and turn west on Briceland Road. Proceed for approximately 26 miles to Needle Rock Visitor Center. Park and hike along Needle Rock Beach Trail for 0.2 mile to the beach.

Parking: Free parking lot.

Hours: Open 24 hours.

Facilities: Rest rooms, picnic tables, and fire rings. There are four campsites for tents at Barn Camp and Stream Side Camp. The fee is $9 per night. No camping reservations.

Contact: For beach information, contact Sinkyone Wilderness State Park at (707) 986-7711.

See number 29 on page 502.

shipped. Wilderness permits are required to hike the Lost Coast Trail between Usal Beach and Bear Harbor. They cost $3 a night, and are obtainable at the Usal Beach Campground or Needle Rock Visitor Center.

Down by the ocean, black sand and coarse gravel beaches lie at the mouths of creeks. Between them, the beach narrows to a thin ribbon of dark volcanic sand. Primitive, beachfront sites are strung out along the Sinkyone shoreline. From south to north, there's **Little Jackass Creek Beach** (visited by as many seals as humans), **Bear Harbor** (good tidepooling), **Needle Rock Beach** (long, hikable shoreline), and **Jones Beach** (cove beach at the end of a steep trail).

For More Information

Contact Sinkyone Wilderness State Park, P.O. Box 245, Whitethorn, CA 95489; (707) 986-7711.

Usal Beach
(a part of Sinkyone Wilderness State Park)

4

Location: Three miles north of Rockport, turn off Highway 1 onto Usal Road (County Route 431). Follow for six miles to Usal Campground. A spur road leads to the beach.

Parking: Free parking lot.

Hours: Open 24 hours.

Facilities: Rest rooms, picnic tables, and fire rings. There are 15 campsites for tents. The fee is $9 per night. No camping reservations.

Contact: For beach information, contact Sinkyone Wilderness State Park at (707) 986-7711.

See number 26 on page 502.

Humboldt County

They call it Humboldt County, but we think a better name would be Humbled County. We certainly were humbled by all there was to do and see in this vast natural wonderland. Perhaps taking a cue from the redwoods, everything seems bigger up here. Not only does Humboldt County claim to have the world's tallest tree—a 388-footer found at the Tall Trees Grove in Redwood National Park—but it's also got 100 miles of coastline; the tallest peak on any continental margin in the U.S. (King Peak, at 4,086 feet, in the King Range National Conservation Area); and the Lost Coast and Coastal trails, which wander along the shoreline for 50 and 30 miles, respectively.

Humboldt County can roughly be thought of as three counties in one. Southern Humboldt County is known as the Lost Coast, a place where mountains rise right out of the ocean and roads swing inland as if afraid to venture near the rugged shoreline. Shelter Cove *(continued on page 538)*

Coastal Humboldt County's Climate

Eureka Averages

	Daily High Temp. (°F)	Daily Low Temp. (°F)	Rainfall (inches)
January	53	41	7.0
February	55	43	5.2
March	54	43	5.1
April	55	44	2.9
May	57	43	1.6
June	59	50	0.6
July	60	52	0.1
August	61	53	0.4
September	62	52	0.9
October	60	48	2.7
November	58	45	5.9
December	55	42	6.2
Yearly Average	**57**	**47**	**38.6**

Source: National Weather Service data, National Oceanographic and Atmospheric Administration.

Humboldt County

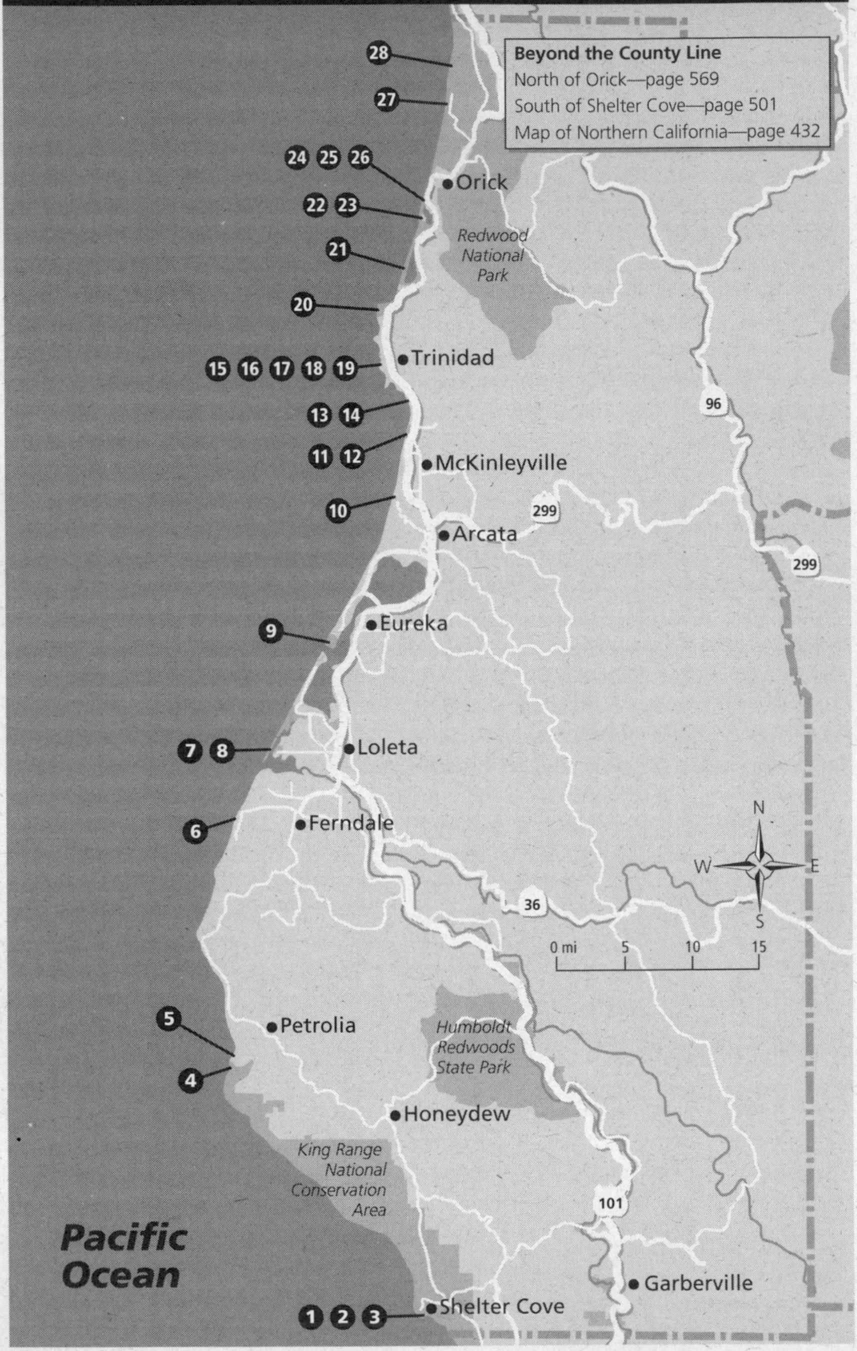

Humboldt County Beaches

Map of Northern California—page 432

(continued from page 535) is the most accessible point on the Lost Coast, but even it requires a 26-mile drive from Highway 101 over curving, narrow, and steeply graded roads. Your reward is a black-sand beach that seems to run to infinity in either direction.

Then there's the middle portion of the county, a land of river valleys, pasture land, embayments, and most of the population centers. Ferndale (a Victorian village), Eureka, Arcata, McKinleyville, and Trinidad are spread out along a 30-mile stretch of Highway 101. Lengthy sand spits and dune-covered beaches can be found in this area. Finally, the northern third of Humboldt is redwood country. Redwood National Park and Prairie Creek Redwoods State Park occupy a big chunk of the coast hereabouts, with little Orick being the only human settlement between Trinidad and the Del Norte County line. West of Orick is Gold Bluffs Beach, one of the most stellar settings for a beach anywhere in the world.

If you come to Humboldt County, allow plenty of time to drink in its immense natural beauty, enjoy the redwoods and beaches, and lose yourself in the foggy mystery of a world apart.

Key to the Symbols

Bike path · Camping · Food and drink · Hiking · Nude

Pier · RVs allowed · Surfing · Volleyball

Crowd Rating

sweet solitude . . . moderate crowds . . . wall-to-wall

Overall Rating

1 don't bother . . . 2 . . . 3 worth a visit . . . 4 . . . 5 beach heaven

Shelter Cove

Location: 220 miles north of San Francisco and 24 miles west of Garberville. From Highway 101, take the Garberville/Redway exit and proceed west to Shelter Cove on paved county roads, following the signs. Shelter Cove is the site of some lengthy black-sand beaches, including a 24-miler known as Black Sands Beach.
Population: 350
Area Code: 707 **Zip Code:** 95589

Shelter Cove lies at the heart of the Lost Coast, a remote and seldom-visited region comprising Sinkyone Wilderness State Park and the King Range National Conservation Area. While a few home builders have stumbled onto Shelter Cove over the past decade, it still deserves to be described as "lost." It lies a mere 24 miles west of Garberville, but these are 24 of the most trying miles you'll ever drive, particularly approaching the coast. The road is paved but unmarked, and it meanders and curves, ascending and descending. Eventually, it reaches a peak high in the King Range and the ocean pops into view—one of the most mesmerizing first glimpses of the mighty Pacific on the entire West Coast. If it's not shrouded in fog, the ocean glistens brightly in the distance like a diamond choker. Then a long, heart-stopping grade drops down to sea level.

Shelter Cove is spread out on land surrounding a natural harbor between headlands in the King Range. About 400 houses have been built out here in a slow-going development of what used to be a giant sheep ranch. The ranch owner sold his tract back in 1965 for a quarter-of-a-million dollars; it was resold for $900,000 to a development company that subdivided it into 1,300 smallish (given the rural location) lots. The homes that have gone up here are mainly incongruously large dwellings built by retirees from points south. They move to Shelter Cove with the best intentions, get the heebie-jeebies from all the isolation, and then try (often unsuccessfully) to unload their Amityville Horror onto the next ocean-loving retiree.

And isolated it is. Unique on the California coast, you must drive for an hour to get to a bona fide grocery store or a movie house. The King Range, with peaks that rise to heights of 4,000 feet, separates Shelter Cove from civilization. Try as they might to lure people here by putting in a small airstrip while continuing to subdivide and sell as best they can, the area is simply too distant to be attractive to urbanites, even those who toy with the fantasy of fleeing the overcrowded city. Shelter Cove does have two marinas, several small motels, a couple of restaurants, all the solitude you can stand (and then some), and black-sand beaches that will dazzle and delight the intrepid beachcomber.

Beaches

On a sunny day, you'll rarely find a beach more beautiful than **Black Sands Beach**, located at the northwest edge of town and accessible via Humboldt Loop and Beach Road. The sand is coarse, gravelly, and dark. The beach is extremely wide by the parking lot, then narrows up the coast. It continues for 24 miles and is

Black Sands Beach

Location: From the end of Beach Road in Shelter Cove, drive north for 24 miles to the mouth of the Mattole River.
Parking: Free parking lot.
Hours: Open 24 hours.
Facilities: None.
Contact: For beach information, contact the Arcata District Office of the King Range National Conservation Area at (707) 825-2300.

See number 4 on page 536.

firm enough for good hiking. In fact, the beach links up with a trail through the Sinkyone Wilderness to form the nearly 50-mile Lost Coast Trail, which runs from Usal Campground to the Mattole River. If you're in search of plentiful solitude on a true wilderness beach, you can do no better than this stretch of the Lost Coast. Closer to the center of town, a short trail in the vicinity of Pelican's Landing restaurant leads to **Little Black Sands Beach**, a favorite of locals. The sand is, as these beach names suggest, dark and volcanic in origin.

Our own favorite beach, and a shoo-in for a coastal Top Ten list, is **Dead Man's Beach**. This gem sits at the south end of town, beginning at the Shelter Cove Marina and Campground. Park in one of the lots by the marina, follow the cement boat-launch ramp down to the beach, and walk south along the broadly curving cove past some spectacular scenery. Cliffs rise behind the narrow strip of sand, while breakers thunder ashore. Small waterfalls cascade over the sheer rock face to the beach below, slowly carving their way through it.

Dead Man's Beach

5

Location: In Shelter Cove, take Shelter Cove Road to Machi Road, which leads to the Shelter Cove Marina and Campground. Hike south from the marina.

Parking: Free parking lot at Shelter Cove Marina and Campground.

Hours: Open 24 hours.

Facilities: None.

Contact: For beach information, contact the Shelter Cove Information Center at (707) 986-7069 or the Arcata District Office of the King Range National Conservation Area at (707) 825-2300.

See number 1 on page 536.

Little Black Sands Beach

4

Location: In Shelter Cove, at Wave and Dolphin Drives, just north of Point Delgada.

Parking: Free street parking.

Hours: Open 24 hours.

Facilities: None.

Contact: For beach information, contact the Arcata District Office of the King Range National Conservation Area at (707) 825-2300.

See number 3 on page 536.

Shelter Cove

RV 4

Location: 26 miles west of Highway 101. Take the Garberville/Redway exit off Highway 101 in Garberville. Follow Briceland-Thorne Road to Shelter Cove Road and continue to Shelter Cove. Shelter Cove Marina and Campground is at the end of Machi Road in Shelter Cove.

Parking: Free parking lot.

Hours: Open 24 hours.

Facilities: Rest rooms, showers, picnic tables, and fire rings. There are 105 tent and RV campsites, with hookups. Fees are $12 to $22 per night. For camping reservations, call the Shelter Cove Marina and Campground at (707) 986-7474.

Contact: For beach information, contact the Shelter Cove Marina and Campground at (707) 986-7474.

See number 2 on page 536.

Surfers are fond of the waves at Dead Man's Beach about half-a-mile south of the boat launch. They'll drive their Toyota 4x4s (everybody's got one here) along the beach, tide permitting. The tidal exchange can be extreme—as great as eight feet—so consult a tide chart before attempting to walk or drive.

Bunking Down

We put in for the evening at the **Shelter Cove Beachcomber Inn** (7272 Shelter Cove Road, 986-7733, $). It's a small place—really a house divided into individual units—that's comfortable and functional. Rooms include a kitchen, a TV, and enough beds to sleep three to six people. They were in the process of expanding during our last visit, so there should be double the number of units—that is to say, six—by the time you read this. The **Shelter Cove Bed and Breakfast** (148 Dolphin Drive, 986-7161, $$) has two first-floor suites with ocean views and Jacuzzis, two small upstairs rooms with balconies, and a large, though viewless, downstairs room. Upon request (a bow to Shelter Cove's isolation), the owners can arrange home-cooked meals to be delivered to your room. Another lodging alternative is to put in at the **Shelter Cove Marina and Campground** (492 Machi Road, 986-7474, $). It's a veritable RV city here, with people venturing to land's end to deep-sea fish, dive for abalone, and enjoy the solitude.

Coastal Cuisine

The on-premises deli at the **Shelter Cove Campground and Marina** (492 Machi Road, 986-7474, $) serves the best fish-and-chips we've ever had on any coast. Lest this sound like hype, let us assure you we were skeptical. "Are the fish-and-chips any good?" we queried without conviction while peering hungrily at the sandwiches (particularly the hearty Surfer's Sub) in the deli case. "Are you kidding?" the matron behind the counter responded. "We caught it fresh this morning." Indeed, the generic term "fish-and-chips" just can't do justice to the basket of delicious, fried black snapper that had been pulled from the ocean mere hours earlier. They'll ask if you want tartar or cocktail sauce with it, but you really need neither. Just splash on a little malt vinegar, and you'll be halfway to heaven, and all for only $5.49.

For More Information

Contact the Shelter Cove Information Bureau, 412 Machi Road, Shelter Cove, CA 95589; (707) 986-7069.

King Range National Conservation Area

Location: 230 miles north of San Francisco and 70 miles south of Eureka. The vast park is accessible from paved roads originating in the towns of Redway and Ferndale, and from Humboldt Redwoods State Park.

The King Range National Conservation Area is a massive tract of public land administered by the federal Bureau of Land Management (BLM). It occupies 52,000 acres in the southwest corner of Humboldt County, extending for 35 miles between Whale Gulch and the Mattole River, and up to six miles inland from the Pacific Ocean. Indeed, there is little in this corner of the county that isn't federal land—just the town of Shelter Cove and some scattered holdings in the mountains.

Black Sands Beach (also see Shelter Cove) is a lengthy strand of coarse, pitch-black volcanic sand that runs from Shelter Cove to the Mattole River. This primeval North Coast beach is backed by the jagged peaks of the relatively youthful King Range. The rise in elevation from sea level to 4,086 feet—the height of King Peak, the highest point on any shoreline in the continental U.S.—occurs in less than three miles.

Black Sands Beach abuts the steep cliffs of the King Range. Beginning in Shelter Cove, hikers can wander northward along the coast for 24 uninterrupted miles, to the mouth of the Mattole River. This sandy traipse is part of the Lost Coast Trail, and it passes through immensely scenic coastal wilderness.

Backpacking is possible both along inland mountain trails and the beach. For a thrilling experience, hike along the beach north from Shelter Cove for exactly five miles, then pick up Buck Creek Trail, which runs for 2.5 miles in a zigzagging northeast direction before approaching the 3,290-foot summit of Saddle Mountain. Back at sea level, you'll pass offshore rocks inhabited by sea lions, seals, and marine birds. Other sights include the remains of shipwrecks and the abandoned Punta Gorda Lighthouse.

Camping is permitted anywhere on the beach. At the north end, Mattole River Beach (see Petrolia) is the site of a semideveloped campground. Away from the beach, BLM maintains four developed campgrounds within the King Range: Wailaki (9 campsites) and Nadelos (6), which lie east of Shelter Cove near the Humboldt-Mendocino County line, and Tolkan (9) and Horse Mountain (9), which also lie in the southern third of the park, about 1.5 miles inland.

May to October are the best months to come, as the torrential rains of winter wash out roads and spirits. Some parts of the King Range get deluged with 200 inches a year of precipitation. Be mindful of encroaching tides while walking along the beach. High tides can strand unwary hikers in coves, and sleeper waves—waves of extraordinary size that appear out of nowhere—can wash the unsuspecting out to sea. Carry and consult tide tables, available at local stores, and never turn your back on the ocean.

For More Information

Contact the Bureau of Land Management, which has offices in Arcata and Ukiah. The addresses are: (1) Arcata Resource Area, 1125 16th Street, Room 219, Arcata, CA 95521; (707) 825-2300. (2) Ukiah District Office, 555 Leslie Street, Ukiah, CA 95482; (707) 468-4000. Trail maps and campfire permits can be obtained from either office. Maps and general information about the area are available at the Shelter Cove Information Center, 412 Machi Road, Shelter Cove, CA 95489; (707) 986-7069.

Honeydew and Petrolia

Location: Take Highway 101 to the Mattole Road turnoff, and go west 21 miles. Petrolia is 15 miles northwest of Honeydew, along the same road. From Petrolia, Lighthouse Road runs west for five miles, ending at Mattole River Beach, the only easily reached beach on this stretch of the Lost Coast. Continuing north from Petrolia along Mattole Road to Wildcat Road eventually leads to Ferndale, about 30 miles away.
Population: 500 (Honeydew), 400 (Petrolia)
Area Code: 707 **Zip Code:** 95545 (Honeydew), 95558 (Petrolia)

They've paved the road to Honeydew! Okay, stop yawning. This is big news in Humboldt County. You can now make the incomparable, 75-mile drive from Shelter Cove to Honeydew, proceed on to the boomtown of Petrolia (general store, bar/restaurant, diner), and finally land in beautiful, Victorian Ferndale with just a few miles of gravel chewing up your car's paint job. This is one of the great scenic drives in America, passing through forests, farmland, meadows, and mountains. The mailboxes are few and far between. The road is narrow and uneven but driveable.

The road to Honeydew is marked with signs pointing off Shelter Cove Road. The turnoff onto this newly paved road is about halfway between Garberville and Shelter Cove. The opening up of the area to more than four-wheel-drive vehicles is the culmination of an effort to drive (no pun intended) some particularly nasty pot growers out of the area. They were as entrenched in these mountains as rattlesnakes, and shared a similarly reptilian disposition. They were the growers of "Humboldt Gold," an agricultural product much loved by a certain segment of the population. The legalization of marijuana is one issue—and there are good arguments on both sides, neither of which we'll make here. But these guys did whatever it took to keep the outside world at bay. Stories are told of potshots taken at unfamiliar vehicles, and of booby traps strung across hiking trails to scare off (if not injure) narks and even outdoorsmen. A campaign involving helicopters and infrared photography identified the hemp, and the crusty growers were eventually flushed from their fields.

You can still see the remnants of their anti-authoritarian ilk here and there, gazing at passers-by with reddened eyes from the front porches of listing houses. More unsettling is the sight of abandoned cars with bullet holes blown through them that sit by the side of the road. It's probably still a good idea not to look too hard or linger too long. In the way of services, there's a general store at Honeydew and a handful of places to fill up with gas, brew, or supplies in Petrolia. And whatever you do, please drive slow for the sake of the wingless quail who scoot across the roads around here. We very nearly wiped out a little brood of the sweet critters as we rounded a curve outside Petrolia.

Beaches

Much of the drive described herein runs around the interior of southern Humboldt County. But for a six-mile stretch along Mattole Road, just north of Petrolia in the direction of Ferndale, it follows the coast at dune level. And what a stretch of coast it is: gigantic sea stacks, one of which could rival Haystack Rock up in Oregon; extruded basalt formations on the inland side as well; a sea that's colored a tropical foam-green close to shore and a shimmering metallic blue farther out; brown-sand beaches that beg to be walked. This is cattle country, and the beasts have the run of the place, crossing the road at their leisure and looking quizzically at passing cars.

The vistas afforded of the beach, particularly as the road makes a perpendicular turn and dizzying northward ascent toward Ferndale, are the equal of any on the coast. Beach access can be gained along Mattole Road via gated paths that cross private land. You must park beside the road when you can find a bit of dusty shoulder. We couldn't find the reputed pullouts, however, and were content just to vista-cruise past it all.

There's one prominent, accessible beach worth mentioning. At a fork in the road, Petrolia lies off to the right along Mattole Road, while Lighthouse Road continues alongside the Mattole River till it meets the ocean. At the mouth of the river is a beach of humongous proportions. The locals have fenced in the parking lot with gigantic driftwood trunks, silvery and skeletal, to keep ATVs (all-terrain vehicles) from tearing up the beach. A colorful mural of a beach scene includes this legend: "We love our beach. Please respect it. Beaches are important to everyone." Attached is a notation that **Mattole River Beach** has been "adopted by the Mattole Union 3rd, 4th, and 5th grades."

Mattole River Beach

3

Location: Five miles west of Petrolia at the end of Lighthouse Road, by the mouth of the Mattole River.

Parking: Free parking lot.

Hours: Open 24 hours.

Facilities: Rest rooms, picnic tables, and fire rings. There are nine campsites for tents. There is a $5 camping fee; no reservations.

Contact: For beach information, contact the Bureau of Land Management, Arcata Resource Area, at (707) 825-2300.

See number 5 on page 536.

The beach is a wide delta formed by the gravelly river. On a late-summer day, the wind was blowing up fearsome whitecaps, and the lone occupant of the beach was fighting to keep a kite under control. Chalk up one more wild and beautiful beach for the seemingly endless coast of northern California. Mattole River Beach falls within the purview of the King Range National Conservation Area. You are welcome to toss up a tent or park a camper in the open area out here, though facilities are primitive: chemical toilets, picnic tables, and fire rings. You must bring your own water. A so-called "iron ranger" has been installed, and you're asked to pay $5 a night on the honor system. Depending on your perspective, the 24-mile Lost Coast Trail either begins or ends here.

Bunking Down

In Petrolia, the **Lost Inn** (Matthole Road, 629-3394, $$) makes a great getaway for those who crave privacy well off the beaten path. The inn features a three-room suite that includes a glassed-in porch and private garden where guests can sit among the flowers and marvel at the splendid isolation of it all. The Lost Inn is located one block from Petrolia's General Store (you can't miss it) and seven miles from Mattole River Beach (a.k.a. Lighthouse Road Beach). The owners are in the process of adding a second unit, which should be ready by late 1996.

Coastal Cuisine

The **Hideaway Bar and Grill** in Petrolia (Mattole Road, 629-3330, $) is a swell place to duck into for a burger, taco, and/or brew. Not that the competition on the culinary front is so very keen out here. It's located at the Lindley Bridge, on the banks of the sparkling Mattole River.

For More Information

Contact the Garberville-Redway Area Chamber of Commerce, 773 Redwood Drive, P.O. Box 445, Garberville, CA 95542; (707) 923-2613.

Ferndale

Location: 20 miles southwest of Eureka. Take the Fernbridge-Ferndale exit off Highway 101, then proceed west for four miles. Centerville Road leads to Centerville Beach County Park, five miles due west of Ferndale.
Population: 1,420
Area Code: 707 **Zip Code:** 95536

There hadn't been such excitement in Ferndale since the 1992 earthquake. The streets of this tiny village of restored Victorian homes and step-back-in-time stores were jammed with trailers and people. Some were busy building a two-story facade over a one-story building. What gives? Were the townsfolk carrying this Victoriana craze too far? Had we entered the Twilight Zone? Actually, Hollywood had descended upon Ferndale in the summer of '94 to film the medical thriller *Outbreak*, about a virus that runs amok through a rural population. The facade they were building around the local bank read "Monroe County Hospital." It looked so authentic that we had to walk up and touch it to convince ourselves it wasn't weathered brick and mortar.

Celebrity sightings were reported all over Ferndale and nearby Eureka, where cast and crew were staying. Tongues wagged: stars Dustin Hoffman, Carrie Fisher, and Renee Russo were seen eating at Bibo and Bear one night. Over in Eureka, they practiced their lines in the lobby of the Hotel Carter during cocktail hour. Hoffman, it was said, got up at 6:30 AM to play tennis one day. And on and on. The townsfolk were eating it up. And why not? Something like this happens less frequently, as fate would have it, than an earthquake.

Normally, life in Ferndale moves at a snail's pace. All visitors should be prepared to set the clock back. Be advised, though, that you don't lose an hour; you lose a century. You think we're exaggerating? Imagine this: every single structure in Ferndale looks exactly as it did 100 years ago. They are cleaned, polished, and freshly painted right down to their elaborately carved woodwork. The whole town has been designated a state historical landmark (Number 883, to be precise). From the beginning, the primary source of income in these parts was dairy farming, and the local creameries were so productive that Ferndale became known nationally as "Cream City." The wealth that flowed from the cows' udders built and maintained the ornate town-and-country residences nicknamed "Butterfat Palaces," built in the 1880s.

Today, Ferndale has got everything for a weekend getaway. You can bed down at the Gingerbread Mansion—the *ne plus ultra* of bed-and-breakfast inns along the North Coast—and walk a mere block downtown to dine at the exquisite Bibo and Bear restaurant. These two places are reasons enough to come to Ferndale, but there's more. The town is packed with antique stores, art galleries, old-fashioned candy emporiums—just the sort of shopping you'd expect to find in a town swathed in a Victorian mantle. It also has a quaint little museum run by the local historical society. For a $1 entrance fee, you can learn all about the history of the area via exhibits that run the gamut from earthquake seismometers to a reconstructed barbershop. You can also ask for recommendations from the golden girls who run the place. We just hung around and listened to them dish the latest about *Outbreak*. Sample snippet: "Have you been uptown?" "Yes." "Are they doing anything with the movie today?" "They're fixing up the ladies jewelry store and making it a pet store." "That's nice."

On the earthquake front, there was a whole lotta shakin' goin' on in Ferndale and its environs on April 25 and 26, 1992. Between 11:06 AM on April 25 and 4:18 AM on April 26—a span of only 17 hours—three separate earthquakes rocked Cape Mendocino. The first (and largest) measured 7.1 on the Richter scale and had its epicenter five miles southeast of Petrolia. The second and third, which came during the night, measured 6.6 and 6.7, respectively, and were centered off the coast. Geologists rank them among the most powerful quakes ever to shake California, with an acceleration force that was measured at 2.25 G. For comparison's sake, the Loma Prieta earthquake that hit San Francisco and Santa Cruz in 1989 had a peak acceleration force of only 0.646 G and an equivalent Richter scale reading of 7.1. No wonder buildings were toppled and fires were started in the villages of Scotia and Rio Dell.

The marks of the quake can still be seen at the entrance to Centerville Beach County Park, where collapsed farm buildings litter the fields. The naval facility at Centerville Beach is in a similar state. The road leading up to the empty facility offers a beautiful coastal vista at the point where asphalt turns to gravel. There's a pullout and a magnificent overlook onto the beach.

For the discerning viewer, there's also an object lesson in what will eventually happen to beachfront real estate on a young, geologically active coastline (the case throughout California). Study the abandoned roadway, much of which has eroded and crumbled into the ocean. Look at the retreating cliffs. Imagine your own personal beach house perched precariously on the edge and giving way some fateful, storm-wracked evening. As one of our coastal geology professors used to say, "If you can see the ocean, it can see you, too."

Beaches

Centerville Beach County Park, located five miles west of Ferndale, is a sizable swath of sand somewhat incongruously bordered by idyllic farmers' fields. The expansive beach is covered with driftwood and deep, soft, dirty brown sand. We watched thunderous breakers roll ashore on an otherwise calm July afternoon, negating the possibility of water activities other than fishing. It is a great beach for barefoot strolls up the coast, beyond where the eye can see in the salty mist kicked up by the roiling surf. Eerily, upon returning, we noticed that the only footprints in the sand were ours.

It is desolate out here. En route to the beach we came to a complete stop in front of an old, abandoned farmhouse—not to wax nostalgic about the cobwebs on the porch swing, but because a flock of geese chose that very moment to waddle across the road.

Bunking Down

The **Gingerbread Mansion** (400 Berding Street, 786-4000, $$$) is the most striking example of the town's elegantly playful Victorian style. Its eye-popping brown and orange exterior, fanciful wedding-cake moldings, and storybook gardens have made it the best known and most often photographed of all of Ferndale's structures. Owner Ken Forbert is an antiques hound, dating back to his college days in San Francisco, when he'd scavenge thrift shops for old pieces. Now he selectively scours antique stores up and down the coast, replacing old pieces whenever he makes a new purchase. Many rooms have authentic claw-foot bathtubs on raised platforms; one has an old Victorian fainting couch (oh, those days of whalebone corsets!) perched beside it. The feeling of the inn is one of a gracious yet relaxed

Centerville Beach County Park

Location: Five miles west of Ferndale at the end of Centerville Road.

Parking: Free parking lot.

Hours: Open 24 hours.

Facilities: Rest rooms.

Contact: For beach information, contact the Humboldt County Parks Department at (707) 445-7651.

See number 6 on page 536.

ambience. Tea is served at four in the afternoon with various treats set out to nibble on. Breakfast is a real undertaking, served at long, decorated tables at the appointed hour with a hot egg dish complementing the array of fruit, pastries, homemade granola, coffee, and tea. After a hearty breakfast, guests are invited to tool around town on one of the inn's old bikes.

Another lodging option that lets visitors steep themselves in the Victorian flavor of the town is the **Shaw House Bed-and-Breakfast Inn** (703 Main Street, 786-9958, $$). Built by the founder of Ferndale in 1854, the inn is the oldest house in Ferndale, and was modeled after Hawthorne's House of the Seven Gables. The six attractive guest rooms have private baths, and well-tended gardens, gazebo, and fish pond lend visual interest to the one-acre property. In the morning, guests rise and shine with the help of an elaborate breakfast spread.

Coastal Cuisine

Bibo and Bear (460 Main Street, 786-9484, $$$) has brought a dash of gourmet flair to Ferndale. The chef-owner is a former Indiana resident who quit another career to pursue his love of cooking in little Ferndale. The Whiskey Crab Soup is a must-try for openers. Seafood entrées include imaginative daily specials, as well as perennial favorites such as Cajun rock shrimp sautéed with sun-dried tomatoes and artichoke hearts, and a sweet dish of Pacific shrimp cooked with kiwi and amaretto. The kitchen also has a way with duck and lamb, and serves a killer secret-recipe barbecue sauce with their baby-back ribs. Oh, and a word to the wise: save room for dessert.

Another choice for fine dining in Ferndale is the **Victorian Inn** (400 Ocean Avenue, 786-4949, $$), which offers an extensive and varied menu—from salmon to steak, scampi to spanokopita—in an attractive building (ca. 1893) that also does business as a lodging house.

For More Information

Contact the Ferndale Chamber of Commerce, P.O. Box 325, Ferndale, CA 95536; (707) 786-4477.

Loleta

Location: 12 miles south of Eureka, off Highway 101. Due west of Loleta is Crab County Park, which provides access to the Eel River Slough and the ocean.
Population: 800
Area Code: 707 **Zip Code:** 95551

Loleta is a sweet ingenue of a town that will make you say "cheese." It is at the center of Humboldt dairy-farming country, between Ferndale and Eureka. Situated in a valley on the fertile delta of the Eel River, it provides an idyllic setting where cows graze and time passes slowly. The little burg's main calling card is the Loleta Cheese Factory (252 Loleta Drive, 733-5470), where you can tour the facility and sample its wares: award-winning Monterey jack and cheddar cheese, among others. A gift shop sells local wines and aged cheeses.

Beyond this, Loleta is notable mainly for the access that it and the neighboring pin-sized communities of Fernbridge and Beatrice provide to the ocean, bay, and river. Fishermen will go batty over the rock jetty on the **South Spit** (reached from Beatrice via Table Bluff Road), the bayfront beaches of **Crab County Park** (off Cannibal Island Road, west of Loleta), and the delta of the Eel River (accessible from a maze of roads out of Ferndale). For a nice panorama and stroll, take the Hookton Road exit from Highway 101 to Table Bluff County Park. Parking is free and hiking trails afford nice views of the ocean that batters the South Spit of Humboldt Bay.

For More Information

Contact the Loleta Chamber of Commerce, P.O. Box 327, Loleta, CA 95551.

Crab County Park

Location: From Loleta, located 12 miles south of Eureka off Highway 101, take Loleta Drive to Cannibal Island Road and proceed west to the park.
Parking: Free parking lot.
Hours: Open 24 hours.
Facilities: Rest rooms.
Contact: For beach information, contact the Humboldt County Parks Department at (707) 445-7651.

See number 7 on page 536.

South Spit and Jetty

Location: Approximately 10 miles south of Eureka, take Hookton Road (off Highway 101) to Table Bluff Road. Pick up South Jetty Road at Table Bluff County Park and drive north to the jetty.
Parking: Free parking lot.
Hours: Open 24 hours.
Facilities: None.
Contact: For beach information, contact the Humboldt County Parks Department at (707) 445-7651.

See number 8 on page 536.

Eureka

Location: 284 miles north of San Francisco, off Highway 101. Eureka is located on Humboldt Bay and offers beach access at Samoa Dunes.
Population: 28,250
Area Code: 707 **Zip Code:** 95501

Eureka is a Greek word meaning "I've found it!" It's also the state motto of California, one that derives from Gold Rush days. However, if you were to take Highway 101 north into the city of Eureka, especially on one of the gray, overcast days that are not infrequent along the Humboldt Coast, you might suspect Eureka is Greek for "They've lost it."

From the south, the retail corridor leading into Eureka is anything but auspicious. For two miles, the ghastliest sort of roadside flotsam flogs one's sensibilities. One sees signs advertising "Burl Slabs 50 Cents" and attractions like the "World's Largest Hammer." The route is pierced with billboards, guide wires, smoke and fumes from paper mills, motel after motel offering rooms for under $30 (and no bargain at that), and an unrelenting march of strip malls. In some ways, little has changed since 1854, when Ulysses S. Grant, stationed at nearby Fort Humboldt, wrote home, "You do not know how forsaken I feel here!"

This visual madness—an unfair gauge of Eureka's true charms—is all the more jarring after a drive through the Avenue of the Giants, the 31-mile stretch of Highway 101 that passes through the majesty of Humboldt Redwoods State Park just south of here. Happily, there's more to Eureka than initially meets the eye. Rounding the bend on Broadway (Highway 101), one finds the other Eureka—the one that dates from the 1850s, when it was the most important port city for the thousand miles between San Francisco and Seattle.

For a quick and helpful orientation, stop by the Chamber of Commerce (2112 Broadway) or the Visitors Bureau (1034 Second Street). You will, no doubt, be directed to historic Old Town, the bayfront area that has been diligently restored and is surprising in its size and vitality. Armed with a Eureka Visitors Map, you'll happily leave the wheels behind and reenter the age of foot traffic.

A principal site on this walking tour is the Carson Mansion (Second & M Streets), which the Smithsonian calls "one of the most exuberant houses built in 19th-century America." Part Victorian and part fairy-tale castle, the house was constructed for William Carson, the lumber baron whose redwood empire opened up the North Coast. The mansion was erected during lulls in the logging season by the bossman's own lumberjacks and was completed in 1885, after three years of labor. The crazy-quilt array of gables, columns, and ornamental woodwork somehow manages to blend together. Look and admire, but don't enter. It's a private men's club now.

Across the street from Carson's former digs is the Pink Lady (202 M Street), another example of money's-no-object Victoriana. The gaudiness of this Pepto Bismol–pink Queen Anne–style structure may give some viewers visual indigestion. Once a private residence, the Pink Lady is now home to a gallery featuring the work of local artists.

Many other structures in and around Old Town have historic value, representing the period when Eureka was known as the "King of the Pacific Northwoods" and the "Heart of the Redwood Empire." The town got its start in 1850 from the fallout of the Gold Rush. The diggings were slim along the Trinity and Klamath Rivers, but the felling of redwoods provided plenty of work for able-bodied men. Within four years of its founding, Eureka was home to seven sawmills, and 140 schooners were kept busy carting away lumber from Humboldt Bay to points south. In their leisure time the lumbermen came to Eureka, a brawling, boozing, and brothel-filled respite from the monotony of sawing logs.

In some ways, Eureka is still King of the Northwoods. Despite the imperilment of the lumber trade all over the northwest, logging has endured in Eureka, though overforesting and cheap lumber from Canada have taken a toll. If you listen to the lumberjacks, Redwood National Park has frozen out the largest chunk of what trees remain in Humboldt County. It's this area, in fact, that provoked George Bush's specious remarks about "being neck deep in spotted owls."

In recent years, the city has turned elsewhere to fill the economic void. Just in time, an influx of arty types have begun flocking here in growing numbers. Their reasons are varied, but most have grown tired of where they came from and simply want to escape. Eureka, like Mendocino, is set in a gorgeous and non-distracting environment, in which artists feel free to hammer out their visions. Galleries, bookshops, and cultural events thrive in this city, thanks in part to the enlightened presence of Humboldt State University in nearby Arcata. Some of the original art, crafts, and handmade furniture on display in the local galleries are quite striking and unique to this locale, as transplanted, university-trained artists blaze new trails in landscape painting, while local folk artists continue to produce their remarkable handmade oddities.

The best site for the latter is the Wooden Garden (317 Second Street), a menagerie of politically charged pieces created by local sculptor Romano Gabriel over a thirty-year span. Other examples reflect the spirit of the location even more closely; a Native-American gallery is particularly welcome. Some of the art, of course, is also derivative (watercolor egrets on cork) and par for the course in any tourist town.

The city is nestled on the banks of Humboldt Bay, the second largest enclosed bay in California and the center of the region's recreational and commercial fishing—30 million pounds of fish are harvested annually in these waters. The fleet docks at the Woodley Island Marina, just across the Samoa Bridge from Old Town on Route 255. Eureka's water-related history can be explored at the Humboldt Bay Maritime Museum (1410 Second Street, 444-9440), a collection of nautical artifacts housed in a replica of the oldest house in town (ca. 1854). The history of the region's ecology and its Indian peoples can be explored at the Clarke Museum (240 E Street, 443-1947), which has a world-class collection of Native American basketry and artifacts. These items are housed—safely, one can be certain—in the historic Bank of Eureka Building (ca. 1912).

Beaches

The easiest way to explore the Humboldt Bay area is by boat. The best tour is the Humboldt Bay Harbor Cruise, operated by the Maritime Museum. A narrated, 75-minute tour aboard the *M/V Madaket* (the oldest operating pas-

Samoa Dunes Recreation Area

Location: From Eureka, take Highway 255 to the North Spit. Turn left on New Navy Base Road and follow till it ends at Samoa Dunes.

Parking: Free parking lot.

Hours: Open 24 hours.

Facilities: Rest rooms, showers, picnic tables, and fire rings. There are 50 tent and RV campsites. Fees are $8 to $10 per night. For camping reservations, call Samoa Boat Launch County Park at (707) 445-7652.

Contact: For beach information, contact the Bureau of Land Management, Arcata Resource Area, at (707) 825-2300.

See number 9 on page 536.

senger ship on the West Coast, ca. 1910) leaves regularly from the foot of C Street, off Waterfront Drive (444-9440). Woodley Island Marina is a great viewing station for harbor seals and egrets, and the adjoining promenade has a number of interpretive placards.

Nearby Samoa Island is the site of **Samoa Dunes Recreation Area**, a broad expanse of dune fields and beaches at the southern tip of the North Spit, which angles down from Arcata. It is one of the projecting fingers that enfolds and protects Humboldt Bay. A 300-acre parcel of Samoa Dunes falls to the Bureau of Land Management, while Humboldt County maintains a boat launch and a bayside campground.

A stiff breeze often blows off the water, which sculpts the dunes into their sloping, windswept shapes. There's a wide swash zone where the sand is sufficiently hard packed to allow for jogging or easy beach hiking. Kite flying, collecting driftwood, and bird-watching are popular activities out here.

Bunking Down

The celebrated **Hotel Carter** (301 L Street, 444-8062, $$$) actually embraces three properties: the 23-room hotel itself; **Carter House**, the awesome Victorian home that sits cattycorner to the hotel at 1033 Third Street; and **Bell House**, the 1890 cottage adjacent to Carter House (call 445-1390 for information on these two last properties). Hotel Carter is a yellow neo-Victorian with large rooms and all the usual modern amenities. A nightly wine-and-cheese hour is provided for the guests. Carter House, the most traditional of the three buildings, is where the stars of *Outbreak* chose to stay while it was being filmed down the road in Ferndale.

Interestingly, it was built in 1982 as an exact replica of a beloved Victorian inn, the Murphy House in San Francisco, which was razed to make room for a high-rise. It's an attractive place, where the wooden beams and walls in the living area receive and reflect sunlight in a way that is positively magical. (Although the wooden floors can make for some sleepless nights when noisy guests go clopping around in the wee hours.) As in the adjacent Bell House, wine and cheese is set out every evening, followed by tea and cookies a few hours later. Both homes have large living areas and a common kitchen for the use of guests, along with TVs and VCRs in each room. Our room in Bell House broke with the code of Victoriana and, refreshingly, was decorated in a contemporary mode.

The **Eureka Inn** (518 Seventh Street, 442-6441, $$) is a bird of a different feather. The sprawling, Tudor revival–style inn opened in 1922 as a symbol of Eureka's booming fortunes. It has since been designated a National Historic Place. The anomalous English architecture, set in an otherwise nondescript neighborhood, only adds to the its imperturbable grace. The 150-room building carries its age well; constant efforts are made to keep the building in good repair and equipped with modern amenities like a heated pool and hot tubs. The rooms, needless to add, are spacious and comfortable enough for a lord.

Coastal Cuisine

Restaurant 301, the on-premises eatery at Hotel Carter (301 L Street, 444-8062, $$$), is among the most distinctive on the North Coast. Appetizers include Hogg Island oysters topped with a swipe of Smokey Jim's BBQ sauce. The roster of entrees is big on creatively sauced grilled seafood and meats, such as rock cod with hazelnuts, lemon, and dill; and filet mignon glazed with burgundy and served with a peppered cheese sauce. A pungent local zinfandel went well with the sliced breast of duck, served in a fruited wine sauce. The wine list is extensive, with many of California's finest vintners represented.

Founded by a chef who once plied his trade at San Francisco's Stars restaurant and Napa's Domaine Chandon, **Ramone's Restaurant**

(203 E Street, 445-1642, $$) also draws raves from local foodies. A humble café and bakery by day, Ramone's reinvents itself at night to become an incredibly inventive dining experience. The menu changes weekly, but you'll always find fresh lamb, succulent seafood, and waistline-threatening desserts in the line-up. The bittersweet-chocolate soufflé is worth the half-hour advance notice the kitchen demands.

Wherever you dine in Eureka, whether it be in a historic old building or a seafood grill by the water, your surroundings are as vital to the experience as the food itself. Both seem tailored to remind you of the town's hard-working past. Take the **Samoa Cookhouse** (Samoa Road, 442-1659, $$). Located across the bridge on Samoa Island, it is the last surviving cookhouse in the West. Food is served camp style, and though the words "all you can eat" are never mentioned in the literature, you won't leave here hungry. There's no menu. One set price. No à la carte. No wine list.

It starts innocently enough, with salad you toss yourself in a large bowl. This is quickly followed by soup, ladled from a black kettle. Gigantic hunks of bread appear next. Then come bowls full of peas, kidney beans, and mashed potatoes and gravy, trailed closely by fried chicken, sliced ham, or whatever else the main courses happen to be. You'll even be offered seconds. Order iced tea, and an entire pitcher materializes. Warm apple pie baked in a big metal pan was placed on the table at the end of the meal. Actually, this is how (and where) the lumberjacks were fed in Eureka's timber heyday. Prices for lunch and dinner are low, given the quantities of food served. As one whiskered and suspendered old-timer proclaimed, "If you leave here hungry, it's yer own dang fault."

Lazio's Seafood (327 Second Street, 447-9717, $$) is another local institution. It's been serving seafood since 1944, though the family's roots in the fishing industry go back as far as 1889, when Lorenzo Lazio started a wholesale fish operation in San Francisco. Lazio's is filled with sea-faring paraphernalia. Take your time poring over the extensive menu, which includes crab legs Lazio and salmon cannelloni. Don't be afraid to order plain old broiled seafood, as it's fresh enough not to need doctoring with sauces. The broiled salmon is especially fine. Pacific oysters on the half shell are plump and gamy, quite different from their East Coast cousins. We admit they are something of an acquired taste—and we quickly acquired a taste for them.

A more recent arrival on the seafood scene is the **Sea Grill** (316 E Street, 443-7187, $$). It's an Old Town eatery that allows you to choose from a lengthy list of catches and the way you want it prepared (sautéed, grilled, charbroiled, broiled, poached, or deep fried). The fact that sturgeon and Dungeness crab were both on the menu caused our fins to perk up.

Café Marina (Woodley Island Marina, 443-2233, $$) serves up decent food in an above-average setting. It boasts the best view in town, looking across the bay onto Old Town Eureka from Woodley Island. A sheet listing available seafood is handed customers along with a regular menu. You can't go wrong with grilled or broiled petrale sole or ling cod.

If you're fried on seafood, take a different tack at another Old Town favorite, **Smokey Jim's BBQ** (307 Second Street, 443-4554, $). It's a classy hole-in-the-wall with its own character and an absurdly good barbecue sauce (mild or spicy) that's slathered on ribs, chicken, beef brisket, and anything else that ain't moving. Prices are fair and portions are ample.

Night Moves

Club West (535 Fifth Street, 444-2582) is a North Coast approximation of a Southern California dance club. What you get is an eclectic mix of folks who've come to shake their booties. You'll see lonesome cowboys in Garth Brooks hats and loud Western shirts, working girls dragging on cigarettes from barside

 Map of Humboldt County beaches—page 536

perches, a smattering of college kids who have wandered over from Arcata, and well-groomed yuppies out to make the scene. A squadron of burly bouncers serve as security, stalking self-importantly around this harmless club in wireless headsets like Secret Service personnel monitoring the president's public movements.

Like many clubs in this day and age, Club West engages in musical narrow-casting. One night they serve up line dancing to country music. Next, rhythm and blues. Karaoke. Oldies. We strolled in for a beer and an eyeful on a night when two local celebrities (radio jocks, probably) were leading the oldies charge from inside a van whose front end had been painted like a psychedelic bus. They wore long wigs, headbands, and sunglasses like, you know, hippies, whipping up the crowd by banging a cowbell and taking requests. If you had told us that 20 years later people would still be dancing to Bachman-Turner Overdrive and KC and the Sunshine Band, we might have fled to Katmandu. But back to the main point: in Eureka, Club West is the place to party. Pick your night and your music.

Civilized imbibers should head to the smoke-free **Lost Coast Brewery** (617 Fourth Street, 445-4480), which specializes in microbrewery beers on tap (ten of them!), plus the usual complement of sports-bar amenities: pool tables, dart boards, big-screen TVs, lunch and dinner items with hot wings on special at happy hour.

For More Information

Contact the Eureka Chamber of Commerce, 2112 Broadway (Highway 101), Eureka, CA 95501; (707) 442-3738.

Arcata

Location: Six miles north of Eureka at the junction of Highways 101 and 299. The main beach accessible to Arcata is Mad River Beach County Park, about five miles northwest of town.
Population: 15,200
Area Code: 707 **Zip Code:** 95521

Humboldt Bay merges with Arcata Bay at its northern end, where the waters balloon inland. It would be an ideal setting for a small town. But Arcata is not all that small a town, and its fairly nondescript outlying development runs in a rough L shape around the top of the bay and up Highway 101. Like Eureka, Arcata got its start as a depot and base (then called Union) for the Trinity Mountain gold fields. But it quickly became a booming lumber town, and evidence of its past lines the bay shore—warehouses, factories, boarded-up slag heaps, smokestacks, and the like. Close by these industrial eyesores are the boxlike homes of the employees. On a gray day, it resembles a scene from George Orwell's *The Road to Wigan Pier*, his impassioned study of working-class life.

Arcata, however, is not just another burned-out mill town. Rounding the bend away from the factories, the visitor discovers an attractive city in transition and an impressive oasis of higher learning. Humboldt State University, one of the oldest branches of the state system, is located here. The school's academic emphases include forestry management, environmental science, and marine biology. When these programs bloomed on university campuses nationwide, Humboldt State was an early and much-imitated model. The school is also oriented toward the arts—one glance at the student body will tell you that (lots of black clothing commingling with plaid flannel). All in all, the students seem to have found a happy nexus between nature and creativity. No wonder they don't feel the need to pursue MBAs.

The forest is never far from their hearts. The school teams are called the Lumberjacks, and the dorms are the Jolly Giant Commons. The campus itself is set on a large, grassy knoll east of the highway. Its 140 acres afford ample space for 7,500 students to roam, and the public is invited to enjoy their excellent natural-history museum.

The university pumps new blood and innovative ideas into the town. One is the Arcata Community Forest, a 600-acre preserve of second-growth redwoods that is the only city-owned forest in the state. Ten miles of trails crisscross the forest for the benefit of hikers, bicyclists, and horseback riders. Another great idea is the Arcata Marsh and Wildlife Sanctuary, a 75-acre haven created from a former landfill and industrial site (at the foot of I Street). It was transformed from a dump into one of the state's best bird-watching areas, with a hiking trail running through the many different ecosystems (bay, marsh, pond, foothills, streams). This restored marsh is fertilized by the Arcata sewer system, an ingenious way of recycling waste materials into something green and clean.

The town also positively beams with pride over its local artists, whose work is showcased on the premises of many businesses and along a self-guided Mural Tour. Arcata's most intriguing cultural event is the Kinetic Sculpture Race, which takes place each year in late May. It's difficult to explain the rules or purpose of this extravaganza, a 35-mile cross-country race that passes over hills and dunes from Arcata to Ferndale. What sets this race apart from NASCAR events is that to qualify, all vehicles must be navigable pieces of sculpture. Beyond that, whether it's pumped, paddled, or pushed doesn't matter. The Kinetic Sculpture Race, which celebrated its 25th anniversary in 1994, is emblematic of the town's spirit.

From June through October, an open-air Farmers Market takes over Arcata Plaza. The fresh local produce, flowers, and baked goods are enough to make you want to sink your own roots in lovely Arcata.

Beaches

The beach nearest Arcata is as hard to fathom as a piece of kinetic sculpture. **Mad River Beach County Park** is aptly named—at least the "mad" part, because this is an area where sand and sea, rivers, creeks, and lagoons come together with an almost primeval fury. Here the roads are a little out of whack, making the whole experience seem rather mad in the British sense as well. To get there, take the Janes Road exit from Highway 101, then turn right on Heindon Road, left on Iverson Road, and right on Mad River Road. Sounds simple on paper, but all are farm-hugging backroads. Try to follow the signs, because the thrill of the chase is half the fun of finding Mad River Beach.

At the end of Mad River Road, the beach overwhelms lucky visitors with its size and beauty, extending in both directions as far as the eye can see. The undertow here is treacherous, but the fishing is good. We watched gaggles of anglers standing around driftwood fires while their spindly, unattended poles stood upright in the sand. Oh yes, be sure to memorize the route you took getting here, or you

Mad River Beach County Park

3

Location: Take Janes Road exit off Highway 101 north of Arcata, then carefully follow signs to the park.

Parking: Free parking lot.

Hours: Open 24 hours.

Facilities: Rest rooms, picnic tables, and fire pits.

Contact: For beach information, contact the Humboldt County Parks Department at (707) 445-7651.

See number 10 on page 536.

may wind up making an unintentionally lengthy side trip through the dairy lands west of Arcata, as we did.

The Lanphere-Christensen Dunes Preserve is located just south of here, at the west end of Lanphere Road. It's part of the Mad River Slough. No fee is charged for access to either.

Bunking Down

The **Hotel Arcata** (708 Ninth Street, 826-0217, $$) is a good, centrally located place to drop your bags. Unveiled as the town plaza's showplace in 1915, the Hotel Arcata was one of the finest inns of its size on the coast. But when a financial downturn hit the town in the 1980s, the hotel fell into disrepair. The likable three-story structure has been restored to its original state of grace and has been augmented with hot tubs, a sauna, and a swimming pool.

At the north end of town, on Valley West Boulevard (off Highway 101), there's a strip of motels and restaurants bearing dependable, franchised names. Among the nicer ones in the former category is the **North Coast Inn** (4975 Valley West Road, 822-4861, $$), an erstwhile Travelodge that has comfortable, well-maintained rooms and a health-club area whose centerpiece is an expansive, heated indoor pool.

Coastal Cuisine

Try **Abruzzi** (780 Eighth Street, 826-2345, $$$) for Italian and **Folie Douce** (1551 G Street, 822-1042, $$) for creative fine dining. The nice thing about both places is that they have less expensive options than the high-end dinner entrées, if you're looking to economize. Folie Douce, for instance, serves wonderful, wood-fired pizzas. Abruzzi specializes in fresh fish and pasta dishes inspired by the cuisine of Abruzzi, a region in central Italy. Should you want something simpler—appetizers, sandwiches, or grilled fare—the **Plaza Grill** (780 Seventh Street, 826-0860) is located upstairs at the same address.

Night Moves

The heart of Arcata is its Plaza, a square formed by G and H and Ninth and 10th Streets. Here you'll find the restored Arcata Hotel; restaurants, cafés, and coffeehouses; record stores; a village green where Arcatans sit cross-legged and contemplate the passing scene; and an assortment of bars and nightclubs. There's live music to be found at the **Alibi** (744 Ninth Street, 822-3731), the **Plaza Grill** (780 Seventh Street, 826-0860), and **Jambalaya** (915 H Street, 822-4766), where something's going on seven nights a week.

We caught a local band at the Alibi called Barking Dogma, whose lineup included four women (two of whom played sax), a drummer, and a wheelchair-bound guitarist who looked like Frank Zappa and composed all the music. The crowd danced vigorously to their witty, complex compositions, hanging tough even through frequent meter changes. The band was having as good a time as the crowd. Nights like these up and down the California coast helped restore our faith in rock and roll, which had been flagging of late.

On weekends, students have been known to engage in a colorful ritual known as "ring around the plaza." It involves downing a beer, a margarita, or some other libation in each of the bars that surround the plaza. Of course, the raised drinking age has greatly reduced the number of legal contestants. In summer, nightlife is notably less frenetic. Still, there's the delightful Minor Theatre, a lavishly restored 1915 structure with three screens showing current, classic, and art films. And even those weary fans who have rightfully grown sick of professional baseball should check out the Humboldt Crabs, a semipro team that plays its home games at Arcata Ballpark (Ninth and F Streets).

For More Information

Contact the Arcata Chamber of Commerce, 1062 G Street, Arcata, CA 95521; (707) 822-3619.

McKinleyville

Location: 10 miles north of Eureka on Highway 101. McKinleyville is the home of Clam Beach County Park.
Population: 10,800
Area Code: 707 **Zip Code:** 95521

Once called Minorsville—after Isaac Minor, owner of the local general store—the town of McKinleyville took its present name in 1901, after President McKinley's assassination. This is a town that fancies itself a holdover from the Wild West. It's got a tradition in which horses have the right of way, and the annual rodeo is the biggest event in town.

Behind the macho image, however, McKinleyville offers little to the traveler, lying well off the highway and consisting mainly of drab dwellings and a homely town center. Don't be fooled by the "Tourist Information" signs pointing toward McKinleyville from Highway 101. It's a bum steer to a little A-frame info stand way the heck off the highway.

Beaches

West of McKinleyville is the first spot above San Francisco where Highway 101 runs directly beside the ocean. Two beach access points sit right off the highway. **Clam Beach County Park** is a sizable swath of sand with 100 RV and tent sites for camping and picnicking areas at its north and south ends.

Getting to the beach is no easy matter. A short path over tall dunes reveals a broad expanse of mostly flat, grassy dune fields extending to the ocean. A small creek must be forded, and logs have been laid across it for that purpose, serving as wooden stepping-stones.

Solitary figures press against the wind as they make their way across the desolate landscape. Though you can comb for driftwood and dig for razor clams, the real appeal of Clam Beach is for the equestrian set. Hitching posts have been provided at various spots off the road that runs through the park. Dogs, too, enjoy charging around the stark expanse, such as the pair of St. Bernards we saw emerging from the creek completely soaked and sandy, but happy.

Little River State Beach is more of the same: 112 undeveloped acres of dunes, driftwood, and hard-packed sand. At the north end, Little River trickles through the sand, creating

Clam Beach County Park

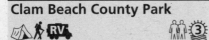

Location: 3.5 miles north of McKinleyville, take the Clam Beach exit off Highway 101.
Parking: Free parking lot.
Hours: Open 24 hours.
Facilities: Rest rooms and picnic tables. There are 100 tent and RV campsites. Fees are $8 to $10 per night. No camping reservations.
Contact: For beach information, contact the Humboldt County Parks Department at (707) 445-7651.

See number 11 on page 536.

Little River State Beach

Location: Four miles north of McKinleyville off Highway 101, on the south side of the bridge over Little River.
Parking: Free parking lot.
Hours: Open 24 hours.
Facilities: None.
Contact: For beach information, contact the North Coast Redwoods District of the California Department of Parks and Recreation at (707) 445-6547.

See number 12 on page 536.

a boundary between this beach and Trinidad's Moonstone Beach.

Coastal Cuisine

Typical of McKinleyville's Old West mind-set is **Stanton's Barn** (2145 Central Avenue, 839-3341, $), a large, friendly restaurant with an American flag proudly waving out front. The menu brags that "we serve only 100-percent ground beef."

There's another restaurant on the edge of town, **Brahma's** (1300 Central Avenue, 839-1400, $$). If you're feeling carnivorous, come here for steak and game such as wild boar, elk, and buffalo.

For More Information

Contact the McKinleyville Chamber of Commerce, 2196 Central Avenue, McKinleyville, CA 95521; (707) 839-2449.

Trinidad

Location: 20 miles north of Eureka, off Highway 1. There are coves and beaches all over the Trinidad area, with Trinidad State Beach being the most accessible.
Population: 432
Area Code: 707 **Zip Code:** 95570

Summer in Trinidad is like spring in many other places. The air is crisp and clean, the sky is a sweet baby blue, the wind blows like March's proverbial lion, and the ground is covered with a colorful carpet of wildflowers. It never really heats up to a summer swelter here in Trinidad.

Actually, the phrase "here in Trinidad" is misleading. Trinidad is not so much a single place you can point to as a jumble of hills, headlands, coves, and coastline that meander at crazy angles. As a result, there is a tremendous diversity of beaches and headlands to explore, making Trinidad an ideal place to bring both hiking shoes and beach blankets.

Briefly, Trinidad and its natural harbor were first sighted by the Portuguese explorer Sebastian Cermeno in 1595. He did not come close to land for fear of the pointed rocks. The Tsurai (pronounced *CHEReye*) Indians who inhabited the region were probably just as glad he kept his distance. On June 11, 1775, they weren't so lucky: the Spanish explorer Hezeta anchored in the bay, came ashore, and promptly declared that all his eye beheld belonged to Spain. It was Trinity Sunday when he staked his claim, and thus the area was called La Santisima Trinidad.

During Gold Rush days, the town boomed, reaching a population of 3,000 and serving as the seat of what was then Klamath County. Trinidad flourished again as a mill town in the 1870s, and once more in the 1920s as a whaling port. When each of these industries bit the dust, so did the town.

Today, Trinidad is home to artists and other lovers of solitude. With its abundant natural beauty—stunning and variegated beaches, rocks, coves, and headlands—it is not hard to understand its appeal to those with creative temperaments and folks with a yen for the outdoors.

Beaches

The beaches begin north of the Little River Bridge, along Scenic Drive. Starting at the river, **Moonstone Beach** sits below Merryman's, a restaurant that enjoys one of the most picture-perfect locations on the California coast. A small spur, Moonstone Beach Road, runs right past Merryman's and down to the beach, where there is parking in a gravel lot and posted warnings not to build bonfires. (The residents above get nervous, you see.)

Moonstone Beach falls under county jurisdiction, and it's plenty popular with an eclectic mix of beachgoers. Located on the large, sandy delta over which the Little River meanders before meeting the sea, it's studded with onshore and offshore sea stacks. Families come to picnic on the beach behind the rocks, which afford protection from the wind. Kids swim and play in the shallow creek waters, which are safer and warmer than the ocean. Surfers hungrily eye the waves that form off the point. We even saw a bicyclist pedaling on the hard-packed sand at water's edge.

Moving up Scenic Drive, there are two more named beaches along the five-mile stretch between Moonstone and the in-town shopping area. **Indian Beach** and **Luffenholtz Beach** are cove beaches at the bases of eroding bluffs. The best beaches are often the hardest to reach, and Indian Beach is a case in point. We never did figure out how to get down to it, but it makes quite a photo op from the road high above it. A giant, gumdrop-shape sea stack right in the surf zone parts incoming waves before they reach the beach. The walls of crashing water wrap around the rock from opposite sides and then meet at a perpendicular angle on the beach. We've never seen anything quite like it. Luffenholtz Beach has a marked parking area on Scenic Drive, and a sign points to a beach-access trail. Unfortunately, the original path has been declared off-limits. A new trail has been carved into the bluffs 200 yards up the road—which means walking along one-lane, cliff-hugging Scenic Drive, with its hidden curves and vehicles that come hurrying around them. Be careful.

In town, a natural harbor has been formed by **Trinidad Head**, a minimountain that has withstood the sea's pounding over countless millennia. An inviting calm-water beach occupies one edge of the harbor. There's a large parking lot, outlined by discarded boat tires,

Agate Beach (a part of Patrick's Point State Park)

5

Location: Five miles north of Trinidad, take the Patrick's Point Drive exit off Highway 101 and follow signs to the park.

Parking: $5 entrance fee per vehicle.

Hours: 7 AM to 8 PM.

Facilities: Rest rooms, showers, picnic tables, and fire pits. There are 124 tent and RV campsites. Fees are $12 to $14 per night. For camping reservations, call Destinet at (800) 444-7275.

Contact: For beach information, contact Patrick's Point State Park at (707) 677-3570.

See number 20 on page 536.

Baker Beach

4

Location: In Trinidad, take Main Street to Scenic Drive, and proceed south for one mile. Marked trailheads lead down the bluffs to Baker Beach.

Parking: Free roadside parking.

Hours: Sunrise to sunset.

Facilities: None.

Contact: For beach information, contact the Humboldt North Coast Land Trust, P.O. Box 457, Trinidad, CA 95570.

See number 15 on page 536.

as well as an old seafood restaurant of long-standing (the 1953 vintage Seascape), a bait shop, and a boat launch. The trailhead for paths leading up and around Trinidad Head lies at the far end of the lot.

Trails encircle the monolith, with dead-end spurs shooting off to vista points along the way. Stay on the main trail—named the Tsurai Trail—proceeding in a counterclockwise direction, and you can hike the whole thing in under an hour. There's plenty of benches strategically placed along the way to allow walkers to savor the views. Even when the area is shrouded in fog, you can sit and listen to sea lions barking like foghorns in the distance. At the top of Trinidad Head, a concrete cross commemorates the original explorers who landed here. There's also a giant Coast Guard satellite dish. At this point, the trip back down is an easy jaunt along a gravel road that meets smooth asphalt on its way to the bottom.

On the ocean-facing side, at the base of Trinidad Head, is a beach on which we sat and ate an impromptu lunch of smoked salmon and albacore. We purchased it just up the road at Katy's Smokehouse, which enjoys an unsurpassed reputation with those who know smoked fish.

A trail leads from here to **Trinidad State Beach**. Alternatively, you can park closer, at the lot just above the beach, and hike down a well-graded trail. In either case, no entrance fee is charged. It's a fairly lengthy strand for this torturous part of the coast, especially when low tide allows beachgoers to walk from one cove beach to another. Watch the sea very carefully, though, and keep track of tides. An unwary walker can easily get trapped in a cove or sea cave with no route out. Be advised that the tide can turn quickly. This is no joke. We easily walked to a couple of coves on wet sand. As we returned five minutes later, the same cove beaches were a half foot under quickly rising water.

One of the most popular beaches in the area is **College Cove**. It's been known for years

Big Lagoon County Park

Location: Seven miles north of Trinidad, off Highway 101 at the south end of Big Lagoon.

Parking: $3 entrance fee per vehicle.

Hours: Open 24 hours.

Facilities: Rest rooms, picnic tables, and fire pits. There are 22 tent and RV campsites. The fee is $10 per night. No camping reservations.

Contact: For beach information, contact the Humboldt County Parks Department at (707) 445-7651.

See number 21 on page 536.

College Cove

Location: In Trinidad, take Main Street west and turn right onto Stagecoach Road. Proceed for 0.25 mile and turn into a dirt parking lot on the left. The trail at the south end of the parking lot leads to College Cove South, a mostly nude beach, and the trail at the north end of the parking lot leads to College Cove North, a mostly clothed beach.

Parking: Free parking lot.

Hours: Sunrise to sunset.

Facilities: None.

Contact: For beach information, contact the North Coast Redwoods District of the California Department of Parks and Recreation at (707) 445-6547.

See number 19 on page 536.

as a clothing-optional beach, but if nudity is an option, no one was exercising it on the warm summer weekend that we ventured out. It's a gorgeous cove that's plenty wide at low tide, reachable from a gravel parking lot from which a trail leads into the woods. Where the trail splits, one fork goes to the beach, descending 130 steps. The other heads out to Elk Point and eventually connects with Trinidad State Beach, passing through fern canyons and Sitka spruce forests that are cool and dark even at the height of summer.

At College Cove, one can sunbathe, play volleyball—yes, a net was set up and a game was in progress—or just walk and wade along the water. Two young boys were totally wet, tossing a stick into the waves and trying to be the first to grab it as it washed ashore. Total immersion, however, is only for the young and hardy or the old and foolhardy, in our estimation. The tidal exchange here is fairly extreme, as a comparison between low tide and the uppermost watermarks in the sand demonstrate. Waves buffet the cliffs at their bases during stormy winter months. Let the hiker beware.

The prize gem of all the beaches in the Trinidad vicinity is **Agate Beach**, located at the northwest edge of Patrick's Point State Park. The park itself is worth exploring in its entirety, but Agate Beach is a treasure that ranks among California's most memorable. Like most Trinidad-area beaches, the cliffs drop so steeply to the beach that you must descend a long bank of stairs to get to it. The view from the top is worth enjoying for a few minutes before taking the stairs down. Observe how the beach extends past the point where the cliffs give out, forming a sand bar that encloses **Big Lagoon**, just to the north. Big Lagoon is the site of a county park with a boat launch, picnic tables, and 22 primitive campsites.

Indian Beach

Location: In Trinidad, follow the marked trailhead to Indian Beach at the intersection of Edwards and Main Streets.

Parking: Free roadside parking.

Hours: Sunrise to sunset.

Facilities: None.

Contact: For beach information, contact the Humboldt North Coast Land Trust, P.O. Box 457, Trinidad, CA 95570.

See number 16 on page 536.

Luffenholtz Beach

Location: From Main Street in Trinidad, proceed south on Scenic Drive for two miles. Marked trails lead down the bluffs to Luffenholtz Beach.

Parking: Free roadside parking.

Hours: Sunrise to sunset.

Facilities: None.

Contact: For beach information, contact the Humboldt County Parks Department at (707) 445-7651.

See number 14 on page 536.

Moonstone Beach

Location: In Trinidad, follow Scenic Drive from its intersection with Main Street south to Moonstone Beach Road, a short spur that leads to Moonstone Beach.

Parking: Free parking lot.

Hours: Sunrise to sunset.

Facilities: None.

Contact: For beach information, contact the Humboldt County Parks Department at (707) 445-7651.

See number 13 on page 536.

The hike from Agate Point to the end of Big Lagoon Spit is three miles—and worth every footstep. Along this stretch of coastline, one can hunt for bits of agate and jade. The chances of striking it rich fall somewhere between slim and none, but the scenery is ample compensation. The cliffs overlooking Agate Beach are not completely vertical, which allows vegetation to grow on them. At the bottom, a little creek empties onto the beach and seeps into the sand before reaching the ocean. In summer, breakers wash ashore, and the beach remains plenty wide throughout the tidal cycle.

Numerous sea stacks sit offshore from Patrick's Point, affording a habitat to sea lions, whose barking fills the air day and night. Rock outcroppings found in the park's interior belong to an earlier generation of sea stacks, now high and dry due to geologic uplift. The largest stacks are Ceremonial Rock (287 feet) and Lookout Rock (250 feet). Trails lead out to Mussel Rock, a stack that's barely connected to the mainland. Visitors can climb all over this unusual formation. Looking out to sea, observe the line of wave-formed ooze that follows the undulating shoreline.

Camping at Patrick's Point is some of the finest to be found in any of California's coastal parks. The 123 sites are large and private, shaded by spruce and protected from the wind. A popular new addition to the park is Sumeg, a re-created Yurok Indian village that offers some virtual reality to go along with its artifacts. A visit to Patrick's Point State Park should be mandatory if you venture up this way.

Bunking Down

Any number of rustic lodges and attractive bed-and-breakfasts line Patrick's Point Drive along the five-mile stretch between Trinidad and Patrick's Point State Park. We have a favorite in both categories.

The **Lost Whale Bed & Breakfast Inn** (3452 Patrick's Point Drive, 677-3425, $$$), located only a half mile from Patrick's Point, is one of the few B&Bs that encourages families to stay. The inn was constructed in 1988 and since the owners were starting from scratch, they were able to build in reinforcement and soundproofing, which made the place sturdy enough to withstand the patter of little feet. Warm woods and comfortable furniture fill the common living area downstairs.

The rooms at the back of the house have balconies and windows that look out over the ocean—as marvelous a view as you could hope

Trinidad Head

4

Location: West end of Edwards Street in Trinidad.
Parking: Free parking lot.
Hours: 7 AM to 5 PM.
Facilities: Rest rooms.
Contact: For beach information, contact Trinidad Harbor at (707) 677-3625.

See number 17 on page 536.

Trinidad State Beach

5

Location: In Trinidad, follow signs leading west into the park at the intersection of Stagecoach Road and Main Street.
Parking: Free parking lot.
Hours: Sunrise to sunset.
Facilities: Rest rooms, picnic tables, and fire pits.
Contact: For beach information, contact the North Coast Redwoods District of the California Department of Parks and Recreation at (707) 445-6547.

See number 18 on page 536.

to enjoy. Moms and dads have a bed of their own, while the kiddies can ascend a ladder to a loft fitted with mattresses. Co-owner Lee Miller, a innkeeper-cum-musician who escaped L.A. for the tranquillity of the North Coast, has built a stairway leading several hundred feet down to the beach. (If you're lucky, one of their cats will escort you to the beach.) Wine and snacks are served in the afternoon, and a full breakfast is placed on the table promptly at 8:30 AM. The Millers are in the process of putting together their own recipe and lodging guidebook. Judging from the taste evinced by their lovely inn, they're the right couple to do it.

A fine cottage court can be found at the **Bishop Pine Lodge** (1481 Patrick's Point Drive, 677-3314, $$), where rustic cabins are spread on shaded grounds. Each unit has a full kitchen and a TV. A card informs you that the management will store your game and fish in their deep freeze. Moreover, the management reports that "well-behaved pets" are welcome. The Bishop Pine Lodge is a restful, out-of-the-way spot charging reasonable rates. If longevity is any indication, this is the place to stay, as the Bishop Pine Lodge has been in business since 1927.

Coastal Cuisine

The **Larrupin' Café** (1658 Patrick's Point Drive, 677-0230, $$$) is hard to miss, and once you've eaten here, you'll take pains to return. Painted a bold mustard yellow and trimmed in red, this former dwelling retained its homey feeling when it made the transition to gourmet restaurant. The menu is heavy on items grilled on the mesquite broiler (filet mignon, fish kabobs, pork ribs, etc.). A few dishes from the oven (chicken in phyllo pastry, spanokopita) are thrown in for good measure. Larrupin's grilled garlic plate makes a terrific appetizer, and you also can't go wrong with barbecued oysters or mussels steamed in white wine and tomatoes. A favorite entrée is the hot 'n' spicy snapper, a sizable serving of Pacific red snapper coated in ground pepper and grilled to a turn. Portions are generous, but leave room for dessert; the chocolate pecan pie in hot buttered rum sauce is worth all the hiking you'll have to do the next morning to work it off. Larrupin' Café is open for dinner six nights a week from Memorial Day to Labor Day, and from Thursday through Sunday during the rest of the year.

Fresh seafood can be found at the **Seascape Restaurant** (Trinidad Harbor, 677-3762, $$), located beside the town's pier. It bustles with tourists and fishermen, serving three meals daily. It's been here for 35 years, so they must be doing something right. **Merryman's** (110 Moonstone Beach Road, 677-3111, $$$) is located directly above beautiful, secluded Moonstone Beach. They offer what the management humbly describes as "exquisite dining" and enforce a dress code (which, in Trinidad, simply means you must wear clothes). The menu is a short, simple list of beef and seafood dishes, not unreasonably priced. And the view....

For More Information

Contact the Greater Trinidad Chamber of Commerce, P.O. Box 356, Trinidad, CA 95570; (707) 677-0591. For state-park information, contact Patrick's Point State Park, 41250 Patrick's Point Drive, Trinidad, CA 95570; (707) 677-3570.

Humboldt Lagoons State Park: Dry Lagoon and Stone Lagoon

Location: 13 miles north of Trinidad and 31 miles north of Eureka, on Highway 101.

You ask, "What is a lagoon?" We answer: "A lagoon is produced from the combined action of wind and water. Ocean currents carry sand parallel to the coastline, and winds mold it into barriers that separate shallow coastal waters from the deep blue sea. Behind the barrier lies a marshy, landlocked wetland—to wit, a lagoon."

Humboldt Lagoons State Park offers camping and fishing opportunities galore. You might inquire about them at the visitors center at the main south entrance, though it's open only from 10 AM to 2 PM (and was, in fact, closed when we dropped by at 1:45 PM—someone skip out early?). The south end includes the spit and a marsh known as **Dry Lagoon**, where you'll find four picnic tables and six walk-in tent sites.

The more intriguing section of the park is **Stone Lagoon**, a short distance north off Highway 101. The road down to it is a bumpy roller-coaster ride that makes a precipitous final dip. Picnic tables and campsites are nestled in thickets, and the parking lot is an unimproved gravel field. This is an archeological resource area, and visitors are urged not to dig for or cart off artifacts. No problem—there's plenty of good fishing to keep everyone occupied. Incidentally, various points along Highway 101 through the area offer wonderful overlooks of the lagoon and the sandy, straight-edged bar that divides it from the sea.

For More Information

Contact Humboldt Lagoons State Park, 15336 Highway 101, Trinidad, CA 95570; (707) 488-2041.

Dry Lagoon (a part of Humboldt Lagoons State Park)

Location: 13 miles north of Trinidad, off Highway 101.

Parking: $2 entrance fee per vehicle.

Hours: Sunrise to sunset.

Facilities: Rest rooms, picnic tables, and fire rings. There are six campsites for tents. Fees are $7 to $9 per night. No camping reservations.

Contact: For beach information, contact Humboldt Lagoons State Park at (707) 488-2041.

See number 22 on page 536.

Stone Lagoon (a part of Humboldt Lagoons State Park)

Location: 14.5 miles north of Trinidad, off Highway 101.

Parking: $2 entrance fee per vehicle.

Hours: Sunrise to sunset.

Facilities: Rest rooms, picnic tables, and fire rings. There are 20 campsites for tents. Fees are $7 to $9 per night. No camping reservations.

Contact: For beach information, contact Humboldt Lagoons State Park at (707) 488-2041.

See number 23 on page 536.

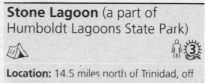

Redwood National Park: Freshwater Lagoon, Redwood Creek Beach, and Orick Fishing Access

Location: North of Trinidad, Redwood National Park occupies 40 miles of coastline along Highway 101 between Orick and Crescent City.

Approaching Orick from the south, Highway 101 descends a hill and rounds a turn, at which point you'll see an amazing site: a centipede-like line of RVs parked by the side of the road just inside Redwood National Park. The area is known as **Freshwater Lagoon**, after the pristine blue lagoon east of the highway.

The ground rules are simple. You may park your RV on the ocean side of the highway, no fewer than 30 feet west of its paved edge. You can stay up to 15 consecutive nights, and as many as 30 total nights in a calendar year. After a 15-day run, you must vacate the site for at least 24 hours before returning. No fee is charged, though a donation is requested.

Road warriors come here in droves, attracted by the broad, sandy beach that lies on one side of the highway, and the lagoon and green hills on the other. Not to mention the people-watching opportunities: pulling out the folding chairs and staring at passing traffic seems to be a popular pastime. A loyal fraternity of like-minded RVers makes merry all along the road's shoulder as far as the eye can see. Only in America.

A visitors center for Redwood National Park is located just above Freshwater Lagoon, before Highway 101 takes a swing inland. (It's

Freshwater Lagoon (a part of Redwood National Park)

RV 3

Location: Three miles south of Orick, along Highway 101.

Parking: Free roadside parking.

Hours: Open 24 hours.

Facilities: Rest rooms. There are informal RV campsites along the west side of Highway 101. No fee or camping reservations, but campers must register at the Redwood Information Center, which is one mile north of Freshwater Lagoon.

Contact: For beach information, contact the Redwood Information Center for Redwood National Park at (707) 464-6101, ext. 5265.

See number 24 on page 536.

Orick Fishing Access (a part of Redwood National Park)

1

Location: Two miles west of Orick, at the end of Hufford Road, off Highway 101.

Parking: Free parking lot.

Hours: Open 24 hours.

Facilities: None.

Contact: For beach information, contact the Redwood Information Center for Redwood National Park at (707) 464-6101, ext. 5265.

See number 26 on page 536.

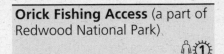

been relocated because coastal erosion claimed the old road in places.) The center is a cubist-style building fashioned from weathered wood, with a walkway leading out to the impressively large **Redwood Creek Beach**. Tell the staff what you have in mind—a short or long hike, viewing elk herds or redwood groves, camping in the backcountry, or simply parking the RV—and they'll set you up with maps and advice. A stop here is a must if you're coming up from the south. Those driving from the north will want to stop at Park Headquarters in Crescent City, where you'll receive the same sort of orientation. We found the staff at both places to be helpful and knowledgeable.

The town of Orick falls outside Redwood National Park, encompassing a string of gas stations, cheap motels, and roadside stands selling "Burl Slabs" and "Redwood Creations," including huge rearing bears, steely-eyed eagles, and grizzled sea captains, which local artisans have carved using chain saws. One stand posts a sign inviting you to "Come See What We Saw." You may come see, but you probably won't stay in Orick unless you've got a wild hair to bunk down at the self-designated "world famous" **Palm Motel and Café** (Highway 101, 488-3381, $), a humble but vaguely appealing roadside complex—motel, pool, restaurant, lounge—that's got character, not to mention an eye-catching mural painted down one side.

For the truly adventurous, a turnoff onto Hufford Road carries you out to **Orick Fishing Access**, at which point you've reentered Redwood National Park. The road quickly morphs into a bumpy one-lane curvathon, hemmed in on both sides by barbed-wire fences to hold back grazing cattle. At the end of the road is a gravel parking lot that looks out upon Redwood Creek's winding egress into the ocean. Anglers cast for salmon and steelhead in the diked waters here. They don't call Orick "Fisherman's Paradise" for nothing.

For More Information

Contact Redwood National Park, 1111 Second Street, Crescent City, CA 95531; (707) 464-6101.

Redwood Creek Beach (a part of Redwood National Park)

Location: Two miles south of Orick, off Highway 101.

Parking: Free parking lot.

Hours: Open 24 hours.

Facilities: Restrooms and picnic tables.

Contact: For beach information, contact the Redwood Information Center for Redwood National Park at (707) 464-6101, ext. 5265.

See number 25 on page 536.

Prairie Creek Redwoods State Park: Gold Bluffs Beach

Location: From Orick, take Highway 101 north for five miles, then take the left fork onto Drury Scenic Parkway. Prairie Creek Visitor Center is one mile north on the left. To get to Gold Bluffs Beach from Orick, take Highway 101 three miles north to Davison Road. Turn left and continue four miles to the beach.

One of the most beautiful beaches on the North Coast (and therefore, anywhere), **Gold Bluffs Beach** lies inside the boundaries of Prairie Creek Redwoods State Park, which itself is surrounded by Redwood National Park. In other words, it is a beach within a state park within a national park.

To get to Gold Bluffs Beach, take Davison Road, a spur off Highway 101 three miles north of Orick that passes through a portion of Redwood National Park. It's a winding little passageway—narrow, unpaved, and hazardous—and trailers are prohibited. After four miles of bumping, bouncing, and shouting "Watch out for that van!," you're there. Park the car, get out, draw in a deep breath.

And look around. Steep sandstone walls rise behind the beach. Forested bluffs overlook the beach. The ocean's thrashing kicks up a refreshing mist that bathes the beach in ghostly, low-lying sheets of white. Waves break and roll slowly across the shore, pushing a line of sea foam ahead of them. The salt-and-pepper sand is flecked with gold specks that gleam brightly in the overwash.

The beach is a couple hundred yards wide, a vast, desertlike expanse virtually devoid of humanity, unchoked by seaweed or litter. It extends farther than the eye can see in either direction. This is an ideal beach for kicking off shoes and walking along the ocean's edge, ankle deep in the bracing sea water. (An exhibit in the parking lot warns beachcombers to keep an eye out for sleeper waves, so be careful.) If you con-

Gold Bluffs Beach
(a part of Prairie Creek Redwoods State Park)

RV 5

Location: Three miles north of Orick, take the Davison Road turnoff from Highway 101 and drive to the beach.

Parking: $5 entrance fee per vehicle.

Hours: Sunrise to sunset.

Facilities: Rest rooms, showers, picnic tables, and fire pits. There are 25 tent and RV campsites. Fees are $12 to $14 per night. No camping reservations.

Contact: For beach information, contact Prairie Creek Redwoods State Park at (707) 488-2171.

See number 27 on page 536.

Carruthers Cove Beach

4

Location: Five miles north of Orick, turn from Highway 101 onto Drury Scenic Parkway (Old Highway 101). Follow for approximately seven miles and then take a left fork onto Coastal Drive. Look for signs for Carruthers Cove Trail, which leads to the beach.

Parking: Free roadside parking.

Hours: Open 24 hours.

Facilities: None.

Contact: For beach information, contact Prairie Creek Redwoods State Park at (707) 488-2171.

See number 28 on page 536.

tinue driving north along Gold Bluffs Beach, you'll reach Fern Canyon in another four miles. There are good camping, hiking, beachcombing, and picnicking opportunities all along this stretch of coastal road. Gold Bluffs Beach Campground is a 25-siter at ocean's edge. A larger campground (Elk Prairie, 75 sites) is located inland, near park headquarters. A note to hikers: The Coastal Trail, which runs for roughly 30 miles from Orick to Crescent City, reaches a point on the north side of Prairie Creek Redwoods State Park, just above Butler Creek, that is passable only at low tide. The northernmost beach within Prairie Creek Redwoods State Park is one of the most secluded on the North Coast. **Carruthers Cove Beach** can be reached by walking north along the Coastal Trail from Fern Canyon. (A beautiful, 0.8-mile loop trail circles this flat-floored, steep-sided canyon, which itself is a spectacle not to be missed.) Alternatively, Carruthers Cove can be accessed from the north via the Carruthers Cove Trail, which leads to the beach from the cliff-hugging Coastal Drive. It's a narrow, isolated beach, and it's unlikely you'll see anybody there—all the more reason to seek it out.

The 14,000-acre state park is also home to a herd of about 30 Roosevelt elk. Generally, they can be seen grazing by the side of the road, and signs warn when you're in an "Elk Crossing Area." Tune in 1610 AM to receive information about where best to spot the creatures and to learn the do's and don'ts of elk-watching. We learned, for instance, that these critters have chased people at speeds of up to 50 miles per hour, and that "elks will not tolerate dogs."

We have one complaint about this otherwise splendid park. Davison Road really needs to be paved. It bears a heavy volume of traffic, which kicks up an unholy cloud of dust. This dust storm coats all vegetation in the vicinity, leaving the ferns and trees photosynthetically deprived. It also blinds drivers, chokes the throat, and irritates the eyes and lungs. If you are driving through here, travel no faster than the posted speed of 15 mph. You won't kick up as much dust, nor will you imperil your fellow driver by forcing him or her over the edge when you meet on a curve, as very nearly happened to us.

For More Information

Contact Prairie Creek Redwoods State Park, Drury Scenic Parkway, Orick, CA 95555; (707) 488-2171.

Del Norte County

As North Coast counties go, Del Norte owns a relatively small chunk of coastline. Compared to its neighbor, Humboldt County, it's but a sliver of sandy real estate. With 27,000 residents, Del Norte isn't heavily populated, nor is it very prosperous, although the arrival of a hard-core maximum security jail north of Crescent City in 1989—the infamous Pelican Bay State Prison—has lightened welfare rolls in these parts. Yet while Del Nortians might not be rich in monetary terms, they've inherited a wealth of natural splendor.

From towering redwoods, preserved in the state and national parks that take up so much of the county, to pristine beaches that run for miles along its craggy coastline, Del Norte County offers no end of things to do in the outdoors. It's no secret that Del Norte County is an angler's paradise, boasting big rivers, such as the Klamath and the Smith, and numerous creeks that are ideal spots to land steelhead and salmon. The Del Norte coastline is less well known, since it is somewhat *(continued on page 572)*

Coastal Del Norte County's Climate

Redwood National Park Averages

	Daily High Temp. (°F)	Daily Low Temp. (°F)	Rainfall (inches)
January	53	41	12.0
February	55	42	9.0
March	55	42	8.0
April	57	43	4.0
May	60	47	3.0
June	62	50	1.0
July	64	51	0.3
August	64	52	0.8
September	65	51	2.0
October	62	48	4.0
November	58	45	9.0
December	54	42	12.0
Yearly Average	**59**	**46**	**65.1**

Source: National Weather Service data, National Oceanographic and Atmospheric Administration.

Del Norte County

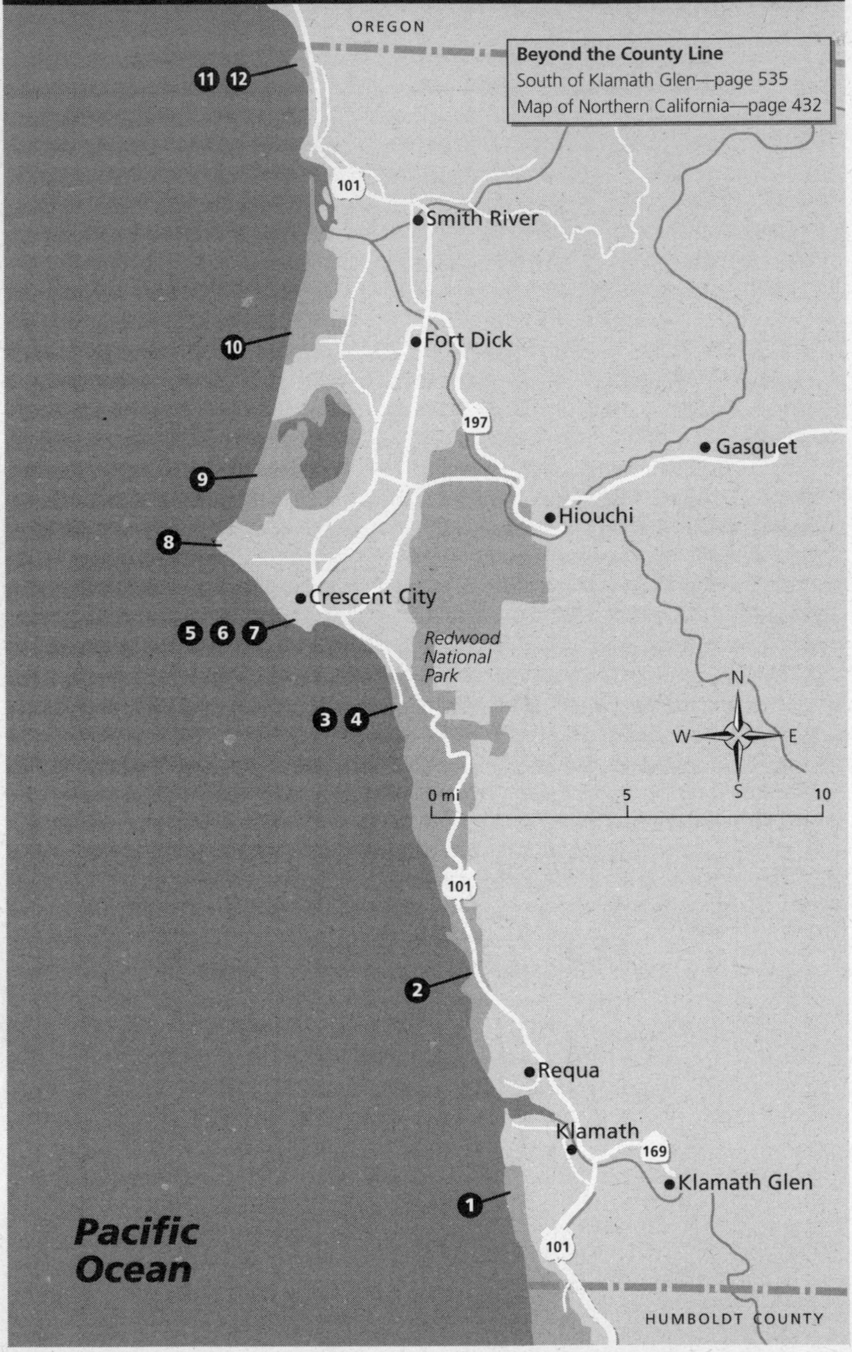

OREGON
Beyond the County Line
South of Klamath Glen—page 535
Map of Northern California—page 432
11 12
101
Smith River
10
Fort Dick
197
Gasquet
9
Hiouchi
8
Crescent City
5 6 7
Redwood National Park
3 4
N
W
E
S
0 mi
5
10
101
2
Requa
Klamath
169
Klamath Glen
1
Pacific Ocean
101
HUMBOLDT COUNTY

Del Norte County Beaches

Map of Northern California—page 432

(continued from page 569) overshadowed by the redwoods, which rightly claim so much attention. But there are oceanside drives and trails that shouldn't be missed: the Coastal Trail, Enderts Beach Road, Requa Road, and Pebble Beach Drive. All follow the coastline, offering spectacular overlooks and beach access. The beaches themselves are alluring and underrated, from the indescribable isolation of High Bluff Beach, below Klamath, to the desolate dune fields of Kellogg Beach, above Crescent City.

Key to the Symbols

Bike path · Camping · Food and drink · Hiking · Nude

Pier · RVs allowed · Surfing · Volleyball

Crowd Rating

sweet solitude . . . moderate crowds . . . wall-to-wall

Overall Rating

1 don't bother . . . 3 worth a visit . . . 5 beach heaven

Redwood National Park: High Bluff Beach

Location: One mile south of Klamath, below Coastal Drive.

How about a little piece of Hawaii—in appearance, if not temperature—on the North Coast of California? Such is the look of magnificent **High Bluff Beach**, which lies below a cliff-hugging wonder known as Coastal Drive. To get to it from the south, disengage from Highway 101 onto the Drury Scenic Parkway and then turn onto Coastal Drive. From the north, reach Coastal Drive via Alder Camp Road, a right turn off Highway 101 just south of the Golden Bear Bridge over the Klamath River.

Coastal Drive runs for eight miles, alternating paved and unpaved sections. The road is not in the best condition, but the scenery is so spectacular that it's worth the effort (especially if you're driving a rented car—ha-ha!). This road used to be Highway 101, before washouts and erosion necessitated its relocation east. Breathtaking glimpses of the ocean below are found around every turn. High Bluff Picnic Area and the beach below are the overlooked gems of Redwood National Park. It is well worth pausing to ponder the vista from the picnic area, and hardier souls with a yen for wilderness beaches will want to hike down to the beach itself.

To reach the beach, visitors must walk a half mile along a trail that passes through cool forests before making a final descent in a series of switchbacks. A log ladder with a handrail of rope leads down to some planking that must be carefully negotiated. Then you're on muddy rocks, crawling and crab-walking until a final heave-ho lands you on the beach. The sand is soft, light brown, and volcanic in origin. Waves overwash footprints at high tide, giving the area a virgin, unvisited appearance every 12 hours. On a sunny day, this secluded cove resembles some sort of hidden tropical paradise, lacking only palm trees and balmy water to complete the scene. It's an illusion, but not such a far-fetched one if you're soaking up the sun's rays here on a warm, cloudless day (of which there are many from June through September).

For More Information

Contact Redwood National Park, 1111 Second Street, Crescent City, CA 95531; (707) 464-6101.

High Bluff Beach (a part of Redwood National Park)

Location: From the south end of the Golden Bear Bridge over the Klamath River, turn west onto Alder Camp Road and continue to Coastal Drive. Proceed south along Coastal Drive to the High Bluff Picnic Area. A half-mile trail leads to the beach.

Parking: Free parking lot.

Hours: Open 24 hours.

Facilities: Picnic tables.

Contact: For beach information, contact Redwood National Park at (707) 464-6101, ext. 5064.

See number 1 on page 570.

Klamath

Location: 65 miles north of Eureka, on Highway 101. The closest beach access is Wilson Creek Beach, north of Klamath inside Redwood National Park.
Population: 1,500
Area Code: 707 **Zip Code:** 95548

One of the fundamental laws of physics, Heisenberg's Uncertainty Principle, applies to travel. A statement about the limited precision of scientific measurement, it says, in essence, that one can specify either the position of a physical particle or its momentum at any given point in time, but not both. Therefore, because one of the variables is unknown, its value could be anything. With this equation, the physicist is telling us that nothing is impossible. Or, put another way, anything is possible.

The same holds true on the road. For instance, while driving the desolate North Coast of California, one might think it unlikely to come upon a 49-foot-tall replica of Paul Bunyan standing in a clearing in the redwoods, with a 17-ton blue ox named Babe beside him. But it is no illusion. Paul and Babe are the gatekeepers and world's largest lawn jockeys for a tourist attraction called the Trees of Mystery (see sidebar, "Trees of Mystery").

Though hard to find, Klamath is a special place, one that a physicist, mapmaker, tourist, and travel writer could all find baffling. It's everywhere and nowhere, diffused over a seven-mile stretch on both sides of Highway 101; along the inland valleys, canyons, and glens of the Klamath River; atop coastal bluffs and on the beaches below; squirreled away in the dark, spooky forests. There is no place that can be pointed to as the town center. It is difficult to say if the town is growing or dwindling, whether there is an actual town or just a scattering of RV parks, motels, restaurants, shops selling redwood gifts and knickknacks, salmon-jerky stands, and the Trees of Mystery. In the case of Klamath, both position *and* momentum are unclear.

There's a good reason for this. The seemingly quiet, salmon-filled waters of the Klamath River conceal a terrible secret. Del Norte County is flood country, and a confluence of factors can turn the river into a raging monster. In 1964, the right—or terribly wrong—combination of factors occurred. A cold, wet winter blanketed the surrounding mountains with a dense pack of snow and ice. Then a fast-moving storm front passed through, inundating the area with rain. Finally warm, high winds melted 10 feet of frozen precipitation in 24 hours. It sent a 90-foot wall of water rushing down the canyon. With boulders and timber as battering rams, the flood wiped the unsuspecting town of Klamath off the map and out to sea.

Klamath was born in the mid-1800s during the fevered Gold Rush that swept California. It was a typical story of greed run amok in the wilderness. Mining camps sprang up along the Klamath River. The miners harassed and depleted the native Yurok Indians' numbers, while the riverbed became so silted with the detritus of their gold digging that the salmon stopped running. Klamath City was a thriving lumber port for most of this century, until the virgin forests were cleared. And then came the December 1964 flood, nature's angriest retort.

Before the flood Klamath was a highfalutin town, flush with prosperity when timber was king and the river was kind. In its heyday, 20 bars lined its rough-and-ready Main Street. The flood left nothing standing but a small church and the massive golden bears that greeted visitors at the edge of town. The U.S. Army Corps of Engineers cleared an area to rebuild Klamath north of the river, at an elevation five feet above the river's highest recorded level. But the citizens of Klamath, most of them anyway, never

 Map of Del Norte County beaches—page 570

Trees of Mystery

Trees of Mystery celebrates the majesty of the coast redwoods and Sitka spruce that grow to fantastic heights and often phantasmagoric shapes in this neck of the rain forest. Located 16 miles south of Crescent City beside Highway 101 in Klamath, "Trees" is hard to miss, thanks to the gargantuan likenesses of Paul Bunyan and Babe the Blue Ox that hail passersby from the side of the road. It's a worthwhile operation—educational, informative, and environmentally responsible, which is a winning combination in our book.

Before investigating the backcountry trails of Redwood National Park, you should take a crash course on the tall trees at Trees of Mystery. A $6 admission fee ($3 for children 6 to 12, free for kids under 6) gains you access to this private redwood forest and its "Trail of Mysterious Trees." Redwoods are awesome to contemplate in any setting, but the stand at Trees of Mystery is especially impressive. Native Americans believed that the area was haunted with evil spirits, causing the trees to grow in crazy ways: twisting, turning, running horizontally, sprouting out of each other. It's really nothing more than good old biological Darwinism on overdrive, with the behemoth redwoods and spruces fighting for all the sunlight they can lay their limbs on, employing ingenious adaptive and reproductive techniques in the quiet struggle for survival. A highlight is the Cathedral Tree—nine redwoods growing in a perfect semicircle out of one root structure. As many as 40 weddings a year are held in the natural altar formed by the trees, and a crackly recording of Nelson Eddy crooning "Trees" plays continuously.

Trees of Mystery is run by a family of Klamath natives that exhibits a scholarly interest in and appreciation for Native American culture. Their on-site museum houses the largest private collection of Native American baskets, pots, ornaments, and apparel in the West. The final attraction is the "Trail of Tall Tales," a half-mile walk that retells the myths and legends of Paul Bunyan and his brawny logging crew in wood. Kids, of course, will be in log heaven, but adults also will get something out of the 50 gigantic chain-saw sculptures and carvings, completed in a period of six months by a talented local artisan (now deceased) named Kenyon Kaiser. There is evidence of primitive genius in his work. His *Pooped Lumberman* is an American classic, kind of a Wild West version of Rodin's *The Thinker*. For more information, contact Trees of Mystery, Highway 101, P.O. Box 96, Klamath, CA 95548; (707) 482-2251.

returned. The new town site is now occupied only by a mobile homes, and the original town is utterly abandoned. The foundations of old homes and businesses have been overgrown by weeds and reclaimed by nature. As for the bears, a pair of them guards each end of the rebuilt Highway 101 bridge over the Klamath River.

If Klamath is more of a bear than a bull these days, it's still an inviting place for visitors with an appreciation of serene, unspoiled nature. Between fishing the Klamath River, camping and hiking in Redwood National Park, and combing isolated beaches, there is plenty to do in and around Klamath. The number-one item on the agenda is fishing. The Klamath is the second largest river in California and one of the best in the world for fishing silver and chinook salmon, steelhead trout, and sturgeon, drawing anglers from far afield during their yearly runs. From the salmon's point of view, the angler-mania that the Klamath inspires is not all fair play. The mouth of the Klamath River used to be known as Suicide Row, because skiff-fishers would tie their boats together to form an impenetrable line against which the salmon, returning to spawn in their natal streams, didn't stand a chance. Dwindling salmon runs caused this practice to be outlawed.

An equally controversial method that yields similar results—catching so many fish that few survive to reproduce—has been the Native American practice of gill-netting. Anglers string a monofilament net across the river, trapping the returning salmon in a mesh that forces their gills together until they suffocate. Today, Yurok Indians alone employ gill-netting techniques for subsistence fishing in the Klamath, having won the right to do so in a controversial federal lawsuit in the mid-1980s.

Somehow, the fish continue to spawn in sufficient numbers to return year after year, though they are beleaguered by greedy outlaw anglers, Native American gill-netters, and various environmental affronts. Many anglers roll into Klamath with little more than a hook, line, and sinker. Three thousand RV and tent campsites are hidden around Klamath, and they fill up quickly when word gets out that the salmon and steelhead runs have begun in late fall and early winter. Nested around bends in the river, out of sight of the highway, the RV parks metamorphose into busy fish camps overnight. Klamath celebrates the fishing frenzy that keeps it flush with a Salmon Festival on the last Sunday in June.

Beaches

There's more to be caught from the waters around Klamath than salmon, as any surf caster can tell you. Shore anglers pull in ling cod, black snapper, cabezon, flounder, perch, smelt, and sea trout. Dungeness crabs and razor clams are also taken. Miles of sandy beaches and rocky shoreline beg to be fished or hiked. They can also be admired from vista points on the highway. In the words of a man who grew up here, "When the sun's shining, this is one of the most beautiful spots in the world." That is not just an idle boast from a prideful local; it is the honest truth, as anyone who's ever seen the sun set from the Klamath Overlook—a turnout off Requa Road, west of Highway 101—can attest.

The most accessible beach in the area is **Wilson Creek Beach**, which is one of those rare points where Highway 101 flirts with the ocean's edge on the north coast. Located five miles north of Klamath, it is a wide, sandy beach in an area known as False Klamath Cove. Less than a mile away is Lagoon Creek, where you'll find a freshwater lagoon, a bluff-top trail, and picnic tables.

Wilson Creek Beach

4

Location: 5.5 miles north of Klamath, at the end of Wilson Creek Road off Highway 101.

Parking: Free parking lot.

Hours: Sunrise to sunset.

Facilities: Rest rooms, picnic tables, and fire pits. There are 45 tent and RV sites at Mill Creek Campground. Fees are $12 to $14 per night. For camping reservations, call Destinet at (800) 444-7275. There are also 10 primitive hike-in sites at De Martin Beach Campground. The fee is $3 per night. No camping reservations.

Contact: For beach information, contact Del Norte Coast Redwoods State Park at (707) 464-9533.

See number 2 on page 570.

Bunking Down

Directly across the street from Trees of Mystery, where Paul Bunyan gives passersby the high five, is a neatly kept motor court by the name of **Motel Trees** (15495 Highway 101 South, P.O. Box 309, 482-3152, $). Its 23 units are clean and comfortable, offering such diversions as cable TV and a tennis court on the grounds. You'll sleep like a Babe in this rustic setting, with the only possible disturbance being the odd, wandering bear who decides to leave his paw prints on your bathroom window.

Up on a hill overlooking the Klamath River and the beaches that flank it is a restored hotel called the **Requa Inn** (451 Requa Road, 482-8205, $). This two-story white wonder is open year-round, except in winter, when it does business only on weekends. Dating back to 1885, it has witnessed fire, flood, and the economic collapse of what used to be a thriving community. Somehow, the inn has managed to survive it all.

Coastal Cuisine

At **Steelhead Lodge** (330 Terwer Riffle Road, 482-8145, $$), the chef of long standing tends a barbecue pit, grilling salmon, Pacific snapper, ribs, and other charbroiled delights. The mountainous margaritas served here are guaranteed to chase away the gray skies, and the rustic lodge atmosphere will have you feeling fit and full of the outdoors. Located several scenic miles up the Klamath River, with the river views becoming more photogenic en route, the Steelhead Lodge opens around the Fourth of July and shuts down for the winter.

Dinner is served nightly at the historic **Requa Inn** (451 Requa Road, 482-8205, $$). Seafood is abundant on the menu, with salmon, halibut, and plump Pacific oysters getting high marks. They also serve steak, chicken, and (on weekends) prime rib.

Babe's Iron Tender (15495 Highway 101 South, 482-3152, $), named after the blue ox who was Paul Bunyan's companion, is adjacent to Motel Trees. They offer a standard surf-and-turf menu at night (with a bit more emphasis on the turf—the steaks are great) and a menu of sandwiches and lighter dishes at lunch. Breakfasts are big and hearty, too, making Babe's the most convenient place to put on the feedbag between Eureka and Crescent City.

Night Moves

If you've got a thirst for something stronger than a can of Coke, head to **Paul's Cannery** (17635 Highway 101 South, 482-4591) for a mug of draft and a hunk of their world's best salmon jerky, along with a complimentary helping of local color.

For More Information

Contact the Klamath Chamber of Commerce, P.O. Box 476, Klamath, CA 95548; (707) 482-7165.

Del Norte Coast Redwoods, Jedediah Smith Redwoods, and Lakes Earl & Talawa State Park

Location: Del Norte Coast Redwoods State Park is located 5.5 miles north of Klamath along Highway 101. Jedediah Smith Redwoods State Park is located seven miles east of Crescent City via Highway 199. To get to Lakes Earl and Talawa, follow Northcrest Drive north from its junction with Highway 101 in Crescent City. Northcrest turns into Lake Earl Drive, and the lakes lie off of it five miles north of town. Beach access can be gained from either Sand Hill Road or Palo Road. Try to get a map of Crescent City before negotiating the maze of roads that lead to these beaches.

Federal and state parks protect a continuous strip of coastland from Stone Lagoon (in Humboldt County) to Crescent Beach (in Crescent City). In Del Norte County, three state parks divvy up the coastline and redwood forests with Redwood National Park. These are:

Del Norte Coast Redwoods State Park—One of the first parks in the state system, it dates back to a deed of land made in 1926. Its 6,375 acres include eight miles of coastline. Mill Creek Campground is located 2.5 miles east of Highway 101. A good bit closer to the ocean is De Martin Campground, a primitive 10-siter overlooking Wilson Creek on the Coastal Trail. It's a half mile from the trailhead, on Highway 101 on the north end of Wilson Creek Bridge. At the bottom of a long hill lies Wilson Creek Beach, which extends for about a half a mile from the creek mouth south to an imposing point where a line of rocks runs out to sea with near-ruler straightness. Locals like to park here and fish or catch some rays. We even saw some people splashing around in the frigid water. Look, ma, no wet suit! How do they do it?

Jedediah Smith Redwoods State Park—The park's namesake was a mountain man who led the first party of white explorers overland into California. Among other things, his 1826–28 travel journals include the first description of coast redwoods. Nowadays he's remembered with a 10,000-acre park set in old-growth redwood forest along the Smith River. The park offers 30 miles of hiking trails, fishing and canoeing in the river, and a 108-site campground.

Lakes Earl & Talawa State Park—Located in the extreme northwest corner of Del Norte County, these two lakes form the centerpiece of the **Lake Earl Wildlife Area**, a 5,000-acre refuge that includes a variety of terrain: wetlands, woodlands, meadows, dune fields, and

Lake Earl Wildlife Area Beaches

Location: Trails lead to the beach from the west side of Lake Earl at parking areas along Sand Hill Road and Crooked Creek.

Parking: Free parking lots.

Hours: Sunrise to sunset.

Facilities: Rest rooms and picnic tables.

Contact: For beach information, contact Del Norte Coast Redwoods State Park at (707) 464-9533. Hand-drawn trail maps of park trails are available at Lake Earl Wildlife Area headquarters, located north of Crescent City at 1375 Elk Valley Road.

See number 9 on page 570.

sand beaches. Bird- and whale watching are both excellent. Twenty miles of trails fall within park boundaries. Within the park is one horse camp and a six-site walk-in campground (neither on the beach). Better yet, it has 7.5 miles of ocean frontage, including a broad, dune-covered strand that runs north into Kellogg Beach County Park (see the entry on page 583).

For More Information

Contact Redwood State Parks, 1375 Elk Valley Road, Crescent City, CA 95531; (707) 464-9533. Or call the state parks at the following numbers: Del Norte Coast Redwoods State Park, (707) 464-9533; Jedediah Smith Redwoods State Park, (707) 458-3310; and Lakes Earl and Talawa, (707) 464-9533.

The Regal Redwoods

Redwood National Park is a 46-by-7-mile preserve for *Sequoia sempervirens* that was established in 1968 by an act of Congress and expanded 10 years later. Straddling both Humboldt and Del Norte Counties, it has been a boon to tourism and a blessing to the sacred trees, though chain saw–crazed timber topplers in these economically beleaguered counties would not agree. Fully half of Del Norte County is state and federal parkland, forever off-limits to logging, and this has taken a painful toll on the ailing economy in this often overlooked corner of the state. While the redwoods draw 600,000 visitors a year, the tourism numbers are still not enough to offset jobs lost in the timber industry. Meanwhile, Del Norte County gamely promotes itself as the "Redwood Gate to the Golden State."

October 1993 marked the 25th anniversary of the park's founding. One of the loftiest stands in the park, the Lady Bird Johnson Grove, commemorates the First Lady whose mission to "beautify America" is one of the better environmental memories of the 1960s. Park information centers are located in downtown Crescent City, at Second and K Streets; in Hiouchi, eight miles east of Crescent City, along Highway 199; and one mile south of Orick, along Highway 101, in Humboldt County.

Three state parks lie within the national park boundaries. Prairie Creek Redwoods State Park (in Humboldt County), Jedediah Smith Redwoods State Park, and Del Norte Coast Redwoods State Park (in Del Norte County) are fully developed, with campsites, hiking trails, information booths, ranger talks, and picnic tables. Considerable beach access is available along stretches of Redwood National Park and at Prairie Creek and Del Norte Coast Redwoods State Parks (see the entry on page 578). Though it's a safe bet you won't want to dive into the frigid waters of the Pacific this far north, swimming in the creeks and rivers that run through these parks is a pleasantly bracing option in the summer months. For more information, contact Redwood National Park, 1111 Second Street, Crescent City, CA; (707) 464-6101 (the phone is answered 24 hours a day).

Redwood National Park: Crescent Beach and Enderts Beach

Location: Two miles south of Crescent City, on Enderts Beach Road.

Surprises await the unsuspecting beach-lover in Redwood National Park. The northernmost section of the park, which touches Crescent City, includes two fine beaches in proximity. **Crescent Beach** is the more accessible of the two, with a beach-level parking lot right off Enderts Beach Road. Picnic tables are strewn about the flat grassy areas behind the beachfront, which itself is wide and littered with drift logs and cobbles (especially along its landward edge).

For a real treat, continue up Enderts Beach Road till it gives out in a parking lot that overlooks Crescent Beach. From here, a 0.6-mile (one-way) trail leads to secluded **Enderts Beach**, the preferred location in terms of scenery, solitude, and beach quality. The beach and trail are part of the "Last Chance" section of the Coastal Trail. Informational signs along the path ask tough questions (i.e., "Seal... Or Sea Lion?"). Approaching the beach, the trail gets steep, and you must slide down some volcanic rock slabs, on feet or fanny, before being deposited on the sand. It is a quarter-mile wilderness beach between rock points. Little Nickel Creek runs into the ocean here, and shorebirds drink from it before returning to sentry duty along the water's edge. As many people come here with books in hand to read or meditate as show up in swimsuits to pursue the usual seaside preoccupations. It's truly a special place that's well worth the side trip.

Bunking Down

For those cycling along the coast, traveling on a shoestring budget, or simply out for new experiences, **Redwood Hostel** (14480 Highway

Crescent Beach (a part of Redwood National Park)

3

Location: South of Crescent City, along Enderts Beach Road off Highway 101.

Parking: Free parking lot.

Hours: Open 24 hours.

Facilities: Rest rooms, picnic tables, and fire pits.

Contact: For beach information, contact Redwood National Park at (707) 464-6101, ext. 5064.

See number 4 on page 570.

Enderts Beach (a part of Redwood National Park)

5

Location: South of Crescent City, at the end of Enderts Beach Road off Highway 101. A half-mile trail leads to the beach.

Parking: Free parking lot.

Hours: Open 24 hours.

Facilities: Rest rooms, picnic tables, and fire pits. There are five free primitive tent campsites at the mouth of Nickel Creek. No camping reservations.

Contact: For beach information, contact Redwood National Park at (707) 464-6101, ext. 5064.

See number 3 on page 570.

101, 482-8265, $) is located in a turn-of-the-century ranch home, the DeMartin House. This 30-room hostel overlooks Wilson Creek from inside Redwood National Park. For $9 a night ($4.50 for children), you'll share dorm-style, bunk-bedded rooms with a host of fellow coastal wayfarers—foreign travelers, city escapees, and footloose free spirits.

For More Information

Contact Redwood National Park, 1111 2nd Street, Crescent City, CA 95531; (707) 464-6101.

Crescent City

Location: 352 miles north of San Francisco via Highway 101. Beaches in the Crescent City area include a length stretch along Pebble Beach Drive from Battery Point to Point St. George.
Population: 8,000
Area Code: 707 **Zip Code:** 95531

A string of road signs along a 10-mile stretch of Highway 101 between Klamath and Crescent City reads: "Daylight Headlight Use." Yes, it's dark enough beneath the roadside canopy of redwoods to require the use of headlights in broad daylight. Crescent City, the last town of any size in California, emerges on the other side of the tree-shrouded darkness.

This city has been defined by two events, one negative and one a mixed blessing. First, on March 28, 1964—only nine months before the calamitous Klamath flood—Crescent City was struck by a tidal wave that destroyed 29 city blocks. A violent Alaskan earthquake measuring 8.8 on the Richter scale sent a tidal surge down the Pacific coast, and it slapped Crescent City silly. It was a sad moment, almost the beginning of the end for a town that at one time bucked to become the capital of California. (That was back in 1854, when the Gold Rush was burning up the north country.)

The second defining event occurred in December 1989, when Pelican Bay State Prison opened its doors. This controversial prison houses California's most hardened felons—gang members, drug dealers, prison-guard assaulters, and cunning criminals in the Hannibal Lechter mold. The hardest of the hardened get thrown into the prison's Security Housing Unit, where they're confined to small, lightless cells for 22.5 hours each day. Already the prison has been the subject of a lawsuit charging excessive force and cruel and unusual punishment, though many would say this particular prison population needs this severe treatment to control them.

The prison was constructed eight miles north of Crescent City, and the arrival of 3,800 prison inmates has had a profound effect upon the town. The prison employs 1,200 and runs on an $86 million annual budget. Still more jobs have been created to serve all the new hires. Formerly, Del Norte County had the lowest per capita income among all of California's 58 counties. Thanks to Pelican Bay, Crescent City has rebounded from the slack-jawed, sad-sack look it wore throughout the 1980s. Something good has come of all of the bad that's been exported up here. City officials are so pleased that they've approached the state about building *another* prison.

Crescent City is booming. At least it looks better than it did when we visited in the pre-prison era. There's a new Kmart, Wal-Mart, and Safeway, and the shopping opportunities are the best between Eureka and the Oregon border. Still, one wonders about the morality of Southern California, which imports what it needs (mainly water) from the north and exports what it doesn't want (mainly criminals) to the north. No wonder there is a movement gaining strength to split California into two, and possibly three, states.

Signs of this discontent could be read between the lines at the county fair, which comes to Crescent City the first week in August. It is not called the Del Norte County Fair, as it logically might be, but the Jefferson State Fair. The fair originates in Sacramento, which is located in Jefferson County. A lot of folks in Northern California would like to see the founding of a 51st state: the state of Jefferson. Can you really blame them?

They may harbor some pretty scary felons at Pelican Bay, but the type of crime that goes on outside the prison walls, as reported in the local paper (the *Triplicate)*, is the sort of small-town shenanigans that can bring a smile to your face. Amid reports of disorderly conduct (good ol' boys having too much to drink and revving their engines or throats), there are such entries as these:

- "A caller from the 600 block of Elk Valley Road reported someone had dumped a fish on her front lawn." (We would have fired up the grill and cooked dinner.)
- "A caller reported smelling something dead on Highway 199 at the second turnout on the left." (Dead skunk in the middle of the road?)
- "A caller reported her baby stolen. She soon remembered that she hired a baby-sitter." ("Never mind.")
- "A caller reported loud music coming from the Seaview Motel." (We were *not* playing that Green Day tape too loud—honest!)

On a more serious note, during our time in the area, a truck negotiating a sharp curve lost a large "rubber bladder" containing 1,800 gallons of gray primer, which spilled into the Smith River. The spill turned the crystal waters white and caused concern about toxic drinking water and fish kills along the river's length.

On our last pass through we noted that Crescent City was "more on the run than in the running." It pleases us to report that the town has made big strides in the right direction during the 1990s. With so much scenic beauty and some of the best stream and surf fishing close at hand, it really deserves to be visited by more people. We certainly look forward to coming back.

Beaches

Crescent City has a bounty of beaches from the harbor north to Point St. George. Starting from the bottom, there's little South Beach, a triangle of sand formed by Highway 101, the Crescent City Harbor, and the ocean. It's protected from the full force of the sea, and plenty of natives spread out on it.

Beachfront Park offers a serene, calm-water beach with a narrow strip of pebbly, dirty sand. People walk their dogs out here. The view across the harbor is pleasant. There's a pier and lighthouse at the end of B Street near where Howe Street gives out at Battery Point. Both Battery Point Vista and Brother Jonathan Point can be excellent spots for whale watching from December through February, when gray whales migrate from the Arctic to Baja, and from March through May, when they return.

The beach makes a perpendicular turn onto Pebble Drive, and the shoreline opens up into all sorts of fascinating shapes and formations. The Pebble Beach Fishing Access marks an in-

Beachfront Park

2

Location: In Crescent City, along the length of Howe Drive.

Parking: Free street parking.

Hours: Open 24 hours.

Facilities: Rest rooms and picnic tables.

Contact: For beach information, contact Crescent City Public Works at (707) 464-9506.

See number 6 on page 570.

teresting divide; the beach is rocky on one side, sandy on the other. Pebble Beach Drive runs along the ocean, giving out at Radio Road, which leads to Point St. George. The coast from **Pebble Beach** to Point St. George is an amazing stretch of gorgeous, undulating shoreline. Sea lions can be heard barking on offshore rocks. We spied a lone surfer trying unsuccessfully to ride the one-foot waves. Parking is available and plentiful along the beach, which was all but deserted on the prettiest summer Saturday of the year.

The land rises to a figurative crescendo at **Point St. George**, a public park that's jointly administered by the California State Wildlife Conservation Board and the Del Norte County Department of Parks and Recreation. The beach here is known to locals as **Radio Beach**, because of the old Coast Guard radio towers at the point. From the parking area, a gravel road leads to the beach. You can also hike a dirt path out to the bluffs, savor the view, and then scramble down to the beach via gullied trails. It is a splendidly scenic coastline, especially on

Kellogg Beach

Location: Eight miles north of Crescent City, turn west from Highway 101 onto Kings Valley Road. Follow the "Coastal Access" signs to Kellogg Beach Park, located at the end of Kellogg Road.

Parking: Free parking lot.

Hours: Sunrise to sunset.

Facilities: None.

Contact: For beach information, contact Del Norte County Parks and Beaches at (707) 464-7237.

See number 10 on page 570.

Pebble Beach

Location: In Crescent City; Pebble Beach can be accessed at several turnouts and stairways along Pebble Beach Drive.

Parking: Free lot and street parking.

Hours: Open 24 hours.

Facilities: Rest rooms and picnic table.

Contact: For beach information, contact Del Norte County Parks and Beaches at (707) 464-7237.

See number 7 on page 570.

Point St. George
(a.k.a. Radio Beach)

Location: From Highway 101 in Crescent City, turn west on Washington Boulevard and continue to its end. Turn right on Radio Road and drive to Point St. George Public Access. Trails lead across bluffs to beach.

Parking: Free parking lot.

Hours: Open 24 hours.

Facilities: None.

Contact: For beach information, contact Del Norte County Parks and Beaches at (707) 464-7237.

See number 8 on page 570.

South Beach

Location: At Crescent City Harbor, south of Anchor Way off Highway 101.

Parking: Free parking lot.

Hours: Open 24 hours.

Facilities: Rest rooms (at Citizens Dock, adjacent).

Contact: For beach information, contact Crescent City Public Works at (707) 464-9506.

See number 5 on page 570.

a clear, sunny day. The terraced bluffs are banded in shades of orange and light brown, and the coast runs in a broad arc for a good distance up to the next rocky point.

Kellogg Beach is the last in the Crescent City–area trove of beaches. It does not start off very encouragingly. Two signs point down the same road. One is a "coastal access" marker; the other shows the way to Pelican Bay State Prison. Fortunately, there is a lot of land out here and the routes to these destinations soon diverge. After a couple of turns the houses thin out and give way to farmer's fields, which in turn give way to dune fields—broad, grassy expanses of them. The beach is wide and windswept, with driftwood scattered about the vast terrain. Winds blow the sand into rippled patterns, making footprints vanish quickly. We spied some RVs parked here, although camping is technically not allowed. It is not a well-developed park, just a mess of big, beautiful beach at the end of the road. Jeeps can continue riding along the beach after the road gives out. Fishing is about the most that can be done out here, unless you (like us) enjoy bundling up in sweatshirts and windbreakers and hiking along an empty beach that's buffeted by wind and waves.

Bunking Down

Some new arrivals have perked up the area, lodging-wise. The **Bayview Inn** (310 Highway 101 South, 465-2050, $) has a freshly painted look to it. It's a trim and tidy three-story Cape Codder that's barely five years old. Rooms at the height of a slow summer season were going for as low as $55, and the view of the bay is the best in Crescent City. The **Holiday Inn Express** (100 Walton Street, 464-3885, $) is another upgraded addition to the lodging scene, offering clean rooms and a free morning breakfast bar for $60 a night and up in season. The **Best Western Northwoods Inn** (655 Highway 101 South, 464-9461, $) has comfortable, modernized rooms and is located across from Crescent City Harbor. Out on Highway 101 west of town, the **Pacific Motor Hotel** (440 Highway 101 North, 464-4141, $) looks out on the county fairgrounds. It's got clean, functional rooms, a separate spa/sauna building, and a liquor store in the lobby.

The **Crescent Beach Motel** (1455 Redwood Highway South, 464-5436, $$) brags of being the only motel on the beach, and its location two miles south of town is another asset. Wooden decks look out over the shoreline and headlands that rise to the south. Finally, there's that perennial curiosity, the **Curly Redwood Lodge** (701 Redwood Highway South, 464-2137, $), which was constructed in its entirety from a single redwood tree that measured 18 feet in diameter and produced 57,000 board-feet of timber. Gadzooks!

Coastal Cuisine

Crescent City still has a ways to go in terms of restaurants, but they are coming around, slowly but surely. The **Good Harvest Café** (700 Northcrest, 465-6028, $) is a health-food emporium serving tasty sandwiches and brunch items in a real café/coffeehouse environment, with rattan chairs and newspapers strewn around for customers to linger over while they sip their French roast. On the sandwich front, menu highlights include "Crescent City's Best Sandwich," a Dagwood-sized creation consisting of sautéed mushrooms, onions, garlic, melted Jack cheese, tomato, sprouts, olives, and sour cream served on a toasted whole-wheat English muffin. All in all, the Good Harvest has added some variety to the dining scene up here in redwood country.

The same can be said of **Shon's** (Ninth and K Streets, 465-3300, $$$), which attempts to bring a touch of gourmet to Crescent City's chicken-fried-steak mentality. It's a surf-and-turf restaurant housed in a turn-of-the-century house. Shon's opened in the spring of '94. Will it take? Depends on whether you can dine here on a prison guard's salary, we guess.

 Map of Del Norte County beaches—page 570

The old reliable in town is the **Harbor House Grotto** (Citizens Dock Road and Starfish Way, 464-3815, $$), a rickety-looking green structure by the harbor. There's nothing fancy about this place, but the full house and lines out the door attest to its consistency and popularity. Seafood items are served either fried or poached. Calamari steak, with or without egg batter, is a good choice. But if you want a little bit of everything, ante up for the Grotto Fisherman's Platter, a heapin' helpin' of fish, oysters, scallops, and shrimp that goes for a very modest $12.50. The upstairs dining rooms have a bird's-eye view of the harbor; come at sunset for the best looks.

Acting on a hot tip from the gals at the Crescent City Information Center, we ate lunch at the **Chart Room** (130 Anchor Way, 464-5993, $). You'd likely overlook it if you didn't know to come here. The locals are certainly in the know, as the place was packed. The seafood preparations are simple, affordable, and delicious. We had the fried seafood combo—fish, shrimp, and scallops the size of hockey pucks—which was as fresh as it could be and nicely complemented by hand-cut French fries and homemade cole slaw. Instead of dessert we bought some pottery by a talented local who used to wait tables here and now displays her work in a case by the register. The prices were insanely low for work of this caliber—$10 for a beautiful handmade Native American vase? This is the kind of restaurant where working folks go, an informal community center where the conversation and the laughter slide down as easily as the home-cooked food. A sign by the clock over the register said it all: "This clock will never be stolen, as the employees are watching it." Flags of many nations hang from the ceiling, with the Stars and Stripes by far the largest, naturally.

Night Moves

Nightlife in a town like this is geared to people who have to drink, as opposed to want to. We found no bar that looked like it had our names written all over it. By and large, Crescent City shuts down early. Most restaurants are closed by 9 PM. The **Apple Peddler** (308 Highway 1 South, 464-5630), however, is open 24 hours, as is the drive-through window at Taco Time.

For More Information

Contact the Crescent City/Del Norte County Chamber of Commerce, 1001 Front Street, Crescent City, CA 95531; (707) 464-9676.

Smith River

Location: 363 miles north of San Francisco and 13 miles south of the Oregon border, along Highway 101. Clifford Kamph Memorial Park provides the best beach access in this area, while Pelican State Beach has the distinction of being the northernmost beach in California.
Population: 600
Area Code: 707 **Zip Code:** 95567

California runs out a few miles past the town of Smith River. There's not much here to eyeball: agricultural fields, sprinkler systems to tend them, last-chance-before-Oregon liquor stores. All that and RV parks, too. The town of Smith River lies off the highway at a point where Highway 101 swings away from the coast. Smith River is the Easter-lily capital of the world. They grow more of them here than anywhere else—90 percent of the nation's commercial lily bulbs, they'll have you know.

It's a small town. When we asked a local what the population was, she replied, "Six hundred. That's including dogs and cats—and two emus." The town is built around the Smith River, one of the prime salmon- and steelhead-fishing rivers in the state. In 1990, the Smith River National Recreation Area, encompassing 300,000 acres, was established to protect the watershed of this Wild and Scenic River. Ample opportunities for recreation exist upriver and along the coast.

Yes, Smith River is the end of the line; four more miles and you slip out of California with little fanfare. After having traveled 1,500 miles of coastline inch-by-inch several times, we always expect some sort of grand reception—a marching band, a 21-gun salute, a token hunk of salmon jerky—when we finally reach the Holy Grail of the state line. But there's not even a sign saying "Goodbye to California" or "Welcome to Oregon." So it goes.

And so as the sun slowly sets in the West on another perfect California day, our pilgrimage up the coast finally comes to an end. We bid you good day, safe passage, and happy beaching.

Beaches

The beaches at California's northern end are interesting to ponder—that is, when you can

Clifford Kamph Memorial Park

Location: Two miles south of the Oregon border off Highway 101.
Parking: Free parking lot.
Hours: Open 24 hours.
Facilities: Rest rooms and picnic tables. There are eight tent campsites; the fee is $5 per night. For reservations, call Del Norte County Parks and Beaches at (707) 464-7237.
Contact: For beach information, contact Del Norte County Parks and Beaches at (707) 464-7237.

See number 11 on page 570.

Pelican State Beach

Location: A half mile south of the Oregon border off Highway 101.
Parking: Free roadside parking.
Hours: Sunrise to sunset.
Facilities: None.
Contact: For beach information, contact Del Norte Coast Redwoods State Park at (707) 464-9533.

See number 12 on page 570.

get to them. Your best shot is **Clifford Kamph Memorial Park**, which sits beside the highway halfway between Smith River and the state line. The park borders someone's home; try to take a picture of the shoreline north to the Oregon border, as we did, and you might just interrupt a backyard cookout. The beach is wide, windswept, and wild. Tenters were encamped in gullies behind dunes and anywhere they could find protection from the wind. An occupied RV near the parking lot serves as the campground host. Anglers cast for ling cod, rockfish, sand dabs, and cabezon here.

California's bounty of beaches ends not with a bang but a whimper at **Pelican State Beach**. It's a spot that's more notable for the symbolism of finality it embodies than for its particular qualities as a beach. Still, this is the last tretch of sand in California, sitting a mere half mile below the Oregon border. Stop to take a snapshot, enjoy a sunset, or bow to Ra, but do something. This is it—California ends here!

Bunking Down

If you're looking to park your RV, car, or carcass for the night, the spot to lay over in Smith River is the **Best Western Ship Ashore** (12370 Highway 101, 487-3141, $). This riverside, ocean-view compound includes a 50-unit motel with hot tubs and an on-premises steak and seafood restaurant. There's also a sizable RV park here that looked to be full to our tired eyes and a museum and gift shop housed in a red, white, and blue ship that sits in the parking lot. Then there's the unpretentious **Pelican Beach Motel** (16855 Highway 101 North, 487-7651, $), which sits at the intersection of Highway 101 and a road that leads to Pelican State Beach, if you're so inclined.

Coastal Cuisine

The **Bayshore Grill** (12451 Highway 101 North, 487-1103, $) is your basic nautical-themed roadside restaurant, serving three meals a day of unfancy home cooking.

Night Moves

Hoist a tall, cool one at the **Captain's Lounge** in the Best Western Ship Ashore Motel (12370 Highway 101, 487-3141). Bottom's up!

For More Information

Contact the Crescent City/Del Norte County Chamber of Commerce, 1001 Front Street, Crescent City, CA 95531, (707) 464-9676.

Beach Bits: Tips, Trends, and Trivia

Toll-Free Phone Numbers at Your Fingertips

Airlines

Aero California	(800) 237-6225
Air Canada	(800) 776-3000
Air Nevada	(800) 634-6377
Alaska Airlines	(800) 426-0333
Aloha Airlines	(800) 367-5250
America West	(800) 247-5692
American Airlines	(800) 433-7300
American Eagle	(800) 433-7300
American Transair	(800) 225-9920
British Airways	(800) 247-9297
Canadian Airlines	(800) 426-7000
Cathay Pacific	(800) 233-2742
Continental Airlines	(800) 525-0280
Delta Airlines	(800) 221-1212
Hawaiian Airlines	(800) 367-5320
Japan Airlines	(800) 525-3663
Mexicana Airlines	(800) 531-7921
Northwest Airlines	(800) 225-2525
Reno Air	(800) 736-6247
Skywest Airlines	(800) 453-9417
Southwest Airlines	(800) 435-9792
TWA	(800) 221-2000
United Airlines	(800) 241-6522
US Air	(800) 428-4322
Virgin Atlantic Airways	(800) 862-8621

Car Rental Agencies

Alamo Rent-a-Car	(800) 327-9633
Avis Rent-a-Car	(800) 831-2847
Budget Car Rental	(800) 527-0700
Dollar Rent-a-Car	(800) 800-4000
Enterprise Rent-a-Car	(800) 325-8007
Hertz Rent-a-Car	(800) 654-3131
National Car Rental	(800) 227-7368
Sears Car Rental	(800) 527-0770
Thrifty Car Rental	(800) 367-2277

Lodgings

Best Western Hotels	(800) 528-1234
Comfort Inns	(800) 228-5150
Courtyard by Marriott	(800) 443-6000
Days Inns	(800) 329-7466
Doubletree Inns	(800) 222-8733
Econo Lodges	(800) 424-4777
Embassy Suites	(800) 362-2779
Fairfield Inns	(800) 228-2800
Fairmont Hotels	(800) 527-4727
Four Seasons Hotels	(800) 332-3442
Friendship Inns	(800) 424-6423
Hampton Inns	(800) 426-7866
Hilton Hotels	(800) 445-8667
Holiday Inns	(800) 465-4329
Howard Johnson's	(800) 446-4656
Hyatt Hotels	(800) 228-9000
Inns by the Sea	(800) 433-4732
Inter-Continental Hotels	(800) 327-0200
Marriott Hotels	(800) 228-9290
Meridien Hotels	(800) 543-4300
Motel 6	(505) 891 6161
Nikko Hotels	(800) 645-5687
Omni Hotels	(800) 843-6664
Quality Inns	(800) 228-5151
Radisson Hotels	(800) 333-3333
Ramada Inns	(800) 272-6232
Red Lion Inns	(800) 733-5166
Red Roof Inns	(800) 843-7663
Residence Inns	(800) 331-3131
Ritz-Carlton Hotels	(800) 241-3333
Sheraton Hotels	(800) 325-3535
Stouffer Hotels	(800) 468-3571
Super 8 Motels	(800) 800-8000
Vagabond Inns	(800) 522-1555
Westin Hotels	(800) 228-3000
Wyndham Hotels	(800) 996-3426

All Aboard, Beach Bums

Despite the profound incursion on its turf by the internal combustion engine, trains still have a lingering, almost mystical appeal. Amtrak, the beleaguered, government-funded passenger service, keeps the barely flickering flame of rail travel alive. In California, Amtrak covers the beaches like a blanket. In some places, the railroad tracks run so close to the ocean that you can actually see the waves break from your coach window.

Amtrak has ocean-hugging routes that allow riders to connect with a myriad of local rail, bus, and trolley lines. The **San Diegan**, launched in 1988, runs between San Diego and Santa Barbara and makes commuter runs between San Diego and Los Angeles. Two years after its inauguration, the San Diegan became the second most popular passenger train in the U.S. It makes stops at the following beach towns: San Diego, Del Mar, Oceanside, San Clemente, San Juan Capistrano, Long Beach, Torrance, Los Angeles, Oxnard, Ventura, and Santa Barbara.

The **Coast Starlight** is a not-to-be-missed ride from San Diego to Seattle that's considered one of the most scenic routes in America. In places, the train follows a seaside route, passing more wilderness beaches than you'd ever see from the highway. And, in what must be the bargain of the century, a round-trip ticket between those two cities was going for only $118 when this book went to press.

A detailed Amtrak booklet—with a timetable, maps, fares, connections, tips, and package deals—is published twice a year. Call Amtrak's toll-free number, 1-800-USA-RAIL, and ask for one. You'll be surprised by what they offer. We were. Anything that's a viable transportation alternative to the automobile is all to the good. And just think: you can leave the driving to them and watch the coast, instead your steering wheel.

Sun Screams: Tips for Skin Protection

In the old days, before the ozone layer was depleted—before anyone knew what ozone *was*—the beach was one gigantic tanning salon. People who hadn't been outdoors in six months had a sudden desire to spend two uninterrupted weeks in the open—on a towel at the beach or in a chaise lounge beside their motel's lima bean–shaped pool. Slathering themselves from forehead to foot-top with greasy lotions and oils, they submitted their bodies to eight hours of slow ultraviolet roasting, oblivious to anything but the fact that by vacation's end they'd have a Coppertone tan and be the envy of friends and co-workers.

But human populations have exploded worldwide in the last quarter century, as has the use of ozone-depleting products, pollutants, car emissions, and toxic industrial emissions. With this assault on the environment has come an increased awareness of what too much sun exposure can do to one's epidermis.

We don't want to spoil your day at the beach, but we'd be irresponsible if we didn't at least mention the latest facts about what is really going on under the sun. You certainly won't get this information from the manufacturers of sunscreens and other expensive lotions designed to make you feel "safe" while you sunbathe. Many of the products on the market misleadingly claim to offer "all-day protection," lulling sun-worshippers into a false sense of security. Here's the reality:

- The fatality rate for malignant melanoma, the skin cancer associated with sun exposure, is rising. According to the National Cancer Institute, it has risen 50 percent for men since 1973. The Environmental Protection Agency estimates there will be 12 million new cases of skin cancer in the next 40 years.

- Pale-skinned, red-haired, and blue-eyed people are no longer the stereotypical targets. Melanomas are now found in Chinese, Japanese, Hawaiians, and Filipinos, populations previously thought immune to them.
- In January 1994, the *Journal of the National Cancer Institute* reported that most sunscreens, while helping to prevent sunburns, did not give the full protection their labels promise. "Protection against sunburn does not necessarily imply protection against other possible UV radiation effects, such as enhanced melanoma growth," the report concluded.

Okay, enough of this. The real culprit is something called UVA radiation, a longer-wave form of sunlight than the UVB radiation that causes sunburn. While UVB radiation does its damage to the outer layer of skin, UVA penetrates the skin's elastic fibers and collagen, causing you to "leather" while you "weather." Even more insidious, UVA radiation is present on cloudy days, too.

As usual, the best defense is preventive maintenance. That is, accept the fact that you can no longer lie out in the sun for eight hours a day, no matter what substances you baste yourself with. Also consider the following measures:

- Avoid the sun's rays between 11 AM and 3 PM, when they are most intense.
- Gradually accustom yourself to the sun by lengthening your exposure a little bit more each day. Don't try to get a perfect tan on the first day out, or you'll inevitably ruin your vacation.
- Always wear a hat, except when you're in the water. The best sort of hat is the broad-brimmed Panama-style variety, which helps deflect the sun from one's eyes. Sunlight has been shown to be a contributing factor in cataract formation.
- Use a sunscreen that claims to block both UVB and UVA radiation. Check the ingredients for avobenzone (a.k.a. Parsol 1789) or bensophenone (a.k.a. oxybenzone). Both are excellent UVA blockers. Brands with these include Photoplex Broad-Spectrum Sunscreen Lotion and Shade UVA Guard.
- Avoid brands of sunscreens that use improperly tested chemicals, some of which are suspected of being carcinogens. Among these are Octyl dimethyl PABA (a.k.a. Padimate-O), diethanolamine (a.k.a. DEA), and triethanolamine (a.k.a. TEA). The best all-around sunscreens (those that block the sun and use the most natural ingredients) on the market are Earth Preserv and Aubrey Organics.
- Apply sunscreen to cool, dry skin about half an hour before going outdoors. These creams cost an arm and a leg, but they could also cost skin if you apply them too thinly. Don't miss those places you never think about until you get burned there: forehead, earlobes, back of the neck, ankles, back of the knees, and (for nudists) all the erogenous zones.
- Use "after sun" lotions/oils that contain sun-protective nutrients. Also helpful—and available as topical ointments—are Vitamin C and Vitamin E. Some naturally occurring substances are good, too, including aloe vera, chamomile, and marigold.

Finally, you aren't going to die just because you didn't know about all this stuff until now. Even the lousy sunscreens and suntan lotions you used in the past gave some protection from ultraviolet radiation. From here on out, just be smart and take added precautions. That way we'll catch you at the beach when we're all in our nineties.

Bare Facts: Clothing-Optional Beaches

It began for us in San Diego County, at Black's Beach, purportedly a mecca for naked beach bums and bunnies. Twice we've visited, twice we saw no naked mermaids. Only a couple of salty dogs wearing ankle socks and deck shoes.

Perhaps most emblematic of our perpetual plight in this regard is a search we made along the Central Coast for Pirate's Cove. It's a place alleged to be so blessed by physical pulchritude as to make grown men weep and grown women swoon. But we never found it. Rather, we found the beach—we always get our beach!—but we never found reclining nudes.

Here are our verbatim notes about the trip to Pirates Cove:

"Said to be a real jewel... between Shell and Avila... take ocean drive to El Portal off Palisades... dead-ends at gate. Climb fence... snag leg... walk along crumbling bluff top... approx. 500 yards... 1,000 yards... don't get too close... they're selling lots out here... how?... land is caving in... bulldozers everywhere... 500 more yds. through tall grass... slashed legs... down gully... down dirt path... hold on to shrubs for support... ends at ledge... whoa Nelly... straight down to small cove with cliffs behind... stub toe on rock.... Can this be Pirate's Cove? Nobody here to ask."

Obviously, this clothing-optional subculture is not for dilettantes or the merely curious. You really have to want to be a "naturist" to make it work. Still, in the interest of journalistic integrity, we offer this admittedly incomplete list of some of the better-known clothing-optional beaches in California:

- **Black's Beach**, San Diego, page 70
- **Boneyard Beach**, San Diego, page 84
- **Palos Verdes Peninsula** (coves near Portuguese Bend), Los Angeles, page 177
- **Nicholas Canyon County Beach**, Malibu, page 220
- **Rincon Beach**, Santa Barbara, page 265
- **Pirate's Cove**, Avila Beach, page 303
- **William R. Hearst Memorial State Beach**, San Simeon, page 319
- **Andrew Molera State Beach**, Big Sur, page 328
- **Garrapata State Park**, Big Sur, page 328
- **Pfeiffer Beach**, Big Sur, page 330
- **Four Mile Beach**, Santa Cruz, page 397
- **Red, White, and Blue Beach,** Santa Cruz, page 398
- **Bonny Doon Beach**, Santa Cruz, page 399
- **Pomponio State Beach**, Santa Cruz, page 412
- **San Gregorio Private Beach**, San Mateo County, page 414
- **North Baker Beach**, San Francisco, page 442
- **Kirby Cove**, Marin County, page 451
- **Muir Beach**, Marin County, page 453
- **Red Rock Beach**, Marin County, page 455
- **Bolinas Beach**, Bolinas, page 459
- **Limantour Beach**, Point Reyes Peninsula, page 463
- **Gualala River**, Gualala, page 506
- **College Cove**, Trinidad, page 559

Spout Spots: Whale Watching on the Coast

Whales migrate south from late November to January, clinging to the coastline during their annual migration to warmer waters. Their migratory route carries them from plankton-rich polar feeding waters to their tropical or subtropical birthing grounds, where there is no food source. They survive the summer's deprivation by subsisting on energy supplies stored in the form of blubber. For their return trip north in the spring they retrace their route, but farther out to sea. Their transoceanic travels carry them 10,000 miles, the longest migration of any mammal. On a typical dive, a whale will plunge 150 feet deep and 1,000 feet forward. The most visible kinds (from the California coast) are filter-feeding baleen-type whales, such as the blue, humpback, and gray whales.

Here are some prime spots for whale watching along the California coast:

- **Point Loma**, San Diego, page 45
- **Torrey Pines State Beach**, La Jolla, page 70
- **San Clemente State Beach**, San Clemente, page 109
- **Point Fermin Park**, San Pedro, page 174
- **San Simeon State Beach**, San Simeon, page 319
- **Julia Pfeiffer Burns State Park**, Big Sur, page 329
- **Pillar Point**, Princeton-by-the-Sea, page 421
- **Montara State Beach**, Pacifica, page 425
- **Point Reyes**, Marin County, page 460
- **Bodega Head**, Bodega Bay, page 479
- **Mendocino Headlands State Park**, Mendocino, page 518
- **MacKerricher State Park**, Fort Bragg, page 529
- **Enderts Beach Cliffs**, Crescent City, page 580
- **Brother Jonathan Vista Point**, Crescent City, page 582

California's Best Bites

Seafood is our first priority when we sit down to eat in a beach town. Our second is local or regional cuisine. If these two elements are combined, we're as happy as clams at high tide. Our favorite dishes on the California coast include:

- **Fish tacos:** Especially the soft wraparound tacos with mahimahi or snapper, found at any authentic Mexican food stand. (*Not* Taco Bell!) Wickedly good surfer food.
- **Chicken quesadillas:** Kind of like Mexican pot pies, they're very filling, and are sloppy, almost soupy, when made correctly.
- **Mesquite-grilled boquetta bass:** It tastes more like lobster than fish. We had it in Carlsbad.
- **Grilled eggplant salad:** You'll never go back to Big Macs.
- **Mesquite-grilled swordfish:** Can't be beat at Las Brisas, in Laguna Beach (see page 127).
- **Valencia oranges:** If picked straight from the tree, they're too juicy to peel and eat without a towel. We raided the tree outside our bungalow at Rancho San Valencia, near Del Mar.
- **Ridiculously healthy fruit muffins:** Especially at Starbucks, our California coastal coffee connection, dependable wherever you find them.
- **Sea-bass ceviche:** Sort of like sushi, except it's "cooked" in a citrus marinade.
- **Popcorn shrimp:** California caught, Cajun cooked.
- **Smoked albacore and salmon:** None better can be had than the Crab Cooker's in Newport Beach (see page 137).
- **Super spuds:** Get them at one of the surfer joints in Sunset Beach.
- **Escolar:** Anywhere, anytime, this uncommon, deep-swimming white fish is a delight.
- **Oak-smoked rabbit:** Especially at the Rio Grill in Carmel (see page 345).
- **Paella Fandango:** It's the signature creation of Chef Pierre Bain at Fandango, in Pacific Grove (see page 354).
- **Fried artichoke hearts:** The Giant Artichoke in Castroville has 'em (see page 371).
- **Calamari Piccata:** Lightly breaded and sautéed. Especially good in restaurants around the Monterey Peninsula.
- **Sushi:** Try the giant, ice-cream-cone-sized "designer" maki-maki at MoBo Sushi in Santa Cruz (see page 394).
- **Scoma's Shellfish Sec:** The starring entrée at Scoma's, one of the busiest restaurants on San Francisco's famous Fisherman's Wharf (see page 445).
- **Shrimp or crab cups:** Speaking of Fisherman's Wharf, you can't leave without trying one of these $4 wonders from the outdoor vendors.
- **Pacific oysters:** Plumper and gamier than their Atlantic counterparts. Try them at River's End in Jenner (see page 489).
- **Fresh steelhead trout:** Try it at St. Orres, in Gualala (see page 507).
- **Pacific Rim Bouillabaisse:** We savored the mix of clams, mussels, and rock shrimp in a lemongrass, tomato, and fennel broth, at the Albion River Inn (see page 514).
- **Hot 'n' spicy sea bass:** A must at the Larrupin' Cafe in Trinidad (see page 562).
- **Charbroiled salmon or steelhead:** A treat at the Steelhead Lodge in Klamath (see page 577).

What's In and What's Out on the California Coast

What's In	What's Out
ATM cards	Credit cards
Blaming others	Personal responsibility
Body piercing	Breast enlargements
Chilean sea bass	Salmon and steelhead
"Chill"	"Have a nice day"
Clint Eastwood	Michael Eisner
Cocooning	Going out at night
Coffee	Alcohol
Computer darts	Foosball
Court TV	MTV
Cyberspace	Greenspace
Dance music	Rock and roll
Dancing	Sex
Earthquake preparedness	"It can't happen here"
Fish tacos (soft)	Beef burritos
Foreclosure	Strip malls
Fresh air	Cigarettes
Golf courses	Nature
Graduate school	Careers
Harleys	Porsches
Merlot	Sauvignon blanc
Mesquite grilled seafood	Fish-and-chips
Mountain bikes with shocks	ATVs and Jet Skis
Olive oil	Real butter
Overpopulation	Quality of life
Pebble Beach (Crescent City)	Pebble Beach (Monterey County)
Planning boards	Military bases
Pool halls	Video arcades
Pragmatists	Democrats/Republicans
Ranch-raised game	Cattle grazed on federal land
Reagan/Nixon Libraries	Literacy
San Luis Obispo	Los Angeles
Starbucks	7-Eleven
Surfer activists	Corporate CEOs
Tattoos	Suntans
Upscale B&Bs	"Homestay" B&Bs
Walking	Driving

Questions for Which We Have No Answers

Why, with an authentic Mexican taco stand on every corner, would anyone in Southern California ever *think* of patronizing Taco Bell?

With the sun shining bountifully year-round, why aren't more homes along the coast equipped with solar panels to capture its power?

What is the purpose of wearing pants that are neither long nor short, but instead fall to some indeterminate middle length somewhere below the knee and above the ankle?

Why are litterers fined $1,000 when murderers go free?

How did the cobbles on the beaches at Leucadia and Carlsbad get there?

Where do all the surfers, slackers, and slummers go when development pushes them off the beachfront?

How can people adapt to living in a place where on any given day the very ground beneath them may give way?

When the grunion run, where do they run to?

Why is synthesized dance music still popular in clubs frequented by young people who ought to know better?

Why is valet parking necessary and, at many restaurants and nightclubs, mandatory?

In the endless faux-adobe sprawl of Orange County, how do people tell one house from another?

How can hotels get away with charging 75 cents for a local phone call?

Why do people fail to comprehend that when too many people crowd in on paradise, it is no longer paradise?

Beach Trends

A bigger and better selection of nonalcoholic beverages in bars (see page 281).

AARPIES: Over-50s who live like under-30s.

Advertising on every conceivable surface, from Budweiser-emblazoned soccer balls hanging in bars to Snickers banners trailing prop planes in the skies.

B&Bs that provide hotel-style amenities: private bath; large, quiet rooms; pools.

Beach erosion.

Bike trails and boardwalks.

Blue neon script in restaurant windows.

Body piercing.

Boutiquing California's shoreline.

Calls for the division of California into separate states.

CD jukeboxes.

Cocooning as a way of life.

Coffeehouses and espresso bars.

Commuting solo.

Fake New England–style architecture.

Faux everything: faux diners, log cabins, bikers, pool halls, thrift shops, tattoo parlors, dive bars.

'50s-style diners and hamburger joints.

Foreign tourists squeezing the sagging dollar.

Gas stations that take only cash or ATM cards, refusing credit cards.

HARPIES: Middle-aged entrepreneurs who buy $30,000 customized Harleys instead of BMWs.

Insanely high gas prices that have no perceptible effect on gas consumption.

Low-fat, low-cal Mexican food.

Noon checkout times at most hotels and inns—more civilized than 10 or 11 AM.

Rivers that no longer run to the sea but end in beds of dry gravel.

Sports bars as glitzy and noisy as discotheques.

The '70s.

Our Favorite Vanity License Plates

1FASTMB (well, lah-de-dah)

3 AN 2 (a full count in baseball)

AM I BLEU

CA GIRL (spotted on a red convertible driven by a hot blond in La Jolla)

CUNNING

DLMRGRL (Del Mar girl)

EASY KO

EASYGIG

FOGYDAZ (spotted in Northern California, naturally)

GOBABY

INKEPER

KING2B

KIZZES

LAACTR (no doubt an L.A. waiter as well)

LVE ROCK (we "lve" it, too)

NDNLIMO ("Indian Limo," on a run-down car)

OH WELL

SCRIPTR (gotta hand it to him—he's pithy)

TACKEE

TRBLSME (troublesome–at least that gives the police something to look for)

XX GG

Our Favorite Headlines

Ocean Beach: "Two Bodies Found in Ocean"

San Diego: "Border Sewer Plant Will Be Shut Down"

Mission Beach: "Police Break Up Beach Concert"

La Jolla: "An Affordable Apartment Complex for La Jolla? Well, We'll See"

Encinitas: "Smog Season Arrives," "Hot Weather Turns Local Beaches into Human Zoo"

Laguna Beach: "Driver Hits 6 Vehicles, Strips, Climbs Tree"
(According to a police officer, "He is lying down buck naked, he is quoting poetry and Nostradamus, he is the son of God, he is eating dirt and grass and spitting and is totally incoherent.... He is definitely under the influence of something.")

Marina del Rey: "Activist Calls for Help in Dealing With Marina's Homeless Cat Problem"

Montecito: "Zoning Plan Puts Residents at Odds With County" (So what else is new?)

San Luis Obispo: "Slack Key Guitarist to Play Afternoon Gig at Boo-Boo's"

Bodega Bay: "Albatross Sighted—Birders Crow"

Crescent City: "Paint Spill Stains Smith River—Officials Trying to Contain Slow-Moving Mess"

Talkin' Trash: Litter on the Beach

Litter is obnoxious anywhere, but at the beach it's life-threatening. Along American shores, more than 2 million seabirds and 100,000 sea animals die each year from discarded plastic–either from ingesting it or getting caught in it and ending up strangled. And, although plastic takes up to 450 years to decompose, 20 million tons of the stuff is produced each year in the United States alone. (So much for the advice Dustin Hoffman got in *The Graduate*.)

Worldwide, the tonnage of garbage dumped in the ocean outweighs the annual catch of fish—and who the hell wants to eat fish caught in a garbage dump? Joe Six-pack is not the sole cause of this trash, either. Most ocean pollution starts with runoff from landfills, city streets, and farmland. As more people move to coastal areas—and half of the U.S. population already lives within 50 miles of the coast—the land that previously absorbed the runoff is being covered with cement, thus diverting even more untreated runoff to the ocean.

The nitrogen and phosphorus from sewage feeds algae, which then uses up oxygen that other aquatic life needs to live. Fish ingest toxic metals, and we eventually ingest the fish. And so on. The grim drumroll will continue... unless we all decide to stop it. Here are some ways we can help give the coastal waters a break:

- Always buy glass or aluminum instead of plastic or Styrofoam if there's a choice. Buy six-packs with biodegradable plastic holders and, even then, cut up the holders before disposing of them. They make perfect nooses for birds that dive-bomb trash cans.
- Boaters and anglers should never dump anything into the ocean, especially not monofilament fishing lines. (Fish get tangled in them and suffocate.) Boaters who see others dumping garbage in the ocean could do everyone a favor by reporting the violation to the U.S. Coast Guard.
- Campers and hikers should pack in and pack out any disposables they bring to coastal wilderness areas.
- Swimmers and surfers should resist the temptation to urinate in the ocean.
- Smokers should stop thinking of a wide, sandy beach as a gigantic ashtray—all those disgusting butts eventually make their way into the ocean.
- Conserve water by using efficient shower heads and toilets (the most recent models use only a gallon per flush, saving 7,665 gallons per year). The less water flushed, the less runoff will make its way to the ocean.

Every beach community sponsors a beach cleanup. Find out about the one nearest you by contacting the California Coastal Commission, Adopt-A-Beach Program, 45 Fremont Street, Suite 2000, San Francisco, CA 94105; (415) 904-5200. Or, outside of California, write to the Coastal States Organization, 444 North Capitol Street N.W., Washington, D.C. 20001.

For a copy of "A Citizen's Handbook on Water Quality Standards," write to the Natural Resources Defense Council, 1350 New York Avenue N.W., Suite 300, Washington, D.C. 20005.

"A Citizen's Guide to Plastics in the Ocean: More Than a Litter Problem" is available by writing to the Center for Marine Conservation, 1725 DeSales Street N.W., Suite 500, Washington, D.C. 20036.

For more information, contact the following environmental organizations, which work directly on ocean and coastal ecology issues:

- The Cousteau Society, 930 West 21st Street, Norfolk, VA 23517; (804) 627-1144.
- Greenpeace USA, 1436 U Street N.W., Washington, D.C. 20009; (202) 462-1177.
- National Coalition for Marine Conservation, P.O. Box 23298, Savannah, GA 31403.
- The Oceanic Society, 1536 16th Street N.W., Washington, D.C. 20036.

Index

A

C

E

G

H

N

P

Q

R

S

Acknowledgments

We owe a major debt of gratitude to the numerous people who helped us during our travels by imparting wisdom and hospitality. That includes everyone from hotel and restaurant owners to chefs, wait staff, bartenders, and bellhops, as well as 1,001 kind strangers we met on the beaches. A handful of people—namely, Bob Roubian (in Newport Beach), Robert Bussinger (in Big Sur), Jeff Stanford (in Mendocino), and John Thompson (in Klamath)—deserve to be singled out by name for their generosity and friendship. We'd also like to thank John Arnold with the California Department of Parks and Recreation for providing us with orientation and entrée to the state parks and beaches. To our many friends in California, especially our old college roommate Tom Chaltas, we'd like to say thanks and a tip of the beach visor.

We consider ourselves fortunate to have found a publisher as competent, energetic, and fun to work with as Foghorn Press. We are indebted to Judith Pynn, Vicki Morgan, Ann Marie Brown, and Donna Galassi, who believed in our idea and—either by virtue of being visionary or delirious—want more from us. It's been a pleasure working with our unflappable editors, Howard Rabinowitz and Mona Behan, who helped fine-tune the format and provided valuable feedback and suggestions. Thanks also to publishing manager Rebecca Forée for her enthusiasm and Stuart Silberman for his superb design and layout. We appreciate Donna Leverenz's promotional efforts to make this book as indispensable as suntan lotion in the minds of beachgoers. Also, an affectionate salute to our longtime friend and literary agent, Anne Zeman, who found us the kind of publisher that other writers only dream about. Finally, we'd like to thank our friends and families back home for all their continued love and support.

Credits

Publishing Manager	Rebecca Poole Forée
Senior Editor	Howard Rabinowitz
Project Editor	Mona Behan
Designer	Stuart L. Silberman
Production Manager	Michele Thomas
Associate Editor	Karin Mullen
Editorial Assistant	Aimee Larsen
Production Assistant	Alexander Lyon
Proofreader	David Sweet
Acquisitions Editor	Judith Pynn
Cover Design	Stuart L. Silberman
Cover Photo	The Marin Headlands, Marin County, California, by Edward Thomas

About the Authors

RUFUS STANDEFER

PARKE PUTERBAUGH is a music, travel, and environmental writer with a special love of the beach. He has been affiliated with *Rolling Stone* magazine for 17 years, having been a staff writer/editor from 1979–84 and a contributing editor ever since. His writing has also appeared in *Stereo Review*, *USA Today*, *Men's Journal*, *Us*, and *Outside*, as well as such books as *The Rolling Stone Illustrated History of Rock & Roll*. He holds a master's degree in environmental science from the University of North Carolina, where he specialized in the study of developed shorelines. He wants to be a surf-guitar great when he grows up.

ALAN BISBORT is a writer, editor, and researcher who has worked for the Library of Congress for the past 20 years. He is co-author of the annual Literary Companions and Baseball series, as well as a book on the New Deal art projects. His most recent books are *See America First: A History of the American Tourist* and *White Rabbit and Other Delights: East Totem West, A Hippie Company*. His writings have appeared in such periodicals as the *Washington Post*, the *Washingtonian*, *City Paper*, *E Magazine*, *Rolling Stone*, and *Creem*. In his next life, he intends to come back as Duke Kahanamoku.

Bisbort and Puterbaugh met when they were undergraduate English majors at the University of North Carolina in the early 1970s. Bonded by a mutual love of rock music, beat literature, and beer drinking, they pursued good times as avidly as higher education, laying the groundwork for future collaborations as beach writers. *California Beaches* is their third book on the subject. Their prior titles, *Life Is a Beach: A Vacationer's Guide to the West Coast* and *Life Is a Beach: A Vacationer's Guide to the East Coast*, were published by McGraw-Hill. They have been dubbed "America's beach bums" by no less an authority than Larry King.

FOGHORN PRESS

Founded in 1985, Foghorn Press has quickly become one of the country's premier publishers of outdoor recreation guidebooks. Through its unique Books Building Community program, Foghorn Press supports community environmental issues, such as park, trail, and water ecosystem preservation. Foghorn Press is also committed to printing its books on recycled paper.

Foghorn Press books are sold throughout the United States. Call 1-800-FOGHORN (8:30–5:30 PST) for the location of a bookstore near you that carries Foghorn Press titles. If you prefer, you may place an order directly with Foghorn Press using your Visa or MasterCard. All of the titles listed below are now available, unless otherwise noted.

The Complete Guide Series

The Complete Guides are the books that have given Foghorn Press its reputation for excellence. Each book is a comprehensive resource for its subject, from *every* golf course in California to *every* fishing spot in the state of Washington. With extensive cross-references and detailed maps, the Complete Guides offer readers a quick and easy way to get the best recreational information available.

California titles include:

- *California Beaches* (640 pp) $19.95
- *California Boating and Water Sports* (608 pp) $19.95, available 6/96
- *California Camping* (848 pp) $19.95
- *California Fishing* (832 pp) $19.95
- *California Golf* (896 pp) $19.95
- *California Hiking* (856 pp) $18.95
- *California In-Line Skating* (496 pp) $19.95, available 6/96
- *Tahoe* (704 pp) $18.95

Other regional titles include:

- *Alaska Fishing* (640 pp) $19.95
- *Baja Camping* (294 pp) $12.95
- *Pacific Northwest Camping* (720 pp) $19.95
- *Pacific Northwest Hiking* (808 pp) $18.95
- *Rocky Mountain Camping* (576 pp) $14.95
- *Washington Fishing* (528 pp) $19.95

The Easy Series

The Easy books are perfect for families, seniors, or anyone looking for easy, fun weekend adventures. No special effort or advance planning is necessary—just head outdoors, relax, and enjoy. Look for Easy guides to Southern California and other favorite destinations in the winter of 1997.

- *Easy Biking in Northern California* (224 pp) $12.95
- *Easy Camping in Northern California* (240 pp) $12.95
- *Easy Hiking in Northern California* (240 pp) $12.95

The Great Outdoor Getaways Series

For outdoor adventure, nothing beats Foghorn's Great Outdoor Getaways guides. Full of terrific ideas for day trips or weekend journeys, these books point you in the right direction for fun in the Great Outdoors.

- *Great Outdoor Getaways to the Bay Area & Beyond* (632 pp) $16.95
- *Great Outdoor Getaways to the Southwest* (448 pp) $16.95

The Dog Lover's Companion Series

Foghorn's Dog Lover's series is for travelers who want to bring their canine companions along for the ride. Readers will find regional listings of pet-friendly restaurants, hotels, parks, walks, and hikes that will keep their dogs' tails wagging. Watch for guides to Atlanta, Boston, and Florida.

- *The Bay Area Dog Lover's Companion* (352 pp) $13.95
- *The California Dog Lover's Companion* (720 pp) $19.95
- *The Seattle Dog Lover's Companion* (352 pp) $17.95, available 10/96

The National Outdoors Series

- *America's Secret Recreation Areas—Your Recreation Guide to the Bureau of Land Management's Wild Lands of the West* (640 pp) $17.95
- *America's Wilderness—The Complete Guide to More Than 600 National Wilderness Areas* (600 pp) $19.95, available 6/96
- *The Camper's Companion—The Pack-Along Guide for Better Outdoor Trips* (464 pp) $15.95
- *Epic Trips of the West—Tom Stienstra's Ten Best* (208 pp) $9.95
- *Our Endangered Parks—What You Can Do to Protect Our National Heritage* (224 pp) $10.95

A book's page length and availability are subject to change.

For more information, call 1-800-FOGHORN or write to:
Foghorn Press
555 DeHaro Street
The Boiler Room, Suite 220
San Francisco, CA 94107

BOOKS BUILDING COMMUNITY

Foghorn Press is pleased to support environmental and social causes nationwide. In an effort to create an awareness of and support for these worthy causes, the Books Building Community program unites Foghorn's media, bookstore, and outdoor retail partners with nonprofit organizations such as:

The Surfrider Foundation

Surfrider Foundation

The Surfrider Foundation is a nonprofit environmental organization dedicated to the protection and enhancement of the world's oceans, waves, and beaches through conservation, advocacy, research, and education. Surfrider believes that our treasured coasts should be valued and treated by the public as our most precious natural parks. Their mission is threefold: protection, preservation, and restoration.

The foundation was formed in August 1984, when a handful of Malibu surfers, concerned about the worsening conditions of our waves and beaches, met to discuss ways in which we could protect the coastal environment. Led by the visionary Malibu surfer and historian Glenn Hening, the group decided to take action to address those concerns.

The Surfrider Foundation's diverse membership now includes surfers, swimmers, divers, bodyboarders, sailors, sandcastle builders, beachcombers, lawyers, scientists, artists, musicians, teachers, businesspeople, and students. Surfrider is represented by more than 25,000 U.S. members, with 29 U.S. chapters, and affiliates in Australia, Japan, Brazil, Canada, and France. Most of the Surfrider Foundation's environmental work is conducted on the United States' East, Gulf, and West Coasts, and on the coasts of Hawaii and Puerto Rico. Chapter members act as coastal watchdogs within their local communities, adapting Surfrider programs to their local beaches.

Thanks to the organization's members and supporters, the Surfrider Foundation has tallied an impressive record of achievements in areas of coastal protection, water quality, beach access, wave preservation, and community service. Surfrider Foundation members have served as powerful spokespeople for and caretakers of the ocean environment.

The organization and its programs are funded entirely by personal and professional donations. Without these donations, Surfrider would not survive. For more information about the Surfrider Foundation, please call (800) 743-SURF.